Basic Issues of

American Democracy

Basic Issues of
American Democracy

SIXTH EDITION

A Book of Readings Selected and Edited by

HILLMAN M. BISHOP *and* SAMUEL HENDEL

Both of The City College of the City University of New York

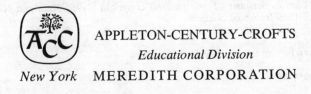

APPLETON-CENTURY-CROFTS

Educational Division

New York MEREDITH CORPORATION

To the Students
of The City College of
the City University of New York

Preface

It is now more than twenty years since our volume first appeared; and it is a source of satisfaction to us that its focus on "basic issues" has commanded wide approval and support in the academic community.

Continuing with this emphasis, we have substantially enlarged and revised our book for its sixth edition; we include nine new topics as follows: Topic 1, an urbane discussion of "politics as a profession" by John F. Kennedy; Topic 16, an analysis of dissent and disorder with an excerpt from the Report of the National Advisory Commission on Civil Disorders; Topic 17, a dispute between Stokely Carmichael and Baynard Rustin over the uses of "black power"; Topic 19, *Miranda* v. *Arizona,* which imposed curbs on police interrogation to accord with "due process"; Topic 21, a critical examination of the role of the electorate in theory and practice; Topic 23, a five-way "debate" over electoral college reform or abolition; Topic 26, contrasting views on the uses and abuses of the "welfare" state by Henry C. Wallich and John Kenneth Galbraith; Topic 28, a discussion of military-industrial power in America, with an excerpt from Dwight D. Eisenhower's farewell address and opposing positions by C. Wright Mills and Daniel Bell; and, finally, Topic 32, some variant conceptions of suitable foreign policies for the United States in its dealings with Red China.

In addition to new topics, a few carried over from the previous edition have been supplemented by new materials or altered by substitutions. Specifically, in Topic 14 we replaced a portion of Studenski and Mort with a "defense" of the federal system by Robert A. Dahl; to Topic 15 we added excerpts from the 1968 decision of the Supreme Court in *Avery* v. *Midland County* which extended the "one man, one vote" principle to the election of local government officials; in Topic 29, we supplemented a curtailed official Soviet evaluation of the U.S.S.R. with Herbert Aptheker's statement. For the rest, a considerable portion of the material found in our previous edition has been retained. Fortunately, it proved unnecessary to make many deletions.

As we have said, our basic premises and objectives remain unchanged. To elaborate, it is our belief that it is desirable to devote considerable attention to the study of fundamental values and persistent issues of our democracy in the introductory, and frequently terminal, American Government and related courses. This view finds support in the statement by Professor Francis O. Wilcox, Chairman of the American Political Science Association's Committee on Undergraduate Instruction who, in the *American Political Science Review,* wrote:

> [It] must be apparent that we have neglected to give adequate attention to the concept of democracy. We speak at great length about the electoral process, the legislature in action, the Constitution, the courts and the executive, but nowhere do we pause to ponder the real meaning of democracy. Yet here, it seems to me, is the all-important question. What is democracy? What are its weaknesses? Wherein lies its strength? What are its chances to survive? What is the real nature of the alternatives to democracy? It is infinitely more important for a student to think about these questions than it is for him to know the steps a bill must go through before it can become a law.

A second conviction that guided our selection of materials is that in dealing with controversial issues it is desirable, within limits of space, to present the most persuasively reasoned or authoritative statements obtainable. We agree with John Stuart Mill that full justice can be done to arguments only if they are presented by persons "who actually believe them; who defend them in earnest, and do their utmost for them," and that the "beliefs we have the most warrant for, have no safeguard to rest on, but a standing invitation to the whole world to prove them unfounded." And it is noteworthy that these principles of selection have meant the inclusion of materials representing some of the truly great names in political science.

Inevitably in making selections out of the vast literature of political discourse, some painful choices proved necessary. It should be noted, too, that since material on one side of a controversy was not ordinarily written in reply to that on another, direct and sharp conflict will not invariably be found. Notwithstanding these reservations, we believe that there is no other book of readings that gives as much emphasis to, and with as great consistency presents, diverse positions on the fundamental values and problems of American government and democracy.

What purposes are served by the emphasis of *Basic Issues?* We believe that this book contributes to a realization of the following: (*a*) It requires the student to analyze conflicting viewpoints, to weigh evidence and arguments, to make value judgments and reach his own conclusions. This experience may assist him in deciding between alternative policies which confront him as a citizen. (*b*) It increases interest in political discussion and may encourage active participation in public affairs outside the classroom. (*c*) It compels the student to reexamine the foundations of his beliefs and brings "clearer perception and livelier impression" to those to which he adheres; particularly, we think, it heightens his understanding of democracy, its values, problems, and dilemmas.

This volume, we suggest, may be adapted to the primary political science course, or to one semester of an integrated social science course, in a number of ways. At some colleges, for purposes of day-to-day classroom discussion, assignments basically consist of selections from these readings; but in addition, students are required to read particular chapters in a standard textbook (or other materials). While many of the textbook chapters are not discussed in the classroom, knowledge of this largely descriptive, factual material is tested in periodic examinations. At other colleges, instructors prefer to rely upon a standard textbook (or other materials), supplemented at appropriate points with required reading from this volume.

We owe a special debt of gratitude to Stephen Ziony who collaborated with us in many ways. He was particularly helpful in preparation of materials for Topic 21, "the role of the voter in theory and practice," Topic 28, "elitism or pluralism," and Topic 32, "China and United States foreign policy." We are, of course, thankful to the authors, editors, and publishers who granted permission to reproduce the materials in this volume. (Specific acknowledgment is made at appropriate points.) Our obligation to members of the department of political science at The City College, past and present, is considerable. We are also grateful to the many members of the profession throughout the country who, over the years, have given us the benefit of their experience and advice.

Samuel Hendel
Hillman M. Bishop

Contents

Contents xiii

He who knows only his own side of the case, knows little of that. His reasons may be good, and no one may have been able to refute them. But if he is equally unable to refute the reasons on the opposite side; if he does not so much as know what they are, he has no ground for preferring either opinion. The rational position for him would be suspension of judgment, and unless he contents himself with that, he is either led by authority, or adopts, like the generality of the world, the side to which he feels most inclination. Nor is it enough that he should hear the arguments of adversaries from his own teachers, presented as they state them, and accompanied by what they offer as refutations. That is not the way to do justice to the arguments, or bring them into real contact with his own mind. He must be able to hear them from persons who actually believe them; who defend them in earnest, and do their very utmost for them. He must know them in their most plausible and persuasive form; he must feel the whole force of the difficulty which the true view of the subject has to encounter and dispose of; else he will never really possess himself of the portion of truth which meets and removes that difficulty.

JOHN STUART MILL—*On Liberty*

Section I

DEMOCRACY AND POLITICS

It is, we think, appropriate that this book designed for basic courses in the study of American government and democracy begin with John F. Kennedy's urbane and witty plea in support of politics as "one of our most neglected, our most abused and our most ignored professions."

As for "democracy" itself, its nature and meaning have been subjects of considerable controversy. To the early Greeks, democracy simply meant rule by the people; a term derived from *dêmos—* people and *kratein—*to rule. But, as Walter Lippmann makes clear, a false conception of democracy may lead to confusion of the ideal and the realizable and to widespread disillusionment.

Definition is further complicated by the fact that radically different regimes have claimed the name and sanction of democracy. Thus, fascist Italy was called a "democracy *par excellence,*" Nazi Germany a "teutonic democracy," the U.S.S.R. the "most thoroughly democratic country in the world," Red China a "peoples' democracy," Burma a "guided democracy," and the United Arab Republic a "presidential democracy." One result might be to cast aside definition as a mere matter of semantics. This would be unfortunate; for disagreement over the nature and meaning of democracy may derive from deep-lying differences over values that manifest themselves in the institutions designed to realize these values.

(For the views of the Founding Fathers on democracy, see the next section. Several other sections deal, in one way or another, with the relation of democratic theory and practice, while a general evaluation of democracy appears in the section titled "Democracy Evaluated.")

1

~~~~TOPIC 1

The Practice of Politics

JOHN F. KENNEDY
Politics as a Profession

Perhaps one of the most dramatic moments of Elihu Root's life came in Utica in 1906 when as Secretary of State he agreed to speak for his party in this state. The opposition had imported a gang of hecklers to make his speech impossible. Having secured copies of his address in advance, they had instructions to start interruptions on particular lines—shouting, for example, on the first reference to the late President McKinley, "Let McKinley rest in peace," with the others roaring their approval. Unfortunately for the hecklers, the meeting was packed with Root admirers and Hamilton College students; and the first one who started to interrupt was pushed in the face, and the rest were bodily threatened. Finally, when a great roar arose from the crowd to throw out one heckler, Root raised his right hand to quell the uproar, and in a powerful voice cried out: "No, let him stay—and learn!"

I trust that all of you will stay—I can only speculate as to how much you will learn—but I will welcome any heckling at the close of these ceremonies. I hope the example of Elihu Root will be an inspiration to all of those whom we honor on this solemn day of Commencement. For them, the pleasures, the values and the friendships of college days are coming to an end—the identical group sitting here this morning will probably never gather again—and the sands of time will gradually erase most of the memories which seem so important today.

But what concerns us most on these occasions is not what you graduates leave behind but what you take with you, what you will do with it, what contribution you can make. I am assuming, of course, that you are taking something with you, that you do not look upon this university as Dean Swift regarded Oxford. Oxford, he said, was truly a great seat of learning; for all freshmen who entered were required to bring some learning with them in order to meet the standards of admission—but no senior, when he left the university, ever took any learning away; and thus it steadily accumulated.

The high regard in which your education at Syracuse is held is evidenced by the intensive competition which rages between those hoping to benefit from it. Your campus is visited by prospective employers ranging from corporation

President of the United States from January 20, 1961 to November 22, 1963. Author of *Profiles in Courage*. The selection is from a speech delivered by President Kennedy at Syracuse University on June 3, 1957.

3

vice-presidents to professional football coaches. Great newspaper advertisements offer inducements to chemists, engineers, and electronic specialists. High public officials plead for more college graduates to follow scientific pursuits. And many of you will be particularly persuaded by the urgent summons to duty and travel which comes from your local draft board.

But in the midst of all these pleas, plans and pressures, few, I dare say, if any, will be urging upon you a career in the field of politics. Some will point out the advantages of civil service positions. Others will talk in high terms of public service, or statesmanship, or community leadership. But few, if any, will urge you to become politicians.

Mothers may still want their favorite sons to grow up to be President, but, according to a famous Gallup poll of some years ago, they do not want them to become politicians in the process. They may be statesmen, they may be leaders of their community, they may be distinguished law-makers—but they must never be politicians. Successful politicians, according to Walter Lippmann, are "insecure and intimidated men," who "advance politically only as they placate, appease, bribe, seduce, bamboozle, or otherwise manage to manipulate" the views and votes of the people who elect them. It was considered a great joke years ago when the humorist Artemas Ward declared: "I am not a politician, and my other habits are good also." And, in more recent times, even the President of the United States, when asked at a news conference early in his first term how he liked "the game of politics," replied with a frown that his questioner was using a derogatory phrase. Being President, he said, is a "very fascinating experience . . . but the word 'politics' . . . I have no great liking for that."

Politics, in short, has become one of our most neglected, our most abused and our most ignored professions. It ranks low on the occupational list of a large share of the population; and its chief practitioners are rarely well or favorably known. No education, except finding your way around a smoke-filled room, is considered necessary for political success. "Don't teach my boy poetry," a mother recently wrote the headmaster of Eton; "Don't teach my boy poetry, he's going to stand for Parliament." The worlds of politics and scholarship have indeed drifted apart.

Unfortunately, this disdain for the political profession is not only shared but intensified in our academic institutions. To many universities and students we politicians represent nothing but censors, investigators and perpetrators of what has been called the "swinish cult of anti-intellectualism." To others, we are corrupt, selfish, unsavory individuals, manipulating votes and compromising principles for personal and partisan gain.

Teachers as well as students, moreover, find it difficult to accept the differences between the laboratory and the legislature. In the former, the goal is truth, pure and simple, without regard to changing currents of public opinion; in the latter, compromises and majorities and procedural customs and rights affect the ultimate decision as to what is right or just or good. And even when they realize the difference, most intellectuals consider their chief function to be that of the critic—and politicians are sensitive to critics (possibly because we have so many of them). "Many intellectuals," Sidney Hook has said, "would rather 'die' than agree with the majority, even on the rare occasions when the majority is right." Of course, the intellectual's attitude is partly defensive—for he has been regarded with so much suspicion and hostility by political figures and their constituents that a recent survey of American intellectuals by a national magazine elicited from one of our foremost literary figures the guarded response, "I ain't no intellectual."

But this mutual suspicion was not always the case—and I would ask those of you who look with disdain and disfavor upon the possibilities of a political career to remember that our nation's first great politicians were traditionally our ablest, most respected, most talented leaders, men who moved from one field to another with amazing versatility and vitality. A contemporary described Thomas Jefferson as "A gentleman of 32, who could calculate an eclipse, survey an estate, tie an artery, plan an edifice, try a cause, break a horse, dance a minuet, and play the violin."

Daniel Webster could throw thunderbolts at Hayne on the Senate Floor and then stroll a few steps down the corridor and dominate the Supreme Court as the foremost lawyer of his time. John Quincy Adams, after being summarily dismissed from the Senate for a notable display of independence, could become Boylston Professor of Rhetoric and Oratory at Harvard and then become a great Secretary of State. (Those were the happy days when Harvard professors had no difficulty getting Senate confirmation.)

This versatility also existed on the frontier. Missouri's first Senator, Thomas Hart Benton, the man whose tavern brawl with Jackson in Tennessee caused him to flee the state, was described with these words in his obituary: "With a readiness that was often surprising, he could quote from a Roman Law or a Greek philosopher, from Virgil's Georgics, The Arabian Nights, Herodotus or Sancho Panza; from the Sacred Carpets, the German reformers or Adam Smith; from Fenelon or Hudibras, from the financial reports of Necca or the doings of the Council of Trent, from the debates on the adoption of the Constitution or intrigues of the kitchen cabinet or from some forgotten speech of a deceased Member of Congress."

This link between American scholarship and the American politician remained for more than a century. A little more than one hundred years ago, in the Presidential campaign of 1856, the Republicans sent three brilliant orators around the campaign circuit: William Cullen Bryant, Henry Wadsworth Longfellow and Ralph Waldo Emerson. (Those were the carefree days when the "egg-heads" were all Republicans.)

I would urge therefore that each of you, regardless of your chosen occupation, consider entering the field of politics at some stage in your career. It is not necessary that you be famous, that you effect radical changes in the government or that you be acclaimed by the public for your efforts. It is not even necessary that you be successful. I ask only that you offer to the political arena, and to the critical problems of our society which are decided therein, the benefit of the talents which society has helped to develop in you. I ask you to decide, as Goethe put it, whether you will be an anvil—or a hammer. The formal phases of the "anvil" stage are now completed for many of you, though hopefully you will continue to absorb still more in the years ahead. The question now is whether you are to be a hammer—whether you are to give to the world in which you were reared and educated the broadest possible benefits of that education.

It is not enough to lend your talents merely to discussing the issues and deploring their solutions. Most scholars, I know, would prefer to confine their attention to the mysteries of pure scholarship or the delights of abstract discourse. But "Would you have counted him a friend of Ancient Greece," as George William Curtis asked a century ago during the Kansas-Nebraska Controversy, "who quietly discussed the theory of patriotism on that Greek summer day through whose hopeless and immortal hours Leonidas and his three hundred stood at Thermopylae for liberty? Was John Milton to conjugate Greek verbs in his library, or talk of the liberty of the ancient Shumanites, when the liberty of Englishmen was imperilled?" No, the duty of the scholar—particularly in a republic such as ours—is to contribute his objective views and his sense of liberty to the affairs of his state and nation.

This is a great university, the University of Syracuse. Its establishment and continued functioning, like that of all great universities, has required considerable effort and expenditure. I cannot believe that all of this was undertaken merely to give the school's graduates an economic advantage in the life struggle. "A university," said Professor Woodrow Wilson, "should be an organ of memory for the state for the transmission of its best traditions. Every man sent out from a university should be a man of his nation, as well as a man of his time." And Prince Bismarck was even more specific—one-third of the students of German universities, he once stated, broke down from overwork; another third broke down from dissipation; and the other third ruled Germany. (I leave it to each of you to decide which category you fall in.)

But if you are to be among the rulers of our land, from precinct captain to President, if you are willing to enter the abused and neglected profession of politics, then let me tell you—as one who is familiar with the political world— that we stand in serious need of the fruits of your education. We do not need political scholars whose education has been so specialized as to exclude them from participation in current events—men like Lord John Russell, of whom Queen Victoria once remarked that he would be a better man if he knew a third subject—but he was interested in nothing but the Constitution of 1688 and himself. No, what we need are men who can ride easily over broad fields of knowledge and recognize the mutual dependence of our two worlds.

I do not say that our political and public life should be turned over to college-trained experts who ignore public opinion. Nor would I adopt from the Belgian Constitution of 1893 the provision giving three votes instead of one to college graduates (at least not until more Democrats go to college). Nor would I give the University of Syracuse a seat in the Congress as William and Mary was once represented in the Virginia House of Burgesses.

But I do urge the application of your talents to the public solution of the great problems of our time—increasing farm foreclosures in the midst of national prosperity—record small business failures at a time of record profits— pockets of chronic unemployment and sweatshop wages amidst the wonders of automation—monopoly, mental illness, race relations, taxation, international trade, and, above all, the knotty complex problems of war and peace, of untangling the strife-ridden, hate-ridden Middle East, of preventing man's destruction by nuclear war or, even more awful to contemplate, by disabling through mutations generations yet unborn.

No, you do not lack problems or opportunities—you do not lack the ability or the energy; nor, I have tried to say, do you lack the responsibility to act, no matter what you have heard about the profession of politics. Bear in mind, as you leave this university and consider the road ahead, not the sneers of the cynics or the fears of the purists, for whom politics will never be an attraction—but bear in mind instead these words which are inscribed behind the Speaker's desk high on the Chamber Wall of the United States House of Representatives, inscribed for all to see and all to ponder, these words of the most famous statesman my state ever sent to the Halls of Congress, Daniel Webster: "Let us develop the resources of our land, call forth its power, build up its institutions, promote all its great interests and see whether we also in our day and generation may not perform something worthy to be remembered."

What Is Democracy?

WALTER LIPPMANN
The Phantom Public

The Unattainable Ideal

A false ideal of democracy can lead only to disillusionment and to meddle-some tyranny. If democracy cannot direct affairs, then a philosophy which expects it to direct them will encourage the people to attempt the impossible. . . .

The private citizen today has come to feel rather like a deaf spectator in the back row, who ought to keep his mind on the mystery off there, but cannot quite manage to keep awake. He knows he is somehow affected by what is going on. Rules and regulations continually, taxes annually and wars occasionally, remind him that he is being swept along by great drifts of circumstance.

Yet these public affairs are . . . for the most part invisible. They are managed, if they are managed at all, at distant centers, from behind the scenes, by unnamed powers. As a private person he does not know for certain what is going on, or who is doing it, or where he is being carried. No newspaper reports his environment so that he can grasp it; no school has taught him how to imagine it; his ideals, often, do not fit with it; listening to speeches, uttering opinions and voting do not, he finds, enable him to govern it. He lives in a world which he cannot see, does not understand and is unable to direct. . . .

There is then nothing particularly new in the disenchantment which the private citizen expresses by not voting at all, by voting only for the head of the ticket, by staying away from the primaries, by not reading speeches and documents, by the whole list of sins of omission for which he is denounced. I shall not denounce him further. My sympathies are with him, for I believe that he has been saddled with an impossible task and that he is asked to practice an unattainable ideal. I find it so myself for, although public business is my main interest and I give most of my time to watching it, I cannot find time to do what is expected of me in the theory of democracy; that is, to know what is going on and to have an opinion worth expressing on every question which confronts a self-governing community. And I have not happened to meet any-

Newspaper columnist. Author of *Public Opinion, A Preface to Politics, The Good Society, The Public Philosophy* and numerous other books. The selection is from Walter Lippmann, *The Phantom Public* (New York, The Macmillan Co., 1927), *passim*. By permission.

body, from a President of the United States to a professor of political science, who came anywhere near to embodying the accepted ideal of the sovereign and omnipotent citizen. . . .

The actual governing is made up of a multitude of arrangements on specific questions by particular individuals. These rarely become visible to the private citizen. Government, in the long intervals between elections, is carried on by politicians, officeholders and influential men who make settlements with other politicians, officeholders, and influential men. The mass of people see these settlements, judge them, and affect them only now and then. They are altogether too numerous, too complicated, too obscure in their effects to become the subject of any continuing exercise of public opinion.

Nor in any exact and literal sense are those who conduct the daily business of government accountable after the fact to the great mass of the voters. They are accountable only, except in spectacular cases, to the other politicians, officeholders and influential men directly interested in the particular act. Modern society is not visible to anybody, nor intelligible continuously and as a whole. One section is visible to another section, one series of acts is intelligible to this group and another to that.

Even this degree of responsible understanding is attainable only by the development of fact-finding agencies of great scope and complexity. These agencies give only a remote and incidental assistance to the general public. Their findings are too intricate for the casual reader. They are also almost always much too uninteresting. Indeed the popular boredom and contempt for the expert and for statistical measurement are such that the organization of intelligence to administer modern affairs would probably be entirely neglected were it not that departments of government, corporations, trade unions and trade associations are being compelled by their own internal necessities of administration, and by compulsion of other corporate groups, to record their own acts, measure them, publish them and stand accountable for them. . . .

It may be objected at once that an election which turns one set of men out of office and installs another is an expression of public opinion which is neither secondary nor indirect. But what in fact is an election? We call it an expression of the popular will. But is it? We go into a polling booth and mark a cross on a piece of paper for one or two, or perhaps three or four names. Have we expressed our thoughts on the public policy of the United States? Presumably we have a number of thoughts on this and that with many buts and ifs and ors. Surely the cross on a piece of paper does not express them. It would take us hours to express our thoughts, and calling a vote the expression of our mind is an empty fiction.

A vote is a promise of support. It is a way of saying: I am lined up with these men, on this side. I enlist with them. I will follow. . . . The public does not select the candidate, write the platform, outline the policy any more than it builds the automobile or acts the play. It aligns itself for or against somebody who has offered himself, has made a promise, has produced a play, is selling an automobile. The action of a group as a group is the mobilization of the force it possesses. . . .

I do not wish to labor the argument any further than may be necessary to establish the theory that what the public does is not to express its opinions but to align itself for or against a proposal. If that theory is accepted, we must abandon the notion that democratic government can be the direct expression of the will of the people. We must abandon the notion that the people govern. Instead we must adopt the theory that, by their occasional mobilizations as a majority, people support or oppose the individuals who actually govern. We must say that the popular will does not direct continuously but that it intervenes occasionally. . . .

The attempt has been made to ascribe some intrinsic moral and intellectual virtue to majority rule. It was said often in the nineteenth century that there was a deep wisdom in majorities which was the voice of God. Sometimes this flattery was a sincere mysticism, sometimes it was the self-deception which always accompanies the idealization of power. In substance it was nothing but a transfer to the new sovereign of the divine attributes of kings. Yet the inherent absurdity of making virtue and wisdom dependent on 51 per cent of any collection of men has always been apparent. The practical realization that the claim was absurd has resulted in a whole code of civil rights to protect minorities and in all sorts of elaborate methods of subsidizing the arts and sciences and other human interests so they might be independent of the operation of majority rule.

The justification of majority rule in politics is not to be found in its ethical superiority. It is to be found in the sheer necessity of finding a place in civilized society for the force which resides in the weight of numbers. I have called voting an act of enlistment, an alignment for or against, a mobilization. These are military metaphors, and rightly so, I think, for an election based on the principle of majority rule is historically and practically a sublimated and denatured civil war, a paper mobilization without physical violence.

Constitutional democrats, in the intervals when they were not idealizing the majority, have acknowledged that a ballot was a civilized substitute for a bullet. "The French Revolution," says Bernard Shaw, "overthrew one set of rulers and substituted another with different interests and different views. That is what a general election enables the people to do in England every seven years if they choose." . . . Hans Delbrück puts the matter simply when he says that the principle of majority rule is "a purely practical principle. If one wants to avoid a civil war, one lets those rule who in any case would obtain the upper hand if there should be a struggle; and they are the superior numbers." . . .

To support the Ins when things are going well; to support the Outs when they seem to be going badly, this, in spite of all that has been said about tweedle-dum and tweedledee, is the essence of popular government. Even the most intelligent large public of which we have any experience must determine finally who shall wield the organized power of the state, its army and its police, by a choice between the Ins and Outs. A community where there is no choice does not have popular government. It is subject to some form of dictatorship or it is ruled by the intrigues of the politicians in the lobbies.

Although it is the custom of partisans to speak as if there were radical differences between the Ins and the Outs, it could be demonstrated, I believe, that in stable and mature societies the differences are necessarily not profound.

If they were profound, the defeated minority would be constantly on the verge of rebellion. An election would be catastrophic, whereas the assumption in every election is that the victors will do nothing to make life intolerable to the vanquished and that the vanquished will endure with good humor policies which they do not approve.

In the United States, Great Britian, Canada, Australia and in certain of the Continental countries an election rarely means even a fraction of what the campaigners said it would mean. It means some new faces and perhaps a slightly different general tendency in the management of affairs. The Ins may have had a bias toward collectivism; the Outs will lean toward individualism. The Ins may have been suspicious and non-cooperative in foreign affairs; the Outs will perhaps be more trusting or entertain another set of suspicions. The Ins may have favored certain manufacturing interests; the Outs may favor agricultural interests. But even these differing tendencies are very small as compared with the immense area of agreement, established habit and unavoidable necessity. In fact, one might say that a nation is politically stable when nothing of radical consequence is determined by its elections. . . .

The test of whether the Ins are handling affairs effectively is the presence or absence of disturbing problems. . . . It is my opinion that for the most part the general public cannot back each reformer on each issue. It must choose between the Ins and the Outs on the basis of a cumulative judgment as to whether the problems are being solved or aggravated. The particular reformers must look for their support normally to the ruling insiders.

Education for Democracy

Education has furnished the thesis of the last chapter of every optimistic book on democracy written for one hundred and fifty years. Even Robert Michels, stern and unbending antisentimentalist that he is, says in his "final considerations" that "it is the great task of social education to raise the intellectual level of the masses, so that they may be enabled, within the limits of what is possible, to counteract the oligarchical tendencies" of all collective action. . . .

The usual appeal to education as the remedy for the incompetence of democracy is barren. It is, in effect, a proposal that school teachers shall by some magic of their own fit men to govern after the makers of laws and the preachers of civic ideals have had a free hand in writing the specifications. The reformers do not ask what men can be taught. They say they should be taught whatever may be necessary to fit them to govern the modern world.

The usual appeal to education can bring only disappointment. For the problems of the modern world appear and change faster than any set of teachers can grasp them, much faster than they can convey their substance to a population of children. If the schools attempt to teach children how to solve the problems of the day, they are bound always to be in arrears. The most they can conceivably attempt is the teaching of a pattern of thought and feeling which will enable the citizen to approach a new problem in some useful fashion. But that pattern cannot be invented by the pedagogue. It is the political theorist's business to trace out that pattern. In that task he must not assume that the mass has political genius, but that men, even if they had genius, would give only a little time and attention to public affairs. . . .

At the root of the effort to educate a people for self-government there has, I believe, always been the assumption that the voter should aim to approximate as nearly as he can the knowledge and the point of view of the responsible man. He did not, of course, in the mass, ever approximate it very nearly. But he was supposed to. It was believed that if only he could be taught more facts, if only he would take more interest, if only he would read more and better newspapers, if only he would listen to more lectures and read more reports, he would gradually be trained to direct public affairs. The whole assumption is false. It rests upon a false conception of public opinion and a false conception of the way the public acts. No sound scheme of civic education can come of it. No progress can be made toward this unattainable ideal.

This democratic conception is false because it fails to note the radical difference between the experience of the insider and the outsider; it is fundamentally askew because it asks the outsider to deal as successfully with the substance of a question as the insider. He cannot do it. No scheme of education can equip him in advance for all the problems of mankind; no device of publicity, no machinery of enlightenment, can endow him during a crisis with the antecedent detailed and technical knowledge which is required for executive action. . . .

The fundamental difference which matters is that between insiders and outsiders. Their relations to a problem are radically different. Only the insider can make decisions, not because he is inherently a better man but because he is so placed that he can understand and can act. The outsider is necessarily ignorant, usually irrelevant and often meddlesome, because he is trying to navigate the ship from dry land. That is why excellent automobile manufacturers, literary critics and scientists often talk such nonsense about politics. Their congenital excellence, if it exists, reveals itself only in their own activity. The aristocratic theorists work from the fallacy of supposing that a sufficiently excellent square peg will also fit a round hole. In short, like the democratic theorists, they miss the essence of the matter, which is, that competence exists only in relation to function; that men are not good, but good for something; that men cannot be educated, but only educated for something. . . .

Democracy, therefore, has never developed an education for the public. It has merely given it a smattering of the kind of knowledge which the responsible man requires. It has, in fact, aimed not at making good citizens but at making a mass of amateur executives. It has not taught the child how to act as a member of the public. It has merely given him a hasty, incomplete taste of what he might have to know if he meddled in everything. The result is a bewildered public and a mass of insufficiently trained officials. The responsible men have obtained their training not from the courses in "civics" but in the law schools and law offices and in business. The public at large, which includes everybody outside the field of his own responsible knowledge, has had no coherent political training of any kind. Our civic education does not even begin to tell the voter how he can reduce the maze of public affairs to some intelligible form. . . .

Education for citizenship, for membership in the public, ought, therefore to be distinct from education for public office. Citizenship involves a radically different relation to affairs, requires different intellectual habits and different methods of action. The force of public opinion is partisan, spasmodic, simple-minded and external. It needs for its direction . . . a new intellectual method which shall provide it with its own usable canons of judgment. . . .

The Role of the Public

If this is the nature of public action, what ideal can be formulated which shall conform to it?

We are bound, I think, to express the ideal in its lowest terms, to state it not as an ideal which might conceivably be realized by exceptional groups now and then or in some distant future but as an ideal which normally might be taught and attained. In estimating the burden which a public can carry, a sound political theory must insist upon the largest factor of safety. It must understate the possibilities of public action. . . .

We cannot, then, think of public opinion as a conserving or creating force directing society to clearly conceived ends, making deliberately toward socialism or away from it, toward nationalism, an empire, a league of nations or any other doctrinal goal. . . .

The work of the world goes on continually without conscious direction from public opinion. At certain junctures problems arise. It is only with the crises of some of these problems that public opinion is concerned. And its object in dealing with a crisis is to help allay that crisis.

I think this conclusion is inescapable. For though we may prefer to believe that the aim of popular action should be to do justice or promote the true, the beautiful and the good, the belief will not maintain itself in the face of plain experience. The public does not know in most crises what specifically is the truth or the justice of the case, and men are not agreed on what is beautiful and good. Nor does the public rouse itself normally at the existence of evil. It is aroused at evil made manifest by the interruption of a habitual process of life. And finally, a problem ceases to occupy attention not when justice, as we happen to define it, has been done but when a workable adjustment that overcomes the crisis has been made. . . .

Thus we strip public opinion of any implied duty to deal with the substance of a problem, to make technical decisions, to attempt justice or impose a moral precept. And instead we say that the ideal of public opinion is to align men during the crisis of a problem in such a way as to favor the action of those individuals who may be able to compose a crisis. The power to discern those individuals is the end of the effort to educate public opinion. The aim of research designed to facilitate public action is the discovery of clear signs by which these individuals may be discerned.

The signs are relevant when they reveal by coarse, simple and objective tests which side in a controversy upholds a workable social rule, or which is attacking an unworkable rule, or which proposes a promising new rule. By following such signs the public might know where to align itself. In such an alignment it does not, let us remember, pass judgment on the intrinsic merits. It merely places its force at the disposal of the side which, according to objective signs, seems to be standing for human adjustments according to a clear rule of behavior and against the side which appears to stand for settlement in accordance with its own unaccountable will.

Public opinion, in this theory, is a reserve of force brought into action during a crisis in public affairs. Though it is itself an irrational force, under favorable institutions, sound leadership and decent training the power of public opinion might be placed at the disposal of those who stood for workable law as against brute assertion. In this theory, public opinion does not make the law. But by canceling lawless power it may establish the condition under which law can be made. It does not reason, investigate, invent, persuade, bargain or settle. But, by holding the aggressive party in check, it may liberate intelligence. Public opinion in its highest ideal will defend those who are prepared to act on their reason against the interrupting force of those who merely assert their will. . . .

These in roughest outline are some of the conclusions, as they appear to me, of the attempt to bring the theory of democracy into somewhat truer alignment with the nature of public opinion. I have conceived public opinion to be, not the voice of God, nor the voice of society, but the voice of the interested spectators of action. I have, therefore, supposed that the opinions of the spectators must be essentially different from those of the actors, and that the kind of action they were capable of taking was essentially different too. It has seemed to me that the public had a function and must have methods of its own in controversies, qualitatively different from those of the executive men; that it was a dangerous confusion to believe that private purposes were a mere emanation of some common purpose. . . .

It is a theory which puts its trust chiefly in the individuals directly concerned. They initiate, they administer, they settle. It would subject them to the least possible interference from ignorant and meddlesome outsiders, for in this theory the public intervenes only when there is a crisis of maladjustment, and then not to deal with the substance of the problem but to neutralize the arbitrary force which prevents adjustment. It is a theory which economizes the attention of men as members of the public, and asks them to do as little as possible in matters where they can do nothing very well. It confines the effort of men, when they are a public, to a part they might fulfill, to a part which corresponds to their own greatest interest in any social disturbance; that is, to an intervention which may help to allay the disturbance, and thus allow them to return to their own affairs.

For it is the pursuit of their special affairs that they are most interested in. It is by the private labors of individuals that life is enhanced. I set no great store on what can be done by public opinion and the action of masses.

I have no legislative program to offer, no new institutions to propose. There are, I believe, immense confusions in the current theory of democracy which frustrate and pervert its action. I have attacked certain of the confusions with no conviction except that a false philosophy tends to stereotype thought against the lessons of experience. I do not know what the lessons will be when we have learned to think of public opinion as it is, and not as the fictitious power we have assumed it to be. It is enough if with Bentham we know that "the perplexity of ambiguous discourse . . . distracts and eludes the apprehension, stimulates and inflames the passions."

HAROLD J. LASKI
Equality and Democracy

No definition of democracy can adequately comprise the vast history which the concept connotes. To some it is a form of government, to others a way of social life. Men have found its essence in the character of the electorate, the relation between government and the people, the absence of wide economic differences between citizens, the refusal to recognize privileges built on birth or wealth, race or creed. Inevitably it has changed its substance in terms of time and place. What has seemed democracy to a member of some ruling class has seemed to his poorer fellow citizen a narrow and indefensible oligarchy. Democracy has a context in every sphere of life; and in each of those spheres it raises its special problems which do not admit of satisfactory or universal generalization.

The political aspect of democracy has the earliest roots in time. For the most part it remained a negative concept until the seventeenth century. Men protested against systems which upon one ground or another excluded them from a share in power. They were opposed to an oligarchy which exercised privileges confined to a narrow range of persons. They sought the extension of such privileges to more people on the ground that limitation was not justifiable. They felt and argued that exclusion from privilege was exclusion from benefit; and they claimed their equal share in its gains.

That notion of equality points the way to the essence of the democratic idea —the effort of men to affirm their own essence and to remove all barriers to that affirmation. All differentials by which other men exercise authority or influence they do not themselves possess hinder their own self-realization. To give these differentials the protection of the legal order is to prevent the realization of the wishes and interests of the mass of men. The basis of democratic development is therefore the demand for equality, the demand that the system of power be erected upon the similarities and not the differences between men. Of the permanence of this demand there can be no doubt; at the very dawn of political science Aristotle insisted that its denial was the main cause of revolutions. Just as the history of the state can perhaps be most effectively written in terms of the expanding claims of the common man upon the results of its effort, so the development of the realization of equality is the clue to the problem of democracy. . . .

It is because political equality, however profound, does not permit the full affirmation of the common man's essence that the idea of democracy has spread to other spheres. The discovery that men may be politically equal without attaining a genuine realization of their personalities was seen by not a few during the

Late Professor of Political Science at London School of Economics and Political Science. The selection is from Harold J. Laski, "Democracy," *Encyclopaedia of Social Sciences* (New York, The Macmillan Co., 1942). By permission.

Puritan revolution, and the demand for economic equality was loudly and ably voiced then by Winstanley and his followers. It was only, however, with the French Revolution that economic equality may be said to have become a permanent part of the democratic creed. From that time, particularly in the context of socialist principles, it has been increasingly insisted that in the absence of economic equality no political mechanisms will of themselves enable the common man to realize his wishes and interests. Economic power is regarded as the parent of political power. To make the diffusion of the latter effective, the former also must be widely diffused. To divide a people into rich and poor is to make impossible the attainment of a common interest by state action. Economic equality is then urged as the clue upon which the reality of democracy depends. . . .

The case for democracy is built upon the assumption that in its absence men become the tools of others, without available proof that the common good is inherently involved in this relationship. The case at bottom is an ethical one. It postulates that the right to happiness is inherent in man as a member of society and that any system which denies that right cannot be justified. The main argument in its favor is the important one that in any social order where it has not been accepted a rational analysis finds it difficult to justify the distribution of benefits which occurs. . . .

Socialism and Democracy

Democratic government during the nineteenth century may be said to have been successful so long as it confined its activities to the purely political field. While it occupied itself with matters of religious freedom, formal political equality, the abrogation of aristocratic privilege, its conquests were swift and triumphant. But the attainment of these ends did not solve any of the major social and economic issues. The masses still remained poor; a small number of rich men still exercised a predominant influence in the state. With the grant of the franchise to the workers therefore a movement toward collectivism was inevitable. Political parties had to attract their support; the obvious method was to offer the prospect of social and economic legislation which should alleviate the workers' condition. And from the early days of the French Revolution there had appeared the portent of socialism with its insistence that only in the rigorous democratization of economic power could a solution to the social problem be found. Incoherent at first, the development of trade unions and the growth of doctrines like that of Marx made what seemed visionary utopianism into a movement. By the eighties of the nineteenth century socialism could represent itself as the natural and logical outcome of democratic theory. It could outbid the older parties on ground which universal suffrage had made the inevitable territory of conflict. In the opening years of the twentieth century the central theme of debate had become the power of the state to satisfy the economic wants of the working-class. . . .

If the hypothesis of self-government is valid in the political sphere it must be valid in the economic sphere also; whence is born the insistence upon constitutional government in industry. Not only must the state interfere to this end in the general details of economic life, but it cannot realize its end if the operation of the profit making motive is admitted in any industry of basic importance to the community. The new ideals of democracy therefore foreshadow a functional society in which the older conception of liberty of contract has no place. Any state in which the economic sphere is left largely uncontrolled is necessarily a class society tilted to the advantage of the rich; it lacks that necessary basis of unity which enables men to compose their differences in peace. The claim for the sovereignty of the state no longer rests upon the strong basis provided by the old liberal hypothesis of a society equal in fact because formally equal in political power. Largely the new democratic theory accepts a quasi-Marxian interpretation of the state while refusing to draw therefrom the inference that revolution is its only satisfactory corrective. . . .

[The new democratic theory] regards the right of men to share in the results of social life as broadly equal; and its regards differences of treatment as justifiable only in so far as they can be shown to be directly relevant to the common good. It takes its stand firmly on the need for a close economic equality on the ground that the benefits a man can obtain from the social process are, at least approximately and in general, a function of his power of effective demand, which in turn depends upon the property he owns. It is thus hostile to all economic privilege as being in its nature fatal to the end at which a democratic society must aim. For the new democratic theory liberty is necessarily a function of equality. . . .

One final remark may be made. It is not the view of modern democratic theory that a political man can be constructed whose interest in the public business of the community is assured. It does believe that increased educational opportunity will increase that interest; a belief which further emphasizes the need for equality. It does argue further that the main result of inequality is so to depress the moral character of those at the base of the social pyramid as to minimize their power to get attention for their experience. Again therefore it sees in equality the path to the end democracy seeks to serve.

R. M. MAC IVER
The Role of the People

Democracy cannot mean the rule of the majority or the rule of the masses. This was the manner in which democracy was interpreted by the Greek philosophers, at a time before there was any representative system or any party system—and this fact may help to explain why they on the whole disapproved of it. The meaning of democracy was then obscure. Even today, with all our experience of democracy, it is often misunderstood. Democracy is not a way of governing, whether by majority or otherwise, but primarily a way of determining who shall govern and, broadly, to what ends. The only way in which the

Professor Emeritus of Political Philosophy and Sociology at Columbia University. Author of *Leviathan and the People, The More Perfect Union* and others. From R. M. MacIver, *The Web of Government* (New York, The Macmillan Co., 1947), pp. 198-199. By permission.

people, *all the people,* can determine who shall govern is by referring the question to public opinion and accepting on each occasion the verdict of the polls. Apart from this activity of the people there is no way of distinguishing democracy from other forms of government.

Any kind of government can claim to rest on "the will of the people," whether it be oligarchy or dictatorship or monarchy. One kind of government alone rests on the constitutional exercise of the will of the people. Every other kind prevents the minority—or the majority—from freely expressing opinion concerning the policies of government, or at the least from making that opinion the free determinant of government. Quite possibly in Russia, at the time of writing, a larger proportion of the people approves and supports its government than may be found in democratic countries to support their governments. But that fact is quite irrelevant to the question of democracy. In the Soviet Union, under these conditions, there is no free exercise of opinion on matters of policy, nor any constitutional means by which the changing currents of opinion can find political expression. It would therefore be the sheerest confusion to classify the Soviet system as democratic.

The growth of democracy has always been associated with the free discussion of political issues, with the right to differ concerning them, and with the settlement of the difference, not by *force majeure* but by resort to the counting of votes. It has always been associated with the growing authority of some assembly of the people or of the people's representatives, such as the Greek *ecclesia,* the Roman *comitia,* the English parliament. The right to differ did not end with the victory of the majority but was inherent in the system. It was a necessary condition of democracy everywhere that opposing doctrines remained free to express themselves, to seek converts, to form organizations, and so to compete for success before the tribunal of public opinion. Any major trend of opinion could thus register itself in the character and in the policies of government. . . .

The Function of the Public*

There are those who condemn democracy because, they say, the people are unfit to rule. And there are those who, in a more friendly spirit, deplore the plight of democracy because the people simply cannot undertake the task it imposes on them, the task of coping with all the complex issues of modern government. In one of his earlier books, *The Phantom Public,* Walter Lippmann put forward the plaint that the democratic man was baffled and disenchanted. He could not make his sovereign voice heard concerning a thousand tangled affairs, and how could he? How could he have an effective opinion about the situation in China today and about the sewers of Brooklyn tomorrow, and the next day about the effects of subsidies to agriculture, and the next day about some deal with Yugoslavia, and so on without end? He gave it up. He was dillusioned about democracy. He could not live up to its demands.

If any "man in the street" holds these views about his democratic obligations it is quite proper he should be disillusioned. But not, we hope, about

* From R. M. MacIver: *The Ramparts We Guard,* copyright, 1950, by Robert M. MacIver, and used with the permission of The Macmillan Co., pp. 27-30, 49-51.

democracy. Only about his illusions about democracy. Representative democracy, the only kind that has any meaning under modern conditions, does not put any such impossible strain on the citizen. The people, let us repeat, do not and cannot govern; they control the government. In every live democracy they decide the broad march of politics. They decide whether there is to be more social legislation or less, more collectivization or somewhat more play for private enterprise, more dependence on an international system of security or more self-sufficiency and relative isolation, and so forth. They decide these issues, not one at a time but by voting for an administration favorable to one or another "platform." They decide them partly—and in the last resort—at the polls, and partly by the continuously manifested indications of public sentiment. To make decisions easier there is in every community a sense of alternative directions, marked respectively left and right, and a sway of opinion in one or the other direction. . . .

This incessant activity of popular opinion is the dynamic of democracy. It decides between the larger alternatives of policy-making and in that way has an impact on a thousand issues. Mr. Lippmann, in the book referred to, was clearly off the beam when he suggested that it is not the business of the public to decide the substantive policies of government but merely to see that the government abides by the rules, like a referee who watches the players but takes no part in the game. The great changes in the socio-economic policies of Western European countries in the nineteenth and twentieth centuries—the whole trend toward social legislation and the control of economic power—were due to the swelling currents of public opinion, responsive to changing conditions. Or we may cite the more recent experience of the United States, where a new manifestation of public opinion, opposed by most of the prestige-bearers and of the well-to-do, carried to power and maintained in power the party of the "New Deal."

That is how the citizens of a democracy make their citizenship effective. Not as individuals deciding for themselves the successive problems of politics, each in speculative detachment registering his opinion on every issue. Not merely as units casting their separate votes every few years as election time comes round—the citizens of a democracy are *continuously* engaged in a massive give-and-take of creative opinion-making. Certainly not as experts who must willy-nilly do the job of the administration, that is, by finding the answers to the very specific questions that the administration must face from day to day. No business is run that way, and no government can be. Executive jobs are for executives, whether in business or in government. The public—or the workers or the shareholders—may very well entertain an opinion on whether the management is doing well or badly, but that is a different matter altogether.

We observe in passing that in a democracy there are two stages of decision-making before the *proper* job of the expert begins. First, there is the primary function of policy-making, the choice between directions, the function of the people. Second, there is the delineation of policy by the legislators and the heads of the government—in accordance with the "mandate" thus entrusted to them. Third, there is the implementation of policy. At this third stage the expert finds his place. It is here, and here alone, that he belongs. He is the technician or the craftsman in the art of government.

It is an eminently logical system. The representatives of the people have the authority. They are presumably—they always become at least—more conversant with the ways of governing than are the lay citizens, but they are not experts. They mark out the lines of advance and the experts build the roads. The logic is admirable, but as in all human affairs it is subject to distortion. These three functions are not clear-cut and separable in practice. The limits of each in relation to the others must be discretionary and flexible. Which means also that there may be conflict, confusion, and encroachment between the participants. The legislator may not let the expert do his proper job or, more commonly, he permits the expert to follow his own devices into the area of policy-making. The cabinet officers may ignore the spirit of their mandate, particularly in the screened-off sector of foreign policy. The expert may become a worshipper of routine, a jealous guardian of the secrets of office, a bureaucrat in the less honorable sense of the word.

Such things happen everywhere, and perhaps there is no safeguard except the vigilance of the public, as it becomes better educated in the ways of democracy and armed with fuller knowledge of its practical operation. What indeed appears throughout, as we study democracy at work, is that the defects and shortcomings it exhibits are due not to any inherent weakness in its principle but to the greater responsibilities it imposes on those who carry it out. These responsibilities are in themselves reasonable and never excessive, but interest and pride and office are always at hand, to deflect, to distort, and to betray. The ever-active democratic process checks these tendencies. How effectively it does so is in the keeping of the public, who have the authority and the means to control those whom they entrust with the business of governing. . . .

Democracy and Free Expression

Democracy constitutionally guarantees certain fundamental rights to all citizens. Apart from these rights—the right to think and believe after one's own mind and heart, the right to express one's opinions and to organize for their furtherance, the right to vote according to one's opinions, and so forth—democracy cannot exist. But the rights in question are not the same thing as a form of government. They may properly be made a *test* of its existence but they do not constitute it. . . . Now then we must ask: what kind of order is it that can *constitutionally* assure these rights? We find that both historically and logically it is an order that, to establish the right of opinion, gives free opinion itself a politically creative role. In other words, the government must be dependent on, and responsive to, the changes of public opinion. More closely, each successive administration is voted into office by an election or series of elections at which the people freely express their effective preference for one group of candidates over another group or other groups. In order that this process may be constitutionally possible the law must bind the relations of men in the areas to which it applies but must not bind their opinions in any areas. (We shall not pause here to examine the apparent but not genuine exceptions to this principle that fall under laws relating to libel, slander, incitement to violence, and so forth.) In a democracy those who oppose the policies of the government lose no civil rights and those who support its policies acquire thereby no civil rights. In a democracy minority opinion remains as untrammeled as majority opinion.

The importance of the creative role assigned to public opinion under democracy lies primarily in the fact that if opinion is free then the whole cultural life of man is free. If opinion is free, then belief is free and science is free and art and philosophy and all the variant styles and modes in which men manifest and develop their values and tastes and ways of living—always up to the limit where they endeavor by oppression or violence to deprive their fellowmen of these same prerogatives. Democracy alone assures the citadel of human personality against the deadly invasions of power. If only we could comprehend what this means we would never let our disappointments with the defects and weaknesses that the workings of democracy may reveal blind us to the intrinsic superiority of democracy over all other systems of government. . . .

*"Political" and "Economic" Democracy**

Some recent writers draw a distinction between "political democracy" and "economic democracy." They regard "economic democracy" as either the complement or the fulfillment of "political democracy." Sometimes they treat "political democracy" as less important than "economic democracy." Not infrequently they refer to the Soviet system as embodying this superior form of democracy. Mr. Harold Laski, who follows this line, writes: "If the hypothesis of self-government is valid in the political sphere it must be valid in the economic sphere also." Now when Mr. Laski speaks of "economic democracy" he is not speaking of *democracy* in any sense. He does not mean that the workers should elect by ballot the managers and the executive boards of industrial corporations or banks and decide what policies they should pursue in the conduct of their business. He certainly can offer no evidence that these democratic procedures are applied in Soviet Russia. Moreover, the economic program he is concerned about is one he wants the state to implement. His program is a *political* one. He wants democratic countries to adopt a collectivist system. But he should not identify a collectivist system with democracy, whether "economic" or "political." A democracy may approve a collectivist program or may reject it. It is still a democracy, and either way it is taking action "in the economic sphere." "The economic sphere" can never be separated from "the political sphere." What policy a democracy follows in this sphere depends on the conditions, and immediately on public opinion.

Mr. Laski, like many others, is apt to identify democracy with the things he would like democracy to do. In some of his writings he suggests that if a democracy should adopt a "revolutionary" socialist program it might meet such resistance from the propertied classes that democracy itself would come to an end and dictatorship take its place. It is indeed possible, but where the democratic spirit prevails, as in England, the United States, the self-governing British Dominions, and the Scandinavian countries, it seeks to avoid such drastic alternatives; it prefers to move to its goals by steps, not by one convulsive act. The point, however, is that should such a convulsion take place Mr. Laski's socialist

* R. M. MacIver, *The Web of Government* (New York, The Macmillan Co., 1947), pp. 206-208. By permission.

program would be achieved at the price of democracy. Nor could it reasonably be argued that "economic democracy" had taken the place of "political democracy." There might be greater economic equality, but we have no ground, either in logic or in history, for assuming that collectivist equality, arrived at on such terms, would become the boon companion of democracy.

JOSEPH A. SCHUMPETER
Competition for Political Leadership

Our chief troubles about the classical theory [of democracy]* center in the proposition that "the people" hold a definite and rational opinion about every individual question and that they give effect to this opinion—in a democracy—by choosing "representatives" who will see to it that that opinion is carried out. Thus the selection of the representatives is made secondary to the primary purpose of the democratic arrangement which is to vest the power of deciding political issues in the electorate. Suppose we reverse the roles of these two elements and make the deciding of issues by the electorate secondary to the election of the men who are to do the deciding. To put it differently, we now take the view that the role of the people is to produce a government, or else an intermediate body which in turn will produce a national executive or government. And we define: *the democratic method is that institutional arrangement for arriving at political decisions in which individuals acquire the power to decide by means of a competitive struggle for the people's vote.*

Defense and explanation of this idea will speedily show that, as to both plausibility of assumptions and tenability of propositions, it greatly improves the theory of the democratic process.

First of all, we are provided with a reasonably efficient criterion by which to distinguish democratic governments from others. . . . The classical theory meets with difficulties on that score because both the will and the good of the people may be, and in many historical instances have been, served just as well or better by governments that cannot be described as democratic according to any accepted usage of the term. Now we are in a somewhat better position partly because we are resolved to stress a *modus procedendi* the presence or absence of which it is in most cases easy to verify.[1]

For instance, a parliamentary monarchy like the English one fulfills the requirements of the democratic method because the monarch is practically constrained to appoint to cabinet office the same people as parliament would elect. A "constitutional" monarchy does not qualify to be called democratic because

Late Professor of Economics at Harvard University. Former Austrian Minister of Finance. Author of *The Theory of Economic Development, Business Cycles, Imperialism and Social Classes.* The selection is from *Capitalism, Socialism, and Democracy,* 3rd ed. (New York, Harper & Brothers, 1950), pp. 269-273. By permission.
* The author defines the classical theory of democracy as ". . . that institutional arrangement for arriving at political decisions which realizes the common good by making the people itself decide issues through the election of individuals who are to assemble to carry out its will." [Eds.]
[1] See however the fourth point below.

electorates and parliaments, while having all the other rights that electorates and parliaments have in parliamentary monarchies, lack the power to impose their choice as to the governing committee: the cabinet ministers are in this case servants of the monarch, in substance as well as in name, and can in principle be dismissed as well as appointed by him. Such an arrangement may satisfy the people. The electorate may reaffirm this fact by voting against any proposal for change. The monarch may be so popular as to be able to defeat any competition for the supreme office. But since no machinery is provided for making this competition effective the case does not come within our definition.

Second, the theory embodied in this definition leaves all the room we may wish to have for a proper recognition of the vital fact of leadership. The classical theory did not do this but attributed to the electorate an altogether unrealistic degree of initiative which practically amounted to ignoring leadership. But collectives act almost exclusively by accepting leadership—this is the dominant mechanism of practically any collective action which is more than a reflex. Propositions about the working and the results of the democratic method that take account of this are bound to be infinitely more realistic than propositions which do not. . . .

Third, however, so far as there are genuine group-wise volitions at all—for instance the will of the unemployed to receive unemployment benefit or the will of other groups to help—our theory does not neglect them. On the contrary we are now able to insert them in exactly the role they actually play. Such volitions do not as a rule assert themselves directly. Even if strong and definite they remain latent, often for decades, until they are called to life by some political leader who turns them into political factors. This he does, or else his agents do it for him, by organizing these volitions, by working them up and by including eventually appropriate items in his competitive offering. The interaction between sectional interests and public opinion and the way in which they produce the pattern we call the political situation appear from this angle in a new and much clearer light.

Fourth, our theory is of course no more definite than is the concept of competition for leadership. This concept presents similar difficulties as the concept of competition in the economic sphere, with which it may be usefully compared. In economic life competition is never completely lacking, but hardly ever is it perfect. Similarly, in political life there is always some competition, though perhaps only a potential one, for the allegiance of the people. To simplify matters we have restricted the kind of competition for leadership which is to define democracy to free competition for a free vote. The justification for this is that democracy seems to imply a recognized method by which to conduct the competitive struggle, and that the electoral method is practically the only one available for communities of any size. But though this excludes many ways of securing leadership which should be excluded,[2] such as competition by military in-

[2] It also excludes methods which should not be excluded, for instance, the acquisition of political leadership by the people's tacit acceptance of it or by election *quasi per inspirationem*. The latter differs from election by voting only by a technicality. But the former is not quite without importance even in modern politics; the sway held by a party boss *within his party* is often based on nothing but tacit acceptance of his leadership. Comparatively speaking, however, these are details which may, I think, be neglected in a sketch like this.

surrection, it does not exclude the cases that are strikingly analogous to the economic phenomena we label "unfair" or "fraudulent" competition or restraint of competition. And we cannot exclude them because if we did we should be left with a completely unrealistic ideal.[3] Between this ideal case which does not exist and the cases in which all competition with the established leader is prevented by force, there is a continuous range of variations within which the democratic method of government shades off into the autocratic one by imperceptible steps. But if we wish to understand and not to philosophize, this is as it should be. The value of our criterion is not seriously impaired thereby.

Fifth, our theory seems to clarify the relation that subsists between democracy and individual freedom. If by the latter we mean the existence of a sphere of individual self-government the boundaries of which are historically variable— *no* society tolerates absolute freedom even of conscience and of speech, *no* society reduces that sphere to zero—the question clearly becomes a matter of degree. We [believe] that the democratic method does not necessarily guarantee a greater amount of individual freedom than another political method would permit in similar circumstances. It may well be the other way round. But there is still a relation between the two. If, on principle at least, everyone is free to compete for political leadership[4] by presenting himself to the electorate, this will in most cases though not in all mean a considerable amount of freedom of discussion *for all*. In particular it will normally mean a considerable amount of freedom of the press. This relation between democracy and freedom is not absolutely stringent and can be tampered with. But, from the standpoint of the intellectual, it is nevertheless very important. At the same time, it is all there is to that relation.

Sixth, it should be observed that in making it the primary function of the electorate to produce a government (directly or through an intermediate body) I intended to include in this phrase also the function of evicting it. The one means simply the acceptance of a leader or a group of leaders, the other means simply the withdrawal of this acceptance. This takes care of an element the reader may have missed. He may have thought that the electorate controls as well as installs. But since electorates normally do not control their political leaders in any way except by refusing to reelect them or the parliamentary majorities that support them, it seems well to reduce our ideas about this control in the way indcated by our definition. Occasionally, spontaneous revulsions occur which upset a government or an individual minister directly or else enforce a certain course of action. But they are not only exceptional, they are, as we [believe], contrary to the spirit of the democratic method.

Seventh, our theory sheds much-needed light on an old controversy. Whoever accepts the classical doctrine of democracy and in consequence believes that the democratic method is to guarantee that issues be decided and policies framed according to the will of the people must be struck by the fact that, even if that will were undeniably real and definite, decision by simple majorities would in many cases distort it rather than give effect to it. Evidently the will

---

[3] As in the economic field, *some* restrictions are implicit in the legal and moral principles of the community.

[4] Free, that is, in the same sense in which everyone is free to start another textile mill.

of the majority is the will of the majority and not the will of "the people." The latter is a mosaic that the former completely fails to "represent." To equate both by definition is not to solve the problem. Attempts at real solutions have however been made by the authors of the various plans for Proportional Representation.

These plans have met with adverse criticism on practical grounds. It is in fact obvious not only that proportional representation will offer opportunities for all sorts of idiosyncrasies to assert themselves but also that it may prevent democracy from producing efficient governments and thus prove a danger in times of stress.[5] But before concluding that democracy becomes unworkable if its principle is carried out consistently, it is just as well to ask ourselves whether this principle really implies proportional representation. As a matter of fact it does not. If acceptance of leadership is the true function of the electorate's vote, the case for proportional representation collapses because its premises are no longer binding. The principle of democracy then merely means that the reins of government should be handed to those who command more support than do any of the competing individuals or teams. And this in turn seems to assure the standing of the majority system within the logic of the democratic method, although we might still condemn it on grounds that lie outside of that logic.

[5] The argument against proportional representation has been ably stated by Professor F. A. Hermens in "The Trojan Horse of Democracy," *Social Research* (November, 1938).

❧Section II

SOME FUNDAMENTAL
CONSTITUTIONAL
PRINCIPLES

The Constitutional Convention of 1787 met behind closed doors and very early adopted a rule "that nothing spoken in the House be printed, or otherwise published, or communicated without leave." This made it possible for the Framers to speak with greater frankness than one would find in speeches intended for the general public. The debates over suffrage, the term of office, and method of electing congressmen reveal the attitude of the Founding Fathers toward democracy and representative government.

Apart from Benjamin Franklin, few members of the Convention had the great faith in the ultimate wisdom of the people which was characteristic of Jefferson. Many delegates made reference to their assumption that men in politics were usually motivated by self-interest and ambition. Although accepting Hamilton's dictum that "Real liberty is neither found in despotism or the extremes of democracy, but in moderate governments," they rejected, however, Hamilton's conclusion that "the rich and well born" should be given a permanent check on the turbulence and follies of democracy.

While it is something of an exaggeration to call Madison "the Father of the Constitution," it is certainly true that among the delegates he was the most widely read and profound student of political institutions. No other member contributed more to the success of the Convention. "The principal task of modern legislation," said Madison, "is the regulation of the various and conflicting economic interests." Assuming that "justice" should be the aim of government, Madison concluded that since human beings are most likely to be biased by self-interest, no body of men should be allowed to judge in its own cause. In writing to Jefferson about the Constitution, Madison asked: "If two individuals are under the bias of interest or enmity against a third, the rights of the latter could never be safely referred to the majority of the three. Will two thousand individuals be less apt to oppress one thousand, or two hundred thousand one hundred thousand?" Madison's answer to this question was the same

27

as that given later by de Tocqueville and Lippmann—that in a completely democratic form of government the civil rights and the economic interests of the minority would be at the mercy of the majority. Jefferson's greater faith in the majority is supported by Commager's "In Defense of Majority Rule."

Although the American Constitution has been changed by amendments and modified by more than a century and a half of political practice, it still embodies, to a considerable extent, the philosophy of the Founding Fathers. The great object of the Constitution, said Madison in Number 10 of *The Federalist,* is to secure the public good and private rights against the power of popular majorities "and at the same time preserve the spirit and form of popular government." The ideal of Madison was representative government which would, to a much greater extent than under the Articles of Confederation, be independent of the people and yet sufficiently controlled by the people so that it would not serve the interests of the representatives at the expense of general welfare.

Debates in the Constitutional Convention of 1787

Debate on the House of Representatives

> *Resolution: 4. first clause; "that the members of the first branch of the National Legislature ought to be elected by the people of the several states."* [under consideration]

Mr. Sherman [Roger Sherman of Connecticut] opposed the election by the people, insisting that it ought to be by the State Legislatures. The people, he said, immediately should have as little to do as may be about the Government. They want information and are constantly liable to be misled.

Mr. Gerry [Elbridge Gerry of Massachusetts].* The evils we experience flow from the excess of democracy. The people do not want virtue; but are the dupes of pretended patriots. In Massachusetts it has been fully confirmed by experience that they are daily misled into the most baneful measures and opinions by the false reports circulated by designing men, and which no one on the spot can refute. One principal evil arises from the want of due provision for those employed in the administration of Government. It would seem to be a maxim of democracy to starve the public servants. He mentioned the popular clamor in Massachusetts for the reduction of salaries and the attack made on that of the Governor though secured by the spirit of the Constitution itself. He had he said been too republican heretofore: he was still however republican, but had been taught by experience the danger of the levelling spirit.

Mr. Mason [George Mason of Virginia, author of the Virginia Declaration of Rights]† argued strongly for an election of the larger branch by the people. It was to be the grand depository of the democratic principle of the Government. It was, so to speak, to be our House of Commons—It ought to know and

This selection is taken from James Madison's Journal of the Debates as reprinted in Max Farrand, ed., *Records of the Federal Convention* (New Haven, Yale University Press, 1927), Vol. I, pp. 48-50. By permission of Yale University Press. The Journal of the Debates was originally published in 1840, after all the members of the Convention had died, as part of *The Papers of James Madison*. Farrand's notations indicating additions and corrections made by Madison in his manuscript in later years have been omitted. The spelling has been modernized and most abbreviations spelled out.

* Gerry refused to sign the Constitution and opposed its adoption. [Eds.]

† Mason also refused to sign the Constitution and opposed its adoption. [Eds.]

sympathize with every part of the community; and ought therefore to be taken not only from different parts of the whole republic, but also from different districts of the larger members of it, which had in several instances particularly in Virginia, different interests and views arising from difference of produce, of habits &c. &c.

He admitted that we had been too democratic but was afraid we should incautiously run into the opposite extreme. We ought to attend to the rights of every class of the people. He had often wondered at the indifference of the superior classes of society to this dictate of humanity and policy, considering that however affluent their circumstances, or elevated their situations, might be, the course of a few years, not only might but certainly would distribute their posterity throughout the lowest classes of Society. Every selfish motive therefore, every family attachment, ought to recommend such a system of policy as would provide no less carefully for the rights—and happiness of the lowest than of the highest orders of Citizens.

Mr. Wilson [James Wilson of Pennsylvania, member of the first Supreme Court] contended strenuously for drawing the most numerous branch of the Legislature immediately from the people. He was for raising the federal pyramid to a considerable altitude, and for that reason wished to give it as broad a basis as possible. No government could long subsist without the confidence of the people. In a republican Government this confidence was peculiarly essential. He also thought it wrong to increase the weight of the State Legislatures by making them the electors of the national Legislature. All interference between the general and local Governments should be obviated as much as possible. On examination it would be found that the opposition of States to federal measures had proceeded much more from the Officers of the States, than from the people at large.

Mr. Madison [James Madison of Virginia] considered the popular election of one branch of the national Legislature as essential to every plan of free Government. He observed that in some of the States one branch of the Legislature was composed of men already removed from the people by an intervening body of electors. That if the first branch of the general legislature should be elected by the State Legislatures, the second branch elected by the first—the Executive by the second together with the first; and other appointments again made for subordinate purposes by the Executive, the people would be lost sight of altogether; and the necessary sympathy between them and their rulers and officers, too little felt. He was an advocate for the policy of refining the popular appointments by successive filtrations, but thought it might be pushed too far. He wished the expedient to be resorted to only in the appointment of the second branch of the Legislature, and in the Executive and Judiciary branches of the Government. He thought too that the great fabric to be raised would be more stable and durable if it should rest on the solid foundation of the people themselves, than if it should stand merely on the pillars of the Legislatures.

Mr. Gerry did not like the election by the people. The maxims taken from the British constitution were often fallacious when applied to our situation which was extremely different. Experience he said had shown that the State Legislatures drawn immediately from the people did not always possess their confidence. He had no objection however to an election by the people if it were so qualified that men of honor and character might not be unwilling to be joined in the appointments. He seemed to think that the people might nominate a certain number out of which the State Legislatures should be bound to choose.

Mr. Butler [Pierce Butler of South Carolina] thought an election by the people an impracticable mode.

On the question for an election of the first branch of the national Legislature, by the people; Massachusetts aye, Connecticut divided, New York aye, New Jersey no, Pennsylvania aye, Delaware divided, Virginia aye, North Carolina aye, South Carolina no, Georgia aye. (Ayes—6; noes—2; divided—2.)

Hamilton's Plan for the Constitution
Monday, June 18, In Committee of the Whole

On motion of Mr. Dickinson to postpone the first Resolution in Mr. Patterson's plan, [New Jersey Plan] in order to take up the following, viz: *"that the articles of confederation ought to be revised and amended so as to render the Government of the U.S. adequate to the exigencies, the preservation and the prosperity of the union."* The postponement was agreed to by 10 States, Pennsylvania divided.

Mr. Hamilton. [Alexander Hamilton of New York] Yet, I confess, I see great difficulty of drawing forth a good representation. What, for example, will be the inducements for gentlemen of fortune and abilities to leave their houses and business to attend annually and long? It cannot be the wages; for these, I presume, must be small. Will not the power, therefore, be thrown into the hands of the demagogue or middling politician, who, for the sake of a small stipend and the hopes of advancement, will offer himself as a candidate, and the real men of weight and influence, by remaining at home, add strength to the state governments?

I am at a loss to know what must be done—I despair that a republican form of government can remove the difficulties. Whatever may be my opinion, I would hold it however unwise to change that form of government. I believe the British government forms the best model the world ever produced, and such has been its progress in the minds of the many, that this truth gradually gains ground. This government has for its object *public strength* and *individual security*. It is said with us to be unattainable. If it was once formed it would maintain itself.

All communities divide themselves into the few and the many. The first

The selections from Hamilton's speech originally appeared in *Secret Proceedings and Debates of the Convention Assembled at Philadelphia, in the year 1787, for the purpose of forming the Constitution of the United States of America. From Notes taken by the late Robert Yates, Esq. Chief Justice of New York, and copied by John Lansing, Jun, Esq.* Reprinted in Farrand, *Records,* Vol. I, pp. 298-301. Farrand's *Records* contain three other versions of Hamilton's speech. The first paragraph below is from Madison's Journal as reprinted in Farrand, *Records,* Vol. I, p. 282.

are the rich and well born, the other the mass of the people. The voice of the people has been said to be the voice of God; and however generally this maxim has been quoted and believed, it is not true in fact. The people are turbulent and changing; they seldom judge or determine right. Give therefore to the first class a distinct, permanent share in the government. They will check the unsteadiness of the second, and as they cannot receive any advantage by a change, they therefore will ever maintain good government. Can a democratic assembly, who annually revolve in the mass of the people, be supposed steadily to pursue the public good? Nothing but a permanent body can check the imprudence of democracy. Their turbulent and uncontrolling disposition requires checks.

The senate of New York, although chosen for four years, we found to be inefficient. Will, on the Virginia plan, a continuance of seven years do it? It is admitted that you cannot have a good executive upon a democratic plan. See the excellency of the British executive— He is placed above temptation— He can have no distinct interests from the public welfare. Nothing short of such an executive can be efficient. The weak side of a republican government is the danger of foreign influence. This is unavoidable, unless it is so constructed as to bring forward its first characters in its support. I am therefore for a general government, yet would wish to go the full length of republican principles.

Let one body of the legislature be constituted during good behavior or life.

Let one executive be appointed who dares execute his powers. It may be asked is this a republican system? It is strictly so, as long as they remain elective.

And let me observe, that an executive is less dangerous to the liberties of the people when in office during life, than for seven years.

It may be said this constitutes an elective monarchy? Pray what is a monarchy? May not the governors of the respective states be considered in that light? But by making the executive subject to impeachment, the term monarchy cannot apply. These elective monarchs have produced tumults in Rome, and are equally dangerous to peace in Poland; but this cannot apply to the mode in which I would propose the election. Let electors be appointed in each of the states to elect the executive.

[Yates' notes indicate that here Hamilton produced his plan for the federal "legislature"] to consist of two branches—and I would give them the unlimited power of passing *all laws* without exception. The assembly to be elected for three years by the people in districts—the senate to be elected by electors to be chosen for that purpose by the people, and to remain in office during life. The executive to have the power of negativing all laws—to make war or peace, with the advice of the senate—to make treaties with their advice, but to have the sole direction of all military operations, and to send ambassadors and appoint all military officers, and to pardon all offenders, treason excepted, unless by advice of the senate. On his death or removal, the president of the senate to officiate, with the same powers, until another is elected. Supreme judicial officers to be appointed by the executive and the senate. The legislature to appoint courts in each state, so as to make the state governments unnecessary to it.

All state laws to be absolutely void which contravene the general laws. An officer to be appointed in each state to have a negative on all state laws. All the militia and the appointment of officers to be under the national government.

I confess that this plan and that from Virginia are very remote from the idea of the people. Perhaps the Jersey plan is nearest their expectation. But the people are gradually ripening in their opinions of government—they begin to be tired of an excess of democracy—and what even is the Virginia plan, but *pork still, with a little change of the sauce.*

Debate on the Senate
Tuesday, June 26, In Convention

The duration of the second branch under consideration.

Mr. Gorham [Nathaniel Gorham of Massachusetts] moved to fill the blank with "six years," one third of the members to go out every second year.
Mr. Wilson seconded the motion. . . .
Mr. Madison. In order to judge of the form to be given to this institution, it will be proper to take a view of the ends to be served by it. These were first to protect the people against their rulers: secondly to protect [the people] against the transient impressions into which they themselves might be led. A people deliberating in a temperate moment, and with the experience of other nations before them, on the plan of Government most likely to secure their happiness, would first be aware, that those charged with the public happiness, might betray their trust. An obvious precaution against this danger would be to divide the trust between different bodies of men, who might watch and check each other. In this they would be governed by the same prudence which has prevailed in organizing the subordinate departments of Government where all business liable to abuses is made to pass through separate hands, the one being a check on the other.

It would next occur to such a people, that they themselves were liable to temporary errors, through want of information as to their true interest, and that men chosen for a short term, and employed but a small portion of that in public affairs, might err from the same cause. This reflection would naturally suggest that the Government be so constituted, as that one of its branches might have an opportunity of acquiring a competent knowledge of the public interests. Another reflection equally becoming a people on such an occasion, would be that they themselves, as well as a numerous body of Representatives, were liable to err also, from fickleness and passion. A necessary fence against this danger would be to select a portion of enlightened citizens, whose limited number, and firmness might seasonably interpose against impetuous counsels. It ought finally to occur to a people deliberating on a Government for themselves, that as different interests necessarily result from the liberty meant to be secured, the major interest might under sudden impulses be tempted to commit injustice on the minority. In all civilized Countries the people fall into different classes having a real or supposed difference of interests. There will be creditors and debtors,

The following extracts from Madison's Journal of the Debates are reprinted from Farrand, *Records,* Vol. I, pp. 421-426.

farmers, merchants and manufacturers. There will be particularly the distinction of rich and poor. It was true as had been observed (by Mr. Pinckney) we had not among us those hereditary distinctions of rank which were a great source of contests in the ancient Governments as well as the modern States of Europe, nor those extremes of wealth or poverty which characterize the latter.

We cannot, however, be regarded even at this time, as one homogeneous mass, in which everything that affects a part will affect in the same manner the whole. In framing a system which we wish to last for ages, we should not lose sight of the changes which ages will produce. An increase of population will of necessity increase the proportion of those who will labor under all the hardships of life, and secretly sigh for a more equal distribution of its blessings. These may in time outnumber those who are placed above the feelings of indigence. According to the equal laws of suffrage, the power will slide into the hands of the former. No agrarian attempts have yet been made in this Country, but symptoms of a leveling spirit, as we have understood, have sufficiently appeared in certain quarters to give notice of the future danger.

How is this danger to be guarded against on republican principles? How is the danger in all cases of interested coalitions to oppress the minority to be guarded against? Among other means by the establishment of a body in the Government sufficiently respectable for its wisdom and virtue, to aid, on such emergencies, the preponderance of justice by throwing its weight into the scale. Such being the objects of the second branch in the proposed Government he thought a considerable duration ought to be given to it. He did not conceive that the term of nine years could threaten any real danger; but in pursuing his particular ideas on the subject, he should require that the long term allowed to the 2d. branch should not commence till such a period of life as would render a perpetual disqualification to be re-elected little inconvenient either in a public or private view. He observed that as it was more than probable we were now digesting a plan which in its operation would decide forever the fate of Republican Government we ought not only to provide every guard to liberty that its preservation could require, but be equally careful to supply the defects which our own experience had particularly pointed out.

Mr. Sherman. Government is instituted for those who live under it. It ought therefore to be so constituted as not to be dangerous to their liberties. The more permanency it has the worse if it be a bad Government. Frequent elections are necessary to preserve the good behavior of rulers. They also tend to give permanency to the Government, by preserving that good behavior, because it ensures their re-election. In Connecticut elections have been very frequent, yet great stability and uniformity both as to persons and measures have been experienced from its original establishment, to the present time; a period of more than 130 years. He wished to have provisions made for steadiness and wisdom in the system to be adopted; but he thought six or four years would be sufficient. He should be content with either. . . .

Mr. Gerry wished we could be united in our ideas concerning a permanent Government. All aim at the same end, but there are great differences as to the means. One circumstance He thought should be carefully attended to. There were not 1/1000 part of our fellow citizens who were not against every approach toward Monarchy. Will they ever agree to a plan which seems to make such an approach? The Convention ought to be extremely cautious in what they hold out to the people. Whatever plan may be proposed will be espoused with warmth by many out of respect to the quarter it proceeds from as well as from an approbation of the plan itself. And if the plan should be of such a nature as to rouse a violent opposition, it is easy to foresee that discord and confusion will ensue, and it is even possible that we may become a prey to foreign powers.

He did not deny the position of Mr. Madison that the majority will generally violate justice when they have an interest in so doing; but did not think there was any such temptation in this Country. Our situation was different from that of Great Britain: and the great body of lands yet to be parcelled out and settled would very much prolong the difference. Notwithstanding the symptoms of injustice which had marked many of our public Councils, they had not proceeded so far as not to leave hopes, that there would be a sufficient sense of justice and virtue for the purpose of Government. He admitted the evils arising from a frequency of elections: and would agree to give the Senate a duration of four or five years. A longer term would defeat itself. It never would be adopted by the people. . . .

On the question for 9 years; ⅓ to go out triennially: Massachusetts no, Connecticut no, New York no, New Jersey no, Pennsylvania aye, Delaware aye, Maryland no, Virginia aye, North Carolina no, South Carolina no, Georgia no. (Ayes—3; noes—8.)

On the question for 6 years; ⅓ to go out biennially: Massachusetts aye, Connecticut aye, New York no, New Jersey no, Pennsylvania aye, Delaware aye, Maryland aye, Virginia aye, North Carolina aye, South Carolina no, Georgia no. (Ayes—7; noes—4.)

Debate on Suffrage
Tuesday, August 7th, In Convention

Article IV. Section 1. (Constitution) taken up.

Article IV, Section 1. "The members of the House of Representatives shall be chosen every second year, by the people of the several States comprehended within this Union. The qualifications of the electors shall be the same, from time to time, as those of the electors in the several States, of the most numerous branch of their own legislatures."

Mr. Gouverneur Morris [of Pennsylvania] moved to strike out the last member of the section beginning with the words "qualifications" of "Electors" in order that some other provision might be substituted which would restrain the right of suffrage to freeholders.

Mr. Fitzsimmons [Thomas Fitzsimmons of Pennsylvania] seconded the motion.

The following extracts from Madison's Journal of the Debates are reprinted from Farrand, *Records*, Vol. II, pp. 201-206.

Mr. Williamson [Hugh Williamson of North Carolina] was opposed to it.

Mr. Wilson. This part of the Report was well considered by the Committee, and he did not think it could be changed for the better. It was difficult to form any uniform rule of qualifications for all the States. Unnecessary innovations he thought too should be avoided. It would be very hard and disagreeable for the same persons, at the same time, to vote for representatives in the State Legislature and to be excluded from a vote for those in the National Legislature. . . .

Col. Mason. The force of habit is certainly not attended to by those gentlemen who wish for innovations on this point. Eight or nine States have extended the right of suffrage beyond the freeholders. What will the people there say, if they should be disfranchised? A power to alter the qualifications would be a dangerous power in the hands of the Legislature. . . .

Mr. Dickinson [John Dickinson of Delaware] had a very different idea of the tendency of vesting the right of suffrage in the freeholders of the Country. He considered them as the best guardians of liberty; and the restriction of the right to them as a necessary defense against the dangerous influence of those multitudes without property and without principle, with which our Country like all others, will in time abound. As to the unpopularity of the innovation it was in his opinion chimerical. The great mass of our Citizens is composed at this time of freeholders, and will be pleased with it.

Mr. Ellsworth [Oliver Ellsworth of Connecticut, Chief Justice of the United States 1796–1800]. How shall the freehold be defined? Ought not every man who pays a tax to vote for the representative who is to levy and dispose of his money? Shall the wealthy merchants and manufacturers, who will bear a full share of the public burdens be not allowed a voice in the imposition of them? Taxation and representation ought to go together.

Mr. Gouverneur Morris. He had long learned not to be the dupe of words. The sound of Aristocracy therefore, had no effect on him. It was the thing, not the name, to which he was opposed, and one of his principal objections to the Constitution as it is now before us, is that it threatens this Country with an Aristocracy. The aristocracy will grow out of the House of Representatives. Give the votes to people who have no property, and they will sell them to the rich who will be able to buy them. We should not confine our attention to the present moment. The time is not distant when this Country will abound with mechanics and manufacturers who will receive their bread from their employers. Will such men be the secure and faithful Guardians of liberty? Will they be the impregnable barrier against aristocracy?—He was as little duped by the association of the words, "Taxation and Representation"—The man who does not give his vote freely is not represented. It is the man who dictates the vote. Children do not vote. Why? Because they want prudence, because they have no will of their own. The ignorant and the dependent can be as little trusted with the public interest. He did not conceive the difficulty of defining "freeholders" to be insuperable. Still less that the restriction could be unpopular. $\frac{9}{10}$ of the people are at present freeholders and these will certainly be pleased with it. As to Merchants etc. if they have wealth and value the right they can acquire it. If not they don't deserve it.

Col. Mason. We all feel too strongly the remains of ancient prejudices, and view things too much through a British medium. A Freehold is the qualification in England, and hence it is imagined to be the only proper one. The true idea in his opinion was that every man having evidence of attachment to and permanent common interest with the Society ought to share in all its rights and privileges. Was this qualification restrained to freeholders? Does no other kind of property but land evidence a common interest in the proprietor? Does nothing besides property mark a permanent attachment? Ought the merchant, the monied man, the parent of a number of children whose fortunes are to be pursued in their own Country, to be viewed as suspicious characters, and unworthy to be trusted with the common rights of their fellow Citizens?

Mr. Madison. The right of suffrage is certainly one of the fundamental articles of republican Government, and ought not to be left to be regulated by the Legislature. A gradual abridgment of this right has been the mode in which Aristocracies have been built on the ruins of popular forms. Whether the Constitutional qualification ought to be a freehold would with him depend much on the probable reception such a change would meet with in States where the right was now exercised by every description of people. In several of the States a freehold was now the qualification. Viewing the subject in its merits alone, the freeholders of the Country would be the safest depositories of Republican liberty. In future times a great majority of the people will not only be without landed, but any other sort of property. These will either combine under the influence of their common situation; in which case, the rights of property and the public liberty, will not be secure in their hands; or which is more probable, they will become the tools of opulence and ambition, in which case there will be equal danger on another side. The example of England has been misconceived (by Col. Mason). A very small proportion of the Representatives are there chosen by freeholders. The greatest part are chosen by the Cities and boroughs, in many of which the qualification of suffrage is as low as it is in any one of the U.S. and it was in the boroughs and Cities rather than the Counties, that bribery most prevailed, and the influence of the Crown on elections was most dangerously exerted.

Doctor Franklin. [Benjamin Franklin of Pennsylvania] It is of great consequence that we should not depress the virtue and public spirit of our common people; of which they displayed a great deal during the war, and which contributed principally to the favorable issue of it. He related the honorable refusal of the American seamen who were carried in great numbers into the British Prisons during the war, to redeem themselves from misery or to seek their fortunes, by entering on board the Ships of the Enemies to their Country; contrasting their patriotism with a contemporary instance in which the British seamen made prisoners by the Americans, readily entered on the ships of the latter on being promised a share of the prizes that might be made out of their own Country. This proceeded, he said, from the different manner in which the common people were treated in America and Great Britain. He did not think that the elected had any right in any case to narrow the privileges of the electors. He quoted as arbitrary the British Statute setting forth the danger of tumultuous meetings, and under that pretext, narrowing the right of suffrage to persons having freeholds of a certain value; observing that this Statute was soon followed by another under the succeeding Parliament subjecting the people who had no votes to peculiar labors and hardships. He was persuaded also that such a restriction as was proposed would give great uneasiness in the populous States. The sons of a substantial farmer, not being themselves freeholders, would not be pleased at being disfranchised, and there are a great many persons of that description.

Mr. Mercer. [John Francis Mercer of Maryland] The Constitution is objectionable in many points, but in none more than the present. He objected to the footing on which the qualification was put, but particularly to the *mode of election* by the people. The people can not know and judge of the characters of Candidates. The worst possible choice will be made. He quoted the case of the Senate in Virginia as an example in point— The people in Towns can unite their votes in favor of one favorite; and by that means always prevail over the people of the Country, who being dispersed will scatter their votes among a variety of candidates.

Mr. Rutledge [John Rutledge of South Carolina] thought the idea of restraining the right of suffrage to the freeholders a very ill advised one. It would create division among the people and make enemies of all those who should be excluded.

On the question for striking out as moved by Mr. Gouverneur Morris, from the word "qualifications" to the end of article III: New Hampshire no, Massachusetts no, Connecticut no, Pennsylvania no, Delaware aye, Maryland divided, Virginia no, North Carolina no, South Carolina no, Georgia not present. (Ayes—1; noes—7 divided—1; absent 1.)

*◌◌◌◌*TOPIC 4

The Control of Majority "Factions"

JAMES MADISON
The Union as a Safeguard Against
Domestic Faction

Among the numerous advantages promised by a well-constructed Union, none deserves to be more accurately developed than its tendency to break and control the violence of faction. The friend of popular governments never finds himself so much alarmed for their character and fate, as when he contemplates their propensity to this dangerous vice. He will not fail, therefore, to set a due value on any plan which, without violating the principles to which he is attached, provides a proper cure for it. The instability, injustice, and confusion introduced into the public councils have, in truth, been the mortal diseases under which popular governments have everywhere perished; as they continue to be the favorite and fruitful topics from which the adversaries to liberty derive their most specious declamations.

The valuable improvements made by the American constitutions on the popular models, both ancient and modern, cannot certainly be too much admired; but it would be an unwarrantable partiality, to contend that they have as effectually obviated the danger on this side, as was wished and expected. Complaints are everywhere heard from our most considerate and virtuous citizens, equally the friends of public and private faith, and of public and personal liberty, that our governments are too unstable; that the public good is disregarded in the conflicts of rival parties; and that measures are too often decided, not according to the rules of justice, and the rights of the minor party, but by the superior force of an interested and overbearing majority. However anxiously we may wish that these complaints had no foundation, the evidence of known facts will not permit us to deny that they are in some degree true.

It will be found, indeed, on a candid review of our situation, that some of the distresses under which we labor have been erroneously charged on the operation of our governments; but it will be found, at the same time, that other causes will not alone account for many of our heaviest misfortunes; and, particularly, for that prevailing and increasing distrust of public engagements, and alarm for private rights, which are echoed from one end of the continent to the

The Federalist, No. 10.

39

other. These must be chiefly, if not wholly, effects of the unsteadiness and injustice with which a factious spirit has tainted our public administrations.

By a faction, I understand a number of citizens, whether amounting to a majority or a minority of the whole, who are united and actuated by some common impulse of passion, or of interest, adverse to the rights of other citizens, or to the permanent and aggregate interests of the community.

There are two methods of curing the mischiefs of faction: the one, by removing its causes; the other, by controlling its effects. There are again two methods of removing the causes of faction: the one, by destroying the liberty which is essential to its existence; the other, by giving to every citizen the same opinions, the same passions, and the same interests.

It could never be more truly said than of the first remedy, that it was worse than the disease. Liberty is to faction what air is to fire, an aliment without which it instantly expires. But it could not be less folly to abolish liberty, which is essential to political life, because it nourishes faction, than it would be to wish the annihilation of air, which is essential to animal life, because it imparts to fire its destructive agency.

The second expedient is as impracticable as the first would be unwise. As long as the reason of man continues fallible, and he is at liberty to exercise it, different opinions will be formed. As long as the connection subsists between his reason and his self-love, his opinions and his passions will have a reciprocal influence on each other; and the former will be objects to which the latter will attach themselves. The diversity in the faculties of men, from which the rights of property originate, is not less an insuperable obstacle to a uniformity of interests. The protection of these faculties is the first object of government. From the protection of different and unequal faculties of acquiring property, the possession of different degrees and kinds of property immediately results; and from the influence of these on the sentiments and views of the respective proprietors, ensues a division of the society into different interests and parties.

The latent causes of faction are thus sown in the nature of man; and we see them everywhere brought into different degrees of activity, according to the different circumstances of civil society. A zeal for different opinions concerning religion, concerning government, and many other points, as well of speculation as of practice; an attachment to different leaders ambitiously contending for pre-eminence and power; or to persons of other descriptions whose fortunes have been interesting to the human passions, have, in turn, divided mankind into parties, inflamed them with mutual animosity, and rendered them much more disposed to vex and oppress each other, than to co-operate for their common good. So strong is this propensity of mankind to fall into mutual animosities, that where no substantial occasion presents itself, the most frivolous and fanciful distinctions have been sufficient to kindle their unfriendly passions and excite their most violent conflicts. But the most common and durable source of factions has been the various and unequal distribution of property. Those who hold and those who are without property have ever formed distinct interests in society. Those who are creditors, and those who are debtors, fall under a like discrimination. A landed interest, a manufacturing interest, a mercantile interest, a moneyed interest, with many lesser interests, grow up of necessity in civilized nations, and divide them into different classes, actuated by different sentiments and views. The regulation of these various and interfering interests forms the principal task of modern legislation, and involves the spirit of party and faction in the necessary and ordinary operations of the government.

No man is allowed to be a judge in his own cause, because his interest would certainly bias his judgment and, not improbably, corrupt his integrity. With equal, nay, with greater reason, a body of men are unfit to be both judges and parties at the same time; yet what are many of the most important acts of legislation, but so many judicial determinations, not indeed concerning the rights of single persons, but concerning the rights of large bodies of citizens? And what are the different classes of legislators, but advocates and parties to the causes which they determine? Is a law proposed concerning private debts? It is a question to which the creditors are parties on one side and the debtors on the other. Justice ought to hold the balance between them. Yet the parties are, and must be, themselves the judges; and the most numerous party, or, in other words, the most powerful faction, must be expected to prevail. Shall domestic manu-facturers be encouraged, and in what degree, by restrictions on foreign manu-factures? are questions which would be differently decided by the landed and the manufacturing classes, and probably by neither with a sole regard to justice and the public good. The apportionment of taxes on the various descriptions of property is an act which seems to require the most exact impartiality; yet there is, perhaps, no legislative act in which greater opportunity and temptation are given to a predominant party, to trample on the rules of justice. Every shill-ing with which they overburden the inferior number, is a shilling saved to their own pockets.

It is in vain to say that enlightened statesmen will be able to adjust these clashing interests, and render them all subservient to the public good. Enlight-ened statesmen will not always be at the helm. Nor, in many cases, can such an adjustment be made at all, without taking into view indirect and remote con-siderations, which will rarely prevail over the immediate interest which one party may find in disregarding the rights of another or the good of the whole. The inference to which we are brought is, that the *causes* of faction cannot be removed, and that relief is only to be sought in the means of controlling its *effects*.

If a faction consists of less than a majority, relief is supplied by the repub-lican principle, which enables the majority to defeat its sinister views by regular vote. It may clog the administration, it may convulse the society; but it will be unable to execute and mask its violence under the forms of the Constitution. When a majority is included in a faction, the form of popular government, on the other hand, enables it to sacrifice to its ruling passion or interest both the public good and the rights of other citizens. To secure the public good and pri-vate rights against the danger of such a faction, and at the same time to preserve the spirit and the form of popular government, is then the great object to which our inquiries are directed. Let me add that it is the great desideratum, by which alone this form of government can be rescued from the opprobrium under which it has so long labored, and be recommended to the esteem and adoption of mankind.

By what means is this object attainable? Evidently by one of two only. Either the existence of the same passion or interest in a majority at the same time must be prevented; or the majority, having such coexisting passion or interest, must be rendered, by their number and local situation, unable to concert and carry into effect schemes of oppression. If the impulse and the opportunity be suffered to coincide, we well know that neither moral nor religious motives can be relied on as an adequate control. They are not found to be such on the injustice and violence of individuals, and lose their efficacy in proportion to the number combined together; that is, in proportion as their efficacy becomes needful.

From this view of the subject it may be concluded that a pure democracy, by which I mean a society consisting of a small number of citizens, who assemble and administer the government in person, can admit of no cure for the mischiefs of faction. A common passion or interest will, in almost every case, be felt by a majority of the whole; a communication and concert result from the form of government itself; and there is nothing to check the inducements to sacrifice the weaker party or an obnoxious individual. Hence it is that such democracies have ever been spectacles of turbulence and contention; have ever been found incompatible with personal security, or the rights of property; and have in general been as short in their lives as they have been violent in their deaths. Theoretic politicians, who have patronized this species of government, have erroneously supposed that by reducing mankind to a perfect equality in their political rights, they would at the same time be perfectly equalized and assimilated in their possessions, their opinions, and their passions.

A republic, by which I mean a government in which the scheme of representation takes place, opens a different prospect, and promises the cure for which we are seeking. Let us examine the points in which it varies from pure democracy, and we shall comprehend both the nature of the cure and the efficacy which it must derive from the Union.

The two great points of difference between a democracy and a republic are: first, the delegation of the government, in the latter, to a small number of citizens elected by the rest; secondly, the greater number of citizens, and greater sphere of country, over which the latter may be extended.

The effect of the first difference is, on the one hand, to refine and enlarge the public views, by passing them through the medium of a chosen body of citizens, whose wisdom may best discern the true interests of their country, and whose patriotism and love of justice will be least likely to sacrifice it to temporary or partial considerations. Under such a regulation, it may well happen that the public voice, pronounced by the representatives of the people, will be more consonant to the public good than if pronounced by the people themselves, convened for the purpose. On the other hand, the effect may be inverted. Men of factious tempers, of local prejudices, or of sinister designs, may, by intrigue, by corruption, or by other means, first obtain the suffrages, and then betray the interests of the people. The question resulting is, whether small or extensive republics are more favorable to the election of proper guardians of the public weal; and it is clearly decided in favor of the latter by two obvious considerations.

In the first place, it is to be remarked that, however small the republic may be, the representatives must be raised to a certain number, in order to guard against the cabals of a few; and that, however large it may be, they must be limited to a certain number, in order to guard against the confusion of a multitude. Hence, the number of representatives in the two cases not being in proportion to that of the two constituents, and being proportionally greater in the small republic, it follows that if the proportion of fit characters be not less in the large than in the small republic, the former will present a greater option, and consequently a greater probability of a fit choice.

In the next place, as each representative will be chosen by a greater number of citizens in the large than in the small republic, it will be more difficult for unworthy candidates to practice with success the vicious arts, by which elections are too often carried; and the suffrages of the people, being more free, will be more likely to centre in men who possess the most attractive merit and the most diffusive and established characters.

It must be confessed that in this as in most other cases, there is a mean, on both sides of which inconveniences will be found to lie. By enlarging too much the number of electors, you render the representative too little acquainted with all their local circumstances and lesser interests; as by reducing it too much, you render him unduly attached to these, and too little fit to comprehend and pursue great and national objects. The federal Constitution forms a happy combination in this respect; the great and aggregate interests being referred to the national, the local and particular to the State legislatures.

The other point of difference is, the greater number of citizens and extent of territory which may be brought within the compass of republican than of democratic government; and it is this circumstance principally which renders factious combinations less to be dreaded in the former than in the latter. The smaller the society, the fewer probably will be the distinct parties and interests composing it; the fewer the distinct parties and interests, the more frequently will a majority be found of the same party; and the smaller the number of individuals composing a majority, and the smaller the compass within which they are placed, the more easily will they concert and execute their plans of oppression. Extend the sphere, and you take in a greater variety of parties and interests; you make it less probable that a majority of the whole will have a common motive to invade the rights of other citizens; or if such a common motive exists, it will be more difficult for all who feel it to discover their own strength, and to act in unison with each other. Besides other impediments, it may be remarked that where there is a consciousness of unjust or dishonorable purposes, communication is always checked by distrust in proportion to the number whose concurrence is necessary.

Hence it clearly appears that the same advantage which a republic has over a democracy, in controlling the effects of faction, is enjoyed by a large over a small republic—is enjoyed by the Union over the States composing it. Does the advantage consist in the substitution of representatives, whose enlightened views and virtuous sentiments render them superior to local prejudices, and to schemes of injustice? It will not be denied that the representation of the Union will be most likely to possess these requisite endowments. Does it consist in the greater security afforded by a greater variety of parties, against the event of any one party being able to outnumber and oppress the rest? In an equal degree does the increased variety of parties, comprised within the Union, increase this security? Does it, in fine, consist in the greater obstacles opposed to the concert and accomplishment of the secret wishes of an unjust and interested majority? Here, again, the extent of the Union gives it the most palpable advantage.

The influence of factious leaders may kindle a flame within their particular States, but will be unable to spread a general conflagration through the other States. A religious sect may degenerate into a political faction in a part of the confederacy; but the variety of sects dispersed over the entire face of it must secure the national councils against any danger from that source. A rage for paper money, for an abolition of debts, for an equal division of property, or for any other improper or wicked project will be less apt to pervade the whole body of the Union than a particular member of it; in the same proportion as such a malady is more likely to taint a particular county or district, than an entire State.

In the extent and proper structure of the Union, therefore, we behold a republican remedy for the diseases most incident to republican government. And according to the degree of pleasure and pride we feel in being republicans, ought to be our zeal in cherishing the spirit and supporting the character of federalists.

PUBLIUS

"Since Angels Do Not Govern Men"

JAMES MADISON
Separation of Powers

One of the principal objections inculcated by the more respectable adversaries of the Constitution, is its supposed violation of the political maxim that the legislative, executive, and judiciary departments ought to be separate and distinct. In the structure of the federal government, no regard, it is said, seems to have been paid to this essential precaution in favor of liberty. The several departments of power are distributed and blended in such a manner as at once to destroy all symmetry and beauty of form, and to expose some of the essential parts of the edifice to the danger of being crushed by the disproportionate weight of other parts.

No political truth is certainly of greater intrinsic value, or is stamped with the authority of more enlightened patrons of liberty, than that on which the objection is founded. The accumulation of all powers, legislative, executive, and judiciary, in the same hands, whether of one, a few, or many, and whether hereditary, self-appointed, or elective, may justly be pronounced the very definition of tyranny. Were the federal Constitution, therefore, really chargeable with the accumulation of power, or with a mixture of powers, having a dangerous tendency to such an accumulation, no further arguments would be necessary to inspire a universal reprobation of the system. I persuade myself, however, that it will be made apparent to everyone that the charge cannot be supported, and that the maxim on which it relies has been totally misconceived and misapplied. In order to form correct ideas on this important subject, it will be proper to investigate the sense in which the preservation of liberty requires that the three great departments of power should be separate and distinct.

The oracle who is always consulted and cited on this subject is the celebrated Montesquieu. If he be not the author of this invaluable precept in the science of politics, he has the merit at least of displaying and recommending it most effectually to the attention of mankind. Let us endeavor, in the first place, to ascertain his meaning on this point.

The British Constitution was to Montesquieu what Homer has been to the didactic writers on epic poetry. As the latter have considered the work of the im-

The Federalist, No. 47. Many editions of *The Federalist* credit Hamilton with the authorship of Numbers 47 and 51. Recent research has established that both were written by Madison.

mortal bard as the perfect model from which the principles and rules of the epic art were to be drawn, and by which all similar works were to be judged, so this great political critic appears to have viewed the Constitution of England as the standard, or to use his own expression, as the mirror of political liberty, and to have delivered, in the form of elementary truths, the several characteristic principles of that particular system. That we may be sure, then, not to mistake his meaning in this case, let us recur to the source from which the maxim was drawn.

On the slightest view of the British Constitution we must perceive that the legislative, executive, and judiciary departments are by no means totally separate and distinct from each other. The executive magistrate forms an integral part of the legislative authority. He alone has the prerogative of making treaties with foreign sovereigns, which, when made, have, under certain limitations, the force of legislative acts. All the members of the judiciary department are appointed by him, can be removed by him on the address of the two Houses of Parliament, and form, when he pleases to consult them, one of his constitutional councils. One branch of the legislative department forms also a great constitutional council to the executive chief; as, on another hand, it is the sole depositary of judicial power in cases of impeachment, and is invested with the supreme appellate jurisdiction in all other cases. The judges, again, are so far connected with the legislative department as often to attend and participate in its deliberations, though not admitted to a legislative vote.

From these facts, by which Montesquieu was guided, it may clearly be inferred that in saying "There can be no liberty where the legislative and executive powers are united in the same person or body of magistrates," or, "if the power of judging be not separated from the legislative and executive powers," he did not mean that these departments ought to have no *partial agency* in, or no *control* over, the acts of each other. His meaning, as his own words import, and still more conclusively as illustrated by the example in his eye, can amount to no more than this, that where the *whole* power of one department is exercised by the same hands which possess the *whole* power of another department, the fundamental principles of a free constitution are subverted. This would have been the case in the Constitution examined by him if the King, who is the sole executive magistrate, had possessed also the complete legislative power, or the supreme administration of justice; or if the entire legislative body had possessed the supreme judiciary or the supreme executive authority.

This, however, is not among the vices of that Constitution. The magistrate in whom the whole executive power resides cannot of himself make a law, though he can put a negative on every law; nor administer justice in person, though he has the appointment of those who do administer it. The judges can exercise no executive prerogative, though they are shoots from the executive stock; nor any legislative function, though they may be advised with by the legislative councils. The entire legislature can perform no judiciary act; though by the joints act of two of its branches the judges may be removed from their offices, and though one of its branches is possessed of the judicial power in the last resort. The entire legislature, again, can exercise no executive prerogative, though one of its branches constitutes the supreme executive magistracy, and another, on the impeachment of a third, can try and condemn all the subordinate officers in the executive department.

The reasons on which Montesquieu grounds his maxim are a further demonstration of his meaning. "When the legislative and executive powers are united in the same person or body," says he, "there can be no liberty, because apprehensions may arise lest *the same* monarch or Senate should *enact* tyrannical laws to *execute* them in a tyrannical manner." Again: "Were the power of judging joined with the legislative, the life and liberty of the subject would be exposed to arbitrary control, for the *judge* would then be the *legislator*. Were it joined to the executive power, the *judge* might behave with all the violence of *an oppressor*." Some of these reasons are more fully explained in other passages; but briefly stated as they are here, they sufficiently establish the meaning which we have put on this celebrated maxim of this celebrated author.

If we look into the constitutions of the several States, we find that, notwithstanding the emphatical and in some instances the unqualified terms in which this axiom has been laid down, there is not a single instance in which the several departments of power have been kept absolutely separate and distinct. . . .

[Here the author examines the constitutions of the original thirteen states, excepting those of Rhode Island and Connecticut which were formed prior to the American Revolution.]

What I have wished to evince is that the charge, brought against the proposed Constitution, of violating a sacred maxim of free government, is warranted neither by the real meaning annexed to that maxim by its author nor by the sense in which it has hitherto been understood in America.

PUBLIUS

JAMES MADISON
Checks and Balances

To what expedient, then, shall we finally resort, for maintaining in practice the necessary partition of power among the several departments, as laid down in the Constitution? The only answer that can be given is, that as all these exterior provisions are found to be inadequate, the defect must be supplied, by so contriving the interior structure of the government as that its several constituent parts may, by their mutual relations, be the means of keeping each other in their proper places. Without presuming to undertake a full development of this important idea, I will hazard a few general observations, which may perhaps place it in a clearer light, and enable us to form a more correct judgment of the principles and structure of the government planned by the Convention.

In order to lay a due foundation for that separate and distinct exercise of the different powers of government, which to a certain extent is admitted on all hands to be essential to the preservation of liberty, it is evident that each depart-

The Federalist, No. 51.

ment should have a will of its own; and consequently should be so constituted that the members of each should have as little agency as possible in the appointment of the members of the others. Were this principle rigorously adhered to, it would require that all the appointments for the supreme executive, legislative, and judiciary magistracies should be drawn from the same fountain of authority, the people, through channels having no communication whatever with one another.

Perhaps such a plan of constructing the several departments would be less difficult in practice than it may in contemplation appear. Some difficulties, however, and some additional expense would attend the execution of it. Some deviations, therefore, from the principle must be admitted. In the constitution of the judiciary department in particular, it might be inexpedient to insist rigorously on the principle: first, because peculiar qualifications being essential in the members, the primary consideration ought to be to select that mode of choice which best secures these qualifications; secondly, because the permanent tenure by which the appointments are held in that department must soon destroy all sense of dependence on the authority conferring them.

It is equally evident that the members of each department should be as little dependent as possible on those of the others, for the emoluments annexed to their offices. Were the executive magistrate, or the judges, not independent of the Legislature in this particular, their independence in every other would be merely nominal.

But the great security against a gradual concentration of the several powers in the same department consists in giving to those who administer each department the necessary constitutional means and personal motives to resist encroachments of the others. The provision for defence must in this, as in all other cases, be made commensurate to the danger of attack. Ambition must be made to counteract ambition. The interest of the man must be connected with the constitutional rights of the place. It may be a reflection on human nature, that such devices should be necessary to control the abuses of government. But what is government itself, but the greatest of all reflections on human nature? If men were angels, no government would be necessary. If angels were to govern men, neither external nor internal controls on government would be necessary. In framing a government which is to be administered by men over men, the great difficulty lies in this: you must first enable the government to control the governed; and in the next place oblige it to control itself. A dependence on the people is, no doubt, the primary control on the government; but experience has taught mankind the necessity of auxiliary precautions.

This policy of supplying, by opposite and rival interests, the defect of better motives, might be traced through the whole system of human affairs, private as well as public. We see it particularly displayed in all the subordinate distributions of power, where the constant aim is to divide and arrange the several offices in such a manner as that each may be a check on the other—that the private interest of every individual may be a sentinel over the public rights. These inventions of prudence cannot be less requisite in the distribution of the supreme powers of the State.

But it is not possible to give to each department an equal power of self-defence. In republican government, the legislative authority necessarily predominates. The remedy for this inconveniency is to divide the legislature into different branches; and to render them, by different modes of election and different principles of action, as little connected with each other as the nature of their common functions and their common dependence on the society will admit. It may even be necessary to guard against dangerous encroachments by still further precautions. As the weight of the legislative authority requires that it should be thus divided, the weakness of the executive may require, on the other hand, that it should be fortified. An absolute negative on the legislature appears at first view to be the natural defence with which the executive magistrate should be armed. But perhaps it would be neither altogether safe nor alone sufficient. On ordinary occasions it might not be exerted with the requisite firmness, and on extraordinary occasions it might be perfidiously abused. May not this defect of an absolute negative be supplied by some qualified connection between this weaker department and the weaker branch of the stronger department, by which the latter may be led to support the constitutional rights of the former, without being too much detached from the rights of its own department?

If the principles on which these observations are founded be just, as I persuade myself they are, and they be applied as a criterion to the several State constitutions, and to the federal Constitution, it will be found that if the latter does not perfectly correspond with them, the former are infinitely less able to bear such a test.

There are, moreover, two considerations particularly applicable to the federal system of America, which place that system in a very interesting point of view.

First. In a single republic all the power surrendered by the people is submitted to the administration of a single government, and the usurpations are guarded against by a division of the government into distinct and separate departments. In the compound republic of America, the power surrendered by the people is first divided between two distinct governments, and then the portion allotted to each subdivided among distinct and separate departments. Hence a double security arises to the rights of the people. The different governments will control each other, at the same time that each will be controlled by itself.

Second. It is of great importance in a republic not only to guard the society against the oppression of its rulers, but to guard one part of the society against the injustice of the other part. Different interests necessarily exist in different classes of citizens. If a majority be united by a common interest, the rights of the minority will be insecure. There are but two methods of providing against this evil: the one by creating a will in the community independent of the majority, that is, of the society itself; the other by comprehending in the society so many separate descriptions of citizens as will render an unjust combination of a majority of the whole very improbable, if not impracticable.

The first method prevails in all governments possessing an hereditary or self-appointed authority. This, at best, is but a precarious security; because a power independent of the society may as well espouse the unjust views of the major as the rightful interests of the minor party, and may possibly be turned against both parties. The second method will be exemplified in the federal republic of the United States. Whilst all authority in it will be derived from and dependent on the society, the society itself will be broken into so many parts, interests and classes of citizens, that the rights of individuals, or of the minority, will be in little danger from interested combinations of the majority.

In a free government the security for civil rights must be the same as that for religious rights. It consists in the one case in the multiplicity of interests, and in the other in the multiplicity of sects. The degree of security in both cases will depend on the number of interests and sects; and this may be presumed to depend on the extent of country and number of people comprehended under the same government. This view of the subject must particularly recommend a proper federal system to all the sincere and considerate friends of republican government, since it shows that in exact proportion as the territory of the Union may be formed into more circumscribed confederacies, or States, oppressive combinations of a majority will be facilitated; the best security under republican forms, for the rights of every class of citizens, will be diminished; and, consequently, the stability and independence of some member of the government, the only other security, must be proportionally increased.

Justice is the end of government. It is the end of civil society. It ever has been and ever will be pursued until it be obtained, or until liberty be lost in the pursuit. In a society under the forms of which the stronger faction can readily unite and oppress the weaker, anarchy may as truly be said to reign as in a state of nature, where the weaker individual is not secured against the violence of the stronger; and as in the latter state even the stronger individuals are prompted by the uncertainty of their condition to submit to a government which may protect the weak as well as themselves; so, in the former state, will the more powerful factions or parties be gradually induced, by a like motive, to wish for a government which will protect all parties, the weaker as well as the more powerful.

It can be little doubted that if the State of Rhode Island was separated from the confederacy, and left to itself, the insecurity of rights under the popular form of government within such narrow limits would be displayed by such reiterated oppressions of factious majorities that some power altogether independent of the people would soon be called for by the voice of the very factions whose misrule had proved the necessity of it.

In the extended republic of the United States, and among the great variety of interests, parties, and sects which it embraces, a coalition of a majority of the whole society could seldom take place on any other principles than those of justice and the general good; whilst there being thus less danger to a minor from the will of a major party, there must be less pretext, also, to provide for the security of the former, by introducing into the government a will not dependent on the latter; or, in other words, a will independent of the society itself. It is no less certain than it is important, notwithstanding the contrary opinions which have been entertained, that the larger the society, provided it lie within a practical sphere, the more duly capable it will be of self-government. And happily for the *republican cause,* the practicable sphere may be carried to a very great extent, by a judicious modification and mixture of the *federal principle.*

PUBLIUS

~~~~~TOPIC 6

"Ambition Must Be Made to Counteract Ambition"

Since Madison contributed to The Federalist, *his theory that good government required a system of checks and balances so that ambition would counteract ambition has been subjected to continued theoretical analysis and practical test in the actual process of governing over a period of nearly two centuries. In the ensuing discussion, James MacGregor Burns maintains that Madison's theory has "long outlived him" because, even in his own terms, his "first great protection against naked majority rule was the broader diversity of interests in a large republic and hence the greater difficulty in concerting their 'plans of oppression.'" Why, then, Burns asks, "would not any popular majority representing such a variety of interests perforce become so broad and moderate in its goals as never to threaten any major or even minor or individual interest? Why was it necessary to have what Madison called 'auxiliary precautions' of checks and balances built right into the frame of government?" What is more, he argues, the urgency of our modern problems, and the furious pace of social and economic change throughout the world, make protracted delay in governmental action a luxury we can no longer afford. (These views derive support from Professor Commager's explanation of the reasons he prefers "the checks and balances of democratic politics" as against judicial review.)*

On the other hand, Reinhold Niebuhr maintains that "it may be taken as axiomatic that great disproportions of power lead to injustice," and he adds that "the larger the group the more certainly will it express itself selfishly in the total community." This is because "it will be more powerful and therefore more able to defy any social restraints which might be devised." He insists that "there has never been a scheme of justice in history which did not have a balance of power at its foundation." But he sees dangers also in the balancing of power which "is always pregnant with the possibility of anarchy." He concludes that "a healthy society must seek to achieve the greatest possible equilibrium of power, the greatest possible number of centers of power, the greatest possible social check upon the administration of power, and the greatest possible inner moral check on

51

human ambition, as well as the most effective use of forms of power in which consent and coercion are compounded."

The viewpoint of Professor Thomas Landon Thorson raises some important questions about majority "rule" and minority "rights." He argues that conceptions or justifications of democracy "that elevate either natural (minority) rights or the principle of majority rule to a position of primacy" are "faulty." He holds, instead, that the principles are "mutually interdependent and essentially equal." Accordingly, the obligation they impose on our political system is that those who operate it "be rational!"

JAMES MAC GREGOR BURNS

The Politics of Deadlock

The Theory of Minority Checks

In *The Federalist,* Number 10, Madison came to grips with the crucial problem of breaking and controlling the violence of faction, which he defined as a "number of citizens, whether amounting to a majority or minority of the whole, who are united and actuated by some common impulse of passion, or of interest, adverse to the rights of other citizens, or to the permanent and aggregate interests of the community." The origins of such factions were in the nature of man, in his passions and interests, economic, religious, and otherwise. The cause of faction, Madison wrote, could not and should not be removed, for that cause was liberty, which must never be suppressed. But the effects of faction could be controlled by enlarging the society to be governed, since the larger the society, the greater the "variety of parties and interests" and the less likely that any one faction will have a majority. The greater variety could be found in a broader Republic, with its national Congress representing many sections and groups and hence able to break and control the violence of faction, whether of a popular majority or minority.

Like a careful cook, Madison wanted to dissolve indigestible lumps and fiery spices in the blander waters of a large pot. His crucial assumption here was that the broader republic would overcome faction. Why? If, say, inflationists in one state could get control of the state legislature, why could not inflationists in all states join hands and gain control of the new Congress? Here Madison marshaled his arguments convincingly. For one thing, he said, in a large republic the people would have to delegate decisions to representatives of bigger constituencies, and hence factional feelings would be refined and tempered by carefully chosen leaders whose views were more refined and broad minded than

Professor of Political Science at Williams College. Author of: *Roosevelt: The Lion and the Fox; John Kennedy: A Political Profile; Congress on Trial.* The selection is from *The Deadlock of Democracy,* © 1963 by James MacGregor Burns, pp. 18-23, 1-7, published by Prentice Hall, Inc., Englewood Cliffs, New Jersey. By permission.

factional leaders. To be sure, factional and even sinister representatives might get elected and betray the people, but this would be less likely where representatives had to appeal to a "greater number of citizens in the large than in the small republic." The new Constitution, providing for two layers of government, would be a fine balance, a "happy combination" of local and general representation. But even more important, under a greater variety of parties and interests, "you make it less probable that a majority of the whole will have a common motive to invade the rights of other citizens; or if such a common motive exists, it will be more difficult for all who feel it to discover their own strength, and to act in unison with one another." Thus inflationists in different states could not easily join together because in the broader sphere other differences would keep them apart—for example, Madison had noted prophetically, the basic conflict between North and South.

But Madison still was not satisfied. There was still the possibility that even in the new Union a majority of the people might gang up on the minority. To be sure, Montesquieu's old safeguard might work: divide up national power among different officials, legislative, executive, and judicial, "for the accumulation of powers . . . in the same hands . . . may justly be pronounced the very definition of tyranny." But even this might not be enough, for what if the different officials—Congressmen, President, and federal judges—got together and pooled their power for the interests of some oppressive majority?

The answer to this question became the archpin of the whole constitutional framework. That answer was the system of checks and balances. "The great security against a gradual concentration of the several powers in the same department, consists in giving to those who administer each department the necessary constitutional means and personal motives to resist encroachments of the others," Madison wrote in the fifty-first paper, which rivals the tenth in intellectual sweep and power. ". . . . Ambition must be made to counteract ambition. The interest of the man must be connected with the constitutional rights of the place." Was it a reflection on human nature that such devices should be necessary to control the abuses of government? Yes, Madison admitted, and reverting to his first premise as to the nature of man, he asked: "But what is government itself, but the greatest of all reflections on human nature? If men were angels, no government would be necessary."

"Ambition must be made to counteract ambition"—in these seven words Madison drove straight to the heart of the whole problem; here he showed his genius as a political scientist. For he was not content with a flimsy separation of power that lunging politicians could smash through like paper. He was calling for barricade after barricade against the thrust of a popular majority—and the ultimate and impassable barricade was a system of checks and balances that would use man's essential human nature—his interests, his passions, his ambitions —to control itself. For Madison's ultimate checks and balances were political; they built into the engine of government automatic stabilizing devices that were sure to counterbalance one another because they were powered by separate sources of political energy. The ambitions of Presidents and Senators and Representatives and judges were bound to collide because each was responsible to separate constituencies in the "greater variety of parties and interests of the new federal republic." And each official, of course, had some kind of constitutional weapon

—the President's veto, for example, or the Senators' power over treaties—that could be used against other officials and the sectional or economic or ideological interests they represented.

It was a stunning solution to the Framers' problem of checking the tyranny of the majority. Yet the solution contained a major flaw, or at least inconsistency, in the thinking behind it—a flaw so relevant to our later analysis that we must note it even in the same breath that we pay tribute to this profound scholar and politician.

The trouble was this: if, as Madison said, the first great protection against naked majority rule was the broader diversity of interests in a larger republic and hence the greater difficulty of concerting their "plans of oppression," why was not this enough in itself? Why would not any popular majority representing such a variety of interests perforce become so broad and moderate in its goals as never to threaten any major or even minor or individual interest? Why was it necessary to have what Madison called "auxiliary precautions" of checks and balances built right into the frame of government? Because, he said, experience had taught men the necessity of them. What experience? Madison must have meant the experience of societies so deeply divided between rich and poor, between master and slave, between sections, between religions, that victory for one side meant coercion or annihilation of the other. But the America he knew was not such a society. No ideological conflict racked the nation; as Louis Hartz has shown, Americans were united—to the extent they thought about such things—over the liberal creed of John Locke. No sharp class or religious conflict had torn the country into two warring halves. The same diversity that Madison used as an argument for broader union would have required any majority to appeal to so many interests, to straddle so many issues, that it must act in a moderate, broadly representative fashion.

The key to Madison's thinking is his central aim to stop people from turning easily to government for help. Today, when many people want protection by or through government, and not just protection from government, the power of a minority to stop the majority from acting through government may be as arbitrary as majority rule seemed to Madison. The fact is that Madison believed in a government of sharply limited powers. His efforts at Philadelphia to shift powers from the states to the new national government were intended more to thwart popular majorities in the states from passing laws for their own ends than to empower national majorities to pass laws for *their* ends. For the new national government was supposed to tame and temper popular majorities—which some states had been unable to do. This meant weaker government—but it was Madison, after all, who said that the necessity of any government was a misfortune and a reflection on human nature. Government, in short, was a necessary evil that must be curbed, not an instrument for the realization of men's higher ideals or a nation's broader interests. Hence he could sponsor what Richard Hofstadter has called a harmonious system of mutual frustration.

Still, if Madison was very much a child of his age, his analysis has long outlived him. Because of his brilliant linking of man's basic drives and man's formal institutions, of political forces and governmental mechanisms, Federalist No. 51 is still the best short analysis of the foundations of the American system. How far Madison extended his insights into political dynamics is not wholly clear. His concern—almost obsession—with factions suggests that he well understood the instincts of politicians to collect groups of followers and to build positions of power, for "the interest of the man must be connected with the constitutional rights of the place."

Certainly the implications of Madison's insight are clear today. Around every position established under the new Constitution—around "the interest of the man," whether President, legislator, or even judge or bureaucrat—a circle of sub-leaders and followers would also grow, the size of the circle depending on the importance of the office and the appeal and skills of the leader. Other factions would grow around politicians outside government, trying to get in. And of course the Constitution left intact a proliferation of offices in the states, counties, and localities, which in turn were the centers of thousands of other little circles of political action and influence.

These officeholders, their rivals, and the circles of sub-leaders and personal followers around them comprise a web of influence stretching across the formal governmental system. This is not to deny the importance of political parties and interest groups, of opinion-shaping agencies such as the press, of the thick crust of traditional habits and attitudes, of ideological and social forces, and of other factors. It is to say that, given the stability and durability of our constitutional system, these offices establish the main structure of political combat and governmental power.

Because Madison took the lead in thinking out and articulating this balance of checks, because he helped in masterly fashion to establish it, he stands today as one of the supreme strategists of American politics. . . .

The Politics of the Cave

Behind the fascination with political personalities and election gladiators there is in this country, I think, a vast boredom with politics. Because it has failed to engage itself with the problems that dog us during our working days and haunt our dreams at night, politics has not engaged the best of us, or at least the best in us. If people seem complacent or inert, the cause may lie less in them than in a political system that evades and confuses the real issues rather than sharpening and resolving them. Anyone active in everyday politics knows of concerned, civic-minded people who give hundreds of hours and dollars to fund drives, the Red Cross, and other worthy local causes but will have nothing to do with politics. It frustrates them, alienates them, bores them to tears. They are failing their political obligations—but perhaps politics is failing them.

But never has politics needed them more. We are at the critical stage of a somber and inexorable cycle that seems to have gripped the public affairs of the nation. We have been mired in government deadlock, as Congress blocked or killed most of Mr. Kennedy's bold proposals of 1960, and many planks of the Republican platform as well. Presently we are caught in the politics of drift, as the nation's politicians put off major decisions until after the presidential campaign of 1964. Then we can expect a period of decision, as the voters choose a President, followed by a brief phase of the "politics of the deed," as the President capitalizes on the psychological thrust of his election mandate to put through some bits and pieces of his program. But after the short honeymoon between Congress and President the old cycle of deadlock and drift will reassert itself.

This cycle is one reason for the disenchantment with politics of those most concerned with political issues. It has led to a government by fits and starts, to a statecraft that has not been able to supply the steady leadership and power necessary for the conduct of our affairs. Historically there has been a serious lag— once a near fatal lag—in the speed and effectiveness with which the national government has coped with emerging crises.

The record is a disturbing one. The steady, moderate action on slavery that was so desperately needed in the 1840's and 1850's finally came, immoderately and at a frightful cost, in the 1860's and 1870's. American participation in the first real efforts at collective security came after World War II instead of World War I. The anti-depression measures so critically necessary in the 1930's, if not long before, became governmental and political commitments only in the 1940's and 1950's. The most elementary types of federal control over economic power were delayed for years. The social security and other welfare measures needed to protect men against the insecurities of the modern economy should have been adopted at least by the turn of the century; they had to wait for the New Deal of the 1930's. The economic internationalism that characterized the Marshall Plan and its successor programs in the last fifteen years was missing in the 1920's, when our nationalistic economic policies helped bring on the world depression. Our admirable concern today with the developing countries would have paid off many times over if we had come to it sooner; as it is, we are trying to influence revolutions that in many cases have moved out of the narrow orbit of American influence. The cost of delay has also been high in countless other areas of hardly less importance: urban decline, conservation, tax reform, medical care, governmental organization. We have reacted to change rather than dominated it.

We have often been too late, and we have been too late with too little. Whether we can master depression in peacetime is still in doubt, for we pulled ourselves out of the Great Depression only by the bootstrap of war. Currently baffled by a sluggish economy, we seem unable to promote long, sustained economic growth. Negroes still do not share the basic rights of citizenship promised in the 14th and 15th Amendments. We have done almost nothing about the old dream of a coordinated and vitalized transportation policy. Our social welfare measures are inadequate, especially in medical care. We cannot play our full economic role abroad because of inhibiting forces in Congress. Our structure of transportation is inequitable and archaic. We have hardly begun to adapt our federal and state policymaking machinery to the heavy demands on it.

One can view this drift and delay with a certain philosophical calm. In the end American government, like the belated hero in the horse opera, seems to come to the rescue. Delays may be hard, of course, on certain persons. A man whose working life stretched from 1900 to the mid-thirties might be a bit concerned in retrospect over the delay in federal social welfare programs. A twelve-year-old boy working in a textile mill during the 1920's or even in the 1930's, might wonder, if he had a chance to wonder about such things, how a great nation like the United States had been unable to outlaw child labor despite general condemnation of it, while most of the civilized world had accomplished this primitive reform years earlier. A Negro in the 1960's might not be so detached toward states' rights and congressional obstruction as some of his fellow Americans. Still, most of us could reflect that progress has almost always come in the long run, even if the run has been longer for some than for others. And the slowness of change has meant, perhaps, less tension and disruption of the social fabric.

Today, however, the notion of the beneficent inevitability of gradual progress is open to challenge. For one thing, the furious pace of social and economic change at home and abroad makes delay in government action far riskier than before. We do not enjoy a cushion of time in adjusting to such change, just as we no longer enjoy a cushion of time in coping with enemy attack. We may not possess, for example, an extra decade or two to respond to the demands of a revolution in Africa or Asia or Cuba. Then too, crisis does not seem so productive of federal action as in former days. Judging by the Democratic and Republican platforms of 1960, the campaign speeches of the presidential candidates, and the bulk of opinion in the press, at the pulpit, and in academia, most American opinion leaders agree that the international situation calls for mobilization of educational, scientific, industrial, manpower, health, and physical resources, as well as military strength. But despite this weight of opinion, key domestic proposals of both the Eisenhower and Kennedy administrations in such areas have been stalled in Congress. It is notable that Kennedy's major foreign-policy proposal of 1961—long-term financing of foreign aid—failed at the very time that the nation was aroused over crises in Berlin and Southeast Asia. Perhaps the American people have become so benumbed by constant emergency that a crisis no longer serves the old function of providing broad support for government action.

Another reason that the habit of delay and devitalization may have to be abandoned, however, lies in the nature of the competition that the nation faces. Never before have we confronted an enemy that, over so long a period, challenges so formidably as does Soviet Russia, our ideology, our economic system, our democratic ways, and our international role. It is clear in the 1960's that the nation faces a period of years and perhaps decades during which it must strain every nerve and marshal every resource to maintain its own strength and to nourish that of the free world. Soviet Russia has shaped a governmental and political system that, whatever its failings and terrors and deprivations, has shown itself capable of mobilizing Russians for a sustained effort. The Chinese colossus, imposing perhaps even greater sacrifices, is building up its own hard strength. The question is whether Americans, without harming the substance and the processes of democracy, can empower and invigorate their own society for the long pull.

Yet, serious as these failings are, I have still not expressed the main reason that so many concerned people are aliens to the political process. The main reason, I think, is that politics to them seems dominated by old and sterile issues and appears unable to grapple with the two cardinal problems of late 20th Century civilization. These problems are the style of life of urban man, and the need for fresh and creative ventures in foreign policy.

By 1980, it is expected, over four-fifths of all Americans will be living in metropolitan areas. By the year 2000 a nation of 300,000,000 will embrace vast patches of almost solid urban settlement: the Eastern seaboard; the West Coast; and an urban Midwest fusing the urban and suburban areas of a dozen cities from St. Louis to Buffalo. We have become, as Walter Lippmann has said, in large part a mass society living in congested urban agglomerations. This inexorable trend poses the question of whether men will become further dehumanized and corrupted in megalopolis, or whether a national government sensitive to urban needs can take the leadership, through policy on education, cultural subsidies, television and other mass media, city planning and redevelopment, recreation, transportation, expansion of civil rights, in making megalopolis not only habitable but hospitable to man.

The other problem is how to break out of immobilism in foreign and military policy. However much we may be balked by Russian intransigence in such areas as disarmament and East-West trade, there are other creative possibilities that we have hardly begun to exploit. Vastly stepped up educational and cultural exchange, broadening of the powers of the United Nations, more sophisticated and longer range programs of economic aid to the new nations, the establishment of international universities and cultural centers, increased international collaboration in social and natural science and in space technology, follow-up action to President Kennedy's "declaration of interdependence" of the Western nations and to the Test Ban Treaty—the possibilities are almost limitless.

It is in these two areas, with their exciting potential for creative statesmanship, that our politics has, I think, seemed most crabbed and irrelevant. One wonders, indeed, whether we have advanced much beyond the cave man in the stakes and style of our politics. He fashioned shelter, gathered food, and doled out sustenance to the weaker members of the clan; he and his fellows huddled together in defense against the outside foe. And in Plato's famous allegory of another cave, he often took shadow for substance in trying to grasp the great world beyond his narrow vista. So too we produce and distribute goods and grant welfare to the poor; we huddle with our allies behind our nuclear weapons; and we act politically in a shadowland of old governmental fetters and outworn stereotypes. Politics is still mainly a matter of brute economics and sheer survival.

While the main reason for our political futility and frustration is the political system described in this book, the ultimate source is intellectual. The root trouble, I think, is in our own minds. Like the people in the cave, we have been hypnotized by the shadows of our own political images and by the echoes of our old incantations.

We have been too much entranced by the Madisonian model of government. This model was the product of the gifted men who gathered in Philadelphia over 175 years ago, and it deserves much of the admiration and veneration we have accorded it. But this is also the system of checks and balances and interlocked gears of government that requires the consensus of many groups and leaders before the nation can act; and it is the system that exacts the heavy price of delay and devitalization that I have noted.

In glorifying the Madisonian model we . . . have underestimated the powerful balances and safeguards that are built into a system of majority rule and responsible parties. We have thwarted and fragmentized leadership instead of allowing it free play within the boundaries of the democratic process.

Partly because of these misclaculations, we still underestimate the extent to which our system was designed for deadlock and inaction. We look on the current impasse in Washington as something extraordinary rather than as the inevitable consequence of a system we accept. We look on the failure of the national government to act as the result of poor leadership or bad luck or evil men, and we search for scapegoats. Some conceive that Mr. Johnson today can break the impasse by some magic feat of manipulation or some deft bit of persuasion or by some grand appeal to the people, but they are ignoring the weight of American experience. Typically the Madisonian system has made us go slow; only under extraordinary combinations of circumstances have we moved vigorously ahead on many fronts. Even the strongest and ablest Presidents have been, in the end, more the victims of the Madisonian system than the masters of it.

And so today we face the Madisonian idea built into a system of entrenched power. We face a . . . system that compels government by consensus and coalition rather than a two-party system that allows the winning party to govern and the losers to oppose. While the demands on our government pile up at a feverish pace, the system shows no sign of relaxing its grip on the levers of action. This system is rooted in our constitutional arrangements, electoral behavior, party institutions, and machinery of government.

Above all, it is rooted in our minds. "We are at one of those uncommon junctures of human affairs when we can be saved by the solution of intellectual problems and in no other way," John Maynard Keynes said in the 1930's. So we are today. Our need is not to win an election or a leader; we must win a government. To do this we must disenthrall ourselves of the shadows and echoes that draw us away from reality. We cannot unfreeze our politics until we unfreeze our minds.

REINHOLD NIEBUHR
The Politics of Countervailing Power

All historic forms of justice and injustice are determined to a much larger degree than pure rationalists or idealists realize by the given equilibrium or disproportion within each type of power and by the balance of various types of power in a given community. It may be taken as axiomatic that great disproportions of power lead to injustice, whatever may be the efforts to mitigate it.[1]

Professor Emeritus, Union Theological Seminary. Recipient of Presidential Freedom Medal 1964. Author of *The Children of Light and The Children of Darkness, Moral Man and Immoral Society,* fifteen other books, and numerous articles. This compilation is taken from the writings of Reinhold Niebuhr cited at the end of each selection. For a fuller statement of Niebuhr's political philosophy the student is referred to Harry R. Davis and Robert C. Good, eds., *Reinhold Niebuhr on Politics* (New York, Charles Scribner's Sons, 1960). This volume has been of great assistance in the preparation of this compilation.

[1] *The Nature and Destiny of Man,* Vol. II. *Human Destiny,* p. 262. Copyright 1943 Charles Scribner's Sons. By permission of Charles Scribner's Sons. Cited below as *Human Destiny.*

Though a tremendous amount of illusion about human nature expresses itself in American culture, our political institutions contain many safeguards against the selfish abuse of power which our Calvinist fathers insisted upon.[2]

Ambivalent Nature of Man

Modern developments have proved that there is a more intimate relation between what Madison called man's reason and self-love than the rationalists have assumed. If political issues were really abstract questions of social policy upon which unbiased citizens were asked to commit themselves, the business of voting and the debate which preceded the election might actually be regarded as an educational programme in which a social group discovers its common mind. But the fact is that political questions are inevitably rooted in [self] interest of some kind or other and few citizens can view a social policy without regard to their interest.[3]

"The diversities in the faculties of men," declared James Madison,

> from which the rights of property originate, are . . . an insuperable obstacle to uniformity of interests. The protection of these faculties is the first object of government. From the protection of different and unequal faculties of acquiring property, the possession of different degrees and kinds of property immediately results; and from the influence of these on the sentiments and views of the respective proprietors ensues a division of society into different interests and parties.[*]

This is a correct analysis of the economic basis of political attitudes, except that too great a significance is attached to faculty as the basis of inequality of privilege. Differences in faculty and function do indeed help to originate inequality of privilege but they never justify the degree of inequality created, and they are frequently not even relevant to the type of inequality perpetuated in a social system.[4]

The selfishness of men and nations is a fixed datum of historical science. Election results can be confidently predicted if the economic interests of the voters can be carefully enough analyzed. Yet this human egotism does not belong to nature. The eighteenth-century rationalists were wrong in asserting that men sought their own, just as every animal seeks to preserve its existence. The human self is different from other creatures in two respects: 1) It is able by its freedom to transmute nature's survival impulse into more potent and more destructive, more subtle and more comprehensive, forms of self-seeking than the one-dimensional survival impulse of nature. 2) It is able to envisage a larger good than its own preservation, to make some fitful responses to this more inclusive obligation and to feel itself guilty for its failure to make a consistent

[2] *The Irony of American History,* p. 22. Copyright 1952 Charles Scribner's Sons. By permission of Charles Scribner's Sons.
[3] "Christianity and Humanism," *Messenger,* Vol. XVII (September 9, 1952), p. 7. By permission.
[*] See *The Federalist,* No. 10, in this volume [Eds.].
[4] *Moral Man and Immoral Society.* Copyright 1932 Charles Scribner's Sons. Renewal Copyright 1960 Reinhold Niebuhr. By permission of Charles Scribner's Sons.

response.[5] Man is the kind of lion who both kills the lamb and also dreams of the day when the lion and the lamb shall lie down together.[6]

The real situation is that the human self is strongly inclined to seek its own but that it has a sufficient dimension of transcendence over self to be unable to ascribe this inclination merely to natural necessity. On the other hand, when it strives for a wider good it surreptitiously introduces its own interests into this more inclusive value. This fault may be provisionally regarded as the inevitable consequence of a finite viewpoint. The self sees the larger structure of value from its own standpoint.[7] All human knowledge is tainted with an "ideological" taint. It pretends to be more true than it is. It is finite knowledge, gained from a particular perspective; but it pretends to be final and ultimate knowledge.[8]

This insinuation of the interests of the self into even the most ideal enterprises and most universal objectives, envisaged in moments of highest rationality, makes hypocrisy an inevitable by-product of all virtuous endeavor. It is, in a sense, a tribute to the moral nature of man as well as a proof of his moral limitations; for it is significant that men cannot pursue their own ends with the greatest devotion, if they are unable to attribute universal values to their particular objectives. There is no miracle by which men can achieve a rationality high enough to give them as vivid an understanding of general interests as of their own.[9]

The Marxist interpretation of man's subrational life is of course sharply distinguished from the romantic one. Since the emphasis lies not so much upon the impulses of individuals but upon the common drives of social classes, and since these drives are interpreted primarily in economic terms, the interpretation of man's infrarational life avails itself of materialistc rather than biological concepts.[10]

Marxism understands the spiritual character of dishonesty as little as the spiritual character of the possessive and the power impulse. Its great insights into the ideological character of all cultural enterprises are vitiated by its interpretation of consciousness as merely the reflection and the product of material conditions. Marxism, in other words, attributes the human tendency to hide egoistic interests behind ideals of general validity, to the mere finiteness of the human mind, its dependence upon its environment. But it fails to explain why the human spirit should feel under the necessity of making such pretentions. Why does not man merely seek his own interest as animals do? Precisely because his spirit transcends his impulses of survival sufficiently to envisage a more general realm of value than his own life, he must seem to be loyal to this more inclusive realm even when he is not. The same spiritual capacity which necessitates hypocrisy also adds an element of conscious deception to the errors of unconscious dis-

---

[5] *Faith and History*, pp. 94, 95. Copyright 1949 Charles Scribner's Sons. By permission of Charles Scribner's Sons.

[6] Quoted in June Bingham, *Courage to Change* (New York, Charles Scribner's Sons, 1961), p. 67. Original source unknown.

[7] *Faith and History*, pp. 95, 96.

[8] *The Nature and Destiny of Man*, Vol. I. *Human Nature*, p. 194. Copyright 1941 Charles Scribner's Sons. By permission of Charles Scribner's Sons. Cited below as *Human Nature*.

[9] *Moral Man and Immoral Society*, p. 45.

[10] *Human Nature*, pp. 43, 44.

honesty. The hypocrisy of man is thus an interesting refutation of the doctrine of man's total depravity.[11]

Whenever modern idealists are confronted with the divisive and corrosive effects of man's self-love, they look for some immediate cause of this perennial tendency, usually in some specific form of social organization. One school holds that men would be good if only political institutions would not corrupt them; another believes that they would be good if the prior evil of a faulty economic organization could be eliminated. Or another school thinks of this evil as no more than ignorance, and therefore waits for a more perfect educational process to redeem man from his partial and particular loyalties. But no school asks how it is that an essentially good man could have produced corrupting and tyrannical political organizations or exploiting economic organizations, or fanatical and superstitious religious organizations.[12]

Individual and Collective Morality

There is a basic difference between the morality of individuals and the morality of collectives, whether [parties,] races, classes or nations.[13] Individual men may be moral in the sense that they are able to consider interests other than their own in determining problems of conduct, and are capable, on occasion, of preferring the advantages of others to their own. They are endowed by nature with a measure of sympathy and consideration for their kind, the breadth of which may be extended by astute pedagogy. Their rational faculty prompts them to a sense of justice which educational discipline may refine and purge of egoistic elements until they are able to view a social situation, in which their own interests are involved, with a fair measure of objectivity. But all these achievements are more difficult, if not impossible, for human societies and social groups. In every human group there is less reason to guide and check impulse, less capacity for self-transcendence, less ability to comprehend the needs of others and therefore more unrestrained egoism than the individuals, who compose the group, reveal in their personal relations. [14] The social validity of a moral ideal is progressively weakened as it is applied to more and more intricate, indirect and collective relations.[15]

The group is more arrogant, hypocritical, self-centered and more ruthless in the pursuit of its ends than the individual. An inevitable moral tension between individual and group morality is therefore created.[16] The inevitable hypocrisy, which is associated with all of the collective activities of the human race, springs chiefly from this source: that individuals have a moral code which makes the actions of collective man an outrage to their conscience. They therefore invent romantic and moral interpretations of the real facts, preferring to

[11] Ibid., p. 48.
[12] The Children of Light and the Children of Darkness, p. 17. Copyright 1960 Charles Scribner's Sons. By permission of Charles Scribner's Sons. Cited below as The Children of Light.
[13] Moral Man and Immoral Society, p. ix.
[14] Ibid., p. xi.
[15] Ibid., p. 266, 267.
[16] Human Nature, pp. 208, 209.

obscure rather than reveal the true character of their collective behavior.[17] In the relations of majority and minority racial groups for instance, for which the Negro-white relation is a convenient example, the majority group justifies the disabilities which it imposes upon the minority group on the ground that the subject group is not capable of enjoying or profiting from the privileges of culture or civilization. Yet it can never completely hide, and it sometimes frankly expresses, the fear that the grant of such privileges would eliminate the inequalities of endowment which supposedly justify the inequalities of privilege.[18]

The inferiority of the morality of groups to that of individuals is due in part to the difficulty of establishing a rational social force which is powerful enough to cope with the natural impulses by which society achieves its cohesion; but in part it is merely the revelation of a collective egotism, compounded of the egotistic impulses of individuals, which achieve a more vivid expression and a more cumulative effect when they are *united in a common impulse* than when they express themselves separately and discretely.*[19]

The social group asks for the individual's unconditional loyalty, asserting that its necessities are the ultimate law of the individual's existence. But on the other hand it is a pretension which the individual makes for himself, not as an individual but as a member of his group. Collective egotism does indeed offer the individual an opportunity to lose himself in a larger whole; but it also offers him possibilities of self-aggrandizement beside which mere individual pretensions are implausible and incredible. Individuals "join to set up a god whom each then severally and tacitly identifies with himself, to swell the chorus of praise which each then severally and tacitly arrogates to himself."[20] *In its whole range from pride of family to pride of nation, collective egotism and group pride are a more pregnant source of injustice and conflict than purely individual pride.*[21]

The larger the group the more certainly will it express selfishly in the total community. It will be more powerful and therefore more able to defy any restraints which might be devised. It will also be less subject to internal moral restraints. The larger the group the more difficult it is to achieve a common mind and purpose and the more inevitably will it be united by momentary impulses and immediate and unreflective purposes. The increasing size of the group increases the difficulties of achieving a group self-consciousness, except as it comes in conflict with other groups and is unified by perils and passions. It is a rather pathetic aspect of human social life that conflict is a seemingly unavoidable prerequisite of group solidarity.[22]

[17] *Moral Man and Immoral Society*, pp. 8, 9.

[18] *Human Nature*, p. 198.

* "By a faction, I understand a number of citizens, whether amounting to a majority or a minority of the whole, *who are united and actuated by some common impulse of passion or of interest,* adverse to the rights of other citizens, or to the permanent and aggregate interests of the community." *The Federalist,* No. 10. (Editor's emphasis.)

[19] *Moral Man and Immoral Society*, pp. xii.

[20] *Human Nature*, p. 212. The quotation is from Philip Leon, *The Ethics of Power*, p. 140.

[21] *Human Nature*, p. 213.

[22] *Moral Man and Immoral Society*, pp. 47, 48.

Contending factions in a social struggle require morale; and morale is created by the right dogmas, symbols and emotionally potent oversimplifications.[23] They have to believe more firmly in the justice and probable triumph of their cause, than any impartial science could give them the right to believe, if they are to have enough energy to contest the power of the strong.[24] A too simple social radicalism does not recognize how quickly the poor, the weak, the despised of yesterday, may, on gaining a social victory over their detractors, exhibit the same arrogance and the same will-to-power which they abhorred in their opponents and which they were inclined to regard as a congenital sin of their enemies. Every victim of injustice makes the mistake of supposing that the sin from which he suffers is a peculiar vice of his oppressor.[25] In political struggles there are no saints but only sinners fighting each other.[26]

The relations between groups must therefore always be predominantly political rather than ethical, that is they will be determined by the proportion of power which each group possesses at least as much as any rational and moral appraisal of the comparative needs and claims of each group.[27] The peace of the world is always, as St. Augustine observed, something of an armistice between opposing factions.[28]

The expectation of changing human nature by the destruction of economic privilege to such a degree that no one will desire to make selfish use of power, must probably be placed in the category of romantic illusions. If power remains in society, mankind will never escape the necessity of endowing those who possess it with the largest measure of ethical self-control. But that does not obviate the necessity of reducing power to a minimum, or bringing the remai·.der under the strongest measure of social control; and destroying such typ s of it as are least amenable to social control. For there is no ethical force strong enough to place inner checks upon the use of power if its quantity is inordinate. "The truth is," declared James Madison, "that all men having power ought to be distrusted."[29]

The Moral Ambiguity of Governments

Political power deserves to be placed in a special category, because it results from the ability to use and manipulate other forms of social power for the purpose of organizing and dominating the community.[30] It is obvious that the principle of government, or the organization of the whole realm of social vitalities, stands upon a high plane of moral sanction and social necessity.[31] It

---

[23] *Ibid.*, p. xv.

[24] *Ibid.*

[25] *Human Nature*, p. 226.

[26] "Leaves from the Notebook of a War Bound American," *Christian Century*, Vol. LVI (November 15, 1939), p. 1406. Copyright 1939 Christian Century Foundation. Reprinted by permission.

[27] *Moral Man and Immoral Society*, p. xxiii.

[28] *Discerning the Signs of the Times*, p. 187. Copyright 1946 by Charles Scribner's Sons. By permission of Charles Scribner's Sons.

[29] *Moral Man and Immoral Society*, p. 164. The quotation is from *Papers of James Madison*, edited by H. D. Gilpin, Vol. II, p. 1073.

[30] *Human Destiny*, p. 263.

[31] *Ibid.*, p. 266.

is nevertheless important to recognize that government is also morally ambiguous.

The power of the rulers is subject to two abuses. It may actually be the dominion which one portion of the community exercises over the whole community. But even if government does not express the imperial impulse of one class or group within the community, it would if its pretensions are not checked, generate imperial impulses of its own towards the community. It would be tempted to destroy the vitality and freedom of component elements in the community in the name of order. It would identify its particular form of order with the principle of order itself. This evil can be fully understood only if it is recognized that all governments and rulers derive a part of their power, not only from the physical instruments of coercion at their disposal, but also from the reality and the pretension of "majesty."

The majesty of the state is legitimate in so far as it embodies and expresses both the authority and power of the total community over all its members and the principles of order and justice as such against the perils of anarchy.[32] But there are no historic expressions of the majesty of state and government without an admixture of illegitimate pretensions of majesty and sanctity. These can be most simply defined as the tendency of states and governments to hide and obscure the contingent and partial character of their rule and to claim unconditional validity for it.[33]

John Adams in his warnings to Thomas Jefferson would seem to have had a premonition of this. At any rate, he understood the human situation well enough to have stated:

> Power always thinks it has a great soul and vast views beyond the comprehension of the weak; and that it is doing God's service when it is violating all His laws. Our passions, ambitions, avarice, love and resentment, etc., possess so much metaphysical subtlety and so much overpowering eloquence that they insinuate themselves into the understanding and the conscience and convert both to their party.

Adams' understanding of the power of self's passions and ambitions to corrupt the self's reason is a simple recognition of the facts of life which refute all theories, whether liberal or Marxist, about the possibility of a completely disinterested self.[34]

Every society uses a degree of coercion in achieving cohesion for the simple reason that the human imagination is too limited and egoistic impulses are too powerful for purely voluntary cooperation on a large scale to be attained. Inevitably the force which society uses for this purpose will seek to serve itself more than society. No matter how general the consent which maintains it, the actual social locus from which the initiative of coercion is taken is narrower than the whole of society. Hence in every society there is something like an oligarchy.[35] Modern democracies tend toward a more equal justice partly be-

---

[32] *Ibid.*, p. 267.
[33] *Human Destiny*, p. 268.
[34] *The Irony of American History*, pp. 21, 22. By permission.
[35] "Russia and Karl Marx," *The Nation*, Vol. CXLVI, (May 7, 1938) pp. 530, 531. By permission.

cause they have divorced political power from special social functions. They endowed all men with a measure of it by giving them the right to review the policies of their leaders. This democratic principle does not obviate the formation of oligarchies in society; but it places a check upon their formation, and upon the exercise of their power.[36]

The Balance of Social Forces

The harmony of communities is not simply attained by the authority of law. The social harmony of living communities is achieved by an interaction between the normative conceptions of morality and law and the existing and developing forces and vitalities of the community. Usually the norms of law are compromises between the rational-moral ideals of what ought to be, and the possibilities of the situation as determined by given equilibria of vital forces. The specific legal enactments are, on the one hand, the instruments of the conscience of the community, seeking to subdue the potential anarchy of forces and interests into a tolerable harmony. They are, on the other hand, merely explicit formulations of given tensions and equilibria of life and power, as worked out by the unconscious interactions of social life.

No human community is, in short, a simple construction of conscience or reason. All communities are more or less stable or precarious harmonies of human vital capacities. They are governed by power. The power which determined the quality and harmony is not merely the coercive and organizing power of government. That is only one of the two aspects of social power. The other is the balance of vitalities and forces in any given social situation.[37]

It is our common assumption that political freedom is a simple *summum bonum*. It is not. Freedom must always be related to community and justice. Every community seeks consciously or unconsciously to make social peace and order the first goal of its life. It may pay a very high price in the restriction of freedom so as to establish order; but order is the first desideratum for the simple reason that chaos means non-existence. The situation in the Congo should persuade us of this obvious fact, if we had not been aware of it before.

Order alone can, of course, be bought at a very high price, usually at too high a price from the standpoint of those classes in society who must pay it. The second goal of any society therefore is justice. Aristotle defined justice as "giving each man his due." Since in the long history of Western democracy no one has ever offered accurate criteria by which each man's due is measured, we must come to the conclusion that open societies have solved the problem by allowing a free competition of social forces, which enables every force in society to make its claims upon society and to acquire enough social and political power and prestige to enforce its claims.

And liberty and equality are generally recognized as the twin principles of justice. But abstract radical libertarianism and equalitarianism falsely regard them as simple historical possibilities. They cannot be simple possibilities. Liberty must be measured against the community's need for security against in-

[36] *Human Destiny*, p. 263.
[37] *Ibid.*, p. 257.

ternal and external peril. Equality must be measured against the need for the hierarchy of social function by which a community integrates its life and work. That is why history has refuted both Jacobin libertarianism and Marxist equalitarianism.[38]

There are various possibilities of so managing and equilibrating the balance of social forces in a given community that the highest possible justice may be achieved, and since the organizing principle and power in the community are also subject to indeterminate refinement, communal order and justice can approximate a more perfect brotherhood in varying degree. But each principle of communal organization—the organization of power and the balance of power—contains possibilities of contradicting the law of brotherhood. The organizing principle and power may easily degenerate into tyranny. Again the principle of balance of power is always pregnant with the possibility of anarchy. These twin evils, tyranny and anarchy, or authority and liberty, represent the Scylla and Charybdis between which the frail bark of social justice must sail. It is almost certain to founder upon one rock if it makes the mistake of regarding the other as the only peril.[39]

The domination of one life by another is avoided most successfully by an equilibrium of powers and vitalities, so that weakness does not invite enslavement by the strong.[40] Such a balance, once achieved, can be stabilized, embellished, and even, on occasion, perfected by more purely moral considerations. But there has never been a scheme of justice in history which did not have a balance of power at its foundation.[41] It may be wise for the community to sacrifice something in efficiency for the sake of preserving a greater balance of forces and avoiding undue centralization of power.[42]

But an equilibrium of power is not brotherhood. The restraint of the will-to-power of one member of the community by the counter-pressure of power by another member results in a condition of tension. All tension is covert or potential conflict. The principle of equilibrium of power is thus a principle of justice in so far as it prevents domination and enslavement but it is a principle of anarchy and conflict in so far as its tensions, if unresolved, result in overt conflict. Furthermore social life, when not consciously managed and manipulated, does not develop perfect equilibria of power. Its capricious disproportions of power generate various forms of domination and enslavement. Human society therefore requires a conscious control and manipulation of the various equilibria which exist in it. There must be an organizing center within a given field of social vitalities. This center must arbitrate conflicts from a more impartial perspective than is available to any party of a given conflict; it must manage and manipulate the processes of mutual support so that the tensions inherent in them will not erupt into conflict; it must coerce submission to the social process by superior power whenever the instruments of arbitrating

[38] "Reflections on Democracy as an Alternative to Communism." Reprinted from the *Columbia University Forum* by permission of the publisher Columbia University, Copyright © 1961. Vol. 4 (Summer 1961), pp. 10, 11.

[39] *Human Destiny,* p. 258.

[40] *Ibid.,* p. 265.

[41] *Christianity and Power Politics,* p. 104. Copyright 1940 by Charles Scribner's Sons. By permission of Charles Scribner's Sons.

[42] *The Children of Light,* p. 115.

and composing conflict do not suffice; and finally it must seek to redress the disproportion of power by conscious shifts of the balances whenever they make for injustice.[43]

A healthy society must seek to achieve the greatest possible equilibrium of power, the greatest possible number of centers of power, the greatest possible social check upon the administration of power, and the greatest possible inner moral check on human ambition, as well as the most effective use of forms of power in which consent and coercion are compounded.[44]

The Strategy of Democracy

A free society requires some confidence in the ability of men to reach tentative and tolerable adjustments between competing interests and to arrive at some common notions of justice which transcend all partial interests. A consistent pessimism in regard to man's rational capacity for justice invariably leads to absolutistic political theories; for they prompt the conviction that only preponderant power can coerce the various vitalities of a community into a working harmony. But a too consistent optimism in regard to man's ability and inclination to grant justice to his fellows obscures the perils of chaos which perennially confront every society, including a free society. In one sense a democratic society is particularly exposed to the dangers of confusion. If these perils are not appreciated they may overtake a free society and invite the alternative of tyranny.[45]

The preservation of a democratic civilization requires the wisdom of the serpent and the harmlessness of the dove. The children of light must be armed with the wisdom of the children of darkness but remain free from their malice. They must know the power of self-interest in human society without giving it moral justification. They must have this wisdom in order that they may beguile, deflect, harness and restrain self-interest, individual and collective, for the sake of the community.[46]

The whole development of democratic justice in human society has depended upon some comprehension of these moral ambiguities which inhere in both government and the principle of the equilibrium of power. It is the highest achievement of democratic societies that they embody the principle of resistance to government within the principle of government itself. The citizen is thus armed with "constitutional" power to resist the unjust exactions of government. He can do this without creating anarchy within the community if government has been so conceived that criticism of the ruler becomes an instrument of better government and not a threat to government itself.[47]

Thus the democratic strategy is two-fold. First it contributes to the establishment of order and community through the non-violent arbitration and accommodation of social conflict. Second, it seeks to maintain freedom by making

[43] *Ibid.,* pp. 265, 266.
[44] Niebuhr, "Coercion, Self-Interest and Love," in K. Boulding, *The Organizational Revolution* (New York, Harper & Brothers, 1953), p. 242. By permission.
[45] *The Children of Light,* pp. xii, xiii.
[46] *Ibid.,* pp. 40, 41.
[47] *Human Destiny,* p. 268.

power responsible, checking the authority of government and providing a form of social control over the leaders of society.[48]

Contrary to the belief and expectations of eighteenth-century democrats, a national community is both integrated and divided by many ethnic, cultural, religious and economic groups. Of our early constitutionalists, Madison was realistic enough to recognize the inevitability of factions. But even he tried in every way to circumscribe their development.[49] The best political answer to the problem of accommodating and balancing the interests of competing groups is democracy, which is a permanently valid method of holding all cultural viewpoints under criticism and of achieving an uncoerced harmony among the various social and cultural vitalities.[50] An open society manages through this strategy to draw upon the virtues, and to correct the vices, of various components of the community by countervailing influences of other components. The mind of each religious and cultural group is freed by these democratic pressures in exactly the same way as interest groups of various kinds are purged of the virulence of their bias, by the challenge which they must meet from other groups.[51] In this way a healthy democracy provides for checks and balances upon the pretensions of men and their lust for power.[52]

In this situation the democratic consensus, without which a community cannot survive, must be tentative and precarious; and the required majority, necessary for common action, may be composed from time to time by the various alliances of groups. But history has proved the consequences in justice to be much higher in this freedom than is possible to attain when the "truth" about justice, as defined by any one religious group, [party,] or for that matter, any interest group, remains unchallenged. This is true because the mind by which we define justice is bound, not by ultimate commitments, but by immediate interests. There is no better way of freeing these various minds than the way which has been found in a free society. They would have, if left unchallenged, attempted to dominate the community and provide it with the only ultimate definition of "truth" and "justice."[53]

A free society thus derives general profit from the interested desires of particular groups, each group leaving a deposit of virtue in the community beyond its intentions and interests. *The health and justice of the community is preserved, not so much by the discriminate judgment of the whole community, as by the effect of free criticism in moderating the pretensions of every group and by the weight of competing power in balancing power* which might become inordinate and oppressive. Democracy in short is not a method which is effec-

[48] Harry R. Davis and Robert C. Good, editors, *Reinhold Niebuhr On Politics*, p. 183. Copyright 1960 Charles Scribner's Sons. By permission of Charles Scribner's Sons.

[49] *The Children of Light*, pp. 119, 120.

[50] "The Contribution of Religion to Cultural Unity," Hazen Pamphlet No. 13 (1945), p. 6. By permission.

[51] "The Commitment of the Self and the Freedom of the Mind," in *Religion and Freedom of Thought*, by Perry Miller, Robert L. Calhoun, Nathan M. Pusey and Reinhold Niebuhr. Copyright 1954 by the Union Theological Seminary. Reprinted by permission of Doubleday & Company, Inc. p. 58.

[52] *Christian Realism and Political Problems*, p. 14.

[53] "The Commitment of the Self and the Freedom of the Mind," p. 59.

tive only among virtuous men. It is a method which prevents interested men from following their interests to the detriment of the community—though there must of course be a minimal inclination for justice to furnish a base of community.[54]

The confusions occasioned by the dogmatic assumptions of both Right and Left prove the validity of President Conant's observation that a high degree of empiricism is a basic requirement for democratic health. All sweeping generalizations and assumptions must be eschewed and the questions must be constantly asked, what is the effect of this or that policy in this or that situation; how well does this particular constellation of power satisfy the requirements of justice and freedom? A healthy democracy never gives all power to the proponents of any dogma; it holds all claims to truth under critical review; it balances all social forces, not in an automatic but in a contrived harmony of power. It distills a modicum of truth from a conflict of error. In this way pretensions to wisdom are not supported by a monopoly of power and sweeping generalizations may be refuted by daily experience.[55]

Because reason is something more than a weapon of self-interest it can be an instrument of justice; but since reason is never dissociated from the vitalities of life, individual and collective, it cannot be a pure instrument of justice.[56] *Man's capacity for justice makes democracy possible; but man's inclination to injustice makes democracy necessary.*[57]

Madison the Realist

The early American culture was not bereft of a realistic theory. Two strains of thought, Calvinist and Jeffersonian, have entered into our original American heritage. On the problem of the resolution of political conflicts of interest and power in the community, the strain of thought most perfectly expressed by James Madison combined Christian realism in interpretation of human motives and desires with Jefferson's passion for liberty. . . .

Jefferson, and his coterie including Tom Paine, had a vision of an harmonious society in which government would interfere as little as possible with the economic ambitions of the individual. These ambitions were presumed to be moderate; and their satisfaction without friction with the neighbor would be guaranteed by the wide opportunities of the new continent. The subordination of man to man would be prevented by the simple expedient of preferring agriculture to industry. Jefferson's ideal society conformed perfectly to John Locke's conception of men "mixing their labor" with nature and claiming the fruits thereof as their legitimate property.

Madison feared the potential tyranny of government as much as Jefferson; but he understood the necessity of government much more. The Constitution protects the citizen against abuses of government, not so much by keeping government weak as by introducing the principle of balance of power into government. This balance of power between executive, legislative and judicial

---

[54] *The Self and the Dramas of History*, p. 198. Copyright 1955 by Charles Scribner's Sons. By permission of Charles Scribner's Sons.

[55] *Christian Realism and Political Problems*, p. 51.

[56] *The Children of Light*, p. 72.

[57] *Ibid.*, p. xiii.

functions is one method of preventing the abuse of power. European democracies have found other methods of achieving the same end; and their methods may be less likely to issue in a mutual frustration of a community's governing powers. The important fact is that the necessity of a strong government was recognized. Madison was much more conscious than Jefferson of the peril of what he called "faction" in the community. He had no hope of resolving such conflicts by simple prudence. With the realists of every age he knew how intimately man's reason is related to his interests. "As long as any connection exists," he wrote, "between man's reason and his self-love, his opinions and passions will have a reciprocal influence upon each other." He even anticipated Marx in finding disproportions in the possession of property to be the primary cause of political and social friction: "The most common and durable source of faction," he declared, "has been the various and unequal distribution of property." He regarded this inequality as the inevitable consequence of unequal abilities among citizens. One of Madison's most persuasive arguments for a federal union was his belief that a community of wide expanse would so diffuse interests and passions as to prevent the turbulent form of political strife, to which he regarded small communities subject. The development of parties in America has partly refuted the belief that interests could not be nationally organized. Yet the interests which are organized in the two great parties of America are so diverse as to prevent the parties from being unambiguous ideological instruments. Thus, history has partly justified his conviction.

Equilibrated Power

In any event the political philosophy which underlies our Constitution is characterized by a shrewd awareness of the potential conflicts of power and passion in every community. It knows nothing of a simple harmony in society, analogous to the alleged reciprocity of the free market.

Our political experience has enlarged upon this wisdom without always being in conscious relation to its explicit early formulation. The American labor movement was almost completely bereft of ideological weapons, which the rebellious industrial masses of Europe carried. In its inception it disavowed not only Marxist revolutionary formulas but every kind of political program. It was a pragmatic movement, born of the necessity of setting organized power against organized power in a technical society. Gradually it became conscious of the fact that economic power does try to bend government to its own ends. It has, therefore, decided to challenge a combination of political and economic power with a like combination of its own. These developments have been very recent; but they have also been very rapid.

Naturally, the "semi-official" creed of a bourgeois community, as distinguished from the philosophy which informs our Constitution, was arrayed against this development. The right of collective bargaining was declared to be a violation of the rights of employers to hire or fire whom they would. Supreme Court decisions, directed against the labor movement, were informed by the generally accepted individualistic creed.* But ultimately, in the words

* At the turn of the century a Supreme Court decision declared, "It is the constitutional right of the employer to dispense with the services of an employee because of his membership in a labor union." [Author's footnote.]

of "Mr. Dooley," the court decisions "followed the election returns." Long before the "New Deal" radically changed the climate of American political life the sovereign power of government had been used to enforce taxation laws which embodied social policy as well as revenue necessities; great concentrations of power in industry were broken up by law; necessary monopolies in utilities were brought under political regulation; social welfare, security, and health and other values which proved to be outside the operations of the free market were secured by political policy. More recently, housing and social security have become matters of public and political policy. All this was accomplished on a purely pragmatic basis, without the ideological baggage which European labor carried.

The development of American democracy toward a welfare state has proceeded so rapidly partly because the ideological struggle has not unnecessarily sharpened. It has proceeded so rapidly in fact that the question must be raised in America, as well as in the more collectivist states of Europe, whether the scope of bureaucratic decisions may not become too wide and the room for the automatic balances of unregulated choices too narrow.[58]

The thesis of classical economics was held by the middle classes. The Marxist theory was the weapon of the industrial classes. They both make faulty analysis of the human situation. But the classical theory provides for a multiplicity of powers and the Marxist theory leads to a monopoly of power. All the errors of the first theory are partially relieved by its one virtue; and all the truth in the second theory does not redeem it from this one serious error.[59]

Modern conservatism holds that justice is the inevitable fruit of a free play of economic forces, but fails to recognize that, since these forces are never equally balanced, the disproportions of power actually result in grave injustice. The healthiest Western nations have preserved their economic and political health by following neither the conservative nor the Marxist dogma, but by adopting an empirical wisdom which separates what is true from what is false in each. Thus a political creed which fears the power of the state too much and trusts the automatic balances of the market too uncritically has been balanced by a creed that brings political power to bear upon economic life, though, in its most consistent form, this creed has been too little aware of the peril in a monopoly of political and economic power in the hands of the omnicompetent state.[60]

We have, in short, achieved such justice as we possess in the only way justice can be achieved in a technical society: we have equilibrated power. We have attained a certain equilibrium in economic society itself by setting organized power against organized power. When that did not suffice we used more broadly based political power to redress disproportions and disbalances in the economic society. *A democratic society preserves a modicum of justice by various strategies of distribution and balancing both economic and political power.* [61]

The triumph of the wisdom of common sense over these two types of

[58] *The Irony of American History,* pp. 96-100.
[59] *Christian Realism and Political Problems,* pp. 99, 100.
[60] *Ibid.,* p. 50.
[61] *The Irony of American History,* p. 104.

wisdom is, therefore, primarily the wisdom of democracy itself, which prevents every strategy from being carried through to its logical conclusion. There is an element of truth in each position which becomes falsehood, precisely when it is carried through too consistently. The element of truth in each creed is required to do full justice to man's real situation. For man transcends the social and historical process sufficiently to make it possible and necessary deliberately to contrive common ends of life, particularly the end of justice. He cannot count on inadvertence and the coincidence of private desires alone to achieve common ends. On the other hand, man is too immersed in the welter of interest and passion in history and his survey over the total process is too short-range and limited to justify the endowment of any group or institution of "planners" with complete power. The "purity" of their idealism and the pretensions of their science must always be suspect. Man simply does not have a "pure" reason in human affairs; and if such reason as he has is given complete power to attain its ends, the taint will become the more noxious.

The controversy between those who would "plan" justice and order and those who trust in freedom to establish both is, therefore, an irresolvable one. Every healthy society will live in the tension of that controversy until the end of history; and will prove its health by preventing either side from gaining ultimate victory.[62]

[62] *Ibid.*, pp. 107, 108.

∽∿∽∿∽TOPIC 7

Majority Rule and Minority Rights

HENRY STEELE COMMAGER

In Defense of Majority Rule

It was in America that the doctrine of majority rule was first successfully asserted and effectuated; it was in America that the principle of limited government was first institutionalized and that machinery for maintaining it was first fashioned.

These statements may require some elaboration. What we have here are two fundamental—perhaps the two most fundamental—principles of American politics: the principle that men make government, and the principle that there are limits to the authority of government. The philosophical origins of the first principle may be found in the natural-rights philosophy of the seventeenth century—in the notion that all rights inhered originally in men and that men, living in a state of nature, came together for mutual self-protection and set up government, and that the governments thus instituted derive all their just powers from the consent of the governed. . . .

The second great basic principle—that governments are limited, that there are things no government may do, rights no government may impair, powers no government may exercise—traces its philosophical origins deep into the past but again derives authority from American experience with Parliamentary and royal pretensions. It held, simply enough, that as government was instituted to secure certain rights, its jurisdiction was strictly limited to the fields assigned to it, and that if it over-stepped the bounds of its jurisdiction its acts were not law. In the great words of Samuel Adams, addressed to Shelburne and Rockingham and Camden, "in all free states the constitution is fixed; it is from thence that the legislative derives its authority; therefore it cannot change the constitution without destroying its own foundations." . . .

[The] generation [of the American Revolution], more conscious of the dangers than of the potentialities of government, more concerned with protection against governmental tyranny than with the promotion of majority wel-

Winthrop H. Smith Professor of American History at Amherst College. Author of *The American Mind.* Co-author of *The Growth of the American Republic, The Heritage of America* and other works. Contributor to many journals and periodicals. The selection is from Henry Steele Commager, *Majority Rule and Minority Rights.* © 1943 by Oxford University Press, Inc., Chs. I and III. By permission of author and publisher.

fare, devised cunning mechanisms for putting limitations upon government. When we contemplate the ingenuity of the Fathers in setting up their system of checks and balances we are deeply impressed, almost dismayed. That the limits of governmental authority might not be misunderstood, that authority was described—for the first time—in written constitutions, and to these constitutions were added bills of rights. But this was merely elementary. There were, in addition, the checks and balances of the federal system, of the tripartite division of powers, of the bicameral legislatures, of frequent elections, and of impeachment. And atop all this there developed—I would not say there was established—the practice of judicial review.

But in their laudable zeal to give reality to John Dickinson's description of a free people—"Not those over whom government is reasonably and equitably exercised, but those who live under a government so constitutionally checked and controlled, that proper provision is made against its being otherwise exercised"—the framers of our constitutions confused, it would seem, jurisdiction with power, and the confusion has persisted down to our own day. They failed properly to distinguish between the authority government should have, and the manner in which government might exercise that authority which it did have. They set up limits on the jurisdiction of government, enumerating things no government could do; and this was eminently proper and in harmony with the philosophy of the Revolutionary era. But they went farther. So fearful were they of governmental tyranny that even where they granted to government certain necessary powers they put obstacles in the way of the effective exercise of those powers. They set up not only boundaries to government but impediments in government. Thus they not only made it difficult for government to invade fields denied to it, but they made it difficult for government to operate at all. They created a system where deadlock would be the normal character of the American government—a situation from which political parties rescued us.

So here we have two institutions which are—or would appear to be—fundamentally contradictory. We have first the institutionalization of the principle that men can alter, abolish, and institute governments, can, in short, make government conform to their will. But over against this we have the institutionalization of the principle that governments are limited—that there are things not even a majority may require government to do because they are outside the jurisdiction of any government. If the majority may use government to do its will, is that not an attack upon the inalienable rights of men over against government? if there are limits upon what governments may do, is that not a challenge to or even a denial of the principle of majority rule? Here is a paradox not yet resolved in our political philosophy or our constitutional system.

This paradox is presented in most familiar form in Jefferson's First Inaugural Address: "All, too, will bear in mind this sacred principle, that though the will of the majority is in all cases to prevail, that will to be rightful must be reasonable; that the minority possess their equal rights which equal law must protect, and to violate would be oppression." And throughout our history runs this theme of majority will and minority rights. Jefferson, as we shall see, emphasized majority will, and so did Jefferson's successors, Jackson and Lincoln —Jackson, who brushed aside judicial interposition, Lincoln, who reminded us that

A majority . . . is the only true sovereign of a free people. Whoever rejects it does, of necessity, fly into anarchy or to despotism. Unanimity is impossible; the rule of a minority, as a permanent arrangement, is wholly inadmissible; so that, rejecting the majority principle, anarchy or despotism in some form is all that is left.

But the emphasis since the Civil War has been increasingly on minority rights—an emphasis so marked, between Reconstruction and the New Deal, that it is no great exaggeration to say that tenderness for the minority became the distinguishing characteristic of the American constitutional system.

Underlying this distinction are, of course, the assumptions that majority will and minority rights are antithetical, that majority rule constantly threatens minority rights, and that the principal function of our constitutional system is to protect minority rights against infringement.

So plausible are these assumptions that there has developed, in course of time, the theory of the "tyranny of the majority"—a theory which derived much support abroad as well as here from the misleading observations of Tocqueville. Tocqueville, who leaned heavily for material and authority on that pillar of conservatism, Joseph Story, confessed that "the very essence of democratic government consists in the absolute sovereignty of the majority," and concluded from this that the prospects for American democracy were bleak indeed. His analysis of the consequences that flow from the tyranny of the majority has given comfort, ever since, to those who fear democracy. So persuasive is this theory of the tyranny of the majority that many Americans have come to believe that our constitutional system is not, in fact, based upon the principle of majority rule. And they have found support and consolation in the curious notion that ours is a "republican" form of government, and that a republic is the very opposite of a democracy.

The fear of the tyranny of the majority has haunted many of the most distinguished and respectable American statesmen and jurists since the days of the founding of the Republic; it persists today, after a century and a half of experience. It was first formulated, in elaborate and coherent fashion, by John Adams in his famous *Defense of the Constitutions of Government of the United States of America* (1786). The people, Adams urges, are not to be trusted, nor are their representatives, without an adequate system of checks and balances:

> If it is meant by the people . . . a representative assembly, . . . they are not the best keepers of the people's liberties or their own, if you give them all the power, legislative, executive and judicial. They would invade the liberties of the people, at least the majority of them would invade the liberties of the minority, sooner and oftener than any absolute monarch. . . .

[And in No. 51 of *The Federalist*, the warning was given that]

> It is of great importance in a republic not only to guard the society against the oppression of its rulers, but to guard one part of the society

This was the consistent note—that the people may—and must—be trusted. "No government can continue good," he assured John Adams, "but under the control of the people"; and again, to that doughty opponent of judicial pretensions, Spencer Roane, "Independence can be trusted nowhere but with the people in the mass. They are inherently independent of all but the moral law." "I know of no safe depository of the ultimate powers of the society," he told William Jarvis, "but the people themselves; and if we think them not enlightened enough to exercise their control with a wholesome discretion, the remedy is not to take it from them, but to inform their discretion by education." And recalling Hume's argument that "all history and experience" confounded the notion that "the people are the origin of all just power," Jefferson burst out with uncharacteristic violence: "And where else will this degenerate son of science, this traitor to his fellow men, find the origin of just powers, if not in the majority of the society? Will it be in the minority? Or in an individual of that minority?" And we hear an echo of that question which the First Inaugural submits to the contemporary world: "Sometimes it is said that man can not be trusted with the government of himself. Can he, then, be trusted with the government of others? Or have we found angels in the forms of kings to govern him? Let history answer this question." For himself, Jefferson knew the answer. His devotion to the people was not that of the benevolent despot, the party boss, or the dictator, but of the good citizen, and his whole career is a monument to the sincerity of his confession to Du Pont de Nemours. "We both love the people," he said, "but you love them as infants, whom you are afraid to trust without nurses; and I as adults whom I freely leave to self-government."

To all of this many of Jefferson's contemporaries could have subscribed without reservation: he, assuredly, had no monopoly on faith in popular government. "We of the United States," as he explained simply, "are constitutionally and conscientiously democrats." But in one respect Jefferson went farther than most of his contemporaries, went so far, indeed, that his argument sounds bizarre and almost alien to our ears. That was his advocacy of what we may call the doctrine of the continuing majority. It was easy enough for most Americans to subscribe to the compact theory of government—the compact made, of course, by the original majority—just as it is easy for us to subscribe, now, to the doctrine that we are, all of us, bound by the compact made at Philadelphia in 1787 and ratified by the majority of that time. And just as we have invested that Constitution with sacrosanctity, so—in England, in France, in America of the eighteenth century—there was a tendency to regard the original compact, the product of the Golden Age of the past, with reverence and to invest it with a peculiar sanctity. Such an attitude was foreign to Jefferson. His conviction, however, that each new majority must write its own fundamental law has sometimes been regarded as merely an amusing exaggeration, a whimsey to be indulged along with the whimsey that a little rebellion, now and then, is an excellent thing. But there can be no doubt of Jefferson's sincerity in the matter, nor of his persuasion that the issue was one of fundamental importance.

This problem is more fundamental, and more complex, than might appear at first glance—this problem of the original *versus* the continuing majority. All of us seem to agree that we are bound by the original majority—by the majority of 1787, or that which decreed our state constitutions. But what if the will of the present majority conflicts with that of the original majority? Is majority

against the injustice of the other part. Different interests necessarily e.
in different classes of citizens. If a majority be united by a common
terest, the rights of the minority will be insecure. . . . Justice is the e
of government. It is the end of civil society. . . . In a society under th
forms of which the stronger faction can readily unite and oppress th
weaker, anarchy may as truly be said to reign as in a state of nature
where the weaker individual is not secured against the violence of the
stronger. . . .

Confronted by these different interpretations of the American constitutional system, of democracy and of republicanism, we may turn with some
confidence to Thomas Jefferson. On these questions he is, indubitably, our
leading authority. He helped to create and to establish the new political systems
in America, and he furnished them with a good part of their political philosophy. He never wrote a formal treatise on the subject (as did his old friend
John Adams), but in his public papers and his private letters we can find the
most comprehensive and consistent statement of the nature of American democracy that has come down to us from the generation of the founders.

And it must be observed, first, that Jefferson was by no means unaware of
the dangers inherent in majority rule. . . . [To him] majority rule is neither
anarchy nor absolutism, but government within self-imposed restraints. And
we search in vain through the voluminous writings of Jefferson for any expression of distrust of the virtue or the wisdom of the people. What we do find,
on the contrary, from the beginning to the end of Jefferson's career, is an un-
terrified and unflinching faith in majority rule.

"I am not among those who fear the people," he wrote to Kercheval in
1816; "they and not the rich, are our dependence for continued freedom." . . .
Writing to Madison [he said], . . . "After all, it is my principle that the will
of the majority should prevail." And to another Virginia friend, Colonel Car-
rington, went the same reassurance:

> I am persuaded myself that the good sense of the people will always
> be found to be the best army. They may be led astray for a moment, but
> will soon correct themselves. The people are the only censors of their
> governors; and even their errors will tend to keep these to the true
> principles of their institution.

That the people, if led astray, would "soon correct themselves" was a fixed
conviction and one which, *mirabile dictu,* found confirmation in their tenacious
support of his own administration. Thus to John Tyler in 1804:

> No experiment can be more interesting than that we are now trying,
> and which we trust will end in establishing the fact that man may be
> governed by reason and truth. . . . The firmness with which the people
> have withstood the late abuses of the press, the discernment that they
> have manifested between truth and falsehood, show that they may safely
> be trusted to hear everything true and false, and to form correct judg-
> ment between them. . . .

will valid only for some past generation? The easy answer is that the present majority can, if it chooses, change the original compact by constitutional amendment or by substituting an entirely new constitution. But it takes more than a majority to amend a constitution or to write a new one, and under our present system a determined minority can, if it will, effectively veto any change in the federal document and in most state documents. Not only this, but the courts have pretty consistently held that the current majority may not even interpret the original constitution to accommodate it to felt needs. . . .

Jefferson, as we know, entertained no reverence for the constitutional dogmas of the past. His attitude, set forth in the famous letter to Samuel Kercheval, of July 1816, is too familiar to justify quotation in full:

> Let us [not] weakly believe that one generation is not as capable as another of taking care of itself, and of ordering its own affairs. Let us . . . avail ourselves of our reason and experience, to correct the crude essays of our first and unexperienced, although wise, virtuous and well-meaning counsels. And lastly, let us provide in our Constitution for its revision at stated periods. What these periods should be, nature herself indicates. . . . Each generation is as independent of the one preceding, as that was of all which had gone before. It has, then, like them, a right to choose for itself the form of government it believes most promotive of its own happiness . . . and it is for the peace and good of mankind that a solemn opportunity of doing this every nineteen or twenty years should be provided by the Constitution. . . .

"The People," a distinguished contemporary statesman has said in a phrase already classic, "have no right to do wrong." It is at least suggestive that Eamon de Valera, who has fought pretty consistently for his people and who regards himself as a democrat, should have found it necessary to invoke the techniques of totalitarianism to prevent the people from "doing wrong." And it is a characteristic of almost every anti-democratic philosophy that it purports to serve the welfare of the people but refuses to trust the judgment of the people on questions affecting their welfare. . . .

Our constitutional system, as has already been observed, is one of checks and balances: these have already been noted. It is sometimes forgotten that our political system is one of checks and balances too. Anyone who has followed the slow and tortuous course of a major public issue—the poll tax, for example, or neutrality, through the arena of public opinion, into the party conventions and caucuses, into the halls of Congress and the rooms of appropriate committees, knows how much of delay, of balance, of compromise, is implicit in our political machinery. A good part of our politics, indeed, seems to be concerned with reconciling majority and minority will, class hostilities, sectional differences, the divergent interests of producer and consumer, of agriculture and labor, of creditor and debtor, of city and country, of tax-payer and tax-beneficiary, of the military and the civilian. In small issues as in great, the result is generally a compromise. Democracy, in short, whether from instinct or from necessity, furnishes its own checks and balances—quite aside from such as may be provided in written constitutions.

Indeed it might plausibly be argued that it is one of the major advantages of democracy over other forms of government that it alone can indulge in the luxury of tolerating minority and dissenting groups because it alone has developed the technique for dealing with them. It is sometimes charged as a criticism of democracy that it cannot act speedily and effectively in an emergency—as can totalitarian or despotic governments. The charge is not sound—as witness the efficiency of our own democracy in the spring of 1933 or the winter of 1941–2—but it is true that in a democracy it requires a real emergency to produce prompt and effective action.

But there is this to be said of the checks and balances of democratic politics—that they are natural, not artificial; that they are flexible rather than rigid; that they can yield to public opinion and to necessity. They do, sometimes, enable the majority to ride down the minority; they do, far more frequently, enable the minority to delay and defeat the majority. But the responsibility in all this is with the people themselves—where it belongs. Where they indulge their apathy, their carelessness, their blindness, they pay the price, and it is right that they should pay the price. As the fault is theirs, so, too, the remedy. Where issues appear sufficiently important the majority can have its way even against the recalcitrance of minorities who take refuge in the labyrinths of our party and our legislative systems. But against minorities entrenched in the judiciary there is no effective appeal except through the complicated and slow process of constitutional amendment. Here it is true today as it was in 1801 that the minority can "retire into the judiciary as a stronghold," and "from that battery" beat down the works of republicanism. . . .

This is the crucial objection to judicial nullification of majority will in any field: that "education in the abandonment of foolish legislation is itself a training in liberty." If our democracy is less educated in this respect than we might wish, if our legislatures are less alert to constitutional principles than might seem desirable, a heavy responsibility rests upon the courts. For these, by taking over to themselves, the peculiar guardianship of the Constitution and of civil liberties, have discouraged the people's active and intelligent interest in these matters. Judges—and liberals—have ignored what Professor Chafee finely says, that "the victories of liberty of speech must be won in the mind before they are won in the courts." For in the long run only an educated and enlightened democracy can hope to endure. . . .

Our own experience, I believe, justifies Jefferson's faith that men need no masters—not even judges. It justifies us, too, in believing that majority will does not imperil minority rights, either in theory or in operation. It gives us firm basis for a belief that the people themselves can be trusted to realize that the majority has a vital interest in the preservation of an alert and critical minority and that, conversely, the minority can have no rights fundamentally inimical to the commonwealth. It justifies us in the belief that only in a democracy where there is free play of ideas, where issues are freely fought out in the public forum,—where, in short, the safety valves of public discussion and experimentation and reconsideration are always open—can there be assurance that both majority and minority rights will be served. It is the glory of democracy that it—and it alone—can tolerate dissent. It is the strength of democracy that dissent, where tolerated, is helpful rather than harmful.

ALEXIS DE TOCQUEVILLE

The Tyranny of the Majority

I hold it to be an impious and an execrable maxim that, politically speaking, a people has a right to do whatsoever it pleases, and yet I have asserted that all authority originates in the will of the majority. Am I, then, in contradiction with myself? . . .

A majority taken collectively may be regarded as a being whose opinions, and most frequently whose interests, are opposed to those of another being, which is styled a minority. If it be admitted that a man, possessing absolute power, may misuse that power by wronging his adversaries, why should a majority not be liable to the same reproach? Men are not apt to change their characters by agglomeration; nor does their patience in the presence of obstacles increase with the consciousness of their strength. And for these reasons I can never willingly invest any number of my fellow creatures with that unlimited authority which I should refuse to any one of them. . . .

I am of opinion that some one social power must always be made to predominate over the others; but I think that liberty is endangered when this power is checked by no obstacles which may retard its course, and force it to moderate its own vehemence.

Unlimited power is in itself a bad and dangerous thing; human beings are not competent to exercise it with discretion, and God alone can be omnipotent, because his wisdom and his justice are always equal to his power. But no power upon earth is so worthy of honor for itself, or of reverential obedience to the rights which it represents, that I would consent to admit its uncontrolled and all-predominant authority. When I see that the right and the means of absolute command are conferred on a people or upon a king, upon an aristocracy or a democracy, a monarchy or a republic, I recognize the germ of tyranny, and I journey onward to a land of more hopeful institutions.

In my opinion the main evil of the present democratic institutions of the United States does not arise, as is often asserted in Europe, from their weakness, but from their overpowering strength; and I am not so much alarmed at the excessive liberty which reigns in that country as at the very inadequate securities which exist against tyranny.

When an individual or a party is wronged in the United States, to whom can he apply for redress? If to public opinion, public opinion constitutes the majority; if to legislature, it represents the majority, and implicitly obeys its injunctions; if to the executive power, it is appointed by the majority, and remains a passive tool in its hands; the public troops consist of the majority

Noted French statesman and critic. Author of *The Old Government and the Revolution* and other works on political and social subjects. The selection is from Alexis de Tocqueville, *Democracy in America* (Henry Reeve translation, 1835), Vol. I, Chs. XIII-XV.

under arms; the jury is the majority invested with the right of hearing judicial cases; and in certain States even the judges are elected by the majority. However iniquitous or absurd the evil of which you complain may be, you must submit to it as well as you can. . . .

I do not say that tyrannical abuses frequently occur in America at the present day, but I maintain that no sure barrier is established against them, and that the causes which mitigate the government are to be found in the circumstances and the manners of the country more than its laws. . . .

In America, the majority raises very formidable barriers to the liberty of opinion: within these barriers an author may write whatever he pleases, but he will repent it if he ever step beyond them. Not that he is exposed to the terrors of an *auto-da-fé,* but he is tormented by the slights and persecutions of daily obloquy. His political career is closed forever, since he has offended the only authority which is able to promote his success. . . .

Monarchical institutions have thrown an odium upon despotism; let us beware lest democratic republics should restore oppression, and should render it less odious and less degrading in the eyes of the many, by making it still more onerous to the few.

THOMAS LANDON THORSON
The Logic of Democracy

Majority Rule and Minority Rights

The problem that most democratic theorists would regard as the most difficult and most important one arises because of the ever-present possibility under a democratic governmental structure that the right of the majority to rule will come into conflict with the right of individuals and minorities to assert and register in a formal way their political preferences. If, as most democrats in the Western political tradition would admit, democracy necessarily involves the application and utilization of both the principle of majority rule and the principle of minority rights, the potential conflicts can be placed in two broad categories. The first of these is majority action that deprives a minority of its legitimate role in the democratic decision-making process (e.g., by denying free expression or suffrage). The second is action on the part of a minority that deprives a majority of the legitimate right to rule (e.g., the abuse of the power of judicial review by the United States Supreme Court). This problem in its manifold aspects is one which will be quite familiar to anyone who has had contact with democratic government.

The argument I wish to make is that the role of the political philosopher

Political scientist. Editor of *Plato: Totalitarian or Democrat.* The selection is from *The Logic of Democracy* (New York, Holt, Rinehart and Winston, Inc., 1962), pp. 151-162. By permission.

in dealing with this problem has been vastly overestimated. I do not think that it is legitimately a philosophical problem or even, in one sense of the term, legitimately a theoretical problem. By this I mean that the political philosopher *qua* political philosopher cannot solve it. He *can,* however—and this is quite important—show why it cannot be solved by philosophical means and thus clarify the *nature* of the solution.

There is no single theoretical solution to the problem of majority rule and minority rights; rather, there are solutions of various kinds, the choice of which turns upon the gathering of relevant empirical evidence. The opinion is nonetheless widespread that this is a problem susceptible of theoretical solution. It has in fact been called by reputable authority "the greatest single theoretical controversy about the nature of democracy."[1] That this essentially empirical question should be seen as a theoretical question is, I think, the result of faulty philosophizing.

In one sense, there is an almost infinite variety of writers about democracy, each in one respect or another looking at democracy in a slightly different perspective. However, as was suggested before, so far as the majority rule—minority rights question is concerned, there are two major categories. On the one hand, there are those who see democracy essentially as an instrument for limiting the powers of governmental officials. For them the widest possible freedom for individuals consistent with stable government is the highest value. What they fear most of all is tyranny, and often the sort of tyranny most feared is the tyranny of the majority.[2] To this camp belong the most notable figures in early American democratic thought: surely James Madison, in some measure Thomas Jefferson, and certainly John C. Calhoun. Typically, the philosophical point of departure for democrats of this school is some sort of conception of the natural rights of men. Let us then lump them together under the general rubric "natural rights democrats."

The contrary view, which is generally speaking the more modern one, sees democracy as the method of popular government. The stress here is laid upon popular sovereignty, political equality, and therefore upon majority rule. The test of whether a governmental act is democratic or not is not so much a matter of how it affects individuals as it is of whether the policy has been decided upon by a majority of the citizenry. There is less emphasis upon limiting governmental activity and more emphasis upon allowing the majority to do what it wants. It seems fair to say that this view of democracy is held by jurists such as Felix Frankfurter and Learned Hand and by political scientists such as Austin Ranney and Willmoore Kendall. Such a position can be and has been worked out in a variety of ways. Generally implicit and often explicit in the view, however, is a denial of the possibility of knowing natural law and natural rights and the consequent conclusion that the will of the majority is the only ultimate test in politics. Frankfurter, for example, has had occasion to refer to the Supreme Court as "non-democratic" and "inherently oligarchic,"[3] thus im-

[1] Austin Ranney and Willmoore Kendall, *Democracy and the American Party System* (New York, Harcourt, Brace & World, Inc., 1956), p. 29.
[2] Cf. Robert A. Dahl, *A Preface to Democratic Theory*. Copyright 1956 by the University of Chicago. (Chicago, University of Chicago Press), pp. 4-33.
[3] *AFL v. American Sash and Door Co.,* 335 U.S. 538 (1949), 555.

plying that for him majority rule is the prime element in democracy. . . . These are what we may fairly call "majority rule democrats."

We need to be clear that the difference between "natural rights democrats" and "majority rule democrats," to which I have attempted to call attention, is less a matter of wholly contradictory notions of democracy than a matter of different theoretical casts of mind. All democrats will recognize the need for both majority rule and the protection of minority rights. The difference is a matter of emphasis. As Robert A. Dahl has stated it,[4]

> . . . so far as I am aware, no one has ever advocated, and no one except its enemies has ever defined democracy to mean, that a majority would or should do anything it felt an impulse to do. Every advocate of democracy of whom I am aware, and every friendly definition of it, includes the idea of restraints on majorities. But one central issue is whether these restraints are, or should be, (1) primarily internalized restraints in the individual behavior system, such as the conscience and other products of social indoctrination, (2) primarily social checks and balances of several kinds, or (3) primarily prescribed constitutional checks. Among political systems to which the term "democracy" is commonly applied in the Western world, one important difference is between those which rely primarily on the first two checks, and those like the United States which also employ constitutional checks.

Because of the existence of constitutional checks in the United States, controversy over the proper roles of majority rule and minority rights has flourished among Americans. The questions to confront in this connection are two: (A) should there be constitutional checks at all? (B) Given that constitutional checks exist, how should they be applied?

The affirmative answer to question A classically takes the following form:

1. All men are endowed with certain natural rights. Among these are life, liberty, property, and the pursuit of happiness.

2. The severe deprivation of these natural rights is tyranny.

3. The true or proper purpose of government is the protection of these rights or, to say the same thing another way, the prevention of tyranny.

4. Minorities can be prevented from depriving other members of the society of their natural rights by the operation of the principle of majority rule.

5. Majorities can be prevented from depriving other members of the society of their natural rights by the operation of constitutional checks on their power.

6. Therefore, constitutional checks on the power of majorities should be employed.

There is no need to elaborate the roles of Locke, Madison, Jefferson, and Calhoun in promoting one or another aspect of this view. Considered historically, this argument represents the mainstream of American democratic thought.

One can object to the argument in a number of ways. Professor Dahl, for

[4] Dahl, *op. cit.,* p. 36.

example, is willing in terms of his analysis to grant the natural rights premise but seeks to demonstrate, quite successfully, that the requirement of constitutional checks does not follow on empirical grounds.[5] My quarrel is with the natural rights premise itself. The conception of democracy presented in this argument quite clearly makes natural rights the prime principle and majority rule a secondary one. For this reason its adherents were not content with social and cultural checks upon the power of majorities but demanded constitutional checks as well. Thus, Dahl's argument that constitutional checks do not *necessarily* follow from the premises, while completely accurate as far as it goes, in a certain sense misses a point of great significance. What, most fundamentally, is wrong with this argument is that it identifies the justification of democracy with the justification of natural rights.

The man who sees the protection of natural rights as the very definition of democracy does not need a conclusive demonstration of the necessity of constitutional checks on majorities. For him the likelihood that they will help is enough. But his definition is wrong, because it presumes the existence of a set of qualities or properties that attach to each man. The existence of these qualities or properties is supposedly proved by observation and inductive generalization, or by deductive demonstration from some grand principle—"These truths are self-evident," "All men are endowed with reason," "All men are created in the image of God." We have, I trust, said enough about these lines of argument.

Do not misunderstand my point. My argument is not against constitutional checks on majorities, nor does it suggest that there are no human rights which should be protected. Rather, my contention is that the conception of democracy which holds natural rights to be the prime principle is faulty because it seeks to justify by proof when no proof is possible. When the argument for constitutional checks is contingent upon such proof as it is in the classical argument, it is also faulty.

The contrary theoretical solution to the problem of constitutional checks posed by question A is equally invalid. This position demands, in the words of Professors Ranney and Kendall, that no *"formal* institutional limitations" be placed on the power of popular majorities. This conclusion is said to follow from the definition of democracy in the following way:[6]

1. Political equality and popular sovereignty are principles of democracy.

2. Majority rule alone is compatible with these principles. (Minority rule is incompatible with political equality and popular sovereignty because it violates them by definition, and unanimity is impossible.)

3. Any attempt at formal institutional limitation (e.g., a Supreme Court

---

[5] *Ibid.*, pp. 11-15.

[6] *"Why 'Absolute' Majority Rule?* For the reasons given in the foregoing pages, any attempt to place *formal* institutional limitations upon the 'absolute' power of popular majorities logically results in the establishment of *minority* rule. And from the standpoint of logic, 'absolute' majority rule must be chosen over minority rule as a principle of ideally democratic government, not because there is any magic or omniscience in popular majorities, but because majority rule is more nearly in accord than minority rule with the other principles of democracy that we have previously discussed." Ranney and Kendall, *op. cit.,* pp. 29-37. (Italics in original.)

with the power of judicial review, the requirements for extraordinary majorities) necessarily involves minority rule.

4. Ergo, no formal institutional limitations on the power of majorities are legitimate from a democratic point of view.

This argument seeks by an exercise of "strict logic," as Ranney and Kendall say several times, to solve the problem of constitutional checks by deduction from the basic democratic premises. Again, it may be criticized from several angles. First of all, the conclusion quite simply does not follow from the premises. The conclusion—*no* formal institutional limitations on the power of popular majorities—is too broad. It is quite reasonable to say that, with respect to a wide range of social policy choices, only majority rule is the legitimate democratic principle because of its compatibility with political equality and popular sovereignty. On the other hand, it is hardly reasonable to argue that with respect to majority actions which abrogate political equality and popular sovereignty (e.g., denial of suffrage, free expression, or the opportunity to run for public office) majority rule alone is legitimate because of its compatibility with political equality and popular sovereignty. But this is what the conclusion *"no* constitutional checks" must mean, if it means anything at all. Thus, as an exercise in "strict logic" the argument is a failure.[7]

Because this argument is in large part a modern one, advanced in an era dominated by an empiricist-positivist *Weltanschauung,* questions of philosophical justification are not often explicitly raised in connection with it. Ranney and Kendall, for example, do not explicitly attempt to justify political equality or popular sovereignty; rather, these principles are given. "No one thinks of democracy" without thinking of these two principles.[8] I suspect quite strongly, however, that the implicit justification of the argument is at the core of its inadequacy.

While this argument usually goes by the name "absolute majority rule," it might more precisely be described as absolute "antiminority" rule. The case *for* majority rule is developed wholly from the case *against* minority rule. Here are Ranney and Kendall on this point:[9]

> A policy or procedure, obviously, does not gain in rightness by picking up enough support to justify the claim that it represents the wishes of a majority, or lose in rightness by losing support. But that is not the point at issue, since what the majoritarian asserts is not the superior intelligence or wisdom or even morality of popular majorities, but the wrongness, from the democratic point of view, of a state of affairs where the few are in a position to have their way over the wishes of the many.

But what *is* wrong with minority rule? The immediate answer would surely be that "it violates political equality and popular sovereignty." But why these principles? My guess is that the answer we would get to this question, and

---

[7] See Thomas Landon Thorson, "Epilogue on Absolute Majority Rule," *The Journal of Politics,* vol. XXIII (August, 1961), pp. 557-565.

[8] Ranney and Kendall, *op. cit.,* p. 29.

[9] *Ibid.,* p. 32.

therefore the real answer to the first question, would be a truncated version of the argument from fallibilism. The reasoning would probably be something like this:

1. No man (or group of men) can demonstrate the rightness of his preferences.
2. Therefore, all men must be treated as equal and allowed to rule.
3. Therefore, no minority should be allowed to rule.
4. If not minority rule, then majority rule.

But this argument *is* truncated; it is oversimplified. Fallibilism prescribes no such simple numerical rule but a general directive on leaving the way open for a change in social goals. The so-called "absolute majority rule" argument eliminates the majority rule—minority rights problem by deductive fiat; and as we have seen, the deduction is faulty.

The conclusion to be drawn from all this is that the controversy over constitutional checks is not to be resolved in either direction by abstract reasoning. The decision to have constitutional checks or not to have them can only turn on an estimate of the empirical situation. The categorical of fallibilism demands that the way be kept open for a change in goals. The categorical, as we have seen, implies the maximization of political equality, popular sovereignty, minority political rights, and majority rule. When faced with the problem of actually designing real-world institutions, this ideal procedure is (or should be) a prime value; but the preservation and stability of the society is also a value. The choice between giving majorities free rein or constitutionally checking them can be sensibly made only by assessing the relative costs of the alternatives. Who in this particular society is more likely to abuse power, a majority or a minority? This is the question, and clearly it is an empirical question, not a theoretical or philosophical one.

Treating the majority rule—minority rights problem as essentially resolved by either a natural rights argument or an "absolute majority rule" argument can lead to very important practical consequences. A good deal of American constitutional history can be understood in these terms. It would be beyond the scope of this essay to discuss this history in any detail. Let me instead discuss a hypothetical society, which I suspect will nonetheless sound a bit familiar. This discussion will deal with question B: given that constitutional checks exist, how should they be applied?

Imagine a society with a democratic governmental structure. This democratic structure is provided for in a written constitution that is to be the supreme law of society. To the legislature and the executive is given a general grant of power to promote the general welfare. The legislature and the executive are specifically prohibited from abridging free expression, suffrage, the right to run for public office, and the right peaceably to assemble. The legislature and the executive are also prohibited from expropriating private property without due process of law. A supreme judicial body with the power of judicial review is also provided for. The constitution is very difficult to amend, so that the exercise of the power of judicial review is quite effective.

This is clearly a constitutional-check situation. The supreme judicial body, a minority, is given the power to check the action of majorities. The delegation of this power is anything but clear. When does a legislative act promote the general welfare, and when is it deleterious to the general welfare? What are the limits on free expression? What is a peaceful assembly? What is due process of law? All these questions will require answers from the members of the supreme judicial body, and it is clear that a mere reading of the constitution, no matter how assiduous, cannot provide them. The judges will therefore have to define their role in this democratic process which the constitution attempts to create. How the judges do this will surely in part turn on their conceptions of democracy. Undoubtedly the formation of attitudes on these questions will be the result of a wide variety of environmental factors, including presumably socio-economic class origins, experience prior to appointment, and education. A particular judge's conception of democracy will be here created and there reinforced by these factors, but he is likely to have a conception of democracy at the level of articulation.

Suppose a majority of judges share a natural rights conception of democracy and see democratic government basically as limited government. How are these judges likely to react to cases that involve a conflict between the wishes of the majority as reflected by the legislature and the freedom to act of individuals affected by the statute in question? Surely it would not be surprising to find them using their power of judicial review aggressively—striking down what they consider to be majority infringement on the freedom of individuals. For these judges "the general welfare" would likely be defined in terms of the freedom to act of individuals. For them "due process of law" might come to mean not only a set of regular procedures but also a substantive directive with regard to the wisdom of certain policies. That this conception of democracy might lead to a frustration of majority desires, to a blocking of the possibility of change with respect to social goals, appears rather clear. That statutes limiting child labor, fixing maximum hours and minimum wages, or coercing payment for old-age pensions might be struck down as infringing freedom of contract or as deleterious to the general welfare would not be surprising.

Suppose, on the other hand, that the court majority held a majority rule conception of democracy. Would not this majority be likely to regard its whole position as somewhat tenuous? Might not judges holding this view see the judicial body of which they were a part as "non-democratic" and "inherently oligarchic," to use words written by Mr. Justice Frankfurter in a not dissimilar context. Majority rule democrats on the court might adopt, as the rule of behavior with respect to the use of the power of judicial review, not the aggressiveness of the natural rights democrats but a doctrine of self-restraint toward the preferences of majorities.

If the legislature were to adopt a statute limiting the right to speak and write of a group of social, political, or economic heretics, a judge who held majority rule to be the very definition of democracy might be quite reluctant to employ judicial review against it. If free expression is limited by a frightened and myopic majority, the possibility of changing social goals is blocked to that extent.

My line of argument, I hope, is now clear. Conceptions of democracy, justifications of democracy that elevate either natural rights or the principle of majority rule to a position of primacy, can lead to practical consequences of great importance. We have tried to show that such justifications are faulty, and we call instead for a conception of democracy which makes no institutional principle supreme but which holds that the principles are mutually interdependent and essentially equal. They are the spelling out of the general categorical recommendation "Be rational" when setting up a political system. According to this view, it is quite consistent for judges empowered with judicial review to be self-restrained in the face of majority preferences on general social policy *and* to be aggressive in the use of their power when free expression, suffrage, or the right to run for public office is in question. Thus, thinking through the logic of democracy can be of great importance to actors in the democratic process.

There is no suggestion here that all the problems involved in implementing democracy will be magically solved if "the proper" justification of democracy is adopted. The categorical of rationality is no Euclidean theorem from which the answers to all problems follow by demonstration. Empirical concerns, or matters of fact, are crucial to every political problem; but matters of choice are equally crucial. One of the functions of the political scientist, the economist, the sociologist, the psychologist, and the anthropologist is to find and present the facts relevant to these problems.

The political philosopher, on the contrary, is not a superscientist. The definition of his task does not include the possession of a superior insight into the way the world *is*. He tries instead to think through matters of choice, often of ultimate choice, for citizens who have not the time or resources to do it for themselves. Unless one is willing to adopt the metaphysic that human beings are Pavlovian dogs whose behavior is *entirely* to be understood as a set of responses to irrational stimuli, this is a task of greatest importance, and it should not be rejected because political philosophers have at times been far too pretentious or because they have made mistakes. Political philosophy can be good or bad, helpful or useless. If it is wrong, it should be criticized, but it should be criticized in its own terms. It is recommendation, not fact. To criticize political philosophy because it is not fact is no criticism at all. Like all political philosophers, Plato made many mistakes, but he made no mistake when he cast the first political philosophy in the form of a dialogue. Mistakes call for criticism, and if he understands his role, the political philosopher welcomes them.

~~Section III

THE CONSTITUTION: "ROAD OR GATE"?

Marbury v. Madison established the power of the Supreme Court to declare Acts of Congress unconstitutional and unenforceable. The Constitution explicitly provided for the exercise of similar power by the Court with respect to state legislation. Thus the limits of both federal and state power have been determined, in the final analysis, by the Supreme Court except in those rare instances where the Constitution has been changed by amendment. That the Court has enjoyed considerable discretion in defining those limits is illustrated by the cases in this section.

McCulloch v. Maryland, in which Chief Justice Marshall gave elastic scope to Congressional power generally under the Constitution, is not merely of historic interest but proved of great importance in helping to sustain much of the New Deal legislation and continues as the foundation of broad federal authority.

On the other hand, the Schechter case, in which the Supreme Court unanimously invalidated the National Industrial Recovery Act, reflects a restricted view of delegated congressional power. This was one of several blows to New Deal legislation which led President Roosevelt in 1937 to seek to reorganize the Supreme Court. Wickard v. Filburn, decided in the decade of the 40's, is representative of sweeping extensions of federal power over the economy upheld by the Court in its greatly expanded view of Congressional prerogative under the Constitution.

Similarly, with respect to the power of the state to legislate in the interests of the health, safety, and welfare of its inhabitants (the so-called police power), the Court for many decades, beginning in the late 1800's, while reflecting a dominant *laissez faire* philosophy, often invoked general clauses of the Constitution, such as the due process and contract clauses, to curb social legislation. However, during President Roosevelt's second term, in the midst of depression, the Court began to give expanded scope to the police power of the states; and this liberal attitude toward social legislation has characterized the decisions of the Supreme Court ever since. The due process (like the equal protection) clause has now served chiefly as a restraint upon state action in denigration of civil liberties and civil rights.

[Further discussion of the role of the Court will be found in the section titled "Judicial Review."]

Foundation of Judicial Review

The Judicial Power

MARBURY *V.* MADISON

1 Cranch 137 (1803)

> *On March 2, 1801, two days before the close of his term, President John Adams appointed William Marbury, among others, as a justice of the peace in the District of Columbia. Through some inadvertence the commission was left on the desk of the Secretary of State when President Adams' term expired at midnight, March 3rd. Upon Thomas Jefferson's accession to the presidency, he directed his Secretary of State, James Madison, to refuse delivery of the commission. Marbury applied to the Supreme Court, sitting as a court of original jurisdiction, for a writ of mandamus to compel delivery of the commission. This specfic writ was sought under section 13 of the Judiciary Act of 1789.*

The following opinion of the court was delivered by the CHIEF JUSTICE [Marshall]. . . .

The first object of inquiry is, Has the applicant a right to the commission he demands? . . . Mr. Marbury, then, since his commission was signed by the President and sealed by the Secretary of State, was appointed; and as the law creating the office gave the officer a right to hold for five years, independent of the executive, the appointment was not revocable, but vested in the officer legal rights, which are protected by the laws of his country. To withhold his commission, therefore, is an act deemed by the court not warranted by law, but violative of a vested legal right.

This brings us to the second inquiry, which is, 2d. If he has a right, and that right has been violated, do the laws of his country afford him a remedy? . . .

It is then the opinion of the court,

1st. That by signing the commission of Mr. Marbury, the President of the United States appointed him a justice of peace for the county of Washington, in the District of Columbia; and that the seal of the United States, affixed thereto by the Secretary of State, is conclusive testimony of the verity of the signature, and of the completion of the appointment; and that the appointment conferred on him a legal right to the office for the space of five years.

2dly. That, having this legal title to the office, he has a consequent right to the commission; a refusal to deliver which is a plain violation of that right, for which the laws of his country afford him a remedy.

It remains to be inquired whether, 3dly. He is entitled to the remedy for which he applies. This depends on,

1st. The nature of the writ applied for; and 2dly. The power of this court.

[As to the 1st, in light of the facts, this was held to be] a plain case for a mandamus, either to deliver the commission, or a copy of it from the record; and it only remains to be inquired, whether it can issue from this court.

[The Court then decided that the portion of Section 13 of the Judiciary Act of 1789 which provided that "The Supreme Court . . . shall have power to issue . . . writs of mandamus in cases warranted by the principles and usages of law, to any persons holding office, under the authority of the United States," was in conflict with the constitution as an attempt to enlarge the original jurisdiction of the Supreme Court beyond that provided by Article III, Section 2 of the Constitution of the United States which reads in part as follows: "In all cases affecting ambassadors, other public ministers and consuls, and those in which a State shall be Party, the Supreme Court shall have *original jurisdiction.*"]

[Chief Justice Marshall continued:] The question, whether an act, repugnant to the constitution, can become the law of the land, is a question deeply interesting to the United States; but, happily, not of an intricacy proportioned to its interest. It seems only necessary to recognize certain principles, supposed to have been long and well established, to decide it. That the people have an original right to establish, for their future government, such principles as, in their opinion shall most conduce to their own happiness, is the basis on which the whole American fabric has been erected. The exercise of this original right is a very great exertion; nor can it, nor ought it, to be frequently repeated. The principles, therefore, so established, are deemed fundamental; and as the authority from which they proceed is supreme, and can seldom act, they are designed to be permanent.

This original and supreme will organizes the government, and assigns to different departments their respective powers. It may either stop here, or establish certain limits not to be transcended by those departments. The government of the United States is of the latter description. The powers of the legislature are defined and limited; and that those limits may not be mistaken, or forgotten, the constitution is written. To what purpose are powers limited, and to what purpose is that limitation committed to writing, if these limits may, at any time, be passed by those intended to be restrained? The distinction between a government with limited and unlimited powers is abolished, if those limits do not confine the persons on whom they are imposed, and if acts prohibited and acts allowed, are of equal obligation. It is a proposition too plain to be contested, that the constitution controls any legislative act repugnant to it; or that the legislature may alter the constitution by an ordinary act.

Between these alternatives, there is no middle ground. The constitution is either a superior paramount law, unchangeable by ordinary means, or it is on a level with ordinary legislative acts, and, like other acts, is alterable when the legislature shall please to alter it. If the former part of the alternative be true, then a legislative act, contrary to the constitution, is not law; if the latter part be true, then written constitutions are absurd attempts, on the part of the people, to limit a power, in its own nature, illimitable.

Certainly, all those who have framed written constitutions contemplate them as forming the fundamental and paramount law of the nation, and consequently, the theory of every such government must be, that an act of the legislature, repugnant to the constitution, is void. This theory is essentially attached to a written constitution, and is, consequently, to be considered, by this court, as one of the fundamental principles of our society. It is not, therefore, to be lost sight of, in the further consideration of this subject.

If an act of the legislature, repugnant to the constitution, is void, does it, notwithstanding its invalidity, bind the courts, and oblige them to give it effect? Or, in other words, though it be not law, does it constitute a rule as operative as if it was a law? This would be to overthrow, in fact, what was established in theory; and would seem, at first view, an absurdity too gross to be insisted on. It shall, however, receive a more attentive consideration.

It is, emphatically, the province and duty of the judicial department, to say what the law is. Those who apply the rule to particular cases, must of necessity expound and interpret that rule. If two laws conflict with each other, the courts must decide on the operation of each. So, if a law be in opposition to the constitution; if both the law and the constitution apply to a particular case, so that the court must either decide that case, conformably to the law, disregarding the constitution; or conformably to the constitution, disregarding the law; the court must determine which of these conflicting rules governs the case; this is of the very essence of judicial duty. If then, the courts are to regard the constitution, and the constitution is superior to any ordinary act of the legislature, the constitution, and not such ordinary act, must govern the case to which they both apply.

Those, then, who controvert the principle, that the constitution is to be considered, in court, as a paramount law, are reduced to the necessity of maintaining that courts must close their eyes on the constitution, and see only the law. This doctrine would subvert the very foundation of all written constitutions. It would declare that an act which, according to the principles and theory of our government, is entirely void, is yet, in practice, completely obligatory. It would declare, that if the legislature shall do what is expressly forbidden, such act, notwithstanding the express prohibition, is in reality effectual. It would be giving to the legislature a practical and real omnipotence, with the same breath which professes to restrict their powers within narrow limits. It is prescribing limits, and declaring that those limits may be passed at pleasure. That it thus reduces to nothing, what we have deemed the greatest improvement on political institutions, a written constitution, would of itself, be sufficient, in America, where written constitutions have been viewed with so much reverence, for rejecting the construction.

But the peculiar expressions of the constitution of the United States furnish additional arguments in favor of its rejection. The judicial power of the United States is extended to all cases arising under the constitution. Could it be the intention of those who gave this power, to say, that in using it, the constitution should not be looked into? That a case arising under the constitution should be decided, without examining the instrument under which it arises? This is too extravagant to be maintained. In some cases, then, the constitution must be looked into by the judges. And if they can open it at all, what part of it are they forbidden to read or to obey?

There are many other parts of the constitution which serve to illustrate this subject. It is declared, that "no tax or duty shall be laid on articles exported from any state." Suppose, a duty on the export of cotton, of tobacco, or of flour; and a suit instituted to recover it. Ought judgment to be rendered in such a case? ought the judges to close their eyes on the constitution, and only see the law?

The constitution declares "that no bill of attainder or *ex post facto* law shall be passed." If, however, such a bill should be passed, and a person should be prosecuted under it; must the court condemn to death those victims whom the constitution endeavors to preserve?

"No person," says the constitution, "shall be convicted of treason, unless on the testimony of two witnesses to the same overt act, or on confession in open court." Here, the language of the constitution is addressed especially to the courts. It prescribes, directly for them, a rule of evidence not to be departed from. If the legislature should change that rule, and declare one witness, or a confession out of court, sufficient for conviction, must the constitutional principle yield to the legislative act?

From these, and many other selections which might be made, it is apparent, that the framers of the constitution contemplated that instrument as a rule for the government of courts, as well as of the legislature. Why otherwise does it direct the judges to take an oath to support it? This oath certainly applies in an especial manner, to their conduct in their official character. How immoral to impose it on them, if they were to be used as the instruments, and the knowing instruments, for violating what they swear to support!

The oath of office, too, imposed by the legislature, is completely demonstrative of the legislative opinion on this subject. It is in these words: "I do solemnly swear, that I will administer justice, without respect to persons, and do equal right to the poor and to the rich; and that I will faithfully and impartially discharge all the duties incumbent on me as ——, according to the best of my abilities and understanding, agreeably to the constitution and laws of the United States." Why does a judge swear to discharge his duties agreeably to the constitution of the United States, if that constitution forms no rule for his government? if it is closed upon him, and cannot be inspected by him? If such be the real state of things, this is worse than solemn mockery. To prescribe, or to take this oath, becomes equally a crime.

It is also not entirely unworthy of observation, that in declaring what shall be the supreme law of the land, the constitution itself is first mentioned; and not the laws of the United States, generally, but those only which shall be made in pursuance of the constitution, have that rank.

Thus, the particular phraseology of the constitution of the United States confirms and strengthens the principle, supposed to be essential to all written constitutions, that a law repugnant to the constitution is void; and that courts, as well as other departments, are bound by that instrument.

The rule must be discharged.

Critique of Marbury v. Madison

EAKIN *V*. RAUB

12 Sergeant and Rawle (Pennsylvania Supreme Court) 330 (1825).

GIBSON, J. (dissenting) . . .

I am aware, that a [judicial] right to declare all unconstitutional acts void
. . . is generally held as a professional dogma; but, I apprehend, rather as a
matter of faith than of reason. I admit that I once embraced the same doctrine,
but without examination, and I shall therefore state the arguments that impelled
me to abandon it, with great respect for those by whom it is still maintained.
But I may premise, that it is not a little remarkable, that although the right in
question has all along been claimed by the judiciary, no judge has ventured to
discuss it, except Chief Justice Marshall (in Marbury *v*. Madison, 1 Cranch,
137), and if the argument of a jurist so distinguished for the strength of his
ratiocinative powers be found inconclusive, it may fairly be set down to the
weakness of the position which he attempts to defend. . . .

The Constitution and the right of the legislature to pass the act, may be in
collision. But is that a legitimate subject for judicial determination? If it be, the
judiciary must be a peculiar organ, to revise the proceedings of the legislature,
and to correct its mistakes; and in what part of the Constitution are we to look
for this proud pre-eminence? Viewing the matter in the opposite direction, what
would be thought of an act of assembly in which it should be declared that the
Supreme Court had, in a particular case, put a wrong construction on the Constitution of the United States, and that the judgment should therefore be reversed? It would doubtless be thought a usurpation of judicial power. But it is
by no means clear, that to declare a law void which has been enacted according to the forms prescribed in the Constitution, is not a usurpation of legislative power. It is an act of sovereignty; and sovereignty and legislative power are
said by Sir William Blackstone to be convertible terms. It is the business of the
judiciary to interpret the laws, not scan the authority of the lawgiver; and
without the latter, it cannot take cognizance of a collision between a law and
the Constitution. So that to affirm that the judiciary has a right to judge of the
existence of such collision, is to take for granted the very thing to be proved.
And, that a very cogent argument may be made in this way, I am not disposed
to deny; for no conclusions are so strong as those that are drawn from the
petitio principii.

But it has been said to be emphatically the business of the judiciary, to
ascertain and pronounce what the law is; and that this necessarily involves a
consideration of the Constitution. It does so: but how far? If the judiciary will
inquire into anything besides the form of enactment, where shall it stop? There
must be some point of limitation to such an inquiry; for no one will pretend

97

that a judge would be justifiable in calling for the election returns, or scrutinizing the qualifications of those who composed the legislature. . . .

In theory, all the organs of the government are of equal capacity; or, if not equal, each must be supposed to have superior capacity only for those things which peculiarly belong to it; and, as legislation peculiarly involves the consideration of those limitations which are put on the law-making power, and the interpretation of the laws when made, involves only the construction of the laws themselves, it follows that the construction of the constitution in this particular belongs to the legislature, which ought therefore to be taken to have superior capacity to judge of the constitutionality of its own acts. But suppose all to be of equal capacity in every respect, why should one exercise a controlling power over the rest? That the judiciary is of superior rank, has never been pretended, although it has been said to be co-ordinate. It is not easy, however, to comprehend how the power which gives law to all the rest, can be of no more than equal rank with one which receives it, and is answerable to the former for the observance of its statutes. . . .

Everyone knows how seldom men think exactly alike on ordinary subjects; and a government constructed on the principle of assent by all its parts, would be inadequate to the most simple operations. The notion of a complication of counter checks has been carried to an extent in theory, of which the framers of the Constitution never dreamt. When the entire sovereignty was separated into its elementary parts, and distributed to the appropriate branches, all things incident to the exercise of its powers were committed to each branch exclusively. The negative which each part of the legislature may exercise, in regard to the acts of the other, was thought sufficient to prevent material infractions of the restraints which were put on the power of the whole; for, had it been intended to interpose the judiciary as an additional barrier, the matter would surely not have been left in doubt. The judges would not have been left to stand on the insecure and ever shifting ground of public opinion as to constructive powers; they would have been placed on the impregnable ground of an express grant. . . .

But the judges are sworn to support the Constitution, and are they not bound by it as the law of the land? In some respects they are. In the very few cases in which the judiciary, and not the legislature, is the immediate organ to execute its provisions, they are bound by it in preference to any act of assembly to the contrary. In such cases, the Constitution is a rule to the courts. But what I have in view in this inquiry, is the supposed right of the judiciary to interfere, in cases where the Constitution is to be carried into effect through the instrumentality of the legislature, and where that organ must necessarily first decide on the constitutionality of its own act.

The oath to support the Constitution is not peculiar to the judges, but is taken indiscriminately by every officer of the government, and is designed rather as a test of the political principles of the man, than to bind the officer in the discharge of his duty: otherwise it were difficult to determine what operation it is to have in the case of a recorder of deeds, for instance, who, in the execution of his office, has nothing to do with the Constitution. But granting it to relate to the official conduct of the judge, as well as every other officer, and not to his political principles, still it must be understood in reference to supporting the Constitution, only as far as that may be involved in his official duty;

and, consequently, if his official duty does not comprehend an inquiry into the authority of the legislature, neither does his oath.

It is worthy of remark here, that the foundation of every argument in favor of the right of the judiciary, is found at last to be an assumption of the whole ground in dispute. Granting that the object of the oath is to secure a support of the Constitution in the discharge of official duty, its terms may be satisfied by restraining it to official duty in the exercise of the ordinary judicial powers. Thus, the Constitution may furnish a rule of construction, where a particular interpretation of a law would conflict with some constitutional principle; and such interpretation, where it may, is always to be avoided. But the oath was more probably designed to secure the powers of each of the different branches from being usurped by any of the rest: for instance, to prevent the House of Representatives from erecting itself into a court of judicature, or the Supreme Court from attempting to control the legislature; and, in this view, the oath furnishes an argument equally plausible against the right of the judiciary. But if it require a support of the Constitution in anything beside official duty, it is in fact an oath of allegiance to a particular form of government; and, considered as such, it is not easy to see why it should not be taken by the citizens at large, as well as by the officers of the government. It has never been thought that an officer is under greater restraint as to measures which have for their avowed end a total change of the Constitution, than a citizen who has taken no oath at all. The official oath, then, relates only to the official conduct of the officer, and does not prove that he ought to stray from the path of his ordinary business to search for violations of duty in the business of others; nor does it, as supposed, define the powers of the officer.

But do not the judges do a positive act in violation of the Constitution, when they give effect to an unconstitutional law? Not if the law has been passed according to the forms established in the Constitution. The fallacy of the question is, in supposing that the judiciary adopts the acts of the legislature as its own; whereas the enactment of a law and the interpretation of it are not concurrent acts, and as the judiciary is not required to concur in the enactment, neither is it in the breach of the Constitution which may be the consequence of the enactment. The fault is imputable to the legislature, and on it the responsibility exclusively rests. . . .

For these reasons, I am of opinion that it rests [ultimately] with the people, in whom full and absolute sovereign power resides, to correct abuses in legislation, by instructing their representatives to repeal the obnoxious act. What is wanting to plenary power in the government, is reserved by the people for their own immediate use; and to redress an infringement of their rights in this respect, would seem to be an accessory of the power thus reserved. It might, perhaps, have been better to vest the power in the judiciary; as it might be expected that its habits of deliberation, and the aid derived from the arguments of counsel, would more frequently lead to accurate conclusions. On the other hand, the judiciary is not infallible; and an error by it would admit of no remedy but a more distinct expression of the public will, through the extraordinary medium of a convention; whereas, an error by the legislature admits of a remedy by an exertion of the same will, in the ordinary exercise of the right of suffrage,—a mode better calculated to attain the end, without popular excitement.

~~~~~~TOPIC 9

The Bases of National Power

"It Is a Constitution We Are Expounding"

MC CULLOUCH *V.* MARYLAND

4 Wheaton 316 (1819)

Congress in 1816 passed an act to incorporate the Bank of the United States, and in the following year the bank established a branch in Baltimore. In 1818 the state of Maryland required all banks not chartered by the state to pay an annual tax of $15,000 or to pay a stamp tax on each bank note issued. McCulloch, the cashier of the Baltimore branch of the Bank of the United States, issued bank notes in violation of the state law whereupon the state of Maryland brought suit against him. The state courts decided in favour of Maryland. McCulloch appealed the case to the United States Supreme Court on a writ of error.

Error to the Court of Appeals of the State of Maryland.

MARSHALL, Chief Justice, delivered the opinion of the court. . . .

The first question made in the cause is, has congress power to incorporate a bank? . . . The power now contested was exercised by the first congress elected under the present constitution. The bill for incorporating the Bank of the United States did not steal upon an unsuspecting legislature, and pass unobserved. Its principle was completely understood, and was opposed with equal zeal and ability. After being resisted, first in the fair and open field of debate, and afterwards in the executive cabinet, with as much persevering talent as any measure has ever experienced, and being supported by arguments which convinced minds as pure and as intelligent as this country can boast, it became a law.

The original act was permitted to expire; but a short experience of the embarrassments to which the refusal to revive it exposed the government, convinced those who were most prejudiced against the measure of its necessity, and induced the passage of the present law. It would require no ordinary share of intrepidity to assert, that a measure adopted under these circumstances, was a bold and plain usurpation, to which the constitution gave no countenance. These observations belong to the cause: but they are not made under the impression that, were the question entirely new, the law would be found irreconcilable with the constitution.

In discussing this question, the counsel for the state of Maryland have deemed it of some importance, in the construction of the constitution, to consider that instrument not as emanating from the people, but as the act of sovereign and independent states. The powers of the general government, it has been said, are delegated by the states, who alone are truly sovereign; and must be exercised in subordination to the states, who alone possess supreme dominion. It would be difficult to sustain this proposition.

The convention which framed the constitution was, indeed, elected by the state legislatures. But the instrument, when it came from their hands, was a mere proposal, without obligation, or pretensions to it. It was reported to the then existing congress of the United States, with a request that it might "be submitted to a convention of delegates, chosen in each state by the people thereof, under the recommendation of its legislature, for their assent and ratification." This mode of proceeding was adopted; and by the convention, by congress, and by the state legislatures, the instrument was submitted to the *people*. They acted upon it, in the only manner in which they can act safely, effectively, and wisely, on such a subject, by assembling in convention. . . . From these conventions, the constitution derives its whole authority. The government proceeds directly from the people; is "ordained and established" in the name of the people; and is declared to be ordained, "in order to form a more perfect union, establish justice, insure domestic tranquility, and secure the blessings of liberty to themselves and to their posterity." . . . The government of the Union, then, is emphatically and truly, a government of the people. In form, and in substance, it emanates from them. Its powers are granted by them, and are to be exercised directly on them, and for their benefit.

This government is acknowledged by all, to be one of enumerated powers. The principle, that it can exercise only the powers granted to it, would seem too apparent, to have required to be enforced by all those arguments, which its enlightened friends, while it was depending before the people, found it necessary to urge; that principle is now universally admitted. But the question respecting the extent of the powers actually granted, is perpetually arising, and will probably continue to arise, as long as our system shall exist. In discussing these questions, the conflicting powers of the general and state governments must be brought into view, and the supremacy of their respective laws, when they are in opposition, must be settled.

If any one proposition could command the universal assent of mankind, we might expect that it would be this—that the government of the Union, though limited in its powers, is supreme within its sphere of action. This would seem to result, necessarily, from its nature. It is the government of all; its powers are delegated by all; it represents all, and acts for all. Though any one state may be willing to control its operations, no state is willing to allow others to control them. The nation, on those subjects on which it can act, must necessarily bind its component parts. But this question is not left to mere reason: the people have, in express terms, decided it, by saying, "this constitution, and the laws of the United States, which shall be made in pursuance thereof," "shall be the supreme law of the land," and by requiring that the members of the state legislatures, and the officers of the executive and judicial departments of the state, shall take the oath of fidelity to it. The government of the United States, then, though limited in its powers, is supreme; and its laws, when made in pursuance of the constitution, form the supreme law of the land, "anything in the constitution or laws of any state, to the contrary notwithstanding."

Among the enumerated powers, we do not find that of establishing a bank or creating a corporation. But there is no phrase in the instrument which, like the articles of confederation, excludes incidental or implied powers; and which requires that everything granted shall be expressly and minutely described. Even the 10th amendment, which was framed for the purpose of quieting the excessive jealousies which had been excited, omits the word "expressly," and declares only that the powers "not delegated to the United States, nor prohibited to the states, are reserved to the states or to the people"; thus leaving the question, whether the particular power which may become the subject of contest, has been delegated to the one government, or prohibited to the other, to depend on a fair construction of the whole instrument.

The men who drew and adopted this amendment had experienced the embarrassments resulting from the insertion of this word in the articles of confederation, and probably omitted it, to avoid those embarrassments. A constitution, to contain an accurate detail of all the subdivisions of which its great powers will admit, and of all the means by which they may be carried into execution, would partake of the prolixity of a legal code, and could scarcely be embraced by the human mind. It would, probably, never be understood by the public. Its nature, therefore, requires, that only its great outlines should be marked, its important objects designated, and the minor ingredients which compose those objects, be deduced from the nature of the objects themselves. That this idea was entertained by the framers of the American constitution, is not only to be inferred from the nature of the instrument, but from the language. Why else were some of the limitations, found in the 9th section of the 1st article, introduced? It is also, in some degree, warranted, by their having omitted to use any restrictive term which might prevent its receiving a fair and just interpretation. In considering this question, then, we must never forget, that it is a *constitution* we are expounding.

Although, among the enumerated powers of government, we do not find the word "bank," or "incorporation," we find the great powers, to lay and collect taxes; to borrow money; to regulate commerce; to declare and conduct war; and to raise and support armies and navies. . . . A government, intrusted with such ample powers, on the due execution of which the happiness and prosperity of the nation so vitally depends, must also be intrusted with ample means for their execution. The power being given, it is the interest of the nation to facilitate its execution. It can never be their interest, and cannot be presumed to have been their intention, to clog and embarrass its execution, by withholding the most appropriate means.

Throughout this vast republic, from the St. Croix to the Gulf of Mexico, from the Atlantic to the Pacific, revenue is to be collected and expended, armies are to be marched and supported. The exigencies of the nation may require, that the treasure raised in the north should be transported to the south, that raised in the east, conveyed to the west, or that this order should be reversed. Is that construction of the constitution to be preferred, which would render these operations difficult, hazardous, and expensive? Can we adopt that construction (unless the words imperiously require it), which would impute to the framers of that instrument, when granting these powers for the public good, the intention of impeding their exercise by withholding a choice of means? If, indeed, such be the mandate of the constitution, we have only to obey; but that instrument does not profess to enumerate the means by which the powers it confers may be executed; nor does it prohibit the creation of a corporation, if the existence of such a being be essential, to the beneficial exercise of those powers. It is, then, the subject of fair inquiry, how far such means may be employed.

It is not denied, that the powers given to the government imply the ordinary means of execution. That, for example, of raising revenue, and applying it to national purposes, is admitted to imply the power of conveying money from place to place, as the exigencies of the nation may require, and of employing the usual means of conveyance. But it is denied, that the government has its choice of means, or, that it may employ the most convenient means, if, to employ them, it be necessary to erect a corporation. . . . The government which has a right to do an act, and has imposed on it the duty of performing that act, must, according to the dictates of reason, be allowed to select the means; and those who contend that it may not select any appropriate means, that one particular mode of effecting the object is excepted, take upon themselves the burden of establishing that exception. . . .

But the constitution of the United States has not left the right of congress to employ the necessary means, for the execution of the powers conferred on the government, to general reasoning. To its enumeration of powers is added, that of making "all laws which shall be necessary and proper, for carrying into execution the foregoing powers, and all other powers vested by this constitution, in the government of the United States, or in any department thereof." . . .

The argument on which most reliance is placed, is drawn from the peculiar language of this clause. Congress is not empowered by it to make all laws, which may have relation to the powers conferred on the government, but only such as may be "necessary and proper" for carrying them into execution. The word "necessary" is considered as controlling the whole sentence, and as limiting the right to pass laws for the execution of the granted powers, to such as are indispensable, and without which the power would be nugatory. That it excludes the choice of means, and leaves to congress, in each case, that only which is most direct and simple.

Is it true, that this is the sense in which the word "necessary" is always used? Does it always import an absolute physical necessity, so strong, that one thing, to which another may be termed necessary, cannot exist without that other? We think it does not. If reference be had to its use, in the common affairs of the world, or in approved authors, we find that it frequently imports no more than that one thing is convenient, or useful, or essential to another. . . . A thing may be necessary, very necessary, absolutely or indispensably necessary. To no mind would the same idea be conveyed by these several phrases. This comment on the word is well illustrated by the passage cited at the bar, from the 10th section of the 1st article of the constitution. It is, we think, impossible to compare the sentence which prohibits a State from laying "imposts, or duties on imports or exports, except what may be absolutely necessary for executing its inspection laws," with that which authorizes congress "to make all laws which shall be necessary and proper for carrying into execution" the powers of the general government, without feeling a conviction, that the convention understood itself to change materially the meaning of the word "necessary" by prefixing the word "absolutely." This word, then, like others, is used in various senses; and, in its construction, the subject, the context, the intention of the person using them, are all to be taken into view.

Let this be done in the case under consideration. The subject is the execution of those great powers on which the welfare of a nation essentially depends. It must have been the intention of those who gave these powers, to insure, as far as human prudence could insure, their beneficial execution. This could not be done, by confining the choice of means to such narrow limits as not to leave it in the power of congress to adopt any which might be appropriate, and which were conducive to the end. This provision is made in a constitution, intended to endure for ages to come, and consequently, to be adapted to the various crises of human affairs. To have prescribed the means by which government should, in all future time, execute its powers, would have been to change, entirely, the character of the instrument, and give it the properties of a legal code. It would have been an unwise attempt to provide, by immutable rules, for exigencies which, if foreseen at all, must have been seen dimly, and which can be best provided for as they occur. To have declared, that the best means shall not be used, but those alone, without which the power given would be nugatory, would have been to deprive the legislature of the capacity to avail itself of experience, to exercise its reason, and to accommodate its legislation to circumstances. If we apply this principle of construction to any of the powers of the government, we shall find it so pernicious in its operation that we shall be compelled to discard it. [The Court here cites the law requiring an oath of office in addition to the oath prescribed by the Constitution.]

So, with respect to the whole penal code of the United States whence arises the power to punish, in cases not prescribed by the constitution? All admit, that the government may, legitimately, punish any violation of its laws; and yet, this is not among the enumerated powers of congress. . . .

If this limited construction of the word "necessary" must be abandoned, in order to punish, whence is derived the rule which would reinstate it, when the government would carry its powers into execution, by means not vindictive in their nature? If the word "necessary" means "needful," "requisite," "essential," "conducive to," in order to let in the power of punishment for the infraction of law; why is it not equally comprehensive, when required to authorize the use of means which facilitate the execution of the powers of government, without the infliction of punishment? . . .

We admit, as all must admit, that the powers of the government are limited, and that its limits are not to be transcended. But we think the sound construction of the constitution must allow to the national legislature that discretion, with respect to the means by which the powers it confers are to be carried into execution, which will enable that body to perform the duties assigned to it, in the manner most beneficial to the people. Let the end be legitimate, let it be within the scope of the constitution, and all means which are appropriate, which are plainly adapted to that end, which are not prohibited, but consist[ent] with the letter and spirit of the constitution, are constitutional.

That a corporation must be considered as a means not less usual, not of higher dignity, not more requiring a particular specification than other means, has been sufficiently proved. . . . If a corporation may be employed, indiscriminately with other means, to carry into execution the powers of the government, no particular reason can be assigned for excluding the use of a bank, if required for its fiscal operations. To use one, must be within the discretion of congress, if it be an appropriate mode of executing the powers of government. That it is a convenient, a useful, and essential instrument in the prosecution of its fiscal operations, is not now a subject of controversy. . . .

After the most deliberate consideration, it is the unanimous and decided opinion of this court, that the act to incorporate the Bank of the United States is a law made in pursuance of the constitution, and is a part of the supreme law of the land.

The branches, proceeding from the same stock, and being conducive to the complete accomplishment of the object, are equally constitutional. . . .

It being the opinion of the court that the act incorporating the bank is constitutional, and that the power of establishing a branch in the state of Maryland might be properly exercised by the bank itself, we proceed to inquire:

2. Whether the State of Maryland may, without violating the constitution, tax that branch?

That the power of taxation is one of vital importance; that it is retained by the States; that it is not abridged by the grant of a similar power to the government of the Union; that it is to be concurrently exercised by the two governments: are truths which have never been denied. But, such is the paramount character of the constitution that its capacity to withdraw any subject from the action of even this power, is admitted. The States are expressly forbidden to lay any duties on imports or exports, except what may be absolutely necessary for executing their inspection laws. If the obligation of this prohibition must be conceded—if it may restrain a State from the exercise of its taxing power on imports and exports; the same paramount character would seem to restrain, as it certainly may restrain, a State from such other exercise of this power, as is in its nature incompatible with, and repugnant to, the constitutional laws of the Union. A law, absolutely repugnant to another, as entirely repeals that other as if express terms of repeal were used. . . .

This great principle is, that the constitution and the laws made in pursuance thereof are supreme; that they control the constitution and laws of the respective States, and cannot be controlled by them. From this, which may be almost termed an axiom, other propositions are deduced as corollaries, on the truth or error of which, and on their application to this case, the cause has been supposed to depend. These are, 1st. That a power to create implies a power to preserve. 2d. That a power to destroy, if wielded by a different hand, is hostile to, and incompatible with these powers to create and to preserve. 3d. That where this repugnancy exists, that authority which is supreme must control, not yield to that over which it is supreme. . . .

The sovereignty of a State extends to everything which exists by its own authority, or is introduced by its permission; but does it extend to those means which are employed by Congress to carry into execution powers conferred on that body by the people of the United States? We think it demonstrable that it does not. Those powers are not given by the people of a single State. They are given by the people of the United States, to a government whose laws, made in pursuance of the constitution, are declared to be supreme. Consequently, the people of a single State cannot confer a sovereignty which will extend over them.

If we measure the power of taxation residing in a State, by the extent of sovereignty which the people of a single State possess, and can confer on its government, we have an intelligible standard, applicable to every case to which the power may be applied. We have a principle which leaves the power of taxing the people and property of a state unimpaired; which leaves to a State the command of all its resources, and which places beyond its reach, all those powers which are conferred by the people of the United States on the government of the Union, and all those means which are given for the purpose of carrying those powers into execution. We have a principle which is safe for the States, and safe for the Union. We are relieved, as we ought to be, from clashing sovereignty; from interfering powers; from a repugnancy between a right in one government to pull down what there is an acknowledged right in another to build up; from the incompatibility of a right in one government to destroy what there is a right in another to preserve. We are not driven to the perplexing inquiry, so unfit for the judicial department, what degree of taxation is the legitimate use, and what degree may amount to the abuse of the power. The attempt to use it on the means employed by the government of the Union, in pursuance of the constitution, is itself an abuse, because it is the usurpation of a power which the people of a single State cannot give. . . .

That the power to tax involves the power to destroy; that the power to destroy may defeat and render useless the power to create; that there is a plain repugnance, in conferring on one government a power to control the constitutional measures of another, which other, with respect to those very measures, is declared to be supreme over that which exerts the control, are propositions not to be denied. . . .

If the States may tax one instrument, employed by the government in the execution of its powers, they may tax any and every other instrument. They may tax the mail; they may tax the mint; they may tax patent rights; they may tax the papers of the customhouse; they may tax judicial process; they may tax all the means employed by the government, to an excess which would defeat all the ends of government. . . .

The Court has bestowed on this subject its most deliberate consideration. The result is a conviction that the States have no power, by taxation or otherwise, to retard, impede, burden, or in any manner control, the operations of the constitutional laws enacted by Congress to carry into execution the powers vested in the general government. This is, we think, the unavoidable consequence of that supremacy which the constitution has declared.

We are unanimously of opinion, that the law passed by the legislature of Maryland, imposing a tax on the Bank of the United States, is unconstitutional and void. . . .

TOPIC 10

National Power Over the Economy

The Commerce Power: A Restricted View
SCHECHTER POULTRY CORP. *V.* UNITED STATES
295 U.S. 495 (1935)

In 1933 Congress passed the National Industrial Recovery Act. In signing the bill President Roosevelt said, "History probably will record the National Industrial Recovery Act as the most important and far-reaching legislation ever enacted by the American Congress." The purpose of the law, according to the President, was to promote re-employment, to shorten hours and increase wages, and to prevent unfair competition.

The first section of the act attempted to provide a constitutional basis for the legislation, stating:

"Section 1. A national emergency productive of widespread unemployment and disorganization of industry, which burdens interstate and foreign commerce, affects the public welfare, and undermines the standards of living of the American people, is hereby declared to exist. It is hereby declared to be the policy of Congress to remove obstructions to the free flow of interstate and foreign commerce which tend to diminish the amount thereof; and to provide for the general welfare by promoting the organization of industry for the purpose of cooperative action among trade groups, to induce and maintain united action of labor and management under adequate competitive practices, to promote the fullest possible utilization of the present productive capacity of industries, to avoid restriction of production (except as may be temporarily required), to increase the consumption of industrial and agricultural products by increasing purchasing power, to reduce and relieve unemployment, to improve standards of labor, and otherwise to rehabilitate industry and to conserve natural resources."

On May 27, 1935 the Supreme Court in a unanimous opinion declared the National Industrial Recovery Act unconstitutional on the grounds that (1), it "attempted delegation of legislative power" and (2), it "attempted regulation of intrastate transactions which affect interstate commerce only indirectly."

107

*In the case at issue, The Schechter Poultry Corporation con-
ducted a wholesale poultry slaughterhouse market in Brooklyn. It
ordinarily purchased live poultry from commission men in New
York City or at the railroad terminals and after slaughtering the
poultry sold it to retail dealers and butchers. The Court stated that
"New York City is the largest live-poultry market in the United
States. Ninety-six per cent of the live poultry there marketed comes
from other States."*

MR. CHIEF JUSTICE HUGHES delivered the opinion of the court.

Penalties are confined to violations of a code provision "in any transaction
in or affecting interstate or foreign commerce." This aspect of the case presents
the question whether the particular provisions of the Live Poultry Code, which
the defendants were convicted for violating and for having conspired to violate,
were within the regulating powers of Congress.

These provisions relate to the hours and wages of those employed by
defendants in their slaughterhouses in Brooklyn and to the sales there made
to retail dealers and butchers.

(1) Were these transactions "in" interstate commerce? Much is made of
the fact that almost all the poultry coming to New York is sent there from
other states. But the code provisions as here applied do not concern the transportation of the poultry from other states to New York, or the transactions of
the commission men or others to whom it is consigned, or the sales made by
such consignees to defendants.

When defendants had made their purchases, whether at the West Washington Market in New York City or at the railroad terminals serving the city,
or elsewhere, the poultry was trucked to their slaughterhouses in Brooklyn for
local disposition. The interstate transactions in relation to that poultry then
ended. Defendants held the poultry at their slaughterhouse markets for slaughter
and local sale to retail dealers and butchers, who in turn sold directly to consumers.

Neither the slaughtering nor the sales by defendants were transactions in
interstate commerce. . . . The undisputed facts thus afford no warrant for
the argument that the poultry handled by defendants at their slaughterhouse
markets was in "current" or "flow" of interstate commerce and was thus subject
to congressional regulation.

The mere fact that there may be a constant flow of commodities into a
state does not mean that the flow continues after the property has arrived and
has become commingled with the mass of property within the state and is there
held solely for local disposition and use. So far as the poultry here in question
is concerned, the flow in interstate commerce had ceased. The poultry had come
to a permanent rest within the state. It was not held, used or sold by defendants in relation to any further transaction in interstate commerce and was not
destined for transportation to other states. Hence, decisions which deal with a
stream of interstate commerce—where goods come to rest within a state temporarily and are later to go forward in interstate commerce—and with the regu-

lations of transactions involved in that practical continuity of movement, are not applicable here. . . .

(2) Did the defendant's transactions directly "affect" interstate commerce so as to be subject to federal regulation? The power of Congress extends not only to the regulation of transactions which are part of interstate commerce, but to the protection of that commerce from injury. It matters not that the injury may be due to the conduct of those engaged in intrastate operations. Thus, Congress may protect the safety of those employed in interstate transportation "no matter what may be the source of the dangers which threaten it." . . .

Defendants have been convicted, not upon direct charges of injury to interstate commerce or of interference with persons engaged in that commerce, but of violations of certain provisions of the Live Poultry Code and of conspiracy to commit these violations. Interstate commerce is brought in only upon the charge that violations of these provisions—as to hours and wages of employes and local sales—"affected" interstate commerce.

In determining how far the federal government may go in controlling intrastate transactions upon the ground that they "affect" interstate commerce, there is a necessary and well-established distinction between direct and indirect effects. The precise line can be drawn only as individual cases arise, but the distinction is clear in principle. . . . [And] where the effect of intrastate transactions upon interstate commerce is merely indirect, such transactions remain within the domain of state power. . . .

The question of chief importance relates to the provision of the Code as to the hours and wages of those employed in defendants' slaughterhouse markets. It is plain that these requirements are imposed in order to govern the details of defendants' management of their local business. The persons employed in slaughtering and selling in local trade are not employed in interstate commerce. Their hours and wages have no direct relation to interstate commerce. . . . If the federal government may determine the wages and hours of employees in the internal commerce of a State, because of their relation to cost and prices and their indirect effect upon interstate commerce, it would seem that a similar control might be exerted over other elements of cost, also affecting prices, such as the number of employees, rents, advertising, methods of doing business, etc. All the processes of production and distribution that enter into cost could likewise be controlled. If the cost of doing an intrastate business is in itself the permitted object of federal control, the extent of the regulation of cost would be a question of discretion and not of power.

The government also makes the point that efforts to enact state legislation establishing high labor standards have been impeded by the belief that, unless similar action is taken generally, commerce will be diverted from the states adopting such standards, and that this fear of diversion has led to demands for federal legislation on the subject of wages and hours. The apparent implication is that the federal authority under the commerce clause should be deemed to extend to the establishment of rules to govern wages and hours in intrastate trade and industry generally throughout the country, thus overriding the authority of the states to deal with domestic problems arising from labor conditions in their internal commerce.

It is not the province of the Court to consider the economic advantages or disadvantages of such a centralized system. It is sufficient to say that the Federal Constitution does not provide for it. Our growth and development have called for wide use of the commerce power of the federal government in its control over the expanded activities of interstate commerce and in protecting that commerce from burdens, interferences, and conspiracies to restrain and monopolize it. But the authority of the federal government may not be pushed to such an extreme as to destroy the distinction, which the commerce clause itself establishes, between commerce "among the several States" and the internal concerns of a State. The same answer must be made to the contention that is based upon the serious economic situation which led to the passage of the Recovery Act,—the fall in prices, the decline in wages and employment, and the curtailment of the market for commodities. Stress is laid upon the great importance of maintaining wage distributions which would provide the necessary stimulus in starting "the cumulative forces making for expanding commercial activity." Without in any way disparaging this motive, it is enough to say that the recuperative efforts of the federal government must be made in a manner consistent with the authority granted by the Constitution.

[The portion of the opinion dealing with the "attempted delegation of legislative power" is omitted.]

MR. JUSTICE CARDOZO, concurring . . .

There is another objection, far-reaching and incurable, aside from any defect of unlawful delegation.

If this code had been adopted by Congress itself, and not by the President on the advice of an industrial association, it would even then be void unless authority to adopt it is included in the grant of power "to regulate commerce with foreign nations and among the several states." United States Constitution, Art. I, Sec. 8 Clause 3.

I find no authority in that grant for the regulation of wages and hours of labor in the intrastate transactions that make up the defendants' business. As to this feature of the case little can be added to the opinion of the court. There is a view of causation that would obliterate the distinction between what is national and what is local in the activities of commerce. Motion at the outer rim is communicated perceptibly, though minutely, to recording instruments at the center. A society such as ours "is an elastic medium which transmits all tremors through its territory; the only question is of their size." Per Learned Hand, J., in the court below. The law is not indifferent to considerations of degree. Activities local in their immediacy do not become interstate and national because of distant repercussions. What is near and what is distant may at times be uncertain. Cf. Board of Trade v. Olsen, 262 U.S. 1. There is no penumbra of uncertainty obscuring judgment here. To find immediacy or directness here is to find it almost everywhere. If centripetal forces are to be isolated to the exclusion of the forces that oppose and counteract them, there will be an end to our federal system.

To take from this code the provisions as to wages and the hours of labor is to destroy it altogether. If a trade or an industry is so predominantly local as to be exempt from regulation by the Congress in respect of matters such as these, there can be no "code" for it at all. This is clear from the provisions of § 7a of the Act with its explicit disclosure of the statutory scheme. Wages and the hours of labor are essential features of the plan, its very bone and sinew. There is no opportunity in such circumstances for the severance of the infected parts in the hope of saving the remainder. A code collapses utterly with bone and sinew gone.

I am authorized to state that MR. JUSTICE STONE joins in this opinion.

[The following year, in Carter *v.* Carter Coal Co., 298 U.S. 238, the Supreme Court took the occasion to say: "Whether the effect of a given activity or condition is direct or indirect is not always easy to determine. The word 'direct' implies that the activity or condition invoked or blamed shall operate proximately—not mediately, remotely, or collaterally—to produce the effect. It connotes the absence of an efficient intervening agency or condition. And the extent of the effect bears no logical relation to its character."]

The Commerce Power: An Expanded View
WICKARD *V.* FILBURN
317 U.S. 111 (1942)

> *The Agricultural Adjustment Act of 1938, as related to wheat, sought to control the volume moving in interstate and foreign commerce in order to avoid surpluses and shortages and consequent abnormalities of price and obstructions to commerce. The Act, as amended, provided procedures which resulted in the fixing of a market quota applicable to each farm and laid a penalty upon any excess brought to market by the farmer. The basic provision of this law was sustained in Mulford v. Smith, 307 U.S. 38 (1939).*
>
> *The question in the instant case is whether Congress may constitutionally regulate production of wheat, not intended in any part for commerce, but wholly for consumption on the farm.*

MR. JUSTICE JACKSON delivered the opinion of the Court. . . .

[Filburn] says that this is a regulation of production and consumption of wheat. Such activities are, he urges, beyond the reach of congressional power under the commerce clause, since they are local in character, and their effects upon interstate commerce are at most "indirect." In answer the government argues that the statute regulates neither production nor consumption, but only marketing; and, in the alternative, that if the Act does go beyond the regulation of marketing it is sustainable as a "necessary and proper" implementation of the power of Congress over interstate commerce.

The government's concern lest the Act be held to be a regulation of production or consumption rather than of marketing is attributable to a few dicta and decisions of this Court which might be understood to lay it down that activities such as "production," "manufacturing," and "mining" are strictly "local' and, except in special circumstances which are not present here, cannot be regulated under the commerce power because their effects upon interstate commerce are, as matter of law, only "indirect." Even today, when this power has been held to have great latitude, there is no decision of this Court that such activities may be regulated where no part of the product is intended for interstate commerce or intermingled with the subjects thereof. We believe that a review of the course of decision under the commerce clause will make plain, however, that questions of the power of Congress are not to be decided by reference to any formula which would give controlling force to nomenclature such as "production" and "indirect" and foreclose consideration of the actual effects of the activity in question upon interstate commerce.

At the beginning Chief Justice Marshall described the federal commerce power with a breadth never yet exceeded. Gibbons *v.* Ogden, 9 Wheat. 1, 194, 195. He made emphatic the embracing and penetrating nature of this power by warning that effective restraints on its exercise must proceed from political rather than from judicial processes. 9 Wheat. at page 197.

For nearly a century, however, decisions of this Court under the commerce clause dealt rarely with questions of what Congress might do in the exercise of its granted power under the clause and almost entirely with the permissibility of state activity which it was claimed discriminated against or burdened interstate commerce. During this period there was perhaps little occasion for the affirmative exercise of the commerce power, and the influence of the clause on American life and law was a negative one, resulting almost wholly from its operation as a restraint upon the powers of the states. In discussion and decision the point of reference instead of being what was "necessary and proper" to the exercise by Congress of its granted power, was often some concept of sovereignty thought to be implicit in the status of statehood. Certain activities such as "production," "manufacturing," and "mining" were occasionally said to be within the province of state governments and beyond the power of Congress under the commerce clause.

It was not until 1887 with the enactment of the Interstate Commerce Act that the interstate commerce power began to exert positive influence in American law and life. This first important federal resort to the commerce power was followed in 1890 by the Sherman Anti-Trust Act and, thereafter, mainly after 1903, by many others. These statutes ushered in new phases of adjudication, which required the Court to approach the interpretation of the commerce clause in the light of an actual exercise by Congress of its power thereunder.

When it first dealt with this new legislation, the Court adhered to its earlier pronouncements, and allowed but little scope to the power of Congress. United States *v.* E. C. Knight Co., 156 U.S. 1. These earlier pronouncements also played an important part in several of the five cases in which this Court later held that acts of Congress under the commerce clause were in excess of its power.

Even while important opinions in this line of restrictive authority were being written, however, other cases called forth broader interpretations of the commerce clause destined to supersede the earlier ones, and to bring about a return to the principles first enunciated by Chief Justice Marshall in Gibbons v. Ogden, *supra.*

Not long after the decision of United States v. E. C. Knight Co., *supra,* Mr. Justice Holmes, in sustaining the exercise of national power over intrastate activity, stated for the Court that "commerce among the states is not a technical legal conception, but a practical one, drawn from the course of business." Swift & Co. v. United States, 196 U.S. 375, 398. It was soon demonstrated that the effects of many kinds of intrastate activity upon interstate commerce were such as to make them a proper subject of federal regulation. In some cases sustaining the exercise of federal power over intrastate matters the term "direct" was used for the purpose of stating, rather than of reaching, a result; in others it was treated as synonymous with "substantial" or "material"; and in others it was not used at all. Of late its use has been abandoned in cases dealing with questions of federal power under the commerce clause.

In the Shreveport Rate Cases (Houston, E. & W T. R. Co. v. United States), 234 U.S. 342, the Court held that railroad rates of an admittedly intrastate character and fixed by authority of the state might, nevertheless, be revised by the federal government because of the economic effects which they had upon interstate commerce. The opinion of Mr. Justice Hughes found federal intervention constitutionally authorized because of "matters having such a close and substantial relation to interstate traffic that the control is essential or appropriate to the security of that traffic, to the efficiency of the interstate service, and to the maintenance of the conditions under which interstate commerce may be conducted upon fair terms and without molestation or hindrance." 234 U.S. at page 351.

The Court's recognition of the relevance of the economic effects in the application of the commerce clause exemplified by this statement has made the mechanical application of legal formulas no longer feasible. Once an economic measure of the reach of the power granted to Congress in the commerce clause is accepted, questions of federal power cannot be decided simply by finding the activity in question to be "production" nor can consideration of its economic effects be foreclosed by calling them "indirect." The present Chief Justice has said in summary of the present state of the law: "The commerce power is not confined in its exercise to the regulation of commerce among the states. It extends to those activities intrastate which so affect interstate commerce or the exertion of the power of Congress over it, as to make regulation of them appropriate means to the attainment of a legitimate end, the effective execution of the granted power to regulate interstate commerce. . . . The power of Congress over interstate commerce is plenary and complete in itself, may be exercised to its utmost extent, and acknowledges no limitations other than are prescribed in the Constitution. . . . It follows that no form of state activity can constitutionally thwart the regulatory power granted by the commerce clause to Congress. Hence the reach of that power extends to those intrastate activities which in a substantial way interfere with or obstruct the exercise of the granted power." United States v. Wrightwood Dairy Co., 315 U.S. 110, 119.

Whether the subject of the regulation in question was "production," "consumption," or "marketing" is, therefore, not material for purposes of deciding the question of federal power before us. That an activity is of local character may help in a doubtful case to determine whether Congress intended to reach it. The same consideration might help in determining whether in the absence of congressional action it would be permissible for the state to exert its power on the subject matter, even though in so doing it to some degree affected interstate commerce. But even if appellant's activity be local and though it may not be regarded as commerce, it may still, whatever its nature, be reached by Congress if it exerts a substantial economic effect on interstate commerce and this irrespective of whether such effect is what might at some earlier time have been defined as "direct" or "indirect."

The parties have stipulated a summary of the economics of the wheat industry. Commerce among the states in wheat is large and important. Although wheat is raised in every state but one, production in most states is not equal to consumption. Sixteen states on average have had a surplus of wheat above their own requirements for feed, seed, and food. Thirty-two states and the District of Columbia, where production has been below consumption, have looked to these surplus-producing states for their supply as well as for wheat for export and carryover.

The wheat industry has been a problem industry for some years. Largely as a result of increased foreign production and import restrictions, annual exports of wheat and flour from the United States during the ten-year period ending in 1940 averaged less than 10 per cent of total production, while during the 1920's they averaged more than 25 per cent. The decline in the export trade has left a large surplus in production which in connection with an abnormally large supply of wheat and other grains in recent years caused congestion in a number of markets; tied up railroad cars; and caused elevators in some instances to turn away grains, and railroads to institute embargoes to prevent further congestion. . . .

In the absence of regulation the price of wheat in the United States would be much affected by world conditions. During 1941 producers who co-operated with the Agricultural Adjustment program received an average price on the farm of about $1.16 a bushel as compared with the world market price of 40 cents a bushel. . . .

The effect of consumption of home-grown wheat on interstate commerce is due to the fact that it constitutes the most variable factor in the disappearance of the wheat crop. Consumption on the farm where grown appears to vary in an amount greater than 20 per cent of average production. The total amount of wheat consumed as food varies but relatively little, and use as seed is relatively constant.

The maintenance by government regulation of a price for wheat undoubtedly can be accomplished as effectively by sustaining or increasing the demand as by limiting the supply. The effect of the statute before us is to restrict the amount which may be produced for market and the extent as well to which one may forestall resort to the market by producing to meet his own needs. That [Filburn's] own contribution to the demand for wheat may be trivial by itself is not enough to remove him from the scope of federal regulation where, as here, his contribution, taken together with that of many others similarly situated, is far from trivial. National Labor Relations Board *v.* Fainblatt, 306 U.S. 601, 606, *et seq.,* 307 U.S. 609; United States *v.* Darby, *supra,* 312 U.S. at page 123.

It is well established by decisions of this Court that the power to regulate commerce includes the power to regulate the prices at which commodities in that commerce are dealt in and practices affecting such prices. One of the primary purposes of the Act in question was to increase the market price of wheat and to that end to limit the volume thereof that could affect the market. It can hardly be denied that a factor of such volume and variability as home consumed wheat would have a substantial influence on price and market conditions. This may arise because being in marketable condition such wheat overhangs the market and, if induced by rising prices, tends to flow in to the market and check price increases. But if we assume that it is never marketed, it supplies a need of the man who grew it which would otherwise be reflected by purchases in the open market. Home-grown wheat in this sense competes with wheat in commerce. The stimulation of commerce is a use of the regulatory function quite as definitely as prohibitions or restrictions thereon. This record leaves us in no doubt that Congress may properly have considered that wheat consumed on the farm where grown if wholly outside the scheme of regulation would have a substantial effect in defeating and obstructing its purpose to stimulate trade therein at increased prices. . . .

[The decision of the lower court is reversed.]

~~Section IV

WHAT LIMITS ON FREE SPEECH?

The age which acclaimed the Declaration of Independence and added a Bill of Rights to the Federal Constitution considered freedom of expression one of the great natural rights which governments were instituted to protect. It believed that this sacred and inalienable right could not be justly impaired by any government, even with the consent of the majority. Today, many "truths" which appeared to Jefferson "self-evident" seem to have less influence on "the opinions of mankind," and the case for freedom of opinion must find a more pragmatic basis.

Most Americans would agree that freedom of speech and of the press is essential to self-government. Many however would have serious doubts whether this freedom should extend so far as to allow the propagation of doctrines which are regarded as false or even loathsome.

The words of the First Amendment are absolute and unqualified: "Congress shall make *no law* . . . abridging the freedom of speech, or of the press. . . ." If taken literally this would seem to prohibit *all* legislation by Congress which in any degree interferes with freedom of expression. However, very few writers have maintained that freedom of speech should be entirely unlimited, and even many libertarian members of the Supreme Court have held that it cannot be an unqualified right.

The cornerstone of most contemporary judicial discussion of freedom of speech is the so-called "clear and present" danger test first enunciated in the case of Schenck *v.* United States. "The question in every case," wrote Mr. Justice Holmes, "is whether the words used are used in such circumstances and are of such a nature as to create a clear and present danger that they will bring about the substantive evils that Congress has a right to prevent." Since, as Mr. Justice Holmes added, "It is a question of proximity and degree," it is not surprising that the Supreme Court justices should frequently disagree in their interpretation and application of this test.

Should freedom of speech include the right to advocate revolution and dictatorship? Should those who seek to destroy constitu-

117

tional liberties be allowed to take advantage of the very liberties which they aim to destroy? The attempt to answer these questions requires an examination of the limits of freedom of discussion, an evaluation of our present loyalty-security program in public service, and related problems of individual liberties.

In the case of Gitlow *v.* New York, 268 U.S. 652, the majority of the Supreme Court took the position that freedom of the press did not include the right to publish a manifesto which contained an "incitement" to violent revolution. In sustaining the Criminal Anarchy law of New York, Mr. Justice Sanford, writing for the majority of the Supreme Court, said in 1925:

"A single revolutionary spark may kindle a fire that, smouldering for a time, may burst into a sweeping and destructive conflagration. It cannot be said that the State is acting arbitrarily or unreasonably when in the exercise of its judgment as to the measures necessary to protect the public peace and safety, it seeks to extinguish the spark without waiting until it has enkindled the flame or blazed into the conflagration."

The dissent of Justice Holmes regarded this decision as a departure from the clear and present danger test enunciated in the Schenck case. He said:

"If what I think is the correct test is applied it is manifest that there was no present danger of an attempt to overthrow the government by force on the part of the admittedly small minority who shared the defendant's view. . . . Whatever may be thought of the redundant discourse before us, it had no chance of starting a present conflagration. If in the long run the beliefs expressed in proletarian dictatorship are destined to be accepted by the dominant forces of the community, the only meaning of free speech is that they should be given their chance and have their way."

Without overruling the Gitlow case, the Supreme Court in the thirties tended to return to the "clear and present danger test" as interpreted by Holmes and Brandeis. The extreme libertarian position was reached by the "Roosevelt Court" in 1941 in the case of Bridges *v.* California, 314 U.S. 252. In a 5-to-4 opinion Mr. Justice Black, writing for the majority, said: "What finally emerges from the 'clear and present danger' cases is a working principle that the substantive evil must be *extremely serious* and the degree of *imminence extremely high* before utterances can be punished." This victory for the extreme libertarian position in the Supreme Court, however, was only temporary.

The case of Dennis *v.* United States, decided in 1951, by a 6-to-2 vote, upheld the constitutionality of the Smith Act which punishes those who "knowingly or willfully advocate" the destruction of "any government in the United States by force or violence." The justices followed at least four different lines of reasoning in reaching their conclusions and none of these opinions was subscribed to by a majority of the Court.

It should be observed that in Yates *v.* United States, decided in 1957 after some changes in its composition, the Court took pains to emphasize that its decision was consistent with that in the Dennis case. However, it is pertinent to inquire whether the Court's narrow construction of the meaning of the word "organize" in the Smith Act and its insistence that advocacy, to serve as a basis for conviction, must be directed toward *action,* do not, in fact, suggest a return to a somewhat more libertarian position.

We suggest, finally, that the ultimate issue is not one of con-stitutionality but of wisdom.

~~~~TOPIC 11

The Dilemmas of Freedom

"Clear and Present Danger"
SCHENCK V. UNITED STATES
249 U.S. 47 (1919)

Error to the District Court of the United States for the Eastern District of Pennsylvania.

MR. JUSTICE HOLMES delivered the opinion of the court.

This is an indictment in three counts. The first charges a conspiracy to violate the Espionage Act of June 15, 1917, c. 30 § 3, 40 Stat. 217, 219, by causing and attempting to cause insubordination, &c., in the military and naval forces of the United States, and to obstruct the recruiting and enlistment service of the United States, when the United States was at war with the German Empire, to-wit, that the defendants wilfully conspired to have printed and circulated to men who had been called and accepted for military service under the Act of May 18, 1917, a document set forth and alleged to be calculated to cause such insubordination and obstruction. The count alleges overt acts in pursuance of the conspiracy, ending in the distribution of the document set forth. The second count alleges a conspiracy to commit an offense against the United States, to-wit, to use the mails for the transmission of matter declared to be non-mailable by Title XII, § 2 of the Act of June 15, 1917, to-wit, the above mentioned document, with an averment of the same overt acts. The third count charges an unlawful use of the mails for the transmission of the same matter and otherwise as above. The defendants were found guilty on all the counts. They set up the First Amendment to the Constitution forbidding Congress to make any law abridging the freedom of speech, or of the press, and bringing the case here on that ground have argued some other points also of which we must dispose. . . .

The document in question upon its first printed side recited the first section of the Thirteenth Amendment, said that the idea embodied in it was violated by the Conscription Act and that a conscript is little better than a convict. In impassioned language it intimated that conscription was despotism in its worst form and a monstrous wrong against humanity in the interest of Wall Street's chosen few. It said, "Do not submit to intimidation," but in form at least confined itself to peaceful measures such as a petition for the repeal of the act.

121

The other and later printed side of the sheet was headed "Assert Your Rights." It stated reasons for alleging that any one violated the Constitution when he refused to recognize "your right to assert your opposition to the draft," and went on, "If you do not assert and support your rights, you are helping to deny or disparage rights which it is the solemn duty of all citizens and residents of the United States to retain." It described the arguments on the other side as coming from cunning politicians and a mercenary capitalist press, and even silent consent to the conscription law as helping to support an infamous conspiracy. It denied the power to send our citizens away to foreign shores to shoot up the people of other lands, and added that words could not express the condemnation such coldblooded ruthlessness deserves, &c., winding up, "You must do your share to maintain, support and uphold the rights of the people of this country." Of course the document would not have been sent unless it had been intended to have some effect, and we do not see what effect it could be expected to have upon persons subject to the draft except to influence them to obstruct the carrying of it out. The defendants do not deny that the jury might find against them on this point.

But it is said, suppose that that was the tendency of this circular, it is protected by the First Amendment to the Constitution. Two of the strongest expressions are said to be quoted respectively from well-known public men. It well may be that the prohibition of laws abridging the freedom of speech is not confined to previous restraints, although to prevent them may have been the main purpose, as intimated in Patterson *v.* Colorado, 205 U.S. 454, 462. We admit that in many places and in ordinary times the defendants in saying all that was said in the circular would have been within their constitutional rights. But the character of every act depends upon the circumstances in which it is done. Aikens *v.* Wisconsin, 195 U.S. 194, 205, 206. The most stringent protection of free speech would not protect a man in falsely shouting fire in a theatre and causing a panic. It does not protect a man from an injunction against uttering words that may have all the effect of force. Gompers *v.* Buck Stove & Range Co., 221 U.S. 418, 439.

The question in every case is whether the words used are used in such circumstances and are of such a nature as to create a clear and present danger that they will bring about the substantive evils that Congress has a right to prevent. It is a question of proximity and degree. When a nation is at war many things that might be said in time of peace are such a hindrance to its effort that their utterance will not be endured so long as men fight and that no Court could regard them as protected by any constitutional right. It seems to be admitted that if an actual obstruction of the recruiting service were proved, liability for words that produced that effect might be enforced. The statute of 1917 in § 4 punishes conspiracies to obstruct as well as actual obstruction. If the act (speaking, or circulating a paper), its tendency and the intent with which it is done are the same, we perceive no ground for saying that success alone warrants making the act a crime. Goldman *v.* United States, 245 U.S. 474, 477. Indeed that case might be said to dispose of the present contention if the precedent covers all *media concludendi.* But as the right to free speech was not referred to specially, we have thought fit to add a few words. . . .

Judgments affirmed.

JUSTICE OLIVER WENDELL HOLMES, JR.
"Free Trade in Ideas"

Persecution for the expression of opinions seems to me perfectly logical. If you have no doubt of your premises or your power and want a certain result with all your heart you naturally express your wishes in law and sweep away all opposition. To allow opposition by speech seems to indicate that you think the speech impotent, as when a man says that he has squared the circle, or that you do not care wholeheartedly for the result, or that you doubt either your power or your premises. But when men have realized that time has upset many fighting faiths, they may come to believe even more than they believe the very foundations of their own conduct that the ultimate good desired is better reached by free trade in ideas—that the best test of truth is the power of the thought to get itself accepted in the competition of the market, and that truth is the only ground upon which their wishes safely can be carried out. That, at any rate, is the theory of our Constitution. It is an experiment, as all life is an experiment. Every year if not every day we have to wager our salvation upon some prophecy based upon imperfect knowledge. While that experiment is part of our system I think that we should be eternally vigilant against attempts to check the expression of opinions that we loathe and believe to be fraught with death, unless they so imminently threaten immediate interference with the lawful and pressing purposes of the law that an immediate check is required to save the country.

I wholly disagree with the argument of the Government that the First Amendment left the common law as to seditious libel in force. History seems to me against the notion. I had conceived that the United States through many years had shown its repentance for the Sedition Act of 1798 by repaying fines that it imposed. Only the emergency that makes it immediately dangerous to leave the correction of evil counsels to time warrants making any exception to the sweeping command, "Congress shall make no law . . . abridging the freedom of speech." Of course I am speaking only of expressions of opinion and exhortations, which were all that were uttered here, but I regret that I cannot put into more impressive words my belief that in their conviction upon this indictment the defendants were deprived of their rights under the Constitution of the United States.

The selection is from his dissenting opinion in Abrams *v.* United States, 250 U.S. 616, 624 (1919).

ALEXANDER MEIKLEJOHN
Free Speech and Self-Government

The First Amendment to the Constitution, as we all know, forbids the federal Congress to make any law which shall abridge the freedom of speech. In recent years, however, the government of the United States has in many ways limited the freedom of public discussion. For example, the Federal Bureau of Investigation has built up, throughout the country, a system of espionage, of secret police, by which hundreds of thousands of our people have been listed as holding this or that set of opinions. The only conceivable justification of that listing by a government agency is to provide a basis for action by the government in dealing with those persons. And that procedure reveals an attitude toward freedom of speech which is widely held in the United States. Many of us are now convinced that, under the Constitution, the government is justified in bringing pressure to bear against the holding or expressing of beliefs which are labeled "dangerous." Congress, we think, may rightly abridge the freedom of such beliefs.

Again, the legislative committees, federal and state, which have been appointed to investigate un-American activities, express the same interpretation of the Constitution. All the inquirings and questionings of those committees are based upon the assumption that certain forms of political opinion and advocacy should be, and legitimately may be, suppressed. And, further, the Department of Justice, acting on the same assumption, has recently listed some sixty or more organizations, association with which may be taken by the government to raise the question of "disloyalty" to the United States. And finally, the President's Loyalty Order, moving with somewhat uncertain steps, follows the same road. We are officially engaged in the suppression of "dangerous" speech.

Now, these practices would seem to be flatly contradictory of the First Amendment. Are they? What do we mean when we say that "Congress shall make no law . . . abridging the freedom of speech . . . ?" What is this "freedom of speech" which we guard against invasion by our chosen and authorized representatives? Why may not a man be prevented from speaking if, in the judgment of Congress, his ideas are hostile and harmful to the general welfare of the nation? Are we, for example, required by the First Amendment to give men freedom to advocate the abolition of the First Amendment? Are we bound to grant freedom of speech to those who, if they had the power, would refuse it to us? The First Amendment, taken literally, seems to answer "Yes" to those questions. It seems to say that no speech, however dangerous, may, for that reason, be suppressed. But the Federal Bureau of Investigation, the un-American Activities Committees, the Department of Justice, the President, are, at the

Former President, Amherst College. Author of *The Liberal College, Freedom and the College* and other works. The selection is from Alexander Meiklejohn, *Free Speech and Its Relation to Self-Government* (New York, Harper & Brothers, 1948), *passim*. Reprinted by permission of author and publisher.

same time, answering "No" to the same question. Which answer is right? What is the valid American doctrine concerning the freedom of speech? . . .

When men govern themselves, it is they—and no one else—who must pass judgment upon unwisdom and unfairness and danger. And that means that unwise ideas must have a hearing as well as wise ones, unfair as well as fair, dangerous as well as safe, un-American as well as American. Just so far as, at any point, the citizens who are to decide an issue are denied acquaintance with information or opinion or doubt or disbelief or criticism which is relevant to that issue, just so far the result must be ill-considered, ill-balanced planning for the general good. *It is that mutilation of the thinking process of the community against which the First Amendment to the Constitution is directed.* The principle of the freedom of speech springs from the necessities of the program of self-government. It is not a Law of Nature or of Reason in the abstract. It is a deduction from the basic American agreement that public issues shall be decided by universal suffrage.

If, then, on any occasion in the United States it is allowable to say that the Constitution is a good document it is equally allowable, in that situation, to say that the Constitution is a bad document. If a public building may be used in which to say, in time of war, that the war is justified, then the same building may be used in which to say that it is not justified. If it be publicly argued that conscription for armed service is moral and necessary, it may likewise be publicly argued that it is immoral and unnecessary. If it may be said that American political institutions are superior to those of England or Russia or Germany, it may, with equal freedom, be said that those of England or Russia or Germany are superior to ours. These conflicting views may be expressed, must be expressed, not because they are valid, but because they are relevant. If they are responsibly entertained by anyone, we, the voters, need to hear them. When a question of policy is "before the house," free men choose to meet it not with their eyes shut, but with their eyes open. To be afraid of ideas, any idea, is to be unfit for self-government. Any such suppression of ideas about the common good, the First Amendment condemns with its absolute disapproval. The freedom of ideas shall not be abridged. . . .

In the course of his argument [in Schenck *v.* United States] Mr. Holmes says, "The question in every case is whether the words used are used in such circumstances and are of such a nature as to create a clear and present danger that they will bring about the substantive evils that Congress has a right to prevent." And to this he adds, a few sentences later, "It seems to be admitted that, if an actual obstruction of the recruiting service were proved, liability for words that produced that effect might be enforced."

As one reads these words of Mr. Holmes, one is uneasily aware of the dangers of his rhetorical skill. At two points the argument seems at first much more convincing than it turns out to be. First, the phrase, "substantive evils that Congress has a right to prevent," seems to settle the issue by presumption, seems to establish the right of legislative control. If the legislature has both the right and the duty to prevent certain evils, then apparently it follows that the legislature must be authorized to take whatever action is needed for the preventing of those evils. But our plan of government by limited powers forbids that that inference be drawn. The Bill of Rights, for example, is a series of denials that the inference is valid. It lists, one after the other, forms of action which, however useful they might be in the service of the general welfare, the legislature is forbidden to take. And, that being true, the "right to prevent evils" does not give unqualifiedly the right to prevent evils. In the judgment of the Constitution, some preventions are more evil than are the evils from which they would save us. And the First Amendment is a case in point. If that amendment means anything, it means that certain substantive evils which, in principle, Congress has a right to prevent, must be endured if the only way of avoiding them is by the abridging of that freedom of speech upon which the entire structure of our free institution rests. . . .

But, second, the "clear and present danger" argument which Mr. Holmes here offers, moves quickly from deliberate obstruction of a law to reasonable protest against it. Taken as it stands, his formula tells us that whenever the expression of a minority opinion involves clear and present danger to the public safety it may be denied the protection of the First Amendment. And that means that whenever crucial and dangerous issues have come upon the nation, free and unhindered discussion of them must stop. If, for example, a majority in Congress is taking action against "substantive evils which Congress has a right to prevent," a minority which opposes such action is not entitled to the freedom of speech of Article I, section 6.* Under that ruling, dissenting judges might, in "dangerous" situations, be forbidden to record their dissents. Minority citizens might, in like situations, be required to hold their peace. No one, of course, believes that this is what Mr. Holmes or the court intended to say. But it is what, in plain words, they did say. The "clear and present danger" opinion stands on the record of the court as a peculiarly inept and unsuccessful attempt to formulate an exception to the principle of the freedom of speech. . . .

Human discourse, as the First Amendment sees it, is not "a mere academic and harmless discussion." If it were, the advocates of self-government would be as little concerned about it as they would be concerned about the freedom of men playing solitaire or chess. The First Amendment was not written primarily for the protection of those intellectual aristocrats who pursue knowledge solely for the fun of the game, whose search for truth expresses nothing more than a private intellectual curiosity or an equally private delight and pride in mental achievement. It was written to clear the way for thinking which serves the general welfare. It offers defense to men who plan and advocate and incite toward corporate action for the common good. On behalf of such men it tells us that every plan of action must have a hearing, every relevant idea of fact or value must have full consideration, whatever may be the dangers which that activity involves. It makes no difference whether a man is advocating conscription or opposing it, speaking in favor of a war or against it, defending democracy or attacking it, planning a communist reconstruction of our economy or criticizing it. So long as his active words are those of participation in public discussion and public decision of matters of public policy, the freedom of those words may not be abridged. That freedom is the basic postulate of a society which is governed by the votes of its citizens.

"If, in the long run, the beliefs expressed in proletarian dictatorship are

* Article I, section 6, of the Constitution defining the duties and privileges of the members of Congress, says, ". . . and for any speech or debate in either House, they shall not be questioned in any other place" [Eds.].

destined to be accepted by the dominant forces of the community, the only meaning of free speech is that they should be given their chance and have their way." [The quote is from Justice Holmes' dissent in Gitlow *v.* New York, 268 U.S. 652 (1925).] That is Americanism. In these wretched days of postwar and, it may be, of prewar, hysterical brutality, when we Americans, from the president down, are seeking to thrust back Communist belief by jailing its advocates, by debarring them from office, by expelling them from the country, by hating them, the gallant, uncompromising words of Mr. Holmes, if we would listen to them, might help to restore our sanity, our understanding of the principles of the Constitution. They might arouse in us something of the sense of shame which the nation so sorely needs. . . .

We Americans, in choosing our form of government, have made, at this point, a momentous decision. We have decided to be self-governed. We have measured the dangers and the values of the suppression of the freedom of public inquiry and debate. And, on the basis of that measurement, having regard for the public safety, we have decided that the destruction of freedom is always unwise, that freedom is always expedient. The conviction recorded by that decision is not a sentimental vagary about the "natural rights" of individuals. It is a reasoned and sober judgment as to the best available method of guarding the public safety. We, the People, as we plan for the general welfare, do not choose to be "protected" from the "search for truth." On the contrary, we have adopted it as our "way of life," our method of doing the work of governing for which, as citizens, we are responsible. Shall we, then, as practitioners of freedom, listen to ideas which, being opposed to our own, might destroy confidence in our form of government? Shall we give a hearing to those who hate and despise freedom, to those who, if they had the power, would destroy our institutions? Certainly, yes! Our action must be guided, not by their principles, but by ours. We listen, not because they desire to speak, but because we need to hear. If there are arguments against our theory of government, our policies in war or in peace, we the citizens, the rulers, must hear and consider them for ourselves. That is the way of public safety. It is the program of self-government.

In his study, *Free Speech in the United States,* Mr. Chafee gives abundant evidence in support of this criticism. . . . The suppression of freedom of speech, he finds, has been throughout our history a disastrous threat to the public safety. As he sums up his results, he takes as a kind of motto the words of John Stuart Mill: "A State which dwarfs its men in order that they may be more docile instruments in its hands even for beneficial purposes, will find that with small men no great thing can really be accomplished." Mr. Chafee tells the story, as he sees it, of the futility and disaster which came upon the efforts of President Wilson in World War I as he was driven, by the threat of clear and present dangers, into the suppressions of the Espionage Act.

President Wilson's tragic failure, according to Mr. Chafee, was his blindness to the imperative need of public information and public discussion bearing on the issues of war and peace. He felt bound to prevent imminent substantive evils which might arise from that discussion. In the attempt to do so, nearly two thousand persons, Mr. Chafee tells us, were prosecuted. The fruits of those prosecutions he sums up as follows: ". . . tens of thousands among those 'forward-looking men and women' to whom President Wilson had appealed in earlier years were bewildered and depressed and silenced by the negation of freedom in the twenty-year sentences requested by his legal subordinates from complacent judges. So we had plenty of patriotism and very little criticism, except of the slowness of ammunition production. Wrong courses were followed like the dispatch of troops to Archangel in 1918, which fatally alienated Russia from Wilson's aims for a peaceful Europe. Harmful facts like the secret treaties were concealed while they could have been cured, only to bob up later and wreck everything." . . .

And the final argument upon which the absoluteness of the First Amendment rests [is that] it does not balance intellectual freedom against public safety. On the contrary, its great declaration is that intellectual freedom is the necessary bulwark of the public safety. That declaration admits of no exceptions. If, by suppression, we attempt to avoid lesser evils, we create greater evils. We buy temporary and partial advantage at the cost of permanent and dreadful disaster. That disaster is the breakdown of self-government. Free men need the truth as they need nothing else. In the last resort, it is only the search for and the dissemination of truth that can keep our country safe.*

* It should be noted that, according to Meiklejohn, the word *liberty* in the due process clause of the Fifth Amendment has been "construed by the Supreme Court to include 'the liberty of speech.' The Fifth Amendment is, then, saying that the people of the United States have a *civil* liberty of speech which, *by due legal process,* the government may limit or suppress." It is Meiklejohn's view, therefore, that the Constitution recognizes "two radically different kinds of utterances." The first—relating to "discussion of public policy"—is in the realm of "absolute freedom of speech." But "the constitutional status of a merchant advertising his wares" and of similar activities "is utterly different" and subject to regulation and limitation. [Eds.]

FREDERICK BERNAYS WIENER
Freedom to Destroy Freedom?

As our legislatures and courts come to closer grips with the nature —and the menace—of world communism, Americans are necessarily forced to inquire whether there is anything in the Constitution of the United States that guarantees immunity, or even possible success, for those who seek to replace the model of government fashioned at Philadelphia in 1787 with the pattern forged at Petrograd in 1917–1918 and since further developed in the Kremlin at Moscow.

To what extent, if at all, is "freedom for the thought that we hate" a principle of our Constitution? Is it the theory of our fundamental law "that the best test of truth is the power of the thought to get itself accepted in the competition of the market"? Is there anything in the Constitution that requires the Government to stay its hand against those who would overthrow it, and to "let them stand undisturbed as monuments of the safety with which error of opinion may be tolerated when reason is left free to combat it"? . . .

Member of the District of Columbia Bar. Professorial Lecturer in Law, George Washington University. Formerly with the Department of Justice. Author of *Effective Appellate Advocacy.* This selection is from Federick Bernays Wiener, " 'Freedom for the Thought That We Hate': Is It a Principle of the Constitution?" *American Bar Association Journal,* Vol. 37 (March 1951). By permission.

Framers Intended to Leave No Scope for Anti-Republican Government

Having fought monarchy for long and hard years in the face of terrible odds, the Framers were not quixotic enough to cast away the prize of independence by providing new sanctuaries where that hated institution might conveniently reappear. They had not turned the other cheek when George III struck at their liberties; now, having secured those liberties, they were not with the other hand preparing to endanger the hard-won prize by providing freedom for the hated thought of monarchy. Indeed, they intended to leave no scope for any antirepublican form of government. For those men of 1787, though they knew nothing of swastikas, or dictatorship of the proletariat, or fascism, or communism, were yet fully aware, good classicists that they were, of the excesses of tyranny in the days of ancient Greece and Rome. And for anti-republican ideas, whether of kings by divine right or of tyrants by irresistible force, of totalitarianism whether in the name of blood unity or in the name of economic interest, they never intended to provide a foothold. They not only presupposed the orthodoxy of republicanism, they guaranteed its continuance.

At this point it will doubtless be urged, however, that the writings of Thomas Jefferson reflect the very ideas that Mr. Justice Holmes expressed, and Mr. Justice Brandeis elaborated, over a century later. Reliance is generally had on the one sentence from Jefferson's First Inaugural:

> If there be any among us who would wish to dissolve this Union or to change its republican form, let them stand undisturbed as monuments of the safety with which error of opinion may be tolerated where reason is left free to combat it.

The hard fact of the matter is, however, that Jefferson is far from being a safe guide on the issues now under consideration. He was not a member of the Constitutional Convention, being at the time Minister to France, and had no access to its records during his lifetime. His letter to Kercheval, written in 1816, in which he deprecates looking at constitutions with sanctimonious reverence, is merely an individual attitude, which is far from representative of the views of those who framed the Constitution in 1787, or of those who in 1795 decided to admit to citizenship only those aliens who were "attached to the principles of the Constitution of the United States."[1] In that connection, it is significant that Madison, then in Congress, opposed the latter requirement. "It was hard to make a man swear that he preferred the Constitution of the United States, or to give any general opinion, because he may, in his own private judgment, think Monarchy or Aristocracy better, and yet be honestly determined to support this Government as he finds it."[2] But Congress adopted the provision over Madison's objections.[3] . . .

Moreover, since Inaugural Addresses traditionally and normally have

[1] Secs. 1 (*Thirdly*) and 2, Act Jan. 29, 1795, c. 20, 1 Stat. 414-415.
[2] 4 *Annals of Congress* 1023.
[3] *Ibid.*

partisan connotations, Jefferson's First Inaugural must be read in the light of the political controversies of the day. It must be read with an eye to the Sedition Act, and to that measure's partisan, even virulent, enforcement by the Federalists; and pre-eminently, it must be read in the light of the vital circumstance, always overlooked by those who uncritically accept that document as constitutional gospel, that Jefferson was the real author of the Kentucky and Virginia Resolutions and hence the spiritual ancestor of nullification and of its progeny, secession.

The Southern leaders of 1860–1861 relied upon the Jeffersonian doctrine of noninterference when they left the Union. But the course of American history did not follow the Jeffersonian view. For if Jefferson was right, if those "who would wish to dissolve this Union" should "stand undisturbed as monuments of the safety with which error of opinion may be tolerated where reason is left free to combat it," then Lincoln was wrong, and the men who fought to preserve the Union were wrong, and we should now be two nations instead of one. Holmes himself asserted the error of the Jeffersonian view at the Marshall centennial in 1901, when, as Chief Justice of Massachusetts, he noted "The fact that time has been on Marshall's side, and that the theory for which Hamilton argued, and he decided, and Webster spoke, and Grant fought, and Lincoln died, is now our cornerstone."[4] Moreover, Holmes, on the United States Supreme Court, wrote the opinions upholding the convictions of Schenck[5] and Frohwerk[6] and Debs,[7] in which the "clear and present danger" test was first enunciated; if Jefferson was right, these persons should never have been convicted, they should have been permitted to stand undisturbed. Indeed, it is not amiss to point out that, much earlier, Jefferson had backtracked also; the treason prosecutions of his Administration indicated a strong disinclination to let Aaron Burr *et al.* pursue their machinations without interference.[8] . . .

We Need Not Follow the Weimar Example

These are not mere theoretical abstractions; the views herein discussed can be illustrated and illustrated by the sorry spectacle of the demise of republican governments elsewhere.

The record in the Knauer denaturalization case[9] showed that Hitler prior to 1923 "never had any intention of trying to obtain political power in Germany except by means of force, except by violence, by a *coup d'état,* or a similar direct action method." It was only after the failure of the 1923 *Putsch* "that he with his advisers decided that the way to do away with democracy in Germany was to use democracy—was to use democratic rights and privileges with the explicit aim of paralyzing democracy and the democratic proce-

[4] Holmes, "John Marshall," in *Collected Legal Papers* 87, 90-91.
[5] Schenck *v.* United States, 249 U.S. 47.
[6] Frohwerk *v.* United States, 249 U.S. 204.
[7] Debs *v.* United States, 249 U.S. 211.
[8] United States *v.* Burr, Fed. Case No. 14693 (C.C.D. Va.); *Ex parte Bollman,* 4 Cranch 75. See also 4 Channing, *History of the United States,* 335-343; 3 Beveridge, *The Life of John Marshall,* 274-545; Channing, *The Jeffersonian System,* 155-168.
[9] Knauer *v.* United States, 328 U.S. 654.

dures. . . .[10] By allowing full "freedom for the thought that we hate," by opening its marketplaces in ideas to "the monstrous and debauching power of the organized lie,"[11] the Germany of the Weimar Republic effectively signed its own death warrant. Nothing in the Constitution of the United States requires us to follow the German example.

The sad history of the second overthrow of Czechoslovakia in 1948 by the Communists illuminates the practical difficulties in the way of applying the "clear and present danger" test to the purposeful underground plottings of organized communism. Those who parrot the Holmes' formula in a vacuum of their own devising—ignoring, by the way, Holmes' warning about the consequences which follow when thoughts become encysted in fine phrases[12]— have yet to indicate the point at which, in their view, the Czechoslovak Government would have been free to move against those who eventually overthrew it. What was said in reply to a similar argument in a treason case affords an ample answer to most of the contentions drawn from a too literal application of "clear and present danger" to the machinations of the Communist Party: "And after this kind of reasoning they will not be guilty till they have success; and if they have success enough, it will be too late to question them."[13] Judge Learned Hand's Dennis opinion[14] blows a welcome breath of fresh realistic air through a good deal of abstract libertarianism. That opinion holds, in substance and effect, that nothing in the Constitution of the United States requires this country to suffer the Czechoslovak experience in the name of freedom of thought. . . .

The truth of the matter is that "freedom for the thought that we hate" is not, certainly in any absolute sense, a principle of our Constitution. And the present paper suggests that it would be well to remember that fact whenever we have occasion to deal with those who seek to use the protections of the Constitution in order to undermine the Constitution, who take advantage of American freedom only that they may be the better able to destroy it.*

[10] Consolidated transcript in Knauer *v.* United States, *supra,* pages 611 *et seq.* (not printed).

[11] Gilbert Murray, quoted in Kimball, "The Espionage Acts and the Limits of Legal Toleration," 33 *Harv. L. Rev.*, 442, 447, note 36, which is an exceptionally well-reasoned defense of Abrams *v.* United States, 250 U.S. 616.

[12] "It is one of the misfortunes of the law that ideas become encysted in phrases and thereafter for a long time cease to provoke further analysis." Holmes, J., dissenting in Hyde *v.* United States, 225 U.S. 347, 384, 391.

"To rest upon a formula is a slumber that, prolonged, means death." Holmes, "Ideals and Doubts," in *Collected Legal Papers,* 303, 306.

[13] Lord Chief Justice Treby in *Trial of Captain Vaughan,* 13 How. St. Tr. 485, 533.

[14] 183 F. (2d) 201 (C.A. 2d), decided August 1, 1950. [See next Topic.] Holmes' dissent in the Abrams case was cited by Dennis *et al.* in their brief some leven times, Brandeis' concurring opinion in the Whitney case no less than nineteen times. Counsel for Dennis *et al.* had not progressed beyond page 14 of the transcript of his oral argument in the Second Circuit before he quoted the sentence beginning, "If there be any among us who would wish to dissolve this Union or to change its republican form," etc.

* For a reply to the above article see Arthur S. Katz, "Freedom for the Thought We Hate," *American Bar Association Journal* (December, 1951), Vol. 37, pp. 901-904. [Eds.]

Freedom to Advocate Revolution?

Democracy May Defend Itself

DENNIS ET AL. *V.* UNITED STATES

341 U.S. 494 (1951)

MR. CHIEF JUSTICE VINSON announced the judgment of the Court and an opinion in which MR. JUSTICE REED, MR. JUSTICE BURTON and MR. JUSTICE MINTON join.

Petitioners were indicted in July, 1948, for violation of the conspiracy provisions of the Smith Act, . . . § 11, during the period of April, 1945, to July, 1948. . . . We granted certiorari, 340 U.S. 863, limited to the following two questions: (1) Whether either § 2 or § 3 of the Smith Act, inherently or as construed and applied in the instant case, violates the First Amendment and other provisions of the Bill of Rights; (2) whether either § 2 or § 3 of the Act, inherently or as construed and applied in the instant case, violates the First and Fifth Amendments because of indefiniteness.

Sections 2 and 3 of the Smith Act, . . . provide as follows:

SEC. 2.

(a) It shall be unlawful for any person—

(1) to knowingly or willfully advocate, abet, advise, or teach the duty, necessity, desirability, or propriety of overthrowing or destroying any government in the United States by force or violence, or by the assassination of any officer of such government;

(3) to organize or help to organize any society, group, or assembly of persons who teach, advocate, or encourage the overthrow or destruction of any government in the United States by force or violence; or to be or become a member of, or affiliate with, any such society, group, or assembly of persons, knowing the purpose thereof. . . .

SEC. 3. It shall be unlawful for any person to attempt to commit, or to conspire to commit, any of the acts prohibited by the provisions of . . . this title.

The indictment charged the petitioners with willfully and knowingly conspiring (1) to organize as the Communist Party of the United States of America a society, group and assembly of persons who teach and advocate the over-

132

throw and destruction of the Government of the United States by force and violence, and (2) knowingly and willfully to advocate and teach the duty and necessity of overthrowing and destroying the Government of the United States by force and violence. The indictment further alleged that § 2 of the Smith Act proscribes these acts and that any conspiracy to take such action is a violation of § 3 of the Act.

The trial of the case extended over nine months, six of which were devoted to the taking of evidence, resulting in a record of 16,000 pages. . . . Petitioners dispute the meaning to be drawn from the evidence, contending that the Marxist-Leninist doctrine they advocated taught that force and violence to achieve a Communist form of government in an existing democratic state would be necessary only because the ruling classes of that state would never permit the transformation to be accomplished peacefully, but would use force and violence to defeat any peaceful political and economic gain the Communists could achieve.

But the Court of Appeals held that the record supports the following broad conclusions: By virtue of their control over the political apparatus of the Communist Political Association,[1] petitioners were able to transform that organization into the Communist Party; that the policies of the Association were changed from peaceful cooperation with the United States and its economic and political structure to a policy which had existed before the United States and the Soviet Union were fighting a common enemy, namely, a policy which worked for the overthrow of the Government by force and violence; that the Communist Party is a highly disciplined organization, adept at infiltration into strategic positions, use of aliases, and double-meaning language; that the Party is rigidly controlled; that Communists, unlike other political parties, tolerate no dissension from the policy laid down by the guiding forces, but that the approved program is slavishly followed by the members of the Party; that the literature of the Party and the statements and activities of its leaders, petitioners here, advocate, and the general goal of the Party was, during the period in question, to achieve a successful overthrow of the existing order by force and violence.

It will be helpful in clarifying the issues to treat next the contention that the trial judge improperly interpreted the statute by charging that the statute required an unlawful intent before the jury could convict. More specifically, he charged that the jury could not find the petitioners guilty under the indictment unless they found that petitioners had the intent "to overthrow the government by force and violence as speedily as circumstances permit. . . ."

The structure and purpose of the statute demand the inclusion of intent as an element of the crime. Congress was concerned with those who advocate and organize for the overthrow of the Government. Certainly those who recruit and combine for the purpose of advocating overthrow intend to bring about that overthrow. We hold that the statute requires as an essential element

[1] Following the dissolution of the Communist International in 1943, the Communist Party of the United States dissolved and was reconstituted as the Communist Political Association. The program of this Association was one of cooperation between labor and management, and, in general, one designed to achieve national unity and peace and prosperity in the post-war period.

of the crime proof of the intent of those who are charged with its violation to overthrow the Government by force and violence. . . .

Nor does the fact that there must be an investigation of a state of mind under this interpretation afford any basis for rejection of that meaning. A survey of Title 18 of the U.S. Code indicates that the vast majority of the crimes designated by that Title require, by express language, proof of the existence of a certain mental state, in words such as "knowingly," "maliciously," "willfully," "with the purpose of," "with intent to," or combinations or permutations of these and synonymous terms. The existence of a *mens rea* is the rule of, rather than the exception to, the principles of Anglo-American criminal jurisprudence. See American Communications Assn. v. Douds, 339 U.S. 382, 411 (1950). . . .

The obvious purpose of the statute is to protect existing Government, not from change by peaceable, lawful and constitutional means, but from change by violence, revolution and terrorism. That it is within the *power* of the Congress to protect the Government of the United States from armed rebellion is a proposition which requires little discussion. Whatever theoretical merit there may be to the argument that there is a "right" to rebellion against dictatorial governments is without force where the existing structure of the government provides for peaceful and orderly change. We reject any principle of governmental helplessness in the face of preparation for revolution, which principle, carried to its logical conclusion, must lead to anarchy. No one could conceive that it is not within the power of Congress to prohibit acts intended to overthrow the Government by force and violence. The question with which we are concerned here is not whether Congress has such *power,* but whether the *means* which it has employed conflict with the First and Fifth Amendments to the Constitution.

One of the bases for the contention that the means which Congress has employed are invalid takes the form of an attack on the face of the statute on the grounds that by its terms it prohibits academic discussion of the merits of Marxism-Leninism, that it stifles ideas and is contrary to all concepts of a free speech and a free press. . . .

The very language of the Smith Act negates the interpretation which petitioners would have us impose on that Act. It is directed at advocacy, not discussion. Thus, the trial judge properly charged the jury that they could not convict if they found that petitioners did "no more than pursue peaceful studies and discussions or teaching and advocacy in the realm of ideas." He further charged that it was not unlawful "to conduct in an American college and university a course explaining the philosophical theories set forth in the books which have been placed in evidence." Such a charge is in strict accord with the statutory language, and illustrates the meaning to be placed on those words. Congress did not intend to eradicate the free discussion of political theories, to destroy the traditional rights of Americans to discuss and evaluate ideas without fear of governmental sanction. Rather Congress was concerned with the very kind of activity in which the evidence showed these petitioners engaged. . . .

We pointed out in Douds, *supra,* that the basis of the First Amendment is the hypothesis that speech can rebut speech, propaganda will answer propaganda, free debate of ideas will result in the wisest governmental policies. It is for this reason that this Court has recognized the inherent value of free discourse. An analysis of the leading cases in this Court which have involved direct limitations on speech, however, will demonstrate that both the majority of the Court and the dissenters in particular cases have recognized that this is not an unlimited, unqualified right, but that the societal value of speech must, on occasion, be subordinated to other values and considerations.

No important case involving free speech was decided by this Court prior to Schenck *v.* United States, 249 U.S. 47 (1919). . . . Writing for a unanimous Court, Justice Holmes stated that the "question in every case is whether the words used are used in such circumstances and are of such a nature as to create a clear and present danger that they will bring about the substantive evils that Congress has a right to prevent." 249 U.S. at 52. But the force of even this expression is considerably weakened by the reference at the end of the opinion to Goldman *v.* United States, 245 U.S. 474 (1918), a prosecution under the same statute. Said Justice Holmes, "Indeed [Goldman] might be said to dispose of the present contention if the precedent covers all *media concludendi,* but as the right of free speech was not referred to specially, we have thought fit to add a few words." 249 U.S. at 52.

The fact is inescapable, too, that the phrase bore no connotation that the danger was to be any threat to the safety of the Republic. The charge was causing and attempting to cause insubordination in the military forces and obstruct recruiting. The objectionable document denounced conscription and its most inciting sentence was, "You must do your share to maintain, support and uphold the rights of the people of this country." 249 U.S. at 51. Fifteen thousand copies were printed and some circulated. This insubstantial gesture toward insubordination in 1917 during war was held to be a clear and present danger of bringing about the evil of military insubordination. . . .

The rule we deduce . . . is that where an offense is specified by a statute in nonspeech or nonpress terms, a conviction relying upon speech or press as evidence of violation may be sustained only when the speech or publication created a "clear and present danger" of attempting or accomplishing the prohibited crime, *e. g.,* interference with enlistment. . . .

Neither Justice Holmes (nor Justice Brandeis) ever envisioned that a shorthand phrase should be crystallized into a rigid rule to be applied inflexibly without regard to the circumstances of each case. Speech is not an absolute, above and beyond control by the legislature when its judgment, subject to review here, is that certain kinds of speech are so undesirable as to warrant criminal sanction. Nothing is more certain in modern society than the principle that there are no absolutes, that a name, a phrase, a standard has meaning only when associated with the considerations which gave birth to the nomenclature. See Douds, 339 U.S. at 397. To those who would paralyze our Government in the face of impending threat by encasing it in a semantic straitjacket we must reply that all concepts are relative.

In this case we are squarely presented with the application of the "clear and present danger" test, and must decide what that phrase imports. We first note that many of the cases in which this Court has reversed convictions by use of this or similar tests have been based on the fact that the interest which the State was attempting to protect was itself too insubstantial to warrant restriction of speecl

Overthrow of the Government by force and violence is certainly a substantial enough interest for the Government to limit speech. Indeed, this is the ultimate value of any society, for if a society cannot protect its very structure from armed internal attack, it must follow that no subordinate value can be protected. If, then, this interest may be protected, the literal problem which is presented is what has been meant by the use of the phrase "clear and present danger" of the utterances bringing about the evil within the power of Congress to punish.

Obviously, the words cannot mean that before the Government may act, it must wait until the *putsch* is about to be executed, the plans have been laid and the signal is awaited. If Government is aware that a group aiming at its overthrow is attempting to indoctrinate its members and to commit them to a course whereby they will strike when the leaders feel the circumstances permit, action by the Government is required. The argument that there is no need for Government to concern itself, for Government is strong, it possesses ample powers to put down a rebellion, it may defeat the revolution with ease needs no answer. For that is not the question. Certainly an attempt to overthrow the Government by force, even though doomed from the outset because of inadequate numbers or power of the revolutionists, is a sufficient evil for Congress to prevent. The damage which such attempts create both physically and politically to a nation makes it impossible to measure the validity in terms of the probability of success, or the immediacy of a successful attempt.

In the instant case the trial judge charged the jury that they could not convict unless they found that petitioners intended to overthrow the Government "as speedily as circumstances would permit." This does not mean, and could not properly mean, that they would not strike until there was certainty of success. What was meant was that the revolutionists would strike when they thought the time was ripe. We must therefore reject the contention that success or probability of success is the criterion.

The situation with which Justices Holmes and Brandeis were concerned in Gitlow was a comparatively isolated event, bearing little relation in their minds to any substantial threat to the safety of the community. Such also is true of cases like Fiske *v*. Kansas, 274 U.S. 380 (1927), and DeJonge *v*. Oregon, 299 U.S. 353 (1937); but cf. Lazar *v*. Pennsylvania, 286 U.S. 532 (1932). They were not confronted with any situation comparable to the instant one—the development of an apparatus designed and dedicated to the overthrow of the Government, in the context of world crisis after crisis.

Chief Judge Learned Hand, writing for the majority below, interpreted the phrase as follows: "In each case [courts] must ask whether the gravity of the 'evil,' discounted by its improbability, justifies such invasion of free speech as is necessary to avoid the danger." 183 F. 2d at 212. We adopt this statement of the rule. As articulated by Chief Judge Hand, it is as succinct and inclusive as any other we might devise at this time. It takes into consideration those factors which we deem relevant, and relates their significances. More we cannot expect from words.

Likewise, we are in accord with the court below, which affirmed the trial court's finding that the requisite danger existed. The mere fact that from the period 1945 to 1948 petitioners' activities did not result in an attempt to overthrow the Government by force and violence is of course no answer to the fact that there was a group that was ready to make the attempt. The formation by petitioners of such a highly organized conspiracy, with rigidly disciplined members subject to call when the leaders, these petitioners, felt that the time had come for action, coupled with the inflammable nature of world conditions, similar uprisings in other countries, and the touch-and-go nature of our relations with countries with whom petitioners were in the very least ideologically attuned, convince us that their convictions were justified on this score. And this analysis disposes of the contention that a conspiracy to advocate, as distinguished from the advocacy itself, cannot be constitutionally restrained, because it comprises only the preparation. It is the existence of the conspiracy which creates the danger. [Citations omitted.] If the ingredients of the reaction are present, we cannot bind the Government to wait until the catalyst is added. . . .

The argument that the action of the trial court is erroneous, in declaring as a matter of law that such violation shows sufficient danger to justify the punishment despite the First Amendment, rests on the theory that a jury must decide a question of the application of the First Amendment. We do not agree.

When facts are found that establish the violation of a statute the protection against conviction afforded by the First Amendment is a matter of law. The doctrine that there must be a clear and present danger of a substantive evil that Congress has a right to prevent is a judicial rule to be applied as a matter of law by the courts. The guilt is established by proof of facts. Whether the First Amendment protects the activity which constitutes the violation of the statute must depend upon a judicial determination of the scope of the First Amendment applied to the circumstances of the case. . . .

The question in this case is whether the statute which the legislature has enacted may be constitutionally applied. In other words, the Court must examine judicially the application of the statute to the particular situation, to ascertain if the Constitution prohibits the conviction. We hold that the statute may be applied where there is a "clear and present danger" of the substantive evil which the legislature had the right to prevent. Bearing as it does, the marks of a "question of law," the issue is properly one for the judge to decide. . . .

Petitioners intended to overthrow the Government of the United States as speedily as the circumstances would permit. Their conspiracy to organize the Communist Party and to teach and advocate the overthrow of the Government of the United States by force and violence created a "clear and present danger" of an attempt to overthrow the Government by force and violence. They were properly and constitutionally convicted for violation of the Smith Act. The judgments of conviction are

Affirmed.

Mr. Justice Clark took no part in the consideration or decision of this case.

Mr. Justice Frankfurter, concurring in affirmance of the judgment.

The First Amendment categorically demands that "Congress shall make no law respecting an establishment of religion, or prohibiting the free exercise thereof; or abridging the freedom of speech, or of the press; or the right of the people peaceably to assemble, and to petition the Government for a redress of grievances." The right of a man to think what he pleases, to write what he thinks, and to have his thoughts made available for others to hear or read has an engaging ring of universality. The Smith Act and this conviction under it no doubt restrict the exercise of free speech and assembly. Does that, without more, dispose of the matter?

Just as there are those who regard as invulnerable every measure for which the claim of national survival is invoked, there are those who find in the Constitution a wholly unfettered right of expression. Such literalness treats the words of the Constitution as though they were found on a piece of outworn parchment instead of being words that have called into being a nation with a past to be preserved for the future. The soil in which the Bill of Rights grew was not a soil of arid pedantry. The historic antecedents of the First Amendment preclude the notion that its purpose was to give unqualified immunity to every expression that touched on matters within the range of political interest.

The Massachusetts Constitution of 1780 guaranteed free speech; yet there are records of at least three convictions for political libels obtained between 1799 and 1803. The Pennsylvania Constitution of 1790 and the Delaware Constitution of 1792 expressly imposed liability for abuse of the right of free speech. Madison's own State put on its books in 1792 a statute confining the abusive exercise of the right of utterance. And it deserves to be noted that in writing to John Adams' wife, Jefferson did not rest his condemnation of the Sedition Act of 1798 on his belief in unrestrained utterance as to political matter. The First Amendment, he argued, reflected a limitation upon Federal power, leaving the right to enforce restrictions on speech to the States.

The language of the First Amendment is to be read not as barren words found in a dictionary but as symbols of historic experience illumined by the presuppositions of those who employed them. Not what words did Madison and Hamilton use, but what was it in their minds which they conveyed? Free speech is subject to prohibition of those abuses of expression which a civilized society may forbid. As in the case of every other provision of the Constitution that is not crystallized by the nature of its technical concepts, the fact that the First Amendment is not self-defining and self-enforcing neither impairs its usefulness nor compels its paralysis as a living instrument. . . .

Absolute rules would inevitably lead to absolute exceptions, and such exceptions would eventually corrode the rules. The demands of free speech in a democratic society as well as the interest in national security are better served by candid and informed weighing of the competing interests, within the confines of the judicial process, than by announcing dogmas too inflexible for the non-Euclidian problems to be solved.

But how are competing interests to be assessed? Since they are not subject to quantitative ascertainment, the issue necessarily resolves itself into asking, who is to make the adjustment?—who is to balance the relevant factors and ascertain which interest is in the circumstances to prevail? Full responsibility for the choice cannot be given to the courts. Courts are not representative bodies. They are not designed to be a good reflex of a democratic society. Their judgment is best informed, and therefore most dependable, within narrow limits. Their essential quality is detachment, founded on independence. History teaches that the independence of the judiciary is jeopardized when courts become embroiled in the passions of the day and assume primary responsibility in choosing between competing political, economic and social pressures.

Primary responsibility for adjusting the interests which compete in the situation before us of necessity belongs to the Congress. The nature of the power to be exercised by this Court has been delineated in decisions not charged with the emotional appeal of situations such as that now before us. We are to set aside the judgment of those whose duty it is to legislate only if there is no reasonable basis for it. [Citations omitted.] . . .

In all fairness, the argument cannot be met by reinterpreting the Court's frequent use of "clear" and "present" to mean an entertainable "probability." In giving this meaning to the phrase "clear and present danger," the Court of Appeals was fastidiously confining the rhetoric of opinions to the exact scope of what was decided by them. We have greater responsibility for having given constitutional support, over repeated protests, to uncritical libertarian generalities.

Nor is the argument of the defendants adequately met by citing isolated cases. Adjustment of clash of interests which are at once subtle and fundamental is not likely to reveal entire consistency in a series of instances presenting the clash. It is not too difficult to find what one seeks in the language of decisions reporting the effort to reconcile free speech with the interests with which it conflicts. The case for the defendants requires that their conviction be tested against the entire body of our relevant decisions. Since the significance of every expression of thought derives from the circumstances evoking it, results reached rather than language employed give the vital meaning. . . .

[After reviewing a number of decisions of the Court, MR. JUSTICE FRANK-FURTER continued:] I must leave to others the ungrateful task of trying to reconcile all these decisions. In some instances we have too readily permitted juries to infer deception from error, or intention from argumentative or critical statements. In other instances we weighted the interest in free speech so heavily that we permitted essential conflicting values to be destroyed. Viewed as a whole, however, the decisions express an attitude toward the judicial function and a standard of values which for me are decisive of the case before us.

First.—Free-speech cases are not an exception to the principle that we are not legislators, that direct policy-making is not our province. How best to reconcile competing interests is the business of legislatures, and the balance they strike is a judgment not to be displaced by ours, but to be respected unless outside the pale of fair judgment. . . .

Second.—A survey of the relevant decisions indicates that the results which we have reached are on the whole those that would ensue from careful weighing of conflicting interests. The complex issues presented by regulation of speech in public places, by picketing, and by legislation prohibiting advocacy of crime have been resolved by scrutiny of many factors besides the imminence and gravity of the evil threatened.

The matter has been well summarized by a reflective student of the Court's work. "The truth is that the clear-and-present-danger test is an oversimplified judgment unless it takes account also of a number of other factors: the relative seriousness of the danger in comparison with the value of the occasion for speech or political activity; the availability of more moderate controls than those which the state has imposed; and perhaps the specific intent with which the speech or activity is launched. No matter how rapidly we utter the phrase 'clear and present danger,' or how closely we hyphenate the words, they are not a substitute for the weighing of values. They tend to convey a delusion of certitude when what is most certain is the complexity of the strands in the web of freedoms which the judge must disentangle." Freund, *On Understanding the Supreme Court,* 27–28. . . .

Bearing in mind that Mr. Justice Holmes regarded questions under the First Amendment as questions of "proximity and degree," Schenck *v.* United States, 249 U.S. at 52, it would be a distortion, indeed a mockery, of his reasoning to compare the "puny anonymities," 250 U.S. at 629, to which he was addressing himself in the Abrams case in 1919 or the publication that was "futile and too remote from possible consequences," 268 U.S. at 673, in the Gitlow case in 1925 with the setting of events in this case in 1950.

"It does an ill-service to the author of the most quoted judicial phrases regarding freedom of speech, to make him the victim of a tendency which he fought all his life, whereby phrases are made to do service for critical analysis by being turned into dogma. 'It is one of the misfortunes of the law that ideas become encysted in phrases and thereafter for a long time cease to provoke further analysis.' Holmes, J., dissenting, in Hyde *v.* United States, 225 U.S. 347, 384, at 391." . . . It were far better that the phrase be abandoned than that it be sounded once more to hide from the believers in an absolute right of free speech the plain fact that the interest in speech, profoundly important as it is, is no more conclusive in judicial review than other attributes of democracy or than a determination of the people's representatives that a measure is necessary to assure the safety of government itself.

Third.–Not every type of speech occupies the same position on the scale of values. There is no substantial public interest in permitting certain kinds of utterances: "the lewd and obscene, the profane, the libelous, and the insulting or 'fighting' words—those which by their very utterance inflict injury or tend to incite an immediate breach of the peace." Chaplinsky *v.* New Hampshire, 315 U.S. 568, 572. We have frequently indicated that the interest in protecting speech depends on the circumstances of the occasion. See Niemotko *v.* Maryland, 340 U.S. at 275–283. It is pertinent to the decision before us to consider where on the scale of values we have in the past placed the type of speech now claiming constitutional immunity.

The defendants have been convicted of conspiring to organize a party of persons who advocate the overthrow of the Government by force and violence. The jury has found that the object of the conspiracy is advocacy as "a rule or principle of action," "by language reasonably and ordinarily calculated to incite persons to such action," and with the intent to cause the overthrow "as speedily as circumstances would permit."

On any scale of values which we have hitherto recognized, speech of this sort ranks low.

Throughout our decisions there has recurred a distinction between the statement of an idea which may prompt its hearers to take unlawful action, and advocacy that such action be taken. The distinction has its root in the conception of the common law that a person who procures another to do an act is responsible for that act as though he had done it himself. . . . We frequently have distinguished protected forms of expression from statements which "incite to violence and crime and threaten the overthrow of organized government by unlawful means." Stromberg *v*. California, 283 U.S. at 369. . . .

The object of the conspiracy before us is clear enough that the chance of error in saying that the defendants conspired to advocate rather than to express ideas is slight. MR. JUSTICE DOUGLAS quite properly points out that the conspiracy before us is not a conspiracy to overthrow the Government. But it would be equally wrong to treat it as a seminar in political theory.

These general considerations underlie decision of the case before us.

On the one hand is the interest in security. The Communist Party was not designed by these defendants as an ordinary political party. For the circumstances of its organization, its aims and methods, and the relation of the defendants to its organization and aims we are concluded by the jury's verdict. The jury found that the Party rejects the basic premise of our political system —that change is to be brought about by nonviolent constitutional process. The jury found that the Party advocates the theory that there is a duty and necessity to overthrow the Government by force and violence. It found that the Party entertains and promotes this view, not as a prophetic insight or as a bit of unworldly speculation, but as a program for winning adherents and as a policy to be translated into action.

In finding that the defendants violated the statute, we may not treat as established fact that the Communist Party in this country is of significant size, well-organized, well-disciplined, conditioned to embark on unlawful activity when given the command. But in determining whether application of the statute to the defendants is within the constitutional powers of Congress, we are not limited to the facts found by the jury. We must view such a question in the light of whatever is relevant to a legislative judgment. We may take judicial notice that the Communist doctrines which these defendants have conspired to advocate are in the ascendency in powerful nations who cannot be acquitted of unfriendliness to the institutions of this country. We may take account of evidence brought forward at this trial and elsewhere, much of which has long been common knowledge. In sum, it would amply justify a legislature in concluding that recruitment of additional members for the Party would create a substantial danger to national security.

In 1947, it has been reliably reported, at least 60,000 members were enrolled in the Party. Evidence was introduced in this case that the membership was organized in small units, linked by an intricate chain of command, and protected by elaborate precautions designed to prevent disclosure of individual identity. There are no reliable data tracing acts of sabotage or espionage directly to these defendants. But a Canadian Royal Commission appointed in 1946 to investigate espionage reported that it was "overwhelmingly established" that "the Communist movement was the principal base within which the espionage network was recruited." The most notorious spy in recent history was led into the service of the Soviet Union through Communist indoctrination. Evidence supports the conclusion that members of the Party seek and occupy positions of importance in political and labor organizations. Congress was not barred by the Constitution from believing that indifference to such experience would be an exercise not of freedom but of irresponsibility.

On the other hand is the interest in free speech. The right to exert all governmental powers in aid of maintaining our institutions and resisting their physical overthrow does not include intolerance of opinions and speech that cannot do harm although opposed and perhaps alien to dominant, traditional opinion. The treatment of its minorities, especially their legal position, is among the most searching tests of the level of civilization attained by a society. It is better for those who have almost unlimited power of government in their hands to err on the side of freedom. We have enjoyed so much freedom for so long that we are perhaps in danger of forgetting how much blood it cost to establish the Bill of Rights. . . .

We must not overlook the value of that interchange. Freedom of expression is the well-spring of our civilization—the civilization we seek to maintain and further by recognizing the right of Congress to put some limitation upon expression. Such are the paradoxes of life. For social development of trial and error, the fullest possible opportunity for the free play of the human mind is an indispensable prerequisite. The history of civilization is in considerable measure the displacement of error which once held sway as official truth by beliefs which in turn have yielded to other truths. Therefore the liberty of man to search for truth ought not to be fettered, no matter what orthodoxies he may challenge. Liberty of thought soon shrivels without freedom of expression. Nor can truth be pursued in an atmosphere hostile to the endeavor or under dangers which are hazarded only by heroes. . . .

It is not for us to decide how we would adjust the clash of interests which this case presents were the primary responsibility for reconciling it ours. Congress has determined that the danger created by advocacy of overthrow justifies the ensuing restriction on freedom of speech. The determination was made after due deliberation, and the seriousness of the congressional purpose is attested by the volume of legislation passed to effectuate the same ends.

Can we then say that the judgment Congress exercised was denied it by the Constitution? Can we establish a constitutional doctrine which forbids the elected representatives of the people to make this choice? Can we hold that the First Amendment deprives Congress of what it deemed necessary for the Government's protection?

To make validity of legislation depend on judicial reading of events still in the womb of time—a forecast, that is, of the outcome of forces at best appreciated only with knowledge of the topmost secrets of nations—is to charge the judiciary with duties beyond its equipment. We do not expect courts to pronounce historic verdicts on bygone events. Even historians have conflicting views to this day on the origin and conduct of the French Revolution. It is as absurd to be confident that we can measure the present clash of forces and their outcome as to ask us to read history still enveloped in clouds of controversy. . . .

Even when moving strictly within the limits of constitutional adjudication, judges are concerned with issues that may be said to involve vital finalities. The too easy transition from disapproval of what is undesirable to condemnation as unconstitutional, has led some of the wisest judges to question the wisdom of our scheme in lodging such authority in courts. But it is relevant to remind that in sustaining the power of Congress in a case like this nothing irrevocable is done. The democratic process at all events is not impaired or restricted. Power and responsibility remain with the people and immediately with their representation. All the Court says is that Congress was not forbidden by the Constitution to pass this enactment and a prosecution under it may be brought against a conspiracy such as the one before us.

The wisdom of the assumptions underlying the legislation and prosecution is another matter. In finding that Congress has acted within its power, a judge does not remotely imply that he favors the implications that lie beneath the legal issues. Considerations there enter which go beyond the criteria that are binding upon judges within the narrow confines of their legitimate authority. . . .

Civil liberties draw at best only limited strength from legal guaranties. Preoccupation by our people with the constitutionality, instead of with the wisdom of legislation or of executive action, is preoccupation with a false value. Even those who would most freely use the judicial brake on the democratic process by invalidating legislation that goes deeply against their grain, acknowledge, at least by paying lip service, that constitutionality does not exact a sense of proportion or the sanity of humor or an absence of fear. Focusing attention on constitutionality tends to make constitutionality synonymous with wisdom. When legislation touches freedom of thought and freedom of speech, such a tendency is a formidable enemy of the free spirit.

Much that should be rejected as illiberal, because repressive and envenoming, may well be not unconstitutional. The ultimate reliance for the deepest needs of civilization must be found outside their vindication in courts of law; apart from all else, judges, howsoever they may conscientiously seek to discipline themselves against it, unconsciously are too apt to be moved by the deep undercurrents of public feeling. A persistent, positive translation of the liberating faith into the feelings and thoughts and actions of men and women is the real protection against attempts to strait-jacket the human mind. Such temptations will have their way, if fear and hatred are not exorcized. The mark of a truly civilized man is confidence in the strength and security derived from the inquiring mind. We may be grateful for such honest comforts as it supports, but we must be unafraid of its uncertitudes. Without open minds there can be no open society. And if society be not open the spirit of man is mutilated and becomes enslaved.

Mr. Justice Jackson, concurring.

This prosecution is the latest of never-ending, because never successful, quests for some legal formula that will secure an existing order against revolutionary radicalism. It requires us to reappraise, in the light of our own times and conditions, constitutional doctrines devised under other circumstances to strike a balance between authority and liberty.

Activity here charged to be criminal is conspiracy—that defendants conspired to teach and advocate, and to organize the Communist Party to teach and advocate, overthrow and destruction of the Government by force and violence. There is no charge of actual violence or attempt at overthrow.

The principal reliance of the defense in this Court is that the conviction cannot stand under the Constitution because the conspiracy of these defendants presents no "clear and present danger" of imminent or foreseeable overthrow.

Communism . . . appears today as a closed system of thought representing Stalin's version of Lenin's version of Marxism. As an ideology, it is not one of spontaneous protest arising from American working-class experience. It is a complicated system of assumptions, based on European history and conditions, shrouded in an obscure and ambiguous vocabulary, which allures our ultrasophisticated intelligentsia more than our hardheaded working people. From time to time it champions all manner of causes and grievances and makes alliances that may add to its foothold in government or embarrass the authorities.

The Communist Party, nevertheless, does not seek its strength primarily in numbers. Its aim is a relatively small party whose strength is in selected, dedicated, indoctrinated, and rigidly disciplined members. From established policy it tolerates no deviation and no debate. It seeks members that are, or may be, secreted in strategic posts in transportation, communications, industry, government, and especially in labor unions where it can compel employers to accept and retain its members. It also seeks to infiltrate and control organizations of professional and other groups. Through these placements in positions of power it seeks a leverage over society that will make up in power of coercion what it lacks in power of persuasion.

The Communists have no scruples against sabotage, terrorism, assassination, or mob disorder; but violence is not with them, as with the anarchists, an end in itself. The Communist Party advocates force only when prudent and profitable. Their strategy of stealth precludes premature or uncoordinated outbursts of violence, except, of course, when the blame will be placed on shoulders other than their own. They resort to violence as to truth, not as a principle but as an expedient. Force or violence, as they would resort to it, may never be necessary, because infiltration and deception may be enough.

Force would be utilized by the Communist Party not to destroy government but for its capture. The Communist recognizes that an established government in control of modern technology cannot be overthrown by force until it is about ready to fall of its own weight. Concerted uprising therefore, is to await that contingency and revolution is seen, not as a sudden episode, but as the consummation of a long process.

The United States, fortunately, has experienced Communism only in its preparatory stages and for its pattern of final action must look abroad. Russia, of course, was the pilot Communist revolution, which to the Marxist confirms the Party's assumptions and points its destiny. But Communist technique in the overturn of a free government was disclosed by the *coup d'état* in which they seized power in Czechoslovakia. There the Communist Party during its preparatory stage claimed and received protection for its freedoms of speech, press, and assembly. Pretending to be but another political party, it eventually was conceded participation in government, where it entrenched reliable members chiefly in control of police and information services. When the government faced a foreign and domestic crisis, the Communist Party had established a leverage strong enough to threaten civil war.

In a period of confusion the Communist plan unfolded and the underground organization came to the surface throughout the country in the form chiefly of labor "action committees." Communist officers of the unions took over transportation and allowed only persons with party permits to travel. Communist printers took over the newspapers and radio and put out only party-approved versions of events. Possession was taken of telegraph and telephone systems and communications were cut off wherever directed by party heads. Communist unions took over the factories, and in the cities a partisan distribution of food was managed by the Communist organization. A virtually bloodless abdication by the elected government admitted the Communists to power, whereupon they instituted a reign of oppression and terror, and ruthlessly denied to all others the freedoms which had sheltered their conspiracy.

The foregoing is enough to indicate that, either by accident or design, the Communist stratagem outwits the anti-anarchist pattern of statute aimed against "overthrow by force and violence" if qualified by the doctrine that only "clear and present danger" of accomplishing that result will sustain the prosecution.

The "clear and present danger" test was an innovation by Mr. Justice Holmes in the Schenck case, reiterated and refined by him and Mr. Justice Brandeis in later cases, all arising before the era of World War II revealed the subtlety and efficacy of modernized revolutionary techniques used by totalitarian parties. In those cases, they were faced with convictions under so-called criminal syndicalism statutes aimed at anarchists but which, loosely construed, had been applied to punish socialism, pacifism, and left-wing ideologies, the charges often resting on far-fetched inferences which, if true, would establish only technical or trivial violations. They proposed "clear and present danger" as a test for the sufficiency of evidence in particular cases.

I would save it, unmodified, for application as a "rule of reason" in the kind of case for which it was devised. When the issue is criminality of a hot-headed speech on a street corner, or circulation of a few incendiary pamphlets, or parading by some zealots behind a red flag, or refusal of a handful of school children to salute our flag, it is not beyond the capacity of the judicial process to gather, comprehend, and weigh the necessary materials for decision whether it is a clear and present danger of substantive evil or a harmless letting off of steam. It is not a prophecy, for the danger in such cases has matured by the time of trial or it was never present.

The test applies and has meaning where a conviction is sought to be based on a speech or writing which does not directly or explicitly advocate a crime but to which such tendency is sought to be attributed by construction or by implication from external circumstances. The formula in such cases favors freedoms that are vital to our society, and, even if sometimes applied too generously, the consequences cannot be grave. But its recent expansion has extended, in particular to Communists, unprecedented immunities. Unless we are to hold our Government captive in a judge-made verbal trap, we must approach the problem of a well-organized, nation-wide conspiracy, such as I have described, as realistically as our predecessors faced the trivialities that were being prosecuted until they were checked with a rule of reason.

I think reason is lacking for applying that test to this case.

If we must decide that this Act and its application are constitutional only if we are convinced that petitioner's conduct creates a "clear and present danger" of violent overthrow, we must appraise imponderables, including international and national phenomena which baffle the best informed foreign offices and our most experienced politicians. We would have to foresee and predict the effectiveness of Communist propaganda, opportunities for infiltration, whether, and when, a time will come that they consider propitious for action, and whether and how fast our existing government will deteriorate. And we would have to speculate as to whether an approaching Communist *coup* would not be anticipated by a nationalistic fascist movement. No doctrine can be sound whose application requires us to make a prophecy of that sort in the guise of a legal decision. The judicial process simply is not adequate to a trial of such far-flung issues. The answers given would reflect our own political predilections and nothing more.

The authors of the clear and present danger test never applied it to a case like this, nor would I. If applied as it is proposed here, it means that the Communist plotting is protected during its period of incubation; its preliminary stages of organization and preparation are immune from the law; the Government can move only after imminent action is manifest, when it would, of course, be too late.

The highest degree of constitutional protection is due to the individual acting without conspiracy. But even an individual cannot claim that the Constitution protects him in advocating or teaching overthrow of government by force or violence. I should suppose no one would doubt that Congress has power to make such attempted overthrow a crime. But the contention is that one has the constitutional right to work up a public desire and will to do what is a crime to attempt. I think direct incitement by speech or writing can be made a crime, and I think there can be a conviction without also proving that the odds favored its success by 99 to 1, or some other extremely high ratio. . . .

As aptly stated by Judge Learned Hand in Masses Publishing Co. *v.* Patten, 244 F. 535, 540: "One may not counsel or advise others to violate the law as it stands. Words are not only the keys of persuasion, but the triggers of action, and those which have no purport but to counsel the violation of law cannot by any latitude of interpretation be a part of that public opinion which is the final source of government in a democratic state."

Of course, it is not always easy to distinguish teaching or advocacy in the sense of incitement from teaching or advocacy in the sense of exposition or explanation. It is a question of fact in each case.

What really is under review here is a conviction of conspiracy, after a trial for conspiracy, on an indictment charging conspiracy, brought under a statute outlawing conspiracy. With due respect to my colleagues, they seem to me to discuss anything under the sun except the law of conspiracy. One of the dissenting opinions even appears to chide me for "invoking the law of conspiracy." As that is the case before us, it may be more amazing that its reversal can be proposed without even considering the law of conspiracy.

The Constitution does not make conspiracy a civil right. The Court has never before done so and I think it should not do so now. Conspiracies of labor unions, trade associations, and news agencies have been condemned, although accomplished, evidenced and carried out, like the conspiracy here, chiefly by letter-writing, meetings, speeches and organization. Indeed, this Court seems, particularly in cases where the conspiracy has economic ends, to be applying its doctrines with increasing severity. While I consider criminal conspiracy a dragnet device capable of perversion into an instrument of injustice in the hands of a partisan or complacent judiciary, it has an established place in our system of law, and no reason appears for applying it only to concerted action claimed to disturb interstate commerce and withholding it from those claimed to undermine our whole Government.

The basic rationale of the law of conspiracy is that a conspiracy may be an evil in itself, independently of any other evil it seeks to accomplish. Thus, we recently held in Pinkerton *v.* United States, 328 U.S. 640, 643–644, "It has been long and consistently recognized by the Court that the commission of the substantive offense and a conspiracy to commit it are separate and distinct offenses. The power of Congress to separate the two and to affix to each a different penalty is well established. . . . And the plea of double jeopardy is no defense to a conviction for both offenses. . . ."

So far does this doctrine reach that it is well settled that Congress may make it a crime to conspire with others to do what an individual may lawfully do on his own. This principle is illustrated in conspiracies that violate the antitrust law as sustained and applied by this Court. Although one may raise the prices of his own products, and many, acting without concert, may do so, the moment they conspire to that end they are punishable. The same principle is applied to organized labor. Any workman may quit his work for any reason, but concerted actions to the same end are in some circumstances forbidden. Labor Management Relations Act, 61 Stat. 136, § 8 (b), 29 U.S.C. § 158 (b).

The reasons underlying the doctrine that conspiracy may be a substantive evil in itself, apart from any evil it may threaten, attempt, or accomplish are peculiarly appropriate to conspiratorial Communism.

> The reason for finding criminal liability in case of a combination to effect an unlawful end or to use unlawful means, where none would exist, even though the act contemplated were actually committed by an individual, is that a combination of persons to commit a wrong, either as an end or as a means to an end, is so much more dangerous, because of its increased power to do wrong, because it is more difficult to guard against and prevent the evil designs of a group of persons than of a single person, and because of the terror which fear of such a combination tends to create in the minds of people.[2]

There is lamentation in the dissents about the injustice of conviction in the absence of some overt act. Of course, there has been no general uprising against the Government, but the record is replete with acts to carry out the conspiracy alleged, acts such as always are held sufficient to consummate the crime where the statute requires an overt act.

[2] Miller on Criminal Law, 110.

But the shorter answer is that no overt act is or need be required. The Court, in antitrust cases, early upheld the power of Congress to adopt the ancient common law that makes conspiracy itself a crime. Through Mr. Justice Holmes, it said: "Coming next to the objection that no overt act is laid, the answer is that the Sherman Act punished the conspiracies at which it is aimed on the common law footing—that is to say, it does not make the doing of any act other than the act of conspiring a condition of liability." Nash *v*. United States, 229 U.S. 373, 378. Reiterated, United States *v*. Socony-Vacuum Oil Co., 310 U.S. 150, 252. It is not to be supposed that the power of Congress to protect the Nation's existence is more limited than its power to protect interstate commerce.

Also, it is urged that since the conviction is for conspiracy to teach and advocate, and to organize the Communist Party to teach and advocate, the First Amendment is violated, because freedoms of speech and press protect teaching and advocacy regardless of what is taught or advocated. I have never thought that to be the law.

I do not suggest that Congress could punish conspiracy to advocate something, the doing of which it may not punish. Advocacy or exposition of the doctrine of communal property ownership, or any political philosophy unassociated with advocacy of its imposition by force or seizure of government by unlawful means could not be reached through conspiracy prosecution. But it is not forbidden to put down force or violence, it is not forbidden to punish its teaching or advocacy, and the end being punishable, there is no doubt of the power to punish conspiracy for the purpose.

The defense of freedom of speech or press has often been raised in conspiracy cases, because, whether committed by Communists, by businessmen, or by common criminals, it usually consists of words written or spoken, evidenced by letters, conversations, speeches or documents. Communication is the essence of every conspiracy, for only by it can common purpose and concert of action be brought about or be proved. However, when labor unions raised the defense of free speech against a conspiracy charge, we unanimously said:

> It rarely has been suggested that the constitutional freedom for speech and press extends its immunity to speech or writing used as an integral part of conduct in violation of a valid criminal statute. We reject the contention now. . . .
>
> Such an expansive interpretation of the constitutional guaranties of speech and press would make it practically impossible ever to enforce laws against agreements in restraint of trade as well as many other agreements and conspiracies deemed injurious to society. Giboney *v*. Empire Storage & Ice Co., 336 U.S. 490, 498, 502. . . .

In conspiracy cases the Court not only has dispensed with proof of clear and present danger but even of power to create a danger: "It long has been settled, however, that a 'conspiracy to commit a crime is a different offense from the crime that is the object of the conspiracy.' Petitioners, for example, might have been convicted here of a conspiracy to monopolize without ever having acquired the power to carry out the object of the conspiracy. . . ." American Tobacco Co. *v*. United States, 328 U.S. 781, 789.

Having held that a conspiracy alone is a crime and its consummation is another, it would be weird legal reasoning to hold that Congress could punish the one only if there was "clear and present danger" of the second. This would compel the Government to prove two crimes in order to convict for one.

When our constitutional provisions were written, the chief forces recognized as antagonists in the struggle between authority and liberty were the Government on the one hand and the individual citizen on the other. It was thought that if the state could be kept in its place the individual could take care of himself.

In more recent times these problems have been complicated by the intervention between the state and the citizen of permanently organized, well-financed, semi-secret and highly disciplined political organizations. Totalitarian groups here and abroad perfected the technique of creating private paramilitary organizations to coerce both the public government and its citizens. These organizations assert as against our Government all of the constitutional rights and immunities of individuals and at the same time exercise over their followers much of the authority which they deny to the Government. The Communist Party realistically is a state within a state, an authoritarian dictatorship within a republic. It demands these freedoms, not for its members, but for the organized party. It denies to its own members at the same time the freedom to dissent, to debate, to deviate from the party line, and enforces its authoritarian rule by crude purges, if nothing more violent.

The law of conspiracy has been the chief means at the Government's disposal to deal with the growing problems created by such organizations. I happen to think it is an awkward and inept remedy, but I find no constitutional authority for taking this weapon from the Government. There is no constitutional right to "gang up" on the Government.

While I think there was power in Congress to enact this statute and that, as applied in this case, it cannot be held unconstitutional, I add that I have little faith in the long-range effectiveness of this conviction to stop the rise of the Communist movement. Communism will not go to jail with these Communists. No decision by this Court can forestall revolution whenever the existing government fails to command the respect and loyalty of the people and sufficient distress and discontent are allowed to grow up among the masses. Many failures by fallen governments attest that no government can long prevent revolution by outlawry. Corruption, ineptitude, inflation, oppressive taxation, militarization, injustice, and loss of leadership capable of intellectual initiative in domestic or foreign affairs are allies on which the Communists count to bring opportunity knocking to their door. Sometimes I think they may be mistaken. But the Communists are not building just for today—the rest of us might profit by their example.

MR. JUSTICE BLACK, dissenting.

At the outset I want to emphasize what the crime involved in this case is, and what it is not. These petitioners were not charged with an attempt to overthrow the Government. They were not charged with overt acts of any kind designed to overthrow the Government. They were not even charged with saying anything or writing anything designed to overthrow the Government. The charge was that they agreed to assemble and to talk and publish certain ideas at a later date: The indictment is that they conspired to organize the Communist Party and to use speech or newspapers and other publications in the future to teach and advocate the forcible overthrow of the Government. No matter how it is worded, this is a virulent form of prior censorship of speech and press, which I believe the First Amendment forbids. I would hold § 3 of the Smith Act authorizing this prior restraint unconstitutional on its face and as applied.

But let us assume, contrary to all constitutional ideas of fair criminal procedure, that petitioners although not indicted for the crime of actual advocacy, may be punished for it. Even on this radical assumption, the other opinions in this case show that the only way to affirm these convictions is to repudiate directly or indirectly the established "clear and present danger" rule. This the Court does in a way which greatly restricts the protections afforded by the First Amendment. The opinions for affirmance indicate that the chief reason for jettisoning the rule is the expressed fear that advocacy of Communist doctrine endangers the safety of the Republic.

Undoubtedly, a governmental policy of unfettered communication of ideas does entail dangers. To the Founders of this Nation, however, the benefits derived from free expression were worth the risk. They embodied this philosophy in the First Amendment's command that Congress "shall make no law abridging . . . the freedom of speech, or of the press. . . ." I have always believed that the First Amendment is the keystone of our Government, that the freedoms it guarantees provide the best insurance against destruction of all freedom. At least as to speech in the realm of public matters, I believe that the "clear and present danger" test does not "mark the furthermost constitutional boundaries of protected expression" but does "no more than recognize a minimum compulsion of the Bill of Rights." Bridges *v.* California, 314 U.S. 252, 263.

So long as this Court exercises the power of judicial review of legislation, I cannot agree that the First Amendment permits us to sustain laws suppressing freedom of speech and press on the basis of Congress' or our own notions of mere "reasonableness." Such a doctrine waters down the First Amendment so that it amounts to little more than an admonition to Congress. The Amendment as so construed is not likely to protect any but those "safe" or orthodox views which rarely need its protection. I must also express my objection to the holding because, as MR. JUSTICE DOUGLAS' dissent shows, it sanctions the determination of a crucial issue of fact by the judge rather than by the jury. . . .

Public opinion being what it now is, few will protest the conviction of these Communist petitioners. There is hope, however, that in calmer times, when present pressures, passions and fears subside, this or some later Court will restore the First Amendment liberties to the high preferred place where they belong in a free society.

MR. JUSTICE DOUGLAS, dissenting.

If this were a case where those who claimed protection under the First Amendment were teaching the techniques of sabotage, the assassination of the

President, the filching of documents from public files, the planting of bombs, the art of street warfare, and the like, I would have no doubts. The freedom to speak is not absolute; the teaching of methods of terror and other seditious conduct should be beyond the pale along with obscenity and immorality. This case was argued as if those were the facts. The argument imported much seditious conduct into the record. That is easy and it has popular appeal, for the activities of Communists in plotting and scheming against the free world are common knowledge.

But the fact is that no such evidence was introduced at the trial. There is a statute which makes a seditious conspiracy unlawful.[3] Petitioners, however, were not charged with a "conspiracy to overthrow" the Government. They were charged with a conspiracy to form a party and groups and assemblies of people who teach and advocate the overthrow of our Government by force or violence and with a conspiracy to advocate and teach its overthrow by force and violence. It may well be that indoctrination in the techniques of terror to destroy the Government would be indictable under either statute. But the teaching which is condemned here is of a different character.

So far as the present record is concerned, what petitioners did was to organize people to teach and themselves teach the Marxist-Leninist doctrine contained chiefly in four books: *Foundations of Leninism* by Stalin (1924), *The Communist Manifesto* by Marx and Engels (1848), *State and Revolution* by Lenin (1917), *History of the Communist Party of the Soviet Union (B)* (1939).[4]

Those books are to Soviet Communism what *Mein Kampf* was to Nazism. If they are understood, the ugliness of Communism is revealed, its deceit and cunning are exposed, the nature of its activities becomes apparent, and the chances of its success less likely. That is not, of course, the reason why petitioners chose these books for their classrooms. They are fervent Communists to whom these volumes are gospel. They preached the creed with the hope that some day it would be acted upon.

The opinion of the Court does not outlaw these texts nor condemn them to the fire, as the Communists do literature offensive to their creed. But if the books themselves are not outlawed, if they can lawfully remain on library shelves, by what reasoning does their use in a classroom become a crime? It would not be a crime under the Act to introduce these books to a class, though that would be teaching what the creed of violent overthrow of the government is. The Act, as construed, requires the element of intent—that those who teach the creed believe in it. The crime then depends not on what is taught but on

---

[3] 18 U.S.C. § 2384 provides: "If two or more persons in any State or Territory, or in any place subject to the jurisdiction of the United States, conspire to overthrow, put down, or to destroy by force the Government of the United States, or to levy war against them, or to oppose by force the authority thereof, or by force to prevent, hinder, or delay the execution of any law of the United States, or by force to seize, take, or possess any property of the United States contrary to the authority thereof, they shall each be fined not more than $5,000 or imprisoned not more than six years, or both."

[4] Other books taught were *Problems of Leninism* by Stalin, *Strategy and Tactics of World Communism* (H. Doc. No. 619, 80th Cong., 2d Sess.), and *Program of the Communist International*.

who the teacher is. That is to make freedom of speech turn not on *what is said,* but on the *intent* with which it is said. Once we start down that road we enter territory dangerous to the liberties of every citizen.

There was a time in England when the concept of constructive treason flourished. Men were punished not for raising a hand against the king but for thinking murderous thoughts about him. The Framers of the Constitution were alive to that abuse and took steps to see that the practice would not flourish here. Treason was defined to require overt acts—the evolution of a plot against the country into an actual project. The present case is not one of treason. But the analogy is close when the illegality is made to turn on intent, not on the nature of the act. We then start probing men's minds for motive and purpose; they become entangled in the law not for what they did but *for what they thought;* they get convicted not for what they said but for the purpose with which they said it. . . .

The vice of treating speech as the equivalent of overt acts of a treasonable or seditious character is emphasized by a concurring opinion, which by invoking the law of conspiracy makes speech do service for deeds which are dangerous to society. The doctrine of conspiracy has served divers and oppressive purposes and in its broad reach can be made to do great evil. But never until today has anyone seriously thought that the ancient law of conspiracy could constitutionally be used to turn speech into seditious conduct. Yet that is precisely what is suggested.

I repeat that we deal here with speech alone, not with speech *plus* acts of sabotage or unlawful conduct. Not a single seditious act is charged in the indictment. To make a lawful speech unlawful because two men conceive it is to raise the law of conspiracy to appalling proportions. That course is to make a radical break with the past and to violate one of the cardinal principles of our constitutional scheme.

Free speech has occupied an exalted position because of the high service it has given our society. Its protection is essential to the very existence of a democracy. The airing of ideas releases pressures which otherwise might become destructive. When ideas compete in the market for acceptance, full and free discussion exposes the false and they gain few adherents. Full and free discussion even of ideas we hate encourages the testing of our own prejudices and preconceptions. Full and free discussion keeps a society from becoming stagnant and unprepared for the stresses and strains that work to tear all civilizations apart.

Full and free discussion has indeed been the first article of our faith. We have founded our political system on it. It has been the safeguard of every religious, political, philosophical, economic, and racial group amongst us. We have counted on it to keep us from embracing what is cheap and false; we have trusted the common sense of our people to choose the doctrine true to our genius and to reject the rest. This has been the one single outstanding tenet that has made our institutions the symbol of freedom and equality. We have deemed it more costly to liberty to suppress a despised minority than to let them vent their spleen. We have above all else feared the political censor. We have wanted a land where our people can be exposed to all the diverse creeds and cultures of the world.

There comes a time when even speech loses its constitutional immunity. Speech innocuous one year may at another time fan such destructive flames that it must be halted in the interests of the safety of the Republic. That is the meaning of the clear and present danger test. When conditions are so critical that there will be no time to avoid the evil that the speech threatens, it is time to call a halt. Otherwise, free speech which is the strengh of the Nation will be the cause of its destruction.

Yet free speech is the rule, not the exception. The restraint to be constitutional must be based on more than fear, on more than passionate opposition against the speech, on more than a revolted dislike for its contents. There must be some immediate injury to society that is likely if speech is allowed. The classic statement of these conditions was made by Mr. Justice Brandeis in his concurring opinion in Whitney *v.* California, 274 U.S. 357, 376-377,

> Fear of serious injury cannot alone justify suppression of free speech and assembly. Men feared witches and burnt women. It is the function of speech to free men from the bondage of irrational fears. To justify suppression of free speech there must be reasonable ground to fear that serious evil will result if free speech is practiced. There must be reasonable ground to believe that the danger apprehended is imminent. There must be reasonable ground to believe that the evil to be prevented is a serious one. Every denunciation of existing law tends in some measure to increase the probability that there will be violation of it. Condonation of a breach enhances the probability. Expressions of approval add to the probability. Propagation of the criminal state of mind by teaching syndicalism increases it. Advocacy of law-breaking heightens it still further. But even advocacy of violation, however reprehensible morally, is not a justification for denying free speech where the advocacy falls short of incitement and there is nothing to indicate that the advocacy would be immediately acted on. The wide difference between advocacy and incitement, between preparation and attempt, between assembling and conspiracy, must be borne in mind. In order to support a finding of a clear and present danger it must be shown either that immediate serious violence was to be expected or was advocated, or that the past conduct furnished reason to believe that such advocacy was then contemplated.
>
> Those who won our independence by revolution were not cowards. They did not fear political change. They did not exalt order at the cost of liberty. To courageous, self-reliant men, with confidence in the power of free and fearless reasoning applied through the processes of popular government, no danger flowing from speech can be deemed clear and present, unless the incidence of the evil apprehended is so imminent that it may befall before there is opportunity for full discussion. *If there be time to expose through discussion the falsehood and fallacies, to avert the evil by the processes of education, the remedy to be applied is more speech, not enforced silence.* [Italics added by Mr. Justice Douglas.]

I had assumed that the question of the clear and present danger, being so critical an issue in the case, would be a matter for submission to the jury. . . .

Yet, whether the question is one for the Court or the jury, there should be evidence of record on the issue.

This record, however, contains no evidence whatsoever showing that the acts charged, *viz.*, the teaching of the Soviet theory of revolution with the hope that it will be realized, have created any clear and present danger to the Nation. The Court, however, rules to the contrary. It says, "The formation by petitioners of such a highly organized conspiracy, with rigidly disciplined members subject to call when the leaders, these petitioners, felt that the time had come for action, coupled with the inflammable nature of world conditions, similar uprisings in other countries, and the touch-and-go nature of our relations with countries with whom petitioners were in the very least ideologically attuned, convince us that their convictions were justified on this score."

That ruling is in my view not responsive to the issue in the case. We might as well say that the speech of petitioners is outlawed because Soviet Russia and her Red Army are a threat to world peace.

The nature of Communism as a force on the world scene would, of course, be relevant to the issue of clear and present danger of petitioners' advocacy within the United States. But the primary consideration is the strength and tactical position of petitioners and their converts in this country. On that there is no evidence in the record. If we are to take judicial notice of the threat of Communists within the nation, it should not be difficult to conclude that *as a political party* they are of little consequence. Communists in this country have never made a respectable or serious showing in any election. I would doubt that there is a village, let alone a city or county or state which the Communists could carry.

Communism in the world scene is no bogey-man; but Communists as a political faction or party in this country plainly is. Communism has been so thoroughly exposed in this country that it has been crippled as a political force. Free speech has destroyed it as an effective political party. It is inconceivable that those who went up and down this country preaching the doctrine of revolution which petitioners espouse would have any success. In days of trouble and confusion when bread lines were long, when the unemployed walked the streets, when people were starving, the advocates of a short-cut by revolution might have a chance to gain adherents. But today there are no such conditions. The country is not in despair; the people know Soviet Communism; the doctrine of Soviet revolution is exposed in all of its ugliness and the American people want none of it.

How it can be said that there is a clear and present danger that this advocacy will succeed is, therefore, a mystery. Some nations less resilient than the United States, where illiteracy is high and where democratic traditions are only budding, might have to take drastic steps and jail these men for merely speaking their creed. But in America they are miserable merchants of unwanted ideas; their wares remain unsold. The fact that their ideas are abhorrent does not make them powerful. . . .

The First Amendment provides that "Congress shall make no law . . . abridging the freedom of speech." The Constitution provides no exception. This does not mean, however, that the Nation need hold its hand until it is in such weakened condition that there is no time to protect itself from incitement to revolution. Seditious conduct can always be punished. But the command of the First Amendment is so clear that we should not allow Congress to call a halt to free speech except in the extreme case of peril from the speech itself.

The First Amendment makes confidence in the common sense of our people and in their maturity of judgment the great postulate of our democracy. Its philosophy is that violence is rarely, if ever, stopped by denying civil liberties to those advocating resort to force. The First Amendment reflects the philosophy of Jefferson "that it is time enough for the rightful purposes of civil government for its officers to interfere when principles break out into overt acts against peace and good order." The political censor has no place in our public debates. Unless and until extreme and necessitous circumstances are shown our aim should be to keep speech unfettered and to allow the processes of law to be invoked only when the provocateurs among us move from speech to action.

Vishinsky wrote in 1948 in *The Law of the Soviet State,* "In our state, naturally there can be no place for freedom of speech, press, and so on for the foes of socialism."

Our concern should be that we accept no such standard for the United States. Our faith should be that our people will never give support to these advocates of revolution, so long as we remain loyal to the purposes for which our Nation was founded.

[Most of the footnotes and many citations to cases have been omitted.]

Distinguishing Forms of Advocacy

YATES ET AL. *V.* UNITED STATES
354 U.S. 298 (1957)

Mr. Justice Harlan delivered the opinion of the Court.

These 14 petitioners stand convicted, after a jury trial in the United States District Court for the Southern District of California, upon a single count indictment charging them with conspiring (1) to advocate and teach the duty and necessity of overthrowing the Government of the United States by force and violence, and (2) to organize, as the Communist Party of the United States, a society of persons who so advocate and teach, all with the intent of causing the overthrow of the Government by force and violence as speedily as circumstances would permit. . . . The conspiracy is alleged to have originated in 1940 and continued down to the date of the indictment in 1951. . . . Upon conviction each of the petitioners was sentenced to five years' imprisonment and a fine of $10,000. . . .

Instructions to the Jury

Petitioners contend that the instructions to the jury were fatally defective in that the trial court refused to charge that, in order to convict, the jury must find that the advocacy which the defendants conspired to promote was of a kind calculated to "incite" persons to action for the forcible overthrow of the Government. It is argued that advocacy of forcible overthrow as mere *abstract doctrine* is within the free speech protection of the First Amendment; that the Smith Act, consistently with that constitutional provision, must be taken as proscribing only the sort of advocacy which incites to illegal *action;* and that the trial court's charge, by permitting conviction for mere advocacy, unrelated to its tendency to produce forcible action, resulted in an unconstitutional application of the Smith Act. The Government, which at the trial also requested the court to charge in terms of "incitement," now takes the position, however, that the true constitutional dividing line is not between inciting and abstract advocacy of forcible overthrow, but rather between advocacy as such, irrespective of its inciting qualities, and the mere discussion or exposition of violent overthrow as an abstract theory. . . .

After telling the jury that it could not convict the defendants for holding or expressing mere opinions, beliefs, or predictions relating to violent overthrow, the trial court defined the content of the proscribed advocacy or teaching in the following terms, which are crucial here:

> Any advocacy or teaching which does not include the urging of force and violence as the means of overthrowing and destroying the Government of the United States is not within the issue of the indictment here and can constitute no basis for any finding against the defendants.
>
> The kind of advocacy and teaching which is charged and upon which your verdict must be reached is not merely a desirability but a necessity that the Government of the United States be overthrown and destroyed by force and violence and not merely a propriety but a duty to overthrow and destroy the Government of the United States by force and violence.

There can be no doubt from the record that in so instructing the jury the court regarded as immaterial, and intended to withdraw from the jury's consideration, any issue as to the character of the advocacy in terms of its capacity to stir listeners to forcible action. Both the petitioners and the Government submitted proposed instructions which would have required the jury to find that the proscribed advocacy was not of a mere abstract doctrine of forcible overthrow, but of action to that end, by the use of language reasonably and ordinarily calculated to incite persons to such action. The trial court rejected these proposed instructions on the ground that any necessity for giving them which may have existed at the time the Dennis case was tried was removed by this Court's subsequent decision in that case. The court made it clear in colloquy with counsel that in its view the illegal advocacy was made out simply by showing that what was said dealt with forcible overthrow and that it was uttered with a specific intent to accomplish that purpose, insisting that all such advocacy was punishable "whether in language of incitement or not." . . .

We are thus faced with the question whether the Smith Act prohibits advocacy and teaching of forcible overthrow as an abstract principle, divorced from any effort to instigate action to that end, so long as such advocacy or teaching is engaged in with evil intent. We hold that it does not.

The distinction between advocacy of abstract doctrine and advocacy directed at promoting unlawful action is one that has been consistently recognized in the opinions of this Court, beginning with Fox *v.* Washington, 236 U.S. 273, and Schenck *v.* United States, 249 U.S. 47. This distinction was heavily underscored in Gitlow *v.* New York, 268 U.S. 652, in which the statute involved was nearly identical with the one now before us. . . . The legislative history of the Smith Act and related bills shows beyond all question that Congress was aware of the distinction between the advocacy or teaching of abstract doctrine and the advocacy or teaching of action, and that it did not intend to disregard it. . . .

In failing to distinguish between advocacy of forcible overthrow as an abstract doctrine and advocacy of action to that end, the District Court appears to have been led astray by the holding in Dennis that advocacy of violent action to be taken at some future time was enough. It seems to have considered that, since "inciting" speech is usually thought of as calculated to induce immediate action, and since Dennis held advocacy of action for future overthrow sufficient, this meant that advocacy, irrespective of its tendency to generate action, is punishable, provided only that it is uttered with a specific intent to accomplish overthrow. In other words, the District Court apparently thought that Dennis obliterated the traditional dividing line between advocacy of abstract doctrine and advocacy of action. . . .

In light of the foregoing we are unable to regard the District Court's charge upon this aspect of the case as adequate. The jury was never told that the Smith Act does not denounce advocacy in the sense of preaching abstractly the forcible overthrow of the Government. We think that the trial court's statement that the proscribed advocacy must include the "urging," "necessity," and "duty" of forcible overthrow, and not merely its "desirability" and "propriety," may not be regarded as a sufficient substitute for charging that the Smith Act reaches only advocacy of action for the overthrow of government by force and violence. The essential distinction is that those to whom the advocacy is addressed must be urged to *do* something, now or in the future, rather than merely to *believe* in something. . . .

Granting . . . that it was not necessary even that the trial court should have employed the particular term "incite," it was nevertheless incumbent on the court to make clear in some fashion that the advocacy must be of action and not merely abstract doctrine. The instructions given not only do not employ the word "incite," but also avoid the use of such terms and phrases as "action," "call for action," "as a rule or principle of action," and so on, all of which were offered in one form or another by both the petitioners and the Government.

What we find lacking in the instructions here is illustrated by contrasting them with the instructions given to the Dennis jury, upon which this Court's sustaining of the convictions in that case was bottomed. There the trial court charged:

In further construction and interpretation of the statute [the Smith Act] I charge you that it is *not the abstract doctrine* of overthrowing or destroying organized government by unlawful means which is denounced by this law, but the teaching and advocacy *of action* for the accomplishment of that purpose, *by language reasonably and ordinarily calculated to incite persons to such action.* Accordingly, you cannot find the defendants or any of them guilty of the crime charged unless you are satisfied beyond a reasonable doubt that they conspired . . . to advocate and teach the duty and necessity of overthrowing or destroying the Government of the United States by force and violence, with the intent that such teaching and advocacy *be of a rule or principle of action* and *by language reasonably and ordinarily calculated to incite persons to such action,* all with the intent to cause the overthrow . . . as speedily as circumstances would permit. (Emphasis added.) 341 U.S., at 511-512.

We recognize that distinctions between advocacy or teaching of abstract doctrines, with evil intent, and that which is directed to stirring people to action, are often subtle and difficult to grasp, for in a broad sense, as Mr. Justice Holmes said in his dissenting opinion in Gitlow, *supra,* at 673: "Every idea is an incitement." But the very subtlety of these distinctions required the most clear and explicit instructions with reference to them, for they concerned an issue which went to the very heart of the charges against these petitioners. . . .

The judgment of the Court of Appeals is reversed, and the case remanded to the District Court for further proceedings consistent with this opinion.

It is so ordered.

[Mr. Justice Burton concurred in the result and agreed with the above portion of the Court's opinion. Justices Brennan and Whittaker took no part in the consideration of this case.]

Mr. Justice Black, with whom Mr. Justice Douglas joins, concurring in part and dissenting in part.

I agree with the Court insofar as it holds that the trial judge erred in instructing that persons could be punished under the Smith Act for teaching and advocating forceful overthrow as an abstract principle. But on the other hand, I cannot agree that the instruction which the Court indicates it might approve is constitutionally permissible. The Court says that persons can be punished for advocating action to overthrow the Government by force and violence, where those to whom the advocacy is addressed are urged "to *do* something, now or in the future, rather than merely to *believe* in something." Under the Court's approach, defendants could still be convicted simply for agreeing to talk as distinguished from agreeing to act. I believe that the First Amendment forbids Congress to punish people for talking about public affairs, whether or not such discussion incites to action, legal or illegal. See Meiklejohn, *Free Speech and Its Relation to Self-Government.* Cf. Chafee, "Book Review," 62 *Harv. L. Rev.* 891. As the Virginia Assembly said in 1785, in its "Statute for Religious Liberty," written by Thomas Jefferson, "it is time enough for the rightful purposes of civil government, for its officers to interfere when principles break out into overt acts against peace and good order. . . ."

MR. JUSTICE CLARK, dissenting. . . .

The conspiracy includes the same group of defendants as in the Dennis case though petitioners here occupied a lower echelon in the party hierarchy. They, nevertheless, served in the same army and were engaged in the same mission. The convictions here were based upon evidence closely paralleling that adduced in Dennis and in United States *v.* Flynn, 216 F. (2d) 354 (C. A. 2d Cir. 1954), both of which resulted in convictions. This Court laid down in Dennis the principles governing such prosecutions and they were closely adhered to here, although the nature of the two cases did not permit identical handling. . . .

I have studied the section of the opinion concerning the instructions and frankly its "artillery of words" leaves me confused as to why the majority concludes that the charge as given was insufficient. I thought that Dennis merely held that a charge was sufficient where it requires a finding that "the Party advocates the theory that there is a duty and necessity to overthrow the Government by force and violence. . . . not as a prophetic insight or as a bit of . . . speculation, but as a program for winning adherents and as a policy to be translated into action" as soon as the circumstances permit. 341 U.S., at 546-547 (concurring opinion). I notice however that to the majority

> The essence of the Dennis holding was that indoctrination of a group in preparation for future violent action, as well as exhortation to immediate action, by advocacy found to be directed to "action for the accomplishment" of forcible overthrow, to violence "as a rule or principle of action," and employing "language of incitement," *id.,* at 511-512, is not constitutionally protected when the group is of sufficient size and cohesiveness, is sufficiently oriented towards action, and other circumstances are such as reasonably to justify apprehension that action will occur.

I have read this statement over and over but do not seem to grasp its meaning for I see no resemblance between it and what the respected Chief Justice wrote in Dennis, nor do I find any such theory in the concurring opinions. As I see it, the trial judge charged in essence all that was required under the Dennis opinions, whether one takes the view of the Chief Justice or of those concurring in the judgment. Apparently what disturbs the Court now is that the trial judge here did not give the Dennis charge although both the prosecution and the defense asked that it be given. Since he refused to grant these requests I suppose the majority feels that there must be some difference between the two charges, else the one that was given in Dennis would have been followed here. While there may be some distinctions between the charges, as I view them they are without material difference. I find, as the majority intimates, that the distinctions are too "subtle and difficult to grasp."

Loyalty and Security

SIDNEY HOOK
Security and Freedom

The quest for security in human life, like the quest for certainty in human knowledge, has many sources. All are rooted in man's finitude in a complex world of danger and mystery. Of the varied methods man has pursued to reduce the dangers and cope with the mysteries, the way of piecemeal knowledge and continuous experiment has been most fruitful. For it is in the fields in which human knowledge has foresworn the quest for absolute certainty, as in the scientific disciplines, that it has proved both reliable and capable of winning universal agreement. On the other hand, in the fields in which the strongest claims to certainty have been made—politics and philosophy—there is the least agreement.

Because absolute certainty in human affairs is impossible, absolute security is impossible. Unless we are aware of this, the price we pay for straining to achieve an impossible ideal may result in netting us less security than would otherwise be attainable. This is not an unusual phenomenon: it is observable in large things and small. The man who strives for absolute health may end up a valetudinarian. The man who won't venture on the highways until they are accident-proof may as well not own an automobile; and if he crawls along playing it supersafe, traffic-enforcement authorities tell us he adds to the dangers of the road.

The real problem, then, is not one of absolute security, or security in general. It is always one of achieving more and better security in meeting specific hazards in a particular area of risk and uncertainty—and meeting them in such a way that we do not lose more by the methods we use than by the disasters we would prevent. . . .

The McCarthy episode in American history was a test of political judgment and political morality. Those who dismissed him as an unimportant phenomenon or extenuated his methods in the light of his goals failed the tests of both judgment and morality. So did those who exaggerated his power, who proclaimed that he had transformed America into a police state, and who fought McCarthy with the weapons of McCarthy instead of the weapons of truth.

Professor, Department of Philosophy, New York University. Author of *Heresy, Yes—Conspiracy, No!; Common Sense and the Fifth Amendment;* and other books. The selection is from *Political Power and Personal Freedom* (New York, Criterion Books, Inc., 1959), pp. 235-249. By permission.

Even at the height of McCarthy's power a more rational view was not impossible. . . .

"Security is like liberty," writes Mr. Justice Jackson in one of his dissenting opinions, "in that many are the crimes that have been committed in its name." Yet he would be the first to admit that this is no more warrant for abandoning the quest for reasonable rules of security than for relinquishing the struggle for a more humane conception of liberty. . . .

After the Seventh Congress of the Communist International, the Communists kidnaped the vocabulary of American liberalism. This "corruption of the word," as I called it then, made it easier for some sentimental liberals to interpret sharp criticisms of Communism as oblique attacks on liberalism, if not a first step towards Fascism. In liberal circles to be an anti-Fascist was always honorable. But to be anti-Communist, especially during the war years, invited distrust. That liberals had a stake in the survival of the democratic system whose defects they could freely criticize under the ground rules of the Bill of Rights was granted, of course. That they therefore also had a stake in preventing the ground rules from being abused, that they had a responsibility to think about the problem, was resolutely ignored. . . .

Instead of offering a viable alternative to eliminate or reduce these injustices, they wrote as if the only problem was to develop more efficient methods of detecting acts of espionage *after* they had been committed. They thereby revealed the extent of their misunderstanding. Not the acts prevented but those which are discovered create public disquietude, because they give the impression that many more remain undiscovered and beyond the reach of prosecution in virtue of the statute of limitations. . . .

Recent experience, or a study of recent history, should make it possible for the liberal to acquire a reliable knowledge of the whole costumer's shop of organizational masks cleverly designed by Communist technicians to take in the unwary until the time comes for the sacrificial slaughter. If he believes that there is a foreign threat to the survival of the liberal community, he cannot withhold assent from the dictum of Roger Baldwin, former head of the American Civil Liberties Union, that "a superior loyalty to a foreign government disqualifies a citizen from service to our own." It does not disqualify the citizen from protection of the Bill of Rights, but the right to government service is not an integral part of the Bill of Rights.

It is the liberal *attitude,* however, which is most crucial in the reasonable administration of a security program. Just as only those who love children can be trusted to discipline them without doing psychological harm, so only those who love freedom can be trusted to devise appropriate safeguards without throttling intellectual independence or smothering all but the mediocre in blankets of regulations. No safeguards are appropriate or even efficient which impose conformity of belief or inhibit intellectual spontaneity. The fresh and unfamiliar solution to difficulties depends on a certain imaginative daring and a receptivity to such solutions by those in a position of authority. A liberal with a sense of history is aware of the possibility that in a specific situation there may be a sharp conflict between the legitimate demands of national security and the freedom of the individual. But on balance, and in perspective, he is convinced that the two are not in opposition. In the very interest of a freely expressed dissent, some security measures are required to protect the institutional processes which, however imperfectly, reflect a freely given consent. At the same time, the faith and practices of freedom, indeed, an almost religious veneration for the *élan* of the free spirit, may generate a sense of security even in the shadows of war. . . .

The argument and evidence can be put briefly. The one unshakeable dogma in the Bolshevik faith is that the Soviet Union is not safe from attack so long as the "capitalistic democracies" of the West—and not only the United States but also countries like Great Britain and France—exist. Let not those who in the past assured us that Hitler's racial myth and ideology of world conquest were "just words" tell us again that ideologies do not count in politics and history. If anything, the Kremlin has gone further than Hitler because it has publicly proclaimed that "encirclement" is a *political*, not a geographical, concept. The Communist parties of the West . . . have as their *first* function the defense of the Soviet Union. Instructions are explicit to all of them to organize secretly (as well as publicly) even in "the freest" and "most democratic" countries and to infiltrate into strategic centers. This type of activity has been extensively carried on for years especially during the days of the popular front struggle against the Nazis. Even during the war which Hitler forced on the Soviets, the Kremlin engaged in the most comprehensive types of espionage against its Allies as part of the underlying struggle which, according to their fanatical conviction, must end either with the victory of the West or the Soviet power.

Because it can count on the devotion *à outrance* of Communist nationals of other countries, many of them highly trained, intelligent and inspired by a misguided idealism which does not see under the flowers of official rhetoric the chains of Soviet control on its own people, the Kremlin possesses an incomparable advantage over the West. For one thing, it is the best informed regime in the world. . . .

Although one would hardly suspect it from present attitudes to security in many circles in those countries, it is from Canadian and British sources that we have the most incontrovertible, if not the weightiest evidence, of how Communist parties are involved in the espionage nets the Soviet Union has spun around the free world.[1]

Since the Kremlin combines this belief in the inevitability of war with a dialectical conception according to which a sudden attack or offense, as in Korea, is the best method of defense and because of the centralized organization of western industrial life, the location of America's undispersed plants, and the evolution of thermonuclear weapons, an attempt at a sudden knockout blow cannot be ruled out as a possibility. Since Bolshevik morality is confessedly subordinate to what will further the victory of the "proletarian dictatorship"—indeed, this is *the whole* of their morality—the possession of information about strategic weakness on the part of the West, or the hope that a sudden

---

[1] Cf. *The Report of the Royal Commission to Investigate the Facts Relating to and Circumstances Surrounding the Communication by Public Officials and Other Persons in Positions of Trust of Secret and Confidential Information to Agents of a Foreign Power* (Ottawa, 1946); also Alexander Foote's *Handbook for Spies* (London, 1949).

blow may prevent instant retaliatory action, may make a decisive difference to the Kremlin in resolving to launch the Blitzkreig which will end "the final struggle." It does not require many persons to betray the key secrets of the radar defense of a nation.

The consequences of less extreme suppositions may be equally disastrous. The free world cannot deploy its defense forces everywhere. Its decisions where to stand, where to fight, once known to the Kremlin, give the latter a flexibility that it can exploit most skillfully to draw the world bit by bit into its orbit. On the other hand, there is no possibility for the free world to build up a counterweight within the Soviet sphere to redress the balance. No democratic Jeffersonian or Millsian International exists with affiliated parties in the Soviet world.

Does it follow that *every* member of the Communist party is an espionage agent ready to do the bidding of his superiors and betray his country? Is it not possible that some members of the Communist party may be loyal to their own government rather than to the Soviet Union? The best answer to these questions was made by Mr. Clement Attlee, Prime Minister at the time when Pontecorvo, scientifically a much more gifted man than Fuchs, fled from England. "There is no way," said Mr. Attlee who never chased a witch in his life, "of distinguishing such people [hypothetically loyal Communists] from those who, if opportunity offered, would be prepared to endanger the security of the state in the interests of another power. The Government has, therefore, reached the conclusion that the only prudent course to adopt is to ensure that no one who is known to be a member of the Communist party, *or to be associated with it in such a way as to raise legitimate doubts about his or her reliability* (my italics), is employed in connection with work, the nature of which is vital to the security of the State." It is well to remember that a clerk in a code office or even those who empty trash baskets may have access to material bearing on national security. Mr. Attlee apparently believes that if we distinguish between legal guilt and *moral* or professional guilt or unfitness, and between association by happenstance and association by cooperation, then there certainly can be and is "guilt by association." . . .

It is the gravest error to imagine that anyone in America, even Senator McCarthy who helped the Communist cause throughout the world, believed for a moment that the Communists constituted a domestic danger. But American public opinion was aroused by a series of incidents over a span of three years which seemed to show that in the international field the position of the American government was being weakened by Soviet agents.

The first was the Hiss case and the revelations that several interlocking rings of Communist conspirators had been active in high places for years. It remains mystifying that many of these individuals continued working in strategic places, one even at the Aberdeen Weapons Proving Grounds, many years after the chief operatives had been identified by former members of the Communist party. The worst of these revelations came after Mr. Truman had dismissed the Hiss case as a "red herring." Following Hiss's conviction, Wadleigh's confession, and a long line of refusals to answer questions about espionage on the ground that a truthful answer would tend to be self-incriminating, the implication was natural, and in part justified, that the government had been lax or indifferent in taking intelligent safeguards. As the Dexter White case shows, the Truman administration feared that its opponents would make political capital out of the presence of Communist espionage agents in the government and tried to hush up matters. This narrow political partisanship by no means warranted the charge of "treason" or of coddling treason hurled by some Republicans against the Democrats. There is no reason to believe that had the former been in power, they would have acted more wisely. But the country never really recovered from the shock of learning that publicly sworn testimony, some of it legally substantiated where the charges were contested, showed that persons holding the following positions were members of the secret Communist underground apparatus:

- an Executive Assistant to the President of the United States
- an Assistant Secretary of the Treasury
- the Director of the Office of Special Political Affairs for the State Department
- the Secretary of the International Monetary Fund
- Head of Latin-American Division of the Office of Strategic Services
- a member of the National Labor Relations Board
- Secretary of the National Labor Relations Board
- Chief Counsel, Senate Subcommittee on Civil Liberties
- Chief, Statistical Analysis Branch, War Production Board
- Treasury Department Representative and Adviser in Financial Control Division of the North African Board of UNRRA, and at the meeting of the Council of Foreign Ministers in Moscow
- Director, National Research Project of the Works Progress Administration

These were not the only, but only the most conspicuous, positions Communists filled. The *actual* amount of damage done, however, is difficult to assess and probably will never be known. But no reasonable person can doubt the existence of a planned pattern of infiltration whose significance can be better gauged by the European reader if he draws up a comparable list of posts in his own government and fills them, in his mind's eye, with Communist espionage agents.

The second series of incidents began with the Fuchs case which broke after several outstanding scientists had dismissed the idea that atomic espionage was possible. "There are no secrets" declared the very scientists who in 1939 and 1940 had imposed upon themselves a voluntary secrecy in publications to prevent Hitler from developing nuclear power. Subsequent trials in the United States of the Communist spies associated with Fuchs produced evidence that there were others deep underground.

All this was still very much in the public mind when Truman announced that the Soviet Union had exploded its first atomic bomb, thus eliminating the monopoly of atomic power which, according to Churchill and other Europeans, had prevented the Red Army from marching west after American and British demobilization. The head of the United States Atomic Energy Commission observed that Soviet espionage had made it possible for the Soviet Union to save years of costly experiment (an observation officially repeated by President

Eisenhower on October 8, 1953, after the U.S.S.R. had exploded a thermo-nuclear bomb).[2]

Finally came the loss of China and the charge that some of the advisors and consultants to the State Department on Far Eastern affairs not only had long records of Communist association but had followed the twists and turns of the Party line. Some like L. Rossinger who fell back on the Fifth Amendment were identified as members of the Communist party. Although there was no legal proof of the identification by Budenz of Lattimore as a top Soviet agent, there could be no reasonable doubt that he was a fellow-traveler whose justification of the Moscow frame-up trials was very brazen. Whatever the degree of their Communism, it seemed indisputable that a group in the State Department had been urging the abandonment of all support to Chiang Kai-shek despite the absence of any alternative to Communist triumph. The defeat of Chiang may have been unavoidable, but the evidence that American Communists and their sympathizers had actively worked for his downfall by attempting to influence official channels was unmistakable.

These events, together with other trials involving Communist espionage and perjury, and the multiplication of cases of refusal to answer questions on the ground that a truthful answer would tend to be self-incriminatory, contributed to the prevalent feeling that the United States was being weakened in the cold war on whose outcome so many things, both domestic and international, depend. The Korean war exacerbated the mood. Had these events, especially the pattern of their succession, occurred in other countries, it is not likely that they would have been met with complacency.

The concern of the American people with the question of Communist penetration, in the light of the evidence, was legitimate enough. Questionable only was the character of the reaction to it on the part of the government. Buffeted by cultural vigilantes on the one side and ritualistic liberals on the other, it swung from one position to another, pleasing no one with its eclecticism. Almost all of the excesses of loyalty and security programs are attributable to the incredible political ignorance and naiveté of the personnel of the Review Boards. It was not the procedures themselves which were at fault, because oddly enough American procedures in crucial respects are fairer than the English. For example, in hearings before English boards, civil servants under investigation are rarely, if ever, told of the evidence against them. They are also denied rights of legal counsel, and even of representation. Nonetheless, American procedures worked hardship and injustices because instead of being administered by knowledgeable men and women with a little common sense who had some political experience, they were entrusted to investment bankers,

---

[2] As early as 1950 some scientists holding high official positions had charged that the Soviet Union had acquired through espionage the "know-how" to make hydrogen bombs. *The New York Times* of July 20, 1950, quoted François Perrin, Joint Commissioner for Atomic Energy in France, as saying that Russia, through its espionage network, had certainly obtained the know-how to make the hydrogen bomb. The same report appeared in *The San Francisco Chronicle* of July 23, 1950. At the time Professor Perrin's co-commissioner was Irene Joliot-Curie, wife of Frederic Joliot-Curie, later dismissed from the post as High Commissioner for Atomic Energy because of his pro-Soviet activities. Frederic Joliot-Curie subsequently charged that the U.S. was waging bacterial germ warfare in Korea and spurned the proposal of a Committee of Nobel Prize Winners to conduct an objective international inquiry into the truth of his charges.

corporation lawyers, army and navy officers, small town officials, or Republican or Democratic party regulars to whom Communist language was gobbledygook, Communist ideas suspiciously like the ideas of socialists, do-gooders and even New Dealers, and Communist organizations with the distinctions between member, sympathizer, front, dupe, innocent, and honest mistaken liberal, as mysterious as the order of beings in the science of angelology.

In the light of the above, the answer to our final question regarding the relative unconcern of other nations to the problem of Communist penetration is not hard to give. The greatest Soviet effort was directed against the United States as the Kremlin's chief and strongest enemy. Since 1939 the United States has been the center of atomic weapons research and development. Its policies are more fateful for the U.S.S.R. than those of any other single nation. To make these policies miscarry, to delay, distort and abort government directives pays rich political dividends. The Kremlin is quite aware of the fact that a defeat or paralysis of the United States would mean the end of the independence of Austria, France and Italy. Further, the Communist movement in the United States is not a mass party and, in all likelihood, will never become one. But it has a solid core of some thousands of hardened "professional revolutionists." From the Soviet viewpoint they are expendable. What is more natural, therefore, than to employ them for all sorts of conspiratorial purposes from direct espionage to the capture of small but key unions, to the seeding of government services with "sleepers"? A few thousand totally dedicated persons, working underground with the help of a sympathetic periphery of several times that size, can cause a great many headaches. Countries like Austria need not worry about the problem, one is tempted to observe, because it wouldn't make a difference if they did. There isn't much the Kremlin can learn from them and an attempt at a Communist putsch on Czechoslovakian lines, so long as the United States is still strong, risks a war for which at the moment the U.S.S.R. is unready. Countries like France and Italy, on the other hand, which have mass Communist parties and where infiltration and underground organization are not inconsiderable can hardly solve the problem without facing crippling strikes and extensive public disorders. Too weak to act they sometimes pretend that there is no need for action. *They can live with the Communist menace only because the United States is free of it and only so long as the United States is strong enough to restrain the Soviet Union from overrunning the free world.*

Only those who are ignorant of the stupendous extent of Soviet infiltration and espionage over the years, the complexity of its patterns and its potential for harm, can sneer at the problems of security in the free world. It is not enough to shout slogans—whether of security or freedom. What is required is creative intelligence to devise just and effective procedures which will protect the free cultures of the world from their hidden enemies without making less free those who are not its hidden enemies. These procedures must be flexible. They cannot be formalized into a code without inviting abuses. They must be devised and administered by civil libertarians who are familiar with Communist theory and who have studied Communist conspiratorial practice. They must be applied discreetly, without fanfare, without developing a climate of public concern. And their primary function must be effective prevention rather than exemplary punishment.

L. A. NIKOLORIĆ
Critique of the Loyalty Program

Established by the President's Executive Order 9835 in March, 1947, the government's loyalty program . . . presents a complex problem: whether, in the name of "loyalty" and "national security," our society is justified in abusing most of the basic tenets of Anglo-American jurisprudence and legal philosophy traditional since the seventeenth century.

The purpose of the program is not to discharge employees expressly because of what they have done in the past. President Truman has stated that it is aimed at "potentially disloyal" persons who, because of attitudes and ideas they entertain today or subscribed to yesterday, might in the future undertake action contrary to the best interests of the United States. The basic concept of the program—to ferret out the "potentially disloyal"—violates a most important principle of Anglo-American law: that one cannot be punished for merely considering the commission of a crime, or for thinking in such a way that a body determines that one might undertake action contrary to the law. . . .

The loyalty program also distorts the concept of equal justice under the law. It assumes that a democratic government may exact from its employees special standards of conduct wholly offensive to constitutional guarantees of freedom and justice as applied to ordinary citizens. We deny two and a half million government employees political and intellectual freedoms in order to protect ourselves from the potentially subversive.

These innovations are spreading not only to some three and a half million state and local employees (the County of Los Angeles, among other local governments, has instituted a loyalty check), but elsewhere. The AFL and the CIO have undertaken to purge the Communists. The Army, the Navy and the Air Force pass on the loyalty of the employees of private contractors who bid successfully on government jobs having to do with classified material. Congressmen have urged that all employees working for industries connected with the national security be subjected to a similar screening. Presumably this concerns the various utilities—in steel, automobile, transportation and others. Teachers and scientists have been discharged for entertaining unpopular ideas. Even veterans' organizations have pledged themselves to loyalty programs. The most liberal of these, the American Veterans Committee, has adopted resolutions directing its officers to purge the Communists.

Since we are rapidly accepting the proposition that American institutions have a right to examine their membership on the basis of their "loyalty," it is appropriate to determine what the government's loyalty program is and how it operates, its ideology, and the concrete effects of its operation. . . .

Washington attorney formerly associated with the firm of Arnold, Fortas and Porter. The selection is from L. A. Nikolorić, "The Government Loyalty Program," *The American Scholar,* Vol. XIX (Summer, 1950). Copyright of United Chapters of Phi Beta Kappa. By permission.

It is the duty of the [Loyalty] Boards to determine the existence of a nebulous state of mind which might lead an employee to commit in the future a disloyal act, either willfully or through an indiscretion. The most important elements of consideration are of necessity the employee's political beliefs, the organizations to which he has belonged, and the associations he has had.

Experience proves that it is not necessary for the employee to have been a member of either a Communist or Fascist organization. He will be found wanting if he has been "sympathetic" to communism or fascism, friendly to persons or organizations that are sympathetic, associated with such persons or organizations, or even "unduly talkative" in the presence of persons who are associated with sympathetic persons. The Boards do not find it necessary to prove any of these matters. They are required only to find "a reasonable doubt."

In order to assist the Boards, the Attorney General, in December, 1947, and by various supplements, designated some 150 organizations—membership in or sympathy for which is held to be indicative of disloyalty. These lists were promulgated without hearings. No explanation for the inclusion of any organization was given. . . .

Although the order provides that the employee is entitled to a charge stating the offense with some particularity, this is limited by the discretion of the agency in the interest of security considerations. Practice has shown that it has been almost impossible for an employee or his lawyer to secure a full or complete statement of the offenses.

Defending against such charges is difficult. The burden is placed on the employee to recall all the persons with whom, and organizations with which, he has ever been in contact, and to explain them. He must also prove affirmatively that he adheres to certain nebulous standards that might be construed by the Board as indicative of so loyal a state of mind that the employee will never commit a disloyal act.

The following quotation demonstrates the position in which an employee finds himself. In this case, Mr. A was faced with an unexplained action of the State Department in dismissing him "for security reasons." A asked the Board to tell him what he had done to justify the action, so that he might defend himself. The Board representative said:

> Well, we realize the difficulty you are in, in this position; on the other hand, I'd suggest that you might think back over your own career and perhaps in your own mind delve into some of the factors that have gone into your career which you think might have been subject to question and see what they are and see whether you'd like to explain or make any statement with regard to any of them. . . .

None of these things could happen in any other court or board proceeding directed against an individual in the United States. Axis Sally and Judith Coplon, who were charged with overt acts of treason and espionage, have received more procedural protection than is accorded the potentially disloyal. A common pickpocket may insist on every traditional and fundamental safeguard. A government employee may not. No one would dream of indicting Axis Sally for merely contemplating broadcasting Nazi propaganda; we would not consider putting a petty thief in jail for thinking about picking his neighbor's pocket. Yet we discharge and publicly smear government employees who have done nothing wrongful, who may not consider committing an act of disloyalty. We fire them because, on the basis of standards of the status quo, the Board suspects that they might do so in the future.

Those who would defend the program argue that the government is not required to secure to its employees procedural safeguards when it fires them. It is said that no citizen has an inherent right to government employment. Thus the government may fire arbitrarily—because it does not like the color of the employee's hair, because he is inefficient, or because the government fears that the employee may become a security risk. The procedural safeguards that are provided—charges and a hearing—are a matter of the sovereign's largess. They do not accrue to the employee as a matter of constitutional right. Therefore, the employee may not ask for other safeguards as a matter of constitutional right.

The opponents have a convincing case. Many judges, notably Mr. Justice Black, have argued that once having been hired, a government employee does secure a vested interest in his job which shall not be taken from him without cause. Cause may not be a matter of speculation; it must be a reality—such as inefficiency or overt acts of disloyalty.

Furthermore, a dismissal for disloyalty entails a permanent brand amounting to treason. Experience has shown that an employee who has been discharged under the loyalty program is unable to get another job; his career is ruined; he loses the respect of the community. Dismissal on loyalty or security grounds transcends the arbitrary right to fire. It amounts to punishment by government, which is protected by the Constitution. If this be the case, an employee who is fired on these grounds does have the constitutional right to traditional due process and safeguards.

Regardless of the coldly legal interpretation of the situation, it is obvious that a loyalty proceeding is a serious matter. On moral grounds, the government should not ruin an employee's career on a conjectural determination that he may in the future become disloyal. It must be remembered that the loyalty program was not designed or intended to punish people who have committed overt acts of disloyalty or treason. Not an employee fired has been charged with the commission of a wrongful act. During a recent public discussion with me, Mr. Seth Richardson, Chairman of the Loyalty Review Board, stated that the loyalty program has not discovered a single instance of espionage or any other overt action contrary to the best interests of the United States.

There are innumerable statutes calculated to deal with persons who are or have been acting contrary to our best interests. They include sanctions against espionage, sabotage, treason or advocacy of the overthrow of the government by force. More important to the inquiry here, any government agency may fire an employee for cause. "Cause" includes everything from simple inefficiency to disagreement with the agency's policy. Every applicant for government employment must sign, under oath, a statement that he does not subscribe to subversive doctrines and does not belong to any organization that does. Failure to make full disclosure is punishable as a criminal offense. . . .

A troublesome question is whether the loyalty program should be retained in the so-called "sensitive" agencies—the Atomic Energy Commission, the Department of Defense, and the State Department. Dr. Klaus Fuchs has done much for the proponents of the argument that in these areas, at least, we must examine employees for potential disloyalty because of the greater dangers involved.

My own view is a minority one. The proponents of the "sensitive agency" argument assume that this program is capable of catching the potentially disloyal. Even if we had the necessary instruments to accomplish this, I believe that if free institutions are to survive, they cannot be compromised in this way. A citizen in the Atomic Energy Commission should not be subjected to arbitrary treatment merely because his contribution is the more sensitive. Once the scientist or State Department official becomes a second class citizen, he will not be alone in this classification for long; he will be joined by the employee who deals in foreign trade and commerce, the expert whose concern is labor in the defense industries, and government men who deal with education and health—all fields fertile for sabotage or infiltration.

But the record speaks for itself. The loyalty program has proved to be a miserable failure as far as security is concerned. It has found no spies or security violations in sensitive areas or otherwise. Nor is it geared to; it is geared to accomplish the impossible—determine who tomorrow's spies will be. Let the FBI attend to the business of sabotage and espionage on the basis of the actual, not the potential—on the basis of acts, not possibilities. Let every agency continue to screen applicants for employment carefully; but let us not, in our fear of the police state, compromise free institutions.

The atmosphere in government is one of fear—fear of ideas and of irresponsible and unknown informers. Government employees are afraid to attend meetings of politically minded groups; they are afraid to read "liberal" publications; they screen their friends carefully for "left-wing" ideas. Government employees are in very real danger of dying intellectually and politically. Everyone knows of someone who has been accused of disloyalty—and it amounts to an accusation of treason—on ridiculous charges. Nobody wants to go through a lengthy "loyalty" investigation. The inclination and inevitable result are simply to restrict one's own freedoms.

All Americans suffer thereby. Political growth and progressive evolution depend on a vital and enthusiastic corps of government workers. Democracy can survive only upon the condition of a constant flexibility in its institutions to meet growing social and economic needs. Good government incorporates varying shades of opinion into a synthesis of action in behalf of the greatest good. Synthesis and flexibility are impossible when dissenters or the unorthodox are ruthlessly stamped out. The suppression of opposition can only mean the retention of outmoded and useless institutions, the impossibility of compromise and adjustment.

History has demonstrated again and again that freedom and the maturity of democratic processes cannot survive when the politically and economically dominant suspend traditional safeguards to the unorthodox. This is true, regardless of whether the suspension is undertaken because of fear of outside forces, or whether it is because a society has frozen in its evolutionary progress toward the fuller dignity of man. Surely it cannot be said that the United States, entering into a period of world leadership and enjoying the greatest prosperity in our history, has ceased growing. Let us not through hysteria and the uncertainty engendered by new responsibilities abdicate the basic standards of freedom which made us great. This is what we have done in the government's loyalty program; and this is what we threaten to do in the extension of that program to other segments of our society.

WALTER GELLHORN
What Limits on the Security Program?

Wholly unrelated to the "sensitive areas," some thirty thousand civilians have professional civil-service ratings in federal agencies as chemists, physicists, meteorologists, entomologists, geologists, bacteriologists, pathologists, astronomers, and so on. To that number must be added the many thousands of supporting technical personnel and the yet further thousands of doctors, dentists, psychologists, and the like who are employed by the Veterans Administration, the Public Health Service, and other departments. Even those scientists who do have access to restricted data possess, for the most part, few real secrets —certainly far fewer than many normally self-assertive men ever permit their acquaintances to suppose. As for the scientists who will be discussed in the present piece, there is no room whatsoever for speculation on this score. They are factually, officially, and unqualifiedly barren of state secrets. They have not the slightest opportunity to deal in restricted data or to magnify their own importance by multiplying the number of hushes in hush-hush.

The inconspicuous ichthyologist of the Fish and Wildlife Service knows many secrets, to be sure, but they are the secrets of the speckled trout rather than the secrets of national defense. The mine safety engineer in the Department of the Interior peers into dark and hidden places, but the information he acquires has no element of confidentiality. The researcher at the National Cancer Institute explores the unknown, but there is certainly no disposition to conceal whatever he may discover. The Liberian scientific mission of the Public Health Service and the Agriculture Department is engaged in work of national importance, but whatever it learns about *Strophanthus sarmentosus* as a ready source of adrenocorticotrophic hormone will not be withheld from the rheumatoid arthritis sufferers of the world. . . . Yet the political views and the associations of all these men, and of others like them, have been a matter of governmental scrutiny almost as though they were entrusted with the latest developments in chemical warfare or rocket design. . . .

In the field of science, the crudities of the loyalty program discourage

Betts Professor of Law at Columbia University. Former Law secretary to Justice Harlan Fiske Stone. Author of *Individual Freedom and Governmental Restraints, American Rights,* and many other books. The selection is from *Security, Loyalty, and Science* (Ithaca, Cornell University Press, 1950), pp. 127-129, 158, 173-174. By permission.

efforts to draw into public service the live-minded and experienced men whose talents are needed in many agencies. The distress occasioned by an unwarranted inquisition by a loyalty board is felt by a wide circle of friends and fellow-workers. Especially in the case of scientists there is a realization that even after a man has been exonerated following a hearing, he may still be subjected to a renewal of the charges and a dusting off of the same evidence if the winds of politics continue to blow strongly. On September 6, 1948, eight of America's great scientists, joining in a message to President Truman and Governor Dewey, deplored the disastrous effects upon scientific recruitment that followed the denunciatory sensationalism of the House Committee on Un-American Activities. . . . [They] concluded that the atmosphere of suspicion surrounding scientists in government was an effective deterrent to procurement and use of their services. What these men said publicly has been echoed privately by scientific men of every level of eminence.

The negative consequences of the Loyalty Order are dramatically realized when able men refuse to engage in public service or choose to leave it for less harassing occupations. All in all, however, the more serious though perhaps more subtle impact is on those who remain in federal service. . . .

Those difficulties would be diminished if we ceased searching for "disloyalty" as a general abstraction and became concerned exclusively with "security." Concededly there are positions outside the "sensitive agencies" that directly involve national safety. Occasionally an entire section or division of an organization may have occasion to deal with classified matters or may be so immediately involved in the formulation of international policy as to render it "sensitive" even though the agency as a whole may not be so. . . .

The solution here is to authorize the head of each department and agency to designate the units or particular positions in his department which he believes to be "sensitive." Persons who may be employed in these sensitive posts may properly be investigated in order that there may be full confidence in them. But as for the rest—the typists in the Veterans Administration or the Federal Housing Administration, the scientists in the Allergen Research Division or the Mycology and Disease Survey of the Bureau of Plant Industry—experience under the Loyalty Order demonstrates that constant peering over their shoulders endangers liberty without enhancing loyalty.

This is the administrative device that has been tried with reasonable success in Great Britain. There the power is lodged in each Minister to decide what parts of his ministry require the equivalent of our security clearance. In all, about 100,000 jobs were identified as having security significance. The Admiralty, as has our Department of the Army, concluded that everyone, from the highest to the lowest, must be cleared. Other ministries found no "sensitive" jobs at all. And this is as it should be, for in the variety of modern governmental activities there is room for both extremes.

If this approach be adopted, it will not mean an abandonment of interest in the probity of "nonsensitive" personnel. It will mean merely that observations will be related to behavior rather than belief. Government employees who improperly discharge their duties, whether motivated by disloyalty or mere slovenliness of habit, should of course be identified and appropriately disciplined. This, however, is a matter of administration rather than of detection.

The supervisory officials of a functioning unit can more readily determine a staff member's misconduct or carelessness than can even the most vigilant agent of the FBI. The responsibility for efficiency should rest squarely on them. They cannot fulfill their responsibility if they tolerate on their staffs employees who are not actively loyal to their jobs. As for misdeeds unrelated to the direct performance of an employee's work, reliance must be placed upon the excellent counterespionage staffs of federal investigating agencies. The thorough work of the Federal Bureau of Investigation has given that bureau the place of public esteem that it occupies. The inherent absurdities of the loyalty program threaten the FBI's deservedly high reputation, for its "loyalty probers" must expend their energies in recording the often ambiguous pettinesses of political expression rather than in uncovering criminality. Releasing the FBI from the thankless and fruitless work to which it is now assigned will enhance the nation's safety. The more broadly we define the limits of our concern with personnel security, the more thinly we must spread attention to it. As has been true so often in matters of public administration, the scattershot of the blunderbuss is less effective than the aimed bullet of the rifle.

More than one hundred and fifty years ago a great friend of American democracy, Edmund Burke, argued that while restraint upon liberty may sometimes be required if liberty itself is to survive, "it ought to be the constant aim of every wise public council to find out by cautious experiments, and cool rational endeavors, with how little, not how much, of this restraint the community can subsist; for liberty is a good to be improved, and not an evil to be lessened." Burke's words are as true today as when he uttered them in 1777. The country will be the stronger for discovering that the restraints of the present loyalty program exceed the needs of national preservation.

✑✑Section V

FEDERALISM

The United States is the first great experiment in federalism. Prior to the framing of the Constitution in 1787, history had witnessed the rise and fall of a number of confederacies, and the world had experienced numberless centralized or unitary states.

Our Constitution establishes a system under which, generally speaking, the federal government, subject to specific prohibitions, enjoys supremacy in the exercise of delegated sovereign powers, while the states, also subject to specific prohibitions and those inferred from grants to the federal government, exercise reserved sovereign powers. Theoretically this distribution of powers can be changed only by constitutional amendment. In actual practice, however, the elastic scope accorded by the Supreme Court to federal power, in spheres previously regarded as reserved to state action, demonstrates that the balance is a changing one.

Although some criticism of our federal structure has been far-reaching, no serious student of politics would suggest the substitution—in our vast and complex land with its long tradition of state sovereignty—of a unitary system of government. The real issues are concerned, rather, with establishing the appropriate spheres of national and state activities. To do this requires regard not only for tradition but for many other considerations including basic democratic values, experience, resources, and changing social needs.

Does federalism contribute to the preservation of democracy? This is the subject of special consideration in this section. So, also, is the controversy over the extent to which the fashioning of state legislative and local governmental districts should be the special if not exclusive prerogative of state legislatures. Concomitantly, there is the question of standards: must such districts conform to the "one-man-one-vote" formula to meet the constitutional requirement that no state shall deny "to any person within its jurisdiction the equal protection of the laws" or may legislative bodies take into account a variety of factors including distinctive history, geography, and the urban-rural distribution of the population?

Centralization and Decentralization

PAUL STUDENSKI *and* PAUL R. MORT
Centralization and Democracy

Theoretically central versus local control is an issue between extreme centralization of government on the one hand, and extreme decentralization of it on the other. In actual practice, however, the issue is generally far
from being so broad in character. It is limited in most cases to a consideration
of whether certain functions of government should be centralized or decentralized, and of the extent to which such centralization or decentralization of
them should be carried. The discussions of these narrower issues are generally
carried on in much more realistic terms than the discussion of the broader
theoretical issues, for they take into account particular situations and problems. . . .

The necessity of complete and direct central control over certain spheres
of public affairs, such as national defense, foreign affairs, and foreign trade, is
admitted by all writers. No one would seriously propose today that these functions be administered locally.

In most spheres of public affairs, however, the sharing of control by the
central and local authorities is generally deemed most advisable. Central and
local control are considered to possess different advantages deemed equally
essential to the national welfare in the administration of public services. This
sharing of control, it is noted, may take the form of (*a*) the exercise by the
central and local governments, respectively, of independent authority over different spheres of the same functions as exemplified by the present control of
most of the federal and state functions, (*b*) the supervision by the central government of the operations of the local governments, as exemplified by state
supervision over local educational administration and, more recently, by federal
supervision over state administration of highways, social security, relief, etc.,
or (*c*) joint or cooperative management by the central government and the

Paul Studenski, former Professor of Economics, New York University. Author
of *The Income of Nations, Financial History of the United States,* and other books
and articles. Paul R. Mort, former Professor of Education, Teachers College, Columbia University. Author of *Principles of School Administration* and other books.
The selection is from Paul Studenski and Paul R. Mort, *Centralized vs. Decentralized Government in Relation to Democracy* (New York, Bureau of Publications,
Teachers College, Columbia University, 1941), *passim* as specially rearranged. By
permission.

local authorities of certain of their affairs as exemplified by the proposals for a joint federal-state management of specific public works. . . .

The national interest can best be served by striking a fair balance between centralization and decentralization so that the advantages of both of those types of control may be maintained and the disadvantages of their extreme manifestations avoided. The exact degree of centralization and decentralization which may be advisable in the case of different countries must necessarily depend on the size of the country, the stage of its economic development, and the particular political, social, and economic situation with which it may be confronted at the moment. . . .

Shortcomings of Decentralization

The principal shortcomings of extreme decentralization may be summarized as follows: (1) it results in an inefficient and an uneconomic management of local affairs; (2) it fosters local autocratic rule by petty officials and powerful minority groups; (3) it breeds narrow parochialism, and produces national and regional disunity and disorganization; (4) it results in extreme inequality in the standards of public service and protection of civil rights throughout the country or the region; (5) central government unifies the nation.

Inefficient and Uneconomic Management of Local Affairs

Central government is in many respects more efficient and economical than are local governments, all other conditions being the same. First of all, central government generally attracts a more competent personnel for its policy-making body and its administrative departments than do local governments. The prestige attached to the holding of a national political office is far greater than that attached to the holding of a local one. The number of leading national offices in the country is smaller than the number of local ones, and the competition for them is therefore much keener. Each national legislator represents a larger area and a larger population, is concerned with more important affairs, and receives wider publicity than does a local councilman. The possibility for elevation to a higher office is greater in the case of a member of the national legislature than in that of a member of a municipal council. The compensation of a national representative is generally greater too. All these circumstances are responsible for the fact that capable men who are willing to devote their time to political affairs, as a rule, more readily aspire to a national political office than to a local one.

The central government has a wider choice of candidates for administrative positions than have local governments. It recruits its personnel wherever it can find suitable material. It is not obligated to employ local men for local offices. It can hire men in one locality and employ them in another. By advertising nationally the vacancies which it wishes to fill, it invites active competition for the positions from applicants all over the country. Inasmuch as the higher positions in the national administration involve greater responsibilities, enjoy greater prestige, and generally offer better pay than do the higher positions in the sphere of local government, they naturally attract more able and ambitious men. The greater opportunities which the national service offers for promotion to higher positions and also the more secure tenure of office it provides tend to secure for the national government a better personnel. In view of all these facts, the national government can afford to be more selective in its choice of employees than can the local governments.

Second, the national government has much wider sources of information than have local governments. It is in a position to collect through its local agents data on existing conditions in the various sections of the country and to base its policies on information of a comparative sort. The national service provides better opportunities to the men engaged therein to acquire wide experience than does the municipal service. The national administrators in the course of their careers are often shifted from one locality to another or travel extensively over the country and in this manner become familiar with the situations in various localities or regions.

Third, the central government can introduce much greater functional specialization in its administrative services than can local governments. It can subdivide the work into minute specialities to a much greater degree and thus can secure greater efficiency and economy of operation.

In the fourth place, the national government affords greater opportunities for centralization of administrative responsibility in a few key offices than does local government. This centralization of responsibility enables the government better to coordinate the activities of its officials. It makes possible quick and decisive action.

In the fifth place, the national government possesses the advantages of large-scale enterprise. One of these advantages, that of division or specialization of labor, has already been noted. The central government is in a better position to employ experts to use elaborate and highly efficient equipment. Moreover, it can execute large projects affecting substantial areas, which the localities in these areas cannot possibly accomplish, separately or jointly, themselves. Large projects of this sort can be executed more economically and are much more efficient than are the smaller projects which local governments can undertake. The central government is able to perform, in cases of this sort, the same amount of work as the local governments with a smaller number of employees. It can eliminate duplicate functions and positions and use its personnel more effectively and economically. . . .

Fostering Local Autocratic Rule by Petty Officials and Powerful Minority Groups

Extreme decentralization fosters local autocratic rule by petty officials and powerful minority groups. The smaller the local area, the more static are likely to be the social, economic, and political conditions therein. Old-time residents cling together in an effort to preserve the traditional policies of the community and lend loyal support to a common leader, an old resident like themselves, who becomes the local dictator in all the spheres of the local public life—political, economic, and the like. Newcomers who have different ideas of the development of the community are not permitted by the dominant local clique to take active part in the management of local affairs. The jobs in the local government are distributed by the local "boss" among his faithful followers, and a job once granted to a follower readily becomes a sinecure. . . .

Narrow Parochialism and National and Regional Disunity and Disorganization

Extreme decentralization results in the disorganization of government in the country or the region. Confusing and conflicting regulations are enacted by the various local governments. Projects conceived in the interest of the entire territory are often blocked by the refusal of a small local area to join in the undertaking or to permit its facilities to be extended through its territory. The officials of the local government are unwilling to cooperate. They fear that intergovernmental cooperation of this sort may bring in its wake the unification of government, the abolition of their local independence, and a loss of their jobs; or that in some other way it may result in the lowering of their prestige and influence in the eyes of their own citizens. . . .

The vesting of excessively wide powers in state governments and of totally inadequate powers in the central government in this country, after the War of Independence, produced disunity and a breakdown of government. As soon as a strong central government was provided under the new constitution, the disintegrating tendencies came to an end. In like manner, in later times the exercise by the states of complete authority over the institution of slavery, over banks, railroads, monopolies and trusts, liquor traffic, and other economic and social matters produced chaos in these spheres of the national economy. With the partial or complete centralization of authority over these spheres in the national government, however, their administration became more orderly in character. The multiplication of local governments in densely populated metropolitan regions has produced serious evils. The small rural governments which, years ago, performed a useful function have become in recent times a bar to governmental and social progress.

Professor Munro refers to the shortcomings of extreme decentralization of government in this country as represented by excessive grants of power to state governments and inadequate grants of them to the Federal authority, as follows:[1]

> In their relation to the problems of American economic and social life, the states have been gradually receding as entities of political action, whether regulative or constructive, until today they are all but powerless in some of the fields ostensibly reserved to them by our scheme of government. . . . When a problem of industry or social welfare becomes too big to be handled by the authorities of the individual states, there are only two alternatives under present conditions. One is to confess our helplessness and bear the evils as best we can; the other is to demand that Washington take the problem in hand, whether it belongs there or not. It is natural that a practical people should prefer the latter alternative. They will continue to prefer it, and no theory of division of powers will

[1] W. B. Munro, "Do We Need Regional Government?" *Forum* (January, 1928), p. 109.

stand in their way. Jurists may sob over the "vanishing rights of the states," but it is a fair guess that these rights will continue to dwindle as our problems keep growing in size. The steady erosion of state powers is bound to go hand in hand with the increasing complexity of our economic and social life. Nothing in the realm of political prophecy can be more certain than that the intrepid rear guards of the states' rights army are fighting for a lost cause. . . .

Extreme Inequality in Standards of Public Service and Protection of Civil Rights

Under an extremely decentralized government, the standards of public service and of the protection of civil rights, it is said, vary greatly from area to area. The maintenance by some areas of high standards benefits the nation or the region. But the maintenance by others of low standards injures the neighboring communities and the country or region as a whole. For the evil conditions resulting from such low standards spread far beyound the boundaries of the areas responsible for them. The low standards maintained by these areas nullify the efforts of the other areas to maintain a high record of performance and eventually cause the latter to relax in their zeal. As a result, the quality of public services throughout the entire country or region is lowered. To prevent this eventuality, the neighboring communities and the state must take some action that would raise the standards of service in the backward areas. . . .

Swift, an American authority on education, points out that:[2]

> . . . a condition essential to democracy is equality of opportunity. . . . Inequalities of educational opportunity in the United States today are directly proportional to the degree of autonomy in matters of school support and control granted to the local communities. Any system which creates, perpetuates, and increases educational inequalities is undemocratic; and these are beyond all doubt the characteristics and results of our decentralized systems.

National Unification and the Service of the National Interest

A properly conceived central government promotes national unity. It provides for the common needs of the population and for the coordinated development of all the social and economic factors upon which the welfare of the nation depends. And it obviously provides for the security of the nation. The centralized government organizes the creative forces of the nation and its resources for the achievement of these important ends. Advocates of centralization strongly emphasize the importance of these unifying functions of the central government. The need for the unification which centralization provides is admitted in many fields of public administration, even by the strongest advocates of local self-government. Thus, it is generally admitted that uniformity of regulation of interstate commerce, throughout the country, is essential for national prosperity, and that the central government, which alone can provide

---

[2] Fletcher H. Swift, *Federal and State Policies in Public School Finance in the United States* (New York, Ginn and Company), p. 85.

uniform regulation over the country as a whole, should exercise jurisdiction over this sphere of the economic life of the people. It is admitted by the advocates of modern centralization that in certain spheres of public affairs there is no need for unified administration and uniformity of regulation.

Central government equalizes the social, economic, and educational opportunities available to the people in various sections of the country. It develops backward territories in accordance with national requirements. It promotes the national economy and the national culture. Well-conceived centralization enables the government to respond quickly to rapid nation-wide social and economic changes. The information which indicates occurrence of such changes and the type of adjustment required to meet them is readily available to the central government. The whole huge machinery of the government may be mobilized at a moment's notice to meet the national emergency or changed situation. Thousands of employees may be shifted from one type of activity to another or from one section of the country to another, as conditions require that this be done.

Proper centralization of government stimulates the civic interest of the people and broadens their civic outlook. It fosters broad national ideals, it gives rise to momentous political issues which profoundly stir the people, and it provides, if the people so desire, its own democratic processes for the consideration of public issues, which are just as effective as the democratic processes provided by the local government for the disposition of local affairs.

A properly conceived central government does not restrict the freedom of the individual. On the contrary, it often proves to be the most effective instrument for safeguarding the civil liberties of the people and their democratic institutions. It endeavors, in a democratic country, to guarantee fundamental civil rights to all the citizens in any portion of the country. Wherever undemocratic local pressure groups gain dominance and deny to some citizens their fundamental civil rights, the national government may intervene and may force upon these pressure groups the observance of these civil rights.

A well-conceived central government enlarges individual freedoms also by guaranteeing to the individuals freedom of enterprise over the entire national territory and by affording them an opportunity for a wider sphere of creative activity. The individual shares, in a democracy, in the determination of the large affairs with which the central government is concerned. The greater the scope of the public affairs, the greater the importance and responsibility of the individuals who share in their disposition. . . .

Some students of political science also emphasize the fact that the country which is exposed to attack requires a more centralized government than one whose natural location affords it relative security. It is significant that the tendencies toward the centralization of government become most pronounced in a country in times of war or when war is imminent.

FRANZ L. NEUMANN
Federalism and Freedom: A Critique

The theoretical argument for federalism revolves around the potential of political power for evil. Federalism is seen as one of the devices to curb the evil use of power by dividing power among a number of competing power-units.

The underlying sentiment—the corruptive influence of power—is often not clearly formulated and the consequences thus not clearly seen. . . .

1. It is Lord Acton's statement on the corruptive effect of political power which appears to have today the greatest influence. Three statements of his on political power are:

> *a.* ". . . power tends to expand indefinitely, and will transcend all barriers, abroad and at home, until met by superior forces."
>
> *b.* "History is not a web woven with innocent hands. Among all the causes which degrade and demoralize men, power is the most constant and the most active."
>
> *c.* To Creighton: "I cannot accept your canon that we are to judge Pope and King unlike other men, with a favorable presumption that they did no wrong. If there is any presumption it is the other way against holders of power, increasing as the power increases. Historic responsibility has to make up for the want of legal responsibility. Power tends to corrupt and absolute power corrupts absolutely. Great men are almost always bad men, even when they exercise influence and not authority: still more when you superadd the tendency or the certainty of corruption by authority. There is no worse heresy than that the office sanctifies the holder of it."

These statements have two aspects. The first one is, indeed, unobjectionable and, of course, not very original. Thucydides said much the same:

> *Melians*—You may be sure that we are as well aware as you of the difficulty of contending against your power and fortune, unless the terms be equal. But we trust that the gods may grant us fortune as good as yours, since we are just men fighting against unjust, and that what we want in power will be made up by the alliance of the Lacedaemonians, who are bound, if only for very shame, to come to the aid of their kindred. Our confidence, therefore, after all is not so utterly irrational.
>
> *Athenians*—When you speak of the favour of the gods, we may as

Late Professor of Public Law and Government, Columbia University. Author of *Behemoth* and other publications. The selection is from Franz L. Neumann, "Federalism and Freedom: A Critique," in A. W. Macmahon, ed., *Federalism: Mature and Emergent* (New York, Doubleday & Co. Inc., 1955), pp. 45-49. By permission of the Trustees of Columbia University.

fairly hope for that as yourselves; neither our pretensions nor our conduct being in any way contrary to what men believe of the gods, or practise among themselves. *Of the gods we believe, and of men we know, that by a necessary law of their nature they rule wherever they can.* And it is not as if we were the first to make this law, or to act upon it when made: we found it existing before us, and shall leave it to exist for ever after us; all we do is to make use of it, knowing that you and everybody else, having the same power as we have, would do the same as we do. (Emphasis supplied.)

And Montesquieu said this even more clearly. According to him power could be checked only by power—a statement that few would be willing to quarrel with. Not ideologies and beliefs but only a counter-power can check power. In this he applies Cartesian principles and stands in the tradition of Spinoza who saw no way of limiting the state's absoluteness (which was a logical consequence of his assumptions and of his geometric method) except by a counter-power.

The Montesquieu generalization is, of course, designed to give his doctrine of the separation of powers an adequate theoretical base. But as little as the theory of separate powers follows from his sociological observation, as little does that of the preferability of the federal state. Bentham rejected the separation of powers not only as incompatible with democracy but also because it could not really maximize freedom if the three organs of government were controlled by the same social group. A quite similar argument can be raised against federalism as a guarantee for liberty. Those who assert that the federal state through the diffusion of *constitutional* powers actually diffuses *political* power often overlook the fact that the real cause for the existence of liberty is the pluralist structure of society and the multi-party (or two-party) system. Federalism is not identical with social pluralism; and neither the two-party nor the multi-party system is the product of the federal state or the condition for its functioning.

2. Whether the federal state does indeed increase freedom cannot be abstractly determined. We have some evidence that the federal state as such (that is, regardless of the form of government) has not fulfilled this role. The German Imperial Constitution certainly created a federal state but there is little doubt that politically it had a dual purpose: to be a dynastic alliance against the forces of liberalism and democracy, and to secure the hegemony of Prussia. One may argue that a unitary state may even have been worse than the federal solution: that is quite possible. Nevertheless one may say, with reason, that the archaic Prussian three-class franchise could not possibly have been introduced as the system for a unitary German state. Thus a unitary German state in all likelihood would have been more progressive than the Bismarckian system. The Austro-Hungarian Dual Monarchy, after the *Ausgleich* of 1867, was an attempt to ensure the rule of the Germans and Magyars over all other nationalities. The Dual Monarchy most certainly did not maximize freedom except for the oligarchies in its two constituent states.

Perhaps more striking are the respective roles of federalism and centralism in the coming to power of National Socialism. Some believe, indeed, that the centralization under the Weimar Republic is wholly or at least partly respon-

sible for the rise of National Socialism. But there is no evidence for this statement—nor indeed for the opposite one. It is certain that Bavaria, with the
strongest states' rights tradition, gave shelter to the National Socialist movement
and it is equally certain that the federal character of the Weimar Republic did
not, after Hitler's appointment, delay the process of synchronization (*Gleich-
schaltung*) of the various state governments. Nor is there any definable relation between democratic conviction and federalist (or unitary) sympathies. The
National Socialists were both centralists and reactionary, as were the Nationalists. Democrats and Social Democrats were antifederalists and committed to
the preservation of political freedom. The Catholic center was not wholeheartedly committed to any position, and the Communists were, in theory, for the
unitary state but did not hesitate, during the revolution of 1918, to advocate the
secession of Brunswick which they believed they had in their pocket.

3. But perhaps what is meant by saying that federalism maximizes freedom is that only in a democracy does the division of constitutional power
among various autonomous territorial units effect a maximum of political liberty; in other words, that democracy and the federal state go together, even that
federalism is necessary for democracy. Literally taken, this statement is most
certainly untrue. The United Kingdom is a proof against it. Weimar Germany
cannot be cited either for or against it. Bavaria—the most states' rights-con-
scious *land*—was certainly the most reactionary; Prussia, the most democratic.
Insofar as the United States is concerned, it seems almost impossible to make
any statement because of the extreme difficulty of attributing to the federal
system—in isolation from other elements—any specific function. There are, perhaps, some tests like the protection of civil liberties. For a criminal, the federal
system has obvious advantages in that it increases his margin of safety from
prosecution. The need for extradition may, in isolated cases, permit a criminal
to escape punishment. It is doubtful, however, that this can be taken as a compliment to federalism. Of real importance would be a study designed to prove
or disprove that the federal nature of American government has strengthened
civil liberties. The criminal syndicalism legislation of the post World War I
period does not permit us to pass a final judgment. The "red hysteria" of that
period "practically assured . . . passage (of this type of legislation) with only
slight examination." The bills were passed with "breath-taking swiftness and
little debate, or with a great outburst of oratory characterized more by passion,
prejudice, and misinformation than by a reasoned effort to get at the facts."
There seemed to be a race among the various states for the most drastic legislation, and vested interests, their influence enhanced by the makeup of the state
legislatures, pushed through the bills. Simultaneously, efforts to enact a federal
bill failed from 1917 to 1920. On the other hand, however, it is possible that
without state laws a federal bill might have been enacted, and it is also true that
in a few states no legislation was enacted. On the whole, one may perhaps say
that the federal system may have speeded up inroads into the civil liberties
rather than have protected them.

The same, perhaps, may be said of the present situation. The evidence is
certainly too slight to be of great value in determining whether the federal system is preferable to the unitary state as an instrument to preserve or enhance
civil liberties. Nor is it likely that convincing evidence can be obtained, since

other factors—the plurality of the social structure, the functioning of a truly competitive party system, the strength of a favorable tradition, the intellectual level of the population, the attitude of the courts—do far more easily permit the formation of a counter-power against forces hostile to civil liberties than does the federal structure of the government.

4. Lord Acton's statements, however, are also concerned with a second aspect: namely, the corruptive influence of power. This brilliant formula that power tends to corrupt and absolute power corrupts absolutely has attained the position of a classical remark; but, inevitably, it has also become a cliché of which neither the meaning nor the validity is ever questioned. The content of the statement is certainly not very original. While Plato's discussion of the same problem shows a much deeper insight, Lord Acton's has the undoubted merits of brevity and of quotability.

Lord Acton asserts that the character of the man who has power is corrupted by the exercise of power, or as the German adage has it: Politics corrupts the character. This is probably a valid generalization—but what is its significance for politics, in general, and for our problem, in particular? A morally evil ruler does not necessarily make a bad ruler—he may accumulate riches, indulge in all kinds of vices—and yet his rule may be beneficial; while the paragon of virtue may lead his country to destruction. But if we turn from monarchy or tyranny to representative government, the applicability of the formula to politics is quite certainly small.

However, we may well redefine the formula to mean that too much power concentrated in any organ of government has evil consequences for the people and that federalism, by dividing power among independent territorial units, checks these evil potentialities.

Thus redefined, the statement is no longer defensible because the opposite may equally be true. It is, indeed, also true: Too little power tends to corrupt and absolute lack of power corrupts absolutely; or, as Edmund Burke put it: "Nothing turns out to be so oppressive and unjust as a feeble government." One can accept Burke's assertion as absolute truth as little as one can Lord Acton's. Both are partially true generalizations, Burke's being, perhaps, a more realistic description of marginal situations than Lord Acton's. If one shares Burke's hatred of revolution, one may keep in mind that modern revolutions such as the French of 1789, the two Russian ones of 1917, and the German of 1918, had their immediate cause in the lack of power of the central governments and not in the excessive use or abuse of power.

It thus seems impossible to attribute to federalism, as such, a value; or to assert that the federal state—as contrasted to the unitary state—enhances political and civil freedom by dividing power among autonomous territorial subdivisions.

ROBERT A. DAHL
The Other Ninety Thousand Governments

The national government is one out of more than ninety thousand governments of all kinds existing within the boundaries of the United States. Of these, more than a third are school districts, although the number of these has declined precipitously since the 1930s. Even if we ignore school and special districts and consider only general territorial governments, the states, counties, municipalities, townships, and towns have numbered altogether close to 38 thousand for the last thirty or forty years. . . .

What contributions do territorial governments below the national level make to the American democracy? If one tries to imagine how the American political system might operate without them, four possible contributions suggest themselves:

1. By reducing the workload of the national government, they make democratic government at the national level more manageable.
2. By permitting diversity, they reduce conflicts at the national level and thus make democratic government at the national level more viable.
3. By providing numerous more or less independent or autonomous centers of power throughout the system, they reinforce the principles of Balanced Authority and Political Pluralism.
4. By facilitating self-government at local levels, they greatly expand the opportunities for learning and practising the ways of democratic government in the United States.

Efficiency, Decentralization, and Democracy

The imagination boggles at the attempt to conceive of the United States as a democratic country operating at the national level by means of elected leaders and competitive political parties and locally through a centralized bureaucracy, federally appointed and controlled, that would administer tasks now carried on by 38 thousand territorial governments. After all, many important self-governing nations are no larger than our larger states. In fact, in 1961 only 28 out of over 125 independent countries were as large as New York or California.

How would a completely centralized system actually function in the United States? On the one hand, the system might be centralized not only in law but *in fact* as well. In this case, would not the weight of the Chief Execu-

Professor of political science, Yale University. Author of: *Congress and Foreign Policy; A Preface to Democratic Theory; Who Governs.* The selection is from Robert A. Dahl, *Pluralist Democracy in the United States: Conflict and Consent* (Chicago, Rand McNally & Company, 1967), Ch. 7. By permission.

tive and the insensitivity of the national bureaucracy to local variation crush out local diversity? What is more, the burdens on national policy-makers—the President, the Congress, the courts, the administrative agencies—would be frightful; to superimpose these new tasks on their present duties (which are already enormous) would surely create a workload well beyond their capacities to handle.

National policy-makers might meet such an impossible work load by either neglecting their duties or delegating decisions to other officials. To the extent that national officials delegated decisions to other officials who were closer to the local scene, the system might become centralized in law but decentralized in fact. National uniformity would doubtless be too rigid and oppressive to remain tolerable for long. National officials would develop strong but informal local ties. Local pressures would be felt. The wise administrator would learn to adapt his policies to local circumstances. Sooner or later, American citizens might conclude that law should conform more closely to fact. In short: If local governments did not exist, they would quickly be invented. . . .

A fairly large number of different indicators do reveal that the role of local governments in American life has actually *expanded* in this century. Evidently what has happened is that all our territorial governments—national, state, and local—have increased their functions; whether it be national, state, or local, every government carries out more tasks today than it did a few generations ago.

For example, the expenditures, revenues, and functions of the state and local governments have steadily grown in recent decades. True, since the high period of the New Deal in 1936, federal expenditures have risen faster than those of the state and local governments. But the lion's share of federal outlays has been consumed by national defense, international relations, space programs, veterans' services, and interest on the public debt. If we eliminate these items, we discover that the difference virtually disappears: In the quarter century from 1938–1963 the expenditures of the federal government increased a little more than eight-fold, the expenditures of state and local governments a little less than eight-fold. In 1962, 'obsolete' state and local governments spent far more than the federal government for education, highways, health and hospitals, public welfare, and housing and community development. Revenues from strictly state and local sources—that is excluding all federal grants, which amount to 7.2 per cent of the total in 1938 and 11.6 per cent in 1963—were six and one-half times greater in 1963 than in 1938. Of about 9.7 million civilians employed by government in 1963, about one in four were federal employees; more than one in six were state employees; and something more than one out of two were employed by local governments.

Far from having lost functions, then, the local governments have been gaining new ones. There is no record that state and local governments spent any funds at all for housing development until 1938, when they spent three million dollars. In 1963 they spent 446 million dollars. The state and local governments are a major factor in the national economy. In 1963 their expenditures for civil functions were equivalent to 11 per cent of the Gross National Product, compared with 4 per cent for the federal government (Table 1).

There are then no valid grounds for doubting that both in fact and in law

TABLE 1. General Expenditure for Civil Functions by All Levels of Government as Percentage of Gross National Product, Selected Years, 1902-63 (Money amounts in billions of dollars)

Year	GNP	Expenditures as Percentage of GNP		
		Federal	State-Local	Total
1902	$ 21.6	1.1	4.7	5.8
1927	96.3	1.5	7.5	9.0
1938	85.2	5.9	10.3	16.2
1948	259.4	3.4	6.8	10.2
1963	583.9	4.0	11.1	15.1

Source: James A. Maxwell, *Financing State and Local Government* (Washington, The Brookings Institution, 1965), Appendix Table A-1, A-3.

Intergovernmental payments are charged to the level of government making final disbursement.

the local territorial governments of the United States assume a huge burden, which in their absence would have to be discharged, somehow, by federal officials. It seems reasonable to conclude that in a country as vast and as complex as the United States, local governments are necessary simply (if for no other reason) in order to achieve a level of efficiency in government high enough to make democracy at the national level tolerable. Without the local governments, democratic institutions at the national level would probably go under from the sheer weight of their burdens.

One might nonetheless wonder whether local governments in the United States operate above some minimum level of tolerability. They may provide enough efficiency to keep the system stumbling along. But are they anything like as efficient as they should be?

Unfortunately, dear though it be to advocates of governmental reform, the criterion of efficiency does not take one very far. For if efficiency is measured by the ratio of valued 'inputs' to valued 'outputs,' then to one who believes strongly in the values of democracy, the efficiency of state and local governments must be measured in large part by comparing their costs, using the term in a very broad sense indeed, against their contributions to democracy. We remain then pretty much in the place from which we started. If efficiency is measured by the ratio between actual output and a theoretically maximum output, how are we to decide what is a theoretical maximum?

It seems perfectly reasonable to ask how well state and local governments perform the various tasks assigned to them by law. Are they efficient administrative units in the narrow sense that they economize, cut costs, act with expertness and dispatch? The question seems reasonable, but it is nonetheless almost impossible to answer. One must first ask a counter-question: With what are we to compare them? If we compared state and local governments with some theoretical ideal, it would be easy to show that like every other human institution they fall very far short of ideal achievement. But we know this much in advance. We can scarcely compare state and local governments with private firms, because neither the inputs nor the outputs of state and local governments are sufficiently like those of private enterprise to make comparisons valid. How can we compare the relative efficiency of the New York police in controlling crime and traffic with the efficiency of General Motors in producing and marketing automobiles? There seems to be little possibility of a useful or even a meaningful comparison; even those intrepid spirits who would contend that General Motors is the more efficient of the two organizations would not propose, I imagine, to turn the police force of New York over to General Motors.

Can we compare the administrative efficiency of state and local governments with that of federal agencies? Here again we run into formidable problems because of the differences in outputs—the services performed. In any case, an adverse comparison would be highly misleading if it led one to conclude that the federal government would perform local functions more 'efficiently,' in the restricted sense, than the local governments themselves.[1] For we need to know what would happen to the present level of efficiency of federal agencies if the federal government were to take on all the additional tasks now performed at local levels; if, in short, the federal civil service bureaucracy were to triple in numbers, from less than one out of twenty-five persons in the civilian labor force to one out of eight.

Perhaps the only way out of this dilemma is to compare similar local units with one another. Yet, given the enormous variety of local governments, even this is a much more formidable enterprise than it might seem.

Thus, despite its glossy appeal, the criterion of efficiency does not take one very far. For appraising governments, 'efficiency' is a concept either too slippery to be meaningful or too precise to be applicable. However, three observations may nevertheless be permissible. First, American state and local governments have generally lagged behind the federal government in introducing reforms thought to contribute to administrative efficiency: in the development of a neutral and expert civil service, an executive budget, a single chief executive with substantial hierarchical control over administrative agencies, an adequate specialized staff for the chief executive, and so on. Corruption seems to occur more frequently, and on a bigger scale, in local units than in the federal government. Pay scales are lower, both at the start and at the end of one's career.

Second, there are enormous variations among the different units of local government. By almost any objective test, the best local government would be as efficient as any found in the federal government; the worst are appalling. Between the best and the worst, there is a whole universe of types. No one can ever judge the quality of local government in the United States by his experience with one or two units.

Third, whatever weight one may give to local governments as instruments of democracy (we shall proceed to that matter at once), it is obvious that American democracy would be a very different system without local governments that enjoy a great measure of autonomy.

[1] From this point forward the term 'local governments' means state and local, except where the context clearly implies the more restricted meaning of a city, town, county, etc. There is no generally accepted word to cover both state and local; local, therefore, will have to do the work of two.

Conflict: Diversity and De-nationalization

If one cannot speak with much confidence about the efficiency of local governments as administrative units, one can say more about their efficiency as instruments of democracy. To begin with, how does the existence of 38 thousand local territorial governments affect the course and severity of political conflicts?

The contributions of local government are, I think, two. Local governments make it possible for different groups of citizens to arrive at different solutions to problems. And they reduce the strain on the national political system by keeping many questions out of the national arena.

It is a great and inescapable defect in any system of rule by majorities that, on all questions in which the policy of a minority conflicts with the policy preferred by a majority, neither can prevail without frustrating the desires of the other. In this respect the hypothetical universe of democracy is rather different from the hypothetical universe of a free market; the hypothetical citizen is not equivalent to the hypothetical consumer. In a model 'free' market it does not matter that in my role as consumer I prefer buying books to phonograph records, while you prefer records to books. Within broad legal limits, we may both spend our incomes as we please, and the market will respond. In the market, differences among individuals in tastes and values need not lead to conflict among them.

Why not, then, substitute the market for the government? The most important reason is that there are a great many matters which the mechanisms of the marketplace are ill equipped to handle—including the sovereign question as to what should and what should not be left to the market. If I as a citizen wish to raise taxes and spend more money in order to construct new schools, and if you prefer lower taxes and no new schools, we cannot both get what we want. We cannot, that is, if we are in exactly the same political system. But if you and the people who think like you are in one political system, while I and other like-minded people are in another, we can perhaps both have what we want. In this way we could both be free to go our own different ways; both our governments might enjoy the full consent of all their citizens. Here is the kernel of truth in Rousseau's belief that small autonomous democracies consisting of like-minded citizens offer the greatest promise of freedom and self-government.

Their local governments permit Americans to take or to keep many questions out of the great arena of national politics, and therefore out of a strictly either-or kind of conflict; they make it possible for Americans to deal with many problems in different ways, ways presumably more in harmony with local tastes and values than any national solution could possibly be. To this extent, the presence of a vast network of local governments with a good deal of autonomy has probably reduced by a considerable margin the severity of conflict that a wholly national system would run into. By *de-nationalizing* many conflicts, local governments can reduce the strain on national political institutions. The importance of de-nationalizing conflicts can hardly be over-estimated, particularly in a large country like the United States where there is great diversity in resources and local problems.

Yet the experience of the United States with the question of the role of the Negro in American life also suggests some limit on the process of denationalizing conflicts. . . . When the question of the place of Negroes in American life became nationalized, as it did in the 1850s and again a century later in the 1940s, that question turned into one of the most explosive issues in American politics. In the first case, nationalizing the conflict led directly to civil war; in the second, to violence and federal troops, to Little Rock, Freedom Riders, murders in Mississippi, demonstrations, Selma, and passage of Civil Rights Acts in 1957, 1960, 1964 and 1965.

This experience reveals some of the limits to the process of de-nationalizing conflicts. It is quite one thing to de-nationalize a dispute by allowing various groups of like-minded people to follow their own desires; but it is quite another to take a dispute out of the national arena in order to hand it over to local despots, as we Americans did in the case of the Negro for all except a few decades in our national history.

The case of the Negro is, admittedly, an extreme one, and it is worth keeping that fact in mind. It is an extreme case partly because as both slave and freeman, the Negro lacked allies, at least in substantial numbers, outside the South. Members of a minority who feel oppressed in their localities would ordinarily search for allies in the national political arena, and they would count on their allies to keep the dispute alive in the Congress and in presidential elections—in short, to prevent the conflict from becoming fully de-nationalized. Today, Southern Negroes have no lack of allies outside the South—nor, for that matter, in the South itself; consequently it would be impossible to de-nationalize that conflict today. . . .

With these reservations in mind, it is nonetheless true that the existence of local government with a considerable measure of autonomy does permit extensive variations among communities in the way they carry on their activities. There are differences in the variety and range of functions. But perhaps more common are differences in levels of expenditure,[2] in emphasis, in administrative and political styles, in the sorts of people who hold office, and in their attitudes. Educational facilities, public health, unemployment compensation, hospital care, city planning, community redevelopment and dozens of other activities vary enormously in quality and quantity from state to state and even from locality to locality. The differences are mainly a function of the resources available; but not entirely. For example, in 1961, state expenditures for public schools were in rough proportion to state income per capita in twenty-seven states, but markedly high in relation to income in eleven states, and markedly

---

[2] *E.g.* in 1961, average payments per recipients under six state welfare programs varied as follows:

U.S. Average	$116.68	$67.85	,73.36	$68.19	$65.13	$33.84
High State	178.57	96.51	126.45	132.90	110.76	42.32
Low State	36.38	35.40	38.43	34.85	12.89	21.24

SOURCE: *Politics in the American States, A Comparative Analysis,* Herbert Jacob and Kenneth N. Vines, eds., Boston, Little, Brown and Company, 1965, Table 4, p. 389.

low in ten states. Or, to take another example from the field of education, in New England private schools, colleges, and universities have played a much more significant part than they do in the Middle West, where resources have been poured almost exclusively into public education.

American local governments have, then, permitted an important measure of local variety and heterogeneity. In so doing, doubtless they have reduced the strain on national institutions. People are able to work out many of their problems in their states and localities, finding solutions which would lead to interminable debate and conflict if they were imposed uniformly throughout the United States. Even though the most pressing questions of the day cannot be denationalized, the existence of local autonomy helps to free the national arena for precisely these 'national' issues.

The Distribution of Power Among Leaders

Alexis de Tocqueville was deeply concerned with discovering the answer to the question: How, if at all, can liberty and democracy be maintained in a society of equals? Tocqueville was both fascinated and repelled by the Janusface of equality. An increasing equality was, he thought, not only inevitable in America and Europe; it was also a necessary condition for democracy. At the same time, Tocqueville, like Aristotle, believed that extensive political, economic, and social equalities created a natural political environment for the tyrant. Thus he formulated a dilemma for democrats: A necessary condition for democracy is also a condition that facilitates despotism. The whole of the two-volume *Democracy in America* can be read as an exploration of the circumstances in which tyranny might be avoided and liberal democracy preserved in a society of equals.

The problem, as Tocqueville saw it, was this: In a society of equals, there are no intermediate institutions or classes with enough power to prevent the rise of a despot. Having eliminated aristocracy, a society of equals needs institutions to perform the political function that Tocqueville attributed, perhaps, over-generously, to a well established aristocracy—some force to stand in the way of the aspiring despot. In a nation of equals, no individual is strong enough to stop the despot; and citizens are incapable of acting as a body except through leaders. Even should citizens want to oppose the despot (Tocqueville thought that they probably would not), in the absence of an intermediate stratum of leaders they would be impotent. It was a haunting and evocative picture that Tocqueville painted of that peculiar tyranny in which democracy might one day culminate, the tyranny of an equal people united under a popular leader, the special tyranny that was appropriate to democracy because it would thrive on the very equality so indispensable to democracy.

I think, then, that the species of oppression by which democratic nations are menaced is unlike anything that ever before existed in the world; our contemporaries will find no prototype of it in their memories. I seek in vain for an expression that will accurately convey the whole of the idea I have formed of it; the old words despotism and tyranny are inappropriate: the thing itself is new, and since I cannot name, I must attempt to define it.

I seek to trace the novel features under which despotism may appear in the world. The first thing that strikes the observation is an innumerable multitude of men, all equal and alike, incessantly endeavoring to procure the petty and paltry pleasures with which they glut their lives. Each of them, living apart, is as a stranger to the fate of all the rest; his children and his private friends constitute to him the whole of mankind. As for the rest of his fellow citizens, he is close to them, but does not see them; he touches them, but does not feel them; he exists only in himself and for himself alone; and if his kindred still remain to him, he may be said at any rate to have lost his country.

Above this race of men stands an immense and tutelary power, which takes upon itself alone to secure their gratifications and to watch over their fate. That power is absolute, minute, regular, provident, and mild. It would be like the authority of a parent if, like that authority, its object was to prepare men for manhood; but it seeks, on the contrary, to keep them in perpetual childhood: it is well content that the people should rejoice, provided they think of nothing but rejoicing. For their happiness such a government willingly labors, but it chooses to be the sole agent and the only arbiter of that happiness; it provides for their security, foresees and supplies their necessities, facilitates their pleasures, manages their principal concerns, directs their industry, regulates the descent of property, and subdivides their inheritances: what remains, but to spare them all the care of thinking and all the trouble of living?

Thus it every day renders the exercise of the free agency of man less useful and less frequent; it circumscribes the will within a narrower range and gradually robs a man of all these uses of himself. The principle of equality has prepared men for these things; it has predisposed men to endure them and often to look on them as benefits.

After having thus successively taken each member of the community in its powerful grasp and fashioned him at will, the supreme power then extends its arm over the whole community. It covers the surface of society with a network of small complicated rules, minute and uniform, through which the most original minds and the most energetic characters cannot penetrate, to rise above the crowd. The will of man is not shattered, but softened, bent, and guided; men are seldom forced by it to act, but they are constantly restrained from acting. Such a power does not destroy, but it prevents existence; it does not tyrannize, but it compresses, enervates, extinguishes, and stupefies a people, till each nation is reduced to nothing better than a flock of timid and industrious animals, of which the government is the shepherd.[3]

In spite of his melancholic vision of the possible fate of democratic societies, Tocqueville was hopeful about the United States—precisely because Americans had not destroyed the intermediate institutions, the democratic

[3] Alexis de Tocqueville, *Democracy in America*, Vol. 2, New York, Vintage Books, 1955, pp. 336-337.

alternatives to aristocracy. Indeed, Americans had not only conserved and strengthened certain old institutions; they had even created some new ones. In the power, autonomy, and self-consciousness of the legal profession, in the freedom of the press, in a variety of private associations, political and non-political, Americans had, he thought, developed their substitutes for the political functions of an aristocracy as an offset to tyranny. Constitutional arrangements themselves had added even more barriers to halt the eager tyrant. Among these constitutionally created barriers were, naturally, the federal system and the tradition of local self-government.

Looking back from our present perspective, what can we say to Tocqueville's judgment? Do state and local governments help to tame our political leaders?

The first and most obvious contribution of local representative institutions is to provide a training ground in which political leaders learn the political arts required in a democratic republic. In Almond's terminology, local institutions carry on the functions of political socialization and recruitment.[4] The enormous number and variety of governments in the United States, many of them with elective offices and many involved in some way with party or factional politics, provide a vast school of politics that turns out a sizeable stratum of sub-leaders with at least modest political skills. Many of the leaders who go into national politics are drawn from this pool of leaders trained in local and state politics; it is this pool, too, that often furnishes the local leaders in moments of emergency—when, for example, a possible unjust local regulation threatens to become a reality and citizens feel the need to act.

Thus, of the twelve men elected President in this century, all except three —Taft, Hoover, and Eisenhower—had previously held elective political office. Of the nine with experience in an elective office, six had held office as governor or member of the state legislature. A large proportion of congressional leaders have also held a state office of some kind, usually an elective office.

Just as being Senator or Governor is the best public position from which to win the Presidency, so, too, the Senate itself recruits a large share of its membership from the House and from state or local offices.

Most state governors first learn their craft in state and local politics. Out of almost one thousand governors elected in the United States from 1870–1950, slightly over half had previously been in the state legislature, a fifth had held local elective office, and nearly a fifth had held some statewide elective office.

The state and local governments also help to provide a secure base to which opposition may retire when it has suffered defeat elsewhere, in order to sally forth and challenge its opponents at the next election. If the two major parties are highly competitive at the national level, perhaps the weaker competition and even the numerous local party monopolies are the price to be paid. In the thirty-six-year period from McKinley's election in 1896 to Franklin Roosevelt's election in 1932, the Democratic party enjoyed only eight years in

---

[4] Gabriel A. Almond, "A Functional Approach to Competitive Politics," in Almond and Coleman, *The Politics of the Developing Areas,* Princeton University Press, Princeton, New Jersey, 1960.

the White House; it had a majority in the Senate during only six years. Yet, thanks to their secure fortress in the South and their bastions in northern cities like New York, Boston, and Chicago, they remained a formidable party at every election and were able to organize the national campaign in 1932 that brought Roosevelt into office for the first of his four terms. The Republicans recovered from the devastation of Roosevelt's famous landslide in 1936 because their state and local party strongholds were never completely over-run. By 1938 they were, in coalition with Southern Democrats, powerful enough to bring further New Deal reforms to a halt. Within individual states the situation is often much the same: The party or faction that controls the state house encounters its toughest opposition in the big cities.

Finally, the state and local governments have helped to maintain the American pattern of pluralistic power. Political power is pluralistic in the sense that there exist many different sets of leaders; each set has somewhat different objectives from the others, each has access to its own political resources, each is relatively independent of the others. There does not exist a single set of all-powerful leaders who are wholly agreed on their major goals and who have enough power to achieve their major goals. Ordinarily, the making of government policies require a coalition of different sets of leaders who have diverging goals. In this situation, it is probably easier for leaders to be effective in a negative way, by blocking other leaders, than in a positive way, by achieving their own goals. Positive leadership generally requires action by the chief executive, the President, governor, or mayor; it is the chief executive who can give impetus and drive to the system, who is the coalition builder and the central coordinator.

The state and local governments have undoubtedly contributed to this pattern, though it is not easy to distinguish the special effects of federalism and local representative institutions. State and local governments have provided a number of centers of power whose autonomy is strongly protected by constitutional and political traditions. A governor of a state or the mayor of a large city may not be the political equal of a President (at least not often); but he is most assuredly not a subordinate. In dealing with a governor or a mayor, a President rarely if ever commands; he negotiates; he may even plead. Here, then, is a part of the intermediate stratum of leadership that Tocqueville looked to as a barrier to tyranny.

The state and local governments have contributed something further to the pluralistic pattern of power. They have increased the options available to citizens. Citizens who find one group of leaders unsympathetic to their wishes can often turn to another group that influences a different level or sector of government. Thus a group that finds its needs ignored at the local level may turn to the state or to the federal government; the system also works the other way round. In its earlier years, for example, the American labor movement, often blocked in its efforts to win national legislation, turned to state governments to lead the way in the regulations of the working day, workmen's compensation, employment of women and children, and unemployment compensation. In recent decades, it has more often concentrated its efforts for positive gains on the national government, where it is assured of more sympathetic attention than in many of the states. At the state level, the labor movement has grown more concerned with occasional negative actions—such as blocking laws limiting the right to strike.

It is permissible, certainly, to argue over the merits of this pluralistic distribution of power. It makes for a politics that depends more upon bargaining than upon hierarchy; that resolves conflicts more by negotiation and compromise than by unilateral decision; that brings about reform more through mutual adjustment and a gradual accumulation of incremental changes than through sweeping programs of comprehensive and coordinated reconstruction. As in other political systems, leaders seek to accumulate power. But the system rarely yields unchecked power to leaders, and rarely leaves any group of citizens powerless. To this extent, the accent of the system is not so much on power as on consent.

Self-Government: The Darker Side

How much do the state and local governments contribute to democracy by enlarging the area of self-government? In particular, to what extent do local elections help citizens to participate in local decisions and to elect leaders responsive to their wishes?

As with the criterion of efficiency, the problem posed by these questions is to find a suitable yardstick with which we can compare local governments.

There can be no question that local governments fall very far short of ideal democracy. But perhaps a more useful comparison is with the national government, since both sets of governments exist within the same general political culture and society. In two respects, local politics in the United States seem to operate at lower levels of performance than national politics. In the first place, party competition is weaker at local levels than at the national level. The frequency of two-party competition, in fact, is roughly correlated with the size of the political unit: it declines from the national arena to statewide contests for U.S. Senator, governor and other statewide elective offices, and declines again from statewide elections to contests in smaller units—congressional districts, cities, and towns. Though we do not have the data one would need to confirm the hunch, there is every reason to suppose that two-party competition is rarest of all in the smallest units: wards, councilmanic districts, state legislative districts, and the like. To overstate the point: Effective contests for office and votes in a larger area do not result from effective electoral contests between the parties in the smaller areas; they are produced by parties that are highly unequal in strength in the smaller units. The smaller the area, evidently, the more difficult it is for oppositions to challenge incumbents by presenting a rival slate at elections.

The principle that the smaller the area the less the chances of two-party competition is quite evident from the data. Nationally, the Democratic and Republican parties are highly competitive. The Presidency is contested vigorously in great nationwide campaigns; the outcome is always to some extent in doubt; over the years the Presidency shifts back and forth from one party to the other. The Congress, too, is the site of considerable party competition. Neither party can take for granted that it will control either the Presidency or the Congress after the next election.

In many states, though by no means all, party competition is a good deal weaker than it is in the national arena. For example, between 1914 and 1954, in six states of the Old South the Republicans did not win a single election for governor, United States Senator, or presidential electors. During the same period, the Democrats won no elections in the northern state of Vermont. In five more southern states and one northern state (Maine), the second party did not win more than one election out of every ten. In another nine states, the second party won fewer than one election out of four. . . .

Using elections for governor and for the members of each house of the legislature from 1946 to 1963, Austin Ranney classified the party systems of the fifty states by averaging:

> four basic figures: (1) the average per cent of the popular vote won by Democratic gubernatorial candidates; (2) the average per cent of the seats in the state senate held by the Democrats; (3) the average per cent of the seats in the state house of representatives held by the Democrats; and (4) the per cent of all terms for governor, senate, and house in which the Democrats had control.

His classification of the fifty states was as follows:

> One-party Democratic (.90 or higher): 8 states.
> Modified one-party Democratic (.70 to .8999): 9 states.
> Two party (.30 to .6999): 25 states.
> Modified one-party Republican (.10 to .2999): 8 states.
> One-party Republican (less than .10): no states.[5]

Not only is competition greater in the national arena than in statewide contests; it is also greater in state-wide elections than in smaller units. Thus in the presidential election of 1960, the Democratic percentage of the vote for President was between 45-55 per cent in two out of three states but in only about one out of three congressional districts. Similarly, elections for U.S. Senator are more closely contested than elections for the House of Representatives.

In the towns, cities, counties, and state legislative districts, party competition is probably even weaker. Unfortunately, we lack good data with which to test this conjecture. But we do know that in a very high proportion of American cities elections are required by law to be nonpartisan. The name of a political party cannot appear on the ballot. In two states, Minnesota and Nebraska, elections to the state legislature are legally non-partisan. In some regions of the country, practically every city over twenty-five thousand requires non-partisan elections for local offices. Even in cities where elections are formally and actually contested by both parties, the second party is often weak and rarely if ever wins the mayor's office or a majority of councilmen.

All this does not mean, of course, that in these states and cities there is no active competition for public office. There is. Where the second party is weak, competition takes place *within* the dominant party. Yet even when intra-party conflict is sharp, it must necessarily occur not between highly or-

[5] "Parties in State Politics," in Jacob and Vines, *op. cit.,* pp. 64-65.

ganized parties but between individuals or loose factions. To be sure, in some one-party states, as in Louisiana over an extended period, two rival factions within the same party may perform many of the functions of political parties. In general, however, the absence of sharp competition for office by organized political parties seems to accentuate the significance of personal qualities and to diminish emphasis on policies.

If local governments fall somewhat short of the national government in the extent to which two or more organized parties compete vigorously to win elections and gain control over the policy-making machinery of government, they also seem to evoke less participation by citizens than the national government. In this respect, the local governments have disappointed the hopes of democratic ideologues like Jefferson who believed that the true centers of American democracy would be the local governments, which would attend to the problems of daily life of most interest and importance to the citizen, and, lying within easy reach, would be his most responsive and responsible instruments of self-government.

So far as one can judge from available data, citizens are less active in state and local elections than in national elections. Although the evidence is by no means all one-sided, one fact is clear: Presidential elections attract a larger number of voters (and probably much more attention) than most elections to state and local offices. Thus in the eighteen largest cities in the period 1948–1952, the vote in mayoralty elections ran from 10 to 30 per cent behind the vote in presidential elections (Table 2).

However, since all contests, including those for the House and Senate in midterm elections, fare badly in comparison with the presidential contest, it may be that participation in state and local elections is about as high as in off-year Congressional elections. . . .

Thus the evidence points to several conclusions, mainly negative. It is not true, as an enthusiastic follower of Rousseau or Jefferson might hold, that the

TABLE 2. *Average Turnout in Mayoralty and Presidential Elections in Large Cities, 1948-1952*

City	Mayoralty	Presidential	City	Mayoralty	Presidential
Chicago	51.5%	71.3%	New Orleans	40.5%	38.6%
Pittsburgh	50.5	61.3	Minneapolis	37.0	63.8
Philadelphia	49.8	63.5	Denver	36.7	66.1
Buffalo	49.1	64.2	Cleveland	34.8	53.0
Cincinnati	49.0	61.2	Detroit	33.8	58.0
Boston	47.0	62.6	Baltimore	31.5	46.2
San Francisco	46.3	60.6	Los Angeles	31.3	58.7
New York	42.3	57.7	St. Louis	30.4	59.2
Indianapolis	41.4	63.1	Kansas City	29.9	59.2

Note: Turnout is here measured as the percentage of all persons of 21 years of age or over who vote in general elections. The figure for the Presidential elections is the average of the 1948 and 1952 turnouts; that for the mayoralty elections is an average of the same period.

Source: Edward C. Banfield and James Q. Wilson, *City Politics* (Cambridge, Mass., Harvard University Press and MIT Press, 1963), Table 13, p. 225.

smaller a political unit is, the more its citizens will participate in political affairs. To the extent that voting is a fair measure of participation, the Rousseau-Jefferson hypothesis is definitely not true today. Although there was probably greater variation in patterns of electoral participation in the first part of the nineteenth century than there is today, the Rousseau-Jefferson hypothesis was not confirmed by experience even then. Nor is it true that participation in state and local elections has fallen off as these units have grown in size and as the role of the national government has expanded.

In short, local territorial governments in the United States are not, and evidently never have been, distinctive sites for high levels of civic participation.

The Case for Self-Government

There is no blinking the fact that local democracy—like national democracy—is highly defective. Yet, to right the balance, one needs to consider what democracy would be like in the United States if representative governments did not exist in the states and localities. While one might argue persuasively that the best alternative to what we have now is more self-government, it would be hard to make a good case that, from a democratic point of view, we would be better off with less.

It may be worth asking, then, how the local governments in the United States compare with the national government as institutions of self-government. Are they markedly worse?

Although a precise answer is impossible, the evidence does support three propositions:

First, citizens seem to be about as concerned with local affairs as with national and international affairs.

Second, except by comparison with voting in presidential elections, citizens participate as much in local as in national politics, if not more.

Third, they probably have greater confidence in their capacity to act effectively at local levels.

Concern

It is possible that the state governments may fall into a kind of limbo, being neither so close to the citizen as the government of his town or city nor so conspicuously important as the national government; but there is some persuasive evidence that Americans are concerned with local affairs. Many of the problems that people regard as urgent and important require action by local governments: education, crime, poverty, racial discrimination, housing, parking, streets and highways, to name a few. In a survey conducted in 1956 in the Detroit area, "which is fairly typical of metropolitan publics . . . 19 per cent said they were very interested in foreign affairs, 32 per cent in national domestic affairs, and 44 per cent in local governmental affairs."[6]

In a survey of registered voters in New Haven, Connecticut in 1959, more people seemed to talk about, worry about, and be concerned with local affairs than with state, national or international affairs.

[6] Samuel J. Eldersveld, *Political Parties, A Behavioral Analysis*, Chicago, Rand McNally, 1964, p. 458.

In a national survey in the 1950s, the percentage of Americans who felt that the local governments had some effect or great effect on their day-to-day lives was actually a shade larger than the percentage who felt this way about the national government. As one might expect, more people thought the national government had *great* effect; but more also thought that local government had *some* effect (Table 3). Similarly the percentage who felt that on the whole the activities of local government "tend to improve conditions in this area" was quite high, though a trifle short of the percentage who felt the same way about the activities of national government.

Participation

The relatively lower turnout in local elections than in presidential elections does not prove that Americans are less involved in local affairs. For one thing, the presidential contest is *sui generis*. As I have already suggested, the turnout

TABLE 3. *Estimated Degree of Impact of National and Local Governments on Daily Life*

	National Government	*Local Governments*
Great effect	41%	35%
Some effect	44	53
No effect	11	10
Other, don't know, etc.	4	2
	100%	100%
Total number of cases	970	970

Source: Gabriel A. Almond and Sidney Verba, *The Civic Culture: Political Attitudes and Democracy in Five Nations* (Princeton, N.J., Princeton University Press, 1963), pp. 80-81.

in elections for mayors and governors may be no lower than for U.S. Senators and Congressmen in midterm elections. In the second place, even if voters were as involved in local affairs as in national affairs, the lower frequency of sharp two-party competition would probably reduce the turnout at elections, partly because the contest itself would be less exciting, partly because the parties would work less vigorously to get out the vote. In elections for governor and U.S. Senator, for example, the turnout from 1956–1960 was considerably higher in the two-party states than in the modified one-party Democratic states; in the modified one-party Democratic states it was more than twice as high as in the one-party Democratic states. In the third place, voting is only one form of participation; some of the other ways of participating in politics are more easily carried on at the local than at the national level: getting in touch with one's councilman about a torn-up street is a good deal easier than getting in touch with one's Congressman or Senator, or the President about the war in Vietnam.

Citizen Effectiveness

Evidence does suggest that Americans look on their local governments as more accessible, more manageable, more responsive. In an exhaustive study of the political attitudes of fifteen lower-middle-class citizens in an Eastern city, Robert Lane found:

> . . . The fact is that these men were pretty discouraged by the idea of doing something about any big problem . . . Eastport's common men find themselves politically impotent on most important specific issues, do not petition or write letters with any frequency, are dubious of the wisdom of the electorate on these issues, see elections as only partially successful instruments for imparting instructions to candidates, find themselves often confused by the complexity of public affairs, and tend to think of elected officials as better judges of policy than they themselves are.

Yet far from being alienated, most of these fifteen men felt that they were politically important. How, Lane asks,

> . . . do they come to have this sense of political importance? One reason is that many of them have political connections and for local matters they have influence, can get close to somebody who may pretend to more authority than he has but who conveys to his circle of acquaintances the sense that they are in communication with important people when they speak to him.[7]

There are also other reasons, of course; but this sense of accessibility and responsiveness may be an important one. The national survey taken in the 1950s, mentioned a moment ago, tends to confirm the hunch that the closeness, accessibility, and comprehensibility of local government enhances the confidence of citizens that they can *do something* about local affairs. Almost two out of three respondents agreed and only a third disagreed with the statement that "politics and government are so complicated that the average man cannot really understand what is going on." Yet the number who said that they understood "local issues in this town or part of the country" very well was three times as large as the number who said they understood "the important national and international issues facing the country" very well. In fact, over half the respondents said that they did not understand national and international issues at all or not so well, compared with only a third who felt this way about local issues (Table 4).

Nor is it only a matter of being able to grasp local issues better; citizens also seem to think that they can act more effectively at the local level. To be sure, not many ever do act at either local or national levels. In fact, seven out of ten respondents in the survey just cited said they had never tried to influence a local decision, while eight out of ten said they had never tried to influence the Congress. Yet many were confident that, if the need arose, they would act and might even be successful. What did they think they could do, they were asked, if a law or regulation which they considered "very unjust or harmful" were being considered by the local government or by Congress? The number who said that it was very likely or moderately likely that they would do some-

---

[7] Robert Lane, *Political Ideology,* p. 165.

TABLE 4. The Sense of Understanding of Issues

	National and International	Local Issues
Very well	7%	21%
Moderately well	38	44
Not so well	37	23
Not at all	14	10
Depends, other, don't know, etc.	4	2
	100%	100%
Total number of cases	970	970

Source: Almond and Verba, *op. cit.*

thing about the law or regulation was slightly larger in the case of a local law (49 per cent) than for a national law (42 per cent). The number who said that it was not at all likely that they would do something about an unjust law or regulation was a little less for local laws (27 per cent) than for national laws (33 per cent). The percentages who expected that they could be successful in their efforts were somewhat higher in the case of the local law (Table 5).

Even if local governments fall a long way short of potential and ideal, they do provide channels through which citizens may express their views on local matters when they have an urge to do so. In the 1959 survey in New Haven, mentioned earlier, a sample of registered voters was asked: "Have you ever contacted any local public officials or politicians to let them know what you

TABLE 5. If you made an effort to change a proposed law or regulation you considered very unjust or harmful, how likely is it that you would succeed?

	Local Regulation	National Law
Very likely or moderately likely	28%	11%
Somewhat unlikely	15	18
Not at all likely, impossible	25	36
Likely only if others joined in	25	24
Other, don't know	6	9
	100%	100%
Total cases	970	970

Source: Almond and Verba, *op. cit.*

were interested in?" More than one out of every four registered voters said they had. Sixteen per cent said they had had some contact with political or governmental officials in New Haven in the past year. In fact, 8 per cent said they had been in touch with the Mayor at some time and 11 per cent with some other city official. Admittedly, these are not the high percentages one might hope for in a democratic polity, but to the extent that local channels do exist and are used by citizens, the domain of self government is enlarged.

"One Man, One Vote"

Legislative Apportionment
REYNOLDS *V.* SIMS
377 U.S. 533 (1964)

In eight cases, decided on June 15, 1964, the apportionment of state legislatures in six states (Alabama, New York, Maryland, Virginia, Delaware and Colorado) was attacked as violative of the provision of the Fourteenth Amendment of the Constitution which provides that "no state shall deny to any person within its jurisdiction the equal protection of the laws." In each case, but one, a gross inequality of population in state legislative districts existed with the result that a vote in one district was, for all practical purposes, worth much more than a vote in other districts.

MR. CHIEF JUSTICE WARREN delivered the opinion of the Court.

Undeniably the Constitution of the United States protects the right of all qualified citizens to vote, in state as well as in federal elections. A consistent line of decisions by this Court in cases involving attempts to deny or restrict the right of suffrage has made this indelibly clear. . . . The right to vote freely for the candidate of one's choice is of the essence of a democratic society, and any restrictions on that right strike at the heart of representative government. And the right of suffrage can be denied by a debasement or dilution of the weight of a citizen's vote just as effectively as by wholly prohibiting the free exercise of the franchise. . . .

In *Baker* v. *Carr,* 369 U.S. 186, we held that a claim asserted under the Equal Protection Clause challenging the constitutionality of a State's apportionment of seats in its legislature, on the ground that the right to vote of certain citizens was effectively impaired since debased and diluted in effect, presented a justiciable controversy subject to adjudication by federal courts. The spate of similar cases filed and decided by lower courts since our decision in *Baker* amply shows that the problem of state legislative malapportionment is one that is perceived to exist in a large number of the States.[1] In *Baker,* a suit

[1] Litigation challenging the constitutionality of state legislative apportionment schemes had been instituted in at least 34 States prior to end of 1962—within nine months of our decision in *Baker v. Carr.*

involving an attack on the apportionment of seats in the Tennessee Legislature, we remanded to the District Court, which had dismissed the action, for consideration on the merits. We intimated no view as to the proper constitutional standards for evaluating the validity of a state legislative apportionment scheme. Nor did we give any consideration to the question of appropriate remedies. Rather, we simply stated:

> Beyond noting that we have no cause at this stage to doubt the District Court will be able to fashion relief if violations of constitutional rights are found, it is improper now to consider what remedy would be most appropriate if appellants prevail at trial. . . .

In *Gray* v. *Sanders,* 372 U.S. 368, we held that the Georgia county unit system, applicable in statewide primary elections, was unconstitutional since it resulted in a dilution of the weight of the votes of certain Georgia voters merely because of where they resided. . . .

In *Wesberry* v. *Sanders,* 376 U.S. 1, decided earlier this Term, we held that attacks on the constitutionality of congressional districting plans enacted by state legislatures do not present nonjusticiable questions and should not be dismissed generally for "want of equity." We determined that the constitutional test for the validity of congressional districting schemes was one of substantial equality of population among the various districts established by a state legislature for the election of members of the Federal House of Representatives.

In that case we decided that an apportionment of congressional seats which "contracts the value of some votes and expands that of others" is unconstitutional, since "the Federal Constitution intends that when qualified voters elect members of Congress each vote be given as much weight as any other vote. . . ." We concluded that the constitutional prescription for election of members of the House of Representatives "by the People," construed in its historical context, "means that as nearly as is practicable one man's vote in a congressional election is to be worth as much as another's." We further stated:

> It would defeat the principle solemnly embodied in the Great Compromise—equal representation in the House for equal numbers of people —for us to hold that, within the States, legislatures may draw the lines of congressional districts in such a way as to give some voters a greater voice in choosing a Congressman than others.

We found further, in *Wesberry,* that "our Constitution's plain objective" was that "of making equal representation for equal numbers of people the fundamental goal. . . ." We conclude by stating:

> No right is more precious in a free country than that of having a voice in the election of those who make the laws under which, as good citizens, we must live. Other rights, even the most basic, are illusory if the right to vote is undermined. Our Constitution leaves no room for classification of people in a way that unnecessarily abridges this right.

Gray and *Wesberry* are of course not dispositive of or directly controlling on our decision in these cases involving state legislative apportionment controversies. Admittedly, those decisions, in which we held that, in statewide and in congressional elections, one person's vote must be counted equally with those of all other voters in a State, were based on different constitutional considerations and were addressed to rather distinct problems. But neither are they wholly inapposite. . . . Our decision in *Wesberry* was of course grounded on that language of the Constitution which prescribes that members of the Federal House of Representatives are to be chosen "by the People," while attacks on state legislative apportionment schemes, such as that involved in the instant cases, are principally based on the Equal Protection Clause of the Fourteenth Amendment. Nevertheless, *Wesberry* clearly established that the fundamental principle of representative government in this country is one of equal representation for equal numbers of people, without regard to race, sex, economic status, or place of residence within a State. Our problem, then, is to ascertain, in the instant cases, whether there are any constitutionally cognizable principles which would justify departures from the basic standards of equality among voters in the apportionment of seats in state legislatures.

A predominant consideration in determining whether a State's legislative apportionment scheme constitutes an invidious discrimination violative of rights asserted under the Equal Protection Clause is that the rights allegedly impaired are individual and personal in nature. . . . Undoubtedly, the right of suffrage is a fundamental matter in a free and democratic society. Especially since the right to exercise the franchise in a free and unimpaired manner is preservative of other basic civil and political rights, any alleged infringement of the right of citizens to vote must be carefully and meticulously scrutinized. Almost a century ago, in *Yick Wo* v. *Hopkins*, 118 U.S. 356, the Court referred to "the political franchise of voting" as "a fundamental political right, because preservative of all rights."

Legislators represent people, not trees or acres. Legislators are elected by voters, not farms or cities or economic interests. As long as ours is a representative form of government, and our legislatures are those instruments of government elected directly by and directly representative of the people, the right to elect legislators in a free and unimpaired fashion is a bedrock of our political system. It could hardly be gainsaid that a constitutional claim had been asserted by an allegation that certain otherwise qualified voters had been entirely prohibited from voting for members of their state legislature. And, if a State should provide that the votes of citizens in one part of the State should be given two times, or five times, or 10 times the weight of votes of citizens in another part of the State, it could hardly be contended that the right to vote of those residing in the disfavored areas had not been effectively diluted. It would appear extraordinary to suggest that a state could be constitutionally permitted to enact a law providing that certain of the state's voters could vote two, five, or 10 times for their legislative representatives, while voters living elsewhere could vote only once. And it is inconceivable that a state law to the effect that, in counting votes for legislators, the votes of citizens in one part of the State would be multiplied by two, five, or 10, while the votes of persons in another area would be counted only at face value, could be constitutionally sustainable. Of course, the effect of state legislative districting schemes which give the same number of representatives to unequal numbers of constituents is identical. Overweighting and overvaluation of the votes of those living here has the certain effect of dilution and undervaluation of the votes of those living there. The resulting discrimination against those individual voters living in disfavored areas is easily demonstrable mathematically. Their right to vote is simply not the same right to vote as that of those living in a favored part of the State. Two, five, or 10 or them must vote before the effect of their voting is equivalent to that of their favored neighbor. Weighting the votes of citizens differently, by any method or means, merely because of where they happen to reside, hardly seems justifiable. One must be ever aware that the Constitution forbids "sophisticated as well as simple-minded modes of discrimination." *Lane* v. *Wilson,* 307 U.S. 268, 275, *Gomillion* v. *Lightfoot,* 364 U.S. 339, 342. . . .

Representative government is in essence self-government through the medium of elected representatives of the people, and each and every citizen has an inalienable right to full and effective participation in the political processes of his State's legislative bodies. Most citizens can achieve this participation only as qualified voters through the election of legislators to represent them. Full and effective participation by all citizens in state government requires, therefore, that each citizen has an equally effective voice in the election of members of his state legislature. Modern and viable state government needs, and the Constitution demands, no less.

Logically, in a society ostensibly grounded on representative government, it would seem reasonable that a majority of the people of a State could elect a majority of that State's legislators. To conclude differently, and to sanction minority control of state legislative bodies, would appear to deny majority rights in a way that far surpasses any possible denial of minority rights that might otherwise be thought to result. Since legislatures are responsible for enacting laws by which all citizens are to be governed, they should be bodies which are collectively responsive to the popular will. And the concept of equal protection has been traditionally viewed as requiring the uniform treatment of persons standing in the same relation to the governmental action questioned or challenged. With respect to the allocation of legislative representation, all voters, as citizens of a State, stand in the same relation regardless of where they live. Any suggested criteria for the differentiation of citizens are insufficient to justify any discrimination, as to the weight of their votes, unless relevant to the permissible purposes of legislative apportionment. Since the achieving of fair and effective representation for all citizens is concededly the basic aim of legislative apportionment, we conclude that the Equal Protection Clause guarantees the opportunity for equal participation by all voters in the election of state legislators. Diluting the weight of votes because of place of residence impairs basic constitutional rights under the Fourteenth Amendment just as much as invidious discriminations based upon factors such as race, *Brown* v. *Board of Education,* 347 U.S. 483, or economic status, *Griffin* v. *Illinois,* 351 U.S. 12, *Douglas* v. *California,* 372 U.S. 353. Our constitutional system amply provides for the protection of minorities by means other than giving them majority control of state legislatures. And the democratic ideals of equality and majority rule, which have served this Nation so well in the past, are hardly of any less significance for the present and the future.

We are told that the matter of apportioning representation in a state legislature is a complex and many-faceted one. We are advised that States can rationally consider factors other than population in apportioning legislative representation. We are admonished not to restrict the power of the States to impose differing views as to political philosophy on their citizens. We are cautioned about the dangers of entering into political thickets and mathematical quagmires. Our answer is this: a denial of constitutionally protected rights demands judicial protection; our oath and our office require no less of us. . . . To the extent that a citizen's right to vote is debased, he is that much less a citizen. The fact that an individual lives here or there is not a legitimate reason for overweighting or diluting the efficacy of his vote. The complexions of societies and civilizations change, often with amazing rapidity. A nation once primarily rural in character becomes predominantly urban.[2] Representation schemes once fair and equitable become archaic and outdated. But the basic principle of representative government remains, and must remain, unchanged —the weight of a citizen's vote cannot be made to depend on where he lives. Population is, of necessity, the starting point for consideration and the controlling criterion for judgment in legislative apportionment controversies. A citizen, a qualified voter, is no more nor no less so because he lives in the city or on the farm. This is the clear and strong command of our Constitution's Equal Protection Clause. This is an essential part of the concept of a government of laws and not men. This is at the heart of Lincoln's vision of "government of the people, by the people, [and] for the people." The Equal Protection Clause demands no less than substantially equal state legislative representation for all citizens, of all places as well as of all races.

We hold that, as a basic constitutional standard, the Equal Protection Clause requires that the seats in both houses of a bicameral state legislature must be apportioned on a population basis. Simply stated, an individual's right to vote for state legislators is unconstitutionally impaired when its weight is in a substantial fashion diluted when compared with votes of citizens living in other parts of the State. . . .

Much has been written since our decision in *Baker* v. *Carr* about the applicability of the so-called federal analogy* to state legislative apportionment arrangements. . . .

Attempted reliance on the federal analogy appears often to be little more than an after-the-fact rationalization offered in defense of maladjusted state apportionment arrangements. The original constitutions of 36 of our States provided that representation in both houses of the state legislatures would be based completely, or predominantly, on population. And the Founding Fathers clearly had no intention of establishing a pattern or model for the apportionment of seats in state legislatures when the system of representation in the Federal Congress was adopted. Demonstrative of this is the fact that the

---

[2] Although legislative apportionment controversies are generally viewed as involving urban-rural conflicts, much evidence indicates that presently it is the fast-growing suburban areas which are probably the most seriously underrepresented in many of our state legislatures.

* Representation according to population in the House and equal representation for each state in the Senate. [Eds.].

Northwest Ordinance, adopted in the same year, 1787, as the Federal Constitution, provided for the apportionment of seats in territorial legislatures solely on the basis of population.

The system of representation in the two Houses of the Federal Congress is one ingrained in our Constitution, as part of the law of the land. It is one conceived out of compromise and concession indispensable to the establishment of our federal republic. Arising from unique historical circumstances, it is based on the consideration that in establishing our type of federalism a group of formerly independent States bound themselves together under one national government. . . . The developing history and growth of our republic cannot cloud the fact that, at the time of the inception of the system of representation in the Federal Congress, a compromise between the larger and smaller States on this matter averted a deadlock in the constitutional convention which had threatened to abort the birth of our Nation. . . .

Political subdivisions of States—counties, cities, or whatever—never were and never have been considered as sovereign entities. Rather, they have been traditionally regarded as subordinate governmental instrumentalities created by the State to assist in the carrying out of state governmental functions. . . .

Since we find the so-called federal analogy inapposite to a consideration of the constitutional validity of state legislative apportionment schemes, we necessarily hold that the Equal Protection Clause requires both houses of a state legislature to be apportioned on a population basis. The right of a citizen to equal representation and to have his vote weighted equally with those of all other citizens in the election of members of one house of a bicameral state legislature would amount to little if States could effectively submerge the equal-population principle in the apportionment of seats in the other house.

If such a scheme were permissible, an individual citizen's ability to exercise an effective voice in the only instrument of state government directly representative of the people might be almost as effectively thwarted as if neither house were apportioned on a population basis. Deadlock between the two bodies might result in compromise and concession on some issues. But in all too many cases the more probable result would be frustration of the majority will through minority veto in the house not apportioned on a population basis, stemming directly from the failure to accord adequate overall legislative representation to all of the State's citizens on a nondiscriminatory basis. In summary, we can perceive no constitutional difference, with respect to the geographical distribution of state legislative representation, between the two houses of a bicameral state legislature.

We do not believe that the concept of bicameralism is rendered anachronistic and meaningless when the predominant basis of representation in the two state legislative bodies is required to be the same—population. A prime reason for bicameralism, modernly considered, is to insure mature and deliberate consideration of, and to prevent precipitate action on, proposed legislative measures. Simply because the controlling criterion for apportioning representation is required to be the same in both houses does not mean that there will be no differences in the composition and complexion of the two bodies. Different constituencies can be represented in the two houses. One body could be composed of single-member districts while the other could have at least some multimember districts. The length of terms of the legislators in the separate bodies could differ. The numerical size of the two bodies could be made to differ, even significantly, and the geographical size of districts from which legislators are elected could also be made to differ. And apportionment in one house could be arranged so as to balance off minor inequities in the representation of certain areas in the other house. In summary, these and other factors could be, and are presently in many States, utilized to engender differing complexions and collective attitudes in the two bodies of a state legislature, although both are apportioned substantially on a population basis.

By holding that as a federal constitutional requisite both houses of a state legislature must be apportioned on a population basis, we mean that the Equal Protection Clause requires that a State make an honest and good faith effort to construct districts, in both houses of its legislature, as nearly of equal population as is practicable. We realize that it is a practical impossibility to arrange legislative districts so that each one has an identical number of residents, or citizens, or voters. Mathematical exactness or precision is hardly a workable constitutional requirement. . . .

A State may legitimately desire to maintain the integrity of various political subdivisions, insofar as possible, and provide for compact districts of contiguous territory in designing a legislative apportionment scheme. Valid considerations may underlie such aims. Indiscriminate districting, without any regard for political or natural or historical boundary lines, may be little more than an open invitation to partisan gerrymandering. Single-member districts may be the rule in one State, while another State might desire to achieve some flexibility by creating multimember or floterial districts. Whatever the means of accomplishment, the overriding objective must be substantial equality of population among the various districts, so that the vote of any citizen is approximately equal in weight to that of any other citizen in the State.

[Mr. Justice Clark and Mr. Justice Stewart substantially disagreed with the reasoning of the majority in *Reynolds* v. *Sims* but concurred in the judgment of the Court. However, these Justices dissented in *Lucas* v. *Colorado* which follows hereafter.]

MR. JUSTICE HARLAN, dissenting.

In these cases the Court holds that seats in the legislatures of six States are apportioned in ways that violate the Federal Constitution. Under the Court's ruling it is bound to follow that the legislatures in all but a few of the other 44 States will meet the same fate. These decisions, with *Wesberry* v. *Sanders,* 376 U.S. 1, involving congressional districting by the States, and *Gray* v. *Sanders,* 372 U.S. 368, relating to elections for statewide office, have the effect of placing basic aspects of state political systems under the pervasive overlordship of the federal judiciary. Once again,[3] I must register my protest.

Today's holding is that the Equal Protection Clause of the Fourteenth

---

[3] See *Baker* v. *Carr,* 369 U.S. 186, 330, and the dissenting opinion of Frankfurter, J., in which I joined, *id.,* at 266; *Gray* v. *Sanders,* 372 U.S. 368, 382; *Wesberry* v. *Sanders,* 376 U.S. 1, 20.

Amendment requires every State to structure its legislature so that all the members of each house represent substantially the same number of people; other factors may be given play only to the extent that they do not significantly encroach on this basic "population" principle. Whatever may be thought of this holding as a piece of political ideology—and even on that score the political history and practices of this country from its earliest beginnings leave wide room for debate (see the dissenting opinion of Frankfurter, J., in *Baker* v. *Carr,* 369 U.S. 186, 266, 301-323)—I think it demonstrable that the Fourteenth Amendment does not impose this political tenet on the States or authorize this Court to do so.

The Court's constitutional discussion, found in its opinion in the Alabama cases is remarkable (as, indeed, is that found in the separate opinions of my Brothers STEWART and CLARK) for its failure to address itself at all to the Fourteenth Amendment as a whole or to the legislative history of the Amendment pertinent to the matter at hand. Stripped of aphorisms, the Court's argument boils down to the assertion that petitioners' right to vote has been invidiously "debased" or "diluted" by systems of apportionment which entitle them to vote for fewer legislators than other voters, an assertion which is tied to the Equal Protection Clause only by the constitutionally frail tautology that "equal" means "equal."

Had the Court paused to probe more deeply into the matter, it would have found that the Equal Protection Clause was never intended to inhibit the States in choosing any democratic method they pleased for the apportionment of their legislatures. This is shown by the language of the Fourteenth Amendment taken as a whole, by the understanding of those who proposed and ratified it, and by the political practices of the States at the time the Amendment was adopted. It is confirmed by numerous state and congressional actions since the adoption of the Fourteenth Amendment, and by the common understanding of the Amendment as evidenced by subsequent constitutional amendments and decisions of this Court before *Baker* v. *Carr, supra,* made an abrupt break with the past in 1962.

The failure of the Court to consider any of these matters cannot be excused or explained by any concept of "developing" constitutionalism. It is meaningless to speak of constitutional "development" when both the language and history of the controlling provisions of the Constitution are wholly ignored. Since it can, I think, be shown beyond doubt that state legislative apportionments, as such, are wholly free of constitutional limitations, save such as may be imposed by the Republican Form of Government Clause (Const., Art. IV, § 4), the Court's action now bringing them within the purview of the Fourteenth Amendment amounts to nothing less than an exercise of the amending power by this Court.

So far as the Federal Constitution is concerned, the complaints in these cases should all have been dismissed below for failure to state a cause of action, because what has been alleged or proved shows no violation of any constitutional right. . . .

[In the appendix to his opinion Mr. Justice Harlan quotes from the speeches of eleven members of the House of Representatives and five members of the Senate to support the view that the purpose of the Fourteenth Amendment was to reduce the number of Representatives in the House and the Electoral College vote of states that denied Negro suffrage. Several of these speakers stated that while they would have preferred an unequivocal guarantee of universal suffrage in the Constitution, they were supporting the Fourteenth Amendment as a step in this direction.]

LUCAS *V.* COLORADO
377 U.S. 713 (1964)

The important distinguishing elements in the Colorado case were that: (1) The parties conceded that one house of the Colorado state legislature was apportioned "as nearly equal in population" as may be practical (while a majority of the other house was elected by 33.2 per cent of the population*), and (2) the whole scheme of districting for both houses was approved by a referendum vote of nearly 2 to 1, with a majority obtained in each county, including those urban counties allegedly discriminated against.

MR. CHIEF JUSTICE WARREN delivered the opinion of the Court. . . .

At the November 1962 general election, the Colorado electorate adopted proposed Amendment No. 7 by a vote of 305,700 to 172,725, and defeated proposed Amendment No. 8 by a vote of 311,749 to 149,822. Amendment No. 8, rejected by a majority of the voters, prescribed an apportionment plan pursuant to which seats in both houses of the Colorado Legislature would purportedly be apportioned on a population basis. Amendment No. 7, on the other hand, provided for the apportionment of the House of Representatives on the basis of population, but essentially maintained the existing apportionment in the Senate, which was based on a combination of population and various other factors. . . .

[Additionally,] this case differs from the others decided this date in that the initiative device provides a practicable political remedy to obtain relief against alleged legislative malapportionment in Colorado. An initiated measure proposing a constitutional amendment or a statutory enactment is entitled to be placed on the ballot if the signatures of 8% of those voting for the Secretary of State in the last election are obtained. No geographical distribution of petition signers is required. Initiative and referendum has been frequently utilized throughout Colorado's history.

We find no significance in the fact that a nonjudicial, political remedy may be available for the effectuation of asserted rights to equal representation in a state legislature. Courts sit to adjudicate controversies involving alleged denials of constitutional rights. While a court sitting as a court of equity might be justified in temporarily refraining from the issuance of injunctive relief in an apportionment case in order to allow for resort to an available political remedy,

---

* The dissenting opinion states the percentage as 36 [Eds.].

such as initiative and referendum, individual constitutional rights cannot be deprived, or denied judicial effectuation, because of the existence of a non-judicial remedy through which relief against the alleged malapportionment, which the individual voters seek, might be achieved. An individual's constitutionally protected right to cast an equally weighted vote cannot be denied even by a vote of a majority of a State's electorate, if the apportionment scheme adopted by the voters fails to measure up to the requirements of the Equal Protection Clause.

Manifestly, the fact that an apportionment plan is adopted in a popular referendum is insufficient to sustain its constitutionality or to induce a court of equity to refuse to act. As stated by this Court in *West Virginia State Bd. of Educ.* v. *Barnette,* 319 U.S. 624, 638, "One's right to life, liberty, and property . . . and other fundamental rights may not be submitted to vote; they depend on the outcome of no elections."[1] A citizen's constitutional rights can hardly be infringed simply because a majority of the people choose to do so. We hold that the fact that a challenged legislative apportionment plan was approved by the electorate is without federal constitutional significance, if the scheme adopted fails to satisfy the basic requirements of the Equal Protection Clause, as delineated in our opinion in *Reynolds* v. *Sims.* And we conclude that the fact that a practicably available political remedy, such as initiative and referendum, exists under state law provides justification only for a court of equity to stay its hand temporarily while recourse to such a remedial device is attempted or while proposed initiated measures relating to legislative apportionment are pending and will be submitted to the State's voters at the next election. . . . Accordingly, we reverse the decision of the court below and remand the case for further proceedings consistent with the views stated here and in our opinion in *Reynolds* v. *Sims.*

It is so ordered.

MR. JUSTICE STEWART, whom JUSTICE CLARK joins, dissenting.*

It is important to make clear at the outset what these cases are not about. They have nothing to do with the denial or impairment of any person's right to vote. Nobody's right to vote has been denied. Nobody's right to vote has been restricted. Nobody has been deprived of the right to have his vote counted. The voting right cases which the Court cites are, therefore, completely wide of the mark. Secondly, these cases have nothing to do with the "weighting" or "diluting" of votes cast within any electoral unit. The rule of *Gray* v. *Sanders,* 372 U.S. 368, is, therefore, completely without relevance here. Thirdly, these cases are not concerned with the election of members of the Congress of the United States, governed by Article I of the Constitution. Consequently, the Court's decision in *Wesberry* v. *Sanders,* 376 U.S. 1, throws no light at all on the basic issue now before us.

The question involved in these cases is quite a different one. Simply stated, the question is to what degree, if at all, the Equal Protection Clause of

---

[1] And, as stated by the court in *Hall* v. *St. Helena Parish School Bd.,* 197 F. Supp. 649, 659 (D. C. E. D. La. 1961), aff'd, 368 U.S. 515, "No plebiscite can legalize an unjust discrimination."

* This dissent applied to both the Colorado and New York cases [Eds.].

the Fourteenth Amendment limits each sovereign State's freedom to establish appropriate electoral constituencies from which representatives to the State's bicameral legislative assembly are to be chosen. The Court's answer is a blunt one, and, I think, woefully wrong. The Equal Protection Clause, says the Court, "requires that the seats in both houses of a bicameral state legislature must be apportioned on a population basis."

After searching carefully through the Court's opinions in these and their companion cases, I have been able to find but two reasons offered in support of this rule. First, says the Court, it is "established that the fundamental principle of representative government in this country is one of equal representation for equal numbers of people. . . ." With all respect, I think that this is not correct, simply as a matter of fact. It has been unanswerably demonstrated before now that this "was not the colonial system, it was not the system chosen for the national government by the Constitution, it was not the system exclusively or even predominantly practiced by the States at the time of adoption of the Fourteenth Amendment, it is not predominantly practiced by the States today."[2] Secondly, says the Court, unless legislative districts are equal in population, voters in the more populous districts will suffer a "debasement" amounting to a constitutional injury. As the Court explains it, "To the extent that a citizen's right to vote is debased, he is that much less a citizen." We are not told how or why the vote of a person in a more populated legislative district is "debased," or how or why he is less a citizen, nor is the proposition self-evident. I find it impossible to understand how or why a voter in California, for instance, either feels or is less a citizen than a voter in Nevada, simply because, despite their population disparities, each of those States is represented by two United States Senators.

To put the matter plainly, there is nothing in all the history of this Court's decisions which supports this constitutional rule. The Court's draconian pronouncement, which makes unconstitutional the legislatures of most of the 50 States, finds no support in the words of the Constitution, in any prior decision of this Court, or in the 175-year political history of our Federal Union. With all respect, I am convinced these decisions mark a long step backward into that unhappy era when a majority of the members of this Court were thought by many to have convinced themselves and each other that the demands of the Constitution were to be measured not by what it says, but by their own notions of wise political theory. The rule announced today is at odds with long-established principles of constitutional adjudication under the Equal Protection Clause, and it stifles values of local individuality and initiative vital to the character of the Federal Union which it was the genius of our Constitution to create.

I

What the Court has done is to convert a particular political philosophy into a constitutional rule, binding upon each of the 50 States, from Maine to

---

[2] *Baker v. Carr,* 369 U.S. 186, 266, 301 (Frankfurter, J., dissenting). See also the excellent analysis of the relevant historical materials contained in MR. JUSTICE HARLAN's dissenting opinion filed this day in these and their companion cases.

Hawaii, from Alaska to Texas, without regard and without respect for the many individualized and differentiated characteristics of each State, characteristics stemming from each State's distinct history, distinct geography, distinct distribution of population, and distinct political heritage. My own understanding of the various theories of representative government is that no one theory has ever commanded unanimous assent among political scientists, historians, or others who have considered the problem. But even if it were thought that the rule announced today by the Court is, as a matter of political theory, the most desirable general rule which can be devised as a basis for the make-up of the representative assembly of a typical State, I could not join in the fabrication of a constitutional mandate which imports and forever freezes one theory of political thought into our Constitution, and forever denies to every State any opportunity for enlightened and progressive innovation in the design of its democratic institutions, so as to accommodate within a system of representative government the interests and aspirations of diverse groups of people, without subjecting any group or class to absolute domination by a geographically concentrated or highly organized majority.

Representative government is a process of accommodating group interests through democratic institutional arrangements. Its function is to channel the numerous opinions, interests, and abilities of the people of a State into the making of the State's public policy. Appropriate legislative apportionment, therefore, should ideally be designed to insure effective representation in the State's legislature, in cooperation with the other organs of political power, of the various groups and interests making up the electorate. In practice, of course, this ideal is approximated in the particular apportionment system of any State by a realistic accommodation of the diverse and often conflicting political forces operating within the State. . . .

I do know enough to be aware of the great variations among the several States in their historic manner of distributing legislative power—of the Governors' Councils in New England, of the broad powers of initiative and referendum retained in some States by the people, of the legislative power which some States give to their Governors, by the right of veto or otherwise, of the widely autonomous home rule which many States give to their cities. The Court today declines to give any recognition to these considerations and countless others, tangible and intangible, in holding unconstitutional the particular systems of legislative apportionment which these States have chosen. Instead, the Court says that the requirements of the Equal Protection Clause can be met in any State only by the uncritical, simplistic, and heavy-handed application of sixth-grade arithmetic.

But legislators do not represent faceless numbers. They represent people, or, more accurately, a majority of the voters in their districts—people with identifiable needs and interests which require legislative representation, and which can often be related to the geographical areas in which these people live. The very fact of geographic districting, the constitutional validity of which the Court does not question, carries with it an acceptance of the idea of legislative representation of regional needs and interests. Yet if geographical residence is irrelevant, as the Court suggests, and the goal is solely that of equally "weighted" votes, I do not understand why the Court's constitutional rule does not require the abolition of districts and the holding of all elections at large.[3]

The fact is, of course, the population factors must often to some degree be subordinated in devising a legislative apportionment plan which is to achieve the important goal of ensuring a fair, effective, and balanced representation of the regional, social, and economic interests within a State. And the further fact is that throughout our history the apportionments of State Legislatures have reflected the strongly felt American tradition that the public interest is composed of many diverse interests, and that in the long run it can better be expressed by a medley of component voices than by the majority's monolithic command. What constitutes a rational plan reasonably designed to achieve this objective will vary from State to State, since each State is unique, in terms of topography, geography, demography, history, heterogeneity and concentration of population, variety of social and economic interests, and in the operation and interrelation of its political institutions. But so long as a State's apportionment plan reasonably achieves, in the light of the State's own characteristics, effective and balanced representation of all substantial interests, without sacrificing the principle of effective majority rule, that plan cannot be considered irrational.

II

This bring me to what I consider to be the proper constitutional standards to be applied in these cases. Quite simply, I think the cases should be decided by application of accepted principles of constitutional adjudication under the Equal Protection Clause. A recent expression by the Court of the principles will serve as a generalized compendium:

> [T]he Fourteenth Amendment permits the States a wide scope of discretion in enacting laws which affect some groups of citizens differently than others. The constitutional safeguard is offended only if the classification rests on grounds wholly irrelevant to the achievement of the State's objective. State legislatures are presumed to have acted within their constitutional power despite the fact that, in practice, their laws result in some inequality. A statutory discrimination will not be set aside if any state of facts reasonably may be conceived to justify it. *McGowan* v. *Maryland*, 366 U.S. 420, 425-426.

These principles reflect an understanding respect for the unique values inherent in the Federal Union of States established by our Constitution. They reflect, too, a wise perception of this Court's role in that constitutional system. The

---

[3] Even with legislative districts of exactly equal voter population, 26% of the electorate (a bare majority of the voters in a bare majority of the districts) can, as a matter of the kind of theoretical mathematics embraced by the Court, elect a majority of the legislature under our simple majority electoral system. Thus, the Court's constitutional rule permits minority rule.

Students of the mechanics of voting systems tell us that if all that matters is that votes count equally, the best vote-counting electoral system is proportional representation in state-wide elections. . . . It is just because electoral systems are intended to serve functions other than satisfying mathematical theories, however, that the system of proportional representation has not been widely adopted.

point was never better made than by Mr. Justice Brandeis, dissenting in *New State Ice Co.* v. *Leibmann,* 285 U.S. 262, 280. The final paragraph of that classic dissent is worth repeating here:

> To stay experimentation in things social and economic is a grave responsibility. Denial of the right to experiment may be fraught with serious consequences to the Nation. It is one of the happy incidents of the federal system that a single courageous State may, if its citizens choose, serve as a laboratory; and try novel social and economic experiments without risk to the rest of the country. This Court has the power to prevent an experiment. We may strike down the statute which embodies it on the ground that, in our opinion, the measure is arbitrary, capricious or unreasonable. . . . But in the exercise of this high power, we must be ever on our guard, lest we erect our prejudices into legal principles. If we would guide by the light of reason, we must let our minds be bold. 285 U.S., at 311. . . .

Moving from the general to the specific, I think that the Equal Protection Clause demands but two basic attributes of any plan of state legislative apportionment. First, it demands that, in the light of the State's own characteristics and needs, the plan must be a rational one. Secondly, it demands that the plan must be such as not to permit the systematic frustration of the will of a majority of the electorate of the State. I think it is apparent that any plan of legislative apportionment which could be shown to reflect no policy, but simply arbitrary and capricious action or inaction, and that any plan which could be shown systematically to prevent ultimate effective majority rule, would be invalid under accepted Equal Protection Clause standards. But, beyond this, I think there is nothing in the Federal Constitution to prevent a State from choosing any electoral legislative structure it thinks best suited to the interests, temper, and customs of its people. In the light of these standards, I turn to the Colorado . . . plan of legislative apportionment.

III. *Colorado*

The Colorado plan creates a General Assembly composed of a Senate of 39 members and a House of 65 members. The State is divided into 65 equal population representative districts, with one representative to be elected from each district, and 39 senatorial districts, 14 of which include more than one county. In the Colorado House, the majority unquestionably rules supreme, with the population factor untempered by other considerations. In the Senate rural minorities do not have effective control, and therefore do not have even a veto power over the will of the urban majorities. It is true that, as a matter of theoretical arithmetic, a minority of 36% of the voters could elect a majority of the Senate, but this percentage has no real meaning in terms of the legislative process. Under the Colorado plan, no possible combination of Colorado senators from rural districts, even assuming *arguendo* that they would vote as a bloc, could control the Senate. To arrive at the 36% figure, one must include with the rural districts a substantial number of urban districts, districts with substantially dissimilar interests. There is absolutely no reason to assume that this theoretical majority would ever vote together on any issue so as to thwart the wishes of the majority of the voters of Colorado. Indeed, when we eschew the world of numbers, and look to the real world of effective representation, the simple fact of the matter is that Colorado's three metropolitan areas, Denver, Pueblo, and Colorado Springs, elect a majority of the Senate. . . .

The present apportionment was proposed and supported by many of Colorado's leading citizens. The factual data underlying the apportionment were prepared by the wholly independent Denver Research Institute of the University of Denver. Finally, the apportionment was adopted by a popular referendum in which not only a 2-1 majority of all the voters in Colorado, but a majority in each county, including those urban counties allegedly discriminated against, voted for the present plan in preference to an alternative proposal providing for equal representation per capita in both legislative houses. As the District Court said:

> The contention that the voters have discriminated against themselves appalls rather than convinces. Difficult as it may be at times to understand mass behaviour of human beings, a proper recognition of the judicial function precludes a court from holding that the free choice of the voters between two conflicting theories of apportionment is irrational or the result arbitrary.

The present apportionment, adopted overwhelmingly by the people in a 1962 popular referendum as a state constitutional amendment, is entirely rational, and the amendment by its terms provides for keeping the apportionment current. Thus the majority has consciously chosen to protect the minority's interests, and under the liberal initiative provisions of the Colorado Constitution, it retains the power to reverse its decision to do so. Therefore, there can be no question of frustration of the basic principle of majority rule.

AVERY *V.* MIDLAND COUNTY
390 U.S. 474 (1968)

Mr. Justice White delivered the opinion of the Court.

Midland County has a population of about 70,000. The Commissioners Court is composed of five members. One, the County Judge, is elected at large from the entire county, and in practice casts a vote only to break a tie. The other four are chosen from districts. The size of those districts, according to the 1963 population estimates that were relied upon when this case was tried, was respectively 67,906, 852, 414, and 828. This vast imbalance resulted from placing in a single district virtually the entire city of Midland, Midland County's only urban center, in which 95% of the county's population resides. . . .

In Reynolds *v.* Sims the Equal Protection Clause was applied to the apportionment of state legislatures. Every qualified resident, *Reynolds* determined, has the right to a ballot for election of state legislators of equal weight to the vote of every other resident, and that right is infringed when legislators are elected from districts of substantially unequal population. The question now before us is whether the Fourteenth Amendment likewise forbids the election of local government officials from districts of disparate size. As has almost every court which has addressed itself to this question, we hold that it does. . . .

When the State apportions its legislature, it must have due regard for the Equal Protection Clause. Similarly, when the State delegates lawmaking power to local government and provides for the election of local officials from districts specified by statute, ordinance, or local charter, it must insure that those qualified to vote have the right to an equally effective voice in the election process. If voters residing in oversize districts are denied their constitutional right to participate in the election of state legislators, precisely the same kind of deprivation occurs when the members of a city council, school board, or county governing board are elected from districts of substantially unequal populalation. . . .

Institutions of local government have always been a major aspect of our system, and their responsible and responsive operation is today of increasing importance to the quality of life of more and more of our citizens. We therefore see little difference, in terms of the application of the Equal Protection Clause and of the principles of Reynolds *v.* Sims, between the exercise of state power through legislatures and its exercise by elected officials in the cities, towns, and counties. . . .

MR. JUSTICE HARLAN, dissenting.

I could not disagree more with this decision, which wholly disregards statutory limitations upon the appellate jurisdiction of this Court in state cases and again betrays such insensitivity to the appropriate dividing lines between the judicial and political functions under our constitutional system. . . .

The argument most generally heard for justifying the entry of the federal courts into the field of state legislative apportionment is that since state legislatures had widely failed to correct serious malapportionments in their own structure, and since no other means of redress had proved available through the political process, this Court was entitled to step into the picture. . . . While I continue to reject that thesis as furnishing an excuse for' the federal judiciary straying outside its proper constitutional role, and while I continue to believe that it bodes ill for the country and the entire federal judicial system if this Court does not firmly set its face against this loose and short-sighted point of view, the important thing for present purposes is that no such justification can be brought to bear in this instance.

No claim is made in this case that avenues of political redress are not open to correct any malapportionment in elective local governmental units, and it is difficult to envisage how such a situation could arise. Local governments are creatures of the States, and they may be reformed either by the state legislatures, which are now required to be apportioned according to *Reynolds,* or by amendment of state constitutions. In these circumstances, the argument of practical necessity has no force. The Court, then, should withhold its hand until such a supposed necessity does arise, before intruding itself into the business of restructuring local governments across the country. . . .

Despite the majority's declaration that it is not imposing a "strait-jacket" on local governmental units, its solution is likely to have other undesirable "freezing" effects on local government. . . . The "one man, one vote" rule, which possesses the simplistic defects inherent in any judicially imposed solution of a complex social problem, is entirely inappropriate for determining the form of the country's local governments. . . .

MR. JUSTICE FORTAS, dissenting.

I would dismiss the writ in this case as improvidently granted. The Texas Supreme Court held the districting scheme unlawful under the Texas Constitution. It ordered redistricting. In this difficult and delicate area I would await the result of the redistricting so that we may pass upon the final product of Texas' exercise of its governmental powers, in terms of our constitutional responsibility, and not upon a scheme which Texas herself has invalidated. . . .

I believe, as I shall discuss, that in the circumstances of this case equal protection of the laws may be achieved—and perhaps can only be achieved—by a system which takes into account a complex of values and factors, and not merely the arithmetic simplicity of one equals one. . . .

This rule is appropriate to the selection of members of a State Legislature. The people of a State are similarly affected by the action of the State Legislature. Its functions are comprehensive and pervasive. They are not specially concentrated upon the needs of particular parts of the State or any separate group of citizens. As the Court in *Reynolds* said, each citizen stands in "the same relation" to the State Legislature. Accordingly, variations from substantial population equality in elections for the State Legislature take away from the individual voter the equality which the Constitution mandates. They amount to a debasement of the citizen's vote and of his citizenship.

But the same cannot be said of all local governmental units, and certainly not of the unit involved in this case. Midland County's Commissioners Court has special functions—directed primarily to its rural area and rural population. Its powers are limited and specialized, in light of its missions. Residents of Midland County do not by any means have the same rights and interests at stake in the election of the Commissioners. Equal protection of their rights may certainly take into account the reality of the rights and interests of the various segments of the voting population. It does not require that they all be treated alike, regardless of the stark difference in the impact of the Commissioners Court upon them. "Equal protection" relates to the substance of citizens' rights and interests. It demands protection adapted to substance; it does not insist upon, or even permit, prescription by arbitrary formula which wrongly assumes that the interests of all citizens in the elected body are the same. . . .

In sum, the Commissioners Court's functions and powers are quite limited, and they are defined and restricted so that their primary and preponderant impact is on the rural areas and residents. The extent of its impact on the city is quite limited. To the extent that there is direct impact in the city, the relevant powers, in important respects, are placed in the hands of officials elected on a one man-one vote basis. Indeed, viewed in terms of the realities of rights and powers, it appears that the city residents have the power to elect the officials who are most important to them, and the rural residents have the electoral power with respect to the Commissioners Court which exercises powers in which they are primarily interested.

In face of this, to hold that "no substantial variation" from equal population may be allowed under the Equal Protection Clause is to ignore the substance of the rights and powers involved. It denies—it does not implement—substantive equality of voting rights. It is like insisting that each stockholder of a corporation have only one vote even though the stake of some may be $1 and the stake of others $1,000. The Constitution does not force such a result. Equal protection of the law is not served by it. . . .

Mr. Justice Stewart also dissented.

Mr. Justice Marshall took no part in the consideration or decision of this case.

SOCIAL CRISES: THE BLACK REVOLUTION, DISSENT, AND DISORDER

In its report to the nation, the National Advisory Commission on Civil Disorders reported, "This is our basic conclusion: Our nation is moving toward two societies, one black, one white—separate and unequal." It sought to explain the causes of violent disorders which occurred in the summer of 1967, made a series of proposals and outlined strategies intended to avert the destruction and violence "not only in the streets of the ghetto but in the lives of people." Some of the explanations offered and solutions suggested meet with objection, or at least qualification and reservation, in the articles by Ernest van den Haag and James Q. Wilson.

In the discussion that follows, Charles Hamilton and Stokely Carmichael furnish definitions and arguments for "black power" which, in the language of Carmichael, will enable black people to "make and participate in making the decisions which govern their destinies" and help to build a society "in which the spirit of community and humanistic love prevail." Bayard Rustin, on the other hand, maintains that " 'black power' not only lacks any real value for the civil-rights movement, but that its propagation is positively harmful" because "it diverts the movement from a meaningful debate over strategy and tactics, it isolates the Negro community, and it encourages the growth of anti-Negro forces." Rustin advocates, in place of "black power," the maintenance and extension of the liberal-labor-civil rights *coalition* to fight effectively for a more equal and just society for black and white alike.

In the attempt to achieve a more equal social order, some Negro leaders including Martin Luther King (and white supporters) have resorted to and justified "civil disobedience." This has become a weapon used as well by some bitterly disaffected by the Vietnam war and, recently and dramatically, by some students seeking to restructure our colleges and our society. The meaning, uses, limits, and arguments for and against "civil disobedience" are dealt with in this section.

TOPIC 16

Civil Disorders

Report of the National Advisory Commission on Civil Disorders

Introduction

The summer of 1967 again brought racial disorders to American cities, and with them shock, fear and bewilderment to the nation.

The worst came during a two-week period in July, first in Newark and then in Detroit. Each set off a chain reaction in neighboring communities.

On July 28, 1967, the President of the United States established this Commission and directed us to answer three basic questions:

What happened?

Why did it happen?

What can be done to prevent it from happening again?

To respond to these questions, we have undertaken a broad range of studies and investigations. We have visited the riot cities; we have heard many witnesses; we have sought the counsel of experts across the country.

This is our basic conclusion: Our nation is moving toward two societies, one black, one white—separate and unequal.

Reaction to last summer's disorders has quickened the movement and deepened the division. Discrimination and segregation have long permeated much of American life; they now threaten the future of every American.

This deepening racial division is not inevitable. The movement apart can be reversed. Choice is still possible. Our principal task is to define that choice and to press for a national resolution.

To pursue our present course will involve the continuing polarization of

The Commission consisted of Fred R. Harris, U.S. Senator from Oklahoma; Edward W. Brooke, U.S. Senator from Massachusetts; James C. Corman, Member of House of Representatives from California; William M. McCulloch, Member of House of Representatives from Ohio; I. W. Abel, President, United Steelworkers of America; Charles B. Thornton, Chairman of the Board of Litton Industries, Inc.; Roy Wilkins, Executive Director, National Association for the Advancement of Colored People; Katherine Graham Peden, Commissioner of Commerce of State of Kentucky; Herbert Jenkins, Chief of Police, Atlanta, Georgia; Vice Chairman John V. Lindsay, Mayor of New York City; and Chairman Otto Kerner, Governor of Illinois. This selection is from the Summary of the Report, pp. 1-29 *passim* and Chapter II, "Patterns of Disorder," pp. 127-150 *passim*. Extensive footnotes omitted.

the American community and, ultimately, the destruction of basic democratic values.

The alternative is not blind repression or capitulation to lawlessness. It is the realization of common opportunities for all within a single society.

This alternative will require a commitment to national action—compassionate, massive and sustained, backed by the resources of the most powerful and the richest nation on this earth. From every American it will require new attitudes, new understanding, and, above all, new will.

The vital needs of the nation must be met; hard choices must be made, and, if necessary, new taxes enacted.

Violence cannot build a better society. Disruption and disorder nourish repression, not justice. They strike at the freedom of every citizen. The community cannot—it will not—tolerate coercion and mob rule.

Violence and destruction must be ended—in the streets of the ghetto and in the lives of people.

Segregation and poverty have created in the racial ghetto a destructive environment totally unknown to most white Americans.

What white Americans have never fully understood—but what the Negro can never forget—is that white society is deeply implicated in the ghetto. White institutions created it, white institutions maintain it, and white society condones it.

It is time now to turn with all the purpose at our command to the major unfinished business of this nation. It is time to adopt strategies for action that will produce quick and visible progress. It is time to make good the promises of American democracy to all citizens—urban and rural, white and black, Spanish-surname, American Indian, and every minority group.

Our recommendations embrace three basic principles:

- To mount programs on a scale equal to the dimension of the problems:
- To aim these programs for high impact in the immediate future in order to close the gap between promise and performance;
- To undertake new initiatives and experiments that can change the system of failure and frustration that now dominates the ghetto and weakens our society.

These programs will require unprecedented levels of funding and performance, but they neither probe deeper nor demand more than the problems which called them forth. There can be no higher priority for national action and no higher claim on the nation's conscience. . . .

Part I—What Happened?

Profiles of Disorder

The report contains profiles of a selection of the disorders that took place during the summer of 1967. These profiles are designed to indicate how the disorders happened, who participated in them, and how local officials, police forces, and the National Guard responded. An illustrative excerpt follows:

Detroit. . . . A spirit of carefree nihilism was taking hold. To riot and destroy appeared more and more to become ends in themselves. Late Sunday afternoon it appeared to one observer that the young people were "dancing amidst the flames."

A Negro plainclothes officer was standing at an intersection when a man threw a Molotov cocktail into a business establishment at the corner. In the heat of the afternoon, fanned by the 20 to 25 m.p.h. winds of both Sunday and Monday, the fire reached the home next door within minutes. As residents uselessly sprayed the flames with garden hoses, the fire jumped from roof to roof of adjacent two- and three-story buildings. Within the hour the entire block was in flames. The ninth house in the burning row belonged to the arsonist who had thrown the Molotov cocktail. . . .

As the riot alternately waxed and waned, one area of the ghetto remained insulated. On the northeast side the residents of some 150 square blocks inhabited by 21,000 persons had, in 1966, banded together in the Positive Neighborhood Action Committee (PNAC). With professional help from the Institute of Urban Dynamics, they had organized block clubs and made plans for the improvement of the neighborhood. . . .

When the riot broke out, the residents, through the block clubs, were able to organize quickly. Youngsters, agreeing to stay in the neighborhood, participated in detouring traffic. While many persons reportedly sympathized with the idea of a rebellion against the "system," only two small fires were set—one in an empty building.

. . . According to Lt. Gen. Thockmorton and Col. Bolling, the city, at this time, was saturated with fear. The National Guardsmen were afraid, the residents were afraid, and the police were afraid. Numerous persons, the majority of them Negroes, were being injured by gunshots of undetermined origin. The general and his staff felt that the major task of the troops was to reduce the fear and restore an air of normalcy.

In order to accomplish this, every effort was made to establish contact and rapport between the troops and the residents. The soldiers—20 percent of whom were Negro—began helping to clean up the streets, collect garbage, and trace persons who had disappeared in the confusion. Residents in the neighborhoods responded with soup and sandwiches for the troops. In areas where the National Guard tried to establish rapport with the citizens, there was a smaller response.

Patterns of Disorder

The "typical" riot did not take place. The disorders of 1967 were unusual, irregular, complex and unpredictable social processes. Like most human events, they did not unfold in an orderly sequence. However, an analysis of our survey information leads to some conclusions about the riot process.

In general:

- The civil disorders of 1967 involved Negroes acting against local symbols of white American society, authority and property in Negro neighborhoods— rather than against white persons.
- Of 164 disorders reported during the first nine months of 1967, eight (5

percent) were major in terms of violence and damage; 33 (20 percent) were serious but not major; 123 (75 percent) were minor and undoubtedly would not have received national attention as "riots" had the nation not been sensitized by the more serious outbreaks.

- In the 75 disorders studied by a Senate subcommittee, 83 deaths were reported. Eighty-two percent of the deaths and more than half the injuries occurred in Newark and Detroit. About 10 percent of the dead and 38 percent of the injured were public employees, primarily law officers and firemen. The overwhelming majority of the persons killed or injured in all the disorders were Negro civilians.
- Initial damage estimates were greatly exaggerated. In Detroit, newspaper damage estimates at first ranged from $200 million to $500 million; the highest recent estimate is $45 million. In Newark, early estimates ranged from $15 to $25 million. A month later damage was estimated at $10.2 million, over 80 percent in inventory losses.

In the 24 disorders in 23 cities which we surveyed:

- The final incident before the outbreak of disorder, and the initial violence itself generally took place in the evening or at night at a place in which it was normal for many people to be on the streets.
- Violence usually occurred almost immediately following the occurrence of the final precipitating incident, and then escalated rapidly. With but few exceptions, violence subsided during the day, and flared rapidly again at night. The night-day cycles continued through the early period of the major disorders.
- Disorder generally began with rock and bottle throwing and window breaking. Once store windows were broken, looting usually followed.
- Disorder did not erupt as a result of a single "triggering" or "precipitating" incident. Instead, it was generated out of an increasingly disturbed social atmosphere, in which typically a series of tension-heightening incidents over a period of weeks or months became linked in the minds of many in the Negro community with a reservoir of underlying grievances. At some point in the mounting tension, a further incident—in itself often routine or trivial—became the breaking point and the tension spilled over into violence.
- "Prior" incidents, which increased tensions and ultimately led to violence, were police actions in almost half the cases; police actions were "final" incidents before the outbreak of violence in 12 of the 24 surveyed disorders.
- No particular control tactic was successful in every situation. The varied effectiveness of control techniques emphasizes the need for advance training, planning, adequate intelligence systems, and knowledge of the ghetto community.
- Negotiations between Negroes—including young militants as well as older Negro leaders—and white officials concerning "terms of peace" occurred during virtually all the disorders surveyed. In many cases, these negotiations involved discussion of underlying grievances as well as the handling of the disorder by control authorities.
- The typical rioter was a teenager or young adult, a lifelong resident of the city in which he rioted, a high school dropout; he was, nevertheless, some-

what better educated than his nonrioting Negro neighbor, and was usually underemployed or employed in a menial job. He was proud of his race, extremely hostile to both whites and middle-class Negroes and, although informed about politics, highly distrustful of the political system.

- A Detroit survey revealed that approximately 11 percent of the total residents of two riot areas admitted participation in the rioting, 20 to 25 percent identified themselves as "bystanders," over 16 percent identified themselves as "counter-rioters" who urged rioters to "cool it," and the remaining 48 to 53 percent said they were at home or elsewhere and did not participate. In a survey of Negro males between the ages of 15 and 35 residing in the disturbance area in Newark, about 45 percent identified themselves as rioters, and about 55 percent as "noninvolved."
- Most rioters were young Negro males. Nearly 53 percent of arrestees were between 15 and 24 years of age; nearly 81 percent between 15 and 35.
- In Detroit and Newark about 74 percent of the rioters were brought up in the North. In contrast, of the noninvolved, 36 percent in Detroit and 52 percent in Newark were brought up in the North.
- What the rioters appeared to be seeking was fuller participation in the social order and the material benefits enjoyed by the majority of American citizens. Rather than rejecting the American system, they were anxious to obtain a place for themselves in it.
- Numerous Negro counter-rioters walked the streets urging rioters to "cool it." The typical counter-rioter was better educated and had higher income than either the rioter or the noninvolved.
- The proportion of Negroes in local government was substantially smaller than the Negro proportion of population. Only three of the 20 cities studied had more than one Negro legislator; none had ever had a Negro mayor or city manager. In only four cities did Negroes hold other important policy-making positions or serve as heads of municipal departments.
- Although almost all cities had some sort of formal grievance mechanism for handling citizen complaints, this typically was regarded by Negroes as ineffective and was generally ignored.
- Although specific grievances varied from city to city, at least 12 deeply held grievances can be identified and ranked into three levels of relative intensity:

First Level of Intensity

1. Police practices
2. Unemployment and underemployment
3. Inadequate housing

Second Level of Intensity

4. Inadequate education
5. Poor recreation facilities and programs
6. Ineffectiveness of the political structure and grievance mechanisms

Third Level of Intensity

7. Disrespectful white attitudes
8. Discriminatory administration of justice
9. Inadequacy of federal programs

10. Inadequacy of municipal services
11. Discriminatory consumer and credit practices
12. Inadequate welfare programs

• The results of a three-city survey of various federal programs—manpower, education, housing, welfare and community action—indicate that, despite substantial expenditures, the number of persons assisted constituted only a fraction of those in need.

The background of disorder is often as complex and difficult to analyze as the disorder itself. But we find that certain general conclusions can be drawn:

• Social and economic conditions in the riot cities constituted a clear pattern of severe disadvantage for Negroes compared with whites, whether the Negroes lived in the area where the riot took place or outside it. Negroes had completed fewer years of education and fewer had attended high school. Negroes were twice as likely to be unemployed and three times as likely to be in unskilled and service jobs. Negroes averaged 70 percent of the income earned by whites and were more than twice as likely to be living in poverty. Although housing cost Negroes relatively more, they had worse housing—three times as likely to be overcrowded and substandard. When compared to white suburbs, the relative disadvantage is even more pronounced.

A study of the aftermath of disorder leads to disturbing conclusions. We find that, despite the institution of some post-riot programs:

• Little basic change in the conditions underlying the outbreak of disorder has taken place. Actions to ameliorate Negro grievances have been limited and sporadic; with but few exceptions, they have not significantly reduced tensions.
• In several cities, the principal official response has been to train and equip the police with more sophisticated weapons.
• In several cities, increasing polarization is evident, with continuing breakdown of inter-racial communication, and growth of white segregationist or black separatist groups.

Organized Activity

The President directed the Commission to investigate "to what extent, if any, there has been planning or organization in any of the riots." . . .

On the basis of all the information collected, the Commission concludes that:

The urban disorders of the summer of 1967 were not caused by, nor were they the consequence of, any organized plan or "conspiracy."

Specifically, the Commission has found no evidence that all or any of the disorders or the incidents that led to them were planned or directed by any organization or group, international, national or local.

Militant organizations, local and national, and individual agitators, who repeatedly forecast and called for violence, were active in the spring and summer of 1967. We believe that they sought to encourage violence, and that they helped to create an atmosphere that contributed to the outbreak of disorder.

We recognize that the continuation of disorders and the polarization of the races would provide fertile ground for organized exploitation in the future. . . .

Part II—Why Did It Happen?

The Basic Causes

In addressing the question "Why did it happen?" we shift our focus from the local to the national scene, from the particular events of the summer of 1967 to the factors within the society at large that created a mood of violence among many urban Negroes.

These factors are complex and interacting; they vary significantly in their effect from city to city and from year to year; and the consequences of one disorder, generating new grievances and new demands, become the causes of the next. Thus was created the "thicket of tension, conflicting evidence and extreme opinions" cited by the President.

Despite these complexities, certain fundamental matters are clear. Of these, the most fundamental is the racial attitude and behavior of white Americans toward black Americans.

Race prejudice has shaped our history decisively; it now threatens to affect our future.

White racism is essentially responsible for the explosive mixture which has been accumulating in our cities since the end of World War II. Among the ingredients of this mixture are:

- *Pervasive discrimination and segregation* in employment, education and housing, which have resulted in the continuing exclusion of great numbers of Negroes from the benefits of economic progress.
- *Black in-migration and white exodus,* which have produced the massive and growing concentrations of impoverished Negroes in our major cities, creating a growing crisis of deteriorating facilities and services and unmet human needs.
- *The black ghettos* where segregation and poverty converge on the young to destroy opportunity and enforce failure. Crime, drug addiction, dependency on welfare, and bitterness and resentment against society in general and white society in particular are the result.

At the same time, most whites and some Negroes outside the ghetto have prospered to a degree unparalleled in the history of civilization. Through television and other media, this affluence has been flaunted before the eyes of the Negro poor and the jobless ghetto youth.

Yet these facts alone cannot be said to have caused the disorders. Recently, other powerful ingredients have begun to catalyze the mixture:

- *Frustrated hopes* are the residue of the unfulfilled expectations aroused by the great judicial and legislative victories of the Civil Rights Movement and the dramatic struggle for equal rights in the South.
- *A climate that tends toward approval and encouragement of violence* as a form of protest has been created by white terrorism directed against non-violent protest; by the open defiance of law and federal authority by state and local officials resisting desegregation; and by some protest groups engaging in civil disobedience who turn their backs on nonviolence, go beyond the con-stitutionally protected rights of petition and free assembly, and resort to violence to attempt to compel alteration of laws and policies with which they disagree.
- *The frustrations of powerlessness* have led some Negroes to the conviction that there is no effective alternative to violence as a means of achieving re-dress of grievances, and of "moving the system." These frustrations are re-flected in alienation and hostility toward the institutions of law and govern-ment and the white society which controls them, and in the reach toward racial consciousness and solidarity reflected in the slogan "Black Power."
- *A new mood* has sprung up among Negroes, particularly among the young, in which self-esteem and enhanced racial pride are replacing apathy and submission to "the system."
- *The police are not merely a "spark" factor.* To some Negroes police have come to symbolize white power, white racism and white repression. And the fact is that many police do reflect and express these white attitudes. The atmosphere of hostility and cynicism is reinforced by a widespread belief among Negroes in the existence of police brutality and in a "double standard" of justice and protection—one for Negroes and one for whites. . . .

In the summer of 1967, we have seen in our cities a chain reaction of racial violence. If we are heedless, none of us shall escape the consequences. . . .

The Formation Of the Racial Ghettos[1]

Throughout the 20th century the Negro population of the United States has been moving steadily from rural areas to urban and from South to North and West. In 1910, 91 percent of the nation's 9.8 million Negroes lived in the South and only 27 percent of American Negroes lived in cities of 2,500 persons or more. Between 1910 and 1966 the total Negro population more than doubled, reaching 21.5 million, and the number living in metropolitan areas rose more than five-fold (from 2.6 million to 14.8 million). The number outside the South rose eleven-fold (from 880,000 to 9.7 million).

Negro migration from the South has resulted from the expectation of thousands of new and highly paid jobs for unskilled workers in the North and the shift to mechanized farming in the South. However, the Negro migration is small when compared to earlier waves of European immigrants. Even be-

---

[1] The term "ghetto" as used in this report refers to an area within a city charac-terized by poverty and acute social disorganization, and inhabited by members of a racial or ethnic group under conditions of involuntary segregation.

tween 1960 and 1966, there were 1.8 million immigrants from abroad compared to the 613,000 Negroes who arrived in the North and West from the South.

As a result of the growing number of Negroes in urban areas, natural increase has replaced migration as the primary source of Negro population increase in the cities. Nevertheless, Negro migration from the South will continue unless economic conditions there change dramatically.

Basic data concerning Negro urbanization trends indicate that:

- Almost all Negro population growth (98 percent from 1950 to 1966) is occurring within metropolitan areas, primarily within central cities.[2]
- The vast majority of white population growth (78 percent from 1960 to 1966) is occurring in suburban portions of metropolitan areas. Since 1960, white central-city population has declined by 1.3 million.
- As a result, central cities are becoming more heavily Negro while the suburban fringes around them remain almost entirely white.
- The twelve largest central cities now contain over two-thirds of the Negro population outside the South, and one-third of the Negro total in the United States.

Within the cities, Negroes have been excluded from white residential areas through discriminatory practices. Just as significant is the withdrawal of white families from, or their refusal to enter, neighborhoods where Negroes are moving or already residing. About 20 percent of the urban population of the United States changes residence every year. The refusal of whites to move into "changing" areas when vacancies occur means that most vacancies eventually are occupied by Negroes.

The result, according to a recent study, is that in 1960 the average segregation index for 207 of the largest United States cities was 86.2. In other words, to create an unsegregated population distribution, an average of over 86 percent of all Negroes would have to change their place of residence within the city.

Unemployment, Family Structure, and Social Disorganization

Although there have been gains in Negro income nationally, and a decline in the number of Negroes below the "poverty level," the condition of Negroes in the central city remains in a state of crisis. Between 2 and 2.5 million Negroes—16 to 20 percent of the total Negro population of all central cities—live in squalor and deprivation in ghetto neighborhoods.

Employment is a key problem. It not only controls the present for the Negro American but, in a most profound way, it is creating the future as well. Yet, despite continuing economic growth and declining national unemployment rates, the unemployment rate for Negroes in 1967 was more than double that for whites.

Equally important is the undesirable nature of many jobs open to Negroes

[2] A "central city" is the largest city of a standard metropolitan statistical area, that is, a metropolitan area containing at least one city of 50,000 or more inhabitants.

and other minorities. Negro men are more than three times as likely as white men to be in low-paying, unskilled or service jobs. This concentration of male Negro employment at the lowest end of the occupational scale is the single most important cause of poverty among Negroes.

In one study of low-income neighborhoods, the "subemployment rate," including both unemployment and underemployment, was about 33 percent, or 8.8 times greater than the overall unemployment rate for all United States workers.

Employment problems, aggravated by the constant arrival of new unemployed migrants, many of them from depressed rural areas, create persistent poverty in the ghetto. In 1966, about 11.9 percent of the nation's whites and 40.6 percent of its nonwhites were below the "poverty level" defined by the Social Security Administration (currently $3,335 per year for an urban family of four). Over 40 percent of the nonwhites below the poverty level live in the central cities.

Employment problems have drastic social impact in the ghetto. Men who are chronically unemployed or employed in the lowest status jobs are often unable or unwilling to remain with their families. The handicap imposed on children growing up without fathers in an atmosphere of poverty and deprivation is increased as mothers are forced to work to provide support.

The culture of poverty that results from unemployment and family breakup generates a system of ruthless, exploitative relationships within the ghetto. Prostitution, dope addiction, and crime create an environmental "jungle" characterized by personal insecurity and tension. Children growing up under such conditions are likely participants in civil disorder.

Conditions of Life In the Racial Ghetto

A striking difference in environment from that of white, middle-class Americans profoundly influences the lives of residents of the ghetto.

Crime rates, consistently higher than in other areas, create a pronounced sense of insecurity. For example, in one city one low-income Negro district had 35 times as many serious crimes against persons as a high-income white district. Unless drastic steps are taken, the crime problems in poverty areas are likely to continue to multiply as the growing youth and rapid urbanization of the population outstrip police resources.

Poor health and sanitation conditions in the ghetto result in higher mortality rates, a higher incidence of major diseases, and lower availability and utilization of medical services. The infant mortality rate for nonwhite babies under the age of one month is 58 percent higher than for whites; for one to 12 months it is almost three times as high. The level of sanitation in the ghetto is far below that in high income areas. Garbage collection is often inadequate. Of an estimated 14,000 cases of rat bite in the United States in 1965, most were in ghetto neighborhoods.

Ghetto residents believe they are "exploited" by local merchants; and evidence substantiates some of these beliefs. A study conducted in one city by the Federal Trade Commission showed that distinctly higher prices were charged for goods sold in ghetto stores than in other areas.

Lack of knowledge regarding credit purchasing creates special pitfalls for the disadvantaged. In many states garnishment practices compound these difficulties by allowing creditors to deprive individuals of their wages without hearing or trial.

Comparing the Immigrant and Negro Experience

. . . Why have so many Negroes, unlike the European immigrants, been unable to escape from the ghetto and from poverty? We believe the following factors play a part:

- *The Maturing Economy:* When the European immigrants arrived, they gained an economic foothold by providing the unskilled labor needed by industry. Unlike the immigrant, the Negro migrant found little opportunity in the city. The economy, by then matured, had little use for the unskilled labor he had to offer.
- *The Disability of Race:* The structure of discrimination has stringently narrowed opportunities for the Negro and restricted his prospects. European immigrants suffered from discrimination, but never so pervasively.
- *Entry into the Political System:* The immigrants usually settled in rapidly growing cities with powerful and expanding political machines, which traded economic advantages for political support. Ward-level grievance machinery, as well as personal representation, enabled the immigrant to make his voice heard and his power felt.

  By the time the Negro arrived, these political machines were no longer so powerful or so well equipped to provide jobs or other favors, and in many cases were unwilling to share their influence with Negroes.
- *Cultural Factors:* Coming from societies with a low standard of living and at a time when job aspirations were low, the immigrants sensed little deprivation in being forced to take the less desirable and poorer-paying jobs. Their large and cohesive families contributed to total income. Their vision of the future—one that led to a life outside of the ghetto—provided the incentive necessary to endure the present.

  Although Negro men worked as hard as the immigrants, they were unable to support their families. The entrepreneurial opportunities had vanished. As a result of slavery and long periods of unemployment, the Negro family structure had become matriarchal; the males played a secondary and marginal family role—one which offered little compensation for their hard and unrewarding labor. Above all, segregation denied Negroes access to good jobs and the opportunity to leave the ghetto. For them, the future seemed to lead only to a dead end.

Today, whites tend to exaggerate how well and quickly they escaped from poverty. The fact is that immigrants who came from rural backgrounds, as many Negroes do, are only now, after three generations, finally beginning to move into the middle class.

By contrast, Negroes began concentrating in the city less than two generations ago, and under much less favorable conditions. Although some Negroes have escaped poverty, few have been able to escape the urban ghetto.

Part III—What Can Be Done?

The Community Response

Our investigation of the 1967 riot cities establishes that virtually every major episode of violence was foreshadowed by an accumulation of unresolved grievances and by widespread dissatisfaction among Negroes with the unwillingness or inability of local government to respond.

Overcoming these conditions is essential for community support of law enforcement and civil order. City governments need new and more vital channels of communication to the residents of the ghetto; they need to improve their capacity to respond effectively to community needs before they become community grievances; and they need to provide opportunity for meaningful involvement of ghetto residents in shaping policies and programs which affect the community.

The Commission recommends that local governments:

- Develop Neighborhood Action Task Forces as joint community-government efforts through which more effective communication can be achieved, and the delivery of city services to ghetto residents improved.
- Establish comprehensive grievance-response mechanisms in order to bring all public agencies under public scrutiny.
- Bring the institutions of local government closer to the people they serve by establishing neighborhood outlets for local, state and federal administrative and public service agencies.
- Expand opportunities for ghetto residents to participate in the formulation of public policy and the implementation of programs affecting them through improved political representation, creation of institutional channels for community action, expansion of legal services, and legislative hearings on ghetto problems.

In this effort, city governments will require state and federal support. The Commission recommends:

- State and federal financial assistance for mayors and city councils to support the research, consultants, staff and other resources needed to respond effectively to federal program initiatives.
- State cooperation in providing municipalities with the jurisdictional tools needed to deal with their problems; a fuller measure of financial aid to urban areas; and the focusing of the interests of suburban communities on the physical, social and cultural environment of the central city.

Police and the Community

The abrasive relationship between the police and the minority communities has been a major—and explosive—source of grievance, tension and disorder. The blame must be shared by the total society.

The police are faced with demands for increased protection and service in the ghetto. Yet the aggressive patrol practices thought necessary to meet these demands themselves create tension and hostility. The resulting grievances have been further aggravated by the lack of effective mechanisms for handling complaints against the police. Special programs for bettering police-community relations have been instituted, but these alone are not enough. Police administrators, with the guidance of public officials, and the support of the entire community, must take vigorous action to improve law enforcement and to decrease the potential for disorder.

The Commission recommends that city government and police authorities:

- Review police operations in the ghetto to ensure proper conduct by police officers, and eliminate abrasive practices.
- Provide more adequate police protection to ghetto residents to eliminate their high sense of insecurity, and the belief of many Negro citizens in the existence of a dual standard of law enforcement.
- Establish fair and effective mechanisms for the redress of grievances against the police, and other municipal employees.
- Develop and adopt policy guidelines to assist officers in making critical decisions in areas where police conduct can create tension.
- Develop and use innovative programs to ensure widespread community support for law enforcement.
- Recruit more Negroes into the regular police force, and review promotion policies to ensure fair promotion for Negro officers.
- Establish a "Community Service Officer" program to attract ghetto youths between the ages of 17 and 21 to police work. These junior officers would perform duties in ghetto neighborhoods, but would not have full police authority. The federal government should provide support equal to 90 percent of the costs of employing CSOs on the basis of one for every ten regular officers.

Control of Disorder

Preserving civil peace is the first responsibility of government. Unless the rule of law prevails, our society will lack not only order but also the environment essential to social and economic progress.

The maintenance of civil order cannot be left to the police alone. The police need guidance, as well as support, from mayors and other public officials. It is the responsibility of public officials to determine proper police policies, support adequate police standards for personnel and performance, and participate in planning for the control of disorders. . . .

The Commission believes there is a grave danger that some communities may resort to the indiscriminate and excessive use of force. The harmful effects of overreaction are incalculable. The Commission condemns moves to equip police departments with mass destruction weapons, such as automatic rifles, machine guns and tanks. Weapons which are designed to destroy, not to control, have no place in densely populated urban communities. . . .

The Future of the Cities

By 1985, the Negro population in central cities is expected to increase by 72 percent to approximately 20.8 million. Coupled with the continued exodus of white families to the suburbs, this growth will produce majority Negro populations in many of the nation's largest cities.

The future of these cities, and of their burgeoning Negro populations, is grim. Most new employment opportunities are being created in suburbs and outlying areas. This trend will continue unless important changes in public policy are made.

In prospect, therefore, is further deterioration of already inadequate municipal tax bases in the face of increasing demands for public services, and continuing unemployment and poverty among the urban Negro population:

- We can maintain present policies, continuing both the proportion of the nation's resources now allocated to programs for the unemployed and the disadvantaged, and the inadequate and failing effort to achieve an integrated society.
- We can adopt a policy of "enrichment" aimed at improving dramatically the quality of ghetto life while abandoning integration as a goal.
- We can pursue integration by combining ghetto "enrichment" with policies which will encourage Negro movement out of central city areas.

The first choice, continuance of present policies, has ominous consequences for our society. The share of the nation's resources now allocated to programs for the disadvantaged is insufficient to arrest the deterioration of life in central city ghettos. Under such conditions, a rising proportion of Negroes may come to see in the deprivation and segregation they experience, a justification for violent protest, or for extending support to now isolated extremists who advocate civil disruption. Large-scale and continuing violence could result, followed by white retaliation, and, ultimately, the separation of the two communities in a garrison state.

Even if violence does not occur, the consequences are unacceptable. Development of a racially integrated society, extraordinarily difficult today, will be virtually impossible when the present black ghetto population of 12.5 million has grown to almost 21 million.

To continue present policies is to make permanent the division of our country into two societies; one, largely Negro and poor, located in the central cities; the other, predominantly white and affluent, located in the suburbs and in outlying areas.

The second choice, ghetto enrichment coupled with abandonment of integration, is also unacceptable. It is another way of choosing a permanently divided country. Moreover, equality cannot be achieved under conditions of nearly complete separation. In a country where the economy, and particularly the resources of employment, are predominantly white, a policy of separation can only relegate Negroes to a permanently inferior economic status.

We believe that the only possible choice for America is the third—a policy which combines ghetto enrichment with programs designed to encourage integration of substantial numbers of Negroes into the society outside the ghetto.

Enrichment must be an important adjunct to integration, for no matter how ambitious or energetic the program, few Negroes now living in central cities can be quickly integrated. In the meantime, large-scale improvement in the quality of ghetto life is essential.

But this can be no more than an interim strategy. Programs must be developed which will permit substantial Negro movement out of the ghettos. The primary goal must be a single society, in which every citizen will be free to live and work according to his capabilities and desires, not his color.

Recommendations For National Action

Introduction. No American—white or black—can escape the consequences of the continuing social and economic decay of our major cities.

Only a commitment to national action on an unprecedented scale can shape a future compatible with the historic ideals of American society.

The great productivity of our economy, and a federal revenue system which is highly responsive to economic growth, can provide the resources.

The major need is to generate new will—the will to tax ourselves to the extent necessary to meet the vital needs of the nation.

We have set forth goals and proposed strategies to reach those goals. We discuss and recommend programs not to commit each of us to specific parts of such programs but to illustrate the type and dimension of action needed.

The major goal is the creation of a true union—a single society and a single American identity. Toward that goal, we propose the following objectives for national action:

• Opening up opportunities to those who are restricted by racial segregation and discrimination, and eliminating all barriers to their choice of jobs, education and housing.
• Removing the frustration of powerlessness among the disadvantaged by providing the means for them to deal with the problems that affect their own lives and by increasing the capacity of our public and private institutions to respond to those problems.
• Increasing communication across racial lines to destroy stereotypes, to halt polarization, end distrust and hostility, and create common ground for efforts toward public order and social justice.

We propose these aims to fulfill our pledge of equality and to meet the fundamental needs of a democratic and civilized society—domestic and social justice.

Employment. Pervasive unemployment and underemployment are the most persistent and serious grievances in minority areas. They are inextricably linked to the problem of civil disorder.

Despite growing federal expenditures for manpower development and training programs, and sustained general economic prosperity and increasing demands for skilled workers, about two million—white and nonwhite—are permanently unemployed. About ten million are underemployed, of whom 6.5 million work full time for wages below the poverty line.

The 500,000 "hard-core" unemployed in the central cities who lack a basic education and are unable to hold a steady job are made up in large part of Negro males between the ages of 18 and 25. In the riot cities which we surveyed, Negroes were three times as likely as whites to hold unskilled jobs, which are often part time, seasonal, low-paying and "dead end."

Negro males between the ages of 15 and 25 predominated among the rioters. More than 20 percent of the rioters were unemployed, and many who were employed held intermittent, low status, unskilled jobs which they regarded as below their education and ability.

The Commission recommends that the federal government:

• Undertake joint efforts with cities and states to consolidate existing manpower programs to avoid fragmentation and duplication.
• Take immediate action to create 2,000,000 new jobs over the next three years —one million in the public sector and one million in the private sector—to absorb the hard-core unemployed and materially reduce the level of underemployment for all workers, black and white. We propose 250,000 public sector and 300,000 private sector jobs in the first year.
• Provide on-the-job training by both public and private employers with reimbursement to private employers for the extra costs of training the hard-core unemployed, by contract or by tax credits.
• Provide tax and other incentives to investment in rural as well as urban poverty areas in order to offer to the rural poor an alternative to migration to urban centers.
• Take new and vigorous action to remove artificial barriers to employment and promotion, including not only racial discrimination but, in certain cases, arrest records or lack of a high school diploma. Strengthen those agencies such as the Equal Employment Opportunity Commission, charged with eliminating discriminatory practices, and provide full support for Title VI of the 1964 Civil Rights Act allowing federal grant-in-aid funds to be withheld from activities which discriminate on grounds of color or race.

The Commission commends the recent public commitment of the National Council of the Building and Construction Trades Unions, AFL-CIO, to encourage and recruit Negro membership in apprenticeship programs. This commitment should be intensified and implemented.

Education. Education in a democratic society must equip children to develop their potential and to participate fully in American life. For the community at large, the schools have discharged this responsibility well. But for many minorities, and particularly for the children of the ghetto, the schools have failed to provide the educational experience which could overcome the effects of discrimination and deprivation.

This failure is one of the persistent sources of grievance and resentment within the Negro community. The hostility of Negro parents and students toward the school system is generating increasing conflict and causing disruption within many city school districts. But the most dramatic evidence of the relationship between educational practices and civil disorders lies in the high incidence of riot participation by ghetto youth who have not completed high school.

The bleak record of public education for ghetto children is growing worse. In the critical skills—verbal and reading ability—Negro students are falling further behind whites with each year of school completed. The high unemployment and underemployment rate for Negro youth is evidence, in part, of the growing educational crisis.

We support integration as the priority education strategy: it is essential to the future of American society. In this last summer's disorders we have seen the consequences of racial isolation at all levels, and of attitudes toward race, on both sides, produced by three centuries of myth, ignorance and bias. It is indispensable that opportunities for interaction between the races be expanded.

We recognize that the growing dominance of pupils from disadvantaged minorities in city school populations will not soon be reversed. No matter how great the effort toward desegregation, many children of the ghetto will not, within their school careers, attend integrated schools.

If existing disadvantages are not to be perpetuated, we must drastically improve the quality of ghetto education. Equality of results with all-white schools must be the goal.

To implement these strategies, the Commission recommends:

- Sharply increased efforts to eliminate de facto segregation in our schools through substantial federal aid to school systems seeking to desegregate either within the system or in cooperation with neighboring school systems.
- Elimination of racial discrimination in Northern as well as Southern schools by vigorous application of Title VI of the Civil Rights Act of 1964.
- Extension of quality early childhood education to every disadvantaged child in the country.
- Efforts to improve dramatically schools serving disadvantaged children through substantial federal funding of year-round compensatory education programs, improved teaching, and expanded experimentation and research.
- Elimination of illiteracy through greater federal support for adult basic education.
- Enlarged opportunities for parent and community participation in the public schools.
- Reoriented vocational education emphasizing work-experience training and the involvement of business and industry.
- Expanded opportunities for higher education through increased federal assistance to disadvantaged students.
- Revision of state aid formulas to assure more per student aid to districts having a high proportion of disadvantaged school-age children.

The Welfare System. Our present system of public welfare is designed to save money instead of people, and tragically ends up doing neither. This system has two critical deficiencies:

First, it excludes large numbers of persons who are in great need, and who, if provided a decent level of support, might be able to become more productive and self-sufficient. No federal funds are available for millions of men and women who are needy but neither aged, handicapped nor the parents of minor children.

minimum necessary for a decent level of existence, and imposes restrictions that encourage continued dependency on welfare and undermine self-respect.

Second, for those included, the system provides assistance well below the

Civil Disorders

A welter of statutory requirements and administrative practices and regulations operate to remind recipients that they are considered untrustworthy, promiscuous and lazy. Residence requirements prevent assistance to people in need who are newly arrived in the state. Regular searches of recipients' homes violate privacy. Inadequate social services compound the problems.

The Commission recommends that the federal government, acting with state and local governments where necessary, reform the existing welfare system to:

- Establish uniform national standards of assistance at least as high as the annual "poverty level" of income, now set by the Social Security Administration at $3,335 per year for an urban family of four.
- Require that all states receiving federal welfare contributions participate in the Aid to Families with Dependent Children—Unemployed Parents program (AFDC-UP) that permits assistance to families with both father and mother in the home, thus aiding the family while it is still intact.
- Bear a substantially greater portion of all welfare costs—at least 90 percent of total payments.
- Increase incentives for seeking employment and job training, but remove restrictions recently enacted by the Congress that would compel mothers of young children to work.
- Provide more adequate social services through neighborhood centers and family-planning programs.
- Remove the freeze placed by the 1967 welfare amendments on the percentage of children in a state that can be covered by federal assistance.
- Eliminate residence requirements.

As long-range goal, the Commission recommends that the federal government seek to develop a national system of income supplementation based strictly on need with two broad and basic purposes:

- To provide, for those who can work or who do work, any necessary supplements in such a way as to develop incentives for fuller employment:
- To provide, for those who cannot work and for mothers who decide to remain with their children, a minimum standard of decent living, and to aid in the saving of children from the prison of poverty that has held their parents.

A broad system of supplementation would involve substantially greater federal expenditures than anything now contemplated. The cost will range widely depending on the standard of need accepted as the "basic allowance" to individuals and families, and on the rate at which additional income above this level is taxed. Yet if the deepening cycle of poverty and dependence on welfare can be broken, if the children of the poor can be given the opportunity to scale the wall that now separates them from the rest of society, the return on this investment will be great indeed.

Housing. After more than three decades of fragmented and grossly underfunded federal housing programs, nearly six million substandard housing units remain occupied in the United States.

The housing problem is particularly acute in the minority ghettos. Nearly two-thirds of all non-white families living in the central cities today live in neighborhoods marked with substandard housing and general urban blight. Two major factors are responsible.

First: Many ghetto residents simply cannot pay the rent necessary to support decent housing. In Detroit, for example, over 40 percent of the non-white occupied units in 1960 required rent of over 35 percent of the tenants' income.

Second: Discrimination prevents access to many non-slum areas, particularly the suburbs, where good housing exists. In addition, by creating a "back pressure" in the racial ghettos, it makes it possible for landlords to break up apartments for denser occupancy, and keeps prices and rents of deteriorated ghetto housing higher than they would be in a truly free market.

To date, federal programs have been able to do comparatively little to provide housing for the disadvantaged. In the 31-year history of subsidized federal housing, only about 800,000 units have been constructed, with recent production averaging about 50,000 units a year. By comparison, over a period only three years longer, FHA insurance guarantees have made possible the construction of over ten million middle and upper-income units.

Two points are fundamental to the Commission's recommendations:

First: Federal housing programs must be given a new thrust aimed at overcoming the prevailing patterns of racial segregation. If this is not done, those programs will continue to concentrate the most impoverished and dependent segments of the population into the central-city ghettos where there is already a critical gap between the needs of the population and the public resources to deal with them.

Second: The private sector must be brought into the production and financing of low and moderate rental housing to supply the capabilities and capital necessary to meet the housing needs of the nation.

The Commission recommends that the federal government:

- Enact a comprehensive and enforceable federal open housing law to cover the sale or rental of all housing, including single family homes.
- Reorient federal housing programs to place more low and moderate income housing outside of ghetto areas.
- Bring within the reach of low and moderate income families within the next five years six million new and existing units of decent housing, beginning with 600,000 units in the next year.

To reach this goal we recommend:

- Expansion and modification of the rent supplement program to permit use of supplements for existing housing, thus greatly increasing the reach of the program.
- Expansion and modification of the below-market interest rate program to enlarge the interest subsidy to all sponsors and provide interest-free loans to nonprofit sponsors to cover pre-construction costs, and permit sale of projects to nonprofit corporations, cooperatives, or condominiums.
- Creation of an ownership supplement program similar to present rent supplements, to make home ownership possible for low-income families.

- Federal writedown of interest rates on loans to private builders constructing moderate-rent housing.
- Expansion of the public housing program, with emphasis on small units on scattered sites, and leasing and "turnkey" programs.
- Expansion of the Model Cities program.
- Expansion and reorientation of the urban renewal program to give priority to projects directly assisting low-income households to obtain adequate housing.

Conclusion. One of the first witnesses to be invited to appear before this Commission was Dr. Kenneth B. Clark, a distinguished and perceptive scholar. Referring to the reports of earlier riot commissions, he said:

> I read that report . . . of the 1919 riot in Chicago, and it is as if I were reading the report of the investigating committee on the Harlem riot of '35, the report of the investigating committee on the Harlem riot of '43, the report of the McCone Commission on the Watts riot.
> I must again in candor say to you members of this Commission—it is a kind of Alice in Wonderland—with the same moving picture re-shown over and over again, the same analysis, the same recommendations, and the same inaction.

These words come to our minds as we conclude this report.

We have provided an honest beginning. We have learned much. But we have uncovered no startling truths, no unique insights, no simple solutions. The destruction and the bitterness of racial disorder, the harsh polemics of black revolt and white repression have been seen and heard before in this country.

It is time now to end the destruction and the violence, not only in the streets of the ghetto but in the lives of people.

Some Detailed Data

Racial Attitudes. The Detroit and Newark surveys indicate that rioters have strong feelings of racial pride, if not racial superiority. In the Detroit survey, 48.6 percent of the self-reported rioters said that they felt Negroes were more dependable than whites. Only 22.4 percent of the noninvolved stated this. In Newark, the comparable figures were 45.0 and 27.8 percent. The Newark survey data indicate that rioters want to be called "black" rather than "Negro" or "colored" and are somewhat more likely than the noninvolved to feel that all Negroes should study African history and languages.

To what extent this racial pride antedated the riot and to what extent it was produced by the riot is impossible to determine from the survey data. Certainly the riot experience seems to have been associated with increased pride in the minds of many of the participants. This was vividly illustrated by the statement of a Detroit rioter:

> Interviewer: You said you were feeling good when you followed the crowd?
> Respondent : I was feeling proud, man, at the fact that I was a

Negro. I felt like I was a first class citizen. I didn't feel ashamed of my race because of what they did. . . .

Along with increased racial pride there appears to be intense hostility toward whites. Self-reported rioters in both the Detroit and Newark surveys were more likely to feel that civil rights groups with white and Negro leaders would do better without the whites. . . .

Self-reported rioters in Newark were also more likely to agree with the statement, "Sometimes I hate white people." Of the self-reported rioters, 72.4 percent agreed; of the noninvolved, 50.0 percent agreed.

The intensity of the self-reported rioters' racial feelings may suggest that the recent riots represented traditional interracial hostilities. Two sources of data suggest that this intepretation is probably incorrect.

First, the Newark survey data indicate that rioters were almost as hostile to middle-class Negroes as they were to whites. Seventy-one and four-tenths percent of the self-reported rioters, but only 59.5 percent of the noninvolved, agreed with the statement, "Negroes who make a lot of money like to think they are better than other Negroes." Perhaps even more significant, particularly in light of the rioters' strong feelings of racial pride, is that 50.5 percent of the self-reported rioters agreed that "Negroes who make a lot of money are just as bad as white people." Only 35.2 percent of the noninvolved shared this opinion.

Second, the arrest data show that the great majority of those arrested during the disorders were generally charged with a crime relating to looting or curfew violations. Only 2.4 percent of the arrests were for assault and 0.1 percent were for homicide, but 31.3 percent of the arrests were for breaking and entering—crimes directed against white property rather than against individual whites.

Political Attitudes and Involvement. Respondents in the Newark survey were asked about relatively simple items of political information, such as the race of prominent local and national political figures. In general, the self-reported rioters were much better informed than the noninvolved. For example, self-reported rioters were more likely to know that one of the 1966 Newark mayoral candidates was a Negro. Of the rioters, 77.1 percent—but only 61.6 percent of the noninvolved—identified him correctly. The overall scores on a series of similar questions also reflect the self-reported rioters' higher levels of information.

Self-reported rioters were also more likely to be involved in activities associated with Negro rights. At the most basic level of political participation, they were more likely than the noninvolved to talk frequently about Negro rights. In the Newark survey, 53.8 percent of the self-reported rioters, but only 34.9 percent of the noninvolved, said that they talked about Negro rights nearly every day.

The self-reported rioters also were more likely to have attended a meeting or participated in civil rights activity. Of the rioters, 39.3 percent—but only 25.7 percent of the noninvolved—reported that they had engaged in such activity.

TABLE 1. Weighted Comparison of Grievance Categories

	1st Place (4 Points)		2nd Place (3 Points)		3rd Place (2 Points)		4th Place (1 Point)		Total	
	Cities	Points	Cities	Points	Cities	Points	Cities	Points	Cities	Points
Police Practices	8	31½	4	12	0	0	2	2	14	45½
Unemployment & Under-Employment	3	11	7	21	4	7	3	3	17	42
Inadequate Housing	5	18½	2	6	5	9½	2	2	14	36
Inadequate Education	2	8	2	6	2	4	3	3	9	21
Poor Recreation Facilities	3	11	1	2½	4	7½	0	0	8	21
Political Structure and Grievance Mechanism	2	8	1	3	1	2	1	1	5	14
White Attitudes	0	0	1	3	1	1½	2	2	4	6½
Administration of Justice	0	0	0	0	2	3½	1	1	3	4½
Federal Programs	0	0	1	2½	0	0	0	0	1	2½
Municipal Services	0	0	0	0	1	2	0	0	1	2
Consumer and Credit Practices	0	0	0	0	0	0	2	2	2	2
Welfare	0	0	0	0	0	0	0	0	0	0

Note: The total of points for each category is the product of the number of cities times the number of points indicated at the top of each double column except where two grievances were judged equally serious. In these cases the total points for the two rankings involved were divided equally (e.g., in case two were judged equally suitable for the first priority, the total points for first and second were divided and each received 3½ points).

246

In the Newark survey, respondents were asked how much they thought they could trust the local government. Only 4.8 percent of the self-reported rioters, compared with 13.7 percent of the noninvolved, said that they felt they could trust it most of the time; 44.2 percent of the self-reported rioters and 33.9 percent of the noninvolved reported that they could almost never trust the government.

Results of weighted comparison of grievance categories*

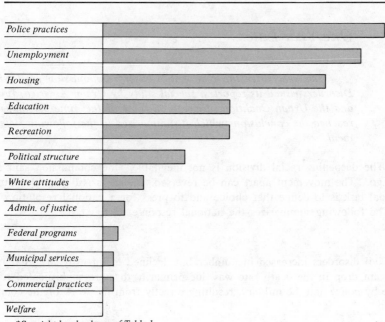

*See right hand column of Table 1

In the Detroit survey, self-reported rioters were much more likely to attribute the riot to anger about politicians and police than were the noninvolved. Of the self-reported rioters, 43.2 percent—but only 19.6 percent of the noninvolved—said anger at politicians had a great deal to do with causing the riot. Of the self-reported rioters, 70.5 percent, compared with 48.8 percent of the noninvolved, believed that anger at the police had a great deal to do with causing the riot.

Perhaps the most revealing and disturbing measure of the rioters' anger at the social and political system was their response to a question asking whether they thought "the country was worth fighting for in the event of a major world war." Of the self-reported rioters, 39.4 percent in Detroit and 52.8 percent in Newark shared the view that it was not. By contrast, 15.5 percent of the noninvolved in Detroit and 27.8 percent of the noninvolved in Newark shared this sentiment. Almost none of the self-reported counter-rioters in Detroit—3.3 percent—agreed with the self-reported rioters.

Some comments of interviewees are worthy of note:

Not worth fighting for—if Negroes had an equal chance it would be worth fighting for.

Not worth fighting for—I am not a true citizen so why should I?

Not worth fighting for—because my husband came back from Vietnam and nothing had changed.

One Year Later

One year after the National Advisory Commission on Civil Disorders issued its report, a special study by Urban America, Inc. and the Urban Coalition (drawing on some of the same personnel) reached the conclusions which it summarized in the following statement.

"The deepening racial division is not inevitable," the commission said a year ago. "The movement apart can be reversed. Choice is still possible. Our principal task is to define that choice and to press for a national resolution." The following summarizes the national response to that task:

1

Civil disorders increased in number but declined in intensity in 1968. A significant drop in the death rate was due primarily to more sophisticated response by police and the military, resulting directly from the work of the commission.

2

A wave of disorder struck the nation's high schools in 1968-69 and is continuing. At the same time, turbulence on college and university campuses has taken on an increasingly racial character.

3

A genuinely alarming increase in crimes of violence contributed to an atmosphere of fear inside and out of the slums and ghettos. There was little evidence of change or reform in the criminal justice system sufficient to stem this increase.

4

Incidents involving the police continued to threaten the civil peace in the slums and ghettos. There was some evidence of a hardening of police attitudes and a weakening of traditional civil controls over their activities.

As reported in the New York Times on February 28, 1969.

5

Structural change in local government to make it more responsive was rare. The number of black elected officials increased substantially throughout the nation and particularly in the South, but remained disproportionately low.

6

There was no evidence that any more than a small minority of the nation's Negro population was prepared to follow militant leaders toward separatism or the tactical use of violence. This minority, however, continued to have an impact beyond its numbers, particularly on the young.

7

There was striking evidence of a deepening of the movement of black pride, black identity, and black control and improvement of ghetto neighborhoods. There were repeated suggestions that efforts toward community control and self-help had been a major contribution to the relative quiet of the summer of 1968.

8

White concern with the problems of the slums and ghettos mounted with the commission report, the assassination of Martin Luther King, and the April disorders. It was subsumed by concern for law and order in the months following the assassination of Senator Robert F. Kennedy, and continued to decline during the Presidential campaign. Outright resistance to slum-ghetto needs and demands intensified during the same months.

9

Black and white Americans remained far apart in their perception of slum-ghetto problems and the meaning of civil disorders. The gap probably had widened by the end of the year.

10

The physical distance between the places where blacks and whites lived did not diminish during the last year and threatens to increase with population growth. The most recent trend showed a virtual stoppage in black immigration and a sharp increase in the rate of white departure; the ghettos, meanwhile, were growing in area while declining in population density. There was an increase in suburban Negro population, but there also were indications of growth in suburban ghettos.

The nation has not reversed the movement apart. Blacks and whites remain deeply divided in the perceptions and experiences of American society. The deepening of concern about conditions in the slums and ghettos on the part of some white persons and institutions has been counterbalanced—perhaps overbalanced—by a deepening of aversion and resistance on the part of others.

The mood of the blacks, wherever it stands precisely in the spectrum between militancy and submission, is not moving in the direction of patience. The black neighborhoods in the cities remain slums, marked by poverty and decay; they remain ghettos, marked by racial concentration and confinement.

The nation has not yet made available—to the cities or the blacks themselves—the resources to improve these neighborhoods enough to make a significant change in their residents' lives. Nor has it offered those who might want it the alternative of escape.

Neither has the nation made a choice among the alternative choices described by the commission, which is the same as choosing what the commission called "present policies." The present policies' alternative, the commission said, "may well involve changes in many social and economic programs—but not enough to produce fundamental alterations in the key factors of Negro concentration, racial segregation, and the lack of sufficient enrichment to arrest the decay of deprived neighborhoods."

It is worth looking again at the commission's description of where the choice would lead:

"We believe that the present policies choice would lead to a larger number of violent incidents of the kind that have stimulated recent major disorders.

"First, it does nothing to raise the hopes, absorb the energies, or constructively challenge the talents of the rapidly growing number of young Negro men in central cities. The proportion of unemployed or underemployed among them will remain very high. These young men have contributed disproportionately to crime and violence in cities in the past, and there is danger, obviously, that they will continue to do so.

"Second, under these conditions, a rising proportion of Negroes in disadvantaged city areas might come to look upon the deprivation and segregation they suffer as proper justification for violent protest or for extending support to now isolated extremists who advocate civil disruption by guerrilla tactics.

"More incidents would not necessarily mean more or worse riots. For the near future, there is substantial likelihood that even an increased number of incidents could be controlled before becoming major disorders, if society undertakes to improve police and national guard forces so that they can respond to potential disorders with more prompt and disciplined use of force.

"In the long run, however, the present policies choice risks a seriously greater probability of major disorders, worse, possibly, than those already experienced.

"If the Negro population as a whole developed even stronger feelings of being wrongly 'penned in' and discriminated against, many of its members might come to support not only riots, but the rebellion now being preached by only a handful. Large-scale violence, followed by white retaliation, could follow. This spiral could quite conceivably lead to a kind of urban apartheid with semimartial law in many major cities, enforced residence of Negroes in segregated areas, and a drastic reduction in personal freedoms for all Americans, particularly Negroes."

The commission description of the immediate consequences of the present policies choice sounds strikingly like a description of the year since its report was issued: some change but not enough; more incidents but less full-scale disorder because of improved police and military response; a decline in expectations and therefore in short-run frustrations.

If the commission is equally correct about the long run, the nation in its neglect may be sowing the seeds of unprecedented future disorders and division. For a year later, we are a year closer to being two societies, black and white, increasingly separate and scarcely less unequal.

ERNEST VAN DEN HAAG
How Not to Prevent Civil Disorders

The Report of the National Advisory Commission on Civil Disorders is so comprehensive as to be useless: the attempt to include everything makes it unselective, though for this very reason, unobjectionable. Nothing is left out, but there is no distinction between the desirable and the possible, and no priorities are given: all things—from changing personal attitudes to rebuilding cities—are to be done (by spending money) at once; wherefore none will be.

Although unwilling to give programmatic priorities, the Commission is unsparing with remonstrances and recriminations addressed to whites; they amount to a misleading "explanation" for last summer's riots. For, if all the grievances of the rioters were justified (and I think most are) they would not "explain" the riots; these were caused by the grievances as much, and no more, as the murder of Jews in Germany, or of capitalists in Russia, was "caused" by grievances against them.

Despite pale disclaimers—riots must not be regarded, after all, as rational or desirable remedies—the Commission clearly suggests that the riots have come as a punishment for our sins, and are to be avoided in the future by repentance and repair. Undoubtedly a religiously orthodox explanation, but not a scientific one. Sins we have committed. Possibly we deserve everything we get and more —I won't argue the point. But the Commission confused sin and punishment with cause and effect: it assumed that whatever deserved punishment *ipso facto* was the cause of the riots, which are felt to be the punishment deserved. Such a theory of crime and punishment does not flow from information and analysis; it has nothing to do with the facts; it was dictated by the guilty consciences of the Commission's members. However, conscience is not a reliable guide to investigate and predict factual matters, nor to determine what means of control would be effective: conscience is a guide only to normative matters, to moral aims, not to the effectiveness of means or of causes.

Pangs of Conscience

There is not a shred of evidence indicating that the riots were caused by our sins—any more than that epidemics of bubonic plague, or the sack of Rome,

Practicing Psychoanalyst. Lecturer at New School for Social Research and Adjunct Professor of Social Philosophy, New York University. Author of *Passion and Social Constraint*. The selection is from "How Not to Prevent Civil Disorders." *The National Review*, Vol. XX, No. 12 (March 26, 1968), pp. 284-287. By permission of National Review, 150 East 35th Street, New York, N. Y. 10016.

were caused by the unquestioned sinfulness of the population. Now, if the Report had mentioned infection, or weakness—but it does not; it cannot, because it is part of both—a symptom rather than a diagnosis of the malaise it was to scrutinize. For the riots—the report notwithstanding—were caused less by our sinfulness than by our attempts to repent for it—to repair the harm done—and by the guilty conscience so dramatically manifested by the Commission.

The Commission believes in a secularized Marxist version of the crime (sin) and punishment theory. Riots occur because white society is rich and allows, or causes, Negroes to be poor in its midst. If the Commission had used more mundane means of investigation—it seems to have used moral generosity exclusively—it might have found that:

> (*a*) the contrast between rich and poor (including Negroes) was greater in the past;
> (*b*) the contrast is greater in most European countries:
> (*c*) the U.S. riots did not occur where Negroes were least well treated;
> (*d*) the contrast is greater in the Soviet Union (if one considers not theory, but consumption, power, and prestige differentials), and
> (*e*) in India and South America.

Morally the contrast may be deplorable. But it neither "explains" nor "caused" the riots.

Negroes have certainly been discriminated against, beginning with slavery. They have suffered from deprivation and lack of opportunity, from unfulfilled promises, and, finally, from demoralization. Yet discrimination has diminished, and conditions have rapidly improved since the Second World War. There has been more improvement in the last twenty years than in the previous two hundred. Thus, the Commission, after stating that white incomes have risen faster than Negro incomes (true for the two aggregate groups, but not for each sub-group), finds (inconspicuously) that "the proportion of Negro families with incomes of $7,000 or more was double in 1966 (28 per cent) of what it was in 1960 [!] and four times greater than the proportion receiving such incomes in 1947" and that "the proportion of Negroes employed in high-skill, high-status and well-paying jobs, rose faster than the comparable proportion among whites from 1960 to 1966." Further, "in 1947, 65 per cent of all Negro families made less than $3,000; in 1966 only thirty-two per cent." A more extended statistical presentation would confirm that, in all material respects, the fate of Negroes has improved faster than ever before, although, as one might expect, some groups benefited more than others.

The riots occurred not despite, but because, of this rapid improvement. The point has been made very well by Alexis de Tocqueville:

> It is natural that the love of equality should constantly increase together with equality itself, and that it should grow by what it feeds on. . . .
>
>   . . . . When a people which has put up with an oppressive rule

over a long period without protest suddenly finds the government relaxing its pressure, it takes up arms against it. . . .

. . . . Experience teaches us that, generally speaking, the most perilous moment for a bad government is one when it seeks to mend its ways. . . .

. . . . *The mere fact that certain abuses have been remedied draws attention to the others and they now appear more galling; people may suffer less, but their sensibility is exacerbated.* . . .

Modern empirical research states these matters less succinctly and elegantly, but confirms them amply. The inevitable is tolerated, the inadequate is not: improvement as a process leads to more dissatisfaction than static misery, for aspiration fueled by the process of improvement pulls ahead of any possible fulfillment.

The Vicious Circle

Although they do not "explain" riots, many external causes for dissatisfaction among Negroes remain. Drawn by economic circumstances, Negroes have migrated to cities which lack facilities to house them. In turn they lack the skills which would allow them to earn a reasonable living there, even in the absence of discrimination. Unions make it both hard to acquire and to utilize skills; and our government does not like to enforce laws against unions. Immigration into the cities, indeed, propinquity—let alone integration—intensifies dissatisfaction by comparison with better-off neighbors. (Thus, Lander[1] states: "when other factors are held constant, delinquency rates are highest in areas of maximum racial heterogeneity", i.e., not in areas tenanted by whites, or by Negroes, and regardless of housing conditions, etc.) Government welfare provisions are marvelously unintelligent: they disorganize Negro families, they cause many to spurn menial and low-paid jobs they could fill, and they humiliate everybody unnecessarily. Welfare provisions defeat any reasonable purpose, and perpetuate the welfare worker, his client, and the misery of both.

Many of these hardships are unavoidable on the way to improvement; other immigrant groups (Negroes, however native, are immigrants to our cities with no fewer problems of acculturation than, say, Italians) have overcome similar hardships without assistance. But some hardships are much worse for Negroes than for other immigrant groups: they are different; and so are the circumstances. (Yet many might be avoided, not necessarily by more money, but by more intelligent ways of using it.)

These external causes—added to many internal ones—have caused Negroes to become more demoralized, hopeless and resentful than any immigrant group ever was. The Commission contributes to this demoralization. No other group has been told so often and so authoritatively what the Commission has now repeated *ex cathedra:* that all their misfortunes are due to others (who therefore must pay for all improvements); and that they are somehow entitled to

[1] *Towards An Understanding of Juvenile Delinquency,* Columbia University Press, 1954.

discharge (at least excused for discharging) their resentment against those who have what they want, by taking it away, or by destroying it.

Not only does the Commission blame the riots on those rioted against—it also proposes to make rioting more rewarding. The equation is: if there are riots, people are dissatisfied; let's satisfy them, for we must be at fault if they were dissatisfied. The conclusion, for anyone dissatisfied or resentful—for good or bad reasons—is obvious: if you riot, you get what you need or want fast; if you don't, you don't, and you may never. It should be obvious that grievances should be remedied according to their merits, but never so as to reward the aggrieved for expressing their resentment by injurious actions. However, it was not obvious to the Commission.

Full of good will and innocent naiveté, empty of historical or sociological knowledge, the Commission treats the riots as the rational phenomenon they are not. By now many Negroes want to fight, and win a victory—even if they could get more material benefits without fighting white authorities. The need to defy, to fight and to win, if you wish, to get things illegally and violently, has become independent of material effects, something desired for its own sake—probably the most important cause of the riots. This need, generated by feelings of humiliation and inadequacy, and by the consequent anger, cannot be satisfied by anything given—only by things taken; not by concessions, only by victories.

Indulgence Is Not the Remedy

Nothing is more pitiful therefore, and sillier, than the stance of the "white liberal": "I know we are at fault; I'll help you, I'll give you anything, just tell me what you want." Negroes are embarrassed. For what they—particularly young Negroes—feel they want, but cannot consciously articulate—though they certainly act it out—might be paraphrased: "We don't want to be given a damn thing by you. Stand up like a man, so we can fight you; we want to beat you up, to express our anger, not to bargain it away for any concessions. Whatever you offer we will ask for more—until you are ready to fight. For the benefits you offer cannot possibly match our fantasies, or make us feel powerful." Such a psychological condition requires specific remedies; indulgence is not among them. (Incidentally, the white liberal attitude is most apparent to Negroes in Jews—and it is a major cause of their antisemitism.)

One thing is certain: if the desire to fight whites, which many young Negroes feel, can be gratified without penalty, if it is rewarded and admired, and victory seems possible, it is not going to weaken. It is not impossible to divert such a desire into harmless, even into productive, channels, provided not only that these channels be made available, but, more important, provided that it be made entirely and credibly clear that the harmful channels are heavily penalized.

Although the demoralization, hysteria, and dissociation from reality of many Negroes is a reaction to external historical events, this reaction, and the attending evils, will not vanish if the external causes are simply removed: the phenomenon is now internal and largely independent of external changes. Meanwhile the demoralized must be prevented from inflicting harm on others, or infecting them.

Considering remedies and preventives, it is essential to distinguish between what is immediately possible and necessary, and what might be useful in the long run. The Commission's remedies are not distinguished by originality, or imagination; nor are they accompanied by evidence of effectiveness, or estimates of feasibility. While some are known to be ineffective, others may be moderately helpful; but practically all are long-run remedies, and in the long run we are all going to be dead unless we provide for the short run first.

Riot Prevention Is Simple

The riots took those in charge of public order by surprise. Attempts to control them therefore were delayed, haphazard, inept, feeble and more harmful to the innocent than to the guilty. Legislation, organization, and training of police departments easily can prevent riots. It is a silly canard that punishment "does not go to the causes of the crime." As the present Attorney General phrases this delusion, "in the long run only the elimination of the [social] causes of crime can make a significant and lasting difference in the incidence of crime."

Mr. Ramsey Clark's view suggests a fireman who declines fire-extinguishing apparatus by pointing out that "in the long run only the elimination of the causes of fire can make a significant and lasting difference in the incidence of fire," and that fire-fighting equipment does not eliminate "the causes"—except that such a fireman would probably not rise to fire chief. Actually, whether fires are checked depends on fire-fighting apparatus, and on the efforts of the firemen using it, no less than on the presence of "the causes": inflammable materials. So with riots. Laws, courts and police actions are no less important in restraining them, than "the causes" are in impelling them. If firemen (or attorneys general) pass the buck, and refuse to use the means available, we may all be burned while waiting for "the long run" and "the elimination of the causes."

Whether any activity—be it lawful or unlawful—takes place depends on whether the desire for it, or for whatever is to be secured by it, is stronger than the desire to avoid the costs involved. Accordingly people work, attend college, riot, go to the movies—or refrain from any of these activities. Attendance at a theater may be high because the show is entertaining and because the price of admission is low. Obviously the attendance depends on both—on the combination of expected gratification and cost. The wish, motive or impulse for doing anything—the experienced or expected gratification—is the cause of doing it; the wish to avoid the cost is the cause of not doing it. One is no more and no less "cause" than the other. Common speech supports this use of "cause" no less than logic. "Why did you go to Jamaica?" "Because it is such a beautiful place." "Why didn't you go to Jamaica?" "Because it is too expensive."—Why do you read *National Review?*" "Because it is so lively and instructive." "Why don't you read *National Review?*" "Because it is too exasperating." In this sense, penalties (costs) are causes of lawfulness, or (if too low or uncertain) of unlawfulness, of crime, including riots or looting.

People commit crimes or riot because, given their condition, the desire for the satisfaction felt, or sought, prevails over the desire to avoid the risk of penalties. They refrain if the desire to avoid the cost prevails. Riots will in-

crease if the penalties are reduced, or the desire is raised. Riots can be decreased by raising the cost, or by reducing the desire. The cost of riots to the
rioters is more easily and swiftly changed than the conditions producing the
inclination to riot. Costs are within the power of the government to change immediately, whereas the conditions producing the propensity to riot will necessarily take a long time to change; some may be altogether beyond the control
of the government. The Commission's one-sided emphasis on these conditions,
and its undue neglect of costs, will contribute to more riots.

What matters in riots is the immediate and stern enforcement of the law;
those who initially engage in unlawful action must be used to deter others, by
immediate apprehension, and if they refuse to surrender, immobilization by the
most effective and least injurious means. To spare lives, it is very important that
the police be armed with immobilizing non-lethal weapons, which permit the
immediate apprehension of looters, stone-throwers, and snipers. Riots spread
like fire and it is important to extinguish the first sparks even at a relatively
high cost. Certainly there should be laws making looting, and incitement to
looting, a specific crime and to punish severely anyone who knowingly disposes
of looted goods. (I have not noticed among the Commission's proposals any
referring to punishments meted out by the states for civil disorders.) The
Commission's major idea for the police is to oppose "the indiscriminate and
excessive use of force" (whoever favors anything "excessive"?) and to condemn "moves to equip police departments with automatic rifles, machine guns
and tanks." Now, a police department should be able to do without these.
However it is obviously reasonable to have such weapons in reserve. (Some
sort of armored car—whether or not it is called a tank—would have been extremely useful in last year's riots.) Meanwhile it is important to have enough
police, to organize them well, and to equip them with means to control crowds
without lasting injury, so that riots will not get into the shooting stage.

In the Medium Run

Medium-run measures, which (mostly) will have effects only some years
from now, include employment, housing, and—largely a long-run matter—
acquisition of skills, and of motivation to acquire them to seek employment.

Negro unemployment is twice as high as white unemployment and that
of Negro adolescents is several times as high as that of white adolescents. This
has little to do with present, though it has much to do with past, discrimination,
which resulted in Negroes often being capable only of unreliable or unskilled
work. It is not true, however, that unskilled work is not available. On the contrary, while unskilled workers and particular adolescents are unemployed, there
are unfilled jobs these workers could fill. They cannot be hired, or they refuse
to take these jobs, because what employers could pay for their services either
is less than what minimum wage laws prescribe, or seems inadequate to maintain a worker properly by current standards. However, prescribing a minimum
wage does not improve matters. It just causes the employer not to hire workers
to whom he would have to pay more than they are worth to him.

Two measures are required:

1. Minimum wage laws which are at best useless, and often harmful to
those supposed to be helped by them, should be eliminated.

2. Welfare payments should supplement inadequate incomes from work, and, above all, should not be reduced, so as to eliminate incentives to earn, once income from work becomes available. The Commission, as have others, makes timid suggestions in this direction but does not go far enough. Too little thought is given to incentives to make "unemployables" employable, and to cause employables to work; too much thought is based on the assumption that they cannot possibly contribute anything to their own welfare. They would, if they were helped to do so. Instead they are helped not to do so, and sometimes helped only on condition that they won't try.

Although noting the high percentage of fatherless families among Negroes and stressing that nearly half of all welfare recipients are dependent children, or those who take care of them, the Commission says nothing about the high fertility rates of the poor. Yet, if "the pill" were made available without prescription—there is no reason whatever not to do so—the fertility rates of the poor would approach those of the rich. I don't think this would foster illicit intercourse; but I'm sure it would reduce illicit conception.

The Commission indicts ghettoes (segregated housing) and slums (bad housing) as causes of riots. This confuses location and cause; it is as though hospitals were indicted as causes of illness. The original Jewish, and the present-day Chinese, ghettoes have not caused riots. There must be a specific element other than segregation, to produce riots in Negro ghettoes. Slums, bad housing, scarcely cause riots either. Surely housing has been worse, and remains so, in many parts of the world.

Nonetheless much could and should be done to improve housing. Yet the Commission proposes nothing that can be taken seriously. Its support for urban renewal (not unjustly nicknamed "Negro removal") is absurd: it is well known that this curious enterprise has destroyed far more dwellings—especially of the poor—than it has replaced.

Although admitting that the cost of building has made it impossible for the poor to find decent dwelling space, the Commission avoids asking why this nation, as it gets richer, seems less able to provide housing. However, the answer is obvious: unions have raised the cost of building so high that people cannot afford the necessary rent. Unions have done so largely by excluding the poor—specifically Negroes—from membership. Our laws, and their selective enforcement, foster and tolerate this monopolistic gouging. The political cost of better housing for the poor appears too high to the government. It would cost the taxpayer nothing. The immense expenses proposed by the Commission, on the other hand, would not begin to solve the problem.

On education the report of the Commission is highly misleading. The low school performance of Negro pupils is largely ascribed to bad textbooks, laboratories, libraries, and to segregation, even though the Coleman Report (which the Commission quotes misleadingly) states explicitly: "The data suggest that variations in school quality are not highly related to variations in achievement of pupils . . . ; the school appears unable to exert independent influence to make achievement levels less dependent on the child's background—and this is true within each ethnic group just as it is between groups" (p. 297). Elsewhere (*The Public Interest*, Fall 1967) James Coleman states: "Even in socially or racially integrated schools a child's family background shows a very high relation to his performance. The findings of the report are quite unambiguous on this score. Even if the school is integrated the heterogeneity of backgrounds with which children enter school is generally preserved in the heterogeneity of their performance when they finish."

Since Coleman wrote, it has become clearer that the deprivation in the background of Negro children is not the main cause of their low scholastic performance. Thus, Morris Gross tested "two Jewish middle class groups" and found that "marked differences in school work were apparent which resemble those uncovered in Negro-white studies . . . the differences between these two Jewish middle class groups parallel those found in different races and classes."[2] The two groups were equally prosperous. Hence deprivation, or, for that matter, race cannot be mainly responsible. An elusive factor—the cultural home ideal—must bear major responsibility. Yet the Commission tirelessly repeats the old (and false) clichés about segregation and deprivation. . . . Another study, by Susan S. Stodolsky and Gerald Lesser, might be mentioned. The authors found: 1) "ethnicity has primary effects upon the organization of mental abilities . . ."; 2) "social class variations within the ethnic group do not alter this."[3]

There are more things involved in differential education achievement than the Commission has dreamt of.

Can anything be done about the whole mess? A great deal, I think. Some things can be done easily with immediate results. Others will take time and are difficult; still others require more research. I have had space only to suggest a few problems and solutions. However, one thing is clear; if we are to make progress we must look at the actual problems and forget about the pathetic handwringing, the pompous threats and reassurances, and the silly clichés the President's Commission has produced.

[2] "Learning Readiness in Two Jewish Groups," Center for Urban Education, New York 1967.

[3] "Learning Patterns in the Disadvantaged," *Harvard Educational Review*, Fall 1967.

JAMES Q. WILSON

Why We Are Having a Wave of Violence

Most theories of collective violence have as their principal defect that they over-predict the phenomenon. Some say Negroes riot because their lot is deplorable—they have nothing to lose but their burdens. But the lot of many Negroes has always been deplorable; indeed, by most standards it is much less deplorable today than 20 years ago.

Professor of Government at Harvard University and a past Director of the M.I.T.-Harvard Joint Center for Urban Studies. Reprinted with permission from *Daedalus*, Journal of the American Academy of Arts and Sciences, Boston, Massachusetts. *Toward The Year 2000:* Work in Progress. The Daedalus Library, Houghton Mifflin Company, 1968. This essay appeared in the *New York Times Magazine* of May 19, 1968.

Others modify the theory by introducing the notion of relative deprivation, or the "revolution of rising expectations." But Negroes have experienced such deprivations and such expectations before—during World War I, World War II and the Korean War, when their incomes rose rapidly, migration to the big cities was heavy and an awareness of and contact with the advantages of white society were widespread. There were no major Negro riots then; the only major riots were begun by *whites* and aimed at Negroes (Chicago in 1919, Detroit in 1943). The only major *Negro* riot took place in Harlem in the depths of the Depression (1935), when presumably there was a "revolution of decreasing expectations."

A third theory is that the riots are caused by conspirators who have recently become organized. There may have been one or two riots that were clearly begun by conspiratorial leaders and there probably have been many attempts by such groups to cause riots, but in the major upheavals—Watts, Detroit, Newark—the activities of the conspirators did not begin in earnest until after the riot had begun from apparently spontaneous causes.

The central problem is not to predict violence, but to explain why violence has occurred during the last two or three years *but not before*. Some commentators, of course, argue that there has always been violence in this country —from the Draft Riots in the eighteen-sixties through the labor riots that began with the railroad strikes of 1877 and continued through the nineteen-thirties (15 men were killed in the Little Steel Strikes of 1937)—and that the Negro rioting today is no worse and perhaps no different from earlier forms of violence. It has even been suggested that violence is in some sense a "normal" and perhaps legitimate political strategy for oppressed groups.

Whether the present riots are any worse than earlier disorders is beside the point; whether they are in some sense legitimate is not beside the point but outside the scope of this paper. What can be said is that they are different. The Draft Riots were popular reactions against a certain concrete public policy, the enforcement of which was resisted by Irishmen and others who were not willing to restrict themselves to "going limp." The violence attending the labor disputes (in 1934 alone, nearly 30 people were killed) was in almost every case the result of an effort by a union to persuade management to recognize it. When management responded by calling in the Pinkertons and the scabs, the workers reacted with violent protest.

Labor-management violence was in the nature of an internal war between two organized opponents struggling over a quite tangible stake. With the winning of union recognition, the incidence of such violence dropped off markedly, though isolated cases recur from time to time, especially in the South.[1] Even the anti-Irish riots of the eighteen-forties and fifties were directed at an "enemy" and resulted in the destruction of "enemy" property; in Philadelphia, two Catholic churches and two parochial schools were burned to the ground; in St. Louis 50 Irish homes were wrecked and looted; in New York a mob marched on City Hall to attack anybody who looked Irish.[2]

[1] Philip Taft, "Violence in American Labor Disputes," Annals, Vol. 364 (March, 1966), pp. 127-140.
[2] Arnold Forster, "Violence on the Fanatical Left and Right," Annals, *op. cit.,* p. 143.

The Negro riots are not apparently aimed at a specific enemy, they do not arise over a specific *issue* (though they may be precipitated by an "incident") and they do not carry the war to the enemy's territory. While it is true that white-owned business establishments are burned and looted, the amount of property owned or occupied by Negroes that is destroyed is often much greater. The Detroit Fire Department listed 477 buildings destroyed or damaged by fire in the 1967 riot. Of these, 103 were single-family and multi-family homes, 30 were apartment buildings and 38 were stores which contained dwelling units. The vast majority were inhabited by Negroes, and many were owned by Negroes. Only five liquor stores, two loan shops, four jewelry stores and one bank were burned, even though these establishments presumably represent "white business" and may be perceived as "white exploitation." Many other, more obvious symbols of white authority—churches, schools, newspaper circulation offices, police buildings—were scarcely touched. To compare these riots with earlier historical examples is like comparing assault to self-flagellation— such pleasure as the latter confers does not depend on the suffering it causes others.

When people destroy their own communities, even at high risk to themselves (43 persons died in Detroit, most from police and National Guard bullets), it is difficult to assert that the riot was an *instrumental* act—that is, an effort to achieve an objective. (The Draft Riots, the anti-Irish riots, the violence practiced by the Ku Klux Klan and the labor-management violence were all to some degree instrumental acts.) The Negro riots are in fact *expressive* acts—that is, actions which are either intrinsically satisfying ("play") or satisfying because they give expression to a state of mind.

Of course, for many people in all riots—whether instrumental or expressive —there are individual gratifications, such as the opportunity for looting, for settling old scores and the like. But these people operate, so to speak, under the cover of the riot and are not obviously the cause of it. To the extent riots are or can be organized, of course, the need to offer incentives to induce people to participate would make the encouragement of looting a prime objective for a riot leader—not only does it get people out on the street in large numbers and put them in an excited state of mind, it disperses and preoccupies police and military forces. There is little evidence yet, however, that it is the desire for loot that precipitates the riot or even plays a very important part in the early hours.

If we are to construct an explanation for what has occurred—and we may never have a testable explanation, for the requirements of experimental or statistical control necessary to test any riot hypothesis are not likely to exist— we must combine attention to the material conditions in which the Negro lives (which on the whole have been improving but are still poor) with the costs and benefits to him of expressing a desire for autonomy, manhood, self-respect and the capacity for independent action.

On the cost side, we note a significant reduction in the willingness of those who command the police to use them with maximum vigor in suppressing disorder. The attention given of late to real and imagined cases of "police brutality" has obscured the fact that, compared to the police response to labor violence even 30 years ago, most big-city police departments, especially in the

North, have recently been less inclined, primarily for political reasons, to use instant and massive retaliatory tactics against any incipient disorder. It would appear that this is one reason the majority of serious riots have occurred in the North, not the South—in the latter region, political constraints on the police are less effective.

One need not deny that police-citizen contacts have often been the spark that triggered a riot, or that many departments have neglected or mismanaged their community relations program, to argue that the police, if they wanted to (that is, if they were willing to pay the price in lives and political support), could make the costs of rioting so high that either there would be no riots at all or there would be a massive convulsion equivalent to civil war.

On the benefits side, persons are coming of age who are several generations away from the rural South and who accordingly have lost their fear of white men without yet having had an opportunity to even scores. Young people are always rebellious; when young people grow up and discover that their elders are *also* rebellious, there is perhaps an urge for even more extreme actions. Just as the sons and daughters of New Deal liberals regard their parents as "square" for confining their demands for change to the rules imposed by the existing political system, so also the sons and daughters of Negroes who have demanded integration and equal opportunity may feel that such demands are not enough because they are based on an acceptance of the distribution of power within the existing social order.

Negro (and some white) leaders, aware of the drift toward violent sentiments, have attempted to take advantage of it by using the threat of violence as a way of increasing their bargaining power; the difficulty, of course, is that the responsible leaders have lacked the capacity either to start or stop a riot while the irresponsible ones have simply lacked the power to stop one.

Furthermore, the mass media—especially television—offer an opportunity for immediate expressive gratification that did not exist even 15 years ago. It is interesting to speculate on what the Know-Nothing violence might have been like if every American could watch in his living room the looting of a convent while it was happening and if every would-be looter could be summoned to the scene by immediate radio coverage of the event.

Finally, young people today, white and Negro, have become quite self-conscious, for reasons I obviously do not understand, about the social functions and therapeutic value of violence. A generation that was absorbed by Camus's intricate analysis of how in existential terms one might have justified the effort to assassinate the czar has given way to a generation some members of which are absorbed by Frantz Fanon's argument for violence: Violence, if practiced by the wretched and oppressed, may be intrinsically valuable as an assertion of self and a reversal of a previous act of violence—slavery—by which self has been denied and subjugation institutionalized.[3]

In short, the few things we know about the riots—that they develop out of a seemingly trivial incident, that they are more expressive than instrumental and that they have thus far occurred primarily in Northern cities or in the more "progressive" Southern cities (such as Atlanta or Nashville)—should lead

[3] Aristide and Vera Zolberg, "The Americanization of Frantz Fanon," *The Public Interest* (Fall, 1967), pp. 49-63.

us to be skeptical of arguments that the riots can be explained entirely or primarily on grounds of *material* deprivation, unresponsive local governments, inadequate poverty programs or the like. No doubt these factors play a part. After all, if the class characteristics of Negroes were identical to those of whites (measured by income, education, mobility and level of political organization), it is hard to imagine that there would be any riots, though there still might be a good deal of discontent. If there were no lower class, there would be fewer riots just as there would be fewer murders. But if class is a necessary explanation, it is not a sufficient one. To material (that is to say, to Marxian) explanations must be added explanations that take into account the role of *ideas* and the role of *force*.

It is hard to discuss such things without being misunderstood. To impute causal power to ideas or to the lack of force seems to imply the desirability of censoring ideas or imposing the most repressive kinds of force. That is not the implication I intend. To try to censor ideas is both wrong and futile; repressive force is neither available nor manageable. The argument here is analytic, not prescriptive, and is designed merely to suggest that we consider the possibility that ideas have consequences.

Theories of social change are often suspect in my eyes because they seem to lead automatically to the policy conclusion favored by their author: It is as if one decided what program one wanted adopted and then decided what "caused" an event in order to justify that remedial program. If one wants a "Marshall Plan" for Negroes, then economic want causes riots; if one wishes the political power of the "Establishment" weakened, then inadequate access and a lack of self-determination are the causes; if one wants Stokely Carmichael and Rap Brown put in jail, then conspirators are the cause. Since almost no one wants (at least publicly) ideas to be controlled, the causal power of ideas is rarely asserted; this theory gets fewer "votes" than it may deserve because it is not in anyone's interest to vote for it.

But if elsewhere ideas are readily conceded to have consequences—"nationalism," "self-determination," "the world community revolution"—might it not be possible that they have consequences here also? Only a fear of being thought illiberal may prevent us from considering that the probability of a riot is increased by demands for "Black Power," by a constant reiteration that white bigotry and racism are at the root of all the problems besetting the Negro, by the reaffirmation of the (untrue) assumption that most Negroes live wretched lives and that matters are going from bad to worse, by constantly predicting apocalyptic violence if "something isn't done" and by "discovering" the non-truth that all Negroes are alike in their hatred of "whitey" and their tacit or open approval of extreme solutions for their plight.

If there is something in the climate of opinion, the mood of a generation or the drift of sentiments that contributes to Negro riots, there is no reason to suppose that only Negroes are affected by these currents. The special and urgent problem of the Negro may lead us to assume, without sufficient reflection, that the Negro case is not only special but unique. But it ought not be taken for granted that 20 million people are affected by ideas that have no effect on the other 180 million living in the same country.

More narrowly, are young Negroes involved in a radical discontinuity in

American history or are they simply at the leading edge of a more general drift toward collective violence? Are we quite confident that there is no connection between Negroes burning down their communities and young whites storming the Pentagon, assaulting Cabinet officers and forcibly occupying university buildings? Or between these acts and the sharp rise in recruitment to the Ku Klux Klan and the emergence of the ominous White Knights and the Minutemen? And if there is a connection, is the entire phenomenon to be put down to "rising expectations" or "unresponsive government"?

I cannot say there is a connection, but I cannot accept without some persuasion the answer that the Negro is wholly a special case. Collective violence was once thought to be an inevitable aspect of the political life of any country, even this one. In 1947, in the second edition of his famous text on political parties, the late V. O. Key Jr. devoted a full chapter to the political role of force. By 1958, when the fourth edition appeared, that chapter had been reduced to a page and a half. And by 1961, when his book on public opinion appeared, there was a chapter on "conflict" but no mention of violent conflict.

Traditionally, one would expect violence whenever there were deep and irreconcilable differences of opinion on fundamental issues in a society where one party had no confidence in the capacity of the other party to govern. (The distrust between the Socialists and Conservatives in prewar Austria was, of course, a classic case; a postwar government was possible only on the basis of a coalition that permitted one party to check the other in the ministries as well as in Parliament—a form of "participatory democracy.") One would also expect violence when, though the nation is not deeply divided, established authority is unwilling to use force to make the costs of violence prohibitively great for any minority unwilling to resign itself to losing in a nonviolent struggle for power.

If the traditional understanding of violence were applied today, one would not expect it to subside once the "demands" of Negroes (or peace marchers, or whatever) were met. One reason is that the demands cannot be met—the competition for leadership among the (largely disorganized) dissident groups will inevitably generate ever more extreme demands faster than less extreme requests are fulfilled.

Another reason is that violent political conflict is only rarely over tangible resources which the government can allocate—it is typically over symbolic values which government either does not control (the sense of equality or human dignity or social acceptance) or does control but cannot redistribute without destroying itself (sending the Irish back to Ireland, abandoning military force as a tool of foreign policy). But primarily violence will not subside because it is the cleavage in opinion which gives rise to it, and concessions sufficient to induce one side to abandon violence (subject to the constraints cited above) might be concessions sufficient to induce the other side to resort to violence.

To cut through the vicious circle, governments historically have increased the application of force to the point that neither side found it rewarding to practice violence, thus inducing both sides to wait for long-term trends to soften or alter the cleavages of opinion. Such increases in force have often required a reduction in the degree to which the use of force was subject to democratic constraints. Parliamentary regimes have been replaced by presidential regimes;

presidential regimes have been replaced by dictatorial regimes. Only when it is clear that *neither* side can gain through violent protest does the resort to such forms of protest cease. The case for dealing with the conditions under which Negroes (or poor whites) live is not, therefore, to be made on the grounds that such efforts will "stop riots"; it can be made only on the grounds that for other, and essentially moral, reasons changing those conditions is right and necessary.

Whether this analysis has any applicability to present-day America is difficult to say. One would first have to estimate the probability of white violence against Negroes (or hawk violence against doves) under various kinds of governmental concessions to Negroes (or doves), and no one is competent to make any confident predictions on these matters. What can be said is that long-term prosperity is no guarantee against political violence of some form. Prosperity cannot by itself eliminate the ideological sources of violence and indeed may weaken the institutional constraints on it so that the effects of the activities of even a few persons with violent intentions may be amplified by an increasingly larger multiplier and thus influence the action of ever larger numbers of persons.

This consequence of prosperity may arise through the dispersal of power and authority that tends to result from the entry of more and more persons into middle-class status and thus into the forms of participation in public life that are reserved for the middle class. Middle-class persons participate in voluntary associations and public affairs more than working-class persons (and certainly more than lower-class persons, who scarcely participate at all). The higher the level of participation, the larger the number and variety of voluntary associations (and social movements) and the more wills which must be concerted in the making of public policy.[4] "Participatory democracy" may be a slogan currently linked with the aspirations of the underprivileged, but in fact participatory democracy has all along been the political style (if not the slogan) of the American middle and upper-middle class. It will become a more widespread style as more persons enter into these classes.

Additionally, continued prosperity will increasingly free young people from the pinch of economic necessity (the need to get a job early in life), place more of them in colleges and universities—where, for better or worse, traditional values are questioned—and increase the number (if not the proportion) of those who find various kinds of personal and political nonconformity attractive.

With participation in greater variety and numbers, the possibility of any one or few organizations dominating the expression of some common interest (civil rights, peace, governmental reform) will be lessened and the competition among such groups will increase. The sensitivity of more and more persons to the substance of issues will reduce the capacity of government to act without regard to these views, and the high (but quite selective) visibility given to governmental acts by television will reduce the capacity of government to act at all in ways (e.g., the use of force or a display of indifference) once employed more readily because less visibly.

---

[4] Cf. Edward C. Banfield and James Q. Wilson, "City Politics" (Cambridge, 1963), esp. concluding chapter.

In short, marches, protests, sit-ins, demonstrations, mass meetings and other forms of direct collective action may become more rather than less common, though it is hard to predict what issues will prove sufficiently salient to generate such activities. How many will be violent no one can say, but it is not unreasonable to assume that if large numbers of people are brought together in public places because of issues about which they feel strongly, a certain though unknown proportion will—either because they seek violence ("confrontation politics") or because they feel provoked by the police or other opponents —take matters into their own hands.

Black Power

CHARLES V. HAMILTON

Definition

Black power has many definitions and connotations in the rhetoric of race relations today. To some people, it is synonymous with premeditated acts of violence to destroy the political and economic institutions of this country. Others equate Black Power with plans to rid the civil-rights movement of whites who have been in it for years. The concept is understood by many to mean hatred of and separation from whites; it is associated with calling whites "honkies" and with shouts of "Burn, baby, burn!" Some understand it to be the use of pressure-group tactics in the accepted tradition of the American political process. And still others say that Black Power must be seen first of all as an attempt to instill a sense of identity and pride in black people.

Ultimately, I suspect, we have to accept the fact that, in this highly charged atmosphere, it is virtually impossible to come up with a single definition satisfactory to all.

Even as some of us try to articulate our idea of Black Power and the way we relate to it and advocate it, we are categorized as "moderate" or "militant" or "reasonable" or "extremist." "I can accept your definition of Black Power," a listener will say to me. "But how does your position compare with what Stokely Carmichael said in Cuba or with what H. Rap Brown said in Cambridge, Md.?" Or, just as frequently, some young white New Left advocate will come up to me and proudly announce: "You're not radical enough. Watts, Newark, Detroit—that's what's happening, man! You're nothing but a reformist. We've got to blow up this society. Read Ché or Debray or Mao." All I can do is shrug and conclude that some people believe that making a revolution in this country involves rhetoric, Molotov cocktails and being under 30.

To have Black Power equated with calculated acts of violence would be very unfortunate. First, if black people have learned anything over the years, it is that he who shouts revolution the loudest is one of the first to run when the action starts. Second, open calls to violence are a sure way to have one's

Professor of urban studies at Columbia University and co-author, with Stokely Carmichael, of *Black Power: The Politics of Liberation in America.* This selection is from "An Advocate of Black Power Defines It," by Charles V. Hamilton. *New York Times Magazine,* April 14, 1968. © 1968 by The New York Times Company. Reprinted by permission.

ranks immediately infiltrated. Third—and this is as important as any reason—violent revolution in this country would fail; it would be met with the kind of repression used in Sharpeville, South Africa, in 1960, when 67 Africans were killed and 186 wounded during a demonstration against apartheid. It is clear that America is not above this. There are many white bigots who would like nothing better than to embark on a program of black genocide, even though the imposition of such repressive measures would destroy civil liberties for whites as well as for blacks. Some whites are so panicky, irrational and filled with racial hatred that they would welcome the opportunity to annihilate the black community. This was clearly shown in the senseless murder of Dr. Martin Luther King Jr., which understandably—but nonetheless irrationally—prompted some black militants to advocate violent retaliation. Such cries for revenge intensify racial fear and animosity when the need—now more than ever—is to establish solid, stable organizations and action programs.

Many whites will take comfort in these words of caution against violence. But they should not. The truth is that the black ghettos are going to continue to blow up out of sheer frustration and rage, and no amount of rhetoric from professors writing articles in magazines (which most black people in the ghettos do not read anyway) will affect that. There comes a point beyond which people cannot be expected to endure prejudice, oppression and deprivation, and they *will* explode.

Some of us can protect our positions by calling for "law and order" during a riot, or by urging "peaceful" approaches, but we should not be confident that we are being listened to by black people legitimately fed up with intolerable conditions. If white America wants a solution to the violence in the ghettos by blacks, then let white America end the violence done to the ghettos by whites. We simply must come to understand that there can be no social order without social justice. "How long will the violence in the summers last?" another listener may ask. "How intransigent is white America?" is my answer. And the answer to that could be just more rhetoric or it could be a sincere response to legitimate demands.

Black power must not be naive about the intentions of white decision-makers to yield anything without a struggle and a confrontation by organized power. Black people will gain only as much as they can win through their ability to organize independent bases of economic and political power—through boycotts, electoral activity, rent strikes, work stoppages, pressure-group bargaining. And it must be clear that whites will have to bargain with blacks or continue to fight them in the streets of the Detroits and the Newarks. Rather than being a call to violence, this is a clear recognition that the ghetto rebellions, in addition to producing the possibility of apartheid-type repression, have been functional in moving *some* whites to see that viable solutions must be sought.

Black Power is concerned with organizing the rage of black people and with putting new, hard questions and demands to white America. As we do this, white America's responses will be crucial to the questions of violence and viability. Black Power must (1) deal with the obviously growing alienation of black people and their distrust of the institutions of this society; (2) work to create new values and to build a new sense of community and of belonging, and (3) work to establish legitimate new institutions that make participants, not recipients, out of a people traditionally excluded from the fundamentally racist processes of this country. There is nothing glamorous about this; it involves persistence and hard, tedious, day-to-day work.

Black Power rejects the lessons of slavery and segregation that caused black people to look upon themselves with hatred and disdain. To be "integrated" it was necessary to deny one's heritage, one's own culture, to be ashamed of one's black skin, thick lips and kinky hair. In their book, "Racial Crisis in America," two Florida State University sociologists, Lewis M. Killian and Charles M. Grigg, wrote: "At the present time, integration as a solution to the race problem demands that the Negro forswear his identity as a Negro. But for a lasting solution, the meaning of 'American' must lose its implicit racial modifier, 'white.' " The black man must change his demeaning conception of himself; he must develop a sense of pride and self-respect. Then, if integration comes, it will deal with people who are psychologically and mentally healthy, with people who have a sense of their history and of themselves as whole human beings.

In the process of creating these new values, Black Power will, its advocates hope, build a new sense of community among black people. It will try to forge a bond in the black community between those who have "made it" and those "on the bottom." It will bring an end to the internal back-biting and suspicious bickering, the squabbling over tactics and personalities so characteristic of the black community. If Black Power can produce this unity, that in itself will be revolutionary, for the black community and for the country.

STOKELY CARMICHAEL
What We Want

Black power can be clearly defined for those who do not attach the fears of white America to their questions about it. We should begin with the basic fact that black Americans have two problems: they are poor and they are black. All other problems arise from this two-sided reality: lack of education, the so-called apathy of black men. Any program to end racism must address itself to that double reality.

Almost from its beginning, SNCC sought to address itself to both conditions with a program aimed at winning political power for impoverished Southern blacks. We had to begin with politics because black Americans are a propertyless people in a country where property is valued above all. We had to work for power, because this country does not function by morality, love, and nonviolence, but by power. Thus we determined to win political power,

Former Director of the Student Nonviolent Coordinating Committee. Co-author with Charles V. Hamilton of *Black Power: The Politics of Liberation in America.* The selection is from Stokely Carmichael, "What We Want," *New York Review of Books,* Vol. VII, No. 4 (September 22, 1966). Reprinted with permission of the Student Nonviolent Coordinating Committee.

with the idea of moving on from there into activity that would have economic effects. With power, the masses could *make or participate in making* the decisions which govern their destinies, and thus create basic change in their day-to-day lives. . . .

Ultimately, the economic foundations of this country must be shaken if black people are to control their lives. The colonies of the United States—and this includes the black ghettoes within its borders, north and south—must be liberated. For a century, this nation has been like an octopus of exploitation, its tentacles stretching from Mississippi and Harlem to South America, the Middle East, southern Africa, and Vietnam; the form of exploitation varies from area to area but the essential result has been the same—a powerful few have been maintained and enriched at the expense of the poor and voiceless colored masses. This pattern must be broken. As its grip loosens here and there around the world, the hopes of black Americans become more realistic. For racism to die, a totally different America must be born.

This is what the white society does not wish to face; this is why that society prefers to talk about integration. But integration speaks not at all to the problem of poverty, only to the problem of blackness. Integration today means the man who "makes it," leaving his black brothers behind in the ghetto as fast as his new sports car will take him. It has no relevance to the Harlem wino or to the cotton-picker making three dollars a day. As a lady I know in Alabama once said, "the food that Ralph Bunche eats doesn't fill my stomach."

Integration, moreover, speaks to the problem of blackness in a despicable way. As a goal, it has been based on complete acceptance of the fact that *in order to have* a decent house or education, blacks must move into a white neighborhood or send their children to a white school. This reinforces, among both black and white, the idea that "white" is automatically better and "black" is by definition inferior. This is why integration is a subterfuge for the maintenance of white supremacy. It allows the nation to focus on a handful of Southern children who get into white schools, at great price, and to ignore the 94 per cent who are left behind in unimproved all-black schools. Such situations will not change until black people have power—to control their own school boards, in this case. Then Negroes become equal in a way that means something, and integration ceases to be a one-way street. Then integration doesn't mean draining skills and energies from the ghetto into white neighborhoods; then it can mean white people moving from Beverly Hills into Watts, white people joining the Lowndes County Freedom Organization. Then integration becomes relevant.

Last April, before the furor over black power, Christopher Jencks wrote in a *New Republic* article on white Mississippi's manipulation of the anti-poverty program:

The war on poverty has been predicated on the notion that there is such a thing as *a community* which can be defined geographically and mobilized for a collective effort to help the poor. This theory has no relationship to reality in the Deep South. In every Mississippi county there are *two* communities. Despite all the pious platitudes of the moderates on both sides, these two communities habitually see their interests in terms of conflict rather than cooperation. Only when the Negro community can muster enough political, economic and professional strength to compete on somewhat equal terms, will Negroes believe in the possibility of true cooperation and whites accept its necessity. En route to integration, the Negro community needs to develop greater independence—a chance to run its own affairs and not cave in whenever "the man" barks . . . Or so it seems to me, and to most of the knowledgeable people with whom I talked in Mississippi. To OEO, this judgment may sound like black nationalism . . .

Mr. Jencks, a white reporter, perceived the reason why America's anti-poverty program has been a sick farce in both North and South. In the South, it is clearly racism which prevents the poor from running their own programs; in the North, it more often seems to be politicking and bureaucracy. But the results are not so different: In the North, non-whites make up 42 per cent of all families in metropolitan "poverty areas" and only 6 per cent of families in areas classified as not poor. SNCC has been working with local residents in Arkansas, Alabama, and Mississippi to achieve control by the poor of the program and its funds; it has also been working with groups in the North, and the struggle is no less difficult. Behind it all is a federal government which cares far more about winning the war on the Vietnamese than the war on poverty; which has put the poverty program in the hands of self-serving politicians and bureaucrats rather than the poor themselves; which is unwilling to curb the misuse of white power but quick to condemn black power . . .

From birth, black people are told a set of lies about themselves. We are told that we are lazy—yet I drive through the Delta area of Mississippi and watch black people picking cotton in the hot sun for fourteen hours. We are told, "If you work hard, you'll succeed"—but if that were true, black people would own this country. We are oppressed because we are black—not because we are ignorant, not because we are lazy, not because we're stupid (and got good rhythm,) but because we're black.

I remember that when I was a boy, I used to go to see Tarzan movies on Saturday. White Tarzan used to beat up the black natives. I would sit there yelling, "Kill the beasts, kill the savages, kill 'em!" I was saying: Kill *me*. It was as if a Jewish boy watched Nazis taking Jews off to concentration camps and cheered them on. Today, I want the chief to beat hell out of Tarzan and send him back to Europe. But it takes time to become free of the lies and their shaming effect on black minds. It takes time to reject the most important lie: that black people inherently can't do the same things white people can do, unless white people help them.

The need for psychological equality is the reason why SNCC today believes that blacks must organize in the black community. Only black people can convey the revolutionary idea that black people are able to do things themselves. Only they can help create in the community an aroused and continuing black consciousness that will provide the basis for political strength. In the past, white allies have furthered white supremacy without the whites involved realizing it—or wanting it, I think. Black people must do things for themselves; they must get poverty money they will control and spend themselves, they must conduct tutorial programs themselves so that black children can identify with black people. This is one reason Africa has such importance: The reality of black men ruling their own natives gives blacks elsewhere a sense of possibility, of power, which they do not now have.

This does not mean we don't welcome help, or friends. But we want the right to decide whether anyone is, in fact, our friend. In the past, black Americans have been almost the only people whom everybody and his momma could jump up and call their friends. We have been tokens, symbols, objects—as I was in high school to many young whites, who liked having "a Negro friend." We want to decide who is our friend, and we will not accept someone who comes to us and says: "If you do X, Y, and Z, then I'll help you." We will not be told whom we should choose as allies. We will not be isolated from any group or nation except by our own choice. We cannot have the oppressors telling the oppressed how to rid themselves of the oppressor. . . .

But our vision is not merely of a society in which all black men have enough to buy the good things of life. When we urge that black money go into black pockets, we mean the communal pocket. We want to see money go back into the community and used to benefit it. We want to see the cooperative concept applied in business and banking. We want to see black ghetto residents demand that an exploiting store keeper sell them, at minimal cost, a building or a shop that they will own and improve cooperatively; they can back their demand with a rent strike, or a boycott, and a community so unified behind them that no one else will move into the building or buy at the store. The society we seek to build among black people, then, is not a capitalist one. It is a society in which the spirit of community and humanistic love prevail. The word love is suspect; black expectations of what it might produce have been betrayed too often. But those were expectations of a response from the white community, which failed us. The love we seek to encourage is within the black community, the only American community where men call each other "brother" when they meet. We can build a community of love only where we have the ability and power to do so: among blacks.

As for white America, perhaps it can stop crying out against "black supremacy," "black nationalism," "racism in reverse," and begin facing reality. The reality is that this nation, from top to bottom, is racist; that racism is not primarily a problem of "human relations" but of an exploitation maintained— either actively or through silence—by the society as a whole. Camus and Sartre have asked, can a man condemn himself? Can whites, particularly liberal whites, condemn themselves? Can they stop blaming us, and blame their own system? Are they capable of the shame which might become a revolutionary emotion?

We have found that they usually cannot condemn themselves, and so we have done it. But the rebuilding of this society, if at all possible, is basically the responsibility of whites—not blacks. We won't fight to save the present society, in Vietnam or anywhere else. We are just going to work, in the way *we* see fit, and on goals *we* define, not for civil rights but for all our human rights.

BAYARD RUSTIN
"Black Power" and Coalition Politics

There are two Americas—black and white—and nothing has more clearly revealed the divisions between them than the debate currently raging around the slogan of "black power." Despite—or perhaps because of—the fact that this slogan lacks any clear definition, it has succeeded in galvanizing emotions on all sides, with many whites seeing it as the expression of a new racism and many Negroes taking it as a warning to white people that Negroes will no longer tolerate brutality and violence. But even within the Negro community itself, "black power" has touched off a major debate—the most bitter the community has experienced since the days of Booker T. Washington and W. E. B. Du Bois, and one which threatens to ravage the entire civil-rights movement. Indeed, a serious split has already developed between advocates of "black power" like Floyd McKissick of CORE and Stokely Carmichael of SNCC on the one hand, and Dr. Martin Luther King of SCLC, Roy Wilkins of the NAACP, and Whitney Young of the Urban League on the other.

There is no question, then, that great passions are involved in the debate over the idea of "black power"; nor, as we shall see, is there any question that these passions have their roots in the psychological and political frustrations of the Negro community. Nevertheless, I would contend that "black power" not only lacks any real value for the civil-rights movement, but that its propagation is positively harmful. It diverts the movement from a meaningful debate over strategy and tactics, it isolates the Negro community, and it encourages the growth of anti-Negro forces.

In its simplest and most innocent guise, "black power" merely means the effort to elect Negroes to office in proportion to Negro strength within the population. There is, of course, nothing wrong with such an objective in itself, and nothing inherently radical in the idea of pursuing it. But in Stokely Carmichael's extravagant rhetoric about "taking over" in districts of the South where Negroes are in the majority, it is important to recognize that Southern Negroes are only in a position to win a maximum of two congressional seats and control of eighty local counties.[1] (Carmichael, incidentally, is in the paradoxical position of screaming at liberals—wanting only to "get whitey off my back"—and simultaneously needing their support: after all, he can talk about Negroes taking over Lowndes County only because there is a fairly liberal federal government to protect him should Governor Wallace decide to eliminate

Executive Director of the A. Philip Randolph Institute. The selection is from " 'Black Power' and Coalition Politics," *Commentary,* Vol. 42, No. 3 (September 1966), pp. 35-40. Reprinted from *Commentary,* by permission; copyright © 1966 by the American Jewish Committee.
[1] See "The Negroes Enter Southern Politics" by Pat Watters, *Dissent,* July-August 1966.

this pocket of black power.) Now there might be a certain value in having two Negro congressmen from the South, but obviously they could do nothing by themselves to reconstruct the face of America. Eighty sheriffs, eighty tax assessors, and eighty school-board members might ease the tension for a while in their communities, but they alone could not create jobs and build low-cost housing; they alone could not supply quality integrated education.

The relevant question, moreover, is not whether a politician is black or white, but what forces he represents. Manhattan has had a succession of Negro borough presidents, and yet the schools are increasingly segregated. Adam Clayton Powell and William Dawson have both been in Congress for many years; the former is responsible for a rider on school integration that never gets passed, and the latter is responsible for keeping the Negroes of Chicago tied to a mayor who had to see riots and death before he would put eight-dollar sprinklers on water hydrants in the summer. I am not for one minute arguing that Powell, Dawson, and Mrs. Motley should be impeached. What I am saying is that if a politician is elected because he is black and is deemed to be entitled to a "slice of the pie," he will behave in one way; if he is elected by a constituency pressing for social reform, he will, whether he is white or black, behave in another way.

Southern Negroes, despite exhortations from SNCC to organize themselves into a Black Panther party, are going to stay in the Democratic party—to them it is the party of progress, the New Deal, the New Frontier, and the Great Society—and they are right to stay. For SNCC's Black Panther perspective is simultaneously utopian and reactionary—the former for the by now obvious reason that one-tenth of the population cannot accomplish much by itself, the latter because such a party would remove Negroes from the main area of political struggle in this country (particularly in the one-party South, where the decisive battles are fought out in Democratic primaries), and would give priority to the issue of race precisely at a time when the fundamental questions facing the Negro and American society alike are economic and social. . . .

The winning of the right of Negroes to vote in the South insures the eventual transformation of the Democratic party, now controlled primarily by Northern machine politicians and Southern Dixiecrats. The Negro vote will eliminate the Dixiecrats from the party and from Congress, which means that the crucial question facing us today is who will replace them in the South. Unless civil-rights leaders (in such towns as Jackson, Mississippi; Birmingham, Alabama; and even to a certain extent Atlanta) can organize grass-roots clubs whose members will have a genuine political voice, the Dixiecrats might well be succeeded by black moderates and black Southern-style machine politicians, who would do little to push for needed legislation in Congress and little to improve local conditions in the South. While I myself would prefer Negro machines to a situation in which Negroes have no power at all, it seems to me that there is a better alternative today—a liberal-labor-civil rights coalition which would work to make the Democratic party truly responsive to the aspirations of the poor, and which would develop support for programs (specifically those outlined in A. Philip Randolph's $100 billion Freedom Budget) aimed at the reconstruction of American society in the interests of greater social justice. The advocates of "black power" have no such programs in mind; what they are in fact arguing for (perhaps unconsciously) is the creation of a *new black establishment.*

Nor, it might be added, are they leading the Negro people along the same road which they imagine immigrant groups traveled so successfully in the past. Proponents of "black power"—accepting a historical myth perpetrated by moderates—like to say that the Irish and the Jews and the Italians, by sticking together and demanding their share, finally won enough power to overcome their initial disabilities. But the truth is that it was through alliances with other groups (in political machines or as part of the trade-union movement) that the Irish and the Jews and the Italians acquired the power to win their rightful place in American society. They did not "pull themselves up by their own bootstraps"—no group in American society has ever done so; and they most certainly did not make isolation their primary tactic.

In some quarters, "black power" connotes not an effort to increase the number of Negroes in elective office but rather a repudiation of non-violence in favor of Negro "self-defense." Actually this is a false issue, since no one has ever argued that Negroes should not defend themselves as individuals from attack.[2] Non-violence has been advocated as a *tactic* for organized demonstrations in a society where Negroes are a minority and where the majority controls the police. Proponents of non-violence do not, for example, deny that James Meredith has the right to carry a gun for protection when he visits his mother in Mississippi; what they question is the wisdom of his carrying a gun while participating in a demonstration.

There is, as well, a tactical side to the new emphasis on "self-defense" and the suggestion that non-violence be abandoned. The reasoning here is that turning the other cheek is not the way to win respect, and that only if the Negro succeeds in frightening the white man will the white man begin taking him seriously. The trouble with this reasoning is that it fails to recognize that fear is more likely to bring hostility to the surface than respect; and far from prodding the "white power structure" into action, the new militant leadership, by raising the slogan of black power and lowering the banner of non-violence, has obscured the moral issue facing this nation, and permitted the President and Vice President to lecture us about "racism in reverse" instead of proposing more meaningful programs for dealing with the problems of unemployment, housing, and education.

"Black power" is, of course, a somewhat nationalistic slogan and its sudden rise to popularity among Negroes signifies a concomitant rise in nationalist sentiment (Malcolm X's autobiography is quoted nowadays in Grenada, Mississippi as well as in Harlem). We have seen such nationalistic turns and withdrawals back into the ghetto before, and when we look at the conditions which brought them about, we find that they have much in common with the conditions of Negro life at the present moment: conditions which lead to despair over the goal of integration and to the belief that the ghetto will last forever.

It may, in the light of the many juridical and legislative victories which

[2] As far back as 1934, A. Philip Randolph, Walter White, then executive secretary of the NAACP, Lester Granger, then executive director of the Urban League, and I joined a committee to try to save the life of Odell Waller. Waller, a sharecropper, had murdered his white boss in self-defense.

have been achieved in the past few years, seem strange that despair should be so widespread among Negroes today. But anyone to whom it seems strange should reflect on the fact that despite these victories *Negroes today are in worse economic shape, live in worse slums, and attend more highly segregated schools than in 1954.* Thus—to recite the appalling, and appallingly familiar, statistical litany once again—more Negroes are unemployed today than in 1954; the gap between the wages of the Negro worker and the white worker is wider; while the unemployment rate among white youths is decreasing, the rate among Negro youths has increased to *32 per cent* (and among Negro girls the rise is even more startling). Even the one gain which has been registered, a decrease in the unemployment rate among Negro adults, is deceptive, for it represents men who have been called back to work after a period of being laid off. In any event, unemployment among Negro men is still twice that of whites, and no new jobs have been created.

So too with housing, which is deteriorating in the North (and yet the housing provisions of the 1966 civil-rights bill are weaker than the antidiscrimination laws in several states which contain the worst ghettos even with these laws on their books). And so too with schools: according to figures issued recently by the Department of Health, Education and Welfare, 65 per cent of first-grade Negro students in this country attend schools that are from 90 to 100 per cent black. (If in 1954, when the Supreme Court handed down the desegregation decision, you had been the Negro parent of a first-grade child, the chances are that this past June you would have attended that child's graduation from a segregated high school.)

To put all this in the simplest and most concrete terms: the day-to-day lot of the ghetto Negro has not been improved by the various judicial and legislative measures of the past decade.

Negroes are thus in a situation similar to that of the turn of the century, when Booker T. Washington advised them to "cast down their buckets" (that is to say, accommodate to segregation and disenfranchisement) and when even his leading opponent, W. E. B. Du Bois, was forced to advocate the development of a group economy in place of the direct-action boycotts, general strikes, and protest techniques which had been used in the 1880's, before the enactment of the Jim-Crow laws. For all their differences, both Washington and DuBois then found it impossible to believe that Negroes could ever be integrated into American society, and each in his own way therefore counseled withdrawal into the ghetto, self-help, and economic self-determination. . . .

The promise of meaningful work and decent wages once held out by the anti-poverty programs has not been fulfilled. Because there has been a lack of the necessary funds, the program has in many cases been reduced to wrangling for positions on boards or for lucrative staff jobs. Negro professionals working for the program have earned handsome salaries—ranging from $14- to $25,000 —while young boys have been asked to plant trees at $1.25 an hour. Nor have the Job Corps camps made a significant dent in unemployment among Negro youths; indeed, the main beneficiaries of this program seem to be the private companies who are contracted to set up the camps.

Then there is the war in Vietnam, which poses many ironies for the Negro community. On the one hand, Negroes are bitterly aware of the fact that more and more money is being spent on the war, while the anti-poverty program is being cut; on the other hand, Negro youths are enlisting in great numbers, as though to say that it is worth the risk of being killed to learn a trade, to leave a dead-end situation, and to join the only institution in this society which seems really to be integrated.

The youths who rioted in Watts, Cleveland, Omaha, Chicago, and Portland are the members of a truly hopeless and lost generation. They can see the alien world of affluence unfold before them on the TV screen. But they have already failed in their inferior segregated schools. Their grandfathers were sharecroppers, their grandmothers were domestics, and their mothers are domestics too. Many have never met their fathers. Mistreated by the local storekeeper, suspected by the policeman on the beat, disliked by their teachers, they cannot stand more failures and would rather retreat into the world of heroin than risk looking for a job downtown or having their friends see them push a rack in the garment district. . . .

The Vietnam war is also partly responsible for the growing disillusion with non-violence among Negroes. The ghetto Negro does not in general ask whether the United States is right or wrong to be in Southeast Asia. He does, however, wonder why he is exhorted to non-violence when the United States has been waging a fantastically brutal war, and it puzzles him to be told that he must turn the other cheek in our own South while we must fight for freedom in South Vietnam.

Thus, as in roughly similar circumstances in the past—circumstances, I repeat, which in the aggregate foster the belief that the ghetto is destined to last forever—Negroes are once again turning to nationalistic slogans, with "black power" affording the same emotional release as "Back to Africa" and "Buy Black" did in earlier periods of frustration and hopelessness. This is not only the case with the ordinary Negro in the ghetto; it is also the case with leaders like McKissick and Carmichael, neither of whom began as a nationalist or was at first cynical about the possibilities of integration.* It took countless beatings and 24 jailings—that, and the absence of strong and continual support from the liberal community—to persuade Carmichael that his earlier faith in coalition politics was mistaken, that nothing was to be gained from working with whites, and that an alliance with the black nationalists was desirable. In the areas of the South where SNCC has been working so nobly, implementation of the Civil Rights Acts of 1964 and 1965 has been slow and ineffective. Negroes in many rural areas cannot walk into the courthouse and register to vote. Despite the voting-rights bill, they must file complaints and the Justice Department must be called to send federal registrars. Nor do children attend integrated schools as a matter of course. There, too, complaints must be filed and the Department of Health, Education and Welfare must be notified. Neither department has been doing an effective job of enforcing the bills. The feeling of isolation increases among SNCC workers as each legislative victory turns out to be only a token victory—significant on the national level, but not affecting the day-to-day lives of Negroes. . . .

It is, in short, the growing conviction that the Negroes cannot win—a con-

* On Carmichael's background, see "Two for SNCC" by Robert Penn Warren in the April 1965 *Commentary*—ED.

viction with much grounding in experience—which accounts for the new popularity of "black power." So far as the ghetto Negro is concerned, this conviction expresses itself in hostility first toward the people closest to him who have
held out the most promise and failed to deliver (Martin Luther King, Roy
Wilkins, etc.), then toward those who have proclaimed themselves his friends
(the liberals and the labor movement), and finally toward the only oppressors
he can see (the local storekeeper and the policeman on the corner). On the
leadership level, the conviction that the Negroes cannot win takes other forms,
principally the adoption of what I have called a "no-win" policy. Why bother
with programs when their enactment results only in "sham"? Why concern
ourselves with the image of the movement when nothing significant has been
gained for all the sacrifices made by SNCC and CORE? Why compromise with
reluctant white allies when nothing of consequence can be achieved anyway?
Why indeed have anything to do with whites at all?

On this last point, it is extremely important for white liberals to understand—as, one gathers from their references to "racism in reverse," the President and the Vice President of the United States do not—that there is all the
difference in the world between saying, "If you don't want me, I don't want
you" (which is what some proponents of black power" have in effect been
saying) and the statement, "Whatever you do, I don't want you" (which is
what racism declares). It is, in other words, both absurd and immoral to equate
the despairing response of the victim with the contemptuous assertion of the
oppressor. It would, moreover, be tragic if white liberals allowed verbal hostility on the part of Negroes to drive them out of the movement or to curtail
their support for civil rights. The issue was injustice before "black power" became popular, and the issue is still injustice.

In any event, even if "black power" had not emerged as a slogan, problems
would have arisen in the relation between whites and Negroes in the civil-rights
movement. In the North, it was inevitable that Negroes would eventually wish
to run their own movement and would rebel against the presence of whites in
positions of leadership as yet another sign of white supremacy. In the South,
the well-intentioned white volunteer had the cards stacked against him from
the beginning. Not only could he leave the struggle any time he chose to do so,
but a higher value was set on his safety by the press and the government—apparent in the differing degrees of excitement generated by the imprisonment or
murder of whites and Negroes. The white person's importance to the movement
in the South was thus an ironic outgrowth of racism and was therefore bound
to create resentment.

But again: however understandable all this may be as a response to objective conditions and to the seeming irrelevance of so many hard-won victories
to the day-to-day life of the mass of Negroes, the fact remains that the quasi-
nationalist sentiments and "no-win" policy lying behind the slogan of "black
power" do no service to the Negro. Some nationalist emotion is, of course, inevitable, and "black power" must be seen as part of the psychological rejection
of white supremacy, part of the rebellion against the stereotypes which have
been ascribed to Negroes for three hundred years. Nevertheless, pride, confidence, and a new identity cannot be won by glorifying blackness or attacking
whites; they can only come from meaningful action, from good jobs, and from

real victories such as were achieved on the streets of Montgomery, Birmingham, and Selma. When SNCC and CORE went into the South, they awakened the country, but now they emerge isolated and demoralized, shouting a slogan that may afford a momentary satisfaction but that is calculated to destroy them and their movement. Already their frustrated call is being answered with counter-demands for law and order and with opposition to police-review boards. Already they have diverted the entire civil-rights movement from the hard task of developing strategies to realign the major parties of this country, and embroiled it in a debate that can only lead more and more to politics by frustration.

On the other side, however—the more important side, let it be said—it is the business of those who reject the negative aspects of "black power" not to preach but to act. Some weeks ago President Johnson, speaking at Fort Campbell, Kentucky, asserted that riots impeded reform, created fear, and antagonized the Negro's traditional friends. Mr. Johnson, according to the New York *Times,* expressed sympathy for the plight of the poor, the jobless, and the ill-housed. The government, he noted, has been working to relieve their circumstances, but "all this takes time."

One cannot argue with the President's position that riots are destructive or that they frighten away allies. Nor can one find fault with his sympathy for the plight of the poor; surely the poor need sympathy. But one can question whether the government has been working seriously enough to eliminate the conditions which lead to frustration-politics and riots. The President's very words, "all this takes time," will be understood by the poor for precisely what they are—an excuse instead of a real program, a cover-up for the failure to establish real priorities, and an indication that the administration has no real commitment to create new jobs, better housing, and integrated schools.

For the truth is that it need only take ten years to eliminate poverty—ten years and the $100 billion Freedom Budget recently proposed by A. Philip Randolph. In his introduction to the budget (which was drawn up in consultation with the nation's leading economists, and which will be published later this month), Mr. Randolph points out: "The programs urged in the Freedom Budget attack all of the major causes of poverty—unemployment and under-employment, substandard pay, inadequate social insurance and welfare payments to those who cannot or should not be employed; bad housing; deficiencies in health services, education, and training; and fiscal and monetary policies which tend to redistribute income regressively rather than progressively. The Freedom Budget leaves no room for discrimination in any form because its programs are addressed to all who need more opportunity and improved incomes and living standards, not to just some of them."

The legislative precedent Mr. Randolph has in mind is the 1945 Full Employment bill. This bill—conceived in its original form by Roosevelt to prevent a postwar depression—would have made it public policy for the government to step in if the private economy could not provide enough employment. . . .

Let me interject a word here to those who say that Negroes are asking for another handout and are refusing to help themselves. From the end of the 19th century up to the last generation, the United States absorbed and provided economic opportunity for tens of millions of immigrants. These people were usually uneducated and a good many could not speak English. They had nothing but their hard work to offer and they labored long hours, often in miserable sweatshops and unsafe mines. Yet in a burgeoning economy with a need for unskilled labor, they were able to find jobs, and as industrialization proceeded, they were gradually able to move up the ladder to greater skills. Negroes who have been driven off the farm into a city life for which they are not prepared and who have entered an economy in which there is less and less need for unskilled labor, cannot be compared with these immigrants of old. The tenements which were jammed by newcomers were way-stations of hope; the ghettos of today have become dead-ends of despair. Yet just as the older generation of immigrants—in its most decisive act of self-help—organized the trade-union movement and then in alliance with many middle-class elements went on to improve its own lot and the condition of American society generally, so the Negro of today is struggling to go beyond the gains of the past and, in alliance with liberals and labor, to guarantee full and fair employment to all Americans.

Mr. Randolph's Freedom Budget not only rests on the Employment Act of 1946, but on a precedent set by Harry Truman when he believed freedom was threatened in Europe. In 1947, the Marshall Plan was put into effect and 3 per cent of the gross national product was spent in foreign aid. If we were to allocate a similar proportion of our GNP to destroy the economic and social consequences of racism and poverty at home today, it might mean spending more than 20 billion dollars a year, although I think it quite possible that we can fulfill these goals with a much smaller sum. It would be intolerable, however, if our plan for domestic social reform were less audacious and less far-reaching than our international programs of a generation ago.

We must see, therefore, in the current debate over "black power," a fantastic challenge to American society to live up to its proclaimed principles in the area of race by transforming itself so that all men may live equally and under justice. We must see to it that in rejecting "black power," we do not also reject the principle of Negro equality. Those people who would use the current debate and/or the riots to abandon the civil-rights movement leave us no choice but to question their original motivation.

If anything, the next period will be more serious and difficult than the preceding ones. It is much easier to establish the Negro's right to sit at a Woolworth's counter than to fight for an integrated community. It takes very little imagination to understand that the Negro should have the right to vote, but it demands much creativity, patience, and political stamina to plan, develop, and implement programs and priorities. It is one thing to organize sentiment behind laws that do not disturb consensus politics, and quite another to win battles for the redistribution of wealth. Many people who marched in Selma are not prepared to support a bill for a $2.00 minimum wage, to say nothing of supporting a redefinition of work or a guaranteed annual income.

It is here that we who advocate coalitions and integration and who object to the "black-power" concept have a massive job to do. We must see to it that the liberal-labor-civil rights coalition is maintained and, indeed, strengthened so that it can fight effectively for a Freedom Budget. We are responsible for the growth of the "black-power" concept because we have not used our own power to insure the full implementation of the bills whose passage we were strong enough to win, and we have not mounted the necessary campaign for winning a decent minimum wage and extended benefits. "Black power" is a slogan directed primarily against liberals by those who once counted liberals among their closest friends. It is up to the liberal movement to prove that coalition and integration are better alternatives.

~~~~TOPIC 18

Civil Disobedience

HUGO A. BEDAU
Meaning of Civil Disobedience

Since I have been unable to find a suitably detailed analysis of what civil disobedience is and of its role in turning dissent into resistance, I have decided to try to provide such an analysis myself. . . .

A dissenter performs an act of civil disobedience only if he acts *illegally;* i.e., if he violates some positive law, because of (one of) the laws, policies, or decisions of his government which he finds objectionable. Acts of protest directed at government, no matter how conscientious or effective, in which no law is violated (as is usually the case with a poster parade, voluntary boycott, or refusal to accept government employment), are not acts of civil disobedience. Civil disobedience, after all, is not just done; it is committed. It is always the sort of thing that can send one to jail. . . .

It is also possible to distinguish between those acts of dissent which, though illegal according to the authorities at hand, are believed by the dissenter to be within his legal rights as defined by the "fundamental law" or constitution as interpreted by the highest courts of the land and those acts which are committed without any belief in their judicial vindication (e.g., helping an escaped slave to keep his freedom in a slave state in the period immediately following the Supreme Court's decision in the Dred Scott case). . . .

Usually, though not always, it is essential to the purpose of the dissenter that both the public and the government should know what he intends to do. At least, it is essential that the government know of his act if it is intended that the government shall change its policy because of the act. This is one reason why the authorities are customarily notified in advance by those intending to commit civil disobedience. More fundamental still is the fact that the dissenter views what he does as a civic act, an act that properly belongs to the public life of the community. This derives from the fact that he thinks of himself as acting to thwart some law, policy, etc., that deviates from the true purpose of government as he sees it. Thus, his act draws attention to something he thinks the whole community should be brought to consider, since the community has as much interest in the act as he does. For these reasons, civil disobedience is necessarily *public.*

Department of Philosophy at Reed College. Editor of *The Death Penalty in America.* The selection is from "On Civil Disobedience," *Journal of Philosophy,* Vol. 58 (1961), pp. 653-661. By permission.

Not every illegal act of public resistance to government, however, is an act of civil disobedience. Anytime the dissenter resists government by deliberately destroying property, endangering life and limb, inciting to riot (e.g., sabotage, assassination, street fighting), he has not committed *civil* disobedience. The pun on 'civil' is essential; only *nonviolent* acts thus can qualify. . . .

Here we meet an important distinction. Some acts of civil disobedience intend to achieve this aim by *directly* violating the objectionable law (e.g., refusing to register for the military draft), whereas other acts, like Thoreau's, intend to achieve this aim by violating some other law and are thus aimed at the objectionable law only *indirectly* (e.g., withholding from payment that portion of one's income taxes used to support the "defense" establishment). . . .

Civil disobedience is, finally, a *conscientious* act. That is, the dissenter proposes to justify his disobedience by an appeal to the incompatibility between his political circumstances and his moral convictions. Usually, this requires that he be convinced that it would be worse for everyone to suffer the consequences of the objectionable law than it would be for everyone to suffer the consequences of his (and, conceivably, of everyone else's) civil disobedience. . . .

In the light of the foregoing examination, I suggest the following definition: Anyone commits an act of civil disobedience if and only if he acts illegally, publicly, nonviolently, and conscientiously with the intent to frustrate (one of) the laws, policies, or decisions of his government.

A GROUP OF CLERGYMEN
Letter to Martin Luther King

We clergymen are among those who, in January, issued "An Appeal for Law and Order and Common Sense," in dealing with racial problems in Alabama. We expressed understanding that honest convictions in racial matters could properly be pursued in the courts, but urged that decisions of those courts should in the meantime be peacefully obeyed.

Since that time there has been some evidence of increased forbearance and a willingness to face facts. Responsible citizens have undertaken to work on various problems which cause racial friction and unrest. In Birmingham, recent public events have given indication that we all have opportunity for a new constructive and realistic approach to racial problems.

However, we are now confronted by a series of demonstrations by some of our Negro citizens, directed and led in part by outsiders. We recognize the natural impatience of people who feel that their hopes are slow in being realized. But we are convinced that these demonstrations are unwise and untimely.

We agree rather with certain local Negro leadership which has called for honest and open negotiation of racial issues in our area. And we believe this

This is the text of the public statement on Negro demonstrations directed to Dr. Martin Luther King Jr. by eight Alabama clergymen, April 12, 1963.

kind of facing of issues can best be accomplished by citizens of our own metropolitan area, white and Negro, meeting with their knowledge and experience of the local situation. All of us need to face that responsibility and find proper channels for its accomplishment.

Just as we formerly pointed out that "hatred and violence have no sanction in our religious and political traditions," we also point out that such actions as incite to hatred and violence, however technically peaceful those actions may be, have not contributed to the resolution of our local problems. We do not believe that these days of new hope are days when extreme measures are justified in Birmingham.

We commend the community as a whole, and the local news media and law enforcement officials in particular, on the calm manner in which these demonstrations have been handled. We urge the public to continue to show restraint should the demonstrations continue, and the law enforcement officials to remain calm and continue to protect our city from violence.

We further strongly urge our own Negro community to withdraw support from these demonstrations, and to unite locally in working peacefully for a better Birmingham. When rights are consistently denied, a cause should be pressed in the courts and in negotiations among local leaders, and not in the streets. We appeal to both our white and Negro citizenry to observe the principles of law and order and common sense.

Signed by:

C. C. J. CARPENTER, D.D., LL.D., *Bishop of Alabama.*

JOSEPH A. DURICK, D.D., *Auxiliary Bishop, Diocese of Mobile-Birmingham*

Rabbi MILTON L. GRAFMAN, *Temple Emanu-El, Birmingham, Alabama*

Bishop PAUL HARDIN, *Bishop of the Alabama-West Florida Conference of the Methodist Church*

Bishop NOLAN B. HARMON, *Bishop of the North Alabama Conference of the Methodist Church*

GEORGE M. MURRAY, D.D., LL.D., *Bishop Coadjutor, Episcopal Diocese of Alabama*

EDWARD V. RAMAGE, *Moderator, Synod of the Alabama Presbyterian Church in the United States*

EARL STALLINGS, *Pastor, First Baptist Church, Birmingham, Alabama*

MARTIN LUTHER KING
Letter From Birmingham City Jail

APRIL 16, 1963

MY DEAR FELLOW CLERGYMEN,

While confined here in the Birmingham City Jail, I came across your recent statement calling our present activities "unwise and untimely." Seldom, if ever, do I pause to answer criticism of my work and ideas. . . . But since I

Late distinguished black leader. Late President of the Southern Christian Leadership Conference; winner of the Nobel Peace Prize for 1964.

feel that you are men of genuine good will and your criticisms are sincerely set forth, I would like to answer your statement in what I hope will be patient and reasonable terms. . . .

I am in Birmingham because injustice is here. Just as the 8th century prophets left their little villages and carried their "thus saith the Lord" far beyond the boundaries of their home town, and just as the Apostle Paul left his little village of Tarsus and carried the gospel of Jesus Christ to practically every hamlet and city of the Graeco-Roman world, I too am compelled to carry the gospel of freedom beyond my particular home town. Like Paul, I must constantly respond to the Macedonian call for aid.

Moreover, I am cognizant of the interrelatedness of all communities and states. I cannot sit idly by in Atlanta and not be concerned about what happens in Birmingham. Injustice anywhere is a threat to justice everywhere. We are caught in an inescapable network of mutuality tied in a single garment of destiny. Whatever affects one directly affects all indirectly. Never again can we afford to live with the narrow, provincial "outside agitator" idea. Anyone who lives inside the United States can never be considered an outsider anywhere in this country.

You deplore the demonstrations that are presently taking place in Birmingham. But I am sorry that your statement did not express a similar concern for the conditions that brought the demonstrations into being. I am sure that each of you would want to go far beyond the superficial social analyst who looks merely at effects, and does not grapple with underlying causes. I would not hesitate to say that it is unfortunate that so-called demonstrations are taking place in Birmingham at this time, but I would say in more emphatic terms that it is even more unfortunate that the white power structure of this city left the Negro community with no other alternative.

In any nonviolent campaign there are four basic steps: 1) collection of the facts to determine whether injustices are alive; 2) negotiation; 3) self-purification; and 4) direct action. We have gone through all of these steps in Birmingham. There can be no gainsaying of the fact that racial injustice engulfs this community. Birmingham is probably the most thoroughly segregated city in the United States. Its ugly record of police brutality is known in every section of this country. Its unjust treatment of Negroes in the courts is a notorious reality. There have been more unsolved bombings of Negro homes and churches in Birmingham than any city in this nation. These are the hard, brutal, and unbelievable facts. On the basis of these conditions Negro leaders sought to negotiate with the city fathers. But the political leaders consistently refused to engage in good faith negotiation. . . .

As in so many experiences of the past, we were confronted with blasted hopes, and the dark shadow of a deep disappointment settled upon us. So we had no alternative except that of preparing for direct action, whereby we would present our very bodies as a means of laying our case before the conscience of the local and national community. We were not unmindful of the difficulties involved. So we decided to go through a process of self-purification. We started having workshops on nonviolence and repeatedly asked ourselves the questions, "Are you able to accept blows without retaliating?" "Are you able to endure the ordeals of jail?" . . .

You may well ask, "Why direct action? Why sit-ins, marches, etc.? Isn't negotiation a better path?" You are exactly right in your call for negotiation. Indeed, this is the purpose of direct action. Nonviolent direct action seeks to create such a crisis and establish such creative tension that a community that has constantly refused to negotiate is forced to confront the issue. It seeks so to dramatize the issue that it can no longer be ignored.

I just referred to the creation of tension as a part of the work of the non-violent resister. This may sound rather shocking. But I must confess that I am not afraid of the word tension. I have earnestly worked and preached against violent tension, but there is a type of constructive nonviolent tension that is necessary for growth. Just as Socrates felt that it was necessary to create a tension in the mind so that individuals could rise from the bondage of myths and half-truths to the unfettered realm of creative analysis and objective appraisal, we must see the need of having nonviolent gadflies to create the kind of tension in society that will help men rise from the dark depths of prejudice and racism to the majestic heights of understanding and brotherhood. So the purpose of the direct action is to create a situation so crisis-packed that it will inevitably open the door to negotiation. We, therefore, concur with you in your call for negotiation. Too long has our beloved Southland been bogged down in the tragic attempt to live in monologue rather than dialogue. . . .

My friends, I must say to you that we have not made a single gain in civil rights without determined legal and nonviolent pressure. History is the long and tragic story of the fact that privileged groups seldom give up their privileges voluntarily. Individuals may see the moral light and voluntarily give up their unjust posture; but as Reinhold Niebuhr has reminded us, groups are more immoral than individuals.

We know through painful experience that freedom is never voluntarily given by the oppressor; it must be demanded by the oppressed. Frankly I have never yet engaged in a direct action movement that was "well timed," according to the timetable of those who have not suffered unduly from the disease of segregation. For years I have heard the word "Wait!" It rings in the ear of every Negro with a piercing familiarity. This "wait" has almost always meant "never." It has been a tranquilizing Thalidomide, relieving the emotional stress for a moment, only to give birth to an ill-formed infant of frustration. We must come to see with the distinguished jurist of yesterday that "justice too long delayed is justice denied." We have waited for more than 340 years for our constitutional and God-given rights. The nations of Asia and Africa are moving with jet-like speed toward the goal of political independence, and we still creep at horse and buggy pace toward the gaining of a cup of coffee at a lunch counter.

I guess it is easy for those who have never felt the stinging darts of segregation to say wait. But when you have seen vicious mobs lynch your mothers and fathers at will and drown your sisters and brothers at whim; when you have seen hate-filled policemen curse, kick, brutalize, and even kill your black brothers and sisters with impunity; when you see the vast majority of your 20 million Negro brothers smothering in an air-tight cage of poverty in the midst of an affluent society; when you suddenly find your tongue twisted and your speech stammering as you seek to explain to your six-year-old daughter why she can't go to the public amusement park that has just been advertised on television, and see tears welling up in her little eyes when she is told that Funtown is closed to colored children, and see the depressing clouds of inferiority begin to form in her little mental sky, and see her begin to distort her little personality by unconsciously developing a bitterness toward white people; when you have to concoct an answer for a five-year-old son asking in agonizing pathos: "Daddy, why do white people treat colored people so mean?"; when you take a cross country drive and find it necessary to sleep night after night in the uncomfortable corners of your automobile because no motel will accept you; when you are humiliated day in and day out by nagging signs reading "white" men and "colored"; when your first name becomes "nigger" and your middle name becomes "boy" (however old you are) and your last name becomes "John," and when your wife and mother are never given the respected title "Mrs."; when you are harried by day and haunted by night by the fact that you are a Negro, living constantly at tip-toe stance never quite knowing what to expect next, and plagued with inner fears and outer resentments; when you are forever fighting a degenerating sense of "nobodiness"—then you will understand why we find it difficult to wait. There comes a time when the cup of endurance runs over, and men are no longer willing to be plunged into an abyss of injustice where they experience the bleakness of corroding despair. I hope, sirs, you can understand our legitimate and unavoidable impatience.

You express a great deal of anxiety over our willingness to break laws. This is certainly a legitimate concern. Since we so diligently urge people to obey the Supreme Court's decision of 1954 outlawing segregation in the public schools, it is rather strange and paradoxical to find us consciously breaking laws. One may well ask, "How can you advocate breaking some laws and obeying others?" The answer is found in the fact that there are two types of laws: There are *just* laws and there are *unjust* laws. I would be the first to advocate obeying just laws. One has not only a legal but a moral responsibility to obey just laws. Conversely, one has a moral responsibility to disobey unjust laws. I would agree with Saint Augustine that "An unjust law is no law at all."

Now what is the difference between the two? How does one determine when a law is just or unjust? A just law is a man-made code that squares with the moral law or the law of God. An unjust law is a mode that is out of harmony with the moral law. To put it in the terms of Saint Thomas Aquinas, an unjust law is a human law that is not rooted in eternal and natural law. Any law that uplifts human personality is just. Any law that degrades human personality is unjust.

All segregation statutes are unjust because segregation distorts the soul and damages the personality. It gives the segregator a false sense of superiority and the segregated a false sense of inferiority. To use the words of Martin Buber, the great Jewish philosopher, segregation substitutes an "I-it" relationship for the "I-thou" relationship, and ends up relegating persons to the status of things. So segregation is not only politically, economically, and sociologically unsound, but it is morally wrong and sinful. Paul Tillich has said that sin is separation. Isn't segregation an existential expression of man's tragic separation, an expression of his awful estrangement, his terrible sinfulness? So I can urge men to obey the 1954 decision of the Supreme Court because it is morally right, and I can urge them to disobey segregation ordinances because they are morally wrong.

Let me give another example of just and unjust laws. An unjust law is a code that a majority inflicts on a minority that is not binding on itself. This is *difference* made legal. On the other hand a just law is a code that a majority compels a minority to follow that it is willing to follow itself. This is *sameness* made legal.

Let me give another explanation. An unjust law is a code inflicted upon a minority which that minority had no part in enacting or creating because they did not have the unhampered right to vote. Who can say the legislature of Alabama which set up the segregation laws was democratically elected? Throughout the state of Alabama all types of conniving methods are used to prevent Negroes from becoming registered voters and there are some counties without a single Negro registered to vote despite the fact that the Negro constitutes a majority of the population. Can any law set up in such a state be considered democratically structured?

These are just a few examples of unjust and just laws. There are some instances when a law is just on its face but unjust in its application. For instance, I was arrested Friday on a charge of parading without a permit. Now there is nothing wrong with an ordinance which requires a permit for a parade, but when the ordinance is used to preserve segregation and to deny citizens the First Amendment privilege of peaceful assembly and peaceful protest, then it becomes unjust.

I hope you can see the distinction I am trying to point out. In no sense do I advocate evading or defying the law as the rabid segregationist would do. This would lead to anarchy. One who breaks an unjust law must do it *openly, lovingly* (not hatefully as the white mothers did in New Orleans when they were seen on television screaming "nigger, nigger, nigger") and with a willingness to accept the penalty. I submit that an individual who breaks a law that conscience tells him is unjust, and willingly accepts the penalty by staying in jail to arouse the conscience of the community over its injustice, is in reality expressing the very highest respect for law.

Of course there is nothing new about this kind of civil disobedience. It was seen sublimely in the refusal of Shadrach, Meschach, and Abednego to obey the laws of Nebuchadnezzar because a higher moral law was involved. It was practiced superbly by the early Christians who were willing to face hungry lions and the excruciating pain of chopping blocks before submitting to certain unjust laws of the Roman Empire. To a degree academic freedom is a reality today because Socrates practiced civil disobedience.

We can never forget that everything Hitler did in Germany was "legal" and everything the Hungarian freedom fighters did in Hungary was "illegal." It was "illegal" to aid and comfort a Jew in Hitler's Germany. But I am sure that, if I had lived in Germany during that time, I would have aided and comforted my Jewish brothers even though it was illegal. If I lived in a Communist country today where certain principles dear to the Christian faith are suppressed, I believe I would openly advocate disobeying these anti-religious laws. . . .

In your statement you asserted that our actions, even though peaceful, must be condemned because they precipitate violence. But can this assertion be logically made? Isn't this like condemning the robbed man because his possession of money precipitated the evil act of robbery? Isn't this like condemning Socrates because his unswerving commitment to truth and his philosophical delvings precipitated the misguided popular mind to make him drink the hemlock? Isn't this like condemning Jesus because His unique God consciousness and never-ceasing devotion to His will precipitated the evil act of crucifixion? We must come to see, as Federal courts have consistently affirmed, that it is immoral to urge an individual to withdraw his efforts to gain his basic constitutional rights because the quest precipitates violence. Society must protect the robbed and punish the robber.

I had also hoped that the white moderate would reject the myth of time. I received a letter this morning from a white brother in Texas which said: "All Christians know that the colored people will receive equal rights eventually, but is it possible that you are in too great of a religious hurry? It has taken Christianity almost 2,000 years to accomplish what it has. The teachings of Christ take time to come to earth." All that is said here grows out of a tragic misconception of time. It is the strangely irrational notion that there is something in the very flow of time that will inevitably cure all ills. Actually time is neutral. It can be used either destructively or constructively. I am coming to feel that the people of ill will have used time much more effectively than the people of good will.

We will have to repent in this generation not merely for the vitriolic words and actions of the bad people, but for the appalling silence of the good people. We must come to see that human progress never rolls in on wheels of inevitability. It comes through the tireless efforts and persistent work of men willing to be co-workers with God, and without this hard work time itself becomes an ally of the forces of social stagnation.

We must use time creatively, and forever realize that the time is always ripe to do right. Now is the time to make real the promise of democracy, and transform our pending national elegy into a creative psalm of brotherhood. Now is the time to lift our national policy from the quicksand of racial injustice to the solid rock of human dignity.

You spoke of our activity in Birmingham as extreme. At first I was rather disappointed that fellow clergymen would see my nonviolent efforts as those of the extremist. I started thinking about the fact that I stand in the middle of two opposing forces in the Negro community. One is a force of complacency made up of Negroes who, as a result of long years of oppression, have been so completely drained of self-respect and a sense of "somebodiness" that they have adjusted to segregation, and of a few Negroes in the middle class who, because of a degree of academic and economic security, and because at points they profit by segregation, have unconsciously become insensitive to the problems of the masses. The other force is one of bitterness and hatred and comes perilously close to advocating violence. It is expressed in the various black nationalist groups that are springing up over the nation, the largest and best known being Elijah Muhammad's Muslim movement. This movement is nourished by the contemporary frustration over the continued existence of racial discrimination.

It is made up of people who have lost faith in America, who have absolutely repudiated Christianity, and who have concluded that the white man is an incurable "devil."

I have tried to stand between these two forces saying that we need not follow the "do-nothingism" of the complacent or the hatred and despair of the black nationalist. There is the more excellent way of love and nonviolent protest. I'm grateful to God that, through the Negro church, the dimension of nonviolence entered our struggle. If this philosophy had not emerged I am convinced that by now many streets of the South would be flowing with floods of blood. And I am further convinced that if our white brothers dismiss us as "rabble rousers" and "outside agitators"—those of us who are working through the channels of nonviolent direct action—and refuse to support our nonviolent efforts, millions of Negroes, out of frustration and despair, will seek solace and security in black nationalist ideologies, a development that will lead inevitably to a frightening racial nightmare.

Oppressed people cannot remain oppressed forever. The urge for freedom will eventually come. This is what has happened to the American Negro. Something within has reminded him of his birthright of freedom; something without has reminded him that he can gain it. Consciously and unconsciously, he has been swept in by what the Germans call the *Zeitgeist,* and with his black brothers of Africa, and his brown and yellow brothers of Asia, South America, and the Caribbean, he is moving with a sense of cosmic urgency toward the promised land of racial justice. Recognizing this vital urge that has engulfed the Negro community, one should readily understand public demonstrations.

The Negro has many pent-up resentments and latent frustrations. He has to get them out. So let him march sometime; let him have his prayer pilgrimages to the city hall; understand why he must have sit-ins and freedom rides. If his repressed emotions do not come out in these nonviolent ways, they will come out in ominous expressions of violence. This is not a threat; it is a fact of history. So I have not said to my people, "Get rid of your discontent." But I have tried to say that this normal and healthy discontent can be channeled through the creative outlet of nonviolent direct action. Now this approach is being dismissed as extremist. I must admit that I was initially disappointed in being so categorized.

But as I continued to think about the matter I gradually gained a bit of satisfaction from being considered an extremist. Was not Jesus an extremist in love? "Love your enemies, bless them that curse you, pray for them that despitefully use you." Was not Amos an extremist for justice—"Let justice roll down like waters and righteousness like a mighty stream." Was not Paul an extremist for the gospel of Jesus Christ—"I bear in my body the marks of the Lord Jesus." Was not Martin Luther an extremist—"Here I stand; I can do none other so help me God." Was not John Bunyan an extremist—"I will stay in jail to the end of my days before I make a butchery of my conscience." Was not Abraham Lincoln an extremist—"This nation cannot survive half slave and half free." Was not Thomas Jefferson an extremist—"We hold these truths to be self evident that all men are created equal."

So the question is not whether we will be extremist but what kind of extremist will we be. Will we be extremists for hate or will we be extremists for love? Will we be extremists for the preservation of injustice—or will we be extremists for the cause of justice? In that dramatic scene on Calvary's hill three men were crucified. We must never forget that all three were crucified for the same crime—the crime of extremism. Two were extremists for immorality, and thus fell below their environment. The other, Jesus Christ, was an extremist for love, truth, and goodness, and thereby rose above His environment. So, after all, maybe the South, the nation, and the world are in dire need of creative extremists. . . .

I hope the Church as a whole will meet the challenge of this decisive hour. But even if the Church does not come to the aid of justice, I have no despair about the future. I have no fear about the outcome of our struggle in Birmingham, even if our motives are presently misunderstood. We will reach the goal of freedom in Birmingham and all over the nation, because the goal of America is freedom. Abused and scorned though we may be, our destiny is tied up with the destiny of America.

Before the pilgrims landed at Plymouth, we were here. Before the pen of Jefferson etched across the pages of history the majestic words of the Declaration of Independence, we were here. For more than two centuries our foreparents labored in this country without wages; they made cotton "king"; and they built the homes of their masters in the midst of brutal injustice and shameful humiliation—and yet out of a bottomless vitality they continued to thrive and develop. If the inexpressible cruelties of slavery could not stop us, the opposition we now face will surely fail. We will win our freedom because the sacred heritage of our nation and the eternal will of God are embodied in our echoing demands.

I must close now. But before closing I am impelled to mention one other point in your statement that troubled me profoundly. You warmly commended the Birmingham police force for keeping "order" and "preventing violence." I don't believe you would have so warmly commended the police force if you had seen its angry violent dogs literally biting six unarmed, nonviolent Negroes. I don't believe you would so quickly commend the policemen if you would observe their ugly and inhuman treatment of Negroes here in the city jail; if you would watch them push and curse old Negro women and young Negro girls; if you would see them slap and kick old Negro men and young Negro boys; if you will observe them, as they did on two occasions, refuse to give us food because we wanted to sing our grace together. I'm sorry that I can't join you in your praise for the police department. . . .

It is true that they have been rather disciplined in their public handling of the demonstrators. In this sense they have been rather publicly "nonviolent." But for what purpose? To preserve the evil system of segregation. Over the last few years I have consistently preached that nonviolence demands that the means we use must be as pure as the ends we seek. So I have tried to make it clear that it is wrong to use immoral means to attain moral ends. But now I must affirm that it is just as wrong, or even more so, to use moral means to preserve immoral ends. . . . T. S. Eliot has said that there is no greater treason than to do the right deed for the wrong reason.

I wish you had commended the Negro sit-inners and demonstrators of Birmingham for their sublime courage, their willingness to suffer, and their amazing discipline in the midst of the most inhuman provocation. One day the South will recognize its real heroes. They will be the James Merediths, courageously and with a majestic sense of purpose, facing jeering and hostile mobs and the agonizing loneliness that characterizes the life of the pioneer. They will be old, oppressed, battered Negro women, symbolized in a 72-year-old woman of Montgomery, Alabama, who rose up with a sense of dignity and with her people decided not to ride the segregated buses, and responded to one who inquired about her tiredness with ungrammatical profundity: "My feets is tired, but my soul is rested." They will be young high school and college students, young ministers of the gospel and a host of the elders, courageously and nonviolently sitting in at lunch counters and willingly going to jail for conscience' sake. One day the South will know that when these disinherited children of God sat down at lunch counters they were in reality standing up for the best in the American dream and the most sacred values in our Judeo-Christian heritage, and thus carrying our whole nation back to great wells of democracy which were dug deep by the founding fathers in the formulation of the Constitution and the Declaration of Independence.

Yours for the cause of Peace and Brotherhood
M. L. KING JR.

JOHN DICKINSON
The Limits of Disobedience

The question of the meaning of sovereignty and legal order takes on special importance in periods where an existing sovereignty begins to be threatened on a significant scale with disobedience to its laws and decrees. At such a time we are faced with the possibility, if not as yet with the certainty, of the break-down and disappearance of sovereignty through increasing disobedience; and only a firm grasp of the significance of sovereignty for legal order will enable us intelligently to balance the cost of obedience.

Suppose, for example, that we do not accept the doctrine of sovereignty. We will then insist that laws do not derive their validity from the stamp of the sovereign, but that a rule may be validly a law which is directly contrary to the rule which the sovereign is seeking to enforce. But if this is the case, and if we must look not to the sovereign but to some other source to assure us what is the law, where else are we to look? Mr. Laski has suggested the only possible answer,—we must look within, each man to his own individual conscience.[1] If we use this method of approach we have no choice but to say that the validity of all law is derived from the conscience of the individual. The question of obe-

Late professor of law, University of Pennsylvania, formerly U.S. Assistant Attorney General. The selection is from pp. 48-59 of "A Working Theory of Sovereignty II," *Political Science Quarterly,* Vol. 43 (1928), pp. 32-63. By permission.

[1] "The individual is ultimately the supreme arbiter of his behaviour; and he most fully realizes the purposes of the state when he offers to it the substance, whatever that may be, of his judgment."—*A Grammar of Politics,* p. 63. "The state is for [the individual] sovereign only where his conscience is not stirred against its performance." —*Authority in the Modern State,* p. 43.

dience or resistance then becomes a simple one. All that is involved is for each individual to set side by side and compare the law as promulgated by the sovereign with what his own conscience tells him is the law, and if there is a discrepancy between the two precepts, then he is not merely morally justified, he is legally authorized, to disobey.

There are but two factors to be taken in account in solving the problem, —the sovereign's pronouncement on the one hand and the individual's own conception of the law,—i.e., of what is right,—on the other. His career as a member of civil society becomes a continuous process of such comparisons, and he stands at every moment on the brink of disobedience and resistance. "The only ground upon which the individual can give or be asked his support for the state is from the conviction that what it is aiming at is, in each particular action, good. . . . It deserves his allegiance, it should receive it, only where it commands his conscience. . . . Its purpose is at each stage subject to examination."[2] The individual is thus invited to assume habitually what Mr. Laski has elsewhere called the "Athanasius attitude."[3]

The doubt which suggests itself in connection with this attitude is that possibly it may be too naïve,—that possibly it may not be sophisticated enough to comprehend the full challenge of civil society. It is the primitive attitude of Antigone,[4] rather than the mature comprehension of Socrates. Its capital defect is that it leaves fundamentally out of account the chief and most difficult factor in the whole problem—the question, namely, of the advantage, not merely to all individuals but to each individual, of having a legally ordered society to live in, and of the price which he must perforce pay to get it. This factor is the thing which really causes all the difficulty; and it is the major factor. If there were no question but of a conflict between two opposing wills, the will of the citizen as one individual and the will of the sovereign as another, the problem would be quite easy; the individual could not fairly be expected to surrender his will until convinced intellectually and morally that he was wrong. But so to state the problem is to simplify it out of all recognition. It is not a question of a

[2] *Ibid.,* p. 46. A more extreme statement is that of Thoreau, "Civil Disobedience," *Writings* (Boston, 1906): "Must the citizen, even for a moment or in the least degree, resign his conscience to the legislator? Why has every man a conscience then? I think we should be men first and subjects afterwards." Vol. IV, p. 358. "There will never be a really free and enlightened state until the state comes to recognize the individual as a higher and independent power from which all its own power and authority are derived and treats him accordingly." *Ibid.,* p. 387.

[3] I would urge against this position the criticism that it reverses the proper order of the burden of proof, that it shifts improperly the presumption of validity. The presumption must be in favor of state action; the burden of proof on the refractory individual. The state must not continually be justifying itself to the individual; the individual must justify himself morally in the exceptional cases when he feels morally compelled to resist the state.

[4] Antigone submits to her punishment, not like Socrates under a sense that it is something owed to civil society, but merely because she must bow to superior force; and she insists on the justice of her position, and protests against the injustice of her punishment, to the bitter end: "What rule of divine justice have I transgressed? . . . It is my piety which wins me the name of impious. But if my death be, as it might seem, the pleasure of the gods, I will suffer death ere I confess that I have sinned; and if, on the other hand, the gods do not approve of my death, and these men are the guilty ones, may they suffer no more woes than they have unjustly done to me."— Sophocles, *Antigone,* lines 921-928.

bare conflict between the individual and the sovereign; the conflict must be regarded as rather between the individual and all the sovereign stands for. The individual may be convinced and reasonably convinced that the sovereign is wrong, unfairly, brutally wrong; but the deeper question must at once arise of what is involved in disobeying the sovereign.

For sovereignty, as we have seen, is a prerequisite of legal order; a prerequisite, that is, of a condition of affairs where the disputes which will honestly and inevitably arise between man and man, and which will as often be due to a real and involuntary difference in intellectual outlook as to a clash between purely selfish purposes, are settled peaceably by a publicly authorized arbiter, and, so far as possible, by impartial rules, rather than by the rough arbitrament of force and chance. The very essence and meaning of civil society is precisely the fact that the former method rather than the latter is the one which habitually prevails; and this essential method of civil society is just the thing which we strike at whenever we disobey or resist the sovereign.

The question of obedience thus raises far more than the mere question of the agreement or disagreement in a particular case between the sovereign's law applying to the case in hand, and what the individual's private conscience tells him the law ought to be; properly approached, it brings dominantly into the foreground the large issues of the desirability of preserving public authority and civil society itself. This is the great truth so clearly put by Socrates, when in answer to Crito's plea for disobedience he represents the City as standing before him and saying, "Tell us, Socrates, what is it you mean to do? Nothing more nor less than to overthrow us by this attempt of yours,—to overthrow the laws and the whole commonwealth so far as in you lies. For do you imagine that a city can stand and not be overthrown, when the decisions of the judges have no power, when they are made of no effect and destroyed by private persons?"

In other words, something of vastly superior consequence is involved than the essential rightness or wrongness in the given case of any particular exercise of sovereign power; what is involved, fundamentally, is the value and validity of civil society in contrast with the freedom, the flexibility, the experimentalism, of anarchy, whether the latter take the form of benevolent cooperation or of forceful competition. Civil society cannot stand when the decisions of the judges are made of no effect by private persons; and the Athanasius attitude, to be defensible, must balance not particular differences of opinion between the individual conscience and the sovereign will, but the value of the end which conscience has at stake as against the value of civil society.[5]

For there are of course ends which from time to time do validly outweigh

[5] This point is often made by Mr. Laski himself, e. g.: "A right to disobedience . . . is . . . reasonably to be exercised only at the margins of political conduct. No community could hope to fulfil its purpose if rebellion became a settled habit of the population."—*A Grammar of Politics*, p. 62. "The real obligation of obedience is to the total interest of our fellow-men."—*Ibid.*, p. 64. "The point at which resistance becomes an expedient factor is not a matter for definition or prophecy; it will vary with the circumstances of each age. All we can say is that at times in the history of a state there may well come a point where the maintenance of order seems to some group of men worthless as an end compared to achieving, by other than constitutional means, some good deemed greater than peace."—*Authority in the Modern State*, pp. 53-54.

the maintenance for the time being of the orderly processes of civil society. Revolution, like war, is no doubt entitled to a place as one of the indispensable ingredients of progress in the existing, and perhaps in any, state of human nature. The only point I am insisting on is that revolution should always be recognized for what it is,—a lapse into anarchy. Only so, in any specific case, can the wisdom of taking the plunge be fairly assessed; only so can the full meaning of the alternative between obedience and resistance be grasped in all its awful implications.[6] The chief defect in the doctrine of the denial of sovereignty is that it glosses over with thin sugarcoating this fundamental alternative. The doctrine that there exists somewhere a law above, and independent of, the law of the sovereign, and capable of being discovered for himself by each private individual so as to justify disobedience to the positive law,[7] carries with it the implication that civil society itself exists, and can exist, apart from and independently of obedience to the sovereign; and that therefore resistance by the individual to the sovereign is not necessarily anything like so serious and ultimate a thing as an assault on civil society is readily seen to be. The essential meaning of resistance is obscured, the price which it entails belittled. And at the same time the price that we must pay for civil society itself is belittled. For the demand which civil society makes that private individual will and purpose be always subordinated to the will of the authorized public representative of the society, on no other and no better ground than merely that the one is private

[6] This was recognized, for example, by Benjamin Constant: "Obedience to law is a duty, but, like all duties, it is not absolute, it is relative; it rests on the supposition that the law emanates from a legitimate source and is confined within just limits. This duty does not cease when the law departs from this rule only in certain respects. We ought to sacrifice a great deal for the sake of the public peace; we should render ourselves guilty in the eyes of morality if, by too inflexible attachment to our rights we should disturb the peace as soon as it seemed to us that they were being infringed upon in the name of law." If we "say that we obey laws only in so far as they are just, we shall find ourselves authorizing resistance to law in the most senseless and culpable instances, and anarchy will reign." . . . This quotation from his *Cours de Politique Constitutionelle* (additions et notes: "Des Droits Individus") are given in Elizabeth W. Schermerhorn, *Benjamin Constant* (Boston and New York, 1924), p. 381. For an excellent statement of the issues involved in disobedience, see T. H. Green, *Lectures on the Principles of Political Obligation,* §§ 143-147, in *Works,* edited by Nettleship (London, 1906), vol. II, pp. 454-459.

[7] This view possesses a perennial appeal for extreme reformers, e. g., the abolitionists before the American Civil War. Thus one of their platforms declares that since slavery is contrary to the natural rights of man, and since "the moral laws of the Creator are paramount to all human laws . . . therefore, Resolved, that we . . . owe it to the Sovereign Ruler of the Universe, as a proof of our allegiance to him, in all our civil relations and offices, whether as private citizens or as public functionaries sworn to support the Constitution of the United States, to regard and to treat the third clause of the second section of the fourth article of that instrument, whenever applied to the case of a fugitive slave, as utterly null and void, and consequently as forming no part of the Constitution of the United States whenever we are called upon or sworn to support it."—*Emancipator Extra,* Tract No. 1, reprinted in K. H. Porter, *National Party Platforms* (New York, 1924), pp. 13-14. . . . This view has naturally been favored by Roman Catholic writers as in accord with the historic position of that body. Thus Orestes A. Brownson, an American Roman Catholic, denied the right of revolution except when the Church "as the representative of the highest authority on earth, determines when resistance is proper and prescribes its forms and extent." *Works,* ed. by Henry F. Brownson (Detroit, 1884), vol. XV, pp. 397-398.

and the other public, is by implication denied, if we accept the doctrine that civil society does not depend for its existence and functioning on obedience to its constituted representative. A view of civil society is thus produced which evades the necessity for political organization,—which tolerates the claim of separate and discrete groups within the state to be independent of the jurisdiction of, and immune from interference by, the state, and which in pursuance of the same conviction is capable of seeing in an unorganized "society of nations" a substantial substitute for an organized League. The theory seeks to have its cake of order without having to pay the price of organization. . . .

Even if we grant the existence of a "law" that is not of men's making, but recognize that room remains for possible differences of opinion as to its specific precepts, we shall still have to admit the need for political organization, the need for a sovereign to "declare" that law authoritatively; and we shall then be driven forward to face the important practical problems incidental to devising a mechanism of organization best adapted to cause the precepts of the sovereign to conform to the precepts of the "higher" law. But this is a task which the doctrine of resistance minimizes and discourages. If each individual is entitled to search in his own conscience for the precept of the higher law applicable to the case in hand, and then to disobey the sovereign should his inquiry lead to a different conclusion from that which that sovereign has reached, the importance of having a sovereign who will reach the right conclusion in the first place is vastly decreased; for if no law made by the sovereign need be obeyed unless it is a good law, the question of whether the sovereign makes bad laws becomes of relatively secondary consequence. From this point of view, therefore, the real guaranty of good government is the "right" of resistance, not the perfecting of the governmental machinery adapted to produce the best results under given circumstances.

In answer to this theory it should be sufficient to point out that the whole history of progress in the art of government has consisted in the gradual substitution of the latter for the former of these guaranties. Revolution was during long ages the only effective way by which the ordinary acts of government could be corrected; the efforts of many centuries have been spent on devising less wasteful and more orderly methods of control. These efforts have proceeded on the assumption that it is not compatible with the existence of civil society to leave to each individual the protection of his own rights; that so long as the normal conditions of civil order prevail, the sovereign, as the organ of the community, must be entitled to the obedience of the individual precisely because, and for no other reason than because, the sovereign *is* the organ of the community; and that therefore the protection of the individual under normal circumstances must be found not in the "right" of resistance, but in the manner and plan whereby sovereign power is organized and constituted.

The fact that in civil society the individual is thus not entitled to set his own idea of the "higher" precepts which the government should follow against the sovereign's version of them, does not mean that there are no such precepts. Whether they constitute a body of "higher law" or not, is of course a wholly different question; but nothing that has been said implies that there are no canons of morality and justice which the sovereign ought to embody in.

his positive laws. On the contrary, the institution of sovereignty exists primarily because of the need of an organ to focus and formulate these fundamental, but more or less vague and disputed, canons into precise and uniform rules which on the one hand have the fixity and generality necessary for a rule of law, and which on the other hand represent the moral conceptions that command acceptance among the most influential members of the community rather than views which are held merely by isolated private thinkers.

In a realm of ideas where there is so much room for differences of opinion as in connection with the precepts of morality, it is absolutely necessary to have such an authoritative declaration of the rule before there can properly be any thought of enforcing it as a rule of community action. It may, and doubtless often will, result that the rule selected by the sovereign for enforcement, precisely because it will be a rule reflecting the morality of the crowd or the morality of the wealthy or military class, will offend the consciences of the individuals who constitute the most enlightened and morally advanced element of the community. Under such circumstances is not the right of this class to resist essential in order to secure moral progress? As a last resort and in extraordinary situations where the stake is sufficiently high, the answer must certainly be, yes; but always with full recognition of the fact that such resistance constitutes rebellion, and entails for the time being a dissolution of the conditions of civil order.

Under a properly adjusted constitution, the necessity should seldom occur, because such a constitution would, on the one hand, provide adequate channels for the views of this class to exert an influence upon the sovereign as far as is compatible with the obvious fact that laws must be made to fit the average rather than the exceptional man; and because, on the other hand, under such a constitution the sovereign would doubtless be wise enough to limit to the narrowest point his interference with those kinds of individual action from which moral improvement can properly be expected to occur.

CHARLES FRANKEL
Is It Ever Right to Break the Law?

During recent months, public events have repeatedly dramatized an old and troublesome problem. A group of students defies the State Department's ban on travel to Cuba; a teachers' union threatens a strike even though a state law prohibits strikes by public employes; advocates of civil rights employ mass demonstrations of disobedience to the law to advance their cause; the Governor of a Southern state deliberately obstructs the enforcement of Federal laws, and declares himself thoroughly within his rights in doing so. . . .

When is it justified for the citizen to act as his own legislator, and to decide that he will or will not obey a given law?

An answer that covers all the issues this question raises cannot be given

Professor of Philosophy at Columbia University. Formerly Assistant Secretary of State for Educational and Cultural Affairs. Author of *The Democratic Prospect* and other books and articles. The selection is from the *New York Times Magazine,* January 12, 1964, printed by the New York Times Company. Reprinted by permission.

here, nor can a set of principles be proposed that will allow anyone to make automatic and infallible judgments concerning the legitimacy or illegitimacy of specific acts of civil disobedience. Such judgments require detailed knowledge of the facts of specific cases, and such knowledge is often unavailable to the outsider. Nevertheless, it is possible to indicate some of the principal issues that are raised by civil disobedience, some of the more common mistakes that are made in thinking about these issues, and, at least in outline, the approach that one man would take toward such issues.

We can begin, it seems to me, by rejecting one extreme position. This is the view that disobedience to the law can never be justified in any circumstances. To take this position is to say one of two things: either every law that exists is a just law, or a greater wrong is always done by breaking the law. The first statement is plainly false. The second is highly doubtful. If it is true, then the signers of the Declaration of Independence, and those Germans who refused to carry out Hitler's orders, committed acts of injustice.

It is possible, however, to take a much more moderate and plausible version of this position, and many quite reasonable people do. Such people concede that disobedience to the law can sometimes be legitimate and necessary under a despotic regime. They argue, however, that civil disobedience can never be justified in a democratic society, because such a society provides its members with legal instruments for the redress of their grievances.

This is one of the standard arguments that is made, often quite sincerely, against the activities of people like supporters of the Congress of Racial Equality, who set about changing laws they find objectionable by dramatically breaking them. Such groups are often condemned for risking disorder and for spreading disrespect for the law when, so it is maintained, they could accomplish their goals a great deal more fairly and patriotically by staying within the law, and confining themselves to the courts and to methods of peaceful persuasion.

Now it is perfectly true, I believe, that there is a stronger case for obedience to the law, including bad law, in a democracy than in a dictatorship. The people who must abide by the law have presumably been consulted, and they have legal channels through which to express their protests and to work for reform. One way to define democracy is to say that it is a system whose aim is to provide alternatives to civil disobedience. Nevertheless, when applied to the kind of situation faced, say, by CORE, these generalizations, it seems to me, become cruelly abstract.

The basic fallacy in the proposition that, in a democracy, civil disobedience can never be justified, is that it confuses the *ideals* or *aims* of democracy with the inevitably less than perfect accomplishments of democracy at any given moment. In accordance with democratic ideals, the laws of a democracy may give rights and powers to individuals which, in theory, enable them to work legally for the elimination of injustices.

In actual fact, however, these rights and powers may be empty. The police may be hostile, the courts biased, the elections rigged—and the legal remedies available to the individual may be unavailing against these evils.

Worse still, the majority may have demonstrated, in a series of free and

honest elections, that it is unwavering in its support of what the minority regards as an unspeakable evil. This is obviously the case today in many parts
of the South, where the white majority is either opposed to desegregation or
not so impatient to get on with it as is the Negro minority. Are we prepared
to say that majorities never err? If not, there is no absolutely conclusive reason
why we must invariably give the results of an election greater weight than considerations of elementary justice.

It is true, of course, that one swallow does not make a summer, and that
the test of legal democratic processes is not this or that particular success or
failure, but rather the general direction in which these processes move over the
long run. Still, the position that violation of the law is never justifiable so long
as there are legal alternatives overstates this important truth. It fails to face at
least three important exceptions to it.

In the first place, dramatic disobedience to the law by a minority may be
the only effective way of catching the attention or winning the support of the
majority. Most classic cases of civil disobedience, from the early Christians
to Gandhi and his supporters, exemplify this truth. Civil disobedience, like
almost no other technique, can shame a majority and make it ask itself just how
far it is willing to go, just how seriously it really is committed to defending the
status quo.

Second, there is the simple but painful factor of time. If a man is holding
you down on a bed of nails, it is all very well for a bystander to say that you
live in a great country in which there are legal remedies for your condition,
and that you ought, therefore, to be patient and wait for these remedies to take
effect. But your willingness to listen to this counsel will depend, quite properly,
on the nature of the injury you are suffering.

Third, it is baseless prejudice to assume that observance of the law is
always conducive to strengthening a democratic system while disobedience to
the law can never have a salutary effect. A majority's complacent acquiescence
in bad laws can undermine the faith of a minority in the power of democratic
methods to rectify manifest evils; yet a vigorous democracy depends on the existence of minorities holding just such a faith.

Disobedience to bad laws can sometimes jolt democratic processes into
motion. Which strengthens one's hope for democracy more—the behavior of
the Negroes in Birmingham who broke municipal ordinances when they staged
their protest marches, or the behavior of the police, using dogs and fire hoses
to assert their legal authority?

Another factor should also be taken into account. In our Federal system,
there are often legitimate doubts concerning the legal validity, under our Constitution, of various state or local ordinances. Disobedience to these laws is in
many cases simply a practical, though painful, way of testing their legality. But
even where no thought of such a test is involved, there is often present a moral
issue which no one can easily dodge—least of all the man whose personal dignity and self-respect are caught up in the issue.

A citizen caught in a conflict between local laws and what he thinks will
be upheld as the superior Federal law can sometimes afford to wait until the
courts have determined the issue for him. But often he cannot afford to wait,

or must take a stand in order to force a decision. This is the situation of many Negro citizens in Southern states as they confront the conflict between local and Federal laws.

Yet there is another side to the story. It would be a mistake to conclude from what has been said that civil disobedience is justified, provided only that it is disobedience in the name of higher principles. Strong moral conviction is not all that is required to turn breaking the law into service to society.

Civil disobedience is not simply like other acts in which men stand up courageously for their principles. It involves violation of the law. And the law can make no provision for its violation except to hold the offender liable to punishment. This is why President Kennedy was in such a delicate position last spring at the time of the Negro demonstrations in Birmingham. He gave many signs that, as an individual, he was in sympathy with the goals of the demonstrators. As a political leader, he probably realized that these goals could not be attained without dramatic actions that crossed the line into illegality. But as Chief Executive he could not give permission or approval to such actions.

We may admire a man like Martin Luther King, who is prepared to defy the authorities in the name of a principle, and we may think that he is entirely in the right; just the same, his right to break the law cannot be officially recognized. No society, whether free or tyrannical, can give its citizens the right to break its laws: To ask it to do so is to ask it to proclaim, as a matter of law, that its laws are not laws.

In short, if anybody ever has a right to break the law, this cannot be a legal right under the law. It has to be a moral right against the law. And this moral right is not an unlimited right to disobey any law which one regards as unjust. It is a right that is hedged about, it seems to me, with important restrictions.

First of all, the exercise of this right is subject to standards of just and fair behavior. I may be correct, for example, in thinking that an ordinance against jaywalking is an unnecessary infringement of my rights. This does not make it reasonable, however, for me to organize a giant sit-down strike in the streets which holds up traffic for a week. Conformity to the concept of justice requires that there be some *proportion* between the importance of the end one desires to attain and the power of the means one employs to attain it.

When applied to civil disobedience, this principle constitutes a very large restriction. Civil disobedience is an effort to change the law by making it impossible to enforce the law, or by making the price of such enforcement extremely high. It is a case, as it were, of holding the legal system to ransom. It can arouse extreme passions on one side or the other, excite and provoke the unbalanced, and make disrespect for the law a commonplace and popular attitude.

Although violence may be no part of the intention of those who practice civil disobedience, the risks of violence are present, and are part of what must be taken into account when a program of civil disobedience is being contemplated.

In short, civil disobedience is a grave enterprise. It may sometimes be justified, but the provocation for it has to be equally grave. Basic principles have to be at issue. The evils being combated have to be serious evils that are likely to endure unless they are fought. There should be reasonable grounds to believe that legal methods of fighting them are likely to be insufficient by themselves.

Nor is this the only limitation on the individual's moral right to disobey the law. The most important limitation is that his cause must be a just one. It was right for General de Gaulle to disobey Marshal Pétain; it was wrong for the commanders of the French Army in Algeria, 20 years later, to disobey General de Gaulle.

Similarly, if it is absolutely necessary, and if the consequences have been properly weighed, then it is right to break the law in order to eliminate inequalities based on race. But it can never be necessary, and no weighing of consequences can ever make it right, to break the law in the name of Nazi principles.

In sum, the goals of those who disobey the law have to lie at the very heart of what we regard as morality before we can say that they have a moral right to do what they are doing.

But who is to make these difficult decisions? Who is to say that one man's moral principles are right and another man's wrong? We come here to the special function that civil disobedience serves in a society. The man who breaks the law on the ground that the law is immoral asks the rest of us, in effect, to trust him, or to trust those he trusts, in preference to the established conventions and authorities of our society.

He has taken a large and visible chance, and implicitly asked us to join him in taking that chance, on the probity of his personal moral judgment. In doing so, he has put it to us whether we are willing to take a similar chance on the probity of our own judgment.

Thomas Hobbes, who knew the trouble that rebels and dissenters convinced of their rectitude can cause, once remarked that a man may be convinced that God has commanded him to act as he has, but that God, after all, does not command other men to believe that this is so. The man who chooses to disobey the law on grounds of principle may be a saint, but he may also be a madman. He may be a courageous and lonely individualist, but he may also merely be taking orders and following his own crowd. Whatever he may be, however, his existence tends to make us painfully aware that we too are implicitly making choices, and must bear responsibility for the ones we make.

This, indeed, may be the most important function of those who practice civil disobedience. They remind us that the man who obeys the law has as much of an obligation to look into the morality of his acts and the rationality of his society as does the man who breaks the law. The occurrence of civil disobedience can never be a happy phenomenon; when it is justified, something is seriously wrong with the society in which it takes place.

But the man who puts his conscience above the law, though he may be right or he may be wrong, does take personal moral responsibility for the social arrangements under which he lives. And so he dramatizes the fascinating and fearful possibility that those who obey the law might do the same. They might obey the law and support what exists, not out of habit or fear, but because they have freely chosen to do so, and are prepared to live with their consciences after having made that choice.

⊷Section VII

JUDICIAL REVIEW

Important decisions of the Supreme Court have often in our history led to extended controversy. In the last few years the most controversial decisions (with sharply divided opinions) have greatly expanded the constitutional protections accorded to individuals accused of crime. Since Chief Justice Marshall's day the Supreme Court has held that the *first Ten Amendments* taken by themselves limit only the Federal Government. Thus the Sixth Amendment provision that "In all criminal prosecutions, the accused shall . . . have the Assistance of Counsel for his defence," does not control the states. However, those provisions of the Federal Bill of Rights which the Supreme Court regards as "fundamental" have in time come to be protected from state infringement by the *due process clause* of the Fourteenth Amendment. In *Powell* v. *Alabama,* decided in 1932, the Supreme Court held that the right to counsel in capital cases was protected from state impairment by the Fourteenth Amendment. In 1963, *Gideon* v. *Wainwright* extended this right to counsel to all indigent defenders accused of serious crimes. *Powell* v. *Alabama* had stated that the right to counsel began at the time of arraignment and until *Escobedo* v. *Illinois* in 1964 this was assumed to be the command of the Constitution. *Miranda* v. *Arizona,* below, decided in 1968, established however that statements made by persons during custodial interrogation may not be placed in evidence against them unless "procedural safeguards effective to secure the privilege against self-incrimination" are utilized. This and a series of related opinions have become the subject of wide controversy over "law and order." They were a prime target in the Senate debate on the confirmation of Justice Fortas as Chief Justice of the United States and became issues in the presidential campaign of 1968.

In the 1968 Omnibus Crime Control Law, Congress attempted to overturn *Miranda* v. *Arizona* and two other recent Supreme Court decisions extending the rights of suspects accused of federal crimes. Title II of this act states that a confession shall be admissible as evidence in federal prosecutions if voluntarily given. The heart of the problem is how to determine whether a confession is voluntary. Past practice had been for the jury to decide this question. The 1968 law modifies this practice by placing the initial responsibility for determining the admissibility of a confession on the trial judge.

Among the circumstances which the law directs the judge to consider are whether the accused was advised of his right to counsel prior to the interrogation, and whether he was informed that he had a constitutional right to refuse to make any statement at the time of the arrest, and that any statement made might be used against him in any criminal prosecution. The 1968 law applies only to federal prosecutions and the constitutionality of the act will have to be determined by the federal courts.

TOPIC 19

Police Interrogation and Due Process

MIRANDA *V*. ARIZONA

384 U.S. 436 (1968)

MR. CHIEF JUSTICE WARREN delivered the opinion of the Court.

The cases before us raise questions which go to the roots of our concepts of American criminal jurisprudence: the restraints society must observe consistent with the Federal Constitution in prosecuting individuals for crime. More specifically, we deal with the admissibility of statements obtained from an individual who is subjected to custodial police interrogation, and the necessity for procedures which assure that the individual is accorded his privilege under the Fifth Amendment to the Constitution not to be compelled to incriminate himself.

We dealt with certain phases of this problem recently in Escobedo *v*. Illinois, 378 US 478 (1964). There, as in the four cases before us, law enforcement officials took the defendant into custody and interrogated him in a police station for the purpose of obtaining a confession. The police did not effectively advise him of his right to remain silent or of his right to consult with his attorney. Rather, they confronted him with an alleged accomplice who accused him of having perpetrated a murder. When the defendant denied the accusation and said "I didn't shoot Manuel, you did it," they handcuffed him and took him to an interrogation room. There, while handcuffed and standing, he was questioned for four hours until he confessed. During this interrogation, the police denied his request to speak to his attorney, and they prevented his retained attorney, who had come to the police station, from consulting with him. At his trial, the State, over his objection, introduced the confession against him. We held that the statements thus made were constitutionally inadmissible. . . .

We start here, as we did in *Escobedo,* with the premise that our holding is not an innovation in our jurisprudence, but is an application of principles long recognized and applied in other settings. We have undertaken a thorough re-examination of the *Escobedo* decision and the principles it announced, and we reaffirm it. That case was but an explication of basic rights that are enshrined in our Constitution—that "No person . . . shall be compelled in any

The majority and minority opinions cover the four cases mentioned on page 305.

criminal case to be a witness against himself," and that "the accused shall . . . have the Assistance of Counsel"—rights which were put in jeopardy in that case through official overbearing. These precious rights were fixed in our Constitution only after centuries of persecution and struggle. And in the words of Chief Justice Marshall, they were secured "for ages to come, and . . . designed to approach immortality as nearly as human institutions can approach it," Cohens *v.* Virginia, 6 Wheat 264, 387 (1821). . . .

Our holding will be spelled out with some specificity in the pages which follow but briefly stated it is this: the prosecution may not use statements, whether exculpatory or inculpatory, stemming from custodial interrogation of the defendant unless it demonstrates the use of procedural safeguards effective to secure the privilege against self-incrimination. By custodial interrogation, we mean questioning initiated by law enforcement officers after a person has been taken into custody or otherwise deprived of his freedom of action in any significant way.[1] As for the procedural safeguards to be employed, unless other fully effective means are devised to inform accused persons of their right of silence and to assure a continuous opportunity to exercise it, the following measures are required. Prior to any questioning, the person must be warned that he has a right to remain silent, that any statement he does make may be used as evidence against him, and that he has a right to the presence of an attorney, either retained or appointed. The defendant may waive effectuation of these rights, provided the waiver is made voluntarily, knowingly and intelligently. If, however, he indicates in any manner and at any stage of the process that he wishes to consult with an attorney before speaking there can be no questioning. Likewise, if the individual is alone and indicates in any manner that he does not wish to be interrogated, the police may not question him. The mere fact that he may have answered some questions or volunteered some statements on his own does not deprive him of the right to refrain from answering any further inquiries until he has consulted with an attorney and thereafter consents to be questioned.

The constitutional issue we decide in each of these cases is the admissibility of statements obtained from a defendant questioned while in custody or otherwise deprived of his freedom of action in any significant way. In each, the defendant was questioned by police officers, detectives, or a prosecuting attorney in a room in which he was cut off from the outside world. In none of these cases was the defendant given a full and effective warning of his rights at the outset of the interrogation process. In all the cases, the questioning elicited oral admissions, and in three of them, signed statements as well which were admitted at their trials. They all thus share salient features—incommunicado interrogation of individuals in a police-dominated atmosphere, resulting in self-incriminating statements without full warnings of constitutional rights.

An understanding of the nature and setting of this in-custody interrogation is essential to our decisions today. The difficulty in depicting what transpires at such interrogations stems from the fact that in this country they have largely taken place incommunicado. . . .

---

[1] This is what we meant in *Escobedo* when we spoke of an investigation which had focused on an accused.

Interrogation still takes place in privacy. Privacy results in secrecy and this in turn results in a gap in our knowledge as to what in fact goes on in the interrogation rooms. A valuable source of information about present police practices, however, may be found in various police manuals and texts which document procedures employed with success in the past, and which recommend various other effective tactics. These texts are used by law enforcement agencies themselves as guides. It should be noted that these texts professedly present the most enlightened and effective means presently used to obtain statements through custodial interrogation. By considering these texts and other data, it is possible to describe procedures observed and noted around the country. . . .

[At this point the opinion quotes from Inbau and Reid, *Criminal Interrogations and Confessions* (1962) and O'Hara, *Fundamentals of Criminal Investigations* (1957) to depict the "most effective psychological stratagems" commonly employed during interrogations. The Chief Justice adds that these two manuals and others cited in footnotes "have had extensive use among law enforcement agencies and among students of police science."]

From these representative samples of interrogation techniques, the setting prescribed by the manuals and observed in practice becomes clear. In essence, it is this: To be alone with the subject is essential to prevent distraction and to deprive him of any outside support. The aura of confidence in his guilt undermines his will to resist. He merely confirms the preconceived story the police seek to have him describe. Patience and persistence, at times relentless questioning, are employed. To obtain a confession, the interrogator must "patiently maneuver himself or his quarry into a position from which the desired objective may be attained." When normal procedures fail to produce the needed result, the police may resort to deceptive stratagems such as giving false legal advice. It is important to keep the subject off balance, for example, by trading on his insecurity about himself or his surroundings. The police then persuade, trick, or cajole him out of exercising his constitutional rights.

Even without employing brutality, the "third degree" or the specific stratagems described above, the very fact of custodial interrogation exacts a heavy toll on individual liberty and trades on the weakness of individuals. . . .

In the cases before us today, given this background, we concern ourselves primarily with this interrogation atmosphere and the evils it can bring. In No. 759, Miranda *v.* Arizona, the police arrested the defendant and took him to a special interrogation room where they secured a confession. In No. 760, Vignera *v.* New York, the defendant made oral admissions to the police after interrogation in the afternoon, and then signed an inculpatory statement upon being questioned by an assistant district attorney later the same evening. In No. 761, Westover *v.* United States, the defendant was handed over to the Federal Bureau of Investigation by local authorities after they had detained and interrogated him for a lengthy period, both at night and the following morning. After some two hours of questioning, the federal officers had obtained signed statements from the defendant. Lastly, in No. 584, California *v.* Stewart, the local police held the defendant five days in the station and interrogated him on nine separate occasions before they secured his inculpatory statement.

In these cases, we might not find the defendant's statements to have been involuntary in traditional terms. Our concern for adequate safeguards to protect precious Fifth Amendment rights is, of course, not lessened in the slightest. In each of the cases, the defendant was thrust into an unfamiliar atmosphere and run through menacing police interrogation procedures. The potentiality for compulsion is forcefully apparent, for example, in *Miranda,* where the indigent Mexican defendant was a seriously disturbed individual with pronounced sexual fantasies, and in *Stewart,* in which the defendant was an indigent Los Angeles Negro who had dropped out of school in the sixth grade. To be sure, the records do not evince overt physical coercion or patent psychological ploys. The fact remains that in none of these cases did the officers undertake to afford appropriate safeguards at the outset of the interrogation to insure that the statements were truly the product of free choice.

It is obvious that such an interrogation environment is created for no purpose other than to subjugate the individual to the will of his examiner. This atmosphere carries its own badge of intimidation. To be sure, this is not physical intimidation, but it is equally destructive of human dignity. The current practice of incommunicado interrogation is at odds with one of our Nation's most cherished principles—that the individual may not be compelled to incriminate himself. Unless adequate protective devices are employed to dispel the compulsion inherent in custodial surroundings, no statement obtained from the defendant can truly be the product of his free choice. . . .

It is impossible for us to foresee the potential alternatives for protecting the privilege which might be devised by Congress or the States in the exercise of their creative rule-making capacities. Therefore we cannot say that the Constitution necessarily requires adherence to any particular solution for the inherent compulsions of the interrogation process as it is presently conducted. Our decision in no way creates a constitutional straitjacket which will handicap sound efforts at reform, nor is it intended to have this effect. We encourage Congress and the States to continue their laudable search for increasingly effective ways of protecting the rights of the individual while promoting efficient enforcement of our criminal laws. However, unless we are shown other procedures which are at least as effective in apprising accused persons of their right of silence and in assuring a continuous opportunity to exercise it, the following safeguards must be observed.

At the outset, if a person in custody is to be subjected to interrogation, he must first be informed in clear and unequivocal terms that he has the right to remain silent. For those unaware of the privilege, the warning is needed simply to make them aware of it—the threshold requirement for an intelligent decision as to its exercise. More important, such a warning is an absolute prerequisite in overcoming the inherent pressures of the interrogation atmosphere. It is not just the subnormal or woefully ignorant who succumb to an interrogator's imprecations, whether implied or expressly stated, that the interrogation will continue until a confession is obtained or that silence in the face of accusation is itself damning and will bode ill when presented to a jury. Further, the warning will show the individual that his interrogators are prepared to recognize his privilege should he choose to exercise it. . . .

The warning of the right to remain silent must be accompanied by the explanation that anything said can and will be used against the individual in court. This warning is needed in order to make him aware not only of the privilege, but also of the consequences of forgoing it. It is only through an awareness of these consequences that there can be any assurance of real understanding and intelligent exercise of the privilege. Moreover, this warning may serve to make the individual more acutely aware that he is faced with a phase of the adversary system—that he is not in the presence of persons acting solely in his interest.

The circumstances surrounding in-custody interrogation can operate very quickly to overbear the will of one merely made aware of his privilege by his interrogators. Therefore, the right to have counsel present at the interrogation is indispensable to the protection of the Fifth Amendment privilege under the system we delineate today. Our aim is to assure that the individual's right to choose between silence and speech remains unfettered throughout the interrogation process. A once-stated warning, delivered by those who will conduct the interrogation, cannot itself suffice to that end among those who most require knowledge of their rights. A mere warning given by the interrogators is not alone sufficient to accomplish that end. Prosecutors themselves claim that the admonishment of the right to remain silent without more "will benefit only the recidivist and the professional." Brief for the National District Attorneys Association as *amicus curiae*, p. 14. Even preliminary advice given to the accused by his own attorney can be swiftly overcome by the secret interrogation process. Cf. Escobedo *v.* Illinois, 378 US 478, 485. Thus, the need for counsel to protect the Fifth Amendment privilege comprehends not merely a right to consult with counsel prior to questioning, but also to have counsel present during any questioning if the defendant so desires.

The presence of counsel at the interrogation may serve several significant subsidiary functions as well. If the accused decides to talk to his interrogators, the assistance of counsel can mitigate the dangers of untrustworthiness. With a lawyer present the likelihood that the police will practice coercion is reduced, and if coercion is nevertheless exercised the lawyer can testify to it in court. The presence of a lawyer can also help to guarantee that the accused gives a fully accurate statement to the police and that the statement is rightly reported by the prosecution at trial. See Crooker *v.* California, 357 US 433, 443–448 (1958) (Douglas, J., dissenting). . . .

Accordingly we hold that an individual held for interrogation must be clearly informed that he has the right to consult with a lawyer and to have the lawyer with him during interrogation under the system for protecting the privilege we delineate today. . . .

In order fully to apprise a person interrogated of the extent of his rights under this system, it is necessary to warn him not only that he has the right to consult with an attorney, but also that if he is indigent a lawyer will be appointed to represent him. Without this additional warning, the admonition of the right to consult with counsel would often be understood as meaning only that he can consult with a lawyer if he has one or has the funds to obtain one. The warning of a right to counsel would be hollow if not couched in terms that would convey to the indigent—the person most often subjected to interrogation—the knowledge that he too has a right to have counsel present. As with the warnings of the right to remain silent and of the general right to counsel, only by effective and express explanation to the indigent of this right can there be assurance that he was truly in a position to exercise it.

Once warnings have been given, the subsequent procedure is clear. If the individual indicates in any manner, at any time prior to or during questioning, that he wishes to remain silent, the interrogation must cease. At this point he has shown that he intends to exercise his Fifth Amendment privilege; any statement taken after the person invokes his privilege cannot be other than the product of compulsion, subtle or otherwise. Without the right to cut off questioning, the setting of in-custody interrogation operates on the individual to overcome free choice in producing a statement after the privilege has been once invoked. If the individual states that he wants an attorney, the interrogation must cease until an attorney is present. At that time, the individual must have an opportunity to confer with the attorney and to have him present during any subsequent questioning. If the individual cannot obtain an attorney and he indicates that he wants one before speaking to police, they must respect his decision to remain silent.

This does not mean, as some have suggested, that each police station must have a "station house lawyer" present at all times to advise prisoners. It does mean, however, that if police propose to interrogate a person they must make known to him that he is entitled to a lawyer and that if he cannot afford one, a lawyer will be provided for him prior to any interrogation.

An express statement that the individual is willing to make a statement and does not want an attorney followed closely by a statement could constitute a waiver. But a valid waiver will not be presumed simply from the silence of the accused after warnings are given or simply from the fact that a confession was in fact eventually obtained. . . .

Our decision is not intended to hamper the traditional function of police officers in investigating crime. See Escobedo v. Illinois, 378 US 478, 492. When an individual is in custody on probable cause, the police may, of course, seek out evidence in the field to be used at trial against him. Such investigation may include inquiry of persons not under restraint. General on-the-scene questioning as to facts surrounding a crime or other general questioning of citizens in the fact-finding process is not affected by our holding. It is an act of responsible citizenship for individuals to give whatever information they may have to aid in law enforcement. In such situations the compelling atmosphere inherent in the process of in-custody interrogation is not necessarily present.

To summarize, we hold that when an individual is taken into custody or otherwise deprived of his freedom by the authorities in any significant way and is subjected to questioning, the privilege against self-incrimination is jeopardized. Procedural safeguards must be employed to protect the privilege, and unless other fully effective means are adopted to notify the person of his right of silence and to assure that the exercise of the right will be scrupulously honored, the following measures are required. He must be warned prior to any questioning that he has the right to remain silent, that anything he says can be used against him in a court of law, that he has the right to the presence of an attorney, and that if he cannot afford an attorney one will be appointed for him prior to any questioning if he so desires. Opportunity to exercise these rights must be afforded to him throughout the interrogation. After such warnings have been given, and such opportunity afforded him, the individual may knowingly and intelligently waive these rights and agree to answer questions or make a statement. But unless and until such warnings and waiver are demonstrated by the prosecution at trial, no evidence obtained as a result of interrogation can be used against him. . . .

Therefore, in accordance with the foregoing, the judgments of the Supreme Court of Arizona in No. 759, of the New York Court of Appeals in No. 760, and of the Court of Appeals for the Ninth Circuit in No. 761 are reversed. The judgment of the Supreme Court of California in No. 584 is affirmed.*

It is so ordered.

MR. JUSTICE CLARK, dissenting in Nos. 759, 760, and 761, and concurring in the result in No. 584.

It is with regret that I find it necessary to write in these cases. However, I am unable to join the majority because its opinion goes too far on too little, while my dissenting brethren do not go quite far enough. Nor can I join in with the Court's criticism of the present practices of police and investigatory agencies as to custodial interrogation. The materials it refers to as "police manuals" are, as I read them, merely writings in this field by professors and some police officers. Not one is shown by the record here to be the official manual of any police department, much less in universal use in crime detection. Moreover, the examples of police brutality mentioned by the Court are rare exceptions to the thousands of cases that appear every year in the law reports. The police agencies—all the way from municipal and state forces to the federal bureaus—are responsible for law enforcement and public safety in this country. I am proud of their efforts, which in my view are not fairly characterized by the Court's opinion.

The ipse dixit of the majority has no support in our cases. Indeed, the Court admits that "we might not find the defendants' statements [here] to have been involuntary in traditional terms." In short, the Court has added more to the requirements that the accused is entitled to consult with his lawyer and that he must be given the traditional warning that he may remain silent and that anything that he says may be used against him. Escobedo v. Illinois, 378 US 478, 490–491 (1964). Now, the Court fashions a constitutional rule that the police may engage in no custodial interrogation without additionally advising the accused that he has a right under the Fifth Amendment to the presence of counsel during interrogation and that, if he is without funds, counsel will be furnished him. When at any point during an interrogation the accused seeks affirmatively or impliedly to invoke his rights to silence or counsel, interrogation must be forgone or postponed. The Court further holds that failure to follow the new procedures requires inexorably the exclusion of any statement by the accused, as well as the fruits thereof. Such a strict constitutional specific

* See page 305. [Eds.]

inserted at the nerve center of crime detection may well kill the patient. Since there is at this time a paucity of information and an almost total lack of empirical knowledge on the practical operation of requirements truly comparable to those announced by the majority, I would be more restrained lest we go too far too fast.

Custodial interrogation has long been recognized as "undoubtedly an essential tool in effective law enforcement." Haynes *v.* Washington, 373 US 503, 515 (1963). Recognition of this fact should put us on guard against the promulgation of doctrinaire rules. Especially is this true where the Court finds that "the Constitution has prescribed" its holding and where the light of our past cases, from Hopt *v.* Utah, 110 US 574 (1884), down to Haynes *v.* Washington, supra, is to the contrary. . . .

The rule prior to today—as Mr. Justice Goldberg, the author of the Court's opinion in *Escobedo,* stated it in Haynes *v.* Washington—depended upon "a totality of circumstances evidencing an involuntary . . . admission of guilt." 373 US, at 514. . . .

I would continue to follow that rule. Under the "totality of circumstances" rule of which my Brother Goldberg spoke in *Haynes,* I would consider in each case whether the police officer prior to custodial interrogation added the warning that the suspect might have counsel present at the interrogation and, further, that a court would appoint one at his request if he was too poor to employ counsel. In the absence of warnings, the burden would be on the State to prove that counsel was knowingly and intelligently waived or that in the totality of the circumstances, including the failure to give the necessary warnings, the confession was clearly voluntary. . . .

MR. JUSTICE HARLAN, whom MR. JUSTICE STEWART and MR. JUSTICE WHITE join, dissenting.

I believe the decision of the Court represents poor constitutional law and entails harmful consequences for the country at large. How serious these consequences may prove to be only time can tell. But the basic flaws in the Court's justification seem to me readily apparent now once all sides of the problem are considered. . . .

Constitutional Premises

It is most fitting to begin an inquiry into the constitutional precedents by surveying the limits on confessions the Court has evolved under the Due Process Clause of the Fourteenth Amendment. This is so because these cases show that there exists a workable and effective means of dealing with confessions in a judicial manner; because the cases are the baseline from which the Court now departs and so serve to measure the actual as opposed to the professed distance it travels; and because examination of them helps reveal how the Court has coasted into its present position.

The earliest confession cases in this Court emerged from federal prosecutions and were settled on a nonconstitutional basis, the Court adopting the common-law rule that the absence of inducements, promises, and threats made a confession voluntary and admissible. Hopt *v.* Utah, 110 US 574; Pierce *v.* United States, 160 US 355. . . .

The second point is that in practice and from time to time in principle, the Court has given ample recognition to society's interest in suspect questioning as an instrument of law enforcement. Cases countenancing quite significant pressures can be cited without difficulty, and the lower courts may often have been yet more tolerant. Of course the limitations imposed today were rejected by necessary implication in case after case, the right to warnings having been explicitly rebuffed in this Court many years ago. Powers *v.* United States, 223 US 303; Wilson *v.* United States, 162 US 613. As recently as Haynes *v.* Washington, 373 US 503, 515, the Court openly acknowledged that questioning of witnesses and suspects "is undoubtedly an essential tool in effective law enforcement." Accord, Crooker *v.* California, 357 US 433, 441. . . .

While the Court finds no pertinent difference between judicial proceedings and police interrogation, I believe the differences are so vast as to disqualify wholly the Sixth Amendment precedents as suitable analogies in the present cases.

The only attempt in this Court to carry the right to counsel into the station house occurred in *Escobedo,* the Court repeating several times that that stage was no less "critical" than trial itself. This is hardly persuasive when we consider that a grand jury inquiry, the filing of a certiorari petition, and certainly the purchase of narcotics by an undercover agent from a prospective defendant may all be equally "critical" yet provision of counsel and advice on that score have never been thought compelled by the Constitution in such cases. The sound reason why this right is so freely extended for a criminal trial is the severe injustice risked by confronting an untrained defendant with a range of technical points of law, evidence, and tactics familiar to the prosecutor but not to himself. This danger shrinks markedly in the police station where indeed the lawyer in fulfilling his professional responsibilities of necessity may become an obstacle to truth-finding. . . .

Policy Considerations

Legal history has been stretched before to satisfy deep needs of society. In this instance, however, the Court has not and cannot make the powerful showing that its new rules are plainly desirable in the context of our society, something which is surely demanded before those rules are engrafted onto the Constitution and imposed on every State and county in the land. . . .

What the Court largely ignores is that its rules impair, if they will not eventually serve wholly to frustrate, an instrument of law enforcement that has long and quite reasonably been thought worth the price paid for it. There can be little doubt that the Court's new code would markedly decrease the number of confessions. To warn the suspect that he may remain silent and remind him that his confession may be used in court are minor obstructions. To require also an express waiver by the suspect and an end to questioning whenever he demurs must heavily handicap questioning. And to suggest or provide counsel for the suspect simply invites the end of the interrogation.

How much harm this decision will inflict on law enforcement cannot fairly be predicted with accuracy. . . . We do know that some crimes cannot be solved without confessions, that ample expert testimony attests to their importance in crime control, and that the Court is taking a real risk with society's welfare in imposing its new regime on the country. The social costs of crime are too great to call the new rules anything but a hazardous experimentation.

While passing over the costs and risks of its experiment, the Court portrays the evils of normal police questioning in terms which I think are exaggerated. Albeit stringently confined by the due process standards interrogation is no doubt often inconvenient and unpleasant for the suspect. However, it is no less so for a man to be arrested and jailed, to have his house searched, or to stand trial in court, yet all this may properly happen to the most innocent given probable cause, a warrant, or an indictment. Society has always paid a stiff price for law and order, and peaceful interrogation is not one of the dark moments of the law.

This brief statement of the competing considerations seems to me ample proof that the Court's preference is highly debatable at best and therefore not to be read into the Constitution. However, it may make the analysis more graphic to consider the actual facts of one of the four cases reversed by the Court. Miranda *v.* Arizona serves best, being neither the hardest nor easiest of the four under the Court's standards.

On March 3, 1963, an 18-year-old girl was kidnapped and forcibly raped near Phoenix, Arizona. Ten days later, on the morning of March 13, petitioner Miranda was arrested and taken to the police station. At this time Miranda was 23 years old, indigent, and educated to the extent of completing half the ninth grade. He had "an emotional illness" of the schizophrenic type, according to the doctor who eventually examined him; the doctor's report also stated that Miranda was "alert and oriented as to time, place, and person," intelligent within normal limits, competent to stand trial, and sane within the legal definition. At the police station, the victim picked Miranda out of a lineup, and two officers then took him into a separate room to interrogate him, starting about 11:30 a.m. Though at first denying his guilt, within a short time Miranda gave a detailed oral confession and then wrote out in his own hand and signed a brief statement admitting and describing the crime. All this was accomplished in two hours or less without any force, threats or promises and—I will assume this though the record is uncertain, without any effective warnings at all.

Miranda's oral and written confessions are now held inadmissible under the Court's new rules. One is entitled to feel astonished that the Constitution can be read to produce this result. These confessions were obtained during brief, daytime questioning conducted by two officers and unmarked by any of the traditional indicia of coercion. They assured a conviction for a brutal and unsettling crime, for which the police had and quite possibly could obtain little evidence other than the victim's identifications, evidence which is frequently unreliable. There was, in sum, a legitimate purpose, no perceptible unfairness, and certainly little risk of injustice in the interrogation. Yet the resulting confessions, and the responsible course of police practice they represent, are to be sacrificed to the Court's own finespun conception of fairness which I seriously doubt is shared by many thinking citizens in this country.

In conclusion: Nothing in the letter or the spirit of the Constitution or in the precedents squares with the heavy-handed and one-sided action that is so precipitously taken by the Court in the name of fulfilling its constitutional responsibilities. The foray which the Court makes today brings to mind the wise and farsighted words of Mr. Justice Jackson in Douglas v. Jeannette, 319 US 157, 181 (separate opinion): "This Court is forever adding new stories to the temples of constitutional law, and the temples have a way of collapsing when one story too many is added."

MR. JUSTICE WHITE, with whom MR. JUSTICE HARLAN and MR. JUSTICE STEWART join, dissenting.

The proposition that the privilege against self-incrimination forbids in-custody interrogation without the warnings specified in the majority opinion and without a clear waiver of counsel has no significant support in the history of the privilege or in the language of the Fifth Amendment. As for the English authorities and the common-law history, the privilege, firmly established in the second half of the seventeenth century, was never applied except to prohibit compelled judicial interrogations. The rule excluding coerced confessions matured about 100 years later, "[b]ut there is nothing in the reports to suggest that the theory has its roots in the privilege against self-incrimination. And so far as the cases reveal, the privilege, as such, seems to have been given effect only in judicial proceedings, including the preliminary examinations by authorized magistrates." Morgan, The Privilege Against Self-Incrimination, 34 Minn L Rev 1, 18 (1949).

That the Court's holding today is neither compelled nor even strongly suggested by the language of the Fifth Amendment, is at odds with American and English legal history, and involves a departure from a long line of precedent does not prove either that the Court has exceeded its powers or that the Court is wrong or unwise in its present re-interpretation of the Fifth Amendment. It does, however, underscore the obvious—that the Court has not discovered or found the law in making today's decision, nor has it derived it from some irrefutable sources; what it has done is to make new law and new public policy in much the same way that it has in the course of interpreting other great clauses of the Constitution.[2] This is what the Court historically has done. Indeed, it is what it must do and will continue to do until and unless there is some fundamental change in the constitutional distribution of governmental powers.

But if the Court is here and now to announce new and fundamental policy to govern certain aspects of our affairs, it is wholly legitimate to examine the mode of this or any other constitutional decision in this Court and to inquire into the advisability of its end product in terms of the long-range interest of the country. At the very least the Court's text and reasoning should withstand analysis and be a fair exposition of the constitutional provision which its opinion interprets. Decisions like these cannot rest alone on syllogism, metaphysics

[2] Of course the Court does not deny that it is departing from prior precedent; it expressly overrules Crooker and Cicenia, ante, at 726, n. 48, and it acknowledges that in the instant "cases we might not find the defendants' statements to have been involuntary in traditional terms," ante, at 713.

or some ill-defined notions of natural justice, although each will perhaps play its part. In proceeding to such constructions as it now announces, the Court should also duly consider all the factors and interests bearing upon the cases, at least insofar as the relevant materials are available; and if the necessary considerations are not treated in the record or obtainable from some other reliable source, the Court should not proceed to formulate fundamental policies based on speculation alone. . . .

The obvious underpinning of the Court's decision is a deep-seated distrust of all confessions. As the Court declares that the accused may not be interrogated without counsel present, absent a waiver of the right to counsel, and as the Court all but admonishes the lawyer to advise the accused to remain silent, the result adds up to a judicial judgment that evidence from the accused should not be used against him in any way, whether compelled or not. This is the not so subtle overtone of the opinion—that it is inherently wrong for the police to gather evidence from the accused himself. And this is precisely the nub of this dissent. I see nothing wrong or immoral, and certainly nothing unconstitutional, in the police's asking a suspect whom they have reasonable cause to arrest whether or not he killed his wife or in confronting him with the evidence on which the arrest was based, at least where he has been plainly advised that he may remain completely silent, see Escobedo v. Illinois, 378 US 478, 499, (dissenting opinion). Until today, "the admissions or confessions of the prisoner, when voluntarily and freely made, have always ranked high in the scale of incriminating evidence." Brown v. Walker, 161 US 591, 596; see also Hopt v. Utah, 110 US 574, 584–585. Particularly when corroborated, as where the police have confirmed the accused's disclosure of the hiding place cf implements or fruits of the crime, such confessions have the highest reliability and significantly contribute to the certitude with which we may believe the accused is guilty. Moreover, it is by no means certain that the process of confessing is injurious to the accused. To the contrary it may provide psychological relief and enhance the prospects for rehabilitation.

This is not to say that the value of respect for the inviolability of the accused's individual personality should be accorded no weight or that all confessions should be indiscriminately admitted. This Court has long read the Constitution to proscribe compelled confessions, a salutary rule from which there should be no retreat. But I see no sound basis, factual or otherwise, and the Court gives none, for concluding that the present rule against the receipt of coerced confessions is inadequate for the task of sorting out inadmissible evidence and must be replaced by the per se rule which is now imposed. Even if the new concept can be said to have advantages of some sort over the present law, they are far outweighed by its likely undesirable impact on other very relevant and important interests.

The most basic function of any government is to provide for the security of the individual and of his property. Lanzetta v. New Jersey 306 US 451, 455. These ends of society are served by the criminal laws which for the most part are aimed at the prevention of crime. Without the reasonably effective performance of the task of preventing private violence and retaliation, it is idle to talk about human dignity and civilized values.

What Role for the Supreme Court?

In the famous case of Marbury v. Madison, *Chief Justice Marshall presented the classic arguments for judicial review. The power of the courts to declare acts of the legislature unconstitutional has long been accepted practice and the legitimacy of the power is today rarely debated. Marshall's case for judicial review assumes that the Court is an objective impersonal body enforcing not its own will but the written commands of the Constitution. Up until 1940 the most persistent critics of the Court were liberals who complained of the predilection of the Court to read into the Constitution its own attachment to laissez-faire economics. Since the Court was "reconstructed" by President Roosevelt, it has tended to defer to legislative judgment in economic matters while following an increasingly libertarian interpretation of the Fourteenth Amendment and the Bill of Rights. What Professor Freund has called the "creative ambiguities" of the due process clause in the Fifth and Fourteenth Amendments give the Court an opportunity for judicial activism.*

The fundamental issue in Constitutional Law today is how the Court should exercise its power to interpret the Constitution. Should the Court act with judicial "self-restraint" and deference to the legislative judgment? The best known proponents of judicial self-restraint were Mr. Justice Holmes and Mr. Justice Frankfurter. On the present court, Mr. Justice John Harlan is the foremost exponent of this point of view.

In the article that follows, Professor Fred Rodell insists that civil liberties should be "given preferred judicial treatment." The very purpose of a Bill of Rights, Rodell believes, was "to guarantee certain fundamental personal rights against *majority rule, because they were deemed so essential to civilized government" and, he adds, the elected majority-minded branches of the government are, by their very nature, less apt to obey those mandates than the Court. Professor Mendelson has characterized this position as the "single-value conditioned reflex." "Shall doubts be resolved by a handful of 'independent' judges whose libertarian or proprietarian preferences happen for the moment to dominate the bench? Or," he queries, "by the people and their elected representatives with a minimum of judicial interference?" "The basic articulate premise of government in the United States," he adds, "is the diffusion of power." The*

Constitution does not give preeminence to any one value. Both majority rule and individual freedom are essential to the democratic process. The special function of the Court, he insists, is to preserve a "constitutional balance between the several elements in a common enterprise."

FRED RODELL
The Case for Judicial Activism

"Of that freedom [freedom of speech] one may say that it is the matrix, the indispensable condition, of nearly every other form of freedom."—Benjamin Cardozo.

"The history of liberty has largely been the history of the observance of procedural safeguards."—Felix Frankfurter.

"What is freedom of speech and of the press; . . . these fundamental canons . . . turn out to be no more than admonitions of moderation."—Learned Hand.

"The idea that they are no more than that has done more to undermine liberty in this country than any other single force."—William O. Douglas.

In the early evening of March 8, 1948, a college student named Irving Feiner was standing on an actual soap box at a street corner in Syracuse, New York, speaking in occasionally abusive language in behalf of Henry Wallace's absurd bid for the United States presidency. Of a crowd of seventy-five or eighty, one or two men threatened Feiner; a policeman thereupon ordered Feiner to shut up and climb down; Feiner refused; he was arrested and sentenced to thirty days in the penitentiary. His conviction, protested up to the Supreme Court, was there upheld, six to three.[1] Said Justice Frankfurter, characteristically, in concurrence: "Where conduct is within the allowable limits of free speech, the police are peace officers for the speaker as well as for his hearers. But . . ."[2] And again: "Enforcement of these [breach-of-peace] statutes calls for public tolerance and intelligent police administration. These, in the long run, must give substance to whatever the Court may say about free speech. But . . ."[3] Said Justice Black, in dissent: "I think this conviction makes a mockery of the free speech guarantees of the First and Fourteenth Amend-

Professor of Law, Yale Law School. Author of *Fifty-five Men: the Story of the Constitution; Woe Unto You, Lawyers; Democracy and the Third Term; Nine Men: A Political History of the Supreme Court from 1790 to 1955;* and of many articles. The selection is from "Judicial Activists, Judicial Self-Deniers, Judicial Review and the First Amendment—Or, How to Hide the Melody of What You Mean Behind the Words of What You say," *Georgetown Law Journal,* Vol. 47 (1959), pp. 483-490.

[1] Feiner v. New York, 340 U.S. 315 (1951).
[2] Id. at 289 (concurring opinion).
[3] Ibid.

ments. . . . I will have no part or parcel in this holding which I view as a long step toward totalitarian authority."[4] There were no But's.

This too-little-noted case—*Feiner v. New York*[5]—along with the head-on-colliding quotes italicized above are here intended to highlight what strikes me as the most meaningful split in constitutional law and theory and practice of the mid-twentieth century. It is a split that stems from the thorny question of *who* is ultimately responsible, under our constitutional system, for the protection of the people's basic liberties, especially those that are guaranteed by the first amendment (and, courtesy of judicial injection, by the fourteenth as well). It is a split that has commonly, if a bit dubiously, been dubbed a conflict between "activists" and "passivists" or "self-deniers," on the bench and in the academic bleachers—and as such, its ramifications reach beyond the first amendment (plus the fourteenth) to the whole of the Bill of Rights and even further still. It is a split whose sources stretch back through at least two thousand years of political theory and whose present manifestations have been known to spawn personal feuds out of ideological differences. In its current intensity, it began to get up steam soon after the clash between the Old Court and the New Deal, or just about twenty years ago.

That, of course, was the approximate point in time when a glorious new epoch in constitutional law seemed to loom immediately and infinitely ahead; an inglorious era of economic overlordship by the Court was at an obvious end; the fat reading of the due process clauses plus the thin reading of the commerce clause, to hobble affirmative government, had been hastily abandoned by the Old Court itself, under the Damoclean sword of the Roosevelt Court plan. Now, new Justices sat in the old seats of power, unanimous in the belief that their predecessors, prior to that quick conversion, had been wrong, wrong, wrong. But how and why had they been wrong? There was the rub whose friction caused the split that has rent the new Court for two decades. And if, in seeking to analyze this split, I should seem too simplistic, too primer-minded for the sophisticated, I offer no apology. The agglutinated gloss of judicial self-justification has grow thicker and stickier with the years; my effort is to cut through those layers of verbal varnish and bare the true grain that lies beneath.

What one group of Old-Court critics said—and are still saying—is that the veto-wielding Nine Old Men of the thirties were wrong to substitute their collective judgment for that of Congress (or, to a lesser extent, for that of state legislatures) on *any* type of issue, under the aegis of *any* constitutional clause. These were and are the passivists, the self-deniers, the apostles' of undifferentiated judicial self-restraint. With rare exceptions—usually involving a conflict of sovereignties under our fifty-governmented federal system—they would leave the commands of the Constitution to legislative hands, with the judiciary keeping a strict hands-off. At the federal government level, they come very close to contending that the Court should never overrule Congress on constitutional grounds—that is, to disavowing the right of judicial review Marshall asserted in *Marbury v. Madison.*[6] Their chief spokesman on the Supreme Court, since the

[4] Id. at 323 (dissenting opinion).
[5] 340 U.S. 315 (1951).
[6] 5 U.S. (1 Cranch) 137 (1803).

death of Justice Jackson, is of course Justice Frankfurter,* who has often bemoaned his inability, self-imposed by self-restraint, to vote to strike down, as unconstitutional, legislation which he finds offensive under the Constitution. Most articulate advocate of this view is the venerable Judge Learned Hand, who has touted the propriety of judicial impotence in the face of legislative arrogance, with special emphasis on the field of civil liberties, in court opinions and in two books—*The Spirit of Liberty*[7] and his recently published Harvard lectures, *The Bill of Rights.*[8] Going further back, the patron saints of the indiscriminate self-deniers include Alexander Hamilton, British jurist John Austin, and Harvard Law Professor Thayer who long preached the doctrine from his lecture platform. Justice Holmes, selectively interpreted to fit the faith, is also claimed as a past adherent—although it is highly doubtful that either Justice Frankfurter or Judge Hand would ever judicially subscribe to such a typical Holmesian statement of his own credo as: "If in the long run the beliefs expressed in proletarian dictatorship are destined to be accepted by the dominant forces of the community, the only meaning of free speech is that they should be given their chance and have their way."[9]

Arrayed against the formidable if somewhat Anglophilic forces of these whole-hog self-deniers are the allegedly illogical and inconsistent activists. They agree that the Old Court was wrong to veto pre-New Deal and New Deal legislation—but they see the error in narrower and more specific terms. They see it in the type of laws that were vetoed—and all were economic regulations—and in the fuzzy imprecision of the constitutional excuses used to cut those laws down. Thus, the "substantive due process" suitcase was expandable enough to give the Court, as Holmes once noted, *carte blanche* to veto at its pleasure, just as a subjective reading of the commerce clause was invited by such Court-bred convolutions as *in*-commerce-or-*affecting*-commerce-*directly*-or-*indirectly*. Not so easily elastic is the bulk of the Bill of Rights—especially the first amendment with its flat and absolute commands. Hence the activists believe the Court can and should diffentiate—that it can and should overrule Congress in the name of the Constitution where the document itself is more precise and, particularly, where the claimed rights at issue are more precious and more personal than those that deal exclusively with matters of money. Chief spokesmen of this view on the current Court, and for many years back, are Justices Black and Douglas. Among its patron saints are Thomas Jefferson, Justice Holmes—differently interpreted than by the self-deniers, with the emphasis here on his civil-liberty dissents—and Justice Stone who, along with his powerful plea for self-restraint in the *Butler* (AAA) case,[10] a strictly economic hassle, also urged in his famous *Carolene Products*[11] footnote that civil liberties be given preferred judicial treatment.

Accused by the self-deniers of result-minded opportunism, the activists

---

* Justice Frankfurter is retired from the Court. The present chief spokesman for this point of view is Justice Harlan. [Eds.]

[7] L. Hand, The Spirit of Liberty (2d ed. 1953).

[8] L. Hand, the Bill of Rights (1958). Judge Hand has since died.

[9] Gitlow v. United States, 268 U.S. 652, 673 (1925) (dissenting opinion).

[10] United States v. Butler, 297 U.S. 1, 78-79 (1936).

[11] United States v. Carolene Prods. Co., 304 U.S. 144, 152-53 (1938).

are asked how they can reconcile judicial supremacy where civil liberties are at stake with legislative supremacy in the regulation of business and wealth. Behind this question lurks the inarticulate major premise that a constitutional policy ought to be conceptually consistent, regardless of the stuff of life with which it deals. But the activists do not believe that logic should rule, rather than serve, the ends of government nor that jurisprudence should be dominated by a syllogism. They believe that our nation, our civilization, our culture, put —or should put—a higher premium on individual dignities and freedoms than on such material matters as the getting and keeping of money. They believe that this simple but exalted scale of values was deliberately implanted into the Constitution by the Bill of Rights (plus the fourteenth amendment) and, further, that it is their duty as judges to militantly uphold it rather than meekly deplore its occasional legislative neglect.

Indeed—to go back briefly to historical roots—why have a written Constitution at all in a republic, or a representative democracy, that is dedicated to majority rule? Why, that is, except to set up the sheer mechanics of government (two senators per state, four-year terms for a president, etc.) and to sketch in the structure by which two overlapping sovereigns—the nation and the states— might operate together? Why a written Bill of Rights—without the assurance of which, incidentally, most of the original states would never have ratified the Constitution? The answer must be plain even to the judicial self-deniers. The purpose was to lay down certain basic rules that even a majority was not to be privileged to violate by vote—to guarantee certain fundamental personal rights and liberties *against* majority rule, because they were deemed so essential to civilized government. These were, and are, the minimum democratic decencies that dictatorships view with scorn, the multifarious protections of individuals and minority groups—especially unpopular individuals and minorities—which range in scope from the first amendment freedoms to the various injunctions of fair treatment and fair trial for every criminal defendant, be he accused of kidnapping or Communism.

And the key question, then—to come back in something of a circle to our starting-point—is *who* is to uphold, under the commands of the Constitution, these uniquely guaranteed liberties of unpopular or even despised people against a lynch-minded, let's-get-them majority. Should it be the legislatures, including Congress, which presumably reflect the current majority will? Or should it perhaps be the courts, especially the Supreme Court, to which the last appeals of those who feel they have been unjustly wronged are regularly taken? It is this old poser in political theory—and in practical day-to-day government as well— that divides, even more than does the logic or illogic of selective self-restraint, the advocates of activism under the Bill of Rights, and most particularly under the first amendment, from the apostles of judicial self-denial. The division has taken on an almost explosive quality during roughly the past dozen years, as "loyalty" and "security" laws and programs have sprouted at every level of government—all of them impinging in some measure on freedom of speech, of press, of association, even of thought in the political realm. Books on the subject have burgeoned, two of the most authoritative, in light of the stature of their authors, being Learned Hand's *The Bill of Rights* and William O. Douglas' *The Right of the People*—both of them published last year.

It is Judge Hand's general thesis, as a lifetime member of the self-denying school, that—with rare and rather fuzzily defined exceptions—the last word should be left by the courts to the legislature, especially to Congress, as much when civil liberties are on the line as when the issue is one of economic regulation. After all, legislators no less than judges take oaths to support the Constitution and should be presumed to consider carefully—though surely this is unrealistic—the constitutionality of whatever laws they pass. Beyond that, though —and this is his basic postulate—Judge Hand sees as inherently undemocratic the whole concept of judicial review (of legislative action) in *any* field; to him, it adds up to rule by judges. "For myself," he says, "it would be most irksome to be ruled by a bevy of Platonic Guardians, even if I knew how to choose them.. . ."[12] Yet Judge Hand must have a twinge of awareness that to equate judicial protection of constitutional liberties, even metaphorically, with rule by a bevy of Platonic Guardians is nonsense. As well call the drafters of the Bill of Rights Platonic Guardians Emeritus. Far more significantly, the judge well knows that the vetoing of laws by courts, on whatever ground, is perforce a negative act, whereas to rule is to act affirmatively in a sovereign fashion— scarcely an attribute of a declaration that this statute or that is void because it runs counter, for instance, to the commands of the first amendment. The fact is that Judge Hand is so absorbed with the abstract theory of judicial review—as well as with defense of his own long-tenanted position—that, despite flashes of the old eloquence, he never hits the crucial, living issues head-on.

By contrast, Justice Douglas faces in his book—as he has in his opinions over a score of years—the fact-situations that call for solution, the competing claims that come before the Court, and the frankly functional nature of his own choices and decisions. Indeed, this approach is the essence of judicial activism. Conceptual consistency about the right of judicial review takes second place to an honest weighing of the ends to be achieved on the scale of democratic values. On this scale, the civil liberties of the Bill of Rights and the fourteenth amendment weigh heaviest, with the freedoms guaranteed by the first amendment— "in terms absolute," as Douglas puts it—outweighing all the rest. Justice Douglas has no doubt that it is the duty of the courts to defend these freedoms militantly against legislative encroachment or disregard, no matter what the calamity-howlers may holler about the evils of judicial supremacy. To him, it is rather a matter of *constitutional* supremacy. Thus, he does not consider the judiciary the only *who* charged with protection of the people's liberties. It is—or should be—equally the job of legislators, executives and administrators as well. But when lawmakers or law-enforcers fall short of their obligation, that does not entitle the judges to bow deferentially out of the picture. It is then their special duty to restore, by vigilant use of the judicial veto, those constitutional rights of which the people have been improperly deprived. On a realistic note—contrasting starkly with Judge Hand's philosophic cerebrations—Justice Douglas recognizes that the two elected, and so majority-minded, branches of government are, by their very nature, less apt to obey those mandates of the Constitution which guarantee minority rights against majority rule. Hence, too often it falls finally to the courts to uphold freedom of speech or press or assembly or religion and all the rest. Tough and unpopular as such decisions frequently are,

12 L. Hand, The Bill of Rights 73 (1958).

Justice Douglas sees them as the judiciary's most challenging and finest achievements.

Such achievements on the part of the Supreme Court were lamentably rare during the decade after World War II, as the Smith Act and the McCarran Acts and the whole congeries of abominations against the Bill of Rights in the name of national security withstood judicial inspection. They were rare because the self-deniers prevailed, because a Court majority meekly manacled itself against overruling Congress—or, in most instances, the legislatures of the states—even in defense of the first amendment. Despite their numerical superiority, there was an air of peevish futility about the self-deniers' explanations. Said Justice Frankfurter, concurring in the *Dennis* decision: "Civic liberties draw at best only limited strength from legal guaranties. . . . The ultimate reliance for the deepest needs of civilization must be found outside their vindication in courts of law. . . ."[13] Of course, the decision itself made these statements temporarily true; but might not the identical words and reasoning be used to uphold lynch law? And Justice Jackson, expatiating on his self-denying philosophy in a post-humously published book, remarked that "any court which undertakes by its legal processes to enforce civil liberties needs the support of an enlightened and vigorous public opinion. . . . I do not think the American public is enlightened on this subject."[14] Which would make an easy out for any government servant seeking to excuse himself from enforcing an unpopular law. These are not vicious men, these self-deniers; they are timid and bothered and bookish men, under whose passive aegis the vicious men—freedom-flouting and conformity-minded—have had their way to the nation's detriment.

Yet even at the lowest ebb in the Court's defense of personal liberties, there were other and braver voices to be heard, albeit in dissent. Thus, John Lord O'Brian, respected and Republican elder statesman of the bar, concluded his book on *National Security and Individual Freedom:* "If and when our leaders in the Executive, Congressional, *and Judicial* departments awaken to their obligation to protect the freedom of the human spirit, they will, like their great predecessors, respond to that obligation. The public, with the issues clarified will *then* also respond. . . ."[15] Thus, Justice Douglas, protesting the Court's approval of New York's Feinberg Law, under which schoolteachers were fired because of their past associations, reminded: "The Framers knew . . . the strength that comes when the mind is free, when ideas may be pursued wherever they lead. *We* forget these teachings of the First Amendment when *we* sustain this law."[16] Thus, Justice Black magnificently ended his *Dennis* dissent: "There is hope, however, that in calmer times, when present pressures, passions and fears subside, this or some later *Court* will restore the First Amendment liberties to the high preferred place where they belong in a free society."[17] In trying to counter these clear calls for active judicial responsibility, the self-deniers might, and some did, go back for support to the Founding Fathers—for

[13] Dennis v. United States, 341 U.S. 494, 555-56 (1951).

[14] Jackson, The Supreme Court in the American System of Government 82 (1955).

[15] O'Brian, National Security and Individual Freedom 83-84 (1955). (Emphasis added.)

[16] Adler v. Board of Educ., 342 U.S. 485, 511 (1952) (dissenting opinion). (Emphasis added.)

[17] 341 U.S. at 581. (Emphasis added.)

instance, to Alexander Hamilton who opposed a Bill of Rights and who opined, in Federalist Paper No. 84, that liberty of the press "must depend on legislative discretion, regulated by public opinion. . . ."[18] But the activists could readily quote in reply James Madison's statement: "If they [civil liberties] are incorporated into the Constitution, independent tribunals of justice will consider themselves in a peculiar manner the guardians of those rights; they will be an impenetrable bulwark against every assumption of power in the legislative or executive; they will be naturally led to resist every encroachment upon rights expressly stipulated for in the Constitution by the declaration of rights."[19] Significantly, Madison gave this strong exposition of judicial activism in the very speech in which he proposed a Bill of Rights to the first Congress.

My less than impartial primer draws to a close. The plain and simple fact is that it is not the dictate of history, long-past or recent, which mainly motivates the self-deniers to decline active judicial defense of the first amendment freedoms. Nor is it a repugnance toward illogic or inconsistency in the exercise of the power of judicial review. Nor is it a faith that if the courts take care of the forms, of the procedure, then the substance of liberty will somehow take care of itself. Nor is it even a decent respect for the prerogatives of the other two branches of government, especially the legislative. All these are factors but they are abstract factors; they are word reasons; they are the gloss upon the underlying grain. The crux of judicial self-denial in the civil liberties field is, in a sense, just as negative as the philosophy it espouses—and it is implicit in the But's that so often follow protestations of devotion to civil liberties. These men, these self-deniers, all believe in the first amendment freedoms; the point is that they do not believe in them enough. They do not believe in them enough to fight officially or effectively for their protection and preservation. Indeed—and here is the essence of it—not one of the self-deniers can say, as can the activists, with Thomas Jefferson: "I have sworn upon the altar of God eternal hostility against every form of tyranny over the mind of man."[20]

[18] The Federalist No. 84, at 538 (Lodge ed. 1888) (Hamilton).
[19] 5 The Writings of James Madison 385 (Hunt ed. 1900).
[20] 10 The Writings of Thomas Jefferson 175 (Library ed. 1903).

WALLACE MENDELSON
The Case for Judicial Restraint

Introduction

> . . . law is always a general statement, yet there are cases which it is not possible to cover in general terms. In matters therefore where, while it is necessary to speak in general terms, it is not possible to do so correctly, the law takes into consideration the majority of cases, although it is not

Professor of Government, University of Texas. Author of *The Constitution and the Supreme Court* and of *Capitalism, Democracy, and the Supreme Court*. The selection is from his *Justices Black and Frankfurter: Conflict in the Court* (Chicago, University of Chicago Press, 1961), pp. VII-IX, 114-131. By permission.

unaware of the error this involves. And this does not make it a wrong law; for the error is not in the law nor in the lawgiver, but in the nature of the case: the material of conduct is essentially irregular.

—ARISTOTLE

The main trouble with the Supreme Court is a general misunderstanding of its role in American government. Without thinking much about such matters, the man in the street assumes that "the law" is crystal clear. He is mistaken. The Constitution comes to us from the eighteenth century. Along with a few later amendments it was written by men wise enough to know they could not prescribe the details of government for an unknowable future. Nor were they in complete accord among themselves on vital issues—just as we are not. And so they often wrote with calculated generality. That is why the Constitution survives while other works of its age—in medicine, engineering, and every other field—have long since passed away. The Founding Fathers, like the amenders, avoided strait-jacketing precision. Their forte was the suggestive, open-ended hint. Not unlike the Delphic oracle, their "meaning" usually depends upon the wisdom of those who contemplate their words.

Even modern legislation is full of ambiguity. Congress dealing merely with present problems on a year-to-year basis cannot anticipate all the eventualities of life. Nor are congressmen, more than the rest of us, known for unanimity on even those issues which they can foresee.

Of course in many contexts the law is clear. To the extent that this is true there is little litigation. What controversy there is will seldom reach the Supreme Court. Cases which go that far generally do so precisely because the law with respect to them is cloudy—and precisely because they involve not a clash of right and wrong, but of competing rights.

That each state shall have two senators is too plain to require judicial interpretation. But what is the meaning of such constitutional terms as "due process of law," "commerce among the several states," or "equal protection of the laws"? These and other basic constitutional phrases have, and doubtless were designed to have, the chameleon's capacity to change their color with changing moods and circumstances. This is why they survive in a world their authors never knew. Short of constitutional amendment, we leave the final burden of "interpreting" such elastic terms to the Supreme Court. This means we expect the judges to solve for us many of the great dilemmas of life. For surely it is plain by now that the old eighteenth-century document does not automatically provide solutions for Atomic Age problems. And so the crucial question is: Where shall the Court find guidance when the light of the law fails? Shall it be past decisions—however out of date? Shall it be the good sense, or moral aspirations of the community, or perhaps natural law? And how may these be ascertained? If none of them, alone or in combination, what then?

We assume, or perhaps we are taught, that somehow the ancient parchment contains within its four corners the answers to all problems. *We* of course cannot read them there, but judges are supposed to have some special vision. Yet, each of us seems convinced that, if a decision does not coincide with his own emotional preference, then the judges must be biased, or worse. The Constitution is infallible, but judges are not—unless they happen to agree with us.

Sooner or later, if our system is to thrive, Americans must recognize that neither the Constitution nor any other legal code provides plain answers to most of the great issues that divide us. Soon or late we must acknowledge that cases which go as far as the Supreme Court usually represent conflicts between highly commendable principles none of which can fully prevail in life on earth. Each is apt to have impressive legal backing. In such conflicts "the law" is far from clear. Yet judges must somehow decide cases. They must solve enigmas that no other agencies of government, nor we ourselves, have been able to solve. This is a fearful responsibility. What Samuel Butler called "the art of life" is also the jurist's art: "to derive sufficient conclusions from insufficient premises."

Until we have a better understanding of the Supreme Court's real function, that institution will be in trouble. For just so long an important element of free government will be in danger. . . .

Justice and Democracy

A little learning is dangerous. Many discovered in the Court crisis of the 1930's that judges do not merely find, but sometimes make, the law. We came to see, as Max Lerner said, that judicial babies are not brought by constitutional storks. This secularization of the Court might have been all to the good, if we had also understood that lawmaking is an inherent and inevitable part of the judicial process. Judges, after all, must be more than mimics. Greatness on the bench, as elsewhere, is creativity. "We shall know," Cardozo said, "that the process of judging is a phase of a never ending movement, and that something more is expected of those who play their part in it than imitative reproduction, the lifeless repetition of a mechanical routine." Or, in the words of Curtis Bok, judging is "the play of an enlightened personality within the boundaries of a system." Of course judges sometimes make law. The great problem is how shall they contribute their bit to the law's growth without overstepping the boundaries of the system. Lord Bryce spoke of the need to reconcile tradition and convenience. Dean Pound referred to the competing claims of stability and change. . . .

"That the courts," Frankfurter once bitterly observed, "are especially fitted to be the ultimate arbiters of policy is an intelligent and tenable doctrine. But let them and us face the fact that five Justices of the Supreme Court *are* conscious molders of policy instead of impersonal vehicles of revealed truth."[1] The English apparently learned the lesson ages ago. They have long since reduced the judge's role to a minimum by rejecting judicial, in favor of parliamentary, supremacy. Either way, some human agency will have the "final" word. We give it to a Supreme Court, they give it to a supreme legislature. Assuming that we are to retain our system, the question is: how far and with what materials shall judges build the law? For build it they must.

Two great traditions provide two quite different approaches to these problems. One finds expression in Taney, Waite, Holmes, Brandeis, Learned Hand, Stone, Cardozo, and Frankfurter. These are the humilitarians, the pragmatists. Recognizing that judicial legislation is inevitable, they would hold it to a minimum. . . .

---

[1] Frankfurter, "Judge Henry W. Edgerton," 43 Cornell Law Quarterly 161 (1957).

The other tradition finds expression in Marshall, Field, Peckham, Fuller, Sutherland, and Black. These are the activists. For them judicial legislation is not incidental, it is the heart of the judicial process. They see great visions and feel compelled to embed them in the law. Or, more mildly, their creative impulses are guided by their ideals. One of Mr. Justice Black's ardent supporters put it this way: "As procedure is the instrument, not the master of law; so law is the instrument, not the master of justice." Law, then, is simply a tool to be manipulated in accordance with the judge's vision of right and wrong.

An old story has it that when Holmes departed to assume his duties on the Supreme Court he was admonished to do Justice. He responded thoughtfully that his job was merely to enforce the law. At best this little tale is incomplete, but it is significant. In an opinion that seems destined to live as long as the ideals of democracy survive, Justice Holmes and Brandeis rejected their colleagues' narrow conception of free speech, yet concurred in the judgment affirming conviction.[2] Though the accused had claimed protection under the appropriate constitutional provision, she had failed at the trial level to raise the "clear and present danger" issue. Raising it in the Supreme Court was futile, thought Holmes and Brandeis, because "Our power of review in this case is limited not only to the question whether a right guaranteed by the Federal Constitution was denied [in the state court] . . . but to the particular claims duly made below and denied." It may be said, of course, that Holmes and Brandeis had "no feel for the dominant issues"; that, preoccupied with "crochet patches of legalism on the fingers of the case," they let a technicality prevail over Justice. Others may suppose the two great judges, well aware of what was at stake, deemed themselves not free to do Justice, but bound to do justice under law, i.e., in accordance with that very special allocation of function and authority which is the essence of Federalism and the Separation of Powers. The point is, one's estimate of a judge hangs on one's conception—articulate or otherwise—of the judicial function.

To those for whom the Supreme Court's first concern is Justice, a great judge on that bench is an activist, one who does not readily permit "technicalities" to frustrate the ultimate. It follows, of course, that in so far as activism prevails the Court is the final governing authority. For, to that extent, its basic job is to impose Justice upon all other agencies of government, indeed upon the community itself. But what is Justice? Not so long ago, activists among the "nine old men" found it in a modified (read perverted) "laissez faire" called rugged individualism. Modern activists see it as a humane and virile libertarianism. Holmes facetiously suggested that its roots are in one's "can't helps."[3]

All this is unacceptable to those who take the more modest view that the Court's chief concern is *justice under law*. For them, the great judge is the humilitarian, the respecter of those "technicalities" which allocate among many agencies different responsibilities in the pursuit of Justice. In this view, the Court's special function is to preserve a constitutional balance between the several elements in a common enterprise. It maintains the ship, others set the course.

While these two views are distinct at their cores, they fuse into one another at their peripheries. Both are deep in American culture. Neither prevails to the

[2] *Whitney* v. *California,* 274 U.S. 357, 372 (1927).
[3] That is, the things which because of their familiarity one can't help believing.

complete exclusion of the other even in the work of a single judge. Eventually, the ardent activist gives way to a rule, just as his counterpart on occasion ignores rules for something deemed transcendental. What is important is the judge's inclination, his view of the nature of his role and the depth of his convictions.

Of the "great dissenters" in the days of "laissez-faire" activism only Harlan Stone remained on the bench to see the new libertarian activism after 1938. He was as unpersuaded by the one as by the other. In his view both entailed abuse of the judicial function. At the close of a long career spanning the two quite different eras of judicial Justice, he wrote a trusted friend,

> My more conservative brethren in the old days [read their preferences into legislation and] into the Constitution as well. What they did placed in jeopardy a great and useful institution of government. The pendulum has now swung to the other extreme, and history is repeating itself. The Court is now in as much danger of becoming a legislative and Constitution-making body, enacting into law its own predilections, as it was then.[4]

As Thomas Reed Powell put it, "Four of the Roosevelt appointees were as determined in *their* direction, as four of their predecessors were determined by attraction to the opposite pole."[5]

Mr. Justice Black's Activism

Where Mr. Justice Sutherland gave a preferred place to dominant economic interests, Mr. Justice Black gives preference to the "underdog." Both positions spring from the same activist premise. Each finds in the law a special tenderness for a chosen (though different) set of values. Judicial idealism of this sort prospers if there is harmony between the judge's Justice and the prevailing ideals of the community. Disharmony brings disaster. The old Court rode high while "laissez faire" was in the air. It destroyed itself by clinging too long to moribund views. But anachronism may not be the most serious risk. Perhaps, in some eras—possibly today—there are no plainly dominant ideals. Maybe society is too perplexed, too pluralistic, too ridden with conflicting values to be captured meaningfully in any ideological common denominator. Moreover, there is always some discrepancy between thought and action. Sometimes the only function of an ideal is to appease the conscience, while institutions take more convenient forms.

Plainly, Mr. Justice Black leans one way when "liberal" values are at stake and another way in the face of "conservative" claims—be the issue one of constitutional law, statutory interpretation, or evaluation of evidence. This tendency no doubt is what critics have in mind when they charge the Court with judicial legislation. For, if at most one colleague goes the whole way with him, Mr. Justice Black is obviously a leader—perhaps the backbone—of the new Court's powerful, "liberal" wing. His humane sympathy for the common man, his

---

4 Quoted in Alpheus T. Mason, *Security through Freedom* (Ithaca, N. Y., Cornell University Press, 1955), pp. 145-46.
5 Powell, *Vagaries and Varieties in Constitutional Law*, p. 82.

courage, creative vigor, and perseverance mark him as a dedicated being in pursuit of utopian ends. But is the bench a proper vehicle to use in pursuing them?

Surely it is an idealized view of the American legislative and constitution-making process that finds the product inevitably favoring New Deal values. It was no less a fantasy, of course, for some of the "nine old men" to find the law so often favoring quite different interests. Activism, whether of the old or new variety, may be consistent with the legislator's function, but is it compatible with the basic judicial job of settling "cases" and "controversies" impartially?

Apologists for the modern version of activist Justice seem to concentrate upon its First Amendment aspects and ignore its economic implications as in the FELA, FLSA, ICC, NLRB, and Sherman Act cases. This permits them to rest upon—or hide behind—the hallowed generalities of democratic dogma. Even so, they do not argue that the Constitution guarantees absolute freedom of expression, or that any explicit limitation can be found in the written document. *Choice then is inevitable.* Yet we are not told why a legislative choice between competing interests here is, *a priori,* less worthy of respect than elsewhere. To put it differently, the activist position assumes that courts are somehow in-herently more competent to achieve a sound balance of interests in First Amendment cases than in others.

Perhaps freedom of expression and religion are so overwhelmingly im-portant that we must weight the scales of justice in their favor. But what of a judge who is also an activist in economic matters? Is there any point in free discussion if its legislative fruits—the accommodations of the democratic way of life—are to be undone by judicial fiat? Surely the free speech that produced the FLSA compromise, for example, was a waste of time, if all judges—like some —were to reject it for one of its extreme components. Ironically, those who are least respectful of a legislative balance of interests in speech cases are the very ones who show least respect for legislative compromise in the economic do-main. A burning faith in democracy and impatience with its results is not a new quality among idealists.

Democracy does not contemplate vast governmental authority in hands that are free both of the legislator's political responsibility and the judge's checkrein of precedent. For a healthy society both stability and change are in-dispensable. Our separation of governmental functions imposes major responsi-bility for the one upon courts; for the other upon legislatures. If the judiciary is to be a free-wheeling, legislative body, it will inevitably forfeit "some of the credit needed to fulfill a role much more unique." For as Professor Jaffe sug-gests:[6]

> Our society *is* a class society, at the least a society of vigorously competing interests. It is also an exceedingly mobile society, richly cre-ating new opportunities, malignantly generating insecurities. It is a society which, in making unprecedented demands on government for change, places a heavy strain on the agencies of stability. To compose the con-stantly clashing demands for new opportunity our society sets up a rep-resentative legislature. To compose the day-to-day differences between

[6] L. L. Jaffe, "Mr. Justice Jackson," 68 Harvard Law Review 940, 994-95 (1955).

man and man, and between man and organized society, it relies upon a nonrepresentative body of professionals. The warrant for their great power is the universal conviction that there is a knowable law which they can and will apply by the exercise of reason. The faith in judicial objectivity is an ultimate source of personal security and social cohesion. But once it comes to be believed by one or another of the great social classes that the Court is an organ of another class, its function is impaired. This is peculiarly the case when the Court is a constitutional one and participates in the very creation of major social premises. To secure wholehearted and widespread acceptance of its pronouncements it has need of all the credit it can amass; to squander it on schemes for social betterment is foolhardy.

In short there are special American reasons for the rejection of Plato's "philosopher-king" in favor of Aristotle's Rule of Law. If the latter is never fully attainable, if "reason" above "personal preference" is an illusion, "to dispel it would cause men to lose themselves in an even greater illusion: the illusion that personal power can be benevolently exercised."[7]

Such creativity destroyed the old Court—and brought the associated state chief justices, among others, to condemn the new one for judicial legislation. But Chief Justice Marshall, too, was condemned for "serving what in his conception [was] the largest good" in his day. To his admirers Hugo Black is another John Marshall: one who—before most of his contemporaries—saw and accommodated the needs of his age. Others see in him the shadow of Sutherland: a wilful judge who with honorable intent abused his power in pursuit of a mirage. Only time can render a true verdict. . . .

Mr. Justice Frankfurter's Restraint

Mr. Justice Frankfurter is deeply humilitarian. Plainly this is an acquired characteristic, a judicial mold superimposed upon a powerfully active and thoroughly libertarian personality. If to some his modesty seems exaggerated —breast-beating it has been called—that may be the measure of the struggle within him or within the Court. Just as Holmes was more skeptical, so he was less vocal in his humility. In any case, there can be no doubt of the deep Holmesian mark upon Mr. Justice Frankfurter. Before he took his seat upon the bench he was the intimate personal and professional confidant of Holmes, as well as Brandeis, during the whole, long course of their struggle against the activism of Sutherland and company. The shared ardors of that contest must have reinforced what Professor Frankfurter was learning as teacher of federal jurisdiction at Harvard; namely, that since the Supreme Court cannot review more than a drop in the floor of American litigation, by long established principle that drop must be selected, not on the basis of Justice to any litigant, but in the interest of balance among the various elements in the governmental structure. Moreover, if the Court takes jurisdiction on the one ground and decides on the other, balance is jeopardized and though Justice (in its then current version) be done for a few, the result is hardly fair to the many whose cases,

[7] T. Arnold, "Professor Hart's Theology," 73 Harvard Law Review 1298, 1311 (1960).

however worthy, cannot for physical limitations hope to reach the judicial summit. What Paul Freund has said of Mr. Justice Brandeis is relevant here.

> [H]e would not be seduced by the quixotic temptation to right every fancied wrong which was paraded before him. The time was always out of joint but he was not [commissioned] to set it right. . . . Husbanding his time and energies as if the next day were to be his last, he steeled himself, like a scientist in the service of man, against the enervating distraction of countless tragedies he was not meant to relieve. His concern for jurisdictional and procedural limits reflected, on the technical level, an essentially Stoic philosophy. For like Epictetus, he recognized "the impropriety of being emotionally affected by what is not under one's control."[8]

The basic articulate premise of government in the United States is the diffusion of power. Ultimate political control is spread broadly among the people. This is the foundation of democracy. Governmental power is divided between nation and states. This is Federalism. What is given to each is parceled out among three branches to accomplish the Separation of Powers. The purpose is not merely (as schoolboys emphasize) to avoid a tyrannical concentration of power. We seek, as well, the alignment of form to special function and, above all, that unique democratic efficiency, the promise that, if decisions be slow, they will be acceptable to those who must live with them.

For Mr. Justice Frankfurter, dispersion of the power to govern is not just a sophomoric slogan. It is the essence of our system. That is why he is so mindful of the political processes, state responsibility and the division of labor between legislative, executive, administrative, and judicial agencies. In Professor Jaffe's thoughtful account, the Justice is "forever disposing of issues by assigning their disposition to some other sphere of competence."

But this is only half the problem. Familiarity obscures for us what to outsiders is a marked characteristic of American government: our habit of dressing up the most intricate social, economic, and political problems in legal jargon and presenting them to the courts for "adjudication." In view of this, a foreign observer long ago concluded that, if asked where he found the American aristocracy, i.e., the governing class, he would reply "without hesitation . . . that it occupies the judicial bench and bar." Perhaps the short of it is that behind and overshadowing our open commitment to the fragmentation of power lies a brooding, inarticulate distrust of popular government. This finds expression in judicial review, or judicial supremacy. Whatever the name, the essence is clear: *concentration in a single agency*—significantly, that farthest removed from the people—of power to override all other elements of government, whether at the national, state, or local level. Neither Congress nor the President, no administrative agency, no governor, no state court or legislature, not a single city or county functionary is immune from the centralized power of judicial review. Indeed, in some eras the Court has been so domineering—in the name of Justice —that from time to time dissenters have felt compelled to remind it that the judiciary is "not the only agency of government that must be assumed to have

[8] *On Understanding the Supreme Court,* p. 65.

capacity to govern." Equally pointed reminders have come from the outside. Most of the great leaders of American democracy, Jefferson, Jackson, Lincoln, Bryan, and the two Roosevelts, among others, have challenged the practice of judicial review. But, except perhaps in some academic circles, the principle has withstood abuse and criticism. It stands only a shade less firmly grounded in our polity than its counterpart, the dispersion of power.

The Supreme Court, then, is caught between basic principles that look in different directions. Mr. Justice Frankfurter seems more sensitive to the pinch than most, though doubtless no one in his position is immune. What is the judge's role in such an impasse? A common "compromise" has been to emphasize diffusion of power or judicial supremacy according to the nature of the interest before the Court. At least since the Civil War some judges have demonstrated a marked propensity to assert their supremacy for the benefit of "private property," while others have shown a tendency to distrust the principle of diffusion only when "personal liberty" is at issue. For Mr. Justice Frankfurter such compromises only underscore the lawless quality of the Court's power. Deeply libertarian in private thought and action, he sees what partisans do not see: that if effective transcendental arguments may be made for the social priority of personal liberty, no less powerful considerations in the abstract would sustain the primacy of economic interests. What Wilmon Sheldon said of philosophers seems relevant to those who hold to either extreme. They are generally right in what they affirm of their own vision and generally wrong in what they deny in the vision of others. There is more subtlety, more depth, and more complexity in our culture than such one-sided polemics dream of. We may be proud of the golden thread of liberalism that runs through American thought, but it is futile to pretend that the "acquisitive instinct" and the old Whiggish concern for property are not as deep in our culture. As Daniel Webster put it long ago, "Life and personal liberty are, no doubt, to be protected by law; but property is also to be protected by law, and is the fund out of which the means for protecting life and liberty are usually furnished." President Hadley of Yale spoke for many when he explained the Constitution as a "set of limitations on the political power of the majority in favor of the political power of the property owner." Such suggestions of the primacy of economic interests are wormwood to libertarians, but the disease is deep. Man must eat and, not less important, he must "know where his next meal is coming from." Our cold war experience in the "backward" areas of the world suggests that those who must choose are far more interested in economic security than in civil liberty.

In any event it is important that neither is fungible and neither in the abstract is ever at stake in litigation. Typically, some finite facet of one or both is imperiled, and certainly in the kind of cases that now reach the Supreme Court the context is often such that intelligent men may differ as to whether a legitimate interest or its abuse is involved. This is what Holmes meant when he said that "general propositions do not decide concrete cases." Or, in Mr. Justice Cardozo's words, "Many an appeal to freedom is the masquerade of privilege or inequality seeking to entrench itself behind the catchword of a principle." For the purpose of settling specific litigation abstract arguments as to the relative importance of personal as against proprietary interests are as futile as medieval arguments about realism and nominalism. They cut no wood. Morris

Cohen has called "attention to the fact that the traditional dilemmas, on which people have for a long time taken opposite stands, generally rest on difficulties rather than real contradictions, and that positive gains . . . can be made not by simply trying to prove that one side or the other is the truth, but by trying to get at the difficulty and determining in what respect and to what extent each side is justified."[9] This principle of polarity is the foundation of Mr. Justice Frankfurter's jurisprudence. He cannot be true to the American tradition and ignore the diffusion of power or judicial supremacy. Least of all can he accept reconciliation which raises now one and then another cluster of interests to a "preferred position" and correspondingly defers others.

Despite unqualified language in some parts of the Bill of Rights, no past or present member of the Court has even suggested that its liberties are unlimited. As with the "rights of property," the basic question always has been how and where to locate boundaries. Brandeis taught us anew, when we were in danger of forgetting it, that law is born of fact. *"Ex facto jus oritur.* That ancient rule must prevail in order that we may have a system of living law." The facts, after all, make up the issue. The precise problem of a minimum wage case,[10] for example, is evaded, not solved, by invoking the abstraction "liberty of contract," just as the *Terminiello* case is not solved by "reiterating generalized approbations of freedom of speech." A Brandeis concern for facts is as relevant in the one situation as in the other, if the Court is to decide real, not hypothetical, cases. It follows for Mr. Justice Frankfurter that judicial intrusion upon governmental policy is permissible only when the special facts of a concrete case leave no room for doubt. Since uncertainty entails choice, constitutional doubt must be resolved in favor of the views of those to whom primary governing authority has been given—and the people to whom they must answer.

This maxim of judicial self-restraint is not limited to constitutional law. It finds expression also in Mr. Justice Frankfurter's doctrine of "expertise" in the administrative law cases; in his willingness to accept legislative compromise —however uninspired—in the statutory interpretation cases; in his constant efforts to prevent federal, judge-made law from intruding upon local management of local affairs; and in his insistence in the *certiorari* cases that the Supreme Court stick to its limited and very special business. In the eyes of one critic, this demonstrates that "Mr. Justice Frankfurter has no feel for the dominant issues; he operates best when weaving crochet patches of legalism on the fingers of the case . . . it is a calamity that his skills happen to be petty skills."[11] Another has written that "the ex-professor . . . remained a rather narrow academician, engrossed in the trivia of formal legal propriety . . . to the disregard of the tough stuff of judicial statesmanship."[12] Obviously these critics are ardent supporters of Mr. Justice Black. It is ironical that the very characteristic which won for Felix Frankfurter an appointment to the bench—

[9] Morris Cohen, *Reason and Nature,* 2d ed. (New York, Harcourt, Brace & Co., 1953), p. 11.

[10] See, for example, *Adkins* v. *Children's Hospital,* 261 U.S. 525 (1923).

[11] Walton Hamilton, quoted in Fred Rodell, *Nine Men* (New York, Random House, 1955), p. 271.

[12] *Ibid.*

his insistence that the "dominant issues," i.e., policy-making, should be left to the democratic process—is now considered a vice by his critics. Obviously they like extensive judicial legislation, provided it is of the "new" libertarian, rather than the old, proprietarian, variety. To put it crudely, much depends upon whose ox is being gored or whose ideals are at stake.

If, as tradition holds, the law is a jealous mistress, it also has the feminine capacity to tempt each devotee to find his own image in her bosom. No one escapes entirely. Some yield blindly, some with sophistication. A few more or less effectively resist—Cardozo, because he could not quite forget that ethic of self-denial which man has never mastered; Holmes, from the hopeful scepticism of an inquiring mind; Frankfurter, largely, perhaps, from remembrance of things past. Surely wilfulness on the bench prior to 1937 was a catalyst in the making of all the "Roosevelt judges." Some of them with appropriate apologetics seemed to fly to an opposite wilfulness. Mr. Justice Frankfurter has tried to subsume will to law and, where the law is vague, judicial will to the will, or conscience, of the community. If he falters, is it that his grasp is short, or that his reach is long? The discrepancy, a poet tells us, is "what a heaven's for." Meanwhile, such a judge must carry a heavier burden than does he whose commitment to proprietarian or libertarian abstractions—whose sense of Justice —is automatically decisive. "Believing it still important to do so," Mr. Justice Frankfurter has

> tried to dispel the age-old illusion that the conflicts to which the energy and ambition and imagination of the restless human spirit give rise can be subdued . . . by giving the endeavors of reason we call law a mechanical or automatic or enduring configuration. Law cannot be confined within any such mold because life cannot be so confined.[13]

The Justice has lived too long with legal problems to be fooled by the simple antinomy. Abraham Lincoln made the point when he cut short the ranting of a northern extremist, "Mr. ———, haven't you lived long enough to know that two men may honestly differ about a question and both be right?" In this paradox lies the genius of our system.

> Often "the American Way of Life" is pictured in terms of rigid adherence to some ideology, ignoring that our search for "a more perfect union" has been directed less to seeking final solutions than at establishing a tolerable balance of conflict among ourselves.[14]

Tolstoi saw that a great leader never leads. Does a great judge? At least for cases that reach the Supreme Court the law is seldom clear. The typical controversy entails a clash of interests, each of which has some, but no plainly proponderant, legal foundation. Yet the Court is expected to give a decision. And so perhaps in the end the intrinsic problem is this: for whom or in what direction shall doubt be resolved? Some have made uncertainty the servant of

---

[13] Frankfurter, *Of Law and Men*, p. 28.
[14] Samuel Lubell, *Revolt of the Moderates* (New York, Harper & Bros., 1956), p. 239.

selected business interests. Others have been guided by more generous considerations. In Mr. Justice Frankfurter's view this "sovereign prerogative of choice" is not for judges. He would resolve all reasonable doubt in favor of the integrity of sister organs of government and the people to whom they must answer. He would adhere, that is, to the deepest of all our constitutional traditions, the dispersion of power—though, as in the "flag salute" cases, the immediate result offend his own generous heart's desire. He is wary of judicial attempts to impose Justice on the community; to deprive it of the wisdom that comes from self-inflicted wounds and the strength that grows with the burden of responsibility. It is his deepest conviction that no five men, or nine, are wise enough or good enough to wield such power over the lives of millions. In his view, humanitarian ends are served best in that allocation of function through which the people by a balance of power seek their own destiny. True to the faith upon which democracy ultimately rests, the Justice would leave to the political processes the onus of building legal standards in the vacuum of doubt. For in his view only that people is free who chooses for itself when choice must be made.

~~Section VIII

POLITICS IN A DEMOCRACY

The Constitution which established the basic framework of our government did not mention political parties. The Framers, to be sure, took cognizance of the potential power of organized public opinion and political parties and attempted to curb their influence through the electoral college, the indirect election of senators, checks and balances and other devices. Yet, today, the force of both public opinion and political parties is recognized as a vital concomitant of our democratic and constitutional system. Some writers, in fact, consider the condition of political parties to be the best index of the vitality of the democracy within any society.

In the literature of political philosophy, some theorists have placed a high value on citizen involvement in the governmental process. Every adult member of the social system, they have declared, is obliged not only to maintain high levels of interest in and knowledge about public affairs, but also to participate energetically in the political activities of the community. Social scientists have established that in the United States most citizens fail to approximate, except in modest degree, this conception of man as a political animal. In the main, the American populace is indifferent to the frequently volatile events of the political arena. Many citizens are not even marginally concerned about the daily transactions linking political parties and interest groups with government. Psychologically detached from public affairs, the man-in-the-street is often appallingly uninformed about political actors and the roles they fulfill. Studies conducted by national survey organizations have revealed that large portions of the American population, ranging from one-fifth to four-fifths, are unable to identify such public figures as members of the President's cabinet, justices of the Supreme Court, and the floor leaders of Congress; cannot describe the current activities of government in civil rights, social welfare, and foreign policy; and lack basic information about the formal structure of major political institutions and, for that matter, about the content of the Bill of Rights. Experiencing little conscious involvement in public affairs, the average citizen—not surprisingly—refrains from most forms of political participation. It is the rare individual indeed who contributes money and labor to the campaigns of candidates for public office, who joins political clubs and civic organizations, or who communicates policy preferences to governmental decision-makers.

For most adult Americans, the instrument of political partici-pation—in many cases, the only instrument—is the act of voting. The process of casting a ballot, of making selections from among competing candidates for public office, represents the principal link between the main body of citizens and government. Yet electoral choice-making does not constitute, at least for most individuals, a highly cerebral activity involving the rigorous evaluation of political parties and their standard-bearers. Indeed, voting is usually a semi-automatic act by which the citizen expresses his loyalty to, or iden-tification with, a party label. In the United States nearly 80 per cent of the electorate claims an affinity for one or the other of the two major parties. This sense of identification, whether with the Democratic or Republican party, is typically "inherited" from one's parents prior to adolescence and, with few exceptions, remains un-changed throughout the years of maturity.

However, partisan identification does not fully account for the voting behavior of all citizens in every election. Short-term variables —the issues and candidate appeals of party leaders—exert an impact on segments of the population. The influence of such factors is most obvious among independent voters, who, of course, do not sub-jectively identify with either party. Among loyalists, though, short-term considerations stemming from the events of a political cam-paign also leave their mark. In every election some Democratic and Republican supporters, particularly voters with a weak sense of allegiance, are drawn across party lines. But for most voters, loyalty to the party standard generally controls the process of electoral choice, even when the issues and candidates tempt them to join the opposition.

Yet, as the article on "Democratic Practice and Democratic Theory" maintains, the democratic system may not depend in any critical sense on the qualifications or the detailed information pos-sessed by the mass of voters. In this view, what helps democracy survive and function in the United States are "certain collective properties that reside in the electorate as a whole and in the political system in which it functions."

TOPIC 21

The Role of the Voter in Theory and Practice

DONALD E. STOKES *and* WARREN E. MILLER

The Uninformed Voter

Any mid-term congressional election raises pointed questions about party government in America. With the personality of the President removed from the ballot by at least a coattail, the public is free to pass judgment on the legislative record of the parties. So the civics texts would have us believe. In fact, however, an off-year election can be regarded as an assessment of the parties' record in Congress only if the electorate possesses certain minimal information about what that record is. The fact of possession needs to be demonstrated, not assumed, and the low visibility of congressional affairs to many citizens suggests that the electorate's actual information should be examined with care.

How much the people know is an important, if somewhat hidden, problem of the normative theory of representation. Implicitly at least, the information the public is thought to have is one of the points on which various classical conceptions of representation divide. Edmund Burke and the liberal philosophers, for example—to say nothing of Hamilton and Jefferson—had very different views about the information the public could get or use in assessing its government. And the period of flood tide in American democracy, especially the Jacksonian and Progressive eras, have been marked by the most optimistic assumptions as to what the people could or did know about their government. To put the matter another way: any set of representative institutions will work very differently according to the amount and quality of information the electorate has. This is certainly true of the institutional forms we associate with government by responsible parties. A necessary condition of party responsibility to the people is that the public have basic information about the parties and their legislative record. Without it, no institutional devices can make responsibility a fact.

The authors are members of the staff of the Survey Research Center and Department of Political Science at the University of Michigan. Mr. Miller is, in addition, Director of the Interuniversity Consortium for Political Research. The essay is from "Party Government and the Saliency of Congress," *Public Opinion Quarterly*, Vol. 26 (Winter, 1962), pp. 531-546. Reprinted by permission.

To explore the information possessed by those who play the legislative and constituent roles in American government, the Survey Research Center of the University of Michigan undertook an interview study of Congressmen and their districts during the mid-term election of Eisenhower's second term. Immediately after the 1958 campaign the Center interviewed a nationwide sample of the electorate, clustered in 116 congressional districts, as well as the incumbent Congressmen and other major-party candidates for the House from the same collection of districts. Through these direct interviews with the persons playing the reciprocal roles of representative government, this research has sought careful evidence about the perceptual ties that bind, or fail to bind, the Congressman to his party and district. We will review some of this evidence here for the light that it throws on the problem of party cohesion and responsibility in Congress.

The Responsible-Party Model and the American Case

What the conception of government by responsible parties requires of the general public has received much less attention than what it requires of the legislative and electoral parties.[1] The notion of responsibility generally is understood to mean that the parties play a mediating role between the public and its government, making popular control effective by developing rival programs of government action that are presented to the electorate for its choice. The party whose program gains the greater support takes possession of the government and is held accountable to the public in later elections for its success in giving its program effect.

Two assumptions about the role of the public can be extracted from these ideas. *First,* in a system of party government the electorate's attitude toward the parties is based on what the party programs are and how well the parties have delivered on them. The public, in a word, gives the parties *programmatic* support. And, in view of the importance that legislative action is likely to have in any party program, such support is formed largely out of public reaction to the legislative performance of the parties, especially the party in power.

Second, under a system of party government the voters' response to the local legislative candidates is based on the candidates' identification with party

[1] For example, the 1950 report of the American Political Science Association's Committee on Political Parties, the closest approach to an official statement of the responsible-party view as applied to American politics, concentrates on the organization of Congress and the national parties and deals only very obliquely with the role of the public. See *Toward a More Responsible Two-party System,* New York, Rinehart, 1950. In general, theoretical and empirical treatments of party government have focused more on the nature of party *appeals*—especially the question of whether the parties present a real "choice"—than on the cognitive and motivational elements that should be found in the *response* of an electorate that is playing its correct role in a system of responsible-party government. For example, see the excellent discussion in Austin Ranney and Wilmoore Kendall, *Democracy and the American Party System,* New York, Harcourt, Brace, 1956, pp. 151-152, 384-385, 525-527.

It should be clear that the data of this report are taken from a particular election of a particular electoral era. We would expect our principal findings to apply to most recent off-year elections, but they are of course subject to modification for earlier or later periods.

programs. These programs are the substance of their appeals to the constituency, which will act on the basis of its information about the proposals and legislative record of the parties. Since the party programs are of dominant importance, the candidates are deprived of any independent basis of support. They will not be able to build in their home districts an electoral redoubt from which to challenge the leadership of their parties.

How well do these assumptions fit the behavior of the American public as it reaches a choice in the off-year congressional elections? A first glance at the relation of partisan identifications to the vote might give the impression that the mid-term election is a triumph of party government. Popular allegiance to the parties is of immense importance in all our national elections, including those in which a President is chosen, but its potency in the mid-term congressional election is especially pronounced. This fact is plain—even stark—in the entries of Table 1, which break down the vote for Congress in 1958 into its component party elements. The table makes clear, first of all, how astonishingly small a proportion of the mid-term vote is cast by political independents. Repeated electoral studies in the United States have indicated that somewhat fewer than 1 American in 10 thinks of himself as altogether independent of the two parties.[2] But in the off-year race for Congress only about a twentieth part of the vote is cast by independents, owing to their greater drop-out rate when the drama and stakes of the presidential contest are missing.

TABLE 1. 1958 Vote for House Candidates, by Party Identification (in per cent)

	Party Identification*			
	Democratic	Independent	Republican	Total
Voted Democratic	53†	2	6	61
Voted Republican	5	3	31	39
Total	58	5	37	100

*The Democratic and Republican party identification groups include all persons who classify themselves as having some degree of party loyalty.

†Each entry of the table gives the per cent of the total sample of voters having the specified combination of party identification and vote for the House in 1958.

Table 1 also makes clear how little deviation from party there is among Republicans and Democrats voting in a mid-term year. The role of party identification in the congressional election might still be slight, whatever the size of the party followings, if partisan allegiance sat more lightly on the voting act. But almost 9 out of every 10 partisans voting in the off-year race support their parties. Indeed, something like 84 per cent of *all* the votes for the House in 1958 were cast by party identifiers supporting their parties. The remaining 16 per cent is not a trivial fraction of the whole—standing, as it did in this case, for 8 million people, quite enough to make and unmake a good many legislative careers. Nevertheless, the low frequency of deviation from party, together with

[2] See Angus Campbell, Philip E. Converse, Warren E. Miller, and Donald E. Stokes, *The American Voter,* New York, Wiley, 1960, p. 124.

the low frequency of independent voting, indicates that the meaning of the mid-term vote depends in large part on the nature of party voting.

The Saliency of the Parties' Legislative Records

If American party voting were to fit the responsible-party model it would be *programmatic* voting, that is, the giving of electoral support according to the parties' past or prospective action on programs that consist (mainly) of legislative measures. There is little question that partisan voting is one of the very few things at the bottom of our two-party system; every serious third-party movement in a hundred years has foundered on the reef of traditional Republican and Democratic loyalties. But there is also little question that this voting is largely nonprogrammatic in nature. A growing body of evidence indicates that party loyalties are typically learned early in life, free of ideological or issue content, with the family as the main socializing agency. Certainly the findings of adult interview studies show that such loyalties are extremely long-lived and, summed across the population, give rise to extraordinarily stable distributions. The very persistence of party identification raises suspicion as to whether the country is responding to the parties' current legislative actions when it votes its party loyalties.

That this suspicion is fully warranted in the mid-term election is indicated by several kinds of evidence from this research. To begin with, the electorate's perceptions of the parties betray very little information about current policy issues. For the past ten years the Survey Research Center has opened its electoral interviews with a series of free-answer questions designed to gather in the positive and negative ideas that the public has about the parties. The answers, requiring on the average nearly ten minutes of conversation, are only very secondarily couched in terms of policy issues. In 1958, for example, more than six thousand distinct positive or negative comments about the parties were made by a sample of 1,700 persons. Of these, less than 12 per cent by the most generous count had to do with contemporary legislative issues. As this sample of Americans pictured the reasons it liked and disliked the parties, the modern battlefields of the legislative wars—aid-to-education, farm policy, foreign aid, housing, aid to the unemployed, tariff and trade policy, social security, medical care, labor laws, civil rights, and other issues—rarely came to mind. The main themes in the public's image of the parties are not totally cut off from current legislative events; the political activist could take the group-benefit and prosperity-depression ideas that saturate the party images and connect them fairly easily with issues before Congress. The point is that the public itself rarely does so.

How little awareness of current issues is embodied in the congressional vote also is attested by the reasons people give for voting Republican or Democratic for the House. In view of the capacity of survey respondents to rationalize their acts, direct explanations of behavior should be treated with some reserve. However, rationalization is likely to increase, rather than decrease, the policy content of reasons for voting. It is therefore especially noteworthy how few of the reasons our respondents gave for their House votes in 1958 had any discernible issue content. The proportion that had—about 7 per cent—was less even than the proportion of party-image references touching current issues.

Perhaps the most compelling demonstration of how hazardous it is to interpret party voting as a judgment of the parties' legislative records is furnished by the evidence about the public's knowledge of party control of Congress. When our 1958 sample was asked whether the Democrats or the Republicans had had more Congressmen in Washington during the two preceding years, a third confessed they had no idea, and an additional fifth gave control of the eighty-fifth Congress to the Republicans. Only 47 per cent correctly attributed control to the Democrats. These figures improve somewhat when nonvoters are excluded. Of those who voted in 1958, a fifth did not know which party had controlled Congress, another fifth thought the Republicans had, and the remainder (61 per cent) correctly gave control to the Democrats. However, when a discount is made for guessing, *the proportion of voters who really knew which party had controlled the eighty-fifth Congress probably is still not more than half.*

It would be difficult to overstate the significance of these figures for the problem of party government. The information at issue here is not a sophisticated judgment as to what sort of coalition had *effective* control of Congress. It is simply the question of whether the country had a Democratic or a Republican Congress from 1956 to 1958. This elementary fact of political life, which any pundit would take completely for granted as he interpreted the popular vote in terms of party accountability, was unknown to something like half the people who went to the polls in 1958.

It is of equal significance to note that the parties' legislative record was no more salient to those who *deviated* from party than it was to those who voted their traditional party loyalty. It might be plausible to suppose that a floating portion of the electorate gives the parties programmatic support, even though most voters follow their traditional allegiances. If true, this difference would give the responsible-party model some factual basis, whether or not the greater part of the electorate lived in darkness. But such a theory finds very little support in these data. In 1958 neither the issue reasons given for the congressional vote nor the awareness of party control of the Eighty-fifth Congress was any higher among those who voted *against* their party identification than it was among those who voted *for* their party, as the entries in Table 2 demonstrate. If anything, correcting perceived party control for guessing suggests

TABLE 2. *Issue Responses and Awareness of Which Party Controlled 85th Congress Among Party Supporters and Voters Who Deviated from Party*

	Of Party Identifiers Who:	
	Voted for Own Party	Voted for Other Party
Per cent aware of party control:		
Uncorrected	61	60
Corrected for guessing*	44	35
Per cent giving issue reasons for House vote	6	7

*This correction deducts from the proportion attributing control to the Democrats a percentage equal to the proportion attributing control to the Republicans.

that voters who deviated from their party in 1958 had poorer information about the course of political events over the preceding two years.

Nor do the perceptions of party control of Congress that *are* found apply a key to understanding the congressional vote. Whatever awareness of control the electorate had in 1958 was remarkably unrelated to its support of candidates for the House. To make this point, Table 3 analyzes deviations from party according to three perceptions held by party identifiers voting in 1958: *first,* whether they thought the country's recent domestic affairs had gone well or badly; *second* (to allow for the complication of divided government), whether they thought Congress or President had the greater influence over what the government did; and, *third,* whether they thought the Democrats or Republicans had controlled Congress. To recreate the basis on which the

TABLE 3. *Percentage of Party Identifiers Voting Against Party in 1958, by Perception of Party Control of Government and Course of Domestic Affairs*

Thought That Domestic Affairs	Thought That More Effective Branch of Government Was Controlled by:	
	Own Party	*Other Party*
	I	II
Had gone well	16	22
	(N = 43)	(N = 46)
	III	IV
Had gone badly	14	13
	(N = 152)	(N = 122)

voter might assign credit or blame to the parties, the second and third of these perceptions may be combined; that is, partisans may be classified according to whether they thought their own party or the opposite party had controlled the more effective branch of government. Crossing this classification with perceptions of whether domestic affairs had gone well yields four groups for analysis, two of which (I and IV) might be expected to show little deviation from party, the other two (II and III) substantially more. In fact, however, the differences between these groups are almost trifling. According to the familiar lore, the groups that thought affairs had gone badly (III and IV) are the ones that should provide the clearest test of whether perceptions of party control are relevant to voting for the House. Moreover, with a recession in the immediate background, most people who could be classified into this table in 1958 fell into one of these two groups, as the frequencies indicate. But when the two groups that felt there had been domestic difficulties are compared, it seems not to make a particle of difference whether the Democrats or Republicans were thought to have controlled the actions of government. And when the two groups (I and II) that felt things had gone well are compared, only a slight (and statistically insignificant) difference appears. Interestingly, even this small rise in the rate of deviation from party (in cell II) is contributed mainly by Democratic identifiers who wrongly supposed that the Congress had been in Republican hands.

The conclusion to be drawn from all this certainly is not that national political forces are without *any* influence on deviations from party in the mid-term year. Clearly these forces do have an influence. Although the fluctuations of the mid-term party vote, charted over half a century or more, are very much smaller than fluctuations in the presidential vote or the congressional vote in presidential years, there is *some* variation, and these moderate swings must be attributed to forces that have their focus at the national level. Even in 1958 one party received a larger share of deviating votes than the other. Our main point is rather that the deviations that *do* result from national forces are not in the main produced by the parties' legislative records and that, in any case, the proportion of deviating votes that can be attributed to national politics is likely to be a small part of the total votes cast by persons deviating from party in a mid-term year. This was specifically true in 1958.

If the motives for deviations from party are not to be found primarily at the national level, the search moves naturally to the local congressional campaign. A third possibility—that deviations are byproducts of state-wide races—can be discounted with some confidence. Despite the popular lore on the subject, evidence both from interview studies and from aggregate election statistics can be used to show that the influence of contests for Governor and Senator on the outcome of House races is slight in mid-term elections, although these contests can have an immense influence on turnout for the House.[3] In our 1958 sample, a majority of those who deviated from party in voting for the House *failed* to deviate also at the state level; more often than not, what had moved them into the other party's column at the House level was dissociated from the contests for Governor or Senator in which they voted. Moreover, the fact that an elector deviates from his party in voting both for the House and some office contested on a state-wide basis is no conclusive evidence that the state race has influenced his choice for the House, rather than the other way round. When the possibility of *reverse* coat-tail effects is allowed for, the reasons for believing that the state-wide race is a potent force on the House vote seem faint indeed. As we search for the motives for deviation from party, analysis of the local congressional race pays greater dividends.

The Saliency of Congressional Candidates

By the standards of the civics text, what the public knows about the candidates for Congress is as meager as what it knows about the parties' legislative records. *Of the people who lived in districts where the House seat was contested in 1958, 59 per cent—well over half—said that they had neither read nor heard anything about either candidate for Congress, and less than 1 in 5 felt that they knew something about both candidates.* What is more, these remarkable proportions are only marginally improved by excluding nonvoters from the calculations. *Of people who went to the polls and cast a vote between rival*

[3] A remarkable fact is that while the total vote for the House increased by 3 million between 1954 and 1958, more than 2 million of this increase was contributed by New York, where Rockefeller sought the governorship; by Ohio, where a fierce referendum battle was fought over the issue of "right-to-work"; and by California, where the fantastic Knight-Knowland-Brown free-for-all was held.

House candidates in 1958, fully 46 per cent conceded that they did so without having read or heard anything about either man. What the other half *had* read or heard is illuminating; we will deal with its policy content presently. Many of our respondents said they knew something about the people contesting the House seat on the basis of very slender information indeed.

The incumbent candidate is by far the better known. In districts where an incumbent was opposed for re-election in 1958, 39 per cent of our respondents knew something about the Congressman, whereas only 20 per cent said they knew anything at all about his nonincumbent opponent. The incumbent's advantage of repeated exposure to the electorate is plain enough. In fact, owing to the greater seniority and longer exposure of Congressmen from safe districts, the public's awareness of incumbents who were unopposed for re-election in 1958 was as great as its awareness of incumbents who had had to conduct an election campaign that year.

The saliency of a candidate is of critical importance if he is to attract support from the opposite party. However little the public may know of those seeking office, any information at all about the rival party's candidate creates the possibility of a choice deviating from party. That such a choice occurs with some frequency is shown by the entries of Table 4, whose columns separate party identifiers in contested districts in 1958 according to whether they were aware of both candidates, the candidate of their own party or the other party only, or neither candidate. The condition of no information leads to fairly unrelieved party-line voting, and so to an even greater degree does the condition of information only about the candidate of the voter's own party. But if partisan

TABLE 4. *Percentage Voting for Own Party Candidate and Other Party Candidate for House in 1958, by Saliency of Candidates in Contested Districts*

Voted for Candidate	Voter Was Aware of:			
	Both Candidates (N = 196)	Own Party Candidate Only (N = 166)	Other Party Candidate Only (N = 68)	Neither Candidate (N = 368)
Of own party	83	98	60	92
Of other party	17	2	40	8
Total	100	100	100	100

voters know something about the opposition's man, substantial deviations from party appear. In fact, if such voters know *only* the opposition candidate, almost half can be induced to cast a vote contrary to their party identification. In the main, recognition carries a positive valence; to be perceived at all is to be perceived favorably. However, some *negative* perceptions are found in our interviews, and when these are taken into account the explanation of deviation from party becomes surer still. For example, if we return to Table 4 and select from the third column only the voters who perceived the candidate of the other party *favorably,* a clear majority is found to have deviated from party allegiance in casting their votes. And if we select from the first column only the handful of voters who perceived the candidate of their own party *negatively* and of the opposite party *positively,* almost three-quarters are found to have deviated from their party loyalty in voting for the House.

What our constituent interviews show about the increment of support that accrues to the salient candidate is closely aligned to what the candidates themselves see as the roots of their electoral strength. Our interviews with incumbent and nonincumbent candidates seeking election to the House explored at length their understanding of factors aiding—or damaging—their electoral appeal. In particular, these interviews probed the candidates' assessment of four possible influences on the result: traditional party loyalties, national issues, state and local contests, and the candidates' own record and personal standing in the district. Caution is in order in dealing with answers to questions that touch the respondent's self-image as closely as these. Specifically, we may expect some overstatement of the candidate's own importance, particularly from the victors, and we may expect, too, that too large a discount will be applied to party allegiance, since this "inert" factor, having little to do with increments of strength, is so easily taken for granted.

After these allowances are made, it is still impressive how heavy a weight the incumbent assigns his personal record and standing. The Congressman's ranking of this and the other factors in the election is shown in Table 5. As the entries of the table indicate, more than four-fifths of the incumbents re-elected in 1958 felt that the niche they had carved out in the awareness of their constituents had substantial impact on the race, a proportion that exceeds by half the percentage who gave as much weight to any of the three other factors. This difference is more than sheer puffing in the interview situation, and the perceptual facts it reveals deserve close attention. Among the forces the Representative feels may enhance his strength at the polls, he gives his personal standing with the district front rank.

TABLE 5. *Relative Importance of Factors in Re-election as Seen by Incumbent Candidates in 1958 (in per cent)*

Perceived As	Personal Record and Standing	National Issues	Traditional Party Loyalties	State and Local Races
Very important	57	26	25	14
Quite important	28	20	21	19
Somewhat important	9	20	24	27
Not very important	3	27	18	19
Not important at all	3	7	12	21
	100	100	100	100

In view of the way the saliency of candidates can move the electorate across party lines, great stress should be laid on the fact that *the public sees individual candidates for Congress in terms of party programs scarcely at all.* Our constituent interviews indicate that the popular image of the Congressman is almost barren of policy content. A long series of open-ended questions asked of those who said they had any information about the Representative produced mainly a collection of diffuse evaluative judgments: he is a good man, he is experienced, he knows the problems, he has done a good job, and the like. Beyond this, the Congressman's image consisted of a mixed bag of impressions, some of them wildly improbable, about ethnicity, the attractiveness of family, specific services to the district, and other facts in the candidate's background. *By the most reasonable count, references to current legislative issues comprised not more than a thirtieth part of what the constituents had to say about their Congressmen.*

The irrelevance of legislative issues to the public's knowledge of Representatives is underscored by the nature of some primary *determinants* of saliency. . . . An excellent example is sex. Both for incumbents and nonincumbents, a candidate property that is related to saliency is gender; one of the best ways for a Representative to be known is to be a Congress*woman*. How irrelevant to policy issues this property is depends on what we make of the causal relation between sex and salience. The fact of being a woman may make a candidate more visible, but a woman may have to be unusually visible (like a Congressman's widow, say) before she can be elected to the House, or even become a serious candidate. If the first of these inferences is even partially right, the salience of the candidate is not likely to be in terms of positions taken on legislative issues.

Given the number of women who run for Congress, the role of sex may seem a trivial example to demonstrate the irrelevance of issue stands to saliency. However, the same point can be made for a much wider set of districts by the greater saliency of candidates who live in the constituent's home community. Just as there is enormous variety in the communities that make up the American nation, so there is the widest possible variation in how well a congressional district coincides with a natural community, and the goodness of this fit is a fundamental way of typing districts. At one extreme is the constituency whose area is lost within one of the country's great metropolitan centers, comprising at best a small fraction of the whole community. At the middle of the range is the district that is itself a natural community, consisting of a single medium-sized city and its environs. At the other extreme is the district whose territory includes a great number of small communities, as well as surrounding open country that goes on, in some cases, for hundreds of miles. In all but the metropolitan districts the salience of the candidate for the voter differs markedly according to whether candidate and voter live in the same community. The fact of common residence—of being "friends and neighbors"—stands for important facts of communication and community identification. Candidates will be joined by formal and informal communication networks to many of the voters living in the same community, and they may also be objects of considerable community pride. . . .

Conclusion

What the public knows about the legislative records of the parties and of individual congressional candidates is a principal reason for the departure of American practice from an idealized conception of party government. On the surface the legislative elections occurring in the middle of the President's term appear to be dominated by two national parties asking public support for their alternative programs. Certainly the electorate whose votes they seek responds to individual legislative candidates overwhelmingly on the basis of their party labels. Despite our kaleidoscopic electoral laws, the candidate's party is the one piece of information every voter is guaranteed. For many, it is the only information they ever get.

However, the legislative events that follow these elections diverge widely from the responsible-party model. The candidates who have presented themselves to the country under two party symbols immediately break ranks. The legislative parties speak not as two voices but as a cacophony of blocs and individuals fulfilling their own definitions of the public good. Party cohesion by no means vanishes, but it is deeply eroded by the pressures external to party to which the Congressman is subject.

The public's information about the legislative record of the parties and of Members of Congress goes far toward reconciling these seemingly contradictory facts. In the congressional election, to be sure, the country votes overwhelmingly for party symbols, but the symbols have limited meaning in terms of legislative policy. The eddies and crosscurrents in Congress do not interrupt a flow of legislation that the public expects but fails to see. The electorate sees very little altogether of what goes on in the national legislature. Few judgments of legislative performance are associated with the parties, and much of the public is unaware even of which party has control of Congress. As a result, the absence of party discipline or legislative results is unlikely to bring down electoral sanctions on the ineffective party or the errant Congressman.

What the public's response to the parties lacks in programmatic support is not made up by its response to local congressional candidates. Although perceptions of individual candidates account for most of the votes cast by partisans against their parties, these perceptions are almost untouched by information about the policy stands of the men contesting the House seat. The increment of strength that some candidates, especially incumbents, acquire by being known to their constituents is almost entirely free of policy content. Were such content present, the Congressman's solidarity with his legislative party would by no means be assured. If the local constituency possessed far greater resources of information than it has, it might use the ballot to pry the Congressman away from his party quite as well as to unite him with it. Yet the fact is that, by plying his campaigning and servicing arts over the years, the Congressman is able to develop electoral strength that is almost totally dissociated from what his party wants in Congress and what he himself has done about it. The relevance of all this to the problem of cohesion and responsibility in the legislative party can scarcely be doubted.

The description of party irresponsibility in America should not be overdrawn. The American system *has* elements of party accountability to the public, although the issues on which an accounting is given are relatively few and the accounting is more often rendered by those who hold or seek the Presidency than by the parties' congressional delegations. Especially on the broad problem of government action to secure social and economic welfare it can be argued that the parties have real differences and that these have penetrated the party images to which the electorate responds at the polls.

Nevertheless, American practice does diverge widely from the model of party government, and the factors underlying the departure deserve close analysis. An implication of the analysis reported here is that the public's contribution to party irregularity in Congress is not so much a matter of encouraging or requiring its Representatives to deviate from their parties as it is of the public having so little information that the irregularity of Congressmen and the ineffectiveness of the congressional parties have scant impact at the polls. Many of those who have commented on the lack of party discipline in Congress have assumed that the Congressman votes against his party because he is forced to by the demands of one of several hundred constituencies of a superlatively heterogeneous nation. In some cases, the Representative may subvert the proposals of his party because his constituency demands it. But a more reasonable interpretation over a broader range of issues is that the Congressman fails to see these proposals as part of a program on which the party—and he himself—will be judged at the polls, because he knows the constituency isn't looking.

WILLIAM H. FLANIGAN
Partisan Identification and Electoral Choice

Partisan Stability

During the past twenty years while there have been landslide elections for both parties in Presidential and Congressional elections, party loyalty has remained almost unchanged. The general sympathy for and identification with the two political parties has shown remarkably little fluctuation during this period of considerable shifting in aggregate voting behavior.

Table 1 presents public opinion survey results from 1940 to 1964. By 1947 the present pattern of partisan preferences is established while prior to that the shift away from the Republican Party occurred. (The 1940 and 1944 percentages for the Republicans appear somewhat exaggerated and the "apoliticals" underestimated.) Presumably this erosion of Republican strength began in the late 1920's and continued with some variation through the thirties, but there are no survey data from that period to document this shifting for individuals. There are two sources of minor variation during this recent period of stability; one is the increase in numbers of Democrats and the other is the further decline in Republican strength. The basic distribution shows that the Democrats and Republicans were almost evenly balanced in the early forties. (With the lower level of turnout among Democrats this would lead to a Republican advantage in normal vote such as we observed in the Congressional elections of 1942 and 1946.) The distribution of the last fifteen years, however, shows a clear advantage to the Democrats with only slightly less than 50 per cent of the electorate as Democrats and slightly over one-fourth as Republicans.

Associate Professor of Political Science and Director of the Political Behavior Laboratory, University of Minnesota. The selection is from William H. Flanigan, *Political Behavior of the Amercan Electorate*, pp. 32-44. Copyrght © 1968 by Allyn and Bacon, Inc., Boston. Reprinted by permission of the author and publisher.

Partisanship

The pioneer studies in voting behavior ignored partisanship because the early emphasis was on social variables like religion and occupation. Since the first major study by Angus Campbell and his colleagues at the Survey Research Center in 1952,[1] party identification has assumed a central role in all voting behavior analysis. Party identification is a relatively uncomplicated measure which arrays responses to the following questions:

"Generally speaking, do you usually think of yourself as a Republican, a Democrat, an Independent, or what? Would you call yourself a strong (R) (D) or not a very strong (R) (D)?"

> Strong Democrat
> Democrat
> Independent
> Republican
> Strong Republican

This self-identification measure of party loyalty is the best indicator of partisanship, and political analysts commonly refer to partisanship and party identification interchangeably. *Partisanship is the most important single influence on political opinions and voting behavior.* Many other influences are at work on voters in our society but none compare in significance with partisanship.[2]

Partisanship represents the feeling of sympathy for and loyalty to a political party an individual acquires (probably) during childhood and which endures (usually) with increasing intensity through his life. Most individuals think of themselves as something politically and this self-image of oneself as a Democrat or a Republican is useful to the individual in a special way. An individual who thinks of himself as a Republican, for example, responds to political information in part by using his party identification to orient himself, to react to new information in such a way that it fits in with the ideals and feelings he already has. A Republican who hears a policy advocated by a Republican Party leader has a basis in his party loyalty for supporting the policy quite apart from other considerations. Or a Democrat may feel favorably toward a candidate for office because he discovers that he is the Democratic candidate. Partisanship may orient the individual in his political environment, but it may also distort his picture of reality.

In order to refine slightly the categories of party identifiers shown in Table 1 in the following analysis, the individuals who have never voted are eliminated from the partisan and independent categories. This does not alter substantially the overall composition of the electorate as illustrated by Table 1,

---

[1] Angus Campbell, Gerald Gurin and Warren Miller, *The Voter Decides* (Evanston: Row, Peterson and Co., 1954).

[2] The most important work on party identification is in Angus Campbell *et al., The American Voter* (New York: John Wiley and Sons, Inc., 1960), pp. 120-67.

TABLE 1. The Party Identification of the Electorate, 1940-1964

	1940	1944	1947	1952	1954	1956	1958	1960	1962	1964
Democrats	41%	41%	45%	47%	47%	44%	47%	46%	47%	51%
Independents	20	20	21	22	22	24	19	23	23	22
Republicans	38	39	27	27	27	29	29	27	27	24
Nothing, Don't Know	1	*	2	4	4	3	5	4	3	2
Total	100%	100%	101%	100%	100%	100%	100%	100%	100%	99%
n =[a]	?	?	1287	1614	1139	1772	1269	3021	1317	1517
	(Gallup)		(NORC)	(Survey			Research			Center)

[a]In this table and most of those which follow, the number of individuals interviewed is given underneath the total percentage for the column. In each table the "n's" give the number of individuals who are represented by the percentages in the column above. In this table the "n's" represent the total sample sizes of many studies, but in most tables the "n's" will represent subsets of a single sample.

Sources: National Opinion Research Center; Survey Research Center, University of Michigan; George Gallup, *The Political Almanac, 1952* (New York: Forbes, 1952) p. 37; A. Campbell et al., *Elections and the Political Order*, p. 13.

but it does change the characteristics of the groups by setting apart the habitual non-voters. This yields five categories of active participants in the electorate according to intensity of partisanship as follows:

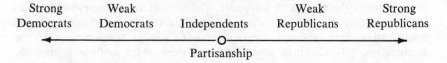

The partisans, strong Democrats and strong Republicans, are loyal to their party and likely to vote in all elections. The sympathizers, weak Democrats and weak Republicans, are less likely to vote and more likely to desert their party occasionally for the other party. The independents have little or no loyalty to either party.

Figure 1 shows how these categories of voters behave in Presidential elections according to the findings of the four major Survey Research Center surveys. Strong Democratic and Republican partisans report a high degree of loyalty to their party's candidates over the years; naturally almost no partisans have consistently voted for the other party and relatively few have ever switched. The independents on the other hand seldom vote consistently for one party—over 50 per cent reporting in all surveys that they have voted for Presidential candidates from both parties.

Figure 2 shows another pattern of voting behavior among partisans and independents in the Presidential elections of 1952, 1956, 1960 and 1964. Over-

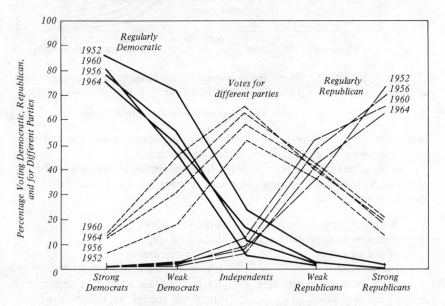

FIGURE 1.   *Party Regularity in Presidential Voting for Partisans and Independents in 1952, 1956, 1960 and 1964.*

Source: Survey Research Center, University of Michigan.

whelmingly strong partisans support the candidate of their party although there are obviously differences in the appeal of candidates. Eisenhower received exceptionally large proportions of the vote in all categories from most Republican to most Democratic, and Goldwater received exceptionally low proportions of the vote in all categories. The turnout varies somewhat in Presidential elections and reveals a slight tendency for the weak partisans to stay at home and a slight tendency for Democrats to stay at home more than the Republicans. (If individuals who never vote were added to these figures, the

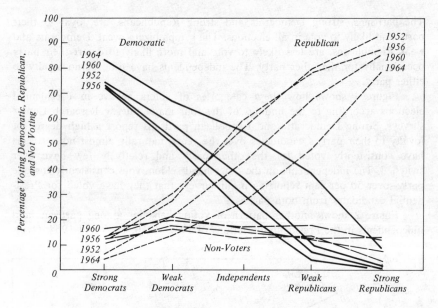

FIGURE 2. *Vote for President by Partisans and Independents in 1952, 1956, 1960 and 1964.*

Source: Survey Research Center, University of Michigan.

Democrats would appear to have even more non-voters; more habitual non-voters consider themselves Democrats than Republicans.)

In the perspective of party strategy these categories of voters must be approached with different purposes in mind. A party has these aims for the respective groups:

VOTER CATEGORY	PARTY STRATEGY
Partisans and sympathizers of the party	—hold their votes and maximize turnout
Independents	—try to win their support
Partisans and sympathizers of the opposition	—try to win their support or appeal to them enough to reduce their turnout
Habitual non-voters	—recruit new voters from potential supporters

It is difficult in practice to isolate these groups and apply a narrow strategy to one type of voter alone. Since political campaigners use appeals that are more or less appropriate for everyone, it might be more correct to say that a general campaign approach is hoped to have rather dissimilar results in different categories of voters. *By making the party's platform and candidates attractive the party intends to improve turnout and fund-raising among its followers, win over independents, and at least increase indifference to the choices among the opposition.*

Partisans

The highly stable patterns of party loyalty and political independence in Tables 2 and 3 are the basis of our description of the national electorate. Throughout this time, the Democrats hold a substantial advantage over the Republicans—an advantage which ranges from three to two in 1956 to a high of two to one in 1964. This means among other things that in the nation as a whole the Democratic Party begins a campaign with many more supporters than the Republican Party. Broadly speaking, the Democrats must try to *hold onto* their following during a campaign while the Republicans must try to *win over* a following.

TABLE 2. The Distribution of Partisans and Independents in 1952, 1956, 1960 and 1964

	1952	1956	1960	1964
Strong Democrats	19%	19%	19%	25%
Weak Democrats	21	20	22	23
Independents	19	21	19	18
Weak Republicans	12	13	13	13
Strong Republicans	13	14	14	11
Never Voted	16	14	11	10
Total	100%	101%	98%	100%
n =	1614	1762	1923	1440

Source: Survey Research Center, University of Michigan.

The advantage the Democrats enjoy nationally is largely a result of the overwhelming majority of Democrats in the South as shown in Table 2. If the South is disregarded where there are comparatively few independents and Republicans, the alignment of Democrats and Republicans outside the South is fairly evenly balanced. To an even greater degree *in the North the independents hold the balance of power between Democrats and Republicans.* Furthermore the most onesided distributions fall in 1964 and reflect an abandonment of the Republican Party resulting from the Goldwater candidacy. In 1964 the Republicans lost support not only in the North but also in the South where their strategy predicted great gains. It is reasonable to anticipate some fall-off from these atypically pro-Democratic distributions in the years following 1964.

TABLE 3. The Distribution of Partisans and Independents for the South and Non-South in 1952, 1956, 1960 and 1964

	South				Non-South			
	1952	1956	1960	1964	1952	1956	1960	1964
Strong Democrats	24%	24%	22%	33%	17%	17%	18%	22%
Weak Democrats	21	25	29	26	21	18	19	21
Independents	8	12	13	11	24	25	23	22
Weak Republicans	4	6	8	7	15	15	16	16
Strong Republicans	5	6	11	8	17	17	17	12
Never Voted	38	26	18	15	7	8	7	8
Total	100%	99%	101%	100%	101%	100%	100%	101%
n =	433	513	645	443	1140	1247	1278	997

Source: Survey Research Center, University of Michigan.

Independents

The independents are the most obvious source of additional votes for either party, given the composition of the national electorate. While loyal supporters of a party sometimes abandon it, as Democrats voted for Eisenhower in large numbers or as Republicans voted for Johnson in preference to Goldwater, year after year the largest bloc of voters available to both parties is the independents. Table 2 shows that independents account for about one-fifth of the national electorate and Table 4 indicates the independents' capacity for shifting back and forth between the major parties. In recent years each party has successfully appealed to the independents on occasion and won over a large majority to its side.

TABLE 4. *The Distribution of Votes for President by Independents from 1940 to 1964*

	1940	1944	1948	1952	1956	1960	1964
Democratic	61%	62%	57%	33%	27%	46%	66%
Republican	39	38	43	67	73	54	34
Total	100%	100%	100%	100%	100%	100%	100%
n =	?	?	?	263	309	298	219
		(Gallup Poll)		(Survey	Research		Center)

Source: George Gallup, *The Political Almanac*, 1952, p. 38, and Survey Research Center, University of Michigan.

It is appropriate to inquire on what basis the independents switch their party preferences. One of the contentions of the major voting studies has been that the popular view of political independents as intelligent, informed, dispassionate evaluators of candidates, parties and issues is mistaken. Studies from the Bureau of Applied Social Research and the Survey Research Center have supported the view that partisans of both parties are better informed and more concerned with politics than the independents. This analysis has been reflected recently in the campaign strategies of both Democratic and Republican organizations. Increasingly the view has become that the available voters, the voters that can be won over to either party, are an uninformed, apathetic group on whom intelligent appeals to issues and reasoned debate would be lost. (Some differences in perspective are involved here. If one is concerned only with the individuals in the electorate who have not made a choice between Presidential candidates, say, by the last two weeks of the campaign, they are indeed an uninformed, apathetic lot and it is difficult to find any basis for their eventual vote choice. If on the other hand one is concerned with all the individuals who are available sometime between one election and the next or who switch preferences between elections, they are not at all uninformed and apathetic in comparison with standpat voters.)[3]

[3] The most extensive analysis of this point is in V. O. Key, Jr., *The Responsible Electorate* (Cambridge: Belknap Press of Harvard University Press, 1966).

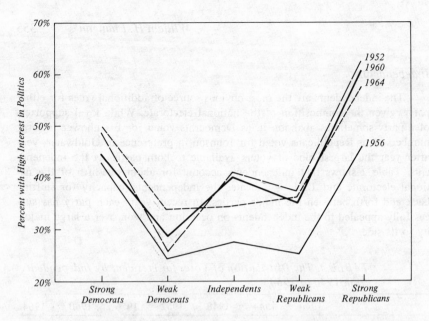

FIGURE 3. *Interest Among Partisans and Independents in 1952, 1956, 1960 and 1964.*

Source: Survey Research Center, University of Michigan.

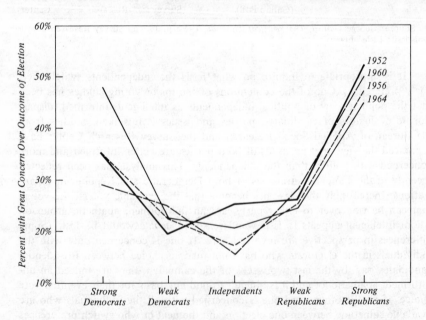

FIGURE 4. *Concern with the Outcome of the Election Among Partisans and Independents in 1952, 1956, 1960 and 1964.*

Source: Survey Research Center, University of Michigan.

The case against the independents has been overstated. It is true that independents are not as interested in campaigns or as concerned with which candidate wins as partisans, and this rather dramatic pattern is shown in Figures 3 and 4. The possibility exists, however, that these measures of "high interest" in the campaign and "great concern" with the outcome of the election are tapping the enthusiasm of the partisans for their party's Presidential candidate rather than a more general interest in politics. Nonetheless Figures 3 and 4 do demonstrate the consistent lack of concern and interest among weak partisans and independents in Presidential campaigns and elections. This is a partial explanation of why it is so difficult to get the attention of the American public during even the most exciting political campaigns. The evidence on general interest in politics shown in Table 5 is inconclusive since strong Republicans appear more interested than others who show similar patterns.

With the other indicators of interest and involvement in politics a different pattern emerges. In the level of ideological conceptualization, or seeing parties and candidates in ideological perspective, there are no differences between partisans and indpendents. The only difference is between Republicans and Democrats; Republicans with their higher level of education are more likely to view politics ideologically. On a sense of political efficacy, that is, how significant

TABLE 5. *Distribution of Interest in Government and Politics Generally According to Partisanship, 1964*

Interested	Strong Demo- crat	Weak Demo- crat	Inde- pendent	Weak Repub- lican	Strong Repub- lican
All the time	29%	27%	33%	31%	51%
Some of the time	46	40	46	46	34
Only now and then	18	20	12	14	12
Hardly at all	7	12	10	9	3
NA	—	*	—	—	—
Total	100%	99%	101%	100%	100%
n =	366	324	262	187	156

Source: Survey Research Center, University of Michigan.

one views his political activities, the same results obtain: there are no differences between independents and partisans but Republicans have a higher sense of political efficacy than Democrats.

It is surprising that with all the political survey research no satisfactory measure of political information has been developed. It has never been ascertained how well-informed different participants are. It is possible, as a substitute for a measure of political information, to report whether or not individuals have opinions on issues and make the assumption that the individuals who have no opinions are poorly informed. Again using this measure, there are no differences between partisans and independents, so by this test there is no basis for saying independents are less well-informed than partisans, using our definitions of independent and partisan.

The most nearly correct view of the independent, I believe, is that independents are not much interested in politics and government and certainly not much concerned with partisan politics—they are not emotionally involved in party clashes. On the other hand independents appear to have the information and the perspective on political affairs necessary for an evaluation of issues and candidates as competent as could be expected of partisans. Independents are no wiser or more virtuous than partisans; nor are they less so. It is not clear whether their lack of involvement means that independents are not easily aroused by political problems demanding their attention or whether their lack of involvement simply means independents are less biased by partisan predispositions. This uncertainty is troublesome because independents may not be sufficiently motivated to play the role of intelligently mediating disputes between Democrats and Republicans. On the other hand the self-perception of playing this mediating role may motivate independents effectively.

Shifting Partisan Sympathy

Most individuals never alter their partisan loyalties and this stability, in party followers, extends over generations. Very few individuals, less than 2 per cent ordinarily, report a change in party identification in the period of a single year. The net gain or loss to one party in a single year is almost always under 1 per cent. *Since 1936 the shifting of party loyalty has worked to the advantage of the Republicans.* Although some individuals in the electorate are moving away from the Republican Party, more are moving toward it. When we combine this characteristic with the pro-Democratic leanings of new members of the electorate, we find that the Democrats are gradually becoming more numerous and Republicans less numerous. *The advantage Democrats enjoy among new voters more than offsets the losses to the Republicans among older voters.*

It is obviously much easier to change the preferences of voters in particular elections than to alter their basic partisan loyalties. The capacity the electorate has demonstrated to shift support from one party to another is essential if there is to be a believable threat to political office holders. If voting patterns were as stable as partisanship, office holders would be relatively secure once elected. In fact during recent decades Americans have varied their voting patterns greatly while providing the parties with a stable base of underlying loyalty which the parties could usually count on when entering electoral contests. On this score the American electorate appears changeable enough nationally to prevent political leaders from taking the public for granted and stable enough to provide both political parties with an effective base of power from which to threaten the other party.

V. O. KEY, JR.
Voting on Substantive Issues

Elections are basic means by which the people of a democracy bend government to their wishes. In both their symbolism and their reality free elections distinguish democratic regimes. They occupy a prominent place in the political faith of democratic orders. The morale of a democracy depends in part on the maintenance of the belief that elections really serve as instruments of popular government, that they are not rituals calculated only to generate the illusion of deference to mass opinion. Since American parties attract the loyalties of persons with considerable similarity of policy views, it might be supposed that elections would merely record the numbers who identify with the major parties. Although the sense of party identification introduces a degree of stability into voting behavior, the looseness of party attachments also assures that at each polling a sector of the electorate considers the alternatives anew. Elections are not occasions at which solid partisan phalanxes march to the polls; they are opportunities for decision, and politicians are not without anxiety as they await their outcome.

The travails of democracies in the past half-century have tarnished the image of elections as an instrument of popular decision. Abortive installations of democratic practices in nations scattered over the world have contributed to this disenchantment, though the moral may be that democratic procedures are workable only under some circumstances and then only by people habituated to their requirements. Yet even American publicists seem to share the global disillusionment with electoral decision. The ancient distrust of democracy gains reinforcement from the indiscriminate projection to mass electoral behavior of the findings of psychology that men's behavior contains an element of irrationality. Dissemination of these views makes it easy for many people to believe that the highbinders of Madison Avenue can humbug the American people in an election.[1] Among some intellectuals doubts about the vitality of the electoral process may flow from sociological interpretations of electoral behavior as but the conditioned by-product of social status, occupational position, or some other deterministic relation. Of the relevance of these factors for electoral behavior there can be no doubt, but of their controlling influence in the

Late Professor of Political Science, Harvard University. Author of *Political Parties, and Pressure Groups, The Responsible Electorate,* and many others. This selection is from *Public Opinion and American Democracy,* by V. O. Key, Jr., pp. 458-466. © Copyright 1961 by V. O. Key, Jr. Reprinted by permission of Alfred A. Knopf, Inc.

[1] It may be doubted that Madison Avenue foisted General Eisenhower off on the American electorate. Probably about all the advertising agencies did was to embellish the image of a presold product. At earlier epochs in American history party managers have found prominent generals both available and capable of election.

political system there must be serious reservation. The American electorate sooner or later belies all predictions on deterministic assumptions.

Obviously one cannot maintain that public opinion is projected through elections with a crystalline clarity to animate governments to actions in accord with patterns it prescribes in precise detail. If such were the reality, governments would be hamstrung. Nevertheless, by elections the people make great decisions, which may have a heavy substantive policy content. Elections probably serve better as instruments for popular decision on broad and great issues; the details and the trivia may be beyond popular control, a fact that at times may lead to a defeat of the majority preferences in the minutiae of administration. The popular decision has components in addition to those of substantive policy. Elections cannot be regarded solely as a conduit for the transmission of policy preferences to government. They also express other judgments and preferences—such as those about candidates and about past performance of government—as well as policy desires. In short, elections matter, and they serve in the political system as a basic connection between public opinion and government. The problem is to indicate how this linkage occurs and on what kinds of questions it seems most clearly controlling.

The despair that leads some analysts to dismiss elections as of no avail in the expression of public opinion comes in part from the simple-minded model against which they test actual elections. That model assumes that elections ought in some way to separate people into two groups: a majority consisting of persons in agreement on a series of propositions to the execution of which their candidate was committed and the minority made up of persons on the other side of the same issues to which position their candidate had committed himself. So stark a model is so remote from reality that its uses are limited in speculation about the place of elections in the political process. Its assumption that the world of opinion is one of blacks and whites does not accord with the existence of gradations of opinion. Nor does the model take into account variations in intensity of opinion from question to question. In it the relative salience of issues for people finds no recognition. Nor does it make allowance for the fact that on many specific questions mass opinion may be uninformed, though most people may have broad sentiments or preferences that may be regarded as logically, if not always practically, controlling of subsidiary issues. Moreover, the model assumes that public opinion is to be regarded as acting prospectively when, in fact, its most forceful expressions may be retrospective judgments about policy and performance.

As has been demonstrated, the citizen's identification with party tends to produce a tie consistent with his policy preferences. To some extent this results from the matching of conscious policy preferences with policy positions taken with some clarity by the parties. To some extent it consists in policy through agency as the citizen perceives his party to be dedicated to the interests of persons like himself. When election day rolls around, though, the citizen may not vote in accord with his party identification. His party attachment is somewhat like his church membership; he regards it as no binding commitment to attend Sunday services. The looseness of their party attachments permits many Americans to bring their voting closer into line with the concerns salient to them at the moment of the election than it would be if undeviating partisan loyalty prevailed. As the voters respond to the changing realities, a fairly impressive correlation prevails between the vote and policy preferences on the salient issues. Moreover, voting decisions inconsistent with party identification often result from policy preferences. The act of voting is by no means devoid of policy content and intent.

Relation Between Vote and Policy Preference

The more conscious the American voter is of policy issues and the more aware he is of party policy, the more likely he is to cast a ballot consistent with his policy preferences. The interpretation runs counter to easy generalizations to the effect that the voter is a boob at the mercy of slick operators. Certainly some voters magnificently fulfill that specification, but the motivations that bring many people to a decision about their presidential vote include a policy component. For some voters substantive policy is far more central than for others; yet few who take the trouble to vote are entirely lacking in policy preferences.

The relationship between policy preferences and vote is neatly demonstrated by Table 1, which merits close examination. That table relates the individual's vote to his perception of the positions of the parties on issues on which he had opinions. Those who had opinions on the issue propositions included in

TABLE 1. Presidential Vote in Relation to Voter's Perception of Closeness of the Parties to His Position on Sixteen Policy Issues [a]

Number of Pro-Democratic Perceptions	Number of Pro-Republican Issue Perceptions			
	0	1-2	3-5	6-16
0	36%	14%	3%	2%
1-2	72	41	16	3
3-5	81	60	33	14
6-16	89	78	b	c

[a] Entries are percentages of those in each cell reporting a Democratic presidential vote in 1956.
[b] Only 12 cases fell in this cell; 8 reported a Democratic vote.
[c] No cases in this cell.
Data Source: Survey Research Center, University of Michigan, 1956.

the 1956 Survey Research Center inquiry were asked whether they thought the government was going too far, about right, or not far enough in each policy field.[2] Some people had no notion of what the government had been doing or no opinion about whether its action was too much or too little; these persons were screened out. Those who survived this test were asked whether the Democrats or Republicans were closer to their preferences on the issue. Response to this inquiry separated out people who saw a distinction between the parties on the issue. A person thus might have a pro-Democratic perception or a pro-Republican perception on from one to sixteen issues. Or he might see the Democrats as closer to him on one issue and the Republicans as closer to his pref-

[2] For text of propositions see Key, Public Opinion & American Democracy, Appendix I.

erences on a dozen issues. Or the predominance of perception and preference might be in the other direction.

The relationships to the reported vote of these perceptions of party positions on issues, shown in Table 1, are startling in their clarity. Of those persons who saw the Republicans as "closer" to what they wanted on from six to sixteen issues and simultaneously gave the Democrats the nod on not a single issue, 98 per cent voted Republican. At the other extreme, of those who saw the Democrats in a comparably favorable issue light, 89 per cent voted Democratic. Between these extremes the division of the vote varied roughly with correspondence between the perceptions of issue positions of the parties and the voters' preferences. Those most concerned with issues, as measured by the numbers of issues on which they had perceptions of party positions, most frequently brought their vote into line with their policy perceptions. The table also clearly indicates that factors in addition to substantive issues enter into the vote decision. Of those who had no impression of party position on any of the sixteen issues, only 36 per cent voted Democratic. If factors other than policy issues had been equal between the parties, a 50:50 split would have been expected in this cell. The other intermediate cells of the table also reflect the net balance of Republican advantage in the nonpolicy influences in this election.[3]

Determination of the political attitudes of a national sample of people and estimation of which attitudes are most relevant to the vote are not operations readily accomplished with imposing precision. One reason, though, why some confidence can be placed in what we have discovered is that alternative procedures yield essentially the same results. In addition to the data on responses to inquiries about specific issues, data are available on issue attitudes expressed in response to open-ended questions. Respondents could indicate what happened to be on their minds as they commented on such questions as: "Is there anything in particular that you like about the Democratic party?" "Is there anything in particular that you don't like about the Democratic party?" In their replies respondents often remarked that they liked a party because of its social security policy, its farm policy, its military policy, or for other reasons with some policy content. From the form of the questions these observations were in approbation or disapproval of a party. When coded, the responses might indicate that a person took a pro-Democratic position in that the number of his pro-Democratic policy comments exceeded the number of pro-Republican comments; a neutral position might be indicated by no policy comments or an equal number of comments in opposite partisan directions; or a person might have a net pro-Republican policy position. When the partisan direction of policy position is determined in this way, a fairly high degree of correspondence prevails between policy outlook and the reported presidential vote. These relationships, in domestic and foreign policy, appear in Table 2.

[3] The technician may be concerned about the numbers in each cell of the table. The o-o cell, those with no perceptions of party positions on policy as measured by the schedule, made up 16 per cent of the sample of voters. (Had nonvoters been included in this tabulation the proportion in the o-o cell probably would have been higher.) The extreme Republican cell, no pro-Democratic perceptions and from six to sixteen pro-Republican perceptions, constituted 18 per cent of the sample of voters. The comparable extreme pro-Democratic cell made up 14 per cent of the sample.

*TABLE 2. Relationship of Issue Position as Determined by
Responses to Open-Ended Questions and Presidential Vote*

Vote	Domestic-Issue Position		
	Pro R	Neutral	Pro D
R	86%	62%	32%
D	14	38	68
	100%	100%	100%
N	338	557	377
	Foreign-Issue Position		
R	82%	51%	32%
D	18	49	68
	100%	100%	100%
N	423	774	75

Data Source: Survey Research Center, University of Michigan, 1956.

The relationships between the direction of vote and policy position do not necessarily mean that people voted Democratic or Republican because of their policy inclinations. Some of them adopted these policy positions because they voted Democratic or Republican. Moreover, probably relatively few persons change their votes at each election to bring them into conformity with their policy preferences. The correlations picture in large part a standing relationship rather than one developed anew at each polling. The relationships also doubtless reflect some misinformation and wishful thinking as people warped their perception of their candidate's position into agreement with their own views. Nevertheless, the parallelism among issue-oriented people between their vote and their perceptions is impressive, however it comes about.[4]

Movement Toward Harmony Between Vote and Policy Preference

The conformity of policy preference with vote does not result from a happenstance association between party choice and policy preference. As people shift their voting position, they tend to bring it into harmony with their policy preferences. The resulting parallelism never achieves completeness, for people have diverse interests and combinations of preferences in politics. Conformity of vote and policy preference is closer on some issues than on others and closer at some times than at other times.

These movements toward conformity are shown to exist by two types of data. They take place through time when a person shifts from a Democratic vote in 1948, say, to a Republican vote in 1952 and by this step brings his vote into line with his policy preferences and his perceptions of the policy orientations of the parties. In another way a person may at a particular election move away from his party identification to vote in a manner that he feels better fits his policy preferences. Thus, a farmer who professes to be a strong Republican

[4] On the relation between issue position and presidential vote in 1952, see Angus Campbell, Gerald Gurin, and Warren E. Miller: "Political Issues and the Vote: November, 1952," *American Political Science Review*, XLVII (1953), 359-85.

may vote for a Democratic candidate because he dislikes Republican farm policy.

Illustrative of the first type of data are findings on shifts of voters from 1928 to 1932. The movements, Republican to Democratic and Democratic to Republican, between these two elections formed a pattern that recurs. From 1928 to 1932 the "more conservative voters tended to move toward the Republican party and the more progressive toward the Democratic." The result of the movement was to increase the attitudinal differences between the party groups. Conservatives who had voted for Al Smith in 1928 tended to become Hoover supporters in 1932; liberals who had voted for Hoover tended to vote for Roosevelt in 1932.

The movement from the candidate of one party to that of another through time does not consist solely of persons motivated by policy considerations. Even in the same individual policy motivations may be mixed with other concerns. From 1948 to 1952 large numbers of Truman voters moved to the support of Eisenhower. These D-R voters were on the average less dedicated to pro-Democratic positions on a series of policy issues than were the faithful who adhered to the Democrats in both 1948 and 1952, a contrast especially marked among the D-R switchers in the South. Yet the D-R group as a whole did not take a pro-Republican policy position in the same degree as did the hard core that voted Republican in both 1948 and 1952. Policy motivations among the D-R shifters were supplemented by their favorable impressions of the Republican candidate.[5] While voters may shift their support from the candidate of one party to that of another for policy reasons, they may also shift for other causes. There is some support for the belief that the group most susceptible to shift through time with the popular tide consists of those individuals completely devoid of policy interests or concerns.

Another illustration of the urge toward congruence of policy and voting preference rests on the tendency of voters to bolt the party with which they are identified when its policies displease them; they consider themselves strong Democrats or strong Republicans but decide to vote for the opposition candidate at a particular election. This process finds illustration in the tendency in 1952 for those Democrats to vote Republican who thought their party had gone too far in the social-welfare field. Of those Democratic identifiers who took a conservative position on welfare policy, 65 per cent voted Republican. Only 10 per cent of those strong Democrats who thought the national government should do more in the welfare field were drawn to Eisenhower by the siren calls of the 1952 campaign. In the other direction, 15 per cent of that small band of weak Republicans favoring broader welfare activity resisted the pressures of the campaign and voted for Stevenson. The details appear in Table 3.

The relation between policy preference and vote appears also in a negative way; that is, the less interest and information a person has about policy, the less likely he is to vote. The greater the policy content of an individual's political concern, the more powerful is this interest in both bringing him to the polls

[5] See Angus Campbell, Gerald Gurin, and Warren E. Miller: *The Voter Decides* (Evanston: Row, Peterson; 1954), 168-72.

TABLE 3. *Presidential Vote in Relation to Party Identification and Opinion on Scope of Social Welfare Activities of Government**

Party Identification	Opinion on Welfare Activities		
	Should do less	Is about right	Should do more
Strong Democratic	35%	85%	90%
Weak Democratic	35	66	68
Independent	10	36	56
Weak Republican	0	6	15
Strong Republican	0	1	2

*Entries are percentages of those in each cell reporting a Democratic vote in 1952. The question was: "Some people think the national government should do more in trying to deal with such problems as unemployment, education, housing, and so on. Others think that the government is already doing too much. On the whole, would you say that what the government has done has been about right, too much, or not enough?"

Data Source: Survey Research Center, University of Michigan, 1952.

and in fixing the direction of his vote. There are other dimensions to autonomous disfranchisement. Some people are so little involved politically that they care not at all how the election comes out.[6] Measures of degree of "care" about election outcomes are crude, but the less a person cares, the less likely he is to vote. The rates of voting in 1952 in relation to response to the question: "Generally speaking, would you say that you personally care a good deal which party wins the presidential election this fall, or that you don't care very much which party wins?" were as follows:

	Per Cent Voting
Care very much	83%
Care somewhat	79
Don't care very much	70
Don't care at all	57

These estimates overstate the actual voting rates, but they doubtless indicate accurately the positive relationship between "care" about outcome and participation.

[6] The extreme of indifference is exemplified by the response of the wife of a Minnesota farm laborer to the question whether she personally cared "which party wins the presidential election" in the fall of 1956. "No difference; didn't know there was an election coming." The interviewer persisted through the lengthy schedule, and about the only political perception gleaned was the thought that the Democrats "are supposed to help the farmers. My husband says so."

BERNARD R. BERELSON, PAUL F. LAZARSFELD, *and*
WILLIAM N. MC PHEE

Democratic Practice and Democratic Theory

We have been studying not how people come to make choices in general but how they make a political choice, and the political content of the study has broad ramifications beyond the technical interests. In the end, of course, we must leave such theoretical questions to the political theorists and the political philosophers. But the fact that they would not be at home in our empirical material has encouraged us to speak at least briefly to their concerns. Both theory and facts are needed. As Schumpeter says in *Capitalism, Socialism and Democracy:* "The question whether [certain] conditions are fulfilled to the extent required in order to make democracy work should not be answered by reckless assertion or equally reckless denial. It can be answered only by a laborious appraisal of a maze of conflicting evidence."

With respect to politics, empirical-analytic theory and normative theory have only recently become truly separated—and often to their mutual disadvantage and impoverishment. . . . If the political theorists do not engage directly in politics, they might explore the relevance, the implications, and the meaning of such empirical facts as are contained in this and similar studies. Political theory written with reference to practice has the advantage that its categories are the categories in which political life really occurs. And, in turn, relating research to problems of normative theory would make such research more realistic and more pertinent to the problems of policy. At the same time, empirical research can help to clarify the standards and correct the empirical presuppositions of normative theory. As a modest illustration, this chapter turns to some of the broad normative and evaluative questions implied in this empirical study.

Requirements for the Individual

Perhaps the main impact of realistic research on contemporary politics has been to temper some of the requirements set by our traditional normative theory for the typical citizen. "Out of all this literature of political observation and analysis, which is relatively new," says Max Beloff, "there has come to exist a picture in our minds of the political scene which differs very considerably from that familiar to us from the classical texts of democratic politics."

Bernard R. Berelson is co-author of *Human Behavior,* and of *The People's Choice.* Paul F. Lazarsfeld is Professor of Sociology, Columbia University, and author of *Academic Mind; Radio and the Printed Page,* and many others. William McPhee is Professor of Sociology, University of Colorado, and author of *Formal Theories of Mass Behavior.* This selection is from *Voting,* Chap. 4. Copyright 1954 University of Chicago Press. Reprinted by permission of the University of Chicago Press.

Experienced observers have long known, of course, that the individual voter was not all that the theory of democracy requires of him. As Bryce put it:

> How little solidity and substance there is in the political or social beliefs of nineteen persons out of every twenty. These beliefs, when examined, mostly resolve themselves into two or three prejudices and aversions, two or three prepossessions for a particular party or section of a party, two or three phrases or catch-words suggesting or embodying arguments which the man who repeats them has not analyzed.

While our data do not support such an extreme statement, they do reveal that certain requirements commonly assumed for the successful operation of democracy are not met by the behavior of the "average" citizen. The requirements, and our conclusions concerning them, are quickly reviewed.[1]

Interest, discussion, motivation

The democratic citizen is expected to be interested and to participate in political affairs. His interest and participation can take such various forms as reading and listening to campaign materials, working for the candidate or the party, arguing politics, donating money, and voting. In Elmira the majority of the people vote, but in general they do not give evidence of sustained interest. Many vote without real involvement in the election, and even the party workers are not typically motivated by ideological concerns or plain civic duty. . . .

An assumption underlying the theory of democracy is that the citizenry has a strong motivation for participation in political life. But it is a curious quality of voting behavior that for large numbers of people motivation is weak if not almost absent. It is assumed that this motivation would gain its strength from the citizen's perception of the difference that alternative decisions made to him. Now when a person buys something or makes other decisions of daily life, there are direct and immediate consequences for him. But for the bulk of the American people the voting decision is not followed by any direct, immediate, visible personal consequences. Most voters, organized or unorganized, are not in a position to foresee the distant and indirect consequences for themselves, let alone the society. The ballot is cast, and for most people that is the end of it. If their side is defeated, "it doesn't really matter."

Knowledge and Principle

The democratic citizen is expected to be well informed about political affairs. He is supposed to know what the issues are, what their history is, what the relevant facts are, what alternatives are proposed, what the party stands for, what the likely consequences are. By such standards the voter falls short. Even when he has the motivation, he finds it difficult to make decisions on the basis of full information when the subject is relatively simple and proximate; how can he do so when it is complex and remote? The citizen is not highly in-

[1] A somewhat more general statement is contained in Bernard Berelson, "Democratic Theory and Public Opinion," *Public Opinion Quarterly*, XVI (Fall, 1952), 313-30.

formed on details of the campaign, nor does he avoid a certain misperception of the political situation when it is to his psychological advantage to do so. The electorate's perception of what goes on in the campaign is colored by emotional feeling toward one or the other issue, candidate, party, or social group.

The democratic citizen is supposed to cast his vote on the basis of principle —not fortuitously or frivolously or implusively or habitually, but with reference to standards not only of his own interest but of the common good as well. Here, again, if this requirement is pushed at all strongly, it becomes an impossible demand on the democratic electorate.

Many voters vote not for principle in the usual sense but "for" a group to which they are attached—their group. The Catholic vote or the hereditary vote is explainable less as principle than as a traditional social allegiance. The ordinary voter, bewildered by the complexity of modern political problems, unable to determine clearly what the consequences are of alternative lines of action, remote from the arena, and incapable of bringing information to bear on principle, votes the way trusted people around him are voting. A British scholar, Max Beloff, takes as the "chief lesson to be derived" from such studies:

> Election campaigns and the programmes of the different parties have little to do with the ultimate result which is predetermined by influences acting upon groups of voters over a longer period. . . . This view has now become a working hypothesis with which all future thinking on this matter will have to concern itself. But if this is admitted, then obviously the picture of the voter as a person exercising conscious choice between alternative persons and alternative programmes tends to disappear.

On the issues of the campaign there is a considerable amount of "don't know"—sometimes reflecting genuine indecision, more often meaning "don't care." Among those with opinions the partisans *agree* on most issues, criteria, expectations, and rules of the game. The supporters of the different sides disagree on only a few issues. Nor, for that matter, do the candidates themselves always join the issue sharply and clearly. The partisans do not agree overwhelmingly with their own party's position, or, rather, only the small minority of highly partisan do; the rest take a rather moderate position on the political considerations involved in an election.

Rationality

The democratic citizen is expected to exercise rational judgment in coming to his voting decision. He is expected to have arrived at his principles by reason and to have considered rationally the implications and alleged consequences of the alternative proposals of the contending parties. Political theorists and commentators have always exclaimed over the seeming contrast here between requirement and fulfilment. Even as sensible and hard-minded an observer as Schumpeter was extreme in his view:

> Even if there were no political groups trying to influence him, the typical citizen would in political matters tend to yield to extra-rational or

irrational prejudice and impulse. The weakness of the rational processes he applies to politics and the absence of effective logical control over the results he arrives at would in themselves suffice to account for that. Moreover, simply because he is not "all there," he will relax his usual moral standards as well and occasionally give in to dark urges which the conditions of private life help him to repress.

Here the problem is first to see just what is meant by rationality. The term, as a recent writer noted, "has enjoyed a long history which has bequeathed to it a legacy of ambiguity and confusion. . . . Any man may be excused when he is puzzled by the question how he ought to use the word and particularly how he ought to use it in relation to human conduct and politics." Several meanings can be differentiated.

It is not for us to certify a meaning. But even without a single meaning—with only the aura of the term—we can make some observations on the basis of our material. In any rigorous or narrow sense the voters are not highly rational; that is, most of them do not ratiocinate on the matter, e.g., to the extent that they do on the purchase of a car or a home. Nor do voters act rationally whose "principles" are held so tenaciously as to blind them to information and persuasion. Nor do they attach efficient means to explicit ends.

The fact that some people change their minds during a political campaign shows the existence of that open-mindedness usually considered a component of rationality. But among whom? Primarily among those who can "afford" a change of mind, in the sense that they have ties or attractions on both sides—the cross-pressured voters in the middle where rationality is supposed to take over from the extremes of partisan feeling. But it would hardly be proper to designate the unstable, uninterested, uncaring middle as the sole or the major possessor of rationality among the electorate. As Beloff points out: "It is likely that the marginal voter is someone who is so inadequately identified with one major set of interests or another and so remote, therefore, from the group-thinking out of which political attitudes arise, that his voting record is an illustration, not of superior wisdom, but of greater frivolity."

The upshot of this is that the usual analogy between the voting "decision" and the more or less carefully calculated decisions of consumers or businessmen or courts, incidentally, may be quite incorrect. For many voters political preferences may better be considered analogous to cultural tastes—in music, literature, recreational activities, dress, ethics, speech, social behavior. Consider the parallels between political preferences and general cultural tastes. Both have their origin in ethnic, sectional, class, and family traditions. Both exhibit stability and resistance to change for individuals but flexibility and adjustment over generations for the society as a whole. Both seem to be matters of sentiment and disposition rather than "reasoned preferences." While both are responsive to changed conditions and unusual stimuli, they are relatively invulnerable to direct argumentation and vulnerable to indirect social influences. Both are characterized more by faith than by conviction and by wishful expectation rather than careful prediction of consequences. The preference for one party rather than another must be highly similar to the preference for one kind of literature or music rather than another, and the choice of the same political party every four years may be parallel to the choice of the same old standards of conduct in new social situations. In short, it appears that a sense of fitness is a more striking feature of political preference than reason and calculation.

If the democratic system depended solely on the qualifications of the individual voter, then it seems remarkable that democracies have survived through the centuries. After examining the detailed data on how individuals misperceive political reality or respond to irrelevant social influences, one wonders how a democracy ever solves its political problems. But when one considers the data in a broader perspective—how huge segments of the society adapt to political conditions affecting them or how the political system adjusts itself to changing conditions over long periods of time—he cannot fail to be impressed with the total result. Where the rational citizen seems to abdicate, nevertheless angels seem to tread.

The eminent judge, Learned Hand, in a delightful essay on "Democracy: Its Presumptions and Reality," comes to essentially this conclusion.

> I do not know how it is with you, but for myself I generally give up at the outset. The simplest problems which come up from day to day seem to me quite unanswerable as soon as I try to get below the surface. . . . My vote is one of the most unimportant acts of my life; if I were to acquaint myself with the matters on which it ought really to depend, if I were to try to get a judgment on which I was willing to risk affairs of even the smallest moment, I should be doing nothing else, and that seems a fatuous conclusion to a fatuous undertaking.

Yet he recognizes the paradox—somehow the system not only works on the most difficult and complex questions but often works with distinction. "For, abuse it as you will, it gives a bloodless measure of social forces—bloodless, have you thought of that?—a means of continuity, a principle of stability, a relief from the paralyzing terror of revolution."

Justice Hand concludes that we have "outgrown" the conditions assumed in traditional democratic theory and that "the theory has ceased to work." And yet, the system that has grown out of classic democratic theory, and, in this country, out of quite different and even elementary social conditions, does continue to work—perhaps even more vigorously and effectively than ever.

That is the paradox. *Individual voters* today seem unable to satisfy the requirements for a democratic system of government outlined by political theorists. But the *system of democracy* does meet certain requirements for a going political organization. The individual members may not meet all the standards, but the whole nevertheless survives and grows. This suggests that where the classic theory is defective is in its concentration on the *individual citizen*. What are undervalued are certain collective properties that reside in the electorate as a whole and in the political and social system in which it functions.

The political philosophy we have inherited, then, has given more consideration to the virtues of the typical citizen of the democracy than to the working of the *system* as a whole. Moreover, when it dealt with the system, it mainly considered the single constitutive institutions of the system, not those general features necessary if the institutions are to work as required. For example, the rule of law, representative government, periodic elections, the party system, and the several freedoms of discussion, press, association, and assembly have all been examined by political philosophers seeking to clarify and to justify the idea of political democracy. But liberal democracy is more than a political system in which individual voters and political institutions operate. For political democracy to survive, other features are required: the intensity of conflict must be limited, the rate of change must be restrained, stability in the social and economic structure must be maintained, a pluralistic social organization must exist, and a basic consensus must bind together the contending parties.

Such features of the system of political democracy belong neither to the constitutive institutions nor to the individual voter. It might be said that they form the atmosphere or the environment in which both operate. In any case, such features have not been carefully considered by political philosophers, and it is on these broader properties of the democratic political system that more reflection and study by political theory is called for. In the most tentative fashion let us explore the values of the political system, as they involve the electorate, in the light of the foregoing considerations.

Requirements for the System

Underlying the paradox is an assumption that the population is homogeneous socially and should be homogeneous politically: that everybody is about the same in relevant social characteristics; that, if something is a political virtue (like interest in the election), then everyone should have it; that there is such a thing as "the" typical citizen on whom uniform requirements can be imposed. The tendency of classic democratic literature to work with an image of "the" voter was never justified. For, as we will attempt to illustrate here, some of the most important requirements that democratic values impose on a system require a voting population that is not homogeneous but heterogeneous in its political qualities.

The need for heterogeneity arises from the contradictory functions we expect our voting system to serve. We expect the political system to adjust itself and our affairs to changing conditions; yet we demand too that it display a high degree of stability. We expect the contending interests and parties to pursue their ends vigorously and the voters to care; yet, after the election is over, we expect reconciliation. We expect the voting outcome to serve what is best for the community; yet we do not want disinterested voting unattached to the purposes and interests of different segments of the community. We want voters to express their own free and self-determined choices; yet, for the good of the community, we would like voters to avail themselves of the best information and guidance available from the groups and leaders around them. We expect a high degree of rationality to prevail in the decision; but were all irrationality and mythology absent, and all ends pursued by the most coldly rational selection of political means, it is doubtful if the system would hold together.

In short, our electoral system calls for apparently incompatible properties—which, although they cannot all reside in each individual voter, can (and do) reside in a heterogeneous electorate. What seems to be required of the electorate as a whole is a *distribution* of qualities along important dimensions. We need some people who are active in a certain respect, others in the middle, and still others passive. The contradictory things we want from the total require that the parts be different. This can be illustrated by taking up a number of important dimensions by which an electorate might be characterized.

Involvement and Indifference

How could a mass democracy work if all the people were deeply involved in politics? Lack of interest by some people is not without its benefits, too. True, the highly interested voters vote more, and know more about the campaign, and read and listen more, and participate more; however, they are also less open to persuasion and less likely to change. Extreme interest goes with extreme partisanship and might culminate in rigid fanaticism that could destroy democratic processes if generalized throughout the community. Low affect toward the election—not caring much—underlies the resolution of many political problems; votes can be resolved into a two-party split instead of fragmented into many parties (the splinter parties of the left, for example, splinter because their advocates are *too* interested in politics). Low interest provides maneuvering room for political shifts necessary for a complex society in a period of rapid change. Compromise might be based upon sophisticated awareness of costs and returns —perhaps impossible to demand of a mass society—but it is more often induced by indifference. Some people are and should be highly interested in politics, but not everyone is or needs to be. Only the doctrinaire would deprecate the moderate indifference that facilitates compromise.

Hence, an important balance between action motivated by strong sentiments and action with little passion behind it is obtained by heterogeneity within the electorate. Balance of this sort is, in practice, met by a distribution of voters rather than by a homogeneous collection of "ideal" citizens.

Stability and Flexibility

A similar dimension along which an electorate might be characterized is stability-flexibility. The need for change and adaptation is clear, and the need for stability ought equally to be (especially from observation of current democratic practice in, say, certain Latin-American countries).

How is political stability achieved? There are a number of social sources of political stability: the training of the younger generation before it is old enough to care much about the matter, the natural selection that surrounds the individual voter with families and friends who reinforce his own inclinations, the tendency to adjust in favor of the majority of the group, the self-perpetuating tendency of political traditions among ethnic and class and regional strata where like-minded people find themselves socially together. Political stability is based upon social stability. Family traditions, personal associations, status-related organizational memberships, ethnic affiliations, socioeconomic strata—such ties for the individual do not change rapidly or sharply, and since his vote is so importantly a product of them, neither does it. In effect, a large part of the study of voting deals not with why votes change but rather with why they do not.

In addition, the varying conditions facing the country, the varying political appeals made to the electorate, and the varying dispositions of the voters activated by these stimuli—these, combined with the long-lasting nature of the political loyalties they instil, produce an important cohesion within the system. For example, the tendencies operating in 1948 electoral decisions not only were built up in the New Deal and Fair Deal era but also dated back to parental and grandparental loyalties, to religious and ethnic cleavages of a past era, and to moribund sectional and community conflicts. Thus, in a very real sense any particular election is a composite of various elections and various political and social events. People vote for a President on a given November day, but their choice is made not simply on the basis of what has happened in the preceding months or even four years; in 1948 some people were in effect voting on the internationalism issue of 1940, others on the depression issues of 1932, and some, indeed, on the slavery issues of 1860.

The vote is thus a kind of "moving average" of reactions to the political past. Voters carry over to each new election remnants of issues raised in previous elections—and so there is always an overlapping of old and new decisions that give a cohesion in time to the political system. Hence the composite decision "smooths out" political change. The people vote *in* the same election, but not all of them vote *on* it.

What of flexibility? Curiously, the voters least admirable when measured against individual requirements contribute most when measured against the aggregate requirement for flexibility. For those who change political preferences most readily are those who are least interested, who are subject to conflicting social pressures, who have inconsistent beliefs and erratic voting histories. Without them—if the decision were left only to the deeply concerned, well-integrated, consistently-principled ideal citizens—the political system might easily prove too rigid to adapt to changing domestic and international conditions.

In fact, it may be that the very people who are most sensitive to changing social conditions are those most susceptible to political change. For, in either case, the people exposed to membership in overlapping strata, those whose former life-patterns are being broken up, those who are moving about socially or physically, those who are forming new families and new friendships—it is they who are open to adjustments of attitudes and tastes. They may be the least partisan and the least interested voters, but they perform a valuable function for the entire system. Here again is an instance in which an individual "inadequacy" provides a positive service for the society: The campaign can be a reaffirming force for the settled majority and a creative force for the unsettled minority. There is stability on both sides and flexibility in the middle.

Progress and Conservation

Closely related to the question of stability is the question of past versus future orientation of the system. In America a progressive outlook is highly valued, but, at the same time, so is a conservative one. Here a balance between the two is easily found in the party system and in the distribution of voters themselves from extreme conservatives to extreme liberals. But a balance between the two is also achieved by a distribution of political dispositions through time. There are periods of great political agitation (i.e., campaigns) alternating with periods of political dormancy. Paradoxically, the former—the campaign period—is likely to be an instrument of conservatism, often even of historical regression.

Many contemporary campaigns must be stabilizing forces that activated past tendencies in individuals and reasserted past patterns of group voting. In 1948, for example, the middle-class Protestants reaffirmed their traditional Republican position, the working-class Protestants reverted toward their position of the 1930's and the working-class Catholics toward their position not only of the 1940's but of a generation or more earlier. In this sense the campaign was a retreat away from new issues back toward old positions.

Political campaigns tend to make people more consistent both socially and psychologically; they vote more with their social groups and agree more with their own prior ideas on the issues. But new ideas and new alignments are in their infancy manifested by inconsistency psychologically and heterogeneity socially; they are almost by definition deviant and minority points of view. To the extent that they are inhibited by pressure or simply by knowledge of what is the proper (i.e., majority) point of view in a particular group, then the campaign period is not a time to look for the growth of important new trends.

This "regressive tendency" may appear as a reaction to intense propaganda during decisive times. The term "regressive" need not imply a reversion to less-developed, less-adaptive behavior; in fact, one might argue that the revival of a Democratic vote among workers was functional for their interests. What it refers to is simply the reactivation of prior dispositions—dispositions in politics that date back years and decades, often to a prior political era.

Its counterpart, of course, is what we believe to be an important potential for progress during the periods of relaxed tension and low-pressure political and social stimuli that are especially characteristic of America between political campaigns. The very tendency for Americans to neglect their political system most of the time—to be "campaign citizens" in the sense that many are "Sunday churchgoers"—is not without its values. Change may come best from relaxation.

Again, then, a balance (between preservation of the past and receptivity to the future) seems to be required of a democratic electorate. The heterogeneous electorate in itself provides a balance between liberalism and conservatism; and so does the sequence of political events from periods of drifting change to abrupt rallies back to the loyalties of earlier years.

Consensus and Cleavage

We have talked much in the text, and perhaps implied more, about consensus and cleavage. Although there were certain clusters of political opinion in Elmira,* at the same time there were a number of opinions that did not break along class or party lines. American opinion on public issues is much too com-

* A study of the effects of campaigning in the presidential election of 1948 in Elmira, New York, showed that 71 percent of the electorate maintained their party preferences throughout while only 29 percent either shifted from their original party loyalty or between such loyalty and neutrality. It was also shown that 64 percent had made their decision by June and an additional 15 percent before the end of August. The study included the comment that "In the end many American families vote as a unit, making joint decisions in voting as in spending parts of the common family income. Indeed it would not be inappropriate to consider the family as the primary unit of voting analysis. . . ." [Eds.]

plex to be designated by such simple, single-minded labels as *the* housewife opinion or *the* young people's opinion or even *the* workers' opinion. If one uses as a base the central Republican-Democratic cleavage, then one finds numerous "contradictions" within individuals, within strata and groups, and within party supporters themselves. There are many issues presented, cafeteria-style, for the voter to choose from, and there are overlaps in opinion in every direction.

Similarly there are required *social* consensus and cleavage—in effect, pluralism—in politics. Such pluralism makes for enough consensus to hold the system together and enough cleavage to make it move. Too much consensus would be deadening and restrictive of liberty; too much cleavage would be destructive of the society as a whole.

Consider the pictures of the hypothetical relationships between political preference (e.g., party support) and a social characteristic as presented in this chart:

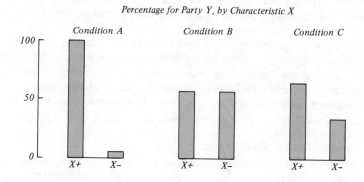

Percentage for Party Y, by Characteristic X

In Condition A there is virtual identity between the characteristic and political preference; all the people of type $X+$ vote one way, and all the people of $X-$ vote the other way. In Condition B the opposite is the case, and there is no relationship between vote and the characteristic; both parties are supported equally by people of the two types. In Condition C there is neither a complete relationship nor a complete absence; more $X+$'s than $X-$'s are partisans of a given side, but there are some members of each type in each political camp.

Now a democratic society in which Condition A was intensified would probably be in danger of its existence. The issues of politics would cut so deeply, be so keenly felt, and, especially, be so fully reinforced by other social identifications of the electorate as to threaten the basic consensus itself. This might be called "total politics"—a conception of politics, incidentally, advanced by such leading theorists of National Socialism and communism as Carl Schmitt and Lenin. This involves the mutual reinforcement of political differences and other social distinctions meaningful to the citizen. The multiplication of Condition B, on the other hand, would suggest a community in which politics was of no "real" importance to the community, in which it was not associated with special interests. Condition C is a combination of Conditions A and B—that is, a situation in which special interests are of some but not of overriding importance. It portrays neither the extremist or fanatical community like A nor the "pure" or utopian community like B.

There is nothing in Elmira that represents Condition A; the closest approximation would be the relationship between vote and religion or minority ethnic status, and even here there are group overlaps in vote amounting to from a quarter to a third of the members. The nearest approximation to Condition B is the relationship between vote and sex, which is another way of saying that there is little relevance of this characteristic to political matters, at least so far as party preference is concerned. The relationships between vote and socioeconomic status or vote and occupation are examples of Condition C.

The social and political correlations we find in places like Elmira (that are not a priori meaningless) are of the C type to a greater or less extent. What this means is that there is a good deal of cross-group and cross-party identification and affiliation within the community. The political lines are drawn in meaningful ways but are not identical with the lines of social groupings. The same social heterogeneity that produces self-interest also produces a cross-cutting and harmonious community interest.

Thus again a requirement we might place on an electoral system—balance between total political war between segments of the society and total political indifference to group interests of that society—translates into varied requirements for different individuals. With respect to group or bloc voting, as with other aspects of political behavior, it is perhaps not unfortunate that "some do and some do not."

Individualism and Collectivism

Lord Bryce pointed out the difficulties in a theory of democracy that assumes that each citizen must himself be capable of voting intelligently:

> Orthodox democratic theory assumes that every citizen has, or ought to have, thought out for himself certain opinions, i.e., ought to have a definite view, defensible by argument, of what the country needs, of what principles ought to be applied in governing it, of the man to whose hands the government ought to be entrusted. There are persons who talk, though certainly very few who act, as if they believed this theory, which may be compared to the theory of some ultra-Protestants that every good Christian has or ought to have . . . worked out for himself from the Bible a system of theology.

In the first place, however, the information available to the individual voter is not limited to that directly possessed by him. True, the individual casts his own personal ballot. But, as we have tried to indicate throughout, that is perhaps the most individualized action he takes in an election. His vote is formed in the midst of his fellows in a sort of group decision—if, indeed, it may be called a decision at all—and the total information and knowledge possessed in the group's present and past generations can be made available for the group's choice. Here is where opinion-leading relationships, for example, play an active role.

Second, and probably more important, the individual voter may not have a great deal of detailed information, but he usually has picked up the crucial *general* information as part of his social learning itself. He may not know the parties' positions on the tariff, or who is for reciprocal trade treaties, or what are the differences on Asiatic policy, or how the parties split on civil rights, or how many security risks were exposed by whom. But he cannot live in an American community without knowing broadly where the parties stand. He has learned that the Republicans are more conservative and the Democrats more liberal—and he can locate his own sentiments and cast his vote accordingly. After all, he must vote for one or the other party, and, if he knows the big thing about the parties, he does not need to know all the little things. The basic role a party plays as an institution in American life is more important to his voting than a particular stand on a particular issue.

It would be unthinkable to try to maintain our present economic style of life without a complex system of delegating to others what we are not competent to do ourselves, without accepting and giving training to each other about what each is expected to do, without accepting our dependence on others in many spheres and taking responsibility for their dependence on us in some spheres. And, like it or not, to maintain our present political style of life, we may have to accept much the same interdependence with others in collective behavior. We have learned slowly in economic life that it is useful not to have everyone a butcher or a baker, any more than it is useful to have no one skilled in such activities. The same kind of division of labor—as repugnant as it may be in some respects to our individualistic tradition—is serving us well today in mass politics. There is an implicit division of political labor within the electorate.

Conclusion

In short, when we turn from requirements for "average" citizens to requirements for the survival of the total democratic system, we find it unnecessary for the individual voter to be an "average citizen" cast in the classic or any other single mold. With our increasingly complex and differentiated citizenry has grown up an equally complex political system, and it is perhaps not simply a fortunate accident that they have grown and prospered together.

But it is a dangerous act of mental complacency to assume that conditions found surviving together are, therefore, positively "functional" for each other. The apathetic segment of America probably has helped to hold the system together and cushioned the shock of disagreement, adjustment, and change. But that is not to say that we can stand apathy without limit. Similarly, there must be some limit to the degree of stability or nonadaptation that a political society can maintain and still survive in a changing world. And surely the quality and amount of conformity that is necessary and desirable can be exceeded, as it has been in times of war and in the present Communist scare, to the damage of the society itself and of the other societies with which it must survive in the world.

How can our analysis be reconciled with the classical theory of liberal political democracy? Is the theory "wrong"? Must it be discarded in favor of empirical political sociology? Must its ethical or normative content be dismissed as incompatible with the nature of modern man or of mass society? That is not our view. Rather, it seems to us that modern political theory of democracy stands in need of revision and not replacement by empirical sociology. The classical political philosophers were right in the direction of their assessment of the virtues of the citizen. But they demanded those virtues in too extreme or doctrinal a form. The voter does have some principles, he does have information and rationality, he does have interest—but he does not have them in the extreme, elaborate, comprehensive, or detailed form in which they were uniformly recommended by political philosophers. Like Justice Hand, the typical citizen has other interests in life, and it is good, even for the political system, that he pursues them. The classical requirements are more appropriate for the opinion leaders in the society, but even they do not meet them directly. Happily for the system, voters distribute themselves along a continuum:

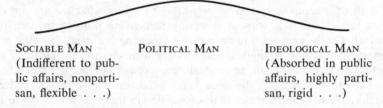

SOCIABLE MAN   POLITICAL MAN   IDEOLOGICAL MAN
(Indifferent to pub-   (Absorbed in public
lic affairs, nonparti-   affairs, highly partisan, flexible . . .)   san, rigid . . .)

And it turns out that this distribution itself, with its internal checks and balances, can perform the functions and incorporate the same values ascribed by some theorists to each individual in the system as well as to the constitutive political institutions!

    Twentieth-century political theory—both analytic and normative—will arise only from hard and long observation of the actual world of politics, closely identified with the deeper problems of practical politics. Values and the behavior they are meant to guide are not distinctly separate or separable parts of life as it is lived; and how Elmirans choose their governors is not completely unrelated to the considerations of how they are *supposed* to choose them. We disagree equally with those who believe that normative theory about the proper health of a democracy has nothing to gain from analytic studies like ours; with those who believe that the whole political tradition from Mill to Locke is irrelevant to our realistic understanding and assessment of modern democracy; or with those like Harold Laski who believe that "the decisions of men, when they come to choose their governors, are influenced by considerations which escape all scientific analysis."

    We agree with Cobban: "For a century and a half the Western democracies have been living on the stock of basic political ideas that were last restated toward the end of the eighteenth century. That is a long time. . . . The gap thus formed between political facts and political ideas has steadily widened. It has taken a long time for the results to become evident; but now that we have seen what politics devoid of a contemporary moral and political theory means, it is possible that something may be done about it."

    To that end we hope this [article] will contribute.

"Responsible" Parties

*A question of major importance, regarding the organization and
functioning of our political parties, was dealt with some years ago
by the Committee on Political Parties of the American Political
Science Association. In 1950, it submitted a Report titled "Toward
a More Responsible Two-Party System." (It was published as a
Supplement in the* American Political Science Review, *Vol. XLIV,
No. 3, Part 2, September, 1950.) The "thesis" of the Committee
was stated as follows:*

*"Historical and other factors have caused the American two-
party system to operate as two loose associations of state and local
organizations, with very little national machinery and very little
national cohesion. As a result, either major party, when in power,
is ill-equipped to organize its members in the legislative and the
executive branches into a government held together and guided by
the party program. Party responsibility at the polls thus tends to
vanish. This is a very serious matter, for it affects the very heartbeat
of American democracy. It also poses grave problems of domestic
and foreign policy in an era when it is no longer safe for the nation
to deal piecemeal with issues that can be disposed of only on the
basis of coherent programs."*

*The Committee categorically insisted that "an effective party
system requires, first, that the parties are able to bring forth programs to which they commit themselves and, second, that the parties
possess sufficient internal cohesion to carry out these programs." It
made a number of specific recommendations designed to realize this
objective.*

*James M. Burns' argument is in essential agreement with the
philosophy of The Committee on Political Parties. On the other
hand, the J. Roland Pennock and Stedman-Sonthoff articles raise
some serious doubts about that philosophy and its proposed implementation.*

JAMES MAC GREGOR BURNS
The Need for Disciplined Parties

Our Multi-Party System

In any democracy a major party seeks control of the government. To achieve that goal it bids for support throughout the community. To gain that support the party must broaden its platform through a series of compromises with organized groups and with unorganized voters. No narrow program will do the job. Constantly searching for the beliefs that bind diverse groups, the party's policy-makers define the issues that transcend the claims of special interests and find response among great masses of the people. Since the politicians attempt to attract as many "customers" as possible, the party system becomes, in the words of Lord Bryce, "the best instrument for the suppression of dissident minorities democracy has yet devised." For in a democracy the parties can hold a minority in check without stifling its creative function in the polity.

In the United States especially, a major party must find the common denominator among a large and varied group of voters, for it hopes to pluck the biggest plum of all at the next election—the Presidency. To elect a Chief Executive it must produce an electoral majority, and in doing so it forces adjustments among minority groups. As Carl Becker has said, "the fundamental compromises are, in the first instance, made not between the major parties but within them." Once having gone through this process of compromise in each of their camps, the two parties can offer the voters a relatively simple "either-or" choice rather than a confused array of alternatives. The two parties take up new ideas and attract new voters in order to survive in rigorous competition, and in doing so they display the inclusiveness that is central to democracy.

Such, ideally, are the benefits of a two-party system. But in the United States we do not enjoy these benefits because our two-party system breaks down in the legislative branch. What we have in Congress might better be called a multi-party system. Instead of a grand encounter between the rallied forces of the two great parties in House and Senate, the legislative battle often degenerates into scuffles and skirmishes among minority groups. On matters of vital public policy the major parties fail to hold their lines. They leave the field in possession of the pressure politicians and other members of Congress who are faithful to a locality or to a special interest but not to the national platform of their party.

A glance at virtually any House or Senate roll call will demonstrate the

Professor of Political Science at Williams College. Formerly Legislative Assistant, United States Congress. Author of *Roosevelt: The Lion and the Fox; John Kennedy: A Political Profile;* and co-author of *Government by the People*. The selection is from James M. Burns, *Congress on Trial* (New York, Harper & Brothers, 1949), pp. 33-44. Copyright, 1949, by Harper & Brothers. By permission.

inability of the party to enforce discipline even if it should try. In recent years the Democratic party has been especially vulnerable to the disruptive effects of bloc voting, but the Republicans too are rarely able to prevent at least a few of their adherents from crossing party lines. Party irresponsibility also affects the shaping of bills in committee and on the floor before the final roll call is reached. Indeed, it is hardly proper even to use the term "party responsibility" in discussing Congress, for the most rudimentary underpinnings of such responsibility do not exist. The party members in Congress have no common political program; as Pendleton Herring has said, "On the majority of issues the party takes no stand." And if there were such a program, little machinery exists in House or Senate to enforce it.

As a result of this situation we have in Congress, as far as public policy is concerned, a group of splinter parties. They are the Southern Democratic party, the Farmers' party, the Labor party, the New Deal party, the Liberal Republican party, the Veterans' party, the Silver party, and many others, along with the faithful adherents of the Republican and Democratic parties. A President of the United States is a Democrat or Republican, but key Senators and Representatives are more than likely to vote as members of a multi-party system.

This congressional patchwork is neither new nor accidental. It is rooted in American political organization. As national institutions, our parties are decrepit. They are coalitions of state and local party organizations, pulling together in awkward harmony every four years in an attempt to elect a President, going their own way the rest of the time.

The bosses who run the party machines are concerned more with private spoils than with public policy. The pressure groups that work through and around the parties are interested in their own designs, which may or may not coincide with the general welfare.

Lacking central control and discipline, the major party cannot hold its congressmen responsible to the broad majority of the voters in the nation who put the party into power. The national committee and chairman of the party have little control over national policy. They can do nothing for the congressman—he feels no responsibility to them.

Senators and Representatives can blithely disregard the national political platform; if they bother to pay it lip service, they usually do so because the program is so broad as to permit the widest leeway. In their states and districts the congressmen are responsible to fragments of the party—fragments that assume a variety of shapes under the impact of economic, sectional, ideological, and other forces.

Britain: Party Government in Action

We have much to learn from the English on this matter of political organization in a democracy. For over the course of many years they have forged a system of party government in the full sense of the term. That system serves three cardinal purposes. It unites the various branches of the government in order to carry out the will of a popular majority. It staves off the thrusts for power of minority groups. And as recent events have made clear, it offers the voters a genuine choice between two fairly distinct programs, rather than the

Tweedledum-Tweedledee alternatives that often characterize political encounters in the United States. . . .

The difference between the British system and ours is not, of course, one of personality, but one of basic political organization. There the party is supreme. Its role in national life is so meaningful and decisive that most Englishmen vote in terms of the party program and record, rather than on the basis of the personality, salesmanship, and promises of the individual candidate.

On first look such a scheme might seem to bear an authoritarian stamp. But in fact the British party system is an almost ideal form of representative government. By forcing candidates for Parliament to run on the national platforms, it gives the voter a real choice between two opposing programs. And the voter expects the successful candidate to support that program once he takes his seat in the Commons, for faithfulness to that cause is part of the bargain between voter, candidate, and party. The parties make no pretense of responding to every ripple of public opinion, or to every pressure of some organized minority. They have the more vital function of expressing the broad political aspirations of a majority of the people. While in this country Congress often seems to represent every group except the majority, in Britain the major parties, operating at the highest level of political organization, give the national welfare right of way over minority interests.

Despite the omnipotence of party in Britain, the legislature is not a dead letter. On the contrary, Parliament enjoys enormous prestige in that country and throughout much of the world. "It has occupied the centre of the political stage for centuries," Jennings has written. "So much of the history of freedom is part of the history of Parliament that freedom and parliamentary government are often considered to be the same thing." . . .

How to explain the contrast between party domination of the legislative in Britain and the constant disruption of party lines in Congress? The answer, in part, lies in the greater homogeneity of the British people that permits a more cohesive political structure. But that is not the whole answer, for Britain too has her sectional rivalries that cut across parties, her special interests that would use either party in their quest for influence. The main reason for that contrast is the organization of political power in Britain as compared with America.

The Conservative Party, and to an even greater extent the Labour Party, are centralized agencies. Ample control over funds, program, and the choice of candidates is lodged in the national office of each party. Because each is responsible for judgment and action on a national scale it requires its parliamentary members to vote in national terms. In contrast to the loose decentralized party structure of the United States, continually disintegrating in Congress under the impact of organized minorities, the British parties have the means of holding their M.P.'s in line.

It is not a matter simply of enforcement machinery. Discipline in the British party rests also on the fact that, except perhaps in times of fast-moving political developments, its program is a genuine compromise among the various groups making up the party. That program is carefully devised not only to consolidate the support of the rank and file but to attract independent voters as well. On the theory that an M.P. is more easily led than driven, it may even make concessions to local and sectional interests. But those concessions are never so fundamental as to endanger seriously the party's loyalty to its national program. It is precisely in this respect—at least as far as discipline in the legislative body is concerned—that the American parties differ so drastically from their British counterparts.

Make-Believe Majorities

Lacking the party rule that invigorates the British parliamentary system, Congress is often unable to furnish majorities for even the most urgent measures. While Parliament automatically musters enough votes to enact the program of the party in power, or else must face dissolution, the majority party in Congress cannot control its own rank and file. Hence bills in Congress get stymied in committee; they survive in one chamber only to stall in the other; a few fail in conference between Senate and House. When measures become marooned somewhere in the winding legislative channels, the villain of the piece may well be a minority group holding a strong position in committee or chamber, and the majority may be powerless to come to the rescue.

How, then, do bills get passed? Partly as a result of the appeals and threats of a President acting as chief legislator as well as chief executive. The President's control of patronage, his means of mobilizing public opinion, the authority of his office often enable him to drive measures through the legislature. In many cases, too, legislation is enacted largely as a result of bi-party coalitions responding to group pressures of some sort. Such important measures as the McNary-Haugen proposals for farm surplus control in the 1920's, the Smoot-Hawley tariff of 1930, the Economy Act of 1933, the National Industrial Recovery Act of the same year, the Employment Act of 1946, the Greek-Turkish aid bill of 1947, to name only a few, were passed by Congress as a result of bi-party support.

Least significant of all in the enactment of legislation seems to be the party as such. Half a century ago A. Lawrence Lowell set out to discover how often more than nine-tenths of the party members in Congress voted on the same side of a question. He found such party cohesion in less than eight per cent of the important bills considered by the Thirty-Eighth Congress, elected in 1862; and party influence on legislation was even less in other samples he studied.

Party cohesion is still slight today. And as for straight party voting—where every Republican lines up on one side of an issue and every Democrat on the opposite side—it would be difficult indeed to find an example of such voting on an important issue (aside from "organizing" the House or Senate) in the last quarter century.

In the absence of party voting Congress at times falls back on curious methods of producing majorities. One of these might be termed the "majority by threat." It is the most primitive of all means of securing a working combination. Rather than agreeing on a common program, blocs theaten to withhold their votes from bills backed by other blocs unless support is forthcoming for their own.

It is a sort of log-rolling in reverse, with the advocates of a measure saying in effect: "If you dare to vote against our bill, we will vote against yours." Thus in 1937 the labor bloc in Congress threatened to oppose agricultural legislation unless farm representatives supported a wages and hours bill. In considering the price control bill of 1942 the majority leader issued a similar warning to the farm group. There is a vast difference between such attempts to win votes through fugitive alliances in reverse, and the effecting of agreement by intra-party action based on awareness of a broad but genuine identity of interest.

Another crude method of achieving joint action on bills is "evasion by delegation"—the consignment of broad powers of decision to the President when congressional blocs cannot agree on a closely defined policy. Not because of the need for administrative discretion but because of its own failure to find a basis for agreement, Congress passes important policy-making powers on to the Chief Executive.

An example of such delegation is found in the consideration of the National Industrial Recovery Act in 1933; protectionist and anti-protectionist Senators were at odds over an embargo provision, and as a "compromise" they left the matter to the discretion of Mr. Roosevelt. This type of delegation is a form of legislative abdication.

Such behavior by congressional majorities should not be confused with genuine majority rule. It is one thing for a party to present its platform and candidates to the voters and, when vested with power, to make specific policies in terms of the approved program. It is quite another matter when bi-party majorities, operating without the endorsement of a majority of the voters, capture the machinery of law-making. Such majorities in Congress raise hob with the representative process. They have little responsibility to the people. They may gain their ends and disappear overnight. Their actions may be good or bad, but in either case the bi-party coalitions can ignore with impunity the national party platforms which, however vague and irresolute, at least must pass some kind of public inspection. Bi-party blocs cannot long provide real majority rule. The fleeting majorities that they muster are often not truly representative of the majority of the voters.

If these coalitions do not provide real majority rule, what does? In a democracy majority rule is assumed to be the best means of discovering and satisfying the "public interest." But what kind of majority? There are many types—the majority required to pass an amendment to the Constitution, that needed to push a bill through Congress, that involved in electing a President, and others.

Virtues of a Popular Majority

The most democratic, stable, and effective type of majority, however, is a popular majority—namely, one half of all the pooled votes throughout the nation, plus one (or more). This is a different sort of majority than that represented by a coalition in Congress responding to minorities organized in the various states and districts. "No public policy could ever be the mere sum of the demands of the organized special interests," says Schattschneider; ". . . the sum of the special interests, especially the organized special interests, is not equal to the total of all interests of the community, for there are vital common interests that cannot be organized by pressure groups."

Not only do pressure groups often fail to represent fairly the interests of many of their own members. Also in the interstices of the pressure groups one finds voting fragments that see their main stake in the well-being of the community at large. The marginal members of pressure groups, those who are not members of pressure groups, and the voters who are torn between allegiance to competing pressure groups—all these have significant weight in a nation-wide popular election, but far less weight in the sum total of local elections. In short, they are far more influential in choosing Presidents (even with the electoral college) than in choosing members of Congress.

Consequently, a popular majority tends to be more representative and democratic than a "segmented" majority. It is more stable too, because it cannot be manipulated by a few pressure politicians who are able to mobilize organized interests in various states and districts. A simple, mass, nation-wide, popular majority is often feared as leading to the "tyranny of the majority." Actually it is the safest kind of majority. Building a nationwide coalition of twenty or more millions of voters is no mean feat. It requires the presidential candidate to find a basis of harmony among diverse groups and to widen his platform to attract those groups and the millions of independent voters. A popular majority, like democratic politics in general, furnishes its own checks and balances.

The nation-wide political party is the natural vehicle for a popular majority. But it is also a rickety one. "Coalition fever" in Congress reflects the weakness of the American parties—their inertia, their slackness, their fear of assuming leadership. Organized interest groups display precisely the traits that the parties should display but do not—discipline over their representatives in office, alertness, the capacity to submerge internal differences in a united drive toward the more decisive group objectives. The special interests operate through either or both major parties with a cynical disregard for the party platform. "In a Republican district I was Republican; in a Democratic district I was a Democrat; and in a doubtful district I was doubtful," said Jay Gould, "but I was always Erie."

Similarly with the organized interests of today. It would be inconceivable for a dairy Senator from Wisconsin, a silver Congressman from Colorado, a cotton Senator from Alabama to desert their respective groups to uphold the party platform or the general welfare. In a Congress lacking sturdy party organization, many of the nation's pressure groups seem to enjoy greater representation than the majority of the voters.

J. ROLAND PENNOCK
Responsibility and Majority Rule

Although, as Lippmann recognized, parties in fact must be judged on the basis of very general and vague standards, it has been widely felt to be the ideal that they should take clear stands on specific issues. Then, of course,

Professor and Chairman, Department of Political Science, Swarthmore College. Author of *Administration and the Rule of Law* and of *Liberal Democracy: Its Merits and Prospects.* The selection is from "Responsiveness, Responsibility, and Majority Rule," *The American Political Science Review,* Vol. XLVI (Sept. 1952), pp. 790-807. By permission.

party members in the executive and legislative branches would have to adhere to these positions; that is to say, they would have to accept party "discipline," for otherwise the whole system would be ineffectual.[1] In other words, those who would stress the role of political parties as instrumentalities of government, as opposed to mere nominating devices, must emphasize the elements of program and discipline.

Now it is clear that party government, in this sense seldom very effective in this country, is today at a low ebb.[2] There are also evidences that voters are both less inclined to vote a straight party ticket and readier to shift their support from one major party to the other than once was the case. The 1950 election in New York City, in which a plurality of the voters supported a Republican candidate for Governor, a Democrat for Senator, and an Independent for Mayor, was a spectacular instance of what appears to be a growing tendency.[3]* It may also be noted that, even apart from the controversial literature that the American Political Science Association's committee report, "Toward a More Responsible Two-Party System," has elicited, numerous students of politics have come to question the workability of the party responsibility theory as applied to this country. Witness, for example, Professor Lasswell's statement that "America is far too diversified, articulate, and swift to abide the elephantine routines of party obligation."[4]

These facts pose a real problem. If the theory is sound, the situation must be bad. . . . In the first place, the system of government through the agency of disciplined political parties may run counter to the principle of majority rule, at least in the sense of responsiveness to the majority of the electorate. If the party that controls the legislature and executive submits to group discipline and supports whatever is agreed upon by a majority of its own membership, it is clear that this majority of a majority may itself represent only a minority of the electorate. (This problem can be ameliorated, of course, if the party

[1] There is a very extensive literature setting forth and defending this position. It has, of course, been given its most authoritative recent expression by the Committee on Political Parties of the American Political Science Association in "Toward a More Responsible Two-Party System," Supplement to *The American Political Science Review,* cited above.

[2] See Julius Turner, *Party and Constituency: Pressures on Congress,* The Johns Hopkins University Studies in Historical and Political Science, Series 69, No. 1 (Baltimore, 1951), pp. 28-34, and especially Table 3, p. 28.

[3] It is true that this phenomenon may itself be a consequence of the indeterminate nature of the parties; but it pretty effectively disposes of the argument that strong parties are needed because of the voters' inability to distinguish between individual candidates.

* The 1964 election produced ticket splitting on an unprecedented scale. Republican candidates for governor ran ahead of their party's Presidential candidate by 42% of the vote in Rhode Island, 27% in Massachusetts, 24% in Michigan and behind by 12% in Iowa. In the contest for the U.S. Senate, Republican candidates led their ticket by 32% in Hawaii, 20% in Vermont, 16% in Pennsylvania, 14% in Nebraska, and fell behind by 24% in Virginia and 13% in Florida. The greatest disparity was in the vote for Senator and Governor in Rhode Island and Washington. In order to elect Democratic Senators and Republican Governors at least one third of the voters split their ticket in Washington and over 44% did so in Rhode Island. See *Congressional Quarterly,* Vol. XXII, No. 45 (November 6, 1964). [Eds.]

[4] Harold D. Lasswell, *National Security and Individual Freedom* (New York, 1950), p. 120.

caucus refuses to bind itself by a bare majority vote.) Nor is such a hypothetical case at all improbable. There can be little doubt that it has recently been exemplified in Great Britain. The nationalization of steel is quite clearly an instance, for in 1950 a majority of the voters cast their ballots for candidates who were opposed to this program. It may even be questioned whether most of the nationalization program carried out between 1945 and 1950 had the support of the majority of the voters, in view of the fact that the popular majority for Socialism in 1945 was, at most, a matter of some 65,000 votes, from nearly 25 million.[5] Since the nationalization program was clearly the least popular plank in Labour's platform, their majority, if it is to be counted at all, must be attributed to other factors.*

It may be replied that the British voters cast their ballots with their eyes open and must be presumed to have preferred other parts of the Labour program *with* nationalization to opposition programs *without* it. This is perfectly true. It is also true, however, that to force such a harsh alternative upon the voters might not be necessary under a looser party system. And, furthermore, even with disciplined parties, clear programs, and sharp issues, one must be chary indeed about interpreting the results of national elections in terms of particular issues. Did the British electorate express itself in favor of Labour's nationalization program? In view of the fact that anyone who approved of the rest of Labour's program more than he disapproved of nationalization had no alternative but to vote for the latter along with the former, such a conclusion would clearly be unjustified; yet it is the conclusion called for by the orthodox theory.

As a footnote, we may observe that the system of direct primaries not only makes it more difficult to enforce party regularity in the legislature, but also makes the result of such enforcement more unrepresentative, more contrary to rule by the majority of the voters. And yet—and this, for present purposes, is the significant point—the institution of the direct primary is aimed at the objective of securing responsiveness to the majority will. The potential conflict between party government and majority rule, in other words, is once more indicated.

A second consequence of the party government system may be briefly noted: it encourages sharp reversals of policy. Again the case of British nationalization of the steel industry is in point. Clearly, in this instance, a decision of basic importance was taken, and acted upon, before it had a sufficiently strong basis in public opinion to be stable. While the example of steel is by no means unique,[6] it is exceptional. The reason it is exceptional, however, is that even in Britain parties, although disciplined, are not highly programmatic. More often than not a decision between them does not contribute greatly to the

[5] See the excellent analysis by R. B. McCallum and Alison Readman, *The British General Election of 1945* (London, 1947), pp. 250-253.

* In the election of 1964 the Labour Party, with 44.1% of the popular vote, won a majority of 4 in the House of Commons. The Conservatives polled 43.4% and the Liberal Party 11.2% of the vote. With disciplined parties the re-nationalization of steel may prevail in the House of Commons although the two parties opposing this measure received 54.5% of the vote in the election. [Eds.]

[6] Cf. the account of the effects of changes of governments on housing programs in Britain during the twenties, in Barbara Wootton, *Freedom Under Planning* (Chapel Hill, 1945), pp. 131-133.

clarification of the majority opinion about issues, because the parties hedge, or agree, on the issues. In other words, party responsibility does not necessarily mean greater clarity as to issues, as is frequently assumed to be the case. Under such circumstances accountability is not furthered.

An oft-remarked effect of disciplined parties is to diminish the power and importance of the individual legislator. Insofar as a collective judgment is substituted for individual judgment, the sense of responsibility of the individual legislator tends to be weakened. Furthermore, and this would be particularly true in the United States where legislative membership is not the sole avenue to top executive positions in the government, a system that weakens the position of the individual legislator would make it more difficult to interest able and responsible men in running for legislative office. It is time we looked at the other side of the picture. If the system of strong, programmatic parties tends to conflict with the objective of responsiveness to the will of the majority, encourages instability of policy or avoids this evil only on pain of losing its claimed advantage of greater accountability, and if it diminishes the number of responsible individuals in the legislature, what of the situation with weak parties? Is it unresponsive or irresponsible? Although these questions are too large to be given anything like a complete answer in this article, it is hoped that examination from the point of view of the preceding analysis can suggest partial answers.

The American system of loose and undisciplined parties which vie, on scarcely even terms, with pressure groups and other associations for giving expression to public opinion, is frequently referred to as government by consensus, or by "concurrent majorities." By permitting representatives to regroup themselves from issue to isssue, with relatively little regard for party affiliation, the very looseness of the American system fosters the maximum response to majority will. (It may be observed in passing that the total product of the legislative process under this system is likely to bear more resemblance to a patchwork quilt than to a woven blanket. The significance of this fact will be discussed at a later stage in the argument.) At the same time, the system of checks and balances tends to make it difficult to secure the enactment of legislation unless it is very strongly supported by public opinion generally or, in the absence of such support, at least is not vigorously opposed by any of the great pressure groups. It will be apparent that this second feature of American government considerably modifies the first (the party system itself). The two must be considered together.

What can be said of the legislative process under the system of government prevailing in this country? As Professor Bailey has said, "one generalization is that the process is almost unbelievably complex."[7] A bill is drafted, perhaps by a legislator, more likely by the staff of an administrative agency, a pressure group, or a policy-leading group such as the National Planning Association or the Committee for Economic Development, or by some combination of two or more such agencies. If it is an important bill with substantial backing, it will be the subject of extensive hearings and subsequent executive deliberations by committees in both houses of Congress. The testimony of experts from within and without the government, arguments and persuasive ef-

[7] Stephen Kemp Bailey, *Congress Makes a Law* (New York, 1950), p. 236.

forts of all kinds, the views of concerned administrative agencies and of the President, will all be presented. The staff experts of the congressional committees themselves are likely to play an influential role. There will be abundant opportunities for amendment at various stages along the legislative path in an effort to adjust conflicting interests; and especially if the measure is highly controversial, it is unlikely to emerge from the legislative mill in its original form. The result is typically the product of many minds and many interests, acting with the aid of extensive research facilities to bring to bear the relevant facts and to point out distortions or omissions in each other's arguments and factual presentations. The process is designed to maximize the opportunities for criticism, for fresh ideas and insights, and for achieving a result that will receive the widest possible acceptance. By this same token, however, the product is likely to be quite different from what would have been desired by any of the interested groups in the first instance—perhaps quite different from what any of them would still consider ideal. Final votes in all probability may not divide sharply along party lines. Such a situation, it is sometimes held, is bad because no "recognizable group, interest, or individual" can be held responsible.[8]

Now it seems clear that the legislative process we have just described involves considerable pains to achieve action that is responsible in the sense of being explicable, rationally supportable. Decision follows only after there has been ample opportunity for investigation and deliberation. The issue before us, then, is whether it is to be condemned because of a failure to meet the test of responsibility in the first sense—answerability. With respect to this question, several observations suggest themselves. In the first place, it would appear that the lack of an identifiable group, interest, or individual as responsible for a given act is certainly not *ipso facto* bad, because such a lack may indicate virtually unanimous support. Surely all unanimous-consent legislation is not to be condemned because of the absence of opposition! In other words, the kind of lack of responsibility that can be attributed to the legislative process as described above, as it operated in the enactment of the Employment Act of 1946, for example, is a function of facts that add to the generality of its acceptability. Responsibility for steel nationalization in England was clear; but it was purchased at the price of such low acceptability that the decision did not stick. Nationalization of the mines, not to mention "cradle-to-the-grave" security, on the other hand, had bipartisan support from the outset. It is hard to view with dissatisfaction the consequent diffusion of responsibility.

If we look again at the example of the Employment Act of 1946, it appears that the only way in which responsibility could have been made clearer would have been either to have had a different final Act—for instance, something more like the original bill—or to have had the whole idea defeated. That is to say, if the result had been more pleasing to one or the other of the (relatively) extreme groups, responsibility would have been clearer. Yet such an achievement would have been more displeasing to the defeated groups, less close to modal opinion, and therefore more likely to prove unstable. Certainly it would have been less representative of public opinion.

We must look further, however, at this matter of answerability. Its purpose, of course, is to enable the electorate to control policy. If something is done

[8] Bailey, p. 237.

which the electorate disapproves, there should be a workable way for the voters to express that disapproval and bring about a change. Legislation which has received very general approval, which represents a substantial consensus, is much less likely than bare majority legislation to become the subject of popular disapproval. The very process that beclouds accountability makes it less essential. Nevertheless, the proof of the pudding is in the eating; that which was approved as a bill may be condemned in operation. Suppose, for example, that we are again beset by severe unemployment and that the President and Congress, lacking the spur of the strong words of the original Full Employment Bill, take inadequate steps to meet the crisis. How can those who are concerned about the situation produce a change? Are they any worse-situated in this respect than they would be if the backers of the law that was enacted had all been members of the same political party, or were otherwise easily identifiable? It would not seem so. In any case, through pressure groups, letters to their representatives, and other avenues of opinion expression, the voters will express their demand for action. If satisfaction is not forthcoming before election time, they will demand that candidates at the primaries (and later at the general election) express themselves on the issue. Incumbents who are up for reëlection and have failed to press for action of the kind demanded will have to account for their failure. In all probability, they will have to campaign against candidates who promise to take a different line. It is unusual, in this country, for important legislation to be repealed, for the reason that transient majorities are seldom able to secure enactment of their projects; but the history of any major field of legislation is a history of major enactments followed, from time to time, by modifications in the form of amendatory legislation, frequently produced by just such a process as has been described.[9]

Exclusion (New York, 1950), for an excellent study of a successful repeal movement.

Indeed, the whole theory that the political party is the primary agency for the enforcement of responsibility with respect to particular issues appears to be somewhat outmoded in contemporary America.[10] When issues were relatively few and simple, it made a great deal of sense. Half a century ago, a few great but relatively simple questions, such as those involving tariffs and trusts, were predominant. It calls for no listing of the issues that face Congress today to prove that the present situation is very different. When each of the major parties must give some indication of its position on such issues as the Point Four program, military aid, the Brannan Plan, price and wage control, aid to education, and how to balance the values of security and liberty, it is unlikely that an election can give a clear indication of what a majority of the public wants.[11] Opinions cluster sufficiently to admit of considerable polar differentiation (but not polar opposites) in any given region, and a slight degree of such differentia-

[9] See Fred W. Riggs, *Pressures on Congress; A Study of the Repeal of Chinese*
[10] We may also hazard the guess that even in Great Britain its vitality is on the decline. However, the sharp class-consciousness of British politics contributes greatly to the solidarity of parties and to the difficulty of achieving government by consensus.
[11] It is true, of course, that attitudes on many of these subjects tend to cluster, so that a person's views on health insurance, for instance, may give a very good indication of what his position will be with regard to tax policy. Unless this situation existed, our party system would be completely unworkable. Even after making due allowance for this fact, however, the situation is incompatible with the existence and survival of programmatic major parties.

tion clearly exists nationally; but this is all that can be said. Southern Democrats will vote for a pro-labor presidential candidate only because they can elect Congressmen who will join with Republicans to defeat his policies. Nor is this situation confined to the Democratic Party. The basic condition it reflects has nothing to do with party organization or the form of government; it lies in the number and complexity of issues facing the country and the almost equal number and variety of group interests comprising the electorate. Such a plurality of views cannot be forced into the confines of dichotomous statement.

Moreover, today's public is far more articulate than were the enfranchised masses of half a century ago. Mr. Lippmann's choice between tweedledum and tweedledee is indeed about all that can be expressed in a general election, but this is only the beginning of popular expression in a modern democracy. Or, often enough, it is the last stage, giving formal sanction to policy determinations that represent responses to popular demands more discriminating and more varied than can be expressed at the polls. These determinations are often made in the selection of candidates. Once more, the device of the primary election is only the crude club that, in accordance with Friedrich's "law of anticipated reactions," leads party managers to find candidates who will achieve maximal voter response. Frequently, to be sure, a change in public opinion does not call for a change in the party candidates, much less a change in the party in power; all that is required is a shift in the position of the incumbents. Thus Senator Taft, not generally thought of as one of the most flexible members of Congress, has made numerous changes of tack;[12] one would have to be exceedingly naïve not to see a connection between these changes and Taft's appraisal of popular sentiment in Ohio and in the nation. Certainly readers of this article will need no reminders of the manifold avenues by which public opinions are brought to bear upon policy determinations in this country.[13] They operate at all levels, from the precinct to the administrator; they use all kinds of techniques and all manner of organization. And the difficulties of achieving democratic and responsible policy-making at the legislative level through the sole agency—or even the dominant agency—of the political party are greatly magnified when it comes to the administrative level, where so much of the policy-determining process today takes place.

Before concluding this discussion, we must deal with an objection that is commonly raised against weak political parties. It is said that they facilitate log-rolling in the legislature, since individuals and groups in the legislature are relatively free to shift alignments from issue to issue, and that they encourage competitive bidding for popular support by being free with promises of *largesse*. Since both of these practices might properly be designated as irresponsible, it is pertinent to consider them in the present context; and the two points are closely enough related to be treated together. That both conditions are far too characteristic of the American scene is painfully evident. The question of

[12] See his volume, *A Foreign Policy for Americans* (New York, 1951).

[13] For an excellent account of them, see David B. Truman, *The Governmental Process; Political Interests and Public Opinion* (New York, 1951). See also Riggs, *Pressures on Congress,* for a valuable case study. His discussion of the "catalytic group" is especially interesting (pp. 43-46). Riggs also gives concrete evidence in support of what was said about the effect given to intensity of demand by the American system (*Pressures on Congress,* pp. 197-199).

whether the existence of disciplined political parties, even if it were attainable, would improve the situation, calls for consideration. A glance at the record is enough to raise serious doubts about the proposed remedy. We may look at what happened in the United States during the early period of the New Deal, when President Roosevelt was in an exceedingly strong position with his party. The inconsistencies and contradictions that were involved in the New Deal program are an old story. Combinations in restraint of trade were at once attacked (strengthened anti-trust enforcement) and fostered (N.R.A.); credit was relaxed (Federal Reserve Board policy) and tightened (pressure from Treasury and F.D.I.C. inspectors); efforts were made to stimulate international economic cooperation (trade agreements program) while we wrecked the International Monetary Conference.[14] A relatively strong party leadership did nothing to prevent such mutually contradictory policies then; and there is nothing to indicate that today such leadership would prevent one arm of the government from spending public money to support the prices of agricultural commodities in a time of great farm prosperity, while other arms struggle to keep down wages and prices.

The situation in England is not radically different. The existence of strong parties there did not prevent the Conservatives in the 1951 campaign from promising to cut expenditures, but to maintain the social services and build more houses. Nor did strong parties hinder the Labour Government from pursuing inconsistent objectives, such as seeking to replenish capital goods while greatly expanding consumption, trying to stimulate private investment while threatening nationalization, and opposing nationalization of British interests abroad while pursuing a nationalization policy at home. Surely the vices of bidding for votes by pursuing opposing objectives at the same time are by no means confined to governments lacking disciplined parties.

As long as political parties can hope to defeat their opponents by winning the votes of groups from within the other party, or from independents, they will be tempted to try to do so by promising good things to the groups they are courting. In fact, the stronger is the discipline of a given party, the better it can afford to make such promises even when they run counter to the interests of some of its constituent elements. We are confronted here with a problem of democracy, not a problem of a particular party system.[15]

Moreover, a strongly disciplined, two-party system can be obtained only

[14] In some of these cases the mutually opposing policies were in effect at the same time, while in others they came in fairly rapid succession.

[15] It is not within the province of this article to offer solutions to this problem. It may be pointed out, however, that government by consensus places power in the hands of any major group to secure the modification of policies opposed to its interests. Where inconsistent programs merely defeat each other, no great harm is done to the general public. Where they do have a harmful general effect, other powerful groups are likely to be aroused and to take effective action. Moreover, the process of political education proceeds by experience. It is often discouragingly slow, but it is sometimes surprisingly effective. It is notable that, following the war, we did attain a balanced budget, and even a budget surplus. That the return of a semi-war economy has reversed the situation is hardly a matter for surprise. Whether any government can avoid some form of inflation under such conditions is doubtful. It is not irrelevant to remark, however, that it can come nearer to accomplishing this result if it is able to borrow from abroad.

by creating a sharp division of the population along class-conscious lines.[16] If the parties are evenly balanced, both competitive bidding for votes and frequent reversals of policy (assuming programmatic parties) are the natural results. If one party or the other gains marked ascendancy, the logical outcome is class rule and exploitation, rather than responsible search for the means of achieving the greatest possible general acceptability.

All of this does not mean that political parties are not important. They are one of the kinds of organization essential to the political process. They are indispensable; but without supplementation they would be woefully inadequate. Moreover, I am not concerned to argue whether or not some strengthening might be both possible and desirable. Some of the recommendations of the Committee on Political Parties are undoubtedly advisable. Possibly most of them are. But, and this *is* part of what I am concerned to argue, they would not accomplish as much as the Committee appears to believe; and it would not be desirable that they should. Tightly disciplined and programmatic political parties would be as inadequate for the task of political brokerage in America as the belief that we could create them would be unrealistic.

[16] Conceivably the same result could be obtained by a regional division, with the threat of civil war or national disintegration.

MURRAY S. STEDMAN, JR., *and* HERBERT SONTHOFF
Party Responsibility—A Critical Inquiry

Majority Rule or Consensus?

There may be wide agreement with the assumption in the Report of the Committee on Political Parties of the American Political Science Association[1] that *the present two party system is irresponsible,* although the precise meaning of "irresponsible" may vary greatly. Yet the essence of the assumption is that the American party system is an inadequate mechanism for translating popular wishes into action or specific policy. This charge rests on several beliefs which are open to considerable doubt. It assumes that the problem of popular responsibility is largely the mechanical one of organization, i.e., that responsibility

Dr. Stedman now teaches at Temple University. He formerly taught at Brown and Columbia Universities and Swarthmore and Trinity Colleges. He is the author of *Religion and Politics in America* and co-author of *Discontent at the Polls* and *The Dynamics of Democratic Government.* Herbert Sonthoff formerly taught at Swarthmore College. The selection is from their article "Party Responsibility—A Critical Inquiry," *Western Political Quarterly,* Vol. IV (September, 1951), pp. 454-468, *passim.* By permission.

[1] "Toward A More Responsible Two-Party System." Supplement to *The American Political Science Review,* Vol. XLIV, No. 3 (September, 1950), hereafter referred to as *Report.*

is "effective" only when there exist clear lines of responsibility.[2] If, as the allegation presupposes, responsibility is a matter of discipline, it becomes a fairly narrow and rigid premise. . . .

Centralized Parties

Another assumption is that *more responsible parties would require a very high degree of centralization of the internal party structure.* It has long been noted by students of Congress that party discipline on important issues is either weak or nonexistent. . . . The advocates of party government desire not only to facilitate executive-legislative co-ordination, but also to guarantee such co-ordination through highly centralized national parties.

Such a degree of centralization would be unprecedented in American history. However, only a centralized organization could possibly commit itself to and subsequently execute a specific program. To be successful, the national party would have to control rigidly such matters as patronage, finances, the nominating processes, and local party subsidiary organizations. The locus of power would be at the national rather than at the state or local level, as is the case today.

To make this change in power relationships, the national parties would have to possess sanctions to penalize recalcitrant state and local party leaders whose faith in the national "line" might otherwise waver. Such control would go far beyond the kind envisaged, for example, by the unsuccessful "purges" of 1938, since it would not be limited merely to congressional candidates. It would affect the nominating process generally. Quite logically, therefore, the advocates of party government stress the need for great control over local party organizations, including the power to refuse to seat "disloyal" elements at national conventions, and to exclude such elements from the national committees. Furthermore, as the *Report* states, ". . . consideration should be given to the development of additional means of dealing with rebellious and disloyal state organizations.

From this line of reasoning it follows that only the closed primary could be endorsed, for only if the national party could control the local nominating process could it choose candidates loyal to itself. It is clear that such a change would require tremendous revision of existing primary statutes. For example, the four states of Pennsylvania, New York, California, and Washington all use different procedures to nominate to statewide offices. It is hardly possible to determine objectively which of the four systems produces the best qualified candidates. Yet, most proposals for party centralization imply a drastic change of the primary, perhaps in the face of hostile public opinion.

The logic of the argument carries much further, however, than merely urging the closed primary or some particular form of it. It also implies a threat to the direct primary as an institution. If nominations are to be determined in

---

[2] "Party responsibility is the responsibility of both parties to the general public, as enforced in elections. Party responsibility to the public, enforced in elections, implies that there be more than one party, for the public can hold a party responsible only if it has a choice. . . . Party responsibility also includes the responsibility of party leaders to the party membership, as enforced in primaries, caucuses and conventions." *Report,* p. 2.

accordance with criteria established by the national party, it is difficult to see what, if any, purpose is served by retaining the direct primary. But the abolition of the primary would have particularly serious effects in those states, counties, and cities which are essentially one-party areas. In those localities, the only meaningful choice for the voter is between candidates of the same party. This may be true not only of the choice between candidates, but also of the choice between programs. The net effect of the disappearance of primaries in such a situation would be to take from the voter his only effective weapon for registering protest. In two-party areas the ending of the direct primary would presumably have less serious results, but such an action might create more problems than it would solve.

Proponents of stronger national parties usually contend that such parties would weaken the hold of local bosses and pressure groups, thus achieving a separation of national from local issues. To be sure, if local organizations lost control of the nominating process, their power would be drastically reduced. It does not follow, however, that a greater separation of national from state and local politics would be achieved. Neither as a matter of principle nor as a matter of applied psychology is there any great support for the contention that the national parties would lose interest in local patronage. It is probable that the first of the existing national parties to reorganize itself would be able to extend its patronage power into hitherto sacrosanct areas. In passing, the question may be raised whether the whole idea of party government is compatible with any kind of nonpartisan approach to local government. If the answer is negative, one can visualize a vast new area of spoils opening up for the benefit of national organizations.

The danger of the idea of party government is not that stronger national parties per se would be created. The danger is that the national leaders, in order to build an ever more extensive base for their own operations, might take over, so far as possible, all existing state and local organizations. Such a development would clearly imply more than the death of the direct primary. To propose it raises very serious challenges to the federal pattern itself and to many real advances made in state and local governments during the past half century. Quite possibly, because of its widespread character the centralized type of bossism, even under the name of "party government," might be even more objectionable than the existing local bossism.

In view of the almost proverbial contempt in which many professional students of politics hold party machines, a word in their defense may appear unusual. Still, we need to reflect on the positive services they perform in terms of the organization of local voter interest; and we should also consider the extent to which the usual connotation of the term "politician," which has become almost an expletive, impedes a realistic understanding of the functional role the politician plays in the crystallization of political opinion and in the political process on the grass roots level generally. It is an open question whether greater responsibility of the political party to the voter is obtained by strengthening the internal chains of party command through closer adherence to an obligatory party platform. The role of the local leader also requires examination; for another belief seemingly held by the proponents of stronger parties is that the public will abandon the idea of the politician as a broker. It is urged that the public will prefer an automaton committed beyond all else to the party program, and thus will cast aside the traditional politician's role of middleman. The implications of this line of thought are far-reaching. What is being urged is nothing less than a revolutionary transformation in the role and function of the party, of the candidates, and of the electorate. . . .

Disciplined Parties and Bipartisan Policy

Let us hypothesize a very strong, disciplined party system in this country. Furthermore, let us imagine that for one reason or another the President and one or both houses represent different parties. What might be expected to occur in the highly important area of foreign affairs? Bipartisanship on foreign policy is often criticized on three principal grounds: First, that it is undemocratic in that the minority party by its acquiescence may contribute to its own demise; second, that it is immoral in that a totally false and misleading impression of national unity may be created; third, that it is incompatible with party government.

It is the last charge which concerns us here and needs examination. Under our present party arrangement, with one or two exceptions the major parties have always co-operated in periods of external crisis. Cooperation was never a hundred per cent complete; but a working majority of each major party usually agreed with its counterpart as to the basic policies to be followed. Whatever opposition existed was likewise usually bipartisan; that is, it was not confined to a single party. A most significant demonstration of approval of bipartisan foreign policy, so obvious as often to be overlooked, occurred in the 1948 elections. Whatever else the presidential election of that year showed, it conclusively demonstrated support for Truman's "bipartisan" foreign policy by repudiating the proposals of Henry A. Wallace.

In principle, the proponents of party government are driven to the position that bipartisanship is per se an evil. They condemn the present practice where, instead of aligning themselves solidly on different sides of great policy issues, Senators and Representatives split into pro and con bipartisan blocs. Party allegiance becomes subordinate to sectional and regional interests.

Few would argue that such an arrangement is an unmixed blessing. On the credit side, however, it offers the tremendous advantage of very great flexibility. It does not suffer from the rigidity which the existence of a really strong, well-organized opposition party would entail. The basis of consensus is broad enough to allow for compromise and thus, among other things, plays down any process of aggrandizement by the President at the expense of Congress. Some critics of the existing system express the fear that our traditional form of government may break down as the result of a series of crises in which congressional inability to co-operate with the executive is followed by presidential dictatorship. These fears appear grossly exaggerated. Nevertheless, in the absence of cabinet responsibility under a parliamentary type of government, the prospect of a breakdown in democratic procedures would surely be aggravated rather than lessened by the existence of strongly disciplined and highly dedicated parties. If such a doctrinaire congressional-presidential impasse would be unfortunate in domestic affairs, it could conceivably be disastrous in the area of foreign policy.

✎ Section IX

PRESIDENT AND CONGRESS

The office of the President is the most powerful, responsible, and difficult in the democratic world. Understandably, the process of selecting the President, from nomination to election, has come under increasing scrutiny. In particular, the constitutional device of the electoral college for the selection of the President has been the subject of growing controversy, with proposals ranging from demands for reform to abolition.

The independent selection of the President (unlike the practice prevailing in parliamentary systems where the chief executive officer usually is selected by the party in power) inevitably leads to some tension between the Congress and the executive; tension lessened at times when one political party controls both of these branches of government. However, it is not uncommon for our system to provide a President of one political party and a Congress or one house thereof dominated by another. Furthermore, the role of the President in the legislative process, even when Congress is composed predominantly of members of his own party, is uncertain and varying. A consequence may be stalemate on important issues with responsibility sometimes difficult to fix. Under these circumstances, various measures to improve, or even drastically alter, legislative-executive organization and relations, to make government more responsive to the wishes of a "majority" as expressed in elections, have been advocated.

Among these measures have been suggestions for congressional reform urged by Senator Joseph S. Clark. On the other hand, John Fischer has emphasized the importance of conforming to "the unwritten rules of American politics" which involve an "informal, highly elastic, and generally accepted understanding" by the terms of which "all of the contending interest groups recognize and abide by certain rules of the game." This, he calls, the "Doctrine of the Concurrent Majority."

An issue which has commanded considerable attention in recent years, the uses and abuses of the filibuster, is also discussed in this section.

Electoral College: Reform or Abolition?

According to the Constitution, each state appoints "in such manner as the legislature thereof may direct, a number of electors, equal to the whole number of Senators and Representatives to which the State may be entitled in the Congress." The electors meet in their respective states and vote for President and Vice-President. In theory, although the electors are free to make any choice, in practice, with rare exceptions, all the electoral votes of a state go to the candidates who get the highest votes (pluralities) in the state.

The candidate who receives a majority of the votes in the electoral college for President and Vice-President, respectively, is elected. If no candidate for President receives a majority vote of the whole number of electors, then the House of Representatives chooses the President from the three highest candidates. But in choosing the president, the vote is taken by states, the entire representation from each state having one vote. *If no candidate for Vice-President receives a majority vote of the whole number of electors, then the Senate chooses the Vice-President from the two highest candidates.*

Many proposals have been made to amend the Constitution to reform or abolish the electoral college. The major ones would achieve the following objectives:

(1) The electoral college system would be abolished. The President and Vice-President would be elected at a general election by direct popular vote throughout the nation. If no candidate received at least 40% (according to the American Bar Association proposal) or a majority (according to S. J. Res. 4 in the Ninetieth Congress) of the total number of votes cast, a run-off election between the two highest contenders would take place. This general proposal has the support of Professor Paul A. Freund in the pages that follow.

(2) The office of elector would be abolished and each state would receive the number of electoral votes equal to the combined number of its Senators and Representatives. These electoral votes would be distributed automatically in each state, however, to each candidate in proportion to his share of the popular vote. At least 40% of the total electoral votes throughout the nation would be necessary to elect a candidate. If no candidate obtained 40%, the

399

members of the House and Senate, sitting in joint session and voting individually, would choose between the two highest (one variation specifies the three highest), a majority of the votes cast being necessary for election. This proposal (S. J. Res. 138 in the Ninetieth Congress), formerly known as the Lodge-Gossett amendment, is supported by Senator John Sparkman in the pages that follow.

(3) Each state would choose a number of electors equal to the combined number of its Senators and Representatives. Two of its electors would be elected at large and the balance within single-elector districts established by the legislature of each state. Before being chosen elector, each candidate would officially disclose the persons for whom he will vote for president and vice-president, which would be binding. If no candidate received a majority of all the electoral votes, then the members of the House and Senate, sitting in joint session and voting individually, would choose from among the three highest candidates. This proposal (S. J. Res. 12 in the Ninetieth Congress) is known as the Mundt plan and is supported by Senator Stennis in the pages that follow.

(4) The office of elector would be abolished and there would be cast for the persons receiving a plurality of votes for president and vice-president in each state the number of electoral votes equal to the combined number of its Senators and Representatives. If no candidate obtained a majority of all the electoral votes, then the members of the House and Senate, sitting in joint session and voting individually, would choose from among the three highest candidates. This proposal (S. J. Res. 58 in the Ninetieth Congress) was advanced by the Johnson administration and is supported by former Attorney General Nicholas de B. Katzenbach in the pages that follow.

(5) Finally, there is the proposal put forward in February 1969 by President Nixon which so far as initial distribution of the electoral college vote goes would be satisfied by the proportional plan outlined in (2) above or by the district plan outlined in (3) above. However, under the Nixon plan if no candidate received more than 40% of the electoral vote, a run-off election between the two top candidates would be held.

PAUL A. FREUND
For Direct Election

I support the proposal to eliminate the electoral college and substitute a system of direct popular election of the President and Vice President.
After some hesitation for reasons that I will indicate, I have become a convert
to this position because it seems to me to be right in principle and to have fewer
inequities and risks attached to it than the present system or any suggested
alternative.

It is right in principle because our highest national offices ought to be
filled by the popular choice of their constituency, the country as a whole. Whatever one's views on the problem of legislative districting, whether one approves
or condemns the reapportionment decisions, the presidential election is the
strongest possible case for equality of individual voting power, since it does
not involve representation in a collegial body but the choice of a single leader
of a great national constituency. The burden is on those who would subordinate
this basic principle because of collateral benefits or values that may be promoted by the present system. In fact, the balance of such values and hazards
seems to me to support, rather than to weaken, the case for direct popular vote.

I will not dwell on the historical accidents that have transformed the
electoral college plan into something totally unlike the concept of the framers.
The rise of political parties, with their designated candidates, converted the
electoral college into a group at best of useless ciphers and at worst of dangerous mavericks. Moreover, the other central feature of the present system—
the unit count in each State—came about in contravention of the original understanding, through the unilateral action of the largest States in the early nineteenth century, and a similar response by the smaller States in order to keep
such leverage as they could in the total electoral count.

Beyond the historical anomalies stand the practical inequities and risks
of the system.

1. The one objective that any democratic electoral system must achieve is
to avoid the election of a candidate who secures fewer popular votes than an
opposing candidate. The electoral college system offers no assurance of this,
and in fact three times in our history the election went to a candidate other
than the winner in the popular count. It has been said that this record is a good
one, showing that in 93 percent of our elections the popular winner was the
actual winner. This is like boasting that 93 percent of the planes leaving Washington airport arrive at their destination. . . .

2. The present system rests on an uneasy tension between opposing dis-

Distinguished constitutional scholar. Professor of law, Harvard Law School. Author of *On Understanding the Supreme Court* and *The Supreme Court of the United
States*. The selection is from testimony given by Professor Freund before the subcommittee on constitutional amendments of the committee on the Judiciary of the United
States Senate on May 18, 1967.

tortions of the popular will. On the one hand, the smaller States receive a bonus for their two Senators. On the other hand, the large closely contested industrial States are the chief prizes in the contest, enjoying a focus of attention and influence that is theirs because of the magnified value of even the smallest popular majority in the State.

3. The present system fails to reflect the actual strength of the voter turnout in each State, giving a premium to those States where the turnout is relatively light.

4. The value of an individual's ballot depends upon the State in which he votes. If his vote is for the candidate who loses in his State the vote is in effect discarded at this point. If his vote was for the local winner his vote is in effect multiplied in value. This may or may not affect the outcome but it is a hazard and is wrong in principle, like ballot box stuffing which may or may not change the result.

In the face of these deep-seated objectives, how does one explain any hesitation in supporting a drastic reform? The answer, it seems to me, is two-fold.

First, the electoral college system does serve to maintain the two-party system in making it relatively profitless for a splinter party to enter the race with no real prospect of capturing the electoral vote of one or more States. Thus the system has in fact served to promote an accommodation of interests within the major parties that ought not lightly be abandoned. The proper solution, I submit, lies in finding a means of preserving the values of the two-party system without the hazards and unfairness of the electoral college and its count. In my opinion this is done by a combination of factors. The two-party system rests also on the political structure of Congress, which would not be affected. Moreover, the method of nominating presidential candidates by convention will continue to give importance to diverse State interests and promote accommodations at this stage of the electoral process. For all its tiresome flamboyance, the national convention does serve a useful unifying purpose. Finally, and in my opinion highly important, is the proposal for a runoff election between the two highest candidates in the event no candidate receives 40 percent of the votes cast. This provision should serve as a deterrent to proliferation of political parties, which might amass a fair number of votes in the aggregate but which at best could look forward only to a final contest between the major party candidates. At that point the power of the splinter parties would, in my judgment, be less than in the case of a contingent election in Congress, where a few undecided votes leaning to a splinter party candidate would enjoy undue leverage in the outcome. The provision for a popular runoff seems to me not simply a collateral feature of the proposal but an integral and vital part, exercising a salutary reflex effect on the potentialities of splinter parties in the system as a whole.

The second reason for hesitation over reform has been the feeling that the present system, by giving admittedly excessive weight to small crucial groups in large closely contested States, has served to offset the undue weight of rural interests in a malapportioned House. It is not necessary to believe that the reapportionment decisions will work miracles to perceive that they do have an appreciable effect in strengthening the representation of urban and metropolitan areas. Beyond this, and in the longer view, there is the prospect that the concentration of population in the whole country will inevitably give greater weight to the urban constituency.

This trend was recently pointed out by a significant source—the Committee on Federal Legislation of the Association of the Bar of the City of New York —in endorsing the plan for a direct popular vote.

I may add I understand the association as a whole had the other day accepted the recommendation of its committee.

The committee observed:

"Whatever the system, we doubt that candidates and campaigns appealing primarily to rural or smalltown voters any longer have any real prospect of success in a country in which an increasingly larger majority lives in large cities or suburbs of large cities."

It remains to consider several alternative measures of reform.

The proposal sponsored by the administration at the last session had the merit of eliminating the human element in the electoral college and changing the method of the contingent election in the Congress. But it would have frozen in constitutional form the unit count in each State, thus preserving the inequities of the bonus to smaller States and the undue leverage of crucial groups in the large States.

The plan for election of electors by districts would achieve a closer correspondence between the electoral vote and the popular vote. But it would retain the bonus to smaller States, would retain the premium to States with a light voter turnout, and would still involve the risk that the candidate with the highest vote would not win the election. In addition, it would intensify the importance of district lines and thus aggravate controversy over gerrymandering and other problems of apportionment.

The plan for a proportionate count in each State of the electoral vote according to the distribution of the popular vote would provide a still closer correlation between the two, but would retain the inequitable features inherent in the allotment of electoral votes to the States and again would not take account of voter nonparticipation. Moreover, the arithmetic of the distribution of electoral votes might cause difficulty unless electors were to be fragmented into fractions of themselves.

The details of a popular election procedure are properly left to Congress, including provision for the conduct of a runoff election. The qualification of voters, and entitlement to be placed on the ballot, may be left to the States as at present subject to a reserved power in Congress to prescribe uniform criteria. Age and residence qualifications are the obvious factors which may at some time call for uniform regulation, and these are specified in the proposal as endorsed by the American Bar Association. Nevertheless, it should be understood that other qualifications, such as literacy, are likewise subject to the reserved power of Congress under decisions of the Supreme Court applying the equal protection clause.

If the committee recommends a plan of direct popular vote, it would be well to make clear in its report that specification of age and residence as items within the power of Congress is not meant to negate the authority of Congress to deal with other qualifications as well, where considerations of equal protection so require.

Senator HRUSKA. Mr. Freund, I notice in your statement that—and I say this advisedly and kindly—you speak somewhat disparagingly of the inequities of the bonus to the smaller States of two Senators. Of course, that was an inequity that was not only invited originally by the founders of our Republic, but it was necessary in order to achieve a Republic in the minds of many students of history.

I am wondering—how far would you press that concept of inequities of the bonus of two Senators to each State? Would you go beyond the electoral college? Little by little we are being inched—we smaller States are being inched out of existence, and after a while the lines between States will be of interest only to the Rand McNally Map Co., and that is about all, and to the tourist who will say, "Well, here once was a State, and now it is a part of the United States."

How far would you push that?

Senator BAYH. Would the Senator permit me to be so forward as to suggest that while he is answering that question—that he also answer if there is anything to be gained by the small States to compensate for the loss of the additional two Senators which are added to their popular vote? I think that is very, very significant to Members of the Congress, particularly the Senate.

Senator HRUSKA. The field is open, Professor. You can go as far as you want.

Dr. FREUND. Senator Hruska, in the first place, I certainly have no intention, in the slightest, of questioning the allocation of Senators by States. And when I speak of an inequity in the country, you are right, I am in no way begging the question, because I am assuming that our highest national office ought to be elected by a popular vote of its constituency, which I have assumed to be the United States.

But I would say this in respect to the original plan.

True, the electoral vote from the beginning included the two Senators allotted to each State. But it is not true that from the beginning those two electoral votes were added to the total of the winner in that State. And I think when that practice came about, extraconstitutionally, so to speak, it intensified, it magnified the effect of the two senatorial electoral votes. But I think more fundamentally, Senator, the smaller States have on balance been the loser under the present system. When I spoke of inequities—or distortions—I spoke of the tension between countervailing distortions. It seems to me clear that on balance the advantage given to the closely contested large industrial States under the present system outweighs the apparent bonus, if you will, to the smaller States in the two votes. . . .

It seems to me, however, if I may say so, Senator, that the big point is not the two-man bonus in the count. The big point is the leverage which the large States now have, and which under the direct vote system would presumably yield to a more national appeal on the part of the candidates and even perhaps to a wider range of selection of candidates by the conventions.

I certainly yield to no one in devotion to the federal system. But it seems to me that in the election of the President, we ought not to make our stand for the federal system.

The Presidency is our great single national office, and the importance of State lines, of State responsibilities, of State independence, experimentation, innovation, diversity, and all the rest, profoundly important as they are, seem to me to have a minimum of relevance to the election of the Presidency. And under the direct popular vote, the States would be equalized—that is to say, one man would be the equal of another wherever he resided. The campaigns would be pitched on a more national level.

Voter turnout would be encouraged. Even under the district system, if a district was predominantly of one party, there would continue to be discouragement of minority voting. . . .

It seemed to me that the real issues are the practical issues of the party structure—something that could not have been in the minds of the framers because there were no political parties, and indeed Madison and his colleagues distrusted parties or factions, as they were called.

Our problem really, it seems to me, is the Federal structure of our political parties, which I for one would not like to see lost, because I think our political parties reflect an accommodation of interests that has prevented the growth of ideological polarized splinter parties such as we see in some European countries, and which I, and I think most Americans, would be very very distressed to find taking hold here.

How are we going to preserve the Federal structure of our political parties under a direct popular vote?

It seems to me there are several answers.

One is that the elections for Congress will not be affected. They will continue to be on a statewide or districtwide basis, encouraging the continuance of territorial rather than ideological groups, encouraging, that is, the accommodation of interests under the umbrella of a party.

Furthermore, the national nominating procedure will not be affected, and there the State political organization will continue to have their say, and indeed if the larger States can unite within themselves on a candidate, they will continue to have the influence which they would insist a large State is entitled to, but at the stage of nomination, where there is a great deal of give and take before the candidate is selected.

So I don't think we are headed for nationalization of our political parties in the sense of obliterating the territorial nature which I thoroughly agree has an ameliorating effect on the sharpness of our ideological controversies. . . .

So far as the Negro vote is concerned—and we may as well be perfectly frank in talking of political realities—it seems to me that whatever artificially enhanced leverage they may lose by a change from the present system, they stand to gain by the incentive for a larger voter turnout in States where they have been passive for one reason or another. That is to say, the major parties, under a direct popular vote, will have much more encouragement to bring out a maximum of voting strength, and to appeal to what have been up to now latent votes. And, therefore, I would suppose that such loss as urban Negro groups may suffer in leverage in the big cities will be offset by a larger and more important participation on the part of qualified Negro citizens in States where they have not been appealed to by the major parties.

JOHN SPARKMAN
For Apportioned Distribution of Electoral Votes

I am pleased to have this opportunity to appear in behalf of Senate Joint Resolution 138. The resolution provides for the elimination of presidential electors, or probably better, the electoral college as such. But it provides for the same electoral votes on the same basis as at the present time. Each State would have the same number of electoral votes as provided for in the Constitution now. Each State's electoral votes would be divided among the candidates in proportion to their share of the total popular vote in the State. Of course, Mr. Chairman, you recognize that this is the old Lodge-Gossett resolution. . . .

Mr. Chairman and members of the Subcommittee, electors should be abolished, firstly, because they are outmoded. Our Founding Fathers were concerned and reasonably so, that a citizen in Georgia could not have the opportunity to evaluate the qualifications of a New England candidate whom he did not know and had never seen. They, therefore, interposed the elector, and set up the electoral college, an expectedly well-qualified man who could meet with others, far from the political arena, to select the man most qualified to be President. The development of modern communications, with radio and TV, has removed any need for the elector. Now the voter who reads and listens and watches is as qualified as the elector was 175 years ago.

Secondly, electors and the unit rule should be abolished because the system disfranchises thousands of voters in every presidential election in every State. With the present "winner take all" system, citizens' votes for electors for losing candidates have no real effect.

Thirdly, change is needed because the present system tends to perpetuate one-party government in some States. Under "all or nothing" election results, there is little incentive for the minority party to wage a vigorous campaign in one-party States. Furthermore, the candidates very often do not bother to visit those States at all. The candidates of the dominant party in these States may take them for granted and the opposition candidates may avoid them as being without vote potential.

Fourthly, and perhaps most importantly, the system should be changed because it leads to the focusing of campaigns and issues in a few populous States. Furthermore, the major party candidates are usually nominated from these same States with their large bloc electoral votes.

We in the Congress are certainly able to testify to the fact that presidential campaigns are big-State oriented. The proposals which we consider here in any election year may have limited relevance to the platform planks adopted

United States Senator from Alabama. The selection is from testimony given by Senator Sparkman before the Senate subcommittee on constitutional amendments on March 1, 1966.

by both parties in the summer and to the issues raised by the two major candidates in the fall. Nonetheless, presidential campaigns will be oriented toward the issues and the needs of the heavy voting States—the States with large metropolitan areas—just as long as the "winner take all" system prevails for the counting of State votes for President.

On the other hand, a proportionate division of the electoral vote according to the popular vote in each State would require that candidates give attention to the issues of interest to citizens in all areas of the country.

If the needed change is made, then presidential candidates will give roughly the same attention that the Congress gives to the problems of, for example, the Southeastern States, Rocky Mountain States, Great Plains States, and the States in upper New England.

Mr. Chairman, political science professors and others who have argued against the Lodge-Gossett proposal have lost some of the force of one argument they used to make against it. They once contended that non-urban populations enjoyed disproportionate influence in the House of Representatives and in State legislatures and, therefore, that it was fair for urban areas to enjoy stronger influence in electing the President. If that argument was ever valid, and I certainly do not concede that it was, the Supreme Court has in recent years destroyed it. The Court has adopted a one-man, one-vote rule to direct the reapportionment of both houses of State legislatures and the redistricting of congressional seats. Now, perhaps, the political scientists will agree that populous, urban States have an unfair advantage in the electoral college system. . . .

Senator BAYH. May I ask you to explain your thinking about the criticism that has been levied at this with reference to the small States? If you have a division where it is not a winner take all, then the emphasis is on the spread, is it not? In other words, the width of the margin that exists between the winner and the loser is really more important than the total number of votes, which it seems to me might cause the trend to be away from campaigning in the large States.

For example, I believe it was the 1948 election where President Truman received a wider margin in the State of Georgia than he did in half a dozen of the larger metropolitan States put together. So if he could go into Georgia, for example, and with less effort increase the size of that margin more than you could, say, in New York, would this not create a big tendency away from the popular vote?

Senator SPARKMAN. No; I do not think so, except insofar as campaigning is largely concentrated now in the big populous States—I think it ought to be spread over the entire country.

I agree, I think it is a good political principle to campaign where the votes are most easily obtained, and naturally, the candidates would do that. But it seems to me that now we have a rather heavy concentration of campaign effort in the big populous States, not only the campaign effort, but also the selection of candidates. I think there is a tendency to select candidates from there because they would much rather think of the great bloc of votes from New York State or California rather than to think of the votes that they will get in 6 or 8 or 10 States necessary to make up for that. And under this plan every vote would be counted, big or small.

JOHN STENNIS
For the District System

One of the most long-standing failures of our present electoral college system is that it makes possible the election of a President who did not
receive a majority, and indeed even a plurality, of the popular votes. Thus it is
that on fourteen occasions we have elected a President by a minority vote . . .
amazing as this may seem, almost one-third of our chief executives have not
been the choice of a majority of those voting in these national elections. In
1824, for example, Andrew Jackson received more popular votes and more
electoral votes than his rival, John Quincy Adams, but the election was thrown
into the House of Representatives which chose Adams. And in 1876 and 1888
the person elected received fewer popular votes but more electoral votes than
the candidate of the other major party.

In addition to these three elections in which the candidate elected did not
receive a plurality of the popular votes, there have been eleven other elections
where the person elected received more votes than his closest rival but did not
receive an absolute majority of the total popular vote. These elections (showing
the year, winning candidate and his percentage of the popular vote) are: 1844,
Polk, 49.56%; 1848, Taylor, 47.35%; 1856, Buchanan, 45.63%; 1860, Lincoln,
39.79%; 1880, Garfield, 48.32%; 1884, Cleveland, 48.53%; 1892, Cleveland,
46.04%; 1912, Wilson, 41.85%; 1916, Wilson, 49.26%; 1949, Truman,
49.51%; 1960, Kennedy, 49.48%.

Even when the winning candidate receives a majority of the popular vote
as well as more than half of the electoral votes, the disparity between the
two is often great. In 1936, for example, President Roosevelt received 60% of
the popular vote and 98% of the electoral vote; General Eisenhower received
83% of the electoral vote in 1952 but only 55% of the popular vote. And in
1960, the late President Kennedy's popular vote exceeded that of Vice President Nixon by only two-tenths of 1% of the total vote, but he received 300
electoral votes to 223 for Mr. Nixon. In the State of Illinois, Mr. Kennedy received less than 10,000 votes more than Mr. Nixon out of almost 5 million
votes cast, and yet he received all of the State's 27 electoral votes. If a district
plan similar to that embodied in S.J. Res. 12 had been in effect, and assuming
that the districts would conform substantially to the Congressional districts,
Kennedy would have received 15 electoral votes and Nixon 12 votes.

Endless statistics could be cited, Mr. Chairman, to illustrate the inequity
of the present unit system, but I do not believe this is necessary. Suffice it to
say, history proves that it is not unusual for a President to be elected without
having received a majority of the popular vote throughout the Nation. Such a
situation should not be permitted to exist in a great democratic republic.

United States Senator from Mississippi. The selection is from a statement submitted by Senator Stennis to a Senate subcommittee on March 1, 1966.

The unit method of casting electoral votes also has the effect of disfranchising those voters who mark their ballot for the losing candidate. In the election of 1944, for example, Mr. Dewey received 49.1% of the popular vote in Michigan but, because President Roosevelt received 50.1%, not one single electoral vote went in Dewey's column. The popular vote of Mr. Dewey was not translated into electoral votes, which actually determine the winner, and so the ballot of all of these people who voted for Dewey, in effect, were not counted.

The two evils of the unit system which I have just described are serious, Mr. Chairman, but I believe there is an even greater danger inherent in this system. This third pitfall has developed because of the great concentration of population in the large industrial states and urban areas of our country. In recent years, hundreds of thousands of our citizens have migrated to these areas with the result that the eleven largest states and any one other state now have a sufficient number of electoral votes to carry a presidential election. These eleven largest states are New York, California, Pennsylvania, Illinois, Ohio, Texas, Michigan, New Jersey, Florida, Missouri, and Indiana.

Before discussing the influence which these large states have on our national election, let me emphasize that I do not suggest that the major population centers should be denied proper representation. It would be just as undemocratic to take from these areas their proportionate electoral vote as it would be to continue using the present system. But I believe a system can be devised which will more nearly guarantee proper representation to all areas but which will also insure that the total electoral vote accurately reflects the total national popular vote. An examination of the most recent presidential election substantiates this contention.

In 1964, there were approximately 69.6 million popular votes cast throughout the Nation. Of this total, 41.5 million votes were cast in the eleven largest states which I have previously mentioned. Under the unit system which now exists in all states, a simple majority or possibly only a plurality of these 41.5 million votes would determine which candidate received the 268 electoral votes to which these eleven states are entitled. Therefore, approximately 20.8 million votes, or less than 30% of the total national vote cast, could have controlled the election. And we must remember also that within these eleven states the total state-wide vote is largely controlled by one or two heavily populated urban areas.

This tremendous concentration of political power in a few states is a relatively recent historical occurrence in our country, but it will continue to be more pronounced and significant as the migration to urban population centers continues. It is not inconceivable that within a few more years only eight or nine states will completely dominate the election of our President and Vice President unless the electoral system is reformed to a significant extent. And, I repeat, this can be accomplished without denying proper representation to any area of the nation.

I have been deeply concerned with this problem since I was first elected to the Senate in 1947 and for a number of years have cosponsored with Senator Mundt and others a proposal which is popularly known as the "district plan." This proposal is embodied in Senate Joint Resolution 12 which is now before this committee for consideration. I believe this proposal presents a fair, just and workable alternative to the system under which we now select our President and Vice President.

Under this proposal, each state would continue to be entitled to a number of electors equal to its representatives in Congress. The people of each State would be guaranteed the right of choosing these electors, two of whom would be elected from the state-at-large and a number equal to its Representatives in the House would be elected within single-elector districts. The resolution provides that these single-elector districts, which shall be established by the respective state legislatures, must be composed of compact and contiguous territory and must contain as nearly as practicable the number of persons which entitle the state to one Representative in the Congress. The electors shall be pledged in advance to specific candidates for President and Vice President.

The adoption of the district plan would result in a much more representative division of the electoral vote on a nation-wide basis than now occurs under the unit system. A state's entire electoral vote would not go to the candidate receiving a plurality of the popular vote, but would be divided according to the vote in each district. This would reduce to a significant degree the size of the voting unit and therefore more accurately reflect voter opinion. In those states with more clearly defined divisions of thought, and this is where the greatest inequities appear under the unit system, the district plan would be particularly effective. In the election of 1960, for example, the electoral vote in New York would have been split 25-20, in California 19-13, in Illinois 15-12, in Pennsylvania 17-15, and in Michigan 10-10. Each of these states would retain the same total number of electors to which it is rightfully entitled, but a bare majority or even a plurality of voters could not control the entire electoral vote.

I am aware of the argument that the small states have a disproportionate number of electoral votes because of the fact that each state has two electoral votes regardless of the size and population of the State. However, this objection applies to any system which retains the electoral vote principle. I personally believe the writers of the Constitution were wise in adopting this principle and that it should be retained. At any rate, I am confident that neither the Congress nor the respective states would ever agree to eliminating this principle which is so basic and essential to the preservation of our Federal system of government. So this argument is not valid as a specific objection to the district plan.

In addition to accomplishing the basic purpose of establishing a district plan for casting electoral votes, S.J. Res. 12 also incorporates a very important change in the method of choosing the President and Vice President in the event that no candidate for these offices receives an absolute majority of the total number of electoral votes. The 12th Amendment now provides that in such an event the House of Representatives shall choose the President from the three candidates having the highest number of electoral votes. In this election, each state has only one vote. A similar procedure is followed in the Senate if no candidate for Vice President receives a majority of the electoral votes.

S.J. Res. 12 would change this procedure to provide that the House and Senate, meeting jointly with each member having one vote, would select the President and Vice President in the event that no candidate for either office receives a majority of electoral votes. Also, the ultimate selection of these officers would be insured by the requirement that the choice on the fifth ballot, if necessary, shall be between the two persons having the highest number of votes on the fourth ballot.

I believe everyone will agree that these are desired changes in the method of selecting the President and Vice President in the event that no candidate for those offices receives a majority of the electoral vote. It is certainly more democratic to allow each state to cast one vote for each of its congressional members rather than giving each state only one vote, regardless of its population. Likewise, it is highly important to insure the ultimate selection of these officers within a time certain.

NICHOLAS DE B. KATZENBACH
President Johnson's Proposals

The Present System

The manner of selecting the President gave the framers of the Constitution much difficulty. Direct election by the people, it was feared, would produce turmoil and confusion and, in addition, deprive the smaller States of any effective voice. Election either by the Congress or by the State legislatures, on the other hand, was opposed because it would deprive the President of independence. The compromise adopted was to provide for election of the President by an independent body of electors, appointed in each State, in such manner as its legislature might direct, to serve that one function only. It was hoped, as Hamilton noted, that distinguished citizens would be chosen as electors, and that they in turn, exercising an informed and independent judgment free from the stress and excitement of political campaigns, could be counted on to select a person well qualified for the office. The Federalist, No. 68 (Cooke Ed), pages 458-460. The fears of the smaller States were allayed by giving each State an extra two electors regardless of size, and the independence of the President was to be assured by the transience of the electing body.

In practice, of course, the electoral college system never operated in the manner envisioned by its framers. Few voters knew or cared who the electors were, and they were seldom selected in a manner inspiring confidence in their superiority of judgment. Instead, national parties arose and the electors became mere figureheads pledged to cast their votes for the party nominees on whose ticket they ran. State laws providing for the short ballot and related devices institutionalized the practice. See Wilkinson, "The Electoral Process and the Power of the States," 47 A.B.A.J. 251, 253-254 (1961). The end result was the system we know today, with the people voting directly for the President and Vice President and with all of each State's electoral votes being cast automatically for the candidate receiving the greatest number of the popular votes in that State.

Formerly Attorney-General of the United States in the Johnson Administration. The selection is from testimony given by Mr. Katzenbach before a Senate subcommittee on March 9, 1966.

Deficiencies

The system thus evolved, though not the original intent of the framers, has by now become deeply imbedded in our system of government. For the most part, it has worked well. Its most serious deficiency is simply its lack of constitutional sanction, a lack which makes it both dependent on the voluntary action of the States and subject to possible manipulation by the electors.

The risk that a State or its electors will depart from established custom and exploit the constitutional independence of the electors is not fanciful. In 1948, a Tennessee elector, running on both the Democratic and States Rights tickets, voted for the States Rights candidate even though the Democratic candidate had a substantial plurality in the State. In 1960, Alabama and Mississippi elected 14 unpledged electors who then voted for a person who was not even a presidential candidate—as did also an Oklahoma elector who had been elected on the Republican ticket. New York Times Election Handbook 1964, page 122. To be sure, such departures from the customary practice have been rare. But so long as there exists the possibility of unpledged electors, or of electors who ignore their pledge, there will always be a grave risk that their constitutional independence will be exploited and that their votes, however few, will be manipulated in a close race to block the election of a major candidate in order to throw the election into the House of Representatives.

The constitutional independence of the electors would create a particularly acute problem, moreover, were a candidate to die after the November elections but before the electors voted in December, as did Horace Greeley in 1872. The result would be to free the electors from their pledge and leave them free to vote as they might choose: they could vote for their party's candidate for Vice President or some other person designated by their party; they could vote for someone of their choosing; or they could simply scatter their votes among the other candidates, as did most of the Horace Greeley electors. If no other candidate had a majority of the electoral votes, the result would be to place the balance of power in the selection of a President in a group of men who had been elected merely as figureheads.

The electoral college system of electing a President having been replaced in practice by a direct popular election, there can be no justification for continuing the constitutional powers of the electors, powers which today perform no legitimate function but nevertheless remain as a potential means of frustrating the will of the people.

Senate Joint Resolution 58

Senate Joint Resolution 58 would remedy that defect in the existing Constitution by abolishing the office of elector and requiring the electoral votes of each State to be cast automatically for the candidates receiving the greatest number of votes in that State. Thus it would do no more than write into the Constitution the system that now exists in practice but without constitutional protection. The electoral votes given to each State would be unchanged and, as now, they would be cast as a unit for the candidates winning a plurality of that State's popular vote. The only effect would be to eliminate the latent power of a State or of an individual elector to depart from the customary practice. The need for that change is, I think, almost universally conceded, and it is the very minimum that is required to protect presidential elections from the grave risks to which they are now exposed.

Other Proposals

The other proposals before the subcommittee would go much further. Instead of merely giving constitutional protection to the existing system of electing the President, they would change the basic system itself. The proponents of such changes, it seems to me, have a heavy burden. The existing system is familiar and has worked well, and there does not now exist any widespread sentiment in favor of a change in its basic structure. Any change in the distribution of electoral power must inevitably create new forces that would significantly influence our political institutions. The effects of such changes can never be fully predicted; and those that can be seem to me undesirable. On a matter of such basic importance to the welfare of our country, we ought not abandon the familiar and workable for the new and untried without the clearest sort of demonstration of its inadequacies, and in my judgment no such demonstration has been made.

1. One of the most popular plans—which, indeed, once passed the Senate in 1950, although a motion in the House to suspend the rules for its consideration was overwhelmingly defeated—is the "proportional" plan, introduced by Senators Sparkman and Saltonstall. Under it, the electoral votes of a State, instead of being cast as a unit for whoever received a plurality of the popular vote in that State, would be divided among the candidates in proportion to each candidate's share of the popular vote. The effect would be similar to a national plebiscite in that each voter's vote would directly affect the final national tally; it would differ in that the weight accorded each vote would differ from State to State, for example, a voter in Alaska would in effect cast one twenty-thousandth of an electoral vote.

There are at least two major predictable effects that such a proposal would have. First, it would greatly reduce the importance of the States in the election and work a significant shift in political power from the States with large urban populations, where the two-party system is strongly competitive, to the rural States and perhaps to those few States with historically a one-party political structure. The extra two electoral votes given to each State regardless of population already give the smaller States power disproportionate to population, but it is now counterbalanced somewhat by the effect of the unit rule.

Were the unit rule to be abolished while retaining the present distribution of the electoral votes, the imbalance would be greatly magnified. Moreover, the small rural States now enjoy an advantage disproportionate to population in representation in the legislative branch, and depriving the large urban States of the power they exercise in presidential elections would leave them with too little influence in our political system.

Considering the legislative and executive branches together, the present system has produced a delicate balance of power among the States. Whatever its defects in theory, it has proved satisfactory in practice, and it can be tampered with only at a grave risk of seriously upsetting the balance with results we cannot foresee.

The second predictable effect of the proposal is that it would weaken the two-party system and encourage the development of splinter groups. At present, minor parties can have little effect on presidential elections, since they must capture an entire State's electoral votes to have any impact on the final outcome.

Under a proportional system, however, just as under a national plebiscite, each vote for any candidate would enter into the final tally, thus permitting a relatively small minority vote, distributed among a number of States, to block the election of either of the major candidates. Even were the requirements of an absolute majority of the electoral vote to be relaxed—as some have proposed—there would remain a much increased incentive for the development of splinter groups or a third party.

In theory, of course, there may be arguments in favor of a multi-party system. Once again, however, I would take experience as our guide, and the experience of countries with multiparty systems can hardly be reassuring. The two-party system works and works well, and I would view with the greatest concern any change in the method of electing the President that would tend to weaken or undermine that system.

Because it would both seriously affect the existing balance of power among the States and jeopardize the two-party system, therefore, the proportional plan seems to me to be clearly objectionable.

During the 1956 debates on electoral college reform, Senator Kennedy summarized the disadvantages to proportional voting plans as follows (102 Congressional Record 5251):

> The importance of State lines in presidential elections would be severely reduced; the likelihood of Presidents being elected with less popular votes than their opponent would be greatly increased; the prospects for obtaining a President with broad experience in a large State would be reduced; the overrepresentation in the Government of the small rural areas of the country would be tremendously increased; the effective electoral strength of most States would be greatly distorted; voting interest in those States would be sharply reduced; the one-party system in other States would be greatly intensified, with incentive for fraud and additional franchise restrictions; Federal voting standards would be invited; splinter parties would be greatly encouraged; hairbreadth elections, with all of their divisive effects, would be made more frequent; the chances for victory of the Republican Party, and consequently the strength of the two-party system, would be permanently ended, and the election of a President and Vice President from different parties would again be made possible.

2. A slightly different proposal is the "national-election" plan under which electoral votes, and the role of the States, would be eliminated entirely and the President would be elected directly by the people in a nationwide election. . . . Since it differs from the "proportional" plan only in that votes in every State

would have the same weight, the same basic objections are applicable to it. Since the discard of the unit rule would be accompanied by an elimination of the disproportionate number of electoral votes given smaller States, the shift of power from the larger urban States might be somewhat less, but it would still be subtantial, and, if anything, the plan would weaken the two-party system even more than the proportional plan. Indeed, I would say that it almost assures splinter parties.

An additional feature of the national-election plan that would probably be objectionable to most States is that there would be strong pressures on the States to lower voter qualifications. While I am in favor of eliminating obstacles to the franchise, the national-election plan would also increase the pressure for national voting standards. With the popular vote in each State being translated into a fixed number of electoral votes regardless of the number of persons voting, differences in voting qualifications among the States do not directly affect the ultimate outcome. But with the popular vote being counted on a national basis, the number of persons voting in each State would directly determine the influence of that State's voters on the final outcome.

Unless uniform voting qualifications were adopted, therefore, the States with more restrictive qualifications would be disadvantaged. Moreover, if the election is to be a truly national one, with State boundaries otherwise playing no part, it would be difficult to justify permitting 18-year-olds, for example, to vote in one State but not in another. While I would not object to having 18-year-olds vote, many State legislatures do not as yet share that view.

Apart from these objections, it is most unlikely that this plan, regardless of its theoretical appeal, will be adopted since it deprives the small States of the advantage they now enjoy of having two extra electoral votes (for their two Senators) regardless of their population. The subcommittee will recall that in 1956, the Senate decisively defeated a proposed amendment embodying the direct-election plan—the vote was 66 to 17.

3. The third proposal for changing the method of electing the President is the "district" plan, an example of which is embodied in Senate Joint Resolution 12, introduced by Senator Mundt and eight cosponsors. Under that proposal, each State would continue to have the same total number of electoral votes, but only two of them would be cast on the basis of a statewide election and the others would be cast on the basis of an election in each congressional (or equivalently sized) district.*

To some extent, the district plan would move in the opposite direction from the national-election and proportional plans. Whereas the latter would enlarge the unit in which popular elections are held from the State to the Nation, Senate Joint Resolution 12 would narrow it from the State to the congressional districts. Instead of focusing on national problems in a national campaign, the emphasis would to a considerable degree be shifted to matters of local concern within a particular district.

I see no point to localizing a national election. The principal effect of Senate Joint Resolution 12 would be, I judge, to expand the influence of rural

* Senate Joint Resolution 12 would not abolish the office of elector, but the electors would be constitutionally bound to vote for the candidate on whose ticket they ran, producing the same effect.

areas at the expense of the cities. To some, of course, that is its virtue, but to others it is a vice. Certainly, however, there is not now a consensus in the country that the rural areas are underrepresented in the government, at either the State or National level.

Senate Joint Resolution 12, to be sure, requires the "elector" districts to be "compact and contiguous" and to be as equal as practicable in population. But even assuming that restriction could be enforced, there would remain an almost infinite number of ways in which a State could be divided into compact and contiguous districts.

Senator Kefauver, after a careful study of the matter, concluded that even with requirements of compactness and contiguity, boundaries could "still be drawn for political advantages." And while, as he also noted, "neither party has a monopoly on this sort of thing," densely populated metropolitan areas "are obviously more vulnerable to this divide-and-conquer partitioning." Kefauver, "The Electoral College: Old Reforms Take on a New Look," 27 Law & Contemp. Prob. 188, 199 (1962).

Finally, since a minority or splinter party would need to capture only a district to influence the final outcome, the district plan, like the other plans—though perhaps to a somewhat lesser extent—would encourage the development of third parties or splinter groups and weaken the two-party system. I have already voiced my concern at any such development, and that objection is likewise applicable to the district system.

In addition to those specific objections to the plans to change the method of electing the President, I should like to reemphasize the point that any change in so delicate a matter is likely to have influences, for good or ill, that cannot wholly be foreseen. That alone is enough to counsel against any such change until the demonstrated need for it has become overwhelming, which surely is not the case today. I would add one practical point: Whatever their theoretical merits, I think it clear that there is not now, nor is there likely to be, any consensus in favor of one of the competing plans for fundamental changes.

In my judgment, the reforms proposed by Senate Joint Resolution 58 are the most there can be any hope of having adopted. Those reforms are urgently needed and their desirability, as far as they go, is almost universally conceded. While I respect the views of those who like to have more thoroughgoing reforms, it is my hope that their advocacy of more drastic changes will not be at the expense of jeopardizing the attainment of the beneficial objectives of Senate Joint Resolution 58, for which there is both a great need and overwhelming public support.

The Contingent Election

The second area in which reform is needed is in the method of selecting the President and Vice President when the popular vote is indecisive—i.e., when no candidate receives a majority of the electoral votes cast on the basis of the popular vote. To be sure, an election has actually been thrown into the House only twice in our history—in 1800 and 1824—and the first instance was attributable to a defect that has since been corrected by the 12th amendment.

The threat is ever present, however, and in 1948 a contingent election was avoided by only the narrowest of margins: a change of less than 0.6 percent of the votes for Mr. Truman in two States would have made the electoral vote indecisive and thrown the election into the House. On so crucial a matter as the election of the President, even remote contingencies should be provided for. Notwithstanding the relatively slight likelihood of an indecisive electoral vote, therefore—at least under Senate Joint Resolution 58—we should take care to correct, also, whatever deficiencies exist in the contingent election system.

At present, if no candidate received a majority of the electoral vote, the President would be selected from among the three leading candidates by the House, with each State delegation having one vote (decided by a plurality vote of its members) and with an absolute majority being necessary to a choice. The Vice President would be selected from among the three leading candidates by the Senate, with each Senator having one vote and an absolute majority again being required.

The most objectionable feature of that system is the equal vote given to each State. It gives a State with a population of 250,000 the same power in the election of the President as a State with a population of over 17 million. The practice was sharply criticized by both Jefferson and Madison as early as 1823. Endorsing Jefferson's criticism, Madison concluded that—

> The present rule of voting for President by the House of Representatives is so great a departure from the Republican principle of numerical equality, and even from the Federal rule, which qualifies the numerical by a State equality, and is so pregnant also with a mischievous tendency in practice, that an amendment to the Constitution on this point is justly called for by all its considerate and best friends.

Voting by States in a contingent election is not only unjust and undemocratic but also anomalous, for there can be no justification for the distribution of power among the States in a contingent election being different from that in the popular election. The very existence of that difference, moreover, may give an incentive to attempt to cause the election to be thrown into the House, where the influence of some States would be greatly increased.

Another defect arises from the present requirement of an absolute majority for election. That requirement makes possible—indeed, likely—a deadlock among the three candidates. Were the deadlock to continue beyond Inauguration Day—a mere 17 days after Congress convenes—the Nation would be left without a President. The Vice President or, if his election were also deadlocked, the Speaker could, of course, act as President until a President was chosen, but the tenure of an Acting President in those circumstances would be of the most precarious sort and he could exercise no real leadership or authority. The breaking of the deadlock, moreover, would almost inevitably be accompanied, at least in appearance if not in reality, with the making of "political deals" in exchange for votes. The prospect of reliving the election of 1800, when the country suffered through 36 ballots in the House and was alive with rumors of political intrigue and machination, is surely not one that can be viewed with equanimity. And once again, the possibility is illustrated by recent history: It is said that, if the 1948 election had been thrown into the

House, the delegations of four States which had been carried by the State's Rights candidate could have deadlocked the election.*

A final defect of the present system is that, since the House would elect the President while the Senate would elect the Vice President, there would be a substantial likelihood of the President and the Vice President being elected from different parties. Harmonious working relationships between the President and the Vice President require that they share a common political philosophy, and it is today generally agreed that the election of a split ticket would be highly undesirable.

Senate Joint Resolution 58 would remedy those defects by having both the President and the Vice President elected by the Senate and the House of Representatives sitting in a joint session, with each Member casting one vote. A quorum of three-fourths of the Members of both Houses would be required, but a plurality of the votes cast would be sufficient for election. Since the representation of each State in the joint session would be exactly equal to the number of its electoral votes, the contingent election under that proposal would be fully as representative as is the popular election.

With the same body electing both officers, the likelihood of a split ticket being elected would be diminished. And with a plurality being sufficient for election, the possibility of a deadlock would be avoided. Those changes are, in my judgment, much to be desired, and I strongly support them.

* Committee Print, "The Electoral College," a Memorandum prepared by the Staff of the Subcommittee on Constitutional Amendments of the Senate Judiciary Committee, 87th Cong., first sess., p. 19 (1961).

RICHARD MILHOUS NIXON
President Nixon's Proposals

One hundred and sixty-five years ago, Congress and the several states adopted the 12th Amendment to the United States Constitution in order to cure certain defects—underscored by the election of 1800—in the Electoral College method of choosing a President.

Today, our Presidential selection mechanism once again requires overhaul to repair defects spotlighted by the circumstances of 1968.

The reforms that I propose are basic in need and desirability. They are changes which I believe should be given the earliest attention by the Congress.

I have not abandoned my personal feeling, stated in October and November, 1968, that the candidate who wins the most popular votes should become President. However, practicality demands recognition that the electoral system is deeply rooted in American history and federalism.

Approval by '72 Doubted

Many citizens, especially in our smaller states and their legislatures, share the belief stated by President Johnson in 1965 that "our present system of com-

Thirty-seventh President of the United States. The selection is a special message of President Nixon to Congress on February 20, 1969.

puting and awarding electoral votes by states is an essential counterpart of our Federal system and the provisions of our Constitution which recognize and maintain our nation as a union of states."

I doubt very much that any constitutional amendment proposing abolition or substantial modification of the electoral vote system could win the required approval of three-quarters of our 50 states by 1972.

For this reason, and because of the compelling specific weaknesses focused in 1968, I am urging Congress to concentrate its attention on formulating a system that can receive the requisite Congressional and state approval.

I realize that experts on constitutional law do not think alike on the subject of electoral reform. Different plans for reform have been responsibly advanced by members of Congress and distinguished private groups and individuals. These plans have my respect and they merit serious consideration by the Congress.

I have in the past supported the proportional plan of electoral reform. Under this plan the electoral vote of a state would be distributed among the candidates for President in proportion to the popular vote cast. But I am not wedded to the details of this plan or any other specific plan.

I will support any plan that moves toward the following objectives: First, the abolition of individual electors; second, allocation to Presidential candidates of the electoral vote of each state and the District of Columbia in a manner that may more closely approximate the popular vote than does the present system; third, making a 40 per cent electoral vote plurality sufficient to choose a President.

Runoff Election Asked

The adoption of these reforms would correct the principal defects in the present system. I believe the events of 1968 constitute the clearest proof that priority must be accorded to Electoral College reform.

Next, I consider it necessary to make specific provision for the eventuality that no Presidential slate receives 40 per cent or more of the electoral vote in the regular election. Such a situation, I believe, is best met by providing that a runoff election between the top two candidates shall be held within a specified time after the general election, victory going to the candidate who receives the largest popular vote.

We must also resolve some other uncertainties:

First, by specifying that if a Presidential candidate who has received a clear electoral vote plurality dies before the electoral votes are counted, the Vice President-elect should be chosen President.

Second, by providing that in the event of the death of the Vice President-elect, the President-elect should, upon taking office, be required to follow the procedures otherwise provided in the 25th Amendment for filling the unexpired term of the Vice President.

Third, by giving Congress responsibility, should both the President-elect and Vice President-elect die or become unable to serve during this interim, to provide for the selection—by a new election or some other means—of persons to serve as President and Vice President.

And finally, we must clarify the situation presented by the death of a candidate for President or Vice President prior to the November general election.

Many of these reforms are noncontroversial. All are necessary. Favorable action by Congress will constitute a vital step in modernizing our electoral process and reaffirming the flexible strength of our constitutional system.

[The Nixon proposals were criticized by Senator Birch Bayh, chairman of the Subcommittee on Constitutional Amendments and spokesman for electoral reform as "a retreat to expediency," according to the New York Times of February 22, 1969. "In my view," he said, "the adoption of the changes recommended by the President would not only not correct the principal defects in the present system but would introduce new and more disturbing defects." "I suggest," he added, "that if the people are capable of making the choice in the runoff then they are equally capable of participating in the initial election." Senator Bayh also criticized the President for calling on Congress to adopt not the best plan but the one most likely to be ratified by state legislatures.]

Congressional Reform ?

JOSEPH S. CLARK
"Tyranny of the Minorities"

Prologue to Reform

The customs, manners, rules and procedures of the Congress owe much to the American tradition of thinking in sectional and local social, economic and political terms. Americans, like most human beings, share a conviction that "The Lord helps those who help themselves." Until recently we were content to protect ourselves from alleged governmental restraint on our personal activities by Congressional devices designed to give minority interests (other than the Negro) a veto on the legislative process. The durability of these devices is also a tribute to the curious notion that to do nothing does not constitute a decision. The fear that the creation of a national legislature with the capacity to act might produce wrong decisions overlooks the fact that to do nothing in the modern world may itself represent a decision as disastrous as any affirmative action.

This strain of negativism runs deep. One may recall the interminable delays in enacting the constitutional amendments providing for the income tax, the direct election of Senators and woman suffrage; and how long we waited for child labor legislation, unemployment compensation and a host of economic and social welfare measures passed a generation earlier in most other Western democracies.

While Congressional political lag has always existed—indeed, through failure to solve the slavery question it played its part in bringing on the Civil War —it did not become glaringly apparent until the Great Depression of the 1930s. Prior to that time the system worked tolerably well. Each section got its interests taken care of by logrolling. Our wealth made the price supportable. World affairs did not require decisive action by the Congress. The really vital interests of the nation were not adversely affected. The system operated through a national legislature so organized that sectional and economic interests were able to protect themselves from objectionable government policy during a period in which no vigorous government policy of any kind was required in the national interest.

United States Senator from Pennsylvania. The selection is from *Congress: The Sapless Branch* by Senator Joseph S. Clark. Copyright © 1964 by Joseph S. Clark. Reprinted with the permission of Harper & Row, Publishers, Incorporated.

A governmental system that is not capable of producing a coherent legislative program is not likely to appear deficient to a people imbued with a firm distaste for strong government and not confronted with crisis. It produced a government that did not interfere with the expanding economy, which was then the main interest of most influential Americans. Understandably, it was not then perceived that an arrangement which gave minority interests a stranglehold on national policy through control over Congressional procedures might, when crisis arrived, prove to be inoperable.

It is in the nature of minorities, as Joseph Chamberlain once said, "to devise some ingenious machinery by which [they] may be saved from the natural consequences of being outnumbered." Such ingenious machinery is the very nerve center of the present control of the Congress. It will not do to defend this machinery as a protection against "the tyranny of the majority," for it is nothing of the sort. It is a built-in defense for maintaining a status quo no longer tenable in the face of present conditions at home and abroad. And it violates every principle of popular rule on which free governments are based. It is the "tyranny of the minorities" we suffer from.

The central defect of the modern Congress is that it permits a minority determined on inaction to frustrate the will of the majority which desires to act. All the majority wants to do is to work the will of the people it represents. Minority obstructionism has merely reinforced that Congressional lag which gets us into trouble. We can reflect soberly today on the results of the bitterest Senate filibuster of the nineteenth century, which in 1890-91 defeated a bill, already passed by the House, to give the federal government supervision over Congressional elections. How much rancor and discord in our century would have been avoided had the majority in the Senate been able to pass this bill, aimed at eliminating Negro disqualification and intimidation in the South.

Those who delight in the fear of "majority tyranny" should seek election to a major governmental post under conditions of genuine political competition. They would soon learn how varied are the interests that must be conciliated if success is to be achieved at the polls. There is nothing monolithic and therefore no basis for "tyranny" in the majorities put together by Congressmen from two-party states and districts today. Potential tyranny is a characteristic of minorities like the John Birch Society or the Communists, not the mark of the representatives of a major party seeking the support of a national electorate.

It is the dynamics of democratic politics, not the erection of legal barriers to action, that make for moderation in our public life and provide the real protection from majority tyranny. In fact, while both major parties have extremists in their ranks, those extremists have never represented orthodoxy in the parties to which they belonged. Their very power emerged from their exploitation of devices aimed at protecting the minority. Huey Long and his one-man filibusters, or Joe McCarthy arrogating to himself the investigatory power of the Senate and temporarily usurping executive prerogatives, never seriously threatened to assume leadership of either party. There is an old saying in England that the House of Commons has more sense than anyone in it. The same thing can be said of any legislative body where a consensus is permitted to develop and take action. It is, therefore, a grave error not to establish procedures which permit the good sense of a majority to prevail.

Congressional preoccupation with legal checks on the majority is super-imposed on functional checks implicit in the separation of powers, including the Presidential veto. Moreover, our strongly held respect for minorities gives them additional protection. It is the strength of that tradition which provides the moral support for the effort to integrate the Negro into American life. It is indeed ironic that this effort on behalf of our most disadvantaged minority is frustrated by devices ostensibly aimed at preventing "majority tyranny."

The obstructionist policies encouraged by those same devices are in the long run self-defeating. In 1925 Vice President Dawes advised the Senate that "under the inexorable laws of human nature and human reaction, the Senate rules, unless changed, could only lessen the effectiveness, prestige, and dignity of that body." There can be no doubt that the Dawes warning was prophetic, if unheeded. A legislature which denies itself the power to act, particularly when the obstacles to action are so obvious and so publicly demeaning as the filibus-ter, merits only disrespect and the loss of popular esteem it has achieved.

Max Lerner's harsh description is a typical reaction:

> Congress has become a problem child of the American governmental family. It is noisy, volatile, vulnerable to pressure groups and lobbies, often parochial in its outlook, jealous of its prerogatives, insecure about its position, implacable in its vendettas, bewildered by its mounting tasks. It has lost its reputation for great debate, has become intractable to party leadership and discipline and incapable of disciplining itself, and in re-cent generations it has developed fewer examples of the great leadership it once possessed.

Vesting the veto power in a minority goes far to destroy that spirit of desirable compromise which is one of the hallmarks of a democratic legislative assembly. A minority bent on inaction finds it unnecessary to compromise with a majority which is powerless to act. The Congress of the United States is, within very broad limits, favorably disposed to accommodate a wide spectrum of opinion. There is no compulsion to agree on moderate and reasonable action, however, when the rules offer hope that nothing at all need be agreed to. Defi-ance by the minority breeds in the end vindictiveness in the majority. Neither sentiment is congenial to useful action.

The risk of tyranny by the majority over the minority is today small in-deed. Tocqueville's fears of democracy have proved groundless. It is a minority, not a majority, which imposes sterile uniformity. Today the Negro minority is tyrannized by a white minority. National democracy has had no fair chance to do justice. . . .

As Henry Steele Commager has noted,

> For well over a century now, this pernicious doctrine [states' rights] has been invoked for two major purposes . . . to weaken government and to endanger freedom. A states' rights philosophy which is never inspired by generosity, never excited by a passion for freedom or for justice, never exalted by magnanimity but takes refuge in narrowness, selfishness and vindictiveness, exhausts its claim to tolerance.

There is no greater nonsense circulated today than the theory that the states are the defenders of freedom and the national government its enemy. The fact is just the opposite. The growth of the power of the national government has secured an increase in individual freedom, social, economic and political. The effect of national power has been benign, not malign. It is a shame that the Congress has not sensed this basic political truth until long after it occurred to both the Supreme Court and the President. The use of states' rights as a rallying cry for those who desire to perpetuate an inept Congress unable to deal with pressing national problems is a cry to perpetuate plutocracy and greed and to protect those who are today violating civil rights and civil liberties with impunity. To rely upon the states for a solution of problems essentially national in their scope, such as education, unemployment, and social security, is to insure that these problems will not be solved. Those who advocate states' rights are, therefore, in the vanguard of the opponents of Congressional reform. As long as they can keep Congress negative their status quo philosophy is safe. It is state debt and state government employment which have risen almost astronomically in the postwar years, not the federal government's. Yet this enormous increase has not been sufficient to make appreciable inroads toward solution of the domestic problems which beset us. Letting the states do it is tantamount to letting the problems remain unsolved.

Closely related to the states' rights argument is the nightmare of "federal control" over individual liberties which haunts the dreams of our conservative friends. This is a sheer hallucination. I cannot think of one current program in which the "heavy hand of the federal government reaching out into our private lives" has actually been restrictive of our personal freedoms or detrimental to our economy—if, that is, one accepts the need for a justly organized society in a civilized world. The problem of protecting liberty against the demands of society is difficult and delicate, as John Stuart Mill made clear long ago. "Government, like dress," said Tom Paine, "is the badge of lost innocence." Sometimes the choice between liberty and order is difficult. In the great struggle for civil rights for all Americans, for example, it has been argued that equal access to public accommodations is an infringement on the liberty of the individual who owns or manages the facility. I would argue that the individual right of every American to the use of that facility is an *expansion* of basic liberty, not a *denial* of liberties. But the question is not easy.

The concern over minority rights and regional interests is understandable enough in view of our history. For the descendants of Southern planters, steerage immigrants, British convicts, African slaves and New England Puritans to live and work in peace and harmony, and pursue happiness together, is no easy thing. No other nation has had to attempt it. On the whole we have been successful, but we still have some miles to go on the road to the good society.

The motto carved on the new Senate Office Building is "The Senate Is the Living Symbol of the Union of the States." That pretty well sums up the Congressional attitude. But time and history and world responsibility have made us a nation, and it is time that in our thinking an l in our behavior we recognized contemporary fact. We must move toward national federalism, accepting the federal structure, but emphasizing the national.

There are many who persist in the mistaken view that the problems of Congress, like the poor, will always be with us. But the Congress has not always been as incapable of action as it is now, and majority rule has not always been so successfully thwarted. Like the tradition of Jim Crow in the South, which is not nearly so old as it is iniquitous, there is a tendency to accept as age-old and hallowed traditions the habits of a few decades. Most of the unfortunate traditions of Congress are not very old and not very hallowed. In a culture confronted with constant change it is surprising that so many still believe change in Congress is not possible.

Procedural reform in the Congress has a history at least as old as the practices which led to it. In the past hundred years, important procedural reforms have often been successfully accomplished as the need became clear. . . .

[Senator Clark then points out, with respect to the House of Representatives, that in 1860 "a largely technical revision of the rules in the interest of clarity was adopted" and that, in 1880, the 167 rules were consolidated into 44 "thus securing 'accuracy in business, economy of time, order, uniformity and impartiality.' " In 1890, the Reed Rules were adopted which "placed the speaker in control of the House with almost dictatorial powers." In 1910, however, drastic reform destroyed "a large part of the system of strong party government, party discipline and majority rule."

With respect to the Senate, in 1913, new rules "gave a majority of a committee authority to call meetings and dispose of pending business, a power hitherto vested in the chairman. They placed in the majority power to name subcommittees, to elect conferees to meet with Representatives of the House and generally democratized Senate procedures."

Under the Legislative Reorganization Act of 1946, the committee structure of both Houses was simplified but "some of the most important recommendations" for reform were defeated. Senator Clark quotes the language of this Legislative Committee Report as "prophetic":

"Devised to handle the simpler task of an earlier day, our legislative machinery and procedures are by common consent no longer competent to cope satisfactorily with the grave and complex problems of the post-war world. They must be modernized if we are to avoid an imminent breakdown of the legislative branch of the national government. . . . Democracy itself is in grave danger of disintegrating from internal dissensions under the terrific pressures of the post-war world."

Senator Clark concludes: "So it is again today."]

Internal Reforms for Congress

The main objectives of internal Congressional reform are, specifically, four:

1. To change the party leadership structure so that within both parties and in both houses a majority will decide party policy and enforce party discipline against recalcitrant members.

2. To change the rules and procedures of both houses so that a majority *can* act when it is ready to act.

3. To substitute cooperation for competition in the relations between the two houses, and between the whole Congress and the President.

4. To establish and enforce high ethical standards for members of Congress.

Nothing less than such drastic treatment will restore the Congress to vigorous, working, democratic health. But I am neither so naïve nor so egotistical as to expect my colleagues to agree with me in the absence of a strong popular demand for Congressional reform. I do not think that the Congressional Establishment will respond to the arguments in this book, cast off lethargy and obstructionism and reform itself. A great deal of public prodding is needed. . . .

The question of discipline is necessarily involved and the conference is the place to settle it. Hardly a Senator today would support the old practice of the binding caucus. "King Caucus" is dead in the Congress for the foreseeable future. Moreover, both parties are divided into liberal and conservative blocks so that substantial agreement would be impossible and revolt certain on all controversial measures if an attempt to bind were made.[1] Finally, the Establishment, even with its wings clipped, as I hope in due course they will be, will probably always be strong enough within the legislative committees to prevent dictation of policy by the conference.

Nevertheless, there is a practical area where the conference should exercise discipline. No institution should countenance members who are consistently out of sympathy with its objectives and the Congressional Democratic Conference should be no exception. Senators and Representatives who are unwilling to support the Presidential candidate of their party in the campaign simply have no place in the Congressional Conferences of their party after the election. Congressmen who are unwilling to support the platform planks of their party in the area of jurisdiction of a particular committee have no business serving as members of that party on that committee; and far less should they have the right through seniority to become or remain chairmen of such committees.

There is plenty of precedent for the exercise of such disipline. . . . After the election of 1924, the Republicans in the Senate, in the second session of the Sixty-eighth Congress, passed a resolution that Senators who had campaigned against President Calvin Coolidge that year "be not invited to future Republican conferences and be not named to fill any Republican vacancies on Senate Committees."

Senator LaFollette, who had run for the Presidency against Coolidge, and Senators Ladd, Brookhart and Frazier were expelled from the Republican conference. They were permitted to retain the committee assignments they had theretofore held, but placed at the bottom of the committee seniority list. Senator Ladd was demoted as chairman of the then important Committee on Public Lands and Surveys.

There are other precedents. [After citing several, Senator Clark adds:]

---

[1] This situation should not, however, prevent votes being taken by the conference from time to time to enable the leadership to determine the strength which could be summoned for the passage of particular measures.

In our own day Senator Wayne Morse of Oregon was disciplined by the Republicans for political independence in 1953 by removal from membership on the Armed Services and Labor Committees. When he later joined the Democratic party, he was restored to the Labor Committee, but at the bottom of the list. Later he was placed on the Foreign Relations Committee. In the House the Democratic party conference seems to be even less effective than in the Senate. . . .

There are fewer examples in House history than in the Senate of demotion of committee chairmen and discipline of committee members. The most famous one resulted from the revolt of the Progressives of Wisconsin against the regular conservative Republican leadership in the early 1920's. It came to a head after the Presidential election of 1924 in which Senator Robert LaFollette, a Bull Moose Republican, ran for the Presidency on a third ticket.

In the "lame duck" session of Congress held in December, 1924, after the election of President Calvin Coolidge that November, ten Representatives from Wisconsin who had supported Senator La Follette for the Presidency were deprived of committee posts to which they had previously been chosen as Republicans. . . . In 1949 Speaker Sam Rayburn caused John Rankin of Mississippi and Edward Hébert of Louisiana to be removed from the House Un-American Activities Committee for "antics" which displeased him and, it might be added, most of the country as well.

In each case in both houses these demotions caused enormous controversy. In many cases they have not received the praise of historians. Vengeance was perhaps a motive in some of them. But for an institution, like the Congress, which exalts precedent, the precedents are there. And in each instance the party leadership recommended the action taken by the caucus. . . .

[Senator Clark then recommends a whole series of particular intra-party organizational reforms basically designed to establish the primacy of majority views in each party in the selection of committee members. He adds:]

A major requirement of Congressional reform is a change in the rules, customs, procedures and floor action of the two houses with the end view of making it easier for both bodies to act effectively when a majority is ready for action. The ultimate purpose of rules reform is to remove as many of these obstacles as is feasible while retaining adequate opportunity for careful consideration in committee and full debate on the floor of all bills under serious consideration.

In the House the problem seems simple. Floor action is expeditious and needs no significant change. "Reed's Rules" plus the reforms connected with the overthrow of Speaker Joseph Cannon in 1910 took care of that many years ago.

The problem in the House is to pry loose from the legislative committees and the Rules Committee bills which are part of the program of the President or whose passage is desired by a clear majority of the House. The presently available techniques to solve this problem have proved inadequate in practice.

Three methods of achieving the desired result which worked well in the past but were abandoned might be restored by changes in the House rules. The first would be to reinstate the twenty-one-day rule which resulted in the passage of much important legislation during its short lifetime in the Truman administration.* The second would be to decrease the number of names on a discharge petition required to bring a bill from committee to the calendar from 218, or a majority of the whole House, to 150, which was the requirement from 1924 to 1935. The third would be to remove from the Rules Committee the power to determine whether a bill shall go to conference if one member of the House objects on the floor to a motion to appoint conferees, thus leaving the decision to the whole House.

Of course, even with restricted powers, it is essential to have the Rules Committee an ally and not an enemy of the leadership. The best way to do this would seem to be to demote its chairman and any other members who are unwilling to commit themselves to the winning party's platform and candidate . . . , as well as members of the minority party who are disloyal to their own national leader and platform. While demotion in the case of other committees should be confined to those who are unwilling to support the platform in the area of the committee's jurisdiction, the Rules Committee covers the waterfront, having authority to send to the floor or pickle *any* proposed legislation on *any* subject. This vast power should never be permitted to be exercised by a committee containing members disloyal to the platform of the party to which they ostensibly belong.

The result of these suggested changes would be to democratize committee action in the House and make the committees subject to the will of a majority of that body. Whether the majority of the House would be prepared to follow the platform of the majority party or of the President is quite a different story. The composition of the House might well be such that no such result would follow. But at least so far as internal operations are concerned the President and his party would fight under ground rules which are in the tradition of our American democracy rather than the outmoded result of control of the House by an ancient oligarchical and plutocratic minority unresponsive to the popular will.

Before discussing needed changes in Senate rules and methods of operation something should be said about the custom of seniority, a controversial subject in both houses and in the country at large.

There is an unwritten custom, sometimes violated in practice, that length of service in the House and Senate determines eligibility for appointment to committees, and that the majority senior member of a committee succeeds automatically to a vacancy in the chairmanship. The latter half of the custom is more scrupulously observed than the former. . . .

In the House the Speaker, the Democratic members of the Ways and Means Committees and the Republican Committee on Committees give some weight to factors other than seniority in making initial assignments. This is because there are, with each new Congress, so many new Representatives with equal seniority to be fitted into committee vacancies. Former members returning to the House after an earlier defeat or resignation are usually given priority

---

* Under this rule, the chairman of a legislative committee could call up for action a bill his committee had reported favorably at any time after the lapse of 21 calendar days—if the Rules Committee, in the meantime, had failed to grant a rule. [Eds.]

in the choice of committee posts, but lose for all time their seniority on defeat or resignation.

The seniority rule has come in for much adverse public comment largely because it tends to give power to elderly conservative members of both houses, mostly from the South when the Democrats control the Congress, who are apt to use their power to defeat or delay the enactment of the program of their party and of the President. . . .

When one considers how much the luck of the draw contributes to achieving a committee chairmanship, the geographical distribution in the House is not subject to serious criticism. While there is some overweighting from the South, it must be remembered that the next time the Republicans carry the House these Southern chairmen will be replaced by Northerners and Westerners. On grounds of ideology the story is different. In the area of their committee's jurisdiction four chairmen hold views not in accord with the platform of their party. In terms of age one notes three chairmen over eighty and five more who have seen three score years and ten go by.

The difficulty is not so much in the seniority system itself as in the failure to exercise party discipline in a manner which would require chairmen to conform to the platform of their party in the area of the committee's jurisdiction or resign and seek service on another committee.

Nor is there any apparent correlation between age and ideology. Representatives Cellar and Patman, among the older chairmen, are as liberal as Representatives Smith and Cannon are conservative. And Chairman Cannon, while he delights in cutting the heart out of appropriations recommended by any administration, voted for both the civil rights and tax bills in 1963.

Nevertheless, a rule that would require chairmen to relinquish their positions as such on reaching age seventy or seventy-five while still remaining as members of the committee, as Senator Theodore Francis Green did voluntarily on the Senate Foreign Relations Committee a few years ago, would avoid the embarrassment of the public display of a slowing down of mental agility and energy which are recognized by all save the elderly chairman himself—and which slow down and sometimes prevent the effective conduct of committee business. There would be a few cases where such a rule would deprive the committee of a useful chairman, but there would be many more where the result would be wholly salutary. Such a rule should apply both to the House and to the Senate. . . .

Seniority is a convenient method of eliminating internal politics in both Houses. It is, in a sense, a lazy man's way of avoiding a struggle and a decision. It makes it possible for the most senior Congressman around to get what he wants without a struggle. But it also gives other Congressmen an excuse not to start a fight. The constituents pleading for action to get a committee off dead center can always be told, "What can I do?"

That invariable following of the seniority rule can do great damage to the legislative process is clear beyond doubt. History is full of instances where incompetent or senile men have obstructed the national interest through their positions as committee chairmen attained through seniority. Even worse are the instances, several of which presently exist, where extremely capable men have used their power as committee chairmen, acquired through seniority, to obstruct and often to defeat the programs of their own party and the President that party sent to the White House.

The remedy is not to eliminate seniority, but rather to curb and regulate it. Primarily this could be done by the exercise of party discipline as recommended earlier in this chapter. Another effective step would be always to fill committee vacancies, regardless of seniority, with men known to be in sympathy with party policy in the area of the committee's jurisdiction. This, of course, requires a Steering Committee or Committee on Committees responsive to a party conference prepared to support party programs.

A third reform to curb the evil effects of seniority would be to provide by rule that the chairmen of all standing committees should be chosen at the beginning of each Congress by secret ballot of the committee members of the majority party. Nine times out of ten the choice would be the senior Senator or Representative. But in the tenth case a recalcitrant chairman would be deposed or a prospective recalcitrant candidate for the chairmanship relying on seniority defeated. And in the other nine cases the chairman chosen because of seniority would bend over backward to be fair, to assure his continued tenure against the threat of demotion by his colleagues.

Finally, the evil effects of seniority or indeed of arbitrary action by chairmen could be curbed by enacting by rule a "Committee Bill of Rights." Some committees presently have rules of procedure which are in accord with normal parliamentary practice. Others do not. It would help very much in the latter cases to provide by rule that a majority of the members of a committee could convene meetings, fix the agenda, call up bills for consideration, regulate the conduct of hearings and terminate debate within the committee after a reasonable time. Ordinarily these matters are left to the chairman, and properly so. But the power of the majority to act if the chairman fails to do so should be clearly established.

Because these procedures were followed in the Senate Committee on Interstate and Foreign Commerce, the Public Accommodations title of President Kennedy's Civil Rights Bill was promptly considered and favorably reported in the fall of 1963. Because they were not, much of the rest of the bill was never reported by the Senate Judiciary Committee.

In the House the absence of effective committee procedures enables the chairman of the Interior Committee to pickle indefinitely the Senate-passed Wilderness Bill, and the chairman of the Rules Committee to delay for months major legislation already approved by the appropriate standing committee.

The seniority system, then, is a serious obstacle to effective Congressional performance of duty. But the remedies for the evil are close at hand. All that is needed is to put them into effect and thus bring the system under control. There is no need to throw the baby out with the bath water. Properly regulated, the seniority system has its uses, principally in minimizing internal conflict between members of Congress. . . .

A useful reform would be to prohibit any Senator from holding the floor for more than two hours, except when floor managing a bill or by unanimous consent. We have no time or need in the modern world for marathon speeches. . . . A motion to take up a bill on the calendar made by the Majority Leaders should be determined by vote without debate. At present such a motion is subject to unlimited debate, thus giving the opponents of the bill two chances to filibuster instead of only one, i.e., (1) when the motion to take up is made the pending business and (2) after the motion is finally approved and unlimited debate begins on the bill and amendments.

The Senate should adopt a rule requiring debate to be germane when legislation which the leadership wishes to expedite has been made the pending business. No other legislative body in the world, so far as I have been able to discover, operates without a rule of germaneness. The principle is well laid down in Jefferson's Manual and was originally followed in the Senate: "No one is to speak impertinently or *beside the question,* superfluously or tediously." Some years ago the Parliamentarian ruled Jefferson need no longer be followed. No one can prevent a Senator from being tedious, but it should be possible to require him to stick to the subject. . . .

Rule XXIV of the Senate should be amended by adding a new paragraph reading: "A majority of the Senate members of a committee or conference shall have indicated by their votes their sympathy with the bill as passed and their concurrence in the prevailing opinion of the Senate on matters of disagreement with the House of Representatives which occasion the appointment of the committee."

This sound, democratic principle, which is recognized in Jefferson's Manual, Cleaves' Manual, and the Watkins and Riddick book on Senate procedure, has been violated on a number of important occasions in recent years. Thus the Senate has been represented on particular bills, as it was in 1959 on the question of extending the temporary unemployment compensation law, by Senators who voted against the Senate position and in favor of the House position on the bill as a whole or particular provisions of it.

Under the existing situation, if a Senator wishes to protest that the practices as stated in the manuals are not being adhered to, he must publicly challenge one or more of the conferees. This has been done successfully on several occasions, but for obvious reasons it has usually created personal ill will, which might be avoided if a Senate rule incorporated the principle and it could be invoked by a point of order.

The need for the change at present is largely, but not entirely, confined to instances where the Senate overrules its Finance Committee on a tax bill. In these instances the senior members of the Committee, who would normally be the conferees, would in all likelihood have voted with the minority on the floor.

Perhaps the most important needed change in Senate rules is the liberalization of Rule XXII, which presently provides for terminating debate only on the affirmative vote of two-thirds of the Senators present. . . .

The single most desirable change in the present attitude of both houses, a change which would do more than any other to bring the President and the Congress together on a program for the country, would be passage of a concurrent resolution committing both houses to bring to a vote on its merits any legislative proposal on which the President requests prompt action within six months of the date his proposed legislation is sent down to Capitol Hill. In this way the original intention of the framers of the Constitution could be resuscitated. The Executive would report annually on the State of the Union and how he had performed his duty to see that the laws should be faithfully executed as provided in Article II of the Constitution. He would make his recommendations for needed legislation to the Congress; send down his budget; and the legislative arm would promptly act on those recommendations—accepting some, modifying others, rejecting still others. It would then pass and send to the President for veto or approval such other laws as in its wisdom, exercising its extensive powers under Article I of the Constitution, it thought should be enacted. . . . So might the public business be expeditiously dispatched.

Until the Congress accepts this obligation there is little hope that our tripartite system of checks and balances with all its frustrations, with all its road-blocks to needed action, with all its futilities and with all its callous disregard of the public interest can measure up to the responsibilities placed on it in the modern world. . . .

Walter Lippmann has made a similar suggestion. "To make our system work, it is essential that the initiative of the President be respected by Congress, and when he says a measure is of great national importance, his proposals should be accorded enough priority to bring them to a vote and a decision within a reasonable time—say three months."

Such are my personal recommendations for turning the Congress into an effective working partner with the executive and judicial branches of our federal government. But to convert such a program into reality a very large part of Congress will have to take a serious interest in reform. To rally support and achieve solid results, Senate Concurrent Resolution 1 was introduced early in January, 1963, by thirty Senators. Senator Clifford Case and I were the principal sponsors. Modeled on the La Follette-Monroney resolution of 1945, it called for the creation of a joint Congressional committee of seven members from each House to make an over-all study of needed Congressional reorganization and to report back its recommendations to the Congress within a year of its passage. . . .

The need for such a study is obvious, and I have no doubt some sort of study will be authorized, if not immediately, then in the foreseeable future. . . . One way or another the massive job of Congressional reorganization and reform must get under way before it is too late and Congressional government breaks down under the strain of modern pressures for action.

JOHN FISCHER

Government by Concurrent Majority

Every now and then somebody comes up with the idea that the party system in American politics is absurd because our two great parties don't stand for clearly contrasting principles, and that we would be better off if we had a conservative party and a radical or liberal party. It is a persuasive argument, especially for well-meaning people who have not had much first-hand

Long-time editor of *Harper's Magazine.* Author of *Why They Behave Like Russians,* and many articles on politics. The selection is from John Fischer, "Unwritten Rules of American Politics," *Harper's Magazine Reader* (Chicago, Bantam Books, 1953). Original copyright, 1948, by Harper & Brothers. Reprinted by permission of author and *Harper's Magazine.*

experience in politics. You have probably heard it; it runs something like this:

"Both of the traditional American parties are outrageous frauds. Neither the Republicans nor the Democrats have any fundamental principles or ideology. They do not even have a program. In every campaign the platforms of both parties are simply collections of noble generalities, muffled in the vaguest possible language; and in each case the two platforms are very nearly identical.

"Obviously, then, both parties are merely machines for grabbing power and distributing favors. In their lust for office they are quite willing to make a deal with anybody who can deliver a sizable block of votes. As a result, each party has become an outlandish cluster of local machines and special interest groups which have nothing in common except a craving for the public trough.

"This kind of political system"—so the argument runs—"is clearly meaningless. A man of high principles can never hope to accomplish anything through the old parties, because they are not interested in principle. Moreover, the whole arrangement is so illogical that it affronts every intelligent citizen.

"We ought to separate the sheep from the goats—to herd all the progressives on one side of the fence and all the conservatives on the other. Then politics really will have some meaning; every campaign can be fought over clearly defined issues. The Europeans, who are more sophisticated politically than we simple Americans, discovered this long ago, and in each of their countries they have arranged a neat political spectrum running from Left to Right."

This argument pops up with special urgency whenever a third party appears—Theodore Roosevelt's in 1912, Robert La Follette's in 1924, or Henry Wallace's in 1948. And it sounds so plausible—at least on the surface—that many people have wondered why these splinter parties have always dwindled away after the election was over. Indeed, many veteran third-party enthusiasts have been able to account for their failure only by assuming a perverse and rock-headed stupidity among the American electorate.

There is, however, another possible explanation for the stubborn durability of our seemingly illogical two-party system; that it is more vigorous, more deeply rooted, and far better suited to our own peculiar needs than any European system would be; that it involves a more complex and subtle conception than the crude blacks and whites of the European ideological parties. There is considerable evidence, it seems to me, that our system—in spite of certain dangerous weaknesses—has on the whole worked out more successfully than the European.

Perhaps it is the very subtlety of the American political tradition which is responsible for the almost universal misunderstanding of it abroad. Every practicing American politician grasps its principles by instinct; if he does not, he soon retires into some less demanding profession. Moreover, the overwhelming majority of citizens have a sound working knowledge of the system, which they apply every day of their lives—though many of them might have a hard time putting that knowledge into words. There are almost no foreigners, however (except perhaps D. W. Brogan), who really understand the underlying theory. Even the editors of the London *Economist*—probably the most brilliant and well-informed group of journalists practicing anywhere today—display their bewilderment week after week. To them, and to virtually all other European observers, our whole political scene looks arbitrary, irrational, and dangerous.

Another reason for this misunderstanding lies in the fact that surprisingly little has been written about the rules of American politics during our generation. The newspapers, textbooks, and learned journals are running over with discussions of tactics and mechanics—but no one, so far as I know, has bothered to trace out the basic tradition for a good many years.

The Doctrine of the Concurrent Majority

In fact, the most useful discussion of this tradition which I have come across is the work of John C. Calhoun, published nearly a century ago. Today of course he is an almost forgotten figure, and many people take it for granted that his views were discredited for good by the Civil War. I know of only one writer—Peter F. Drucker—who has paid much attention to him in recent years. It was he who described Calhoun's ideas as "a major if not the only key to the understanding of what is specifically and uniquely American in our political system"; and I am indebted to Mr. Drucker for much of the case set forth here.

Calhoun summed up his political thought in what he called the Doctrine of the Concurrent Majority. He saw the United States as a nation of tremendous and frightening diversity—a collection of many different climates, races, cultures, religions, and economic patterns. He saw the constant tension among all these special interests, and he realized that the central problem of American politics was to find some way of holding these conflicting groups together.

It could not be done by force; no one group was strong enough to impose its will on all the others. The goal could be achieved only by compromise—and no real compromise could be possible if any threat of coercion lurked behind the door. Therefore, Calhoun reasoned, every vital decision in American life would have to be adopted by a "concurrent majority"—by which he meant, in effect, a unanimous agreement of all interested parties. No decision which affected the interests of the slave-holders, he argued, should be taken without their consent; and by implication he would have given a similar veto to every other special interest, whether it be labor, management, the Catholic church, old-age pensioners, the silver miners, or the corngrowers of the Middle West.

Under the goad of the slavery issue, Calhoun was driven to state his doctrine in an extreme and unworkable form. If every sectional interest had been given the explicit, legal veto power which he called for, the government obviously would have been paralyzed. (That, in fact, is precisely what seems to be happening today in the United Nations.) It is the very essence of the idea of "concurrent majority" that it cannot be made legal and official. It can operate effectively only as an informal, highly elastic, and generally accepted understanding.

Moreover, government by concurrent majority can exist only when no one power is strong enough to dominate completely, *and then only when all of the contending interest groups recognize and abide by certain rules of the game.*

Unwritten Rules of American Politics

These rules are the fundamental bond of unity in American political life. They can be summed up as a habit of extraordinary toleration, plus "equality" in the peculiar American meaning of that term which cannot be translated into any other language, even into the English of Great Britain. Under these rules every group tacitly binds itself to tolerate the interests and opinions of every other group. It must not try to impose its views on others, nor can it press its own special interests to the point where they seriously endanger the interests of other groups or of the nation as a whole.

Furthermore, each group must exercise its implied veto with responsibility and discretion; and in times of great emergency it must forsake its veto right altogether. It dare not be intransigent or doctrinaire. It must make every conceivable effort to compromise, relying on its veto only as a last resort. For if any player wields this weapon recklessly, the game will break up—or all the other players will turn on him in anger, suspend the rules for the time being, and maul those very interests he is trying so desperately to protect. That was what happened in 1860, when the followers of Calhoun carried his doctrine to an unbearable extreme. Much the same thing, on a less violent scale, happened to American business interests in 1933 and to the labor unions in 1947.

This is the somewhat elusive sense, it seems to me, in which Calhoun's theory has been adopted by the American people. But elusive and subtle as it may be, it remains the basic rule of the game of politics in this country—and in this country alone. Nothing comparable exists in any other nation, although the British, in a different way, have applied their own rules of responsibility and self-restraint.

It is a rule which operates unofficially and entirely outside the Constitution —but it has given us a method by which all the official and Constitutional organs of government can be made to work. It also provides a means of selecting leaders on all levels of our political life, for hammering out policies, and for organizing and managing the conquest of political power.

The way in which this tradition works in practice can be observed most easily in Congress. Anyone who has ever tried to push through a piece of legislation quickly discovers that the basic units of organization on Capitol Hill are not the parties, but the so-called blocs, which are familiar to everyone who reads a newspaper. There are dozens of them—the farm bloc, the silver bloc, the friends of labor, the business group, the isolationists, the public power bloc— and they all cut across party lines.

They are loosely organized and pretty blurred at the edges, so that every Congressman belongs at different times to several different blocs. Each of them represents a special interest group. Each of them ordinarily works hand-in-hand with that group's Washington lobby. In passing, it might be noted that these lobbies are by no means the cancerous growth which is sometimes pictured in civics textbooks. They have become an indispensable part of the political machine—the accepted channel through which American citizens make their wishes known and play their day-to-day role in the process of government. Nor is their influence measured solely by the size of the bankrolls and propaganda apparatus which they have at their disposal. Some of the smallest and poorest lobbies often are more effective than their well-heeled rivals. For example, Russell Smith, the one-man lobby of the Farmers Union, was largely responsible for conceiving and nursing through Congress the Employment Act of 1946, one of the most far-reaching measures adopted since the war.

Now it is an unwritten but firm rule of Congress that no important bloc shall ever be voted down—under normal circumstances—on any matter which touches its own vital interests. Each of them, in other words, has a tacit right of veto on legislation in which it is primarily concerned. The ultimate expression of this right is the institution—uniquely American—of the filibuster in the Senate. Recently it has acquired a bad name among liberals because the Southern conservatives have used it ruthlessly to fight off civil rights legislation and protect white supremacy. Not so long ago, however, the filibuster was the stoutest weapon of such men as Norris and the La Follettes in defending many a progressive cause.

Naturally no bloc wants to exercise its veto power except when it is absolutely forced to—for this is a negative power, and one which is always subject to retaliation. Positive power to influence legislation, on the other hand, can be gained only by conciliation, compromise, and endless horse-trading.

The farm bloc, for instance, normally needs no outside aid to halt the passage of a hostile bill. As a last resort, three or four strong-lunged statesmen from the corn belt can always filibuster it to death in the Senate. If the bloc wants to put through a measure to support agricultural prices, however, it can succeed only by enlisting the help of other powerful special interest groups. Consequently, it must always be careful not to antagonize any potential ally by a reckless use of the veto; and it must be willing to pay for such help by throwing its support from time to time behind legislation sought by the labor bloc, the National Association of Manufacturers, or the school-teachers' lobby.

The classic alliance of this sort was formed in the early days of the New Deal, when most of the Roosevelt legislation was shoved onto the statute books by a temporary coalition of the farm bloc and urban labor, occasionally reinforced by such minor allies as the public power group and spokesmen for the northern Negroes. Mr. Roosevelt's political genius rested largely on his ability to put together a program which would offer something to each of these groups without fatally antagonizing any of them, and then to time the presentation of each bill so that he would always retain enough bargaining power to line up a Congressional majority. It also was necessary for him to avoid the veto of the business group, which viewed much of this legislation as a barbarous assault upon its privileges; and for this purpose he employed another traditional technique, which we shall examine a little later.

This process of trading blocs of votes is generally known as log-rolling, and frequently it is deplored by the more innocent type of reformer. Such pious disapproval has no effect whatever on any practicing politician. He knows that log-rolling is a sensible and reasonably fair device, and that without it Congress could scarcely operate at all.

In fact, Congress gradually has developed a formal apparatus—the committee system—which is designed to make the log-rolling process as smooth and efficient as possible. There is no parallel system anywhere; the committees of Parliament and of the Continental legislative bodies work in an entirely different way.

Obviously the main business of Congress—the hammering out of a series of compromises between many special interest groups—cannot be conducted satisfactorily on the floor of the House or Senate. The meetings there are too large and far too public for such delicate negotiations. Moreover, every speech delivered on the floor must be aimed primarily at the voters back home, and not at the other members of the chamber. Therefore, Congress—especially the House—does nearly all its work in the closed sessions of its various committees, simply because the committee room is the only place where it is possible to arrange a compromise acceptable to all major interests affected.

For this reason, it is a matter of considerable importance to get a bill before the proper committee. Each committee serves as a forum for a particular cluster of special interests, and the assignment of a bill to a specific committee often decides which interest groups shall be recognized officially as affected by the measure and therefore entitled to a hand in its drafting. "Who is to have standing before the committee" is the technical term, and it is this decision that frequently decides the fate of the legislation.

Calhoun's principles of the concurrent majority and of sectional compromise operate just as powerfully, though sometimes less obviously, in every other American political institution. Our cabinet, for example, is the only one in the world where the members are charged by law with the representation of special interests—labor, agriculture, commerce, and so on. In other countries, each agency of government is at least presumed to act for the nation as a whole; here most agencies are expected to behave as servants for one interest or another. The Veterans' Administration, to cite the most familiar case, is frankly intended to look out for Our Boys; the Maritime Board is to look out for the shipping industry; the National Labor Relations Board, as originally established under the Wagner Act, was explicitly intended to build up the bargaining power of the unions.

Even within a single department, separate agencies are sometimes set up to represent conflicting interests. Thus in the Department of Agriculture under the New Deal the old Triple-A became primarily an instrument of the large-scale commercial farmers, as represented by their lobby, the Farm Bureau Federation; while the Farm Security Administration went to bat for the tenants, the farm laborers, and the little subsistence farmers, as represented by the Farmers Union.

This is one reason why federal agencies often struggle so bitterly against each other, and why the position of the administration as a whole on any question can be determined only after a long period of interbureau squabbling and compromise. Anyone who was in Washington during the war will remember how these goings-on always confused and alarmed our British allies.

Calhoun's laws also govern the selection of virtually every candidate for public office. The mystery of "eligibility" which has eluded most foreign observers simply means that a candidate must not be unacceptable to any important special interest group—a negative rather than a positive qualification. A notorious case of this process at work was the selection of Mr. Truman as the Democrats' Vice Presidential candidate in 1944. As Edward J. Flynn, the Boss of the Bronx, has pointed out in his memoirs, Truman was the one man "who would hurt . . . least" as Roosevelt's running mate. Many stronger men were disqualified, Flynn explained, by the tacit veto of one sectional interest or another. Wallace was unacceptable to the businessmen and to the many local party machines. Byrnes was distasteful to the Catholics, the Negroes, and organ-

ized labor. Rayburn came from the wrong part of the country. Truman, however, came from a border state, his labor record was good, he had not antagonized the conservatives, and—as Flynn put it—"he had never made any 'racial'
remarks. He just dropped into the slot."

The same kind of considerations govern the selection of candidates right
down to the county, city, and precinct levels. Flynn, one of the most successful
political operators of our time, explained in some detail the complicated job
of making up a ticket in his own domain. Each of the main population groups
in the Bronx—Italians, Jews, and Irish Catholics—must be properly represented
on the list of nominees, and so must each of the main geographical divisions.
The result was a ticket which sounded like the roster of the Brooklyn Dodgers:
Loreto, Delagi, Lyman, Joseph, Lyons, and Foley.

Comparable traditions govern the internal political life of the American
Legion, the Federation of Women's Clubs, university student bodies, labor
unions, Rotary Clubs, and the thousands of other quasi-political institutions
which are so characteristic of our society and which give us such a rich fabric
of spontaneous local government.

The stronghold of Calhoun's doctrine, however, is the American party
—the wonder and despair of foreigners who cannot fit it into any of their concepts of political life.

"Not to Divide But to Unite"

The purpose of European parties is, of course, to divide men of different
ideologies into coherent and disciplined organizations. The historic role of the
American party, on the other hand, is not to divide but to unite. That task was
imposed by simple necessity. If a division into ideological parties had been attempted, in addition to all the other centrifugal forces in this country, it very
probably would have proved impossible to hold the nation together. The Founding Fathers understood this thoroughly; hence Washington's warning against
"factions."

Indeed, on the one occasion when we did develop two ideological parties,
squarely opposing each other on an issue of principle, the result was civil war.
Fortunately, that was our last large-scale experiment with a third party formed
on an ideological basis—for in its early days that is just what the Republican
party was.

Its radical wing, led by such men as Thaddeus Stevens, Seward, and Chase,
made a determined and skillful effort to substitute principles for interests as
the foundations of American political life. Even within their own party, however, they were opposed by such practical politicians as Lincoln and Johnson—
men who distrusted fanaticism in any form—and by the end of the Reconstruction period the experiment had been abandoned. American politics then swung
back into its normal path and has never veered far away from it since. Although
Calhoun's cause was defeated, his political theory came through the Civil War
stronger than ever.

The result is that the American party has no permanent program and no
fixed aim, except to win elections. Its one purpose is to unite the largest possible
number of divergent interest groups in the pursuit of power. Its unity is one of

compromise, not of dogma. It must—if it hopes to succeed—appeal to considerable numbers on both the left and the right, to rich and poor, Protestant and Catholic, farmer and industrial worker, native and foreign born.

It must be ready to bid for the support of any group that can deliver a sizable chunk of votes, accepting that group's program with whatever modifications may be necessary to reconcile the other members of the party. If sun worship, or Existentialism, or the nationalization of industry should ever attract any significant following in this country, you can be sure that both parties would soon whip up a plank designed to win it over.

This ability to absorb new ideas (along with the enthusiasts behind them) and to mold them into a shape acceptable to the party's stand-patters is, perhaps, the chief measure of vitality in the party's leadership. Such ideas almost never germinate within the party itself. They are stolen—very often from third parties.

Indeed, the historic function of third parties has been to sprout new issues, nurse them along until they have gathered a body of supporters worth stealing, and then to turn them over (often reluctantly) to the major parties. A glance at the old platforms of the Populists, the Bull Moosers, and the Socialists will show what an astonishingly high percentage of their once-radical notions have been purloined by both Republicans and Democrats—and enacted into law. Thus the income tax, child-labor laws, minimum wages, regulation of railroads and utilities, and old-age pensions have all become part of the American Way of Life.

While each major party must always stand alert to grab a promising new issue, it also must be careful never to scare off any of the big, established interest groups. For as soon as it alienates any one of them, it finds itself in a state of crisis.

During the nineteen-thirties and -forties the Republicans lost much of their standing as a truly national party because they had made themselves unacceptable to labor. Similarly, the Democrats, during the middle stage of the New Deal, incurred the wrath of the business interests. Ever since Mr. Truman was plumped into the White House, the Democratic leadership has struggled desperately—though rather ineptly—to regain the confidence of businessmen without at the same time driving organized labor out of the ranks. It probably would be safe to predict that if the Republican party is to regain a long period of health, it must make an equally vigorous effort to win back the confidence of labor. For the permanent veto of any major element in American society means political death—as the ghosts of the Federalists and Whigs can testify.

Weaknesses of the American Political System

The weaknesses of the American political system are obvious—much more obvious, in fact, than its virtues. These weaknesses have been so sharply criticized for the past hundred years, by a procession of able analysts ranging from Walter Bagehot to Thomas K. Finletter, that it is hardly necessary to mention them here. It is enough to note that most of the criticism has been aimed at two major flaws.

First, it is apparent that the doctrine of the concurrent majority is a negative one—a principle of inaction. A strong government, capable of rapid and decisive action, is difficult to achieve under a system which forbids it to do anything until virtually everybody acquiesces. In times of crisis, a dangerously long period of debate and compromise usually is necessary before any administration can carry out the drastic measures needed. The depression of the early thirties, the crisis in foreign policy which ended only with Pearl Harbor, the crisis of the Marshall program all illustrate this recurring problem.

This same characteristic of our system gives undue weight to the small but well-organized pressure group—especially when it is fighting *against* something. Hence a few power companies were able to block for twenty years the sensible use of the Muscle Shoals dam which eventually became the nucleus of TVA, and—in alliance with the railroads, rail unions, and Eastern port interests—they [held] up development of the St. Lawrence Waterway. An even more flagrant example is the silver bloc, representing only a tiny fraction of the American people. It has been looting the Treasury for a generation by a series of outrageous silver subsidy and purchase laws.

The negative character of our political rules also makes it uncommonly difficult for us to choose a President. Many of our outstanding political operatives—notably those who serve in the Senate—are virtually barred from a Presidential nomination because they are forced to get on record on too many issues. Inevitably they offend some important interest group, and therefore become "unavailable." Governors, who can keep their mouths shut on most national issues, have a much better chance to reach the White House. Moreover, the very qualities of caution and inoffensiveness which make a good candidate—Harding and Coolidge come most readily to mind—are likely to make a bad President.

An even more serious flaw in our scheme of politics is the difficulty in finding anybody to speak for the country as a whole. Calhoun would have argued that the national interest is merely the sum of all the various special interests, and therefore needs no spokesmen of its own—but in this case he clearly was wrong.

In practice, we tend to settle sectional and class conflicts at the expense of the nation as a whole—with results painful to all of us. The labor troubles in the spring of 1946, for instance, could be settled only on a basis acceptable to *both* labor and management: that is, on the basis of higher wages *plus* higher prices. The upshot was an inflationary spiral which damaged everybody. Countless other instances, from soil erosion to the rash of billboards along our highways, bear witness to the American tendency to neglect matters which are "only" of national interest, and therefore are left without a recognized sponsor.

Over the generations we have developed a series of practices and institutions which partly remedy these weaknesses, although we are still far from a complete cure. One such development has been the gradual strengthening of the Presidency as against Congress. As the only man elected by all the people, the President inevitably has had to take over many of the policy-making and leadership functions which the Founding Fathers originally assigned to the legislators. This meant, of course, that he could no longer behave merely as an obedient executor of the will of Congress, but was forced into increasingly frequent conflicts with Capitol Hill.

Today we have come to recognize that this conflict is one of the most important obligations of the Presidency. No really strong executive tries to avoid it—he accepts it as an essential part of his job. If he simply tries to placate the pressure groups which speak through Congress, history writes him down as a failure. For it is his duty to enlist the support of many minorities for measures rooted in the national interest, reaching beyond their own immediate concern —and, if necessary, to stand up against the ravening minorities for the interest of the whole.

In recent times this particular part of the President's job has been made easier by the growth of the Theory of Temporary Emergencies. All of us—or nearly all—have come around to admitting that in time of emergency special interest groups must forego their right of veto. As a result, the President often is tempted to scare up an emergency to secure legislation which could not be passed under any other pretext. Thus, most of the New Deal bills were introduced as "temporary emergency measures," although they were clearly intended to be permanent from the very first; for in no other way could Mr. Roosevelt avoid the veto of the business interests.

Again, in 1939 the threat of war enabled the President to push through much legislation which would have been impossible under normal circumstances.

Elements of Strength

Because we have been so preoccupied with trying to patch up the flaws in our system, we have often overlooked its unique elements of strength. The chief of these is its ability to minimize conflict—not by suppressing the conflicting forces, but by absorbing and utilizing them. The result is a society which is both free and reasonably stable—a government which is as strong and effective as most dictatorships, but which can still adapt itself to social change.

The way in which the American political organism tames down the extremists of both the left and right is always fascinating to watch. Either party normally is willing to embrace any group or movement which can deliver votes—but in return it requires these groups to adjust their programs to fit the traditions, beliefs, and prejudices of the majority of the people. The fanatics, the implacable radicals cannot hope to get to first base in American politics until they abandon their fanaticism and learn the habits of conciliation. As a consequence, it is almost impossible for political movements here to become entirely irresponsible and to draw strength from the kind of demagogic obstruction which has nurtured both Communist and Fascist movements abroad.

The same process which gentles down the extremists also prods along the political laggards. As long as it is in a state of health, each American party has a conservative and a liberal wing. Sometimes one is dominant, sometimes the other—but even when the conservative element is most powerful, it must reckon with the left-wingers in its own family. At the moment the Republican party certainly is in one of its more conservative phases; yet it contains such men as Senators Morse, Aiken, Flanders, and Tobey, who are at least as progressive as most of the old New Dealers.* They, and their counterparts in the Democratic party, exert a steady tug to the left which prevents either party from lapsing into complete reaction.

* This was written in 1948. [Eds.]

The strength of this tug is indicated by the fact that the major New Deal reforms have now been almost universally accepted. In the mid-thirties, many leading Republicans, plus many conservative Democrats, were hell-bent on wiping out social security, TVA, SEC, minimum-wage laws, rural electrification, and all the other dread innovations of the New Deal. Today no Presidential aspirant would dare suggest the repeal of a single one of them. In this country there simply is no place for a hard core of irreconcilable reactionaries, comparable to those political groups in France which have never yet accepted the reforms of the French Revolution.

This American tendency to push extremists of both the left and right toward a middle position has enabled us, so far, to escape class warfare. This is no small achievement for any political system; for class warfare cannot be tolerated by a modern industrial society. If it seriously threatens, it is bound to be suppressed by some form of totalitarianism, as it has been in Germany, Spain, Italy, Russia, and most of Eastern Europe.

In fact, suppression might be termed the normal method of settling conflicts in continental Europe, where parties traditionally have been drawn up along ideological battle lines. Every political campaign becomes a religious crusade; each party is fanatically convinced that it and it alone has truth by the tail; each party is certain that its opponents not only are wrong, but wicked. If the sacred ideology is to be established beyond challenge, no heresy can be tolerated. Therefore it becomes a duty not only to defeat the enemy at the polls, but to wipe him out. Any suggestion of compromise must be rejected as treason and betrayal of the true faith. The party must be disciplined like an army, and if it cannot win by other means it must be ready to take up arms in deadly fact.

Under this kind of political system the best that can be hoped for is a prolonged deadlock between parties which are too numerous and weak to exterminate one another. The classic example is prewar France, where six revolutions or near-revolutions broke out within a century, where cabinets fell every weekend, and no government could ever become strong enough to govern effectively. The more usual outcome is a complete victory for one ideology or another, after a brief period of electioneering, turmoil, and fighting in the streets; then comes the liquidation of the defeated.

Because this sort of ideological politics is so foreign to our native tradition, neither Socialists, Communists, nor Fascists have ever been accepted as normal parties. So long as that tradition retains its very considerable vitality, it seems to me unlikely that any third party founded on an ideological basis can take root. The notion of a ruthless and unlimited class struggle, the concept of a master race, a fascist élite, or a proletariat which is entitled to impose its will on all others—these are ideas which are incompatible with the main current of American political life. The uncompromising ideologist, of whatever faith, appears in our eyes peculiarly "un-American," simply because he cannot recognize the rule of the concurrent majority, nor can he accept the rules of mutual toleration which are necessary to make it work. Unless he forsakes his ideology, he cannot even understand that basic principle of American politics which was perhaps best expressed by Judge Learned Hand: "The spirit of liberty is the spirit which is not too sure that it is right."

⌇⌇⌇⌇TOPIC 25

The Filibuster

JACOB K. JAVITS
The Public Business Must Go Forward

At the opening of the 1959 session of Congress, some Democratic and Republican Senators, including Senator Javits, proposed a substantial change in Senate Rule XXII so that debate could be shut off by a simple majority of the whole Senate membership. The Senate rejected this proposal and adopted a plan by which cloture could be made operative by vote of two-thirds of the senators on the floor. While Javits' argument and that of Lindsay Rogers were addressed to the old Rule, they have retained their essential force insofar as the prevailing Rule still requires an extraordinary majority to impose an end to debate, and remains a source of continuing controversy. One such controversy, in fact, arose in the Senate in 1964 over the civil rights bill. In this instance, after a 75-day filibuster, cloture was achieved by a vote of 71 to 29, the necessary two-thirds margin (with four votes to spare).

After careful study of the hearing testimony and of the historic conceptions of the function of the Senate, I am convinced that rule XXII needs amendment to end its veto power on behalf of a small minority; while at the same time assuring the opportunity for full debate and discussion of any subject in the Senate, which has been called the greatest deliberative body on earth.

I do not believe that the present rule XXII serves the purpose of deliberation within the Senate or of education of the public generally. No one questions those two objectives. What I do question is a delegation of the power and responsibility of the majority to a determined minority, which has been and can be again and again an arbitrary block to action, contrary to the will of the majority of this body and of the people to whom they are responsible. Indeed, it seems to me prophetic that this report is filed at an hour of basic crisis in the defense of our country when the weapons which challenge us are precisely so mortally dangerous because of the speed with which they may be effectively

United States Senator from New York. The selection is from *Proposed Amendments to Rule XXII of the Standing Rules of the Senate* (Senate Report No. 1509, 85th Congress, 2d Session), pp. 9-19. By permission.

used to destroy us. In such a time—and there is nothing temporary about this new frame of reference—there is a justifiable demand for making our organs of decision conform to the challenge. How appropriate, then, to consider now a rule of debate which can and has paralyzed decision in the Senate and which can be used by a determined minority to paralyze it on any subject—not alone civil rights. Rule XXII as now written was archaic long before the first Russian earth satellite was launched and is even more so now.

Careful research on the development of the United States Government from its initial period under the Articles of Confederation, through the Constitutional Convention of 1787, when studied in the light of the contemporaneous writings of the Founding Fathers, convinces me that the power which now stems from rule XXII was not even contemplated at the time. On the contrary, from the expressed views of Madison, Hamilton, and others, a method of parliamentary procedure premised on rule XXII would have been violently opposed had it been suggested.

For the premise of rule XXII violates fundamental parliamentary law. It is at odds with early Senate procedures, British Parliamentary practice, and, almost without exception, is contrary to all our State legislative rules of procedure.

In the early Senate, simple majority cloture was used and the "previous question" as a parliamentary device was available under Senate rules and in Jefferson's Senate Manual to close debates. Even after reference to the "previous question" was dropped from the standing rules (in 1806), the presiding officer's power to rule on questions of relevancy and order could have prevented abuse through unrestrained irrelevancies. The conjunction of the lack of cloture and the lack of enforcement of a rule of relevancy (after 1872) made possible the modern veto-type filibuster.

Its fullest development and its most flagrant abuses have occurred following the Civil War in opposition to civil rights legislation—mostly in the last 35 years. While rule XXII did not prevent enactment of the Civil Rights Act of the last session, I believe it did profoundly affect its final formulation. . . .

The realistic effect of [both the old and new rule XXII] is that a small minority of Senators, if sufficiently determined, can by use of a filibuster absolutely prevent the Senate from taking action (in the only way it can—by voting) even though a great majority of Senators desires to come to a vote. Voting is the final method of resolution of national issues contemplated in the Constitution. Protracted speaking which is not intended to illuminate that decision, but to prevent its occurrence, makes a mockery of freedom of speech by confusing it with freedom to obstruct. It does not require great imagination to grasp the significance of this potential power in the hands of Members bent on influencing enactment or the course of particular proposals, without the necessity for persuasion.

The basic issue underlying the problem of cloture is whether we shall permit the Senate, resting as it does on the premise of majority rule, to function at all; to fulfill its legislative purpose; or whether we shall permit the Congress to be stultified by the undemocratic and, in essence, unparliamentary device of filibuster in the Senate—even though cloaked in the senatorial toga of rule XXII. . . .

The Power of the Filibuster as a Veto, With a Case History of the Civil Rights Bill of 1957

The *ability* to carry on a filibuster can affect the kind of legislation passed by the Senate even though no actual filibuster is undertaken. The incidence of a filibuster or the certain knowledge that a filibuster would be organized has made the majority come to terms before. The mere threat that a filibuster of great length would be undertaken against some proposal or unless amendment to a bill was accepted has in effect resulted in the majority of the Senate acquiescing in changes in legislation which otherwise they would probably not have considered wise or desirable.

Careful study of the legislative background and history of the civil rights bill of 1957 and the changes that occurred during the long Senate debate bears out this conclusion and illustrates the pervasive and subtle effect of rule XXII. . . . It became apparent that a bloc of Senators had selected part III as the most objectionable feature of the bill from their viewpoint; and that they were prepared to use every parliamentary device to prevent the enactment of a law which would contain the authorization for the Attorney General on his own motion to enforce through civil action (as an alternative to criminal prosecutions in existing law) the provisions of the 14th amendment to the Constitution. I believe that a number of Senators, among whom were some who favored the retention of part III, felt that insistence on part III would inevitably force the Senators from the South into a filibuster, with the ensuing possibility that no bill at all might be passed. . . .

I have no doubt that if part III had been retained in the bill the Senate would have faced the necessity of a long filibuster which could be blocked only if a large majority were sufficiently determined to sit out the long dreary months that would have been involved. In that interim, no other business could have been transacted and Congress would have been at a standstill. In these times, with important pending legislation, this was a risk to which, naturally, Members of the Senate should give thoughtful consideration. The determined proponents of part III were fully aware of the consequences of insisting upon it. Schedules were worked out for around-the-clock coverage of the Senate floor, Members had beds installed in their offices, the staff details were worked out for a 24-hour operation. Senator Russell of Georgia, the leader of the southern bloc of Senators, was interviewed on a nationwide television program, Face the Nation, on July 21, 1957. Pertinent excerpts of the interview transcript inserted in the Congressional Record of July 22, 1957, indicate clearly the position of the minority:

> Mr. SHADEL. But, Senator, is there any feeling in the Senate that this bill is going to go through, as is, without modifications?
>
> Senator RUSSELL. Not on my part because I will certainly die fighting it in my tracks before this vicious bill could go through, and I would feel the same way if it were aimed at any section of the country. . . .
>
> Mr. LAWRENCE. Well, would it be the intention of the South, under

the circumstances that I can foresee and that you can foresee at the moment, to talk this bill to death?

Senator RUSSELL. I can't say that, Mr. Lawrence, without seeing the bill and if it has these very vicious provisions in it, well, you may be sure that we will use every means at our command to fight it to the very death because it is a very vicious piece of legislation in its present form.

Decision by ordeal was imminent.

No one who participated in the Senate's deliberations could escape the sense of drama, or the mounting tension and concern over the threat inherent in a filibuster. It was in this atmosphere that crucial decisions were made resulting in a number of changes in the legislation, including the elimination of part III. In closing on this point, I should like to add that Little Rock has demonstrated that the decision taken by the Senate to eliminate part III was unwise and that the risk of a stubborn filibuster should have been faced. . . .

Close observers of the legislative process in Congress are aware of this force—of the filibuster—in other legislative compromises which have been adopted, and could cite other examples of the effect of the filibuster on legislation. Vice President Charles G. Dawes, a keen student of Senate proceedings, described the effect of the filibuster in the following words:

> The right of filibuster does not affect simply legislation defeated but, in much greater degree, legislation passed, continually weaving into our laws, which should be framed in the public interest alone, modifications dictated by personal and sectional interest as distinguished from the public interest.

It is no answer to say, as some do say, that such power prevents or softens bad legislation. Of course, it may do that; because legislative proposals subject to a successful filibuster do not get enacted. If any specific action is bad, inaction may be preferred. If all change were bad, then whatever inhibited it would be wise. But the millennium is not here and events do not wait, even if governments do. The built-in stalemate as a permanent method of procedure is opposed to our American spirit and genius.

If the men who conceived our Constitution had thought we needed the concurrence of the majority of two Houses, the assent of the President, and in addition the forbearance of 33 Senators to make law, I assume they would have said so. If this additional check on governmental action is necessary, let us amend the Constitution. The standing rules of the Senate were not drafted in Philadelphia in 1787. The American people neither concurred in them nor agreed to be bound by them—nor did the States. In each Congress, as adopted or acquiesed in, and, to the extent they are constitutional, they bind our Senate procedure so long as they remain unchanged, but they are not the supreme law. They are not the bulwark of free speech and States rights; nor are they immutable. . . .

One may, of course, argue that the existence of rule XXII by which any substantial group of Senators can conduct a filibuster so as to act as a veto, constitutes a "power" which may be exercised on behalf of the States represented by the filibustering Senators; but it is the power neither of persuasion nor of public education. It is an arbitrary power unsanctioned by the Constitution and indeed in direct conflict with its spirit.

Far from securing any constitutional balance, rule XXII seriously disturbs it. The Constitution, in article I, section 5, clause 1, states that—"A majority of each [House] shall constitute a quorum to do business."

That is, 49 Senators are sufficient for the transaction of legislative business. A majority of this quorum is required to assent to the passage of a normal bill. Yet cloture may not be invoked unless at least 64 Members are present and vote for cloture. Legislation of the most profound national effect requires the assent of fewer than half of those required to bring a filibuster to a reasonable close so that that very legislation may be acted upon. I fail to see what balance is here maintained by continuance of the present rule. Alexander Hamilton in arguing, in the Federalist Papers, for the adoption of the Constitution he had helped frame, set forth the need for a totally different balance (Federalist Papers No. 22):

> To give a minority a negative upon the majority (which is always the case where more than a majority is requisite to a decision), is, in its tendency, to subject the sense of the greater number to that of the lesser. . . . This is one of those refinements which, in practice, has an effect the reverse of what is expected from it in theory. The necessity of unanimity in public bodies, or of something approaching toward it, has been founded upon a supposition that it would contribute to security. But its real operation is to embarrass the administration, to destroy the energy of the Government, and to substitute the pleasure, caprice, or artifices of an insignificant, turbulent, or corrupt junto, to the regular deliberations and decisions of a respectable majority. . . . The public business must, in some way or other, go forward. If a pertinacious minority can control the opinion of a majority respecting the best mode of conducting it, the majority, in order that something may be done, must conform to the views of the minority; and thus the sense of the smaller number will overrule that of the greater, and give a tone to the national proceedings. Hence, tedious delays; continual negotiation and intrigue; contemptible compromises of the public good, and yet, in such a system, it is even happy when such compromises can take place: for upon some occasions things will not admit of accommodation: and then the measures of government must be injuriously suspended, or fatally defeated. It is often, by the impracticability of obtaining the concurrence of the necessary number of votes, kept in a state of inaction. Its situation must savor of weakness, sometimes border upon anarchy. . . .
>
> When the concurrence of a large number is required by the Constitution to the doing of any national act, we are apt to rest satisfied that all is safe, because nothing improper will be likely to be done; but we forget how much good may be prevented, and how much ill may be produced, by the power of hindering the doing what may be necessary; and of keeping affairs in the same unfavorable posture in which they may happen to stand at particular periods.

. . . There was a great question of the proper balance of State representation in the Congress in 1787. A study of the debates of the Constitutional Convention shows very clearly that the decision to establish 2 Houses, one to be based on a reference to population, and the other to have 2 Senators from each State regardless of size or population, was the compromise between the delegates from big States and the delegates from the small States. This was the only basis on which the small States would agree to join the Federal Union. This was the great compromise that gave the small States an equal measure of legislative power with the more populous States in this body.

As far as the big States are concerned, according to Madison and others devoted to the principle of proportional representation, they had given enough and more than enough when they finally agreed that each State should have two votes in the Senate. No one then dreamed that in the future Senators would want to upset this balance and add an additional check by a small minority of one-third upon the power of a majority of the Senate as so constituted. This, of course, was long prior to the time when John C. Calhoun developed his theory of concurrent majorities under which legislation favored by a majority in the country as a whole or in the Congress would be subject to the veto of a majority of each and every sectional interest in the country.

This kind of balance, which the opponents of civil-rights legislation wish to retain in the Senate, is a modern version of Calhoun's "concurrent majorities." It was such a sectional right of veto and interposition that Calhoun and other States-rights advocates urged during the debates, in and out of Congress, that led up to the Civil War. This type of imbalance, however, finds no support in the Constitution nor in current practice outside of rule XXII.[1]

Senator Underwood of Alabama said, with respect to the filibuster against the Dyer anti-lynching bill, as follows:

> We are not disguising what is being done on this side of the Chamber. It must be apparent, not only to the Senate but to the country, that an effort is being made to prevent the consideration of a certain bill, and I want to be perfectly candid about it. It is known throughout the country generally as a "force" bill. . . .
>
> *I do not say that captiously. I think all men here know that under the rules of the Senate when 15 or 20 or 25 men say that you cannot pass a certain bill, it cannot be passed.* . . .
>
> I want to say right now to the Senate that if the majority party insists on this procedure they are not going to pass the bill, and they are not going to do any other business. . . .
>
> You know you cannot pass it. Then let us go along and attend to the business of the country. [Emphasis supplied.]

. . .

Permitting a Senator or a group of Senators to talk for hours and days on any conceivable subject or on no subject in order to consume time and prevent the Senate from voting, affords no dignity to the Senate and adds nothing

[1] The paralyzing effect of the minority veto is clearly evident in the deliberations of the United Nations Security Council.

to its deliberative function. Reading recipes for "pot licker," "fried oysters," quoting from Aesop's Fables,[2] and otherwise talking in utter irrelevancies does nothing to enhance the Senate's standing as a great deliberative body.

Senators have a right—and freely exercise it—to express their views on any question before the Senate or before the country. Without doubt it would be a violation of the letter and the spirit of the Constitution to deny or even seriously abridge the right of debate. But, it is also a most flagrant violation of the spirit of the Constitution to clothe this body with forms of procedure by which it may be blocked in the exercise of the legislative powers, and thereby suspended of every other function except that of speaking. The Senate has a duty to debate, but it is likewise a constitutional duty of a majority of this body to act, and with some reasonable expedition. We are obligated not only to pass laws, but also to pass them in time to meet the public need and the general welfare of the country.

Some observers have declared that, far from enhancing the Senate's deliberative function, the right to filibuster has all but destroyed it. Vice President Dawes, for example, said of the veto power of the filibuster:

> The Senate is not and cannot be a properly deliberative body, giving due consideration to the passage of all laws, unless it allots its time for work according to the relative importance of its duties, as do all other great parliamentary bodies. It has, however, through the right of unlimited debate surrendered to the whim and personal purposes of individuals and minorities its right to allot its own time. Only the establishment of majority cloture will enable the Senate to make itself a properly deliberative body. This is impossible when it must sit idly by and see time needed for deliberation frittered away in frivolous and irrelevant talk, indulged in by individuals and minorities for ulterior purposes.

Yet, the Senators who argue that rule XXII should be retained in its present form support this retention as necessary to its deliberative character. I certainly agree that the Senate is a forum of great debate, deliberation, and revision; but I submit that it owes nothing to rule XXII for achieving this distinction. It has achieved that eminence despite the rule.

[2] During the filibuster against the extension of a skeletonized NRA, Senator Long discussed various recipes at great length. This talk continued for 15½ hours and included the reading of long passages from works of Victor Hugo and a reading and discussion of the United States Constitution, article by article, without any necessary reference to the pending business. (See *Congressional Record,* vol. 79, pt. 8, pp. 9122 et seq.)

On June 20, 1936, Senator Rush D. Holt of West Virginia successfully filibustered against passage of a coal conservation bill by reading Aesop's Fables to the Senate. The Senate finally adjourned, sine die, without ever voting on the bill.

LINDSAY ROGERS
Barrier Against Steamrollers

"The Senate of the United States is the only legislative body in the world which cannot act when its majority is ready for action." Thus Woodrow Wilson early in 1917 when a Senate filibuster killed his proposal to arm American merchant ships. The "little group of willful men" were successful only because we then had "short sessions" of Congress that had to come to an end on March 4. The check was not a catastrophe. The ships were armed under authority conferred by an old statute that had been forgotten.

In 1917 the Senate was powerless to end a debate so long as any senator insisted on holding the floor, but debate can now be ended by a vote of two-thirds of the "Senators duly chosen and sworn." It is this much-debated Rule XXII that the Northern liberals hope to change in order to prevent Southern senators from using a filibuster to prevent the passage of drastic civil-rights legislation.

The Northern liberals propose two amendments. The first of these is that two days after a petition has been filed to end debate, two-thirds of the Senate present and voting may so decree. This is not very important; if such a cloture resolution were up, practically all of the "Senators duly chosen and sworn" would be present and vote. But the Northern liberals have a further proposal: that fifteen days after the filing of a petition to end debate, a majority of the entire Senate may so decree. Garrulity would still be permitted; each senator could speak for an hour, but under such circumstances only the filibusters would do so. Then a vote. No longer could a filibuster interpose a veto as it has sometimes done in the past.

Such a change in the rule would, I think, be a mistake. Not so, says [former] Senator Irving M. Ives (R., New York), who maintains that "the principle of majority rule is at stake." It is only in the Senate of the United States, exclaims Senator Clifford P. Case (R., New Jersey), that an opposition must be beaten down by "physical exhaustion" and where "the medieval practice of trial by ordeal still survives."

With great respect to Senator Ives, the term "majority rule" is meaningless as he uses it. Does he want to amend the Constitution so that the Senate would advise and consent to the ratification of a treaty by a majority instead of a two-thirds vote? Is he uneasy because of the theoretical possibility that the minority which defeats a treaty (or a proposed Constitutional amendment) might come from the seventeen smallest states with a total population less than that of New York? Or that a Senate majority might be drawn from twenty-five states with

Former Professor of Public Law at Columbia University. Author of *The American Senate, Crisis Government, The Pollsters,* and other works. The selection is from "Barrier Against Steamrollers," *The Reporter,* Vol. 20 (January 8, 1959), pp. 21-23. By permission.

a population of less than twenty-nine millions? We elect Presidents not by a national popular majority or even plurality, but by counting the ballots federally; each state's Presidential electors do the choosing. Fifty-one per cent may be a numerical majority, but in many cases it is not the majority that our Constitutional practices contemplate. Our Federal arrangements take account of what has been called "the gravity and the impact of the decision." Thus, when one great section of our country opposes a proposed decision, attention may well be paid to "gravity" and "impact."

And when Senator Case brands the Senate as the only legislative assembly in which verbal avoirdupois plays a role along with numbers, so what? The Northern liberals have sometimes insisted on "trial by ordeal." Senator Paul H. Douglas (D., Illinois) boasts that in 1954 he "spoke for three days against the offshore oil bill and in 1956 for four days against the natural gas bill. In each case, with my colleagues of the so-called liberal group, we kept the discussion going for approximately a month." Mr. Douglas applauds "stunts such as Senator Morse's record-breaking, 22½-hour speech delivered without sitting down or leaving the Chamber." The stunters were not attempting "to prevent a vote from being taken." They simply "believed that in these cases many of our colleagues were not fully acquainted with the real issues which were at stake." This is not a veto, Mr. Douglas insists, but only an endeavor to educate senators who were poorly informed. I would allow a substantial group of senators who are well informed, who come from a great section of the country, and who are united in purpose, to impose a veto unless two-thirds of their colleagues are prepared to overrule them.

Blocking the Steamroller

Gladstone called the Senate "the most remarkable of all the inventions of modern politics," and it has remained remarkable in that, contrary to the fate of practically every other upper chamber, it has not become secondary and suffered a loss of authority either by Constitutional amendment or by custom. It is the only legislative body in the world made up of representatives from commonwealths no one of which without its consent can be deprived of its equal representation and whose rights, even though steadily dwindling, still remain substantial. Where in other assemblies is there anything resembling our Senate's rule that its members must not "refer offensively to any State of the Union"?

The filibuster is a weapon that the Constitutional framers who constructed the Senate failed to anticipate but one that they would view with favor. "A dependence on the people is, no doubt, the primary control on the government," Number 51 of *The Federalist* tells us; "but experience has taught mankind the necessity of auxiliary precautions." The framers sought to have "in the society so many separate descriptions of citizens as will render an unjust combination of the majority of the whole very improbable, if not impracticable." The filibuster is no more than a modern "auxiliary precaution" against what one more than one-third of the senators may consider an "unjust combination" of the majority; and I am not impressed when I am told that no other legislative body in the world allows a minority to have such a formidable weapon of defense.

With us the Executive holds office for a fixed term and never appears before the legislature to account for his actions. Hence, it is "an auxiliary precaution" that there be some place in the congressional system at which a party steamroller will meet an effective barrier. The House of Representatives cannot serve this purpose. There, debate is often more severely limited and freedom of decision is more restricted than in any other legislative chamber in the world. A two-thirds majority can suspend the rules, and after forty minutes of discussion, it can pass a measure with no opportunity to offer amendments. A special order from the Rules Committee can allocate time for debate between the majority and minority and require that the House can say only "Yes" or "No." Since the senators number only ninety-eight and show more qualities of prima donnas than do representatives, they would refuse to shackle themselves as do members of the House when they approve a special order from the Committee on Rules; senators would insist that they be permitted to vote on amendments. But without the possibility of parliamentary obstruction—that is, filibustering—a party steamroller, driven by a President and party leaders, could on occasion move almost as ruthlessly on the Senate side as it does on the House side of the Capitol.

Thirty-odd years ago in a book called *The American Senate,* which now occasionally enjoys what William James called the immortality of a footnote, I argued the case for the filibuster. I began the book during the Harding administration and finished when Coolidge was in the White House—the era of the Teapot Dome scandals. The Republican Party machine was then powerful enough to prevent any investigation by a House committee, and Republicans in the Senate were not anxious to uncover wrongdoing. The Republican leaders knew that Senator Thomas J. Walsh of Montana and other Democrats could hold up important business; hence they had to consent to the thoroughgoing inquiry that was demanded. As to whether the threatened filibuster that brought about this result was in the public interest, it is sufficient to remark that three out of ten cabinet members were permitted or pressed to resign, and that there were several indictments and two suicides.

Those desiring Federal civil-rights legislation talk a great deal about the high-handed behavior of a minority. The Southern senators, it is charged, are able to defy "not only a majority in the Senate, but a majority in the country at large." Probably a majority in the country at large is willing for more civil-rights legislation to be passed, but we must not forget that one of the main reasons the framers of the Constitution provided two senators for each state, large or small, was precisely in order to protect the rights of sections against a majority in the country at large.

December 5, 1958, marked the twenty-fifth anniversary of an event on which the Northern liberals might pause to reflect: the end of national prohibition, which was, perhaps, in President Herbert Hoover's phrase, an experiment "noble in motive" but which was certainly a spectacular and disastrous failure. In 1918, when the state legislatures began to vote on the proposed prohibition amendment, saloons were illegal in approximately ninety per cent of the area of the nation, which contained nearly two-thirds of the population of the country. Temperance societies and the Anti-Saloon League (the most powerful pressure group that ever worked on Congress and state legislatures) insisted that aridity be complete. The "drys" marched to a battle that they won. Then they lost the war.

One concluding observation. Ours is the only major country with a two-party system where the laws that get on the Federal statute books, or that fail to get there, usually have bipartisan support and bipartisan opposition. In academic quarters one sometimes hears laments that American political parties are not "disciplined"; that their leadership is sometimes shadowy or undiscoverable, and that they do not present to the electorate clashing bodies of doctrine. But in a country as vast as the United States, with different sectional interests, a political providence has been good in seeing to it that a party majority does not pass party legislation which is opposed by a powerful and determined party minority; that on policies our parties prefer concessions to Pyrrhic victories. The filibuster is undemocratic if "democracy" means that anywhere, and particularly in a federal system, any majority should be able to do what it wishes on any issue at any time. Do the Northern liberals thus define "democracy"? Federalism was the means of forming the nation and it remains the means of preserving it. Congress, as well as the Supreme Court, is the Federal system's manager, and a Senate filibuster is well worth while if, on occasion, it prevents the Congressional manager from being tyrannical.

WALTER LIPPMANN
Minorities Should Not Be Coerced

Although the question before the Senate is whether to amend the rules, the issue is not one of parliamentary procedure. It is whether there shall be a profound and far-reaching constitutional change in the character of the American government. The proposed amendment to Rule XXII would enable two-thirds of the Senate to close the debate and force any measure, motion, or other matter to a vote.* If the amendment is carried, the existing power of a minority of the states to stop legislation will have been abolished.

"Stripped of all mumbo-jumbo and flag waving," says "The New York Times," the issue "is whether the country's highest legislative body will permit important measures to be kept from a vote through the activities of a few leather-throated, iron-legged members who don't want democratic decision." This is an unduly scornful and superficial way to dispose of a great constitu-

Newspaper columnist. Formerly newspaper editor. Author of *Public Opinion, A Preface to Politics, A Preface to Morals, The Good Society, Public Philosophy,* and numerous other books. The selection is from a column by Walter Lippmann in the *New York Herald Tribune,* March 3, 1949. Copyright, 1949, New York Herald Tribune, Inc. By permission.

* This has reference to a proposal before the Senate in 1949 to enable two-thirds of *all* Senate members to close debate which was, in fact, adopted. In 1959, the rule was liberalized to permit cloture by two-thirds of those present and voting. The proposal presently being urged would enable a simple majority of the Senate membership to terminate debate. [Eds.]

tional problem. For the real issue is whether any majority, even a two-thirds majority, shall now assume the power to override the opposition of a large minority of the states.

In the American system of government, the right of "democratic decision" has never been identified with majority rule as such. The genius of the American system, unique I believe among the democracies of the world, is that it limits all power—including the power of the majority. Absolute power, whether in a king, a president, a legislative majority, a popular majority, is alien to the American idea of "democratic decision."

The American idea of a democratic decision has always been that important minorities must not be coerced. When there is strong opposition, it is neither wise nor practical to force a decision. It is necessary and it is better to postpone the decision—to respect the opposition and then to accept the burden of trying to persuade it.

For a decision which has to be enforced against the determined opposition of large communities and regions of the country will, as Americans have long realized, almost never produce the results it is supposed to produce. The opposition and the resistance, having been overridden, will not disappear. They will merely find some other way of avoiding, evading, obstructing or nullifying the decision.

For that reason it is a cardinal principle of the American democracy that great decisions on issues that men regard as vital shall not be taken by the vote of the majority until the consent of the minority has been obtained. Where the consent of the minority has been lacking, as for example in the case of the prohibition amendment, the "democratic decision" has produced hypocrisy and lawlessness.

This is the issue in the Senate. It is not whether there shall be unlimited debates. The right of unlimited debates is merely a device, rather an awkward and tiresome device, to prevent large and determined communities from being coerced.

The issue is whether the fundamental principle of American democratic decision—that strong minorities must be persuaded and not coerced—shall be altered radically, not by constitutional amendment but by a subtle change in the rules of the Senate.

The issue has been raised in connection with the civil rights legislation. The question is whether the vindication of these civil rights requires the sacrifice of the American limitation on majority rule. The question is a painful one. But I believe the answer has to be that the rights of Negroes will in the end be made more secure, even if they are vindicated more slowly, if the cardinal principle—that minorities shall not be coerced by majorities—is conserved.

For if that principle is abandoned, then the great limitations on the absolutism and tyranny of transient majorities will be gone, and the path will be much more open than it now is to the demagogic dictator who, having aroused a mob, destroys the liberties of the people.

THE WELFARE STATE

In an age of vast and proliferating government enterprise, regulation and control, issues of persistent and increasing importance are: What are the economically efficient and politically democratic limits of what has come to be known as the welfare state? How are we best to cope with the problems of poverty in the midst of plenty? How are we to achieve an appropriate balance between the needs of the public and private sectors of our economy? These issues receive the attention of two scholars in the pages which follow.

ҩ҂ҩ҂ҩ҂ TOPIC 26

The Limits of Intervention

HENRY C. WALLICH
The Cost of Freedom

We must, first of all, remind ourselves why we believe in a free economy. Are our chief grounds that we believe it to be the most productive? Or do we prefer it because it helps safeguard personal freedom? Or, finally, is preference for free enterprise perhaps just a rationalization of personal advantage? If we understand our reasons and motives more clearly, we shall have a better view of the choices before us. We shall see in better perspective the risk and cost of alternative courses of action. And from such materials we can construct a stronger case and project a more persuasive image to present to skeptics at home and abroad. These must be the principal objectives of reexamination. . . .

Change in a Free Economy

The principles by which America works and produces are not of today and yesterday. They have stood the test of time for generations. Yet it would be a mistake to assume that because they are fundamental, they must be changeless. It would be futile in particular to expect that the embodiment they find in our economy could somehow remain static. The only way to progress is to change. Let us look at some of the changes to which our generation has been party.

We have participated in social and economic changes that would have looked strange thirty years ago. In our day, the government has taken on by law the responsibility for keeping the economy stable and growing. Social security and unemployment insurance have become part of daily living for many of us. A heavy tax load, principally for national defense, has descended upon all.

At the same time, this age has seen a great spread in private ownership

Professor of Economics, Yale University. Former member of the President's Council of Economic Advisors. The selection is an abridgment of pp. 15-24, 27-28, 40-43, 129-134, 149-153 (Collier edition) from *The Cost of Freedom* by Henry C. Wallich. Copyright © 1960 by Henry C. Wallich. Reprinted by permission of Harper & Row, Publishers.

and private welfare arrangements. More than half of American families have become home owners, a great majority of adults own life insurance policies, about one-half have savings accounts, a substantial minority hold common stocks. Private health insurance, private retirement plans, even private unemployment compensation are growing all around us.

Private business itself meanwhile has not remained the same. Big business has become even bigger, but big labor has arrived and taken over some of the power and, by implication, the responsibility of leadership. Collective bargaining has firmly established itself. Business is becoming increasingly professionized and "managerial" as the separation of ownership and control advances, and has taken on new social functions in research, education, and community services. To sum up diversity under a few labels: as we have become richer, we have moved toward more government, more welfare—public and private—and more bigness.

These developments have been closely related, each one made possible and perhaps necessary by the others. Bigness has been a necessary condition of growing wealth. High living standards demand mass production, and mass production demands big organizations. We could not hope to get the necessary capital, research, and selling by relying on small units.

The demand for welfare measures reflects both our greater wealth and the social conditions of a highly industrial and predominantly urban community. In our kind of world, many needs that in a simpler age could be taken care of more easily call for special provision. Temporarily unemployed workers cannot go home to the farm and live off the land any more—they need unemployment compensation. The aged can no longer plan to live with their children—they need social security and a retirement plan. Medical protection no longer consists of simple remedies prescribed by a kindly country doctor and available for a few cents—our higher standards call for hospitalization insurance and other forms of protection.

The growing role of government is traceable to the other changes—bigness in the private sphere, greater wealth, and the growing demand for welfare and other services. When business and labor grow and gain in power, it is almost inevitable that government should grow likewise, if it wants to keep the other two in check. Pressure generates counter-pressure. The public interest, confronted with powerful private interests, has responded by building up a big and powerful government.

The social conditions created by industry and the city have likewise abetted the growth of government. The need for social services, where private action proved inadequate or too slow, has called forth public action. So have the economic fluctuations to which this industrial and urban economy has been prone. No longer are we minded to ride out major ups and downs; we have found defenses against them, at the cost of rising government activity.

Growing wealth, too, has become a motive for enlarging the sphere of government in our economy. As our income has risen, we have been able to afford more of everything. But we have not expanded our demands equally in all directions. With basic needs taken care of, it is natural that additional demand should reach out toward newer fields—luxuries, services, education, security. There is no economic law which says that a growing share of such high income needs should be supplied by government. But government abhors a vacuum and will quickly move to fill real or imagined gaps left by private enterprise. In many instances, demand seems to have been elastic in the direction of wants that government could meet, and it has met them.

These, in simplest terms, are the reasons why growing wealth seems to have been accompanied by more bigness, welfare, and government. Is this march into the future a march into socialism? In the face of the buoyant expansion of private activity and ownership, it would take more-than-average pessimism to arrive at this conclusion. The success of capitalism since the war likewise contradicts such fears. To our grandparents, perhaps, we might all appear as dangerous radicals. But a less static appraisal suggests that free enterprise has changed America, and in doing so has also shifted the old signposts.

Those who believe that our traditional values must necessarily be in conflict with such innovations overlook that the application of conservative principles does not depend so much on the "what" as the "how." Continuing social change is inevitable. That is the nature of a dynamic system. If we do not accept this, we are in conflict with the very principles we want to conserve.

Loyalty to our heritage means more than mechanically to repeat what our ancestors began. It would be futile to try to uphold traditional values by doing for the hundredth time what others did for the first. The American tradition is one of constant evolution. If we want to be like those who came before us, we must invite change as they did and break away from old patterns. Conservatism does not mean to substitute imitation for creation. It is expressed in the way in which change is brought about—step by step, relying on experience more than on theory, acting with continuity and responsibility.

This creative attitude toward the past is quite taken for granted in the operation of business enterprise. Businessmen generally are conservatives—their success, power, and responsibility all combine to make them so. Yet in order to become and remain successful, they must also be innovators. Invention, rather than market equilibrium, is the core of capitalism. One cannot revolutionize the processes of production and almost double the standard of living in each generation without setting in motion great social changes.

To try to improve upon the past does not mean to disapprove of it. There are some who, in contrast to the traditionalists, seek to justify capitalism mainly by pointing to its recent improvements. "The capitalism of the nineteenth century," they say, "was harsh, the economy of the 1920's was speculative, but now we have overcome these defects, now we have the right system." In saying so, they do injustice to the past, while also overlooking the certainty of future change. If our basic principles are sound, we may have confidence in their effectiveness today without fear of the inevitable changes, but we likewise must accept their working in the past.

Along this road that leads from the past to the future, men with different temperaments and interests will no doubt want to advance rather different distances. Men tend to be "modern" in the field in which they are specialists, more conservative outside it. This accounts for many of the differences, on social and economic matters, between academics and practical people. But whoever believes himself unalterably opposed to some kind of change has open to him a simple test. He need only ask himself whether he has ever changed his mind on a question of this nature. The world is full of people who at one time were unalterably opposed to labor unions, social security, or a flexible fiscal policy. Yet for most of them the enormities of twenty years ago have become today's matter of course. He who ever has changed his mind must beware of last ditch attitudes.

What matters is that the new propositions be guided by the old principles. We must furnish welfare without destroying initiative and provide security without doing injury to incentives. We must maintain stability without falling into regimentation and seek change without courting discontinuity. To keep initiative and incentives alive, we must be prepared to accept a certain degree of inequality in our economic fortunes, after assuring as much equality of opportunity as we can. To avoid regimentation, we must put up with some degree of uncertainty and risk. To assure continuity, our reforms should be conducted in a spirit of constructiveness and cooperation, without vindictiveness or punitive intent. If these things can be done, forms will change but substance will remain. . . .

The Issues

The substance of the economic beliefs that I would like to reexamine is not exclusively economic; it has a moral tinge. Every principle that wants to command strong allegiance must make a moral case. Men want to feel that what they are doing is useful, but they want also, and mainly, to feel that it is right.

Freedom is one of these principles. It is freedom that gives the image of a market economy, an open economy, so powerful an appeal. The belief in freedom lies at the core of our civilization. It is part of our belief in the dignity of man. Our economic system draws immense strength from this identification with our moral faiths. Because our free economy has given us an unrivaled standard of living, we have concluded, not unnaturally, that our methods are not only the "right" way for a free people, but also the most efficient way. This reaction is understandable, although one cannot help suspecting that it reflects more self-congratulation than soul searching. We should perhaps have asked ourselves whether it is really possible to have the best of everything at once. Economics rests on the proposition that to get a little more of one blessing one must accept a little less of another. Have we fallen into the trap of thinking that because we like something, it must serve us best in all possible respects? . . .

We need recall only what the nation did during two world wars. When maximum output was needed, we shifted to centralized control and direction. When the emergency was over, the shift was reversed—fortunately. The lesson is plain. A free economy can perform very well, as ours has. It can provide a rapidly rising standard of output and consumption. But if absolute maximum of output and growth is wanted there are other methods. The United States, fortunately, has never in peacetime been tempted to sell its birthright of freedom for a mess of production accelerated by forced draft methods. We have viewed economic freedom—the freedom to work and quit, to hire and fire, and to consume as we please—as part of our total freedom. We have believed—rightly, I think—that a free economy buttresses political freedom by assuring that power, freedom's eternal enemy, shall remain widely dispersed. A free economy has seemed to us a good and efficient economy, but even more it has seemed the right economy for a society of free men.

I would wish, however, that these non-material motives could have become more explicit. Freedom loving people pay themselves a poor compliment when they explain their devotion on the grounds that it is profitable. I would rather feel that I held my beliefs for their own sake and perhaps at some sacrifice in material terms. That, I believe, happens to be the truth of the matter. Freedom comes at a cost, not at a profit. . . .

A free economy relies for its success upon the initiative displayed by millions of people and business firms, all of them representing small—sometimes perhaps not so small—centers of decision. To work effectively, these centers of decision must be powered by strong incentives. The need for initiative and incentives thus becomes the second subject of our inquiry. . . .

An incentive economy—even if its rules are softened as I would suggest —is bound to produce economic inequality. To some this will appear as no more than an old fact of economic life. If they are concerned at all, they may feel that equality of opportunity, rather than of shares, is the issue. To others, inequality becomes a matter of conscience more than of economics. How can great inequality of wealth and income be squared with belief in democracy and political equality? How does it stand up before our general ideas of fairness? Inequality of wealth and income will be our final object of inquiry.

This issue has troubled men's minds since time immemorial, and while wise men may debate it, only fools will come to a final decision. To those who regard all inequality as bad, no helpful answer can be given. Others may note, however, that in a dynamic economy inequality acquires a function—it accelerates growth. By facilitating the use of incentives and the accumulation of savings, and so stimulating economic growth, inequality benefits even those who initially appear to be its victims.

In a growing economy, moreover, the parallel of political and economic inequality breaks down. One man's gain in political power is bound to be at the expense of others—his economic gain need not be. This, to my mind, removes a good part of the moral element from the issue.

Meanwhile, the growing similarity of living habits among the higher and lower income groups takes much of the edge off economic inequality. The extreme contrast of rich and poor that characterized early capitalism has vanished, and it would fulfill no function today. Equality of opportunity is also advancing, though much remains to be done.

To say a good word, howsoever qualified, on behalf of inequality nevertheless is an awkward undertaking. In the absence of other considerations, greater equality surely is to be preferred to less. Yet progressive equalization threatens harm not only to economic growth. The trend toward grey flannel conformity testifies to other dangers of equalization. Originality, excellence, and achievement in any field of endeavor are at stake. If we have needed them in the past, we can do even less without them today. The future of a free society depends on the preservation of beliefs that give room to creative inequalities. . . .

Freedom in American Life

Freedom is one of the great words in our language. It stands for one of the great ideas of our civilization. It was in search of freedom that the Pilgrim Fathers left their homes for America. The authors of the Declaration of Independence put freedom directly after life itself. . . .

Today, the lines of debate are drawn around three important issues. The first is the very meaning of freedom. Traditionally, freedom has been thought of in terms of man's freedom from arbitrary government. Now, it is being argued persuasively that to the hungry man this sort of freedom is a mockery. To be free, he needs also financial independence. What are we to think of this "new freedom"?

Second, we have before us the familiar issue of a market economy versus a "controlled" economy. Which will give the better result? On one extreme are the devotees of laissez faire; arrayed against them on the other stand the whole-hearted planners. Most people find their place somewhere in between. The problem is old, but new and conflicting evidence keeps coming in. We must once more define our position.

The third disputed area encompasses the role of a free economy in protecting our political freedom. Some believers in freedom are prepared to concede that under certain conditions, a controlled economy may outperform a free market economy. But they regard controls as too much of a threat to liberty to take this chance. . . . The issue comes to this: Is a free economy necessary —perhaps even sufficient—as a bulwark against arbitrary power? . . .

What makes a free economy? First of all, a free economy is a decentralized economy. Decentralization means that we have millions of centers of initiative, instead of only one. It means variety that stimulates creative thinking. "Crazy ideas" have a chance that might never survive scrutiny by an entrenched bureaucracy. Decentralization means making the fullest use of our individual capacities.

Next, a free economy relies upon free markets to decide what is to be produced, instead of upon a central authority. The market gives the economy high flexibility, and makes it responsive to consumer wishes. If consumer wishes are to rule—and what else should in a free economy?—the free market offers the best means for the allocation of productive resources.

In the third place, a free economy relies heavily on incentives and competition. It offers to reward each according to his contribution, and it holds out exceptional prizes to the exceptional man. Competition stimulates each to do his utmost.

Decentralization, free markets, incentives and competition are the basic mechanisms of a free economy. The more freedom allowed, one must assume, the more intensive and effective will be the work of these mechanisms. It is noteworthy, therefore, that in practice we rather pointedly refrain from pushing freedom as far as it will go. If we felt that no other system had comparable advantages, that presumably is what we ought to do. We would want an economy consisting mainly of very small units, in order to have as many centers of initiative and sources of ideas as possible. This kind of economy would also give us perfectly competitive free markets and would hold out the unique incentive of everybody being able to become his own boss. Is it only perverseness, or the scheming of selfish interests, that blocks such wholesome extension of freedom?

Of course it is not, and most of us are perfectly satisfied to see economic freedom restrained in some respects. The uses of freedom have their limits. Competing with the principle of decentralization is its opposite, organization, as represented by big business. Big business has always been credited with the special advantages arising from mass production. Today, however, big business also claims pre-eminence in two other respects: research, and the ability to finance large investment expenditures to realize upon its research. Much is made of these advantages of big business in contemporary literature. It is refreshing to hear such forthright speech on behalf of a sector of the economy that until recently preferred to keep itself under wraps. But we must be alive to its meaning. The claims of big business severely cramp the style of several familiar figures: the independent inventor in his attic or garage, the young man striking out for himself in a free competitive market, the small business man who is often said to be the backbone of the American economy. They are all manifestations of the freedom we extol in a sense in which big business is not. To the extent that we accept the superiority of the big corporation, we agree that there are economic forces more powerful than sheer freedom.

Especially intriguing is big business' claim to superiority in the financing of capital formation. The claim can hardly be denied. Big business has better access to the capital market, and it often can finance its expenditures from undistributed profits. But in driving home its superiority in capital formation, big business touches the Achilles heel of the free and completely decentralized economy. The speed with which capital is accumulated in such an economy is unpredictable. Rapid accumulation is possible, but it is not part of the logic of the system. The decentralized system can promise a strong flow of inventions, and efficiency in the use of resources. These are, as it were, among its built-in features. Up to a point, inventions also probably set in motion forces that generate additional savings. But in the main, the flow of savings is regulated by the tastes of the people in the community. The system merely interprets these tastes through the market. It is not the fault of the system if people decide to consume all of their income, nor can it claim credit if they save a high proportion. It works just as efficiently in one case as in the other.

A high rate of saving and a high rate of technological advance are the joint promoters of economic progress, with technology probably the senior partner of the firm. Since the decentralized system can promise the second, but not the first, it can guarantee some progress, but not necessarily at the fastest rate. In practice we have enjoyed very satisfactory progress, because invention has been accompanied by a high rate of business saving, and because we have been willing to save as consumers. But the consumer is not entirely reliable as a source of savings. Big business, by reminding us of its superior power of capital formation, points up one of the advantages that a more highly organized system enjoys over a more decentralized.

As it stands today, our economic system is a combination of the elements of decentralization and organization. We have not pushed freedom to its ultimate limits, but have taken it, as a good thing should be taken, in moderation. This poses some ticklish questions. We are pretty sure that our system contains the right ingredients, but how about the proportions? If we had to do it over, would we order "the mixture as before"? And supposing, as I do, that we would, why do we like this particular combination of freedom and organization? Is it because we feel that it is the most productive combination? Or do we prefer it because we like freedom for its own sake, and insist on a certain substantial amount of it even though production could be increased by adding more organization to the formula? In other words, is there one optimum formula if we care mostly about production, and another if we care mostly about freedom? If so, which of the two formulas are we using, the productive or the free? If we are closer to the free formula, how much production are we giving up as the price of freedom? . . .

Equality of Opportunity

For the better part of this section, equality has remained at odds with goals like progress or freedom. One species of equality, however, is not involved in this conflict: equality of opportunity. Capitalism thrives on equality of opportunity. The economy is bound to perform better where jobs are assigned by the merit system—to each according to his capacity—and not by nepotism—to each according to his uncle. Here, for once, equality is on the same team with all the other virtues.

Their common ground is rather narrow, however, and scarcely allows room for unlimited rejoicing. Equality of opportunity is certainly no panacea for all the ills bequeathed by inequality in other respects. Moreover, it would be harder to organize in practice than some of its admirers seem to think. This we shall presently see.

Equality of opportunity must be called a narrow virtue primarily because it seems to envisage human existence as a kind of race. Only if we all have the same goal—to excel, to be successful—does it make sense to demand an even start. In a world where everything is competition and competition is everything, starting position matters—starting inequality is inequity. But inequality ceases to be inequity as soon as we envisage different people following different tracks. The very term "equal opportunity" loses its meaning once we remind ourselves that people may have very different goals. How can we truly equalize Jones' opportunity to live a quiet life close to his family with Smith's to devote himself to intellectual pursuits and Robinson's to make a million dollars? . . .

Each wants to start as close to his objective as he can, and it should be of no great concern to him where travelers with other destinations take off from. In other words, where goals differ, what we seek is optimum rather than equal opportunity.

No unfairness need be involved in providing each man with the best start possible toward his particular dream. . . . If opportunity in this broadest sense is to be maximized, our need is, not for equality, but for freedom. Freedom, first of all, for each to discover what he really wants, free not only from state direction but also from social pressure bent on imposing some homogenized pattern of compulsory felicity. This opportunity to live the good life is something we can all give to ourselves and to each other. If we have not made full use of it, the fault belongs to us and not to our free institutions. . . .

To make sure, however, that opportunity will knock equally often and equally loudly on every man's door is by no means easy. To do it in a literal way, in fact, is not only undesirable but fortunately also quite impossible. To begin with, it would seem obvious that we cannot mean literally equal job and career opportunities for everybody regardless of aptitude. That would lead to some very witless arrangements. Everybody would have to have the same education stuffed down his throat. To make sure that it was really the same, it would have to be of a pretty mediocre grade. . . .

Obviously, no sane society would in this way deprive itself of the services of its most talented members nor deprive those members of the best possible education. Equal opportunity cannot sensibly be interpreted to require equal mediocrity. If what is wanted is the best use of talent, equal opportunity must mean equal chance for equal talent. This, however, would mean very unequal education for the gifted and the less gifted.

On the other side of the fence, equality of opportunity of this more efficient kind is not very helpful if it leads to extreme inequality of results. . . . This implies that people of average ability must have some chance of doing well, and reasonable assurance against doing very badly. . . . And of course some floor must be fitted under the "also-rans"—minimum reward to the unsuccessful—that makes it worth their while to go to the starting post. . . . Perfect equality of opportunity remains beyond reach so long as we do not abolish the family system.

The family, because it reaches beyond the individual, produces one inevitable effect: it polarizes opportunity potentials. To eliminate the unequal effect of the home upon children's development and education, the state would have to take them into its fatherly arms practically as soon as they learned to speak. To keep fathers from using their influence on behalf of their sons when they start their careers, it might prove necessary to destroy all means of family identification at an early age. That we would have to get rid of inheritance, with all this would mean for the willingness to save and for the continuation of our business system, is just a minor incidental. For, in fact, we would have to turn our society inside out. . . . The United States has long regarded itself as the country of opportunity. Do we offer it on terms of equality that deserve to be called acceptable?

But this lack of equal opportunity for the less talented is not all. Racial discrimination is a blemish that, in the areas that it blights, works even greater injustice and waste of human ability. The United States deserves no particular blame for being saddled with a problem that most countries have never known. But our failure to solve it hangs like an albatross around our necks. Until this sin is expiated, we can never feel very sure of what we assert about equality of opportunity in our country. . . .

To sum up our impression on equality of opportunity in the United States: American society has managed to provide equal opportunity wherever it was to the interests of the economy. Able men from all ranks have been pushed ahead by the system, and have found few obstacles in their way. Top jobs thus have generally gone to top men. But we have fewer occasions to pat ourselves on the back when we look at the way the less critical jobs are assigned to the less high-powered citizens. Job performance may matter less in these lower echelons, but the number of lives affected runs far higher. A great deal of work remains to be done here.

Too Many Trivia?

The thesis that public services are neglected and private consumption inflated with trivia has found its most eloquent interpretation in *The Affluent Society* by John Kenneth Galbraith, to whom we were previously indebted for important insights into the workings of American capitalism. Galbraith argues that this imbalance is nourished by advertising, which creates artificial wants. He sees it further accentuated by an obsession with production, which keeps us from realizing that our problems are not those of want, but of affluence. The imbalance is epitomized by our supposed tendency to limit public expenditures to what is strictly essential, while we apply no such criterion to private expenditures.

One may reasonably argue that Galbraith exaggerates the distorting influence of advertising. That would not alter the basic assumption on which his thesis rests—the assumption that there are better wants and worse wants. Scientific detachment notwithstanding. I find it extraordinarily difficult to disagree with this proposition. To rate an attendance at the opera and a visit to an (inexpensive) nightclub as equivalents, because the market puts a similar price on them, goes against my grain. So does the equation of a dollar's worth of education and a dollar's worth of chromium on an automobile. And a plausible case could probably be made, on the basis of the evolution of the species, that opera and education do represent more advanced forms of consumption.

But what consequences, if any, should be drawn from such judgment? Does it yield a basis for trying to discourage the growth of the less "good" expenditures? In a free society, we obviously want to move with the utmost circumspection. It is worth remembering that even Thorstein Veblen, who went to some extreme in deriding the "leisure class" and its "conspicuous consumption," did not take an altogether negative view of all conspicuous waste. In *The Theory of the Leisure Class* he said, "No class of society, not even the most abjectly poor, foregoes all customary conspicuous consumption. . . . There is no class and no country that has yielded so abjectly before the pressure of physical want as to deny themselves all gratification of this higher or spiritual need."

For a fair appraisal of the case against trivia, we would also want to know the approximate size of the bill that is being incurred for various frills and frivolities. Gadgets in cars and homes have drawn the special ire of the critics. It is interesting to note, therefore, that expenditures for all kinds of durable consumer goods, including automobiles, run about 14 per cent of personal consumption. The greater part of this, presumably, goes for the essential parts of fairly essential equipment. What is left for ornaments and gadgets does not loom impressively large.

Whatever our private feelings about the gadgetry in our life, we probably do well not to stress them too hard. It is only too easy for some members of a community to work themselves into a fit of righteousness and to feel tempted to help the rest regulate their existence. In an extreme form, and not very long ago, this happened in the United States with the introduction of prohibition. Some of us may lean toward special taxation of luxuries, but surely no one wants sumptuary legislation banishing from our show windows and homes the offending contrivances. A new puritanism directed against wasteful consumption, however understandable, would make no great contribution to an economy that requires incentive goods to activate competition and free markets. Neither would it be compatible with the freedom that we value.

It is the positive side of the case—the asserted need for more public services—that must chiefly concern us. One can listen with some sympathy to the case and to the account of the biases in our economy that work against public and for private spending. The pressure of $10 billions worth of advertising is a bias of that sort. The natural reluctance of taxpayers to vote taxes the benefits of which will be shared by others is a second. A third is the somewhat vague nature of many public benefits—education, welfare, and health, for instance. They are of a kind that the taxpayer himself might tend to neglect a little were he to purchase them in the market place. Then there is the peculiar relationship of state and local authorities to the federal government, which restrains public expenditures by leaving most of the socially useful expenditures to the former while giving the more productive tax sources to the latter. And finally, there is the American tradition which in the interests of freedom puts a special premium on private activity over public.

But what we are in some danger of overlooking are the biases on the other side—the pressures that work for greater public spending. If advertising promotes sales to individuals, those who supply the public authorities are not without means of their own to promote their wares. If some taxpayers object to taxes that will benefit others besides themselves, there are others who vote for expenditures expecting that they will benefit where they have not contributed. Politicians in general have not been averse to voting funds for well supported worthy causes. Vocal minorities that know what they want often can outmaneuver inarticulate majorities that don't know how to stand up for their own interests. Finally, our tax system itself has a built-in bias to encourage spending, because it collects relatively small amounts per head from taxpayers in the lower brackets, while those in the upper brackets pay a good deal. If the benefits that individuals in different brackets derive from public services are not too disparate, taxpayers in the lower brackets obviously are getting theirs at a bargain. Since they constitute a majority, they are in a position to increase the number of these bargains.

As between the forces that inhibit and those that advance public expenditures, no one can say for sure where the balance lies. But on the evidence that thirty years ago taxes of all kinds added up to less than 10 per cent of the Gross National Product, whereas today they account for well over 25 per cent, we have no reason to suspect that the expansive forces lack vigor—even allowing one-third of the present load for major national security.

Meanwhile, those who would like to see public services taking a still larger share must bear in mind two facts, one economic, the other political. The economic fact is that the free provision of public services paid for by taxation is a very inefficient way of catering to consumer needs. I am not referring to popular suspicions about the efficiency of public administration, but to the manner in which costs and benefits are adjusted to each other, or fail to be adjusted. In private dealings, the consumer purchases the exact amount of the exact product he wants, and so gets the most for his money. The taxpayer voting for certain public services has no means of securing such nice adjustment. He may find himself getting less, or more, or something other than he wanted. He has no incentive, moreover, to economize in the use of many of the services offered— usually they come to him free of charge. Our methods of making public decisions and apportioning public services leave much to be desired as compared with the neat job done by the free market.

The political problem that confronts advocates of larger public expenditures is of a different order. We return here to the point stressed earlier in this section—the tendency of our society to produce a balance of interests that impedes ready shifts among private and public resources. This applies also, of course, to budgetary expenditures. Barring some outward disturbance that shakes the balance of interests, such as a military emergency, the balance of expenditures in the budget will also tend to remain stable. If there are to be budget cuts, they are likely to cut all around. If the purse strings are to be relaxed, they are likely to be relaxed not just in one direction, but in all. That is the result of a balance which makes all interests share burdens and benefits in accordance with their bargaining strength.

The consequences, when larger expenditures are proposed, tend to be those we have often observed. The proponents of new expenditures rarely demand that all forms of public spending be enlarged. They have some particular purposes in mind. But the prevailing balance of interests works against such favors for any one group, extended to the exclusion of all the rest. If one form of expenditures is expanded, political pressures develop for giving everybody else something he wants.

The "balance of interests" effect need not, of course, be taken in its most literal sense. Obviously the proportions among different public expenditures always are shifting in some degree. Some expenditures are subject to factors that cannot be controlled, such as fluctuating interest rates or crop yields. Some have a built-in momentum, as does Social Security. And as public opinion and political constellations shift, so does the balance among public functions. Marginal improvements in particular public programs are never out of reach. Major increases, however, are not likely to occur unless accompanied by major shifts in the balance of interests. With that balance intact, the politics of the case incline toward, not "first come, first served," but "come one, come all."

This imposes a heavy surcharge upon expenditures that intrinsically may have much to recommend them. It alters the practical attractiveness of such proposals. To spend public money for a good program is one thing. To have to loosen up on half a dozen unrelated programs as a condition of expanding one is quite another.

A political surcharge of this kind can make the implicit cost of desirable programs very high. Some may argue that this cost will have to be faced. Nevertheless, it should give pause even to those who feel strongly about their proposals. In a free country, no group can expect to change the balance of interests save as they succeed in swinging some of its components to their side. Once more we must note that freedom has its price.

JOHN KENNETH GALBRAITH
The Affluent Society

The Conventional Wisdom

Through the nineteenth century, liberalism in its classical meaning having become the conventional wisdom, there were solemn warnings of the irreparable damage that would be done by Factory Acts, trade unions, social insurance, and other social legislation. Liberalism was a fabric which could not be raveled without being rent. Yet the desire for protection and security and some measure of equality in bargaining power would not down. In the end it became a fact with which the conventional wisdom could not deal. The Webbs, Lloyd George, LaFollette, Roosevelt, Beveridge, and others crystallized the acceptance of the new fact. The result is what we call the welfare state. The conventional wisdom now holds that these measures softened and civilized capitalism and made it tenable. There have never ceased to be warnings that the break with classical liberalism was fatal.

Another interesting instance of the impact of circumstance on the conventional wisdom was that of the balanced budget in times of depression. Almost from the beginning of organized government the balanced budget or its equivalent has been the *sine qua non* of sound and sensible management of the public purse. The spendthrift tendencies of princes and republics alike were curbed by the rule that they must unfailingly take in as much money as they paid out. The consequences of violating this rule had always been unhappy in the long run and not infrequently in the short. Anciently it was the practice of states to cover the deficit by clipping or debasing the coins and spending the metal so saved. The result invariably was to raise prices and lower national self-esteem. In modern times the issue of paper money or the obtaining of soft loans from banks had led to the same results. As a result, the conventional wisdom had never emphasized anything more strongly than the importance of an annually balanced budget. . . .

Audiences continued to respond to the warnings of the disaster which would befall were this rule not respected. The shattering circumstance was the Great Depression. This led to a severe reduction in the revenues of the federal government; it also brought increased pressure for a variety of relief and welfare expenditures. A balanced budget meant increasing tax rates and reducing

Warburg Professor of Economics at Harvard University; United States Ambassador to India from 1961 to 1963; Chairman of Americans for Democratic Action. His books include *The Great Crash, American Capitalism, The Liberal Hour, The New Industrial State.* This excerpt is from *The Affluent Society* (Boston, Houghton Mifflin Co., 1958). Copyright © 1958 by John Kenneth Galbraith. Reprinted by permission of the publisher, Houghton Mifflin Company.

public expenditure. Viewed in retrospect, it would be hard to imagine a better design for reducing both the private and the public demand for goods, aggravating deflation, increasing unemployment, and adding to the general suffering. In the conventional wisdom, nonetheless, the balanced budget remained of paramount importance. President Hoover in the early thirties called it an "absolute necessity," "the most essential factor to economic recovery," "the imperative and immediate step," "indispensable," "the first necessity of the Nation," and "the foundation of all public and private financial stability."[1] Economists and professional observers of public affairs agreed almost without exception. Almost everyone called upon for advice in the early years of the depression was impelled by the conventional wisdom to offer proposals designed to make things worse. The consensus embraced both liberals and conservatives. The Roosevelt Administration was also elected in 1932 with a strong commitment to reduced expenditures and a balanced budget. In his acceptance speech in 1932 Roosevelt said, "Revenue must cover expenditures by one means or another. Any government, like any family, can for a year spend a little more than it earns. But you and I know that a continuation of that habit means the poorhouse." One of the early acts of his Administration was an economy drive which included a horizontal slash in public pay. Mr. Lewis W. Douglas, through a distinguished life a notable exemplar of the conventional wisdom, made the quest for a balanced budget into a personal crusade and ultimately broke with the Administration on the issue.

In fact, circumstances had already triumphed over the conventional wisdom. By the second year of the Hoover Administration the budget was irretrievably out of balance. In the fiscal year ending in 1932, receipts were much less than half of spending. The budget was never balanced during the depression. But not until 1936 did both the necessities and advantages of this course begin to triumph in the field of ideas. In that year, John Maynard Keynes launched his formal assault in *The General Theory of Employment, Interest and Money*. Thereafter the conventional insistence on the balanced budget under all circumstances and at all levels of economic activity was in retreat. . . .

Nothing in the history of social ideas is more interesting that the treatment of the so-called business cycle in the central tradition of economic thought. Its study was isolated in a separate compartment. (To some extent the quarantine still continues.) Prices, wages, rents and interest, all of which were profoundly affected by depressions, were studied on the assumption that depressions did not occur. Normal conditions were assumed; normal meant stable prosperity. In the separate study of the business cycle emphasis was placed on the peculiar and nonrecurring conditions which lay back of each depression—the retirement of the greenbacks prior to 1873, the readjustments following World War I, the breakdown of international trade and capital movements and the collapse of the stock market in 1929. But, paradoxically, there was an equal emphasis—sometimes in the same work—on the rhythmic and normal character of the succession of good times and bad. The etymology emphasized the rhythm—as noted, the

[1] Arthur M. Schlesinger, Jr., *The Crisis of the Old Order* (Boston: Houghton Mifflin, 1956), p. 232.

study was not of depressions but of the business cycle which served to remind everyone that just as bad times followed good, so good times would follow the bad. . . .

To view the business cycle as a normal rhythm was to regard it as self-correcting. Hence nothing needed to be done about it. Remedies are unnecessary if the patient is certain to recover and they are also unwise. Writing in 1934, Joseph A. Schumpeter, then with Wesley C. Mitchell one of the world's two most eminent authorities on the business cycle, surveyed the experience of the preceding century and concluded, "In *all* cases . . . recovery came of itself. . . . But this is not all: our analysis leads us to believe that recovery is sound only if it does come of itself. For any revival which is merely due to artificial stimulus leaves part of the work of depressions undone and adds, to an undigested remnant of maladjustment, new maladjustments of its own."[2]

Had depressions always remained mild, the notion of a normal rhythm, which wisdom required be undisturbed, would have been reassuring. But as depressions became more violent such a view was the very reverse of reassuring. Workers lost their jobs. Farm prices fell and some farmers lost their farms. Investors lost their savings and some businessmen, more particularly the smaller ones, went bankrupt. And all this was insouciantly described as normal. The conclusion was inevitable: there must be something very wrong with a system in which such faults were normal. . . .

There is little need to stress the consequences. To the lingering fear that poverty might be normal, the increasing conviction that inequality was inevitable and the sense of individual insecurity which was inherent in the competitive model, the orthodox view of the business cycle added a much more general sense of disquiet. This was the insecurity of a householder who is told that in the normal and regular course of events he must expect his house to catch fire and his property to be partially or wholly destroyed. The fire cannot be prevented or arrested for it has its work to do; to call for a fire department is to invite an attempt to drown the flames by drenching them with gasoline.

Such was the legacy of ideas in the great central tradition of economic thought. Behind the façade of hope and optimism there remained the haunting fear of poverty, inequality, and insecurity. . . .

Economic Security

Few matters having to do with economic life have been so much misunderstood as the problem of economic security. And in remarkable degree the misunderstanding persists. . . . The first step in penetrating this bedlam is to recognize that while risk was indeed inherent in the economic society of the central tradition, it has long been regarded with equanimity by almost no one. And all who were subject to insecurity sooner or later set about eliminating it as it affected themselves. In large measure they were successful. . . .

The elimination of economic insecurity was pioneered by the business firm in respect of its own operations. The greatest source of insecurity, as

---

[2] J. A. Schumpeter, *Essays*, ed. by Richard V. Clemence (Cambridge, Mass.: Addison-Wesley, 1951), p. 117. This essay was originally published in 1934 in *The Economics of the Recovery Program* (New York: Whittlesey House, McGraw-Hill). The italics are in the original.

noted, lay in competition and the free and unpredictable movement of competitive market prices. From the very beginning of modern capitalist society, businessmen have addressed themselves to the elimination or the mitigation of this source of insecurity. Monopoly or the full control of supply, and hence of price, by a single firm was the ultimate security. But there were many very habitable halfway houses. Price and production agreements or cartels, price-fixing by law, restrictions on entry of new firms, protection by tariffs or quotas, and many other devices have all had the effect of mitigating the insecurity inherent in the competitive economy. Most important, where the number of firms is small, a characteristic feature of the modern industry, interdependence is recognized and respected, and firms stoutly avoid price behavior which would enhance uncertainty for all. . . .

These efforts have been long and widely remarked. However, the tendency of these measures to focus directly or indirectly on price, which, as stated, is the greatest source of uncertainty, has led economists to regard the management of prices as being of unique importance. And they have far more frequently related such management to the maximization of profits than to the minimization of risks. The specter that has haunted the economist has been the monopoly seeking extortionate gains at the public expense. This has dominated his thoughts. The less dramatic figure, the businessman seeking protection from the vicissitudes of the competitive economy, has been much less in his mind. That is unfortunate, for the development of the modern business enterprise can be understood only as a comprehensive effort to reduce risk. It is not going too far to say that it can be understood in no other terms.

Specifically, it falls within the power of the modern large corporation to mitigate or eliminate (with one exception) every important risk to which business enterprises have anciently been subject. Consumer taste and demand may shift. The modern large corporation protects itself by its advertising. Consumer taste is thereby brought at least partly under its control. Size makes possible a diversified line. This provides further protection. There is danger that technological change will render obsolete a product or method of production. The modern corporation is able, through its research and technological resources, to insure that it will be abreast of such change. Therefore technological change will occur under its own auspices or within its reach. A measure of control over prices means a measure of control over earnings. This means at least partial independence of the capital market for funds. Size, moreover, greatly diversifies the opportunities of the firm in raising money. In the large organization even the risks associated with the selection of leadership are reduced. Organization replaces individual authority; no individual is powerful enough to do much damage. Were it otherwise, the stock market would pay close attention to retirements, deaths, and replacements in the executive ranks of the large corporations. In fact, it ignores such details in tacit recognition that the organization is independent of an individual.

The massive reduction in risk that is inherent in the development of the modern corporation has been far from fully appreciated. This is partly because the corporation, unlike the worker, farmer, or other individual citizen, has been able to reduce its insecurity without overtly seeking the assistance of government. It has required elaborate organization, but this has been the product of continuous evolution from the original entrepreneurial enterprise. Farmers, workers, and other citizens, by contrast, have had to seek the assistance of government or (as in the case of the unions) they have had to organize specially for the purpose of reducing insecurity. Consequently their search for greater security has been notorious. By contrast the corporate executive, whose concern pioneered the escape from insecurity, has been able to suppose that security is something with which only workers or farmers are preoccupied.

Myth has also played a part in concealing the effort of the modern corporation to minimize insecurity. There is a remarkable conviction, even on the part of the executives of the largest business corporations, that they live dangerously. As this is written, no large United States corporation, which is also large in its industry, has failed or been seriously in danger of insolvency in many years. The security of tenure of corporation executives is remarkably high. So is their remuneration. Certainly these bear no resemblance to the insecurity of the fortunes of the business entrepreneur of the competitive model. Individual decisions of corporate management may still turn out to have been wrong. But in the large, diversified corporation—in contrast with the small and more specialized firm—such decisions are rarely fatal. . . .

But the large corporation has been only the leader in the retreat from risk. Nearly everyone else has participated to the best of his ability and ingenuity, and in the thirties there was an especially widespread effort to mitigate the economic perils of the average man. The federal government intervened for the first time with relief and welfare funds to protect the individual from economic misfortune. This was followed by social security—unemployment insurance and old-age and survivors' pensions. Farmers, through public payments and support prices, were protected from some of the insecurity associated with competitive market prices. The unions developed rapidly during this decade. Along with their redress of bargaining power, they provided the worker with protection against capricious or adventitious firing or demotion and thus increased his security in his job. Even the smaller businessman, through the Robinson-Patman Act, the Fair Trade laws, legislation against below-cost selling, and through trade associations, won a measure of security from the uncertainties of market competition for which he shared the universal distaste. . . .

The desire for economic security was long considered the great enemy of increased production. This attitude was firmly grounded in the belief that the insecurity of the competitive model was essential for efficiency. . . . Plainly, however, the notion that economic insecurity is essential for efficiency and economic advance was a major miscalculation—perhaps the greatest in the history of economic ideas. (It was the common miscalculation of both Marxian and orthodox economists. Marx and his followers were deeply persuaded that capitalism would be crippled by efforts to civilize it. To cite one obvious example, unemployment compensation would ruin the operation of the industrial reserve army in regulating wages.) In fact the years of increasing concern for economic security have been ones of unparalleled advance in productivity. Those spokesmen who have been most alarmed over the debilitating effects of the search for security have often remarked most breathlessly on the improvements in productivity which have occurred at the same time. . . .

The data on what has happened to output in the age of security could scarcely be more impressive. In the twenty years prior to the nineteen-thirties, the decade when the concern for security first became a source of uneasiness, labor productivity—national income produced per man-hour—increased from 89.6 cents in 1900 to 113.3 cents in 1929. This was a total of 23.7 cents or at a rate of about 1.2 cents a year. In the ten years following the thirties the total increase was from 131.5 cents to 179.2 cents or by 47.7 cents. This was by an average of 4.8 cents a year or four times the amount of the earlier period. The increases continued in the decade of the fifties. Plainly the increased concern for security, so far from being in conflict with increased productivity, was consistent with a greatly accelerated rate of advance. The most impressive increases in output in the history of both the United States and other western countries have occurred since men began to concern themselves with reducing the risks of the competitive system. . . .

The Paramount Position of Production

There is another respect in which our concern for production is traditional and irrational. We are curiously unreasonable in the distinctions we make between different kinds of goods and services. We view the production of some of the most frivolous goods with pride. We regard the production of some of the most significant and civilizing services with regret.

Economists in calculating the total output of the economy—in arriving at the now familiar Gross National Product—add together the value of all goods and all services of whatever sort and by whomsoever produced. No distinction is made between public and privately produced services. An increased supply of educational services has a standing in the total not different in kind from an increased output of television receivers. Nothing, however, could be more in conflict with popular attitudes, and indeed it is rather surprising that economists have not been reproached by the rather considerable number of individuals who, if they fully understood the nature of the calculation, would regard the inclusion of government spending as subversive. . . .

[In such eyes,] at best public services are a necessary evil; at worst they are a malign tendency against which an alert community must exercise eternal vigilance. Even when they serve the most important ends, such services are sterile. "Government is powerless to create anything in the sense in which business produces wealth. . . ."[3]

Such attitudes lead to some interesting contradictions. Automobiles have an importance greater than the roads on which they are driven. We welcome expansion of telephone services as improving the general well-being but accept curtailment of postal services as signifying necessary economy. We set great store by the increase in private wealth but regret the added outlays for the police force by which it is protected. Vacuum cleaners to insure clean houses are praiseworthy and essential in our standard of living. Street cleaners to insure clean streets are an unfortunate expense. Partly as a result our houses are generally clean and our streets generally filthy. . . .

Not surprisingly, modern economic ideas incorporated a strong suspicion

[3] Francis X. Sutton, Seymour E. Harris, Carl Kaysen, and James Tobin, *The American Business Creed* (Cambridge, Mass.: Harvard University Press, 1956), p. 195.

of government. The goal of nineteenth-century economic liberalism was a state which did provide order reliably and inexpensively and which did as little as possible else. Even Marx intended that the state should wither away. These attitudes have persisted in the conventional wisdom. And again events have dealt them a series of merciless blows. Once a society has provided itself with food, clothing, and shelter, all of which so fortuitously lend themselves to private production, purchase, and sale, its members begin to desire other things. And a remarkable number of these things do not lend themselves to such production, purchase, and sale. They must be provided for everyone if they are to be provided for anyone, and they must be paid for collectively or they cannot be had at all. Such is the case with streets and police and the general advantages of mass literacy and sanitation, the control of epidemics, and the common defense. There is a bare possibility that the services which must be rendered collectively, although they enter the general scheme of wants after the immediate physical necessities, increase in urgency more than proportionately with increasing wealth. This is more likely if increasing wealth is matched by increasing population and increasing density of population. Nonetheless these services, although they reflect increasingly urgent desires, remain under the obloquy of the unreliability, incompetence, cost, and pretentious interference of princes. . . .

Finally—also a closely related point—the payment for publicly produced services has long been linked to the problem of inequality. By having the rich pay more, the services were provided and at the same time the goal of greater equality was advanced. This community of objectives has never appealed to those being equalized. Not unnaturally, some part of their opposition has been directed to the public services themselves. By attacking these, they could attack the leveling tendencies of taxation. This has helped to keep alive the notion that the public services for which they pay are inherently inferior to privately produced goods. . . .

The Theory of Social Balance

The final problem of the productive society is what it produces. This manifests itself in an implacable tendency to provide an opulent supply of some things and a niggardly yield of others. This disparity carries to the point where it is a cause of social discomfort and social unhealth. The line which divides our area of wealth from our area of poverty is roughly that which divides privately produced and marketed goods and services from publicly rendered services. Our wealth in the first is not only in startling contrast with the meagerness of the latter, but our wealth in privately produced goods is, to a marked degree, the cause of crisis in the supply of public services. For we have failed to see the importance, indeed the urgent need, of maintaining a balance between the two.

This disparity between our flow of private and public goods and services is no matter of subjective judgment. On the contrary, it is the source of the most extensive comment which only stops short of the direct contrast being made here. In the years following World War II, the papers of any major city—those of New York were an excellent example—told daily of the shortages and shortcomings in the elementary municipal and metropolitan services. The schools were old and overcrowded. The police force was under strength and underpaid. The parks and playgrounds were insufficient. Streets and empty lots were filthy, and the sanitation staff was underequipped and in need of men. Access to the city by those who work there was uncertain and painful and becoming more so. Internal transportation was overcrowded, unhealthful, and dirty. So was the air. Parking on the streets had to be prohibited, and there was no space elsewhere. These deficiencies were not in new and novel services but in old and established ones. Cities have long swept their streets, helped their people move around, educated them, kept order, and provided horse rails for vehicles which sought to pause. That their residents should have a nontoxic supply of air suggests no revolutionary dalliance with socialism. . . .

The family which takes its mauve and cerise, air-conditioned, power-steered, and power-braked automobile out for a tour passes through cities that are badly paved, made hideous by litter, blighted buildings, billboards, and posts for wires that should long since have been put underground. They pass on into a countryside that has been rendered largely invisible by commercial art. (The goods which the latter advertise have an absolute priority in our value system. Such aesthetic considerations as a view of the countryside accordingly come second. On such matters we are consistent.) They picnic on exquisitely packaged food from a portable icebox by a polluted stream and go on to spend the night at a park which is a menace to public health and morals. Just before dozing off on an air mattress, beneath a nylon tent, amid the stench of decaying refuse, they may reflect vaguely on the curious unevenness of their blessings. Is this, indeed, the American genius? . . .

Residential housing also illustrates the problem of the social balance, although in a somewhat complex form. Few would wish to contend that, in the lower or even the middle-income brackets, Americans are munificently supplied with housing. A great many families would like better located or merely more houseroom, and no advertising is necessary to persuade them of this wish. And the provision of housing is in the private domain. At first glance at least, the line we draw between private and public seems not to be preventing a satisfactory allocation of resources to housing.

On closer examination, however, the problem turns out to be not greatly different from that of education. It is improbable that the housing industry is greatly more incompetent or inefficient in the United States than in those countries—Scandinavia, Holland, or (for the most part) England—where slums have been largely eliminated and where *minimum* standards of cleanliness and comfort are well above our own. As the experience of these countries shows, and as we have also been learning, the housing industry functions well only in combination with a large, complex, and costly array of public services. These include land purchase and clearance for redevelopment; good neighborhood and city planning, and effective and well-enforced zoning; a variety of financing and other aids to the housebuilder and owner; publicly supported research and architectural services for an industry which, by its nature, is equipped to do little on its own; and a considerable amount of direct or assisted public construction for families in the lowest-income brackets. The quality of the housing depends not on the industry, which is given, but on what is invested in these supplements and supports.

The case for social balance has, so far, been put negatively. Failure to keep public services in minimal relation to private production and use of goods is a cause of social disorder or impairs economic performance. The matter may now be put affirmatively. By failing to exploit the opportunity to expand public production we are missing opportunities for enjoyment which otherwise we might have had. Presumably a community can be as well rewarded by buying better schools or better parks as by buying bigger automobiles. By concentrating on the latter rather than the former it is failing to maximize its satisfactions. As with schools in the community, so with public services over the country at large. It is scarcely sensible that we should satisfy our wants in private goods with reckless abundance, while in the case of public goods, on the evidence of the eye, we practice extreme self-denial. So, far from systematically exploiting the opportunities to derive use and pleasure from these services, we do not supply what would keep us out of trouble.

The conventional wisdom holds that the community, large or small, makes a decision as to how much it will devote to its public services. This decision is arrived at by democratic process. Subject to the imperfections and uncertainties of democracy, people decide how much of their private income and goods they will surrender in order to have public services of which they are in greater need. Thus there is a balance, however rough, in the enjoyments to be had from private goods and services and those rendered by public authority.

It will be obvious, however, that this view depends on the notion of independently determined consumer wants. In such a world one could with some reason defend the doctrine that the consumer, as a voter, makes an independent choice between public and private goods. But given the dependence effect— given that consumer wants are created by the process by which they are satisfied —the consumer makes no such choice. He is subject to the forces of advertising and emulation by which production creates its own demand. Advertising operates exclusively, and emulation mainly, on behalf of privately produced goods and services. Since management and emulative effects operate on behalf of private production, public services will have an inherent tendency to lag behind. Automobile demand which is expensively synthesized will inevitably have a much larger claim on income than parks or public health or even roads where no such influence operates. The engines of mass communication, in their highest state of development, assail the eyes and ears of the community on behalf of more beer but not of more schools. Even in the conventional wisdom it will scarcely be contended that this leads to an equal choice between the two. . . .

A feature of the years immediately following World War II was a remarkable attack on the notion of expanding and improving public services. During the depression years such services had been elaborated and improved partly in order to fill some small part of the vacuum left by the shrinkage of private production. During the war years the role of government was vastly expanded. After that came the reaction. Much of it, unquestionably, was motivated by a desire to rehabilitate the prestige of private production and therewith of producers. No doubt some who joined the attack hoped, at least tacitly, that it might be possible to sidestep the truce on taxation vis-à-vis equality by having less taxation of all kinds. For a time the notion that our public services had somehow become inflated and excessive was all but axiomatic. Even liberal politicians did not seriously protest. They found it necessary to aver that they were in favor of public economy too.

In this discussion a certain mystique was attributed to the satisfaction of privately supplied wants. A community decision to have a new school means that the individual surrenders the necessary amount, willy-nilly, in his taxes. But if he is left with that income, he is a free man. He can decide between a better car or a television set. This was advanced with some solemnity as an argument for the TV set. The difficulty is that this argument leaves the community with no way of preferring the school. All private wants, where the individual can choose, are inherently superior to all public desires which must be paid for by taxation and with an inevitable component of compulsion.

The cost of public services was also held to be a desolating burden on private production, although this was at a time when the private production was burgeoning. Urgent warnings were issued of the unfavorable effects of taxation on investment—"I don't know of a surer way of killing off the incentive to invest than by imposing taxes which are regarded by people as punitive."[4] This was at a time when the inflationary effect of a very high level of investment was causing concern. The same individuals who were warning about the inimical effects of taxes were strongly advocating a monetary policy designed to reduce investment. However, an understanding of our economic discourse requires an appreciation of one of its basic rules: men of high position are allowed, by a special act of grace, to accommodate their reasoning to the answer they need. Logic is only required in those of lesser rank.

Finally it was argued, with no little vigor, that expanding government posed a grave threat to individual liberties. "Where distinction and rank is achieved almost exclusively by becoming a civil servant of the state . . . it is too much to expect that many will long prefer freedom to security."[5]

With time this attack on public services has somewhat subsided. The disorder associated with social imbalance has become visible even if the need for balance between private and public services is still imperfectly appreciated.

Freedom also seemed to be surviving. Perhaps it was realized that all organized activity requires concessions by the individual to the group. This is true of the policeman who joins the police force, the teacher who gets a job at the high school, and the executive who makes his way up the hierarchy of Du Pont. If there are differences between public and private organization, they are of kind rather than of degree. As this is written the pendulum has in fact swung back. Our liberties are now menaced by the conformity exacted by the large corporation and its impulse to create, for its own purposes, the organization man. This danger we may also survive.

Nonetheless, the postwar onslaught on the public services left a lasting imprint. To suggest that we canvass our public wants to see where happiness can be improved by more and better services has a sharply radical tone. Even public services to avoid disorder must be defended. By contrast the man who devises a nostrum for a nonexistent need and then successfully promotes both remains one of nature's noblemen. . . .

The Benthamite test of public policy was "what serves the greatest happiness of the greatest number," and happiness was more or less implicitly identified with productivity. This is still the official test. In modern times the test has

[4] Arthur F. Burns, Chairman of the President's Council of Economic Advisers, *U. S. News & World Report,* May 6, 1955.
[5] F. A. Hayek, *The Road to Serfdom* (London: George Routledge & Sons, 1944), p. 98.

not been very rigorously applied. We have sensed though we have not recognized the declining importance of goods. Yet even in its deteriorated form we cling to this criterion. It is so much simpler than to substitute the other tests—compassion, individual happiness and well-being, the minimization of community or other social tensions—which now become relevant. . . .

An affluent society, that is also both compassionate and rational, would, no doubt, secure to all who needed it the minimum income essential for decency and comfort. The corrupting effect on the human spirit of a small amount of unearned revenue has unquestionably been exaggerated as, indeed, have the character-building values of hunger and privation. To secure to each family a minimum standard, as a normal function of the society, would help insure that the misfortunes of parents, deserved or otherwise, were not visited on their children. It would help insure that poverty was not self-perpetuating. Most of the reaction, which no doubt would be almost universally adverse, is based on obsolete attitudes. When poverty was a majority phenomenon, such action could not be afforded. A poor society, as this essay has previously shown, had to enforce the rule that the person who did not work could not eat. And possibly it was justified in the added cruelty of applying the rule to those who could not work or whose efficiency was far below par. An affluent society has no similar excuse for such rigor. It can use the forthright remedy of providing for those in want. Nothing requires it to be compassionate. But it has no high philosophical justification for callousness.

Nonetheless any such forthright remedy for poverty is beyond reasonable hope. Also, as in the limiting case of the alcoholic or the mental incompetent, it involves difficulties. To spend income requires a minimum of character and intelligence even as to produce it. By far the best hope for the elimination, or in any case the minimization, of poverty lies in less direct but, conceivably, almost equally effective means.

The first and strategic step in an attack on poverty is to see that it is no longer self-perpetuating. This means insuring that the investment in children from families presently afflicted be as little below normal as possible. If the children of poor families have first-rate schools and school attendance is properly enforced; if the children, though badly fed at home, are well nourished at school; if the community has sound health services, and the physical well-being of the children is vigilantly watched; if there is opportunity for advanced education for those who qualify regardless of means; and if, especially in the case of urban communities, law and order are well enforced and recreation is adequate—then there is a very good chance that the children of the very poor will come to maturity without grave disadvantage. In the case of insular poverty this remedy requires that the services of the community be assisted from outside. Poverty is self-perpetuating because the poorest communities are poorest in the services which would eliminate it. To eliminate poverty efficiently we should invest more than proportionately in the children of the poor community. It is there that high-quality schools, strong health services, special provision for nutrition and recreation are most needed to compensate for the very low investment which families are able to make in their own offspring.

The effect of education and related investment in individuals is to enable them either to contend more effectively with their environment, or to escape it and take up life elsewhere on more or less equal terms with others. The role of education as an antidote to the homing instinct which crowds people into the areas of inadequate opportunity and frustration is also clear. However, in the strategy of the attack on insular poverty a place remains for an attack on the frustrations of the environment itself. This is particularly clear in the case of the slum. Slum clearance and expansion of low and middle-income housing removes a comprehensive set of frustrations and greatly widens opportunity. There is a roughly parallel opportunity in the rural slum. By identifying a land use which is consistent with a satisfactory standard of living, and by assisting with the necessary reorganization of land and capital, public authority can help individuals to surmount frustrations to which they are now subject. The process promises to be expensive and also time-consuming. But the question is less one of feasibility than of will. . . .

Nor is case poverty in the contemporary generation wholly intransigent. Much can be done to treat those characteristics which cause people to reject or be rejected by the modern industrial society. Educational deficiencies can be overcome. Mental deficiencies can be treated. Physical handicaps can be remedied. The limiting factor is not knowledge of what can be done. Overwhelmingly it is our failure to invest in people.

It will be clear that to a remarkable extent the requirements for the elimination of poverty are the same as for social balance. (Indeed a good deal of case poverty can be attributed to the failure to maintain social balance.) The myopic preoccupation with production and material investment has diverted our attention from the more urgent questions of how we are employing our resources and, in particular, from the greater need and opportunity for investing in persons.

Here is a paradox. When we begin to consider the needs of those who are now excluded from the economic system by accident, inadequacy, or misfortune—we find that the normal remedy is to make them or their children productive citizens. This means that they add to the total output of goods. We see once again that even by its *own terms* the present preoccupation with material as opposed to human investment is inefficient. The parallel with investment in the supply of trained and educated manpower will be apparent.

But increased output of goods is not the main point. Even to the most intellectually reluctant reader it will now be evident that enhanced productive efficiency is not the *motif* of this volume. The very fact that increased output offers itself as a by-product of the effort to eliminate poverty is one of the reasons. No one would be called upon to write at such length on a problem so easily solved as that of increasing production. The main point lies elsewhere. Poverty—grim, degrading, and ineluctable—is not remarkable in India. For few the fate is otherwise. But in the United States the survival of poverty is remarkable. We ignore it because we share with all societies at all times the capacity for not seeing what we do not wish to see. Anciently this has enabled the nobleman to enjoy his dinner while remaining oblivious to the beggars around his door. In our own day it enables us to travel in comfort through south Chicago and the South. But while our failure to notice can be explained, it cannot be excused. "Poverty," Pitt exclaimed, "is no disgrace but it is damned annoying." In the contemporary United States it is not annoying but it is a disgrace.

✐✐ Section XI

DEMOCRACY EVALUATED

That governments derive "their just powers from the consent of the governed" appears to many Americans so self-evident as to require no demonstration. But in a world in which democracy as understood and valued in the West is under challenge, it is essential to subject this premise to continuing examination.

The section begins with a thought-provoking selection from Norman L. Stamps' book, *Why Democracies Fail,* in which he presents and analyzes what he considers to be serious and disturbing weaknesses in traditional democratic assumptions and practices.

These assumptions and practices are also the subject of rigorous debate between C. Wright Mills and Daniel Bell. Mills argues that "the history of modern society may readily be understood as the story of the enlargement and the centralization of the means of power—in economic, in political, and in military institutions" and that, in America, "at the top there has emerged an elite whose power probably exceeds that of any small group of men in world history," while the mass of the people lack power to make meaningful and important decisions. Contrariwise, Bell maintains that competition within our system is high among various and different interests. "The growing complexity of society necessarily multiplies those interests, regional or functional, and in an open society the political arena— unless there is a conflict to overthrow the system—is a place where different interests fight it out for advantage." "The theory of the 'power elite,' " he concludes, "implies a unity of purpose and community of interest among the elite that is not proven or demonstrated. It is simply asserted."

This discussion is followed by Lenin's critique of capitalist democracy which reflects a point of view which, it must be recognized, commands acceptance in a vast area of the world. Lenin also provides a description of socialist and communist society as envisaged before the Bolshevik revolution. What actually happened is the subject of conflicting analyses by Herbert Aptheker and an official Soviet view, on the one hand, and Reinhold Niebuhr, on the other. H. B. Mayo then presents the affirmative case for democracy. (Earlier in this volume, consideration was given to the value and limits of free expression. It is well to mention that the case for free speech is obviously an integral part of the case for democracy and arguments in support of one will ordinarily support the other.)

The Decline of Democracy

NORMAN L. STAMPS
Why Democracies Fail

At the end of World War I it appeared as though democracy had reached its greatest triumph. Lord Bryce in his *Modern Democracies,* first published in 1921, pointed out that "A century ago there was in the Old World only one tiny spot in which the working of democracy could be studied."[1] This was in "a few of the ancient rural cantons of Switzerland" but "nowhere else in Europe did the people rule." However, within a hundred years "nearly all the monarchies of the Old World have been turned into democracies," twenty new republics have sprung up in the Western hemisphere, and five new democracies developed out of colonies within the British dominions. Lord Bryce added that more than a hundred representative assemblies were at work legislating for self-governing communities but that the most significant change in the last hundred years was "the universal acceptance of democracy as the normal and natural form of government." The word, democracy, which had formerly awakened dislike or fear, was now a word of praise; and the old question as to what is the best form of government had become almost obsolete.[2]

This almost universal confidence in the ultimate triumph of popular government was not merely the mood of this generation but was instead the climax of an ever-widening and deepening conviction that democracy was the predestined form of government for all civilized nations. Jeremy Bentham, James and John Stuart Mill, Thomas Paine, and Thomas Jefferson believed that, given widespread educational opportunities, the whole world would eventually become democratic. . . .

Even W. E. H. Lecky, whose own misgivings concerning democracy effectively protected him against any suspicion of wishful thinking, wrote in 1896:

> I do not think that anyone who seriously considers the force and universality of the movement of our generation in the direction of democracy

Late Professor of Government at Rutgers University. The selection is from *Why Democracies Fail* (Notre Dame, Indiana, University of Notre Dame Press, 1957), *passim.* By permission.

[1] James Bryce, *Modern Democracies* (New York, 1924), I, 3.
[2] *Ibid.,* pp. 3-4.

can doubt that this conception of government will necessarily, at least for a considerable time, dominate in all civilized countries, and the real question for politicians is the form it is likely to take, and the means by which its characteristic evils can be best mitigated.[3]

The World War increased, rather than diminished, belief in the irresistible triumph of popular government. Woodrow Wilson gradually became convinced that the selfish ambition of irresponsible kings and military rulers was a major cause of the conflict. When America entered the war the absolute Tsarist regime in Russia had been replaced by a provisional government committed to the selection of a constituent assembly, and Wilson announced in his message to Congress that a major aim of the allied cause was to "make the world safe for democracy." At the end of the war military defeat had brought an end to the reign, not only of the Romanov, but also to the Hapsburg and Hohenzollern dynasties; and the victory of the Entente powers was attributed partially to the democratic spirit of their peoples. Thus the return of peace coincided with the establishment of democratic constitutions all over Europe.

It was hardly expected that a rapid spread of dictatorship should begin at this time; yet there were signs of approaching danger. . . . A few close students of government noted that the universal acceptance of democracy was not a tribute to the smoothness of its working and that discontent was everywhere rife. For example, Lord Bryce, writing in 1921, concluded that there were few countries "in which freedom seems safe for a century or two ahead";[4] but such statements were exceptional at this time. Although a provisional government committed to the election of a constituent assembly had triumphed over Russian Tsarism in March, 1917, a Communist dictatorship of the proletariat under Lenin soon took its place. In 1922 Mussolini made his famous "march on Rome" and began the gradual consolidation of power which was eventually to turn Italy into a totalitarian state. However, defenders of democracy, for the most part, were undisturbed by these developments. It was explained that party government had never taken root in Italy or Russia and that these countries had merely turned from one form of dictatorship to another. . . . By 1938 all of central and eastern Europe and all Mediterranean countries were under dictatorial rule. . . .

Empirical Causes of Dictatorship

There is perhaps no single set of causes for dictatorship. In modern Europe absolutism has appeared in very different countries, under different cir-

[3] William Edward Hartpole Lecky, *Democracy and Liberty* (New York, 1913), I, 256.

[4] *Modern Democracies* (1921), II, 603. *The New Democratic Constitutions of Europe* (London, 1929). In 1913 A. Lawrence Lowell had written: "Many people feel that because popular government is new it must be lasting. They know it is a vital part of the spirit of the age, which they assume to be permanent. But that is the one thing the spirit of the age never is. It would not deserve its name if it were; and when any spirit of the age has become universally recognized, it is time to scan the horizon for signs of a new era." *Public Opinion and Popular Government* (New York, 1913), p. 303.

cumstances, and for very different reasons. Although in each country it was imposed to deal with a crisis of some kind, there was no similarity in social structure, economic organization, national tradition, or race. . . .

Executive Impotence

Perhaps the greatest operational weakness of popular government has been its inability to provide effective political leadership within the traditional institutional framework. In the eighteenth and nineteenth centuries there was a reaction against executives, and during this period legislatures everywhere gained in power. The struggle was first an attempt to establish parliaments as a counterpoise to the Crown and then, as election came to be looked upon as the primary basis of authority, to dominate the executive and bring the specialized bureaucracy under parliamentary control. Thus the memory of an old regime of executive absolutism caused the assembly to be jealous of its power and to be constantly on the alert against the new executive in order to prevent its reversion to the old type.

Today there is a reaction against weak executive power because social and economic conditions are of such a nature as to demand swift and drastic executive action. Perhaps one of the most dramatic cleavages between constitutional intent and political reality has been that legislative supremacy has so frequently led to the establishment of dictatorship. This is because government requires the concentration of political power in a small compact group. A multi-membered assembly, torn by party dissensions and subject to the fluctuating moods of public opinion, is incapable of governing. The most such an assembly can do is control the government it places in the chair of authority. It is an interesting fact that in no European country has the aggrandizement of a strong constitutional executive led towards authoritarian rule. It is instead a weak executive, incapable of providing effective government, that has been replaced by a strong executive free from legislative control.

In Italy the country was faced with serious economic difficulties. There was mounting unemployment, economic dislocation brought about by the war, a seething discontent not only on the part of workers but also of veterans who returned home to find that they had no jobs and that the sacrifices they had made benefited the profiteers. The socialists, who had opposed the war, benefited from the general disappointment felt in the peace treaties and Italy's failure to secure the colonial territories she had expected. Although the cost of living was still rising, employers sought to reduce wages on the theory that labor costs had increased during the war far beyond their real value. The government apparently, because of successive splits in the party system, was unable to agree upon a consistent policy of any kind. . . . Although there was chaos and an obvious need for drastic action, the government did nothing. Although Mussolini had only thirty-five deputies in the Chamber, he finally challenged the government itself. It was only then that the cabinet decided to take action, but it was too late. The king, upon being advised that the Fascists had infiltrated the army and the police, refused to permit the government to declare martial law, accepted the cabinet's resignation, and asked Mussolini to become premier.

Party Stalemate

The major cause of executive impotence has been party deadlock in the legislature. Since parliamentary government makes the executive dependent upon and responsible to a majority in the representative assembly, all governmental activity becomes paralyzed if the assembly becomes divided into so many factions that there cannot be found a stable majority for the executive's support. For example, there were twelve parties in the Italian Parliament before the Fascist revolution and fifteen in the German Reichstag in 1928. As this paralysis crept in, the people in country after country lost hope that effective action ever would be produced and "parliamentarism" became a by-word for inefficiency and inaction.

This fact raises a number of fundamental issues concerning the party system and its functions in the governmental system. In the first place, what is the purpose of parties and what should be the subject of party controversy? Acting alone the individual citizen can do nothing, and it appears obvious that a principal aim of political parties is to organize the chaotic public will and educate the private citizen to political responsibility. However, not everything can be the subject of party controversy. By following obstruction tactics a party can paralyze the work of an assembly and sabotage parliamentary institutions. Even though a minority and regularly defeated when votes are taken, such a party can delay debates and prevent the majority from bringing them to a conclusion, hurl insults, resort to disorderly conduct and a program of violence, and employ other techniques designed to prevent the normal operation of democratic institutions. Obviously a government must remove such obstacles; for it will otherwise be unable to act decisively and its opponents may profit from the chaos and confusion which they have caused; yet if the government goes too far in cutting off the fringes of dissent, it will have thereby destroyed the very principles upon which democracy is based. Democracy assumes that the minority will accept the rule of the majority and that the majority, in turn, will not rule too oppressively. In other words, both the majority and minority have rights but they also have obligations. It is the duty of the majority as represented in the government to govern and of the minority to confine its opposition to appeals to public opinion. Although the *raison d'être* of the opposition is to discuss and criticize and thereby educate public opinion, it does not have the right to follow obstructionist tactics.

There is also the question concerning how to correlate party responsibility with executive action. For example, the multiple party system in Germany was furthered by proportional representation so that there were regularly between ten and fifteen parties in the Reichstag. The result was that no government could command a majority in the legislature and that any combination of parties for the assumption of responsibility could always be defeated by a combination of those in opposition. Moreover, the electoral system discouraged a spirit of moderation and cooperation among the parties, not only because it gave representation to extremist groups, but also because each party was able to win seats on its own program without compromising its position and without taking into consideration the marginal voter. . . .

Party stalemate also raises a question concerning the proper function of the legislature. A parliament is an admirable instrument for the expression of grievances and for the discussion of large principles. Its purpose is to discuss and guide the general conduct of the government, but it does not exist in order to govern. As a matter of fact, it may be argued that a legislative assembly is too numerous and too incoherent even to legislate directly and that it is bound by its nature to accept or reject proposals offered to it by the executive power. This is the view set forth by John Stuart Mill in a famous passage of *Representative Government:*

> Instead of the function of governing, for which it is radically unfit, the proper office of a representative assembly is to watch and control the government: . . . to be at once the nation's Committee of Grievances and its Congress of Opinions. . . . Nothing but the restriction of the function of representative bodies within these rational limits, will enable the benefits of popular control to be enjoyed in conjunction with the no less important requisites (growing ever more important as human affairs increase in scale and complexity) of skilled legislation and administration.[5]

In any case, a legislative chamber composed of five or six hundred people of divergent political outlook cannot really govern; but it can prevent the government from doing so. . . .

Lack of Agreement on Fundamental Matters

Democracy is a delicate form of government which rests upon conditions which are rather precarious. For representative institutions to function successfully there must be a wide area of agreement on fundamental matters and a willingness to compromise on others. The great advantage which the British government had during the nineteenth century was that the differences which divided the two parties were on methods of action rather than on deep-seated principles. The Whigs and Tories, Liberals and Conservatives were united in their desire to preserve the monarchy, the established Church, and the main tenets of the economic system. . . . In other words, the two parties were in agreement as to the kind of state they wanted, and there was little difference in their social composition. Being in agreement on the broad and general principles which ought to guide the policies of government, they could proceed to disagree on the best means of achieving the aims or goals they both had in common. There were, of course, differences of opinion, but they were concerned primarily with matters of degree and emphasis rather than with the fundamental structure of society or the form of government. Under such circumstances government by discussion and majority vote works best because compromise is possible at all pivotal points and because the minority can meet defeat at the polls in good temper since it need not regard the decision as either a fatal or a permanent surrender of its vital interests.

It is impossible to overestimate the extent to which the success of parliamentary government is dependent upon a considerable measure of agreement on fundamentals. The device of alternating government and opposition is possible only because the minority consents to lose and is willing to accept the

---

[5] *Representative Government* (Everyman's Library; New York, 1936) pp. 239-241.

rule of the majority. The opposition party is willing to do this because it can, when it comes to office again, take up the threads of its activity more or less where it left them. It is prepared to accept the risks of the next election because it knows that in the meantime the fundamental contours of the state will remain unchanged and that eventually it is certain of office again.

When differences of opinion within a state become irreconcilable and passionate and when individuals or groups refuse peaceably to lose, constitutional government breaks down. For example, in Portugal a substantial portion of the people refused to accept the republic and wanted a monarchy. Under such circumstances it was impossible for the republican system to operate because the government was compelled, in order to maintain the regime, to cut off the fringes of dissent and thus itself became authoritarian. Under such circumstances the dominant interest in the state establishes control by force and governs by coercion rather than by consent.[6] Only a firmly established government is capable of being constitutionalized. . . .

Constitutionalism imposes limitations on the organs of government and diffuses powers in order to prevent a dangerous concentration at the top. This limitation may be enforced in a number of ways. For example, in some countries it is partially enforced by a supreme court which acts as the guardian of the constitution and repels encroachments by other agencies of the government. In other countries there are special administrative courts which prevent the executive from exceeding and abusing such powers as he has. Sometimes the existence of a federal system helps curtail and balance the powers of the central government, and sometimes this limitation is enforced by the different political groups which together exercise supreme guardianship in the legislature. However, in all countries reliance must ultimately be based upon a nation's sense of its heritage, upon a common understanding that certain things are not done, and upon an insistence that the time-honored procedure must be followed. In other words, all legal and theoretical rules rest on the expectation that every major group in the country will agree to be bound by the constitution and will not attempt to force its will beyond these limits. In the last analysis this agreement must be voluntary; for a state either collapses or becomes a dictatorship when a considerable number of people refuse to accept the constitution.

A voluntary agreement of this kind is possible only when the contending political forces within a country are not too far apart on fundamental principles. This does not mean that there cannot be spirited debates over important issues for the electorate to decide; but when mutual animosity and differences of opinion reach the point "where one political party feels that its very life is threatened by the possible victory of another important party, then constitutional barriers are easily brushed aside and the grim struggle for political, and sometimes physical, survival begins."[7]

[6] One of the techniques used by most dictators is to distinguish between the "real" and the empiric. There is an underlying something which is the real country and which the party will bring forth. Thus the "real" Portugal is altogether different from the existing Portugal. Both the Russian and the German, as well as most other, dictatorships have used this device. For example, Lenin said that the peasants are ignorant and probably would rush back into private property, but the "real" Russia is crying to be communized.

[7] Neumann, *European and Comparative Government*, p. 593.

Political Inexperience and Exploitation

It is impossible to operate a democratic government when the people are not interested in public affairs and when people have not had experience in self-government. There must be not only a passion for liberty but also a desire to preserve the conditions of liberty. This means that the people must possess enough of the common to sustain the common weal against the fierce conflicts of interests and factions. When class lines are strongly held and when a sense of class exploitation reaches deep into the masses of the population, democratic institutions are hard to establish and maintain. In Italy and Germany proportional representation made it possible for political parties representing narrow class interests to secure a larger representation in the legislature; and although political parties even in Germany did not have a strict class basis in the Marxian sense, they did tend to reflect narrow group interests and to develop platforms appealing to specific local, economic, or occupational interests to a much greater extent than in hardly any other country.[8] . . .

Marxist parties, unlike the Labor party in England, are not inclined to advocate a gradual approach to socialism.

> They oppose "reform" and believe in revolution. When they become powerful they regard the political conflict as a sheer struggle between themselves and the reactionary right, in which latter category they tend to include all who do not share their own allegiance. Marxism and fascism breed one another and in the clash, whichever wins, democracy loses.[9]

The situation that developed in Spain prior to the civil war is only one of many illustrations that could be given. Democracy puts the common interest, and not merely some majority interest, above the divisive interests of all groups.

Democracy requires a process of maturation. Where its spirit has long been awake, as in Switzerland, Scandinavia, England, and the United States, the movement towards dictatorship has never succeeded. It may be that these countries were not so profoundly shaken by the universal crisis and that, if pressure had been further intensified, they too would have followed the same road. There are catastrophic conditions under which democracy cannot flourish or even endure. On the other hand, in immature republics, such as Weimar Germany, where there was no established democratic tradition, there was a greater willingness to follow the leader and to submit to authority. In these countries the people, faced with an economic and spiritual crisis, were more inclined to vote for political parties pledged to change not merely the government but the whole system of government.

Nature of Constitutional Development

There can be little doubt that conditions prevailing in the nineteenth century presented a more favorable environment for the operation of parliamentary institutions. The problems of government were simpler than they are today;

---

[8] Hermens, *Democracy or Anarchy?*, pp. 35-43, 241-244, 290-292.
[9] MacIver, *The Web of Government*, p. 191.

public opinion was more homogeneous; agriculture was still the predominant occupation of men; and the representation of geographical areas had a meaning it has since lost. The electorate was then smaller, and an elaborate party organization was not needed. The issues discussed in the nineteenth century were of a character which the average man found interesting and intelligible without the possession of special knowledge, and lent themselves to eloquent debate in the legislature.[10]

Today the character of discussion has changed. It is indeed difficult to dramatize or to interest public opinion in matters such as the details of industrial reorganization, currency reform, grants-in-aid for housing, and other matters of this kind which require a special knowledge not available to the ordinary man. Moreover, as life becomes more technical and complicated it becomes increasingly difficult for legislators to understand thoroughly the details of the legislation concerning which they are called upon to pass; yet the amount of legislation passed each year has increased to such an extent that representatives are overwhelmed with work and find it increasingly difficult to find the time for adequate discussion of legislative projects. The broad outlines of legislative procedure were laid down at a time when the main tasks of the state were few in number and negative in character. There was a suspicion of too much government, and legislative procedure developed forms which were designed to prevent a majority from riding roughshod over its opponents. Hence the amplitude of debate, the resentment of an assembly against steps designed to limit its initiative or freedom of discussion, and the power of a minister to make any question, no matter how insignificant, a question of confidence. Moreover, the very nature of political democracy precludes the possibility of swift and comprehensive action. Based as it is on a process of discussion, new measures cannot be undertaken until they have received the support of public opinion; a political party is naturally hesitant to promote novel ideas because of the possibility of defeat; and the number of interests to be consulted and the time required to do so is always great. . . .

A democratic party system is based upon the idea that man is a rational animal capable of intelligent choice and that, having heard the arguments, he will make a wise decision; but when emotion takes the place of reason, when party organization reaches the point where party spirit completely dominates his mind, or when there is no longer the possibility that he will exercise a choice, then the democratic process tends to break down. It is undoubtedly true that the number of independent voters who record the general movements of opinion by changing their votes from time to time is always small; but party organization can become so intensive that it precludes a reasonable opportunity for all groups to appeal to the electorate and to influence its judgment by intellectual argument. Under such circumstances the electorate tends to become fixed in its allegiances and inflexible in its attitudes. There can be no swing of the pendulum but a constant stalemate with the added threat of civil war. The

---

[10] Professor Harold J. Laski, *Democracy in Crisis* (Chapel Hill, 1933), p. 70, says: "The debates of the nineteenth century did not, I think, arouse greater interest or secure wider publicity because their level was higher; it was rather because their subject matter was, in itself, calculated to arrest the attention of a non-technical audience."

cry is then heard for a party above parties, for a "movement" which will encompass all others and bring about a "new unity."

Democracy is based upon the assumption that the party can penetrate the associations to which an individual belongs, that it can teach its programmes, and that the individual will consider the alternatives with an open mind; but the total party attempts to indoctrinate its members thoroughly, to cover the whole of men's minds, and to mold their minds so as to leave them in no position to exercise a free choice. When parties become emotional absolutes, they cease to be a part of the system of rational discussion. . . .

Material Conditions for Democracy

Democracy is a delicate form of government which rests upon conditions that are rather precarious. It makes certain assumptions about the capacities and virtues of men, and it presumes the presence of certain material and intellectual conditions favorable to the exercise of these capacities and virtues. John Stuart Mill, whose devotion to liberty cannot be doubted, pointed out that a people might desire liberty and yet be unable or unwilling to fulfill its conditions.[11] There must be a wide range of interest and a capacity to relate one's own immediate interest to a more general pattern. The only possible government is some kind of oligarchy when people are deeply divided by racial, religious, or other differences. . . .

Economic Theories of Dictatorship

1. The Marxian explanation. Perhaps the most popular explanation for the rise of dictatorship has been derived from Marxian philosophy. According to this view, every state has a class basis. Political democracy, therefore, is nothing more than a concealed dictatorship which permits the capitalists to delude the workers; and so long as it can be carried on it is, from the capitalist point of view, the most efficient and acceptable form of government. However, the growth of working-class organizations and universal suffrage have produced a clash between the working-class and the owners of property, and the capitalist is compelled to resort to open force to maintain his position. Thus fascism is an effort to save capitalism and give it a longer life by preventing the establishment of socialism. "The creation of a fascist party is, then, a desperate expedient only resorted to by a capitalist class in the face of the most urgent danger from the workers."[12] . . .

2. Polarization of an authoritarian left and right. It has also been contended that certain conditions inherent in democracy itself create an anti-democratic spirit and that as time goes on there is a tendency for the adherents of democracy to decrease and for the supporters of dictatorship to increase. This is because the left develops a fear of majority rule believing that if the decision were left to the ballot box they would lose. There is no government more conservative than a democratic regime because the people are by

[11] See his *Representative Government* (Everyman's Library, New York, 1936), esp. pp. 175-184, 218-227.
[12] John Strachey, *The Coming Struggle for Power* (New York, 1933), p. 262; see also by the same author, *The Menace of Fascism* (New York, 1933).

nature suspicious of change and because drastic reforms cannot be undertaken until the great body of the people has become convinced of the need for change. The result is that the left begins to despair of winning a majority at the polls and the demand for and a readiness to accept a dictatorship on the Russian pattern are greatly enhanced. On the other hand, the middle classes also fear majority rule because it means the enthronement of the "have-nots." With the development of communication and education, there is a constant increase in the number of people whose ideas are anti-democratic. Out of this situation will come an authoritarian movement, either from the left or from the right and probably from both, which will sap the democratic structure.[13] . . .

The Propaganda Theory

To prove their assertion that fascism was a gigantic capitalist plot, Marxian writers are compelled to fall back upon the propaganda theory which asserts that the masses were manipulated by the clever use of propaganda. They are encouraged in this view by many statements made by leading Fascists and Nazis themselves. As is well known, Hitler was particularly interested in propaganda techniques. *Mein Kampf* is largely a treatise on the art of political propaganda; and, along with Dr. Joseph Goebbels, Hitler became the world's foremost exponent of propaganda as a method of controlling opinion. The Nazis carefully employed most of the devices discovered by modern psychology and drew upon the experience made available by modern advertising. Nazi theory proceeded upon the assumption that man is not a rational animal, that he is subject to emotion rather than to reason, that political pronouncements should not be deliberative but present exclusively the idea or view which they are designed to advance, and that propaganda was useful mainly to manipulate opinion and as a weapon in the struggle for power. . . .

The Nature of Modern Society

Although it has been fashionable in recent years to speak of dictatorship as an incomprehensible freak and as a reaction against the whole trend of western civilization, conditions inherent in the very nature of modern industrial society pose new problems and help explain the contemporary crisis of democracy. In many countries dictatorship has emerged after the breakdown of established institutions. In other countries it represents a protest against what has become a questionable economic system, a shattered social order, or the injustice of the preceding system. Thus dictatorship has grown out of democracy, is not completely divorced from the past, and is a reaction to modern conditions. The question arises as to what factors inherent in the nature of modern society have contributed to the decline of democracy and the establishment of dictatorship.

Isolation of the Individual

The rise of capitalism destroyed the old medieval social system together with the stability and relative security it offered. Although the individual was

[13] See Hans Kelsen, "The Party Dictatorship," *Politica,* II (March, 1936), 19-32; Charles E. Merriam, *The New Democracy and the New Despotism* (New York, 1939), p. 197.

freed from the authority of the medieval church and the absolutist state, he was also uprooted with a consequent feeling of insecurity and reduced to becoming a mere cog in a vast machine. Modern man is unable to make decisions affecting the most important aspects of his life, and his feeling of isolation and powerlessness is enhanced by the fear of mass unemployment and the threat of war.

Everywhere he goes and in everything he does he comes into contact with vast impersonal forces. Although he lives in a large city together with thousands of others, he is not integrated into the community and has a terrible feeling of frustration and isolation. At his job he is merely a small part of a vast operation. When he goes to the department store, no one is particularly happy because he came. The clerks who wait on him are employees of a large concern; and, unlike the proprietor of a small store, they do not care whether he buys anything or not. If he joins a trade union to further his economic interests, the union is also likely to be a huge organization in which he cannot play an important role. The individual, therefore, stands alone, confused, frustrated, and overawed by a consciousness of his lack of importance and powerlessness.

Erich Fromm has shown how every aspect of modern life is calculated to produce a sense of insecurity, doubt, aloneness, and anxiety and that such feelings exist among all classes. The paradox of contemporary society is that "as man becomes more independent, self-reliant and critical he becomes more isolated, alone and afraid" and hence more susceptible to "any custom and any belief, however absurd and degrading, if it only connects the individual with others." Dr. Fromm says that the appeal of fascism can be partially explained by the desire to "escape into submission" from the heavy burden and strain of freedom; for "if we do not see the unconscious suffering of the average atomized person, then we fail to see the danger that threatens our culture from its human basis: the readiness to accept any ideology and any leader, if only he promises excitement and offers a political structure and symbols which allegedly give meaning and order to an individual's life. The despair of the human automaton is fertile soil for the political purposes of Fascism."[14]

It has sometimes been said that men everywhere are desirous of freedom, but an unemotional investigation would subject this statement to considerable doubt. There is, to be sure, the desire for a negative freedom: to be rid of certain oppressions, such as colonial administrators or domestic secret-police forces; but the positive desire to govern oneself and to make constant decisions on matters of public concern is not too widespread in the world. As soon as certain grievances have been eliminated, many people are content to leave the government in the hands of "those who know best."

Increased Burden on the Electorate

Democratic theory assumes that the intellectual qualities of the people are such that they can judge effectively the general quality of the men who seek their votes. Historical experience seems to confirm that the electorate can give a great and simple answer to a great and simple question; but in modern society the number of policies requiring electoral decision have been vastly increased and their nature has become progressively complicated. Hence it has become

[14] *Escape from Freedom* (New York, 1941), p. 256.

increasingly difficult to interpret the meaning of election results. One has only to sample the literature on [British and American elections] to see how many factors play a role and how difficult it is to say precisely what it was that "the people" thought about the matters discussed in the campaign. In a sense this has always been true. Opinions seldom carry weight in pure proportion to their intrinsic merit. The average man has always made his decision on the basis of a general impression; and trivial matters, rather than important questions of principle, have always influenced his vote. Nevertheless it is far more difficult today to say definitely that an election decides anything other than the personnel of key office holders; and in a multi-party country, such as France, it cannot be said that even this issue is decided by an election. The average man is likely to think that parties exist not because there are two sides to every question but because there are two sides to a political office—an inside and an outside; and he is also likely to feel that it is impossible for him to exert an effective influence on the policies of the government.

Growth of Bureaucracy

The assumption of new functions by the state has resulted in the growth of a vast and complicated administrative machine. To deplore and denounce this development is futile; for the economic functions of the modern state cannot be abandoned, have been dictated by public opinion, and have come into being in all modern states as a response to real problems. On the other hand, it is equally ridiculous to ignore this new expansion of administration and argue, as many people do, that because it is necessary, no problem exists.

The increasing complexity of the economic system, the growth of public regulation, the nationalization of industry, and an increasing demand for all kinds of social services have produced a mighty bureaucracy which is highly specialized and which has had professional training in administration. Gone are the days when, as President Jackson said, a government job was either so simple or could be made so simple that the average man could perform it satisfactorily. As administration becomes more and more a closed profession and as the power of this group increases, the ordinary voter is less likely to feel that he lives under a system which makes him one of the governors as well as one of the governed. . . .

Red tape and bureaucratic inefficiency are problems facing all modern governments—democratic and dictatorial as well. A study of the speeches and of the changes made in party rules at the Nineteenth Communist Party Congress held shortly before Premier Stalin's death confirms that most of the evils ordinarily associated with bureaucracy were a matter of chief concern.[15] However, in a democracy there is the added problem of how to keep this huge administration responsible and sensitive to public opinion. Even in Britain this is today a matter of chief concern. It is generally admitted that ministers are more dependent on their permanent civil servants than at any previous time, that ministers probably have little knowledge of what is done in their names or

[15] Harry Schwartz, "Anatomy of the Russian Communist Party," *New York Times Magazine* (March 22, 1953), p. 12; Merle Fainsod, *How Russia Is Ruled* (Cambridge, Mass., 1953), pp. 327-353; Victor Kravchenko, *I Chose Freedom* (New York, 1946), esp. pp. 316-331.

under their nominal responsibility, and that the traditional methods for controlling the administration are far from satisfactory. Members of the House of Commons are finding it increasingly difficult to discuss intelligently much of the highly technical legislation which they are called upon to pass, and they are finding the traditional methods of control over the processes of administration increasingly unsatisfactory. . . .

When one contemplates the size and complexity of the governmental machine in any modern state, it is indeed a tribute to the political capacity of the people if the government can be operated at all within a democratic framework. It is impossible to go on forever piling bureau upon bureau and constantly increasing the number of boards. The individual citizen will become lost in a maze! Yet a way must be found to restore the idea that he is one of the governors as well as one of the governed. It has been suggested that this can perhaps best be done by creating an opportunity for him to participate, at least to some extent, in the decisions of bodies which most intimately affect his daily life. It is no longer a question as to whether "big gover.iment" is a good thing; for the welfare state and its bureaucratic machine are already here. It is instead a question as to whether new administrative techniques can be developed rapidly enough to meet the challenge of the social service state.

Growth of Organized Economic Power

Since the individual standing alone can accomplish nothing, he joins an association to further his interests. Today there are trade unions, employers' organizations, professional societies, agricultural associations, and many other special interest groups. "If we wish to get a correct picture of the social and economic structure of the modern world," Professor E. H. Carr tells us,

> We must think not of a number of individuals cooperating and competing within the framework of a state, but a number of large and powerful groups, sometimes competing, sometimes cooperating, in the pursuit of their group interests, and of a state constantly impelled to increase the strength and scope of its authority in order to maintain the necessary minimum of cohesion in the social fabric. We can no longer base our thinking, like the classical economists, on the isolated independent individual. The subject of modern economics is a man in society, man as a member of a number of collective groups struggling for power, of which the most powerful, the most highly organised and the most broadly based is the state.[16]

The existence of these many groups increases the opportunity for participation by the citizen, but it also raises the question as to what their relationships should be to society as a whole and how these various organizations are to be integrated into community life.

To vast numbers of people political rights have lost their former importance because of the feeling that the unorganized majority of the electorate can accomplish nothing against the overriding force of organized economic power. Even in Great Britain the opinion is growing that politics consist of a bargain-

[16] *Conditions of Peace* (New York, 1943), pp. 74-75.

ing process between the forces representing organized capital and organized labor. It would be an exaggeration to say that the Conservative and Labor parties are nothing more than two machines representing respectively the combined forces of organized capital and organized labor, for electoral considerations compel both major parties to broaden their appeal to include a great deal more than a narrow special group interest. Yet there is considerable evidence to substantiate the charge that political policies are influenced in a major degree by the vested interests who supply the bulk of party funds and only to a minor degree by the opinions of the electorate whom they claim to represent. . . .

Under modern conditions it is more difficult to preserve a sense of community because the individual instead of becoming a civic-minded person is likely to be the supporter of a special interest group. Thus what was formerly a uniform and homogeneous opinion under simpler conditions may become broken up into a number of highly specialized functional organizations. . . .

Exercise of Dictatorial Power Easier

If the nature of modern society has made the emergence of dictatorship psychologically possible, it has also made the exercise of autocratic power easier than in any preceding period. The telephone, telegraph, railways, motor cars, aeroplanes, and other means of transportation and communication make it possible for governments to regulate and control vast areas and huge populations. The military weapons used by a modern army, such as tanks and machine guns, make it possible for a small number of men to dominate a huge population. Gone are the days when an aroused citizenry can take to the streets and overthrow a government which still has the support of the army. The growth of large-scale business organizations has also facilitated centralized governmental control, for it is easier for the state to regulate a small number of huge corporations than to check on a large number of small business men. The emphasis placed upon "scientific management" in modern industry and the development of a huge business bureaucracy have meant that the responsibility for making key decisions has become progressively centered in fewer and fewer hands and that the average person becomes increasingly accustomed to being led by others and gives up his own interpretation of events for those which others give him. The nationalization of industry offers no solution to this problem because in any highly industrial society men are bound to be part of a highly disciplined and authoritative organization. Thus "a modern industrial democratic state has been a house divided against itself, an autocratically governed industry over against a political democracy."[17]

It is impossible to discuss here all the changes brought about by the Industrial Revolution and their psychological effects, but it is easy to see that the cumulative result may be inimical to democracy. Having witnessed how science has conquered terrible diseases, how transportation advances and construction marvels have overcome the former impediments of both distance and space, and how government itself has performed functions previously considered impossible, people no longer feel that the insecurity they experience or

[17] A. D. Lindsay, *The Modern Democratic State* (New York, 1943), pp. 186-187. See also Karl Mannheim, *Man and Society in an Age of Reconstruction* (New York, 1941).

the disasters they fear are due to the uncontrollable forces of nature. They are instead inclined to believe that the government can do anything. Such an attitude is fertile ground for the demagogue because the people are credulous and are not likely to detect that he promises more than he can deliver. Moreover, the electorate is likely to be too impatient because it believes all problems are capable of solution and because it is likely to feel that hardships and inconveniences are due to the greed, selfishness, or incompetence of other men or else to the inadequacies of the economic and political system. Thus the emotionally charged propaganda of the demagogue claiming that a particular group is selfishly causing the trouble and ought to be brought under control has a powerful effect.[18] The spread of industry has brought a higher standard of living together with the increase and diffusion of knowledge, but it may in the long run have the effect of discouraging democratic institutions. As a matter of fact, both fascism and communism are so closely connected with contemporary sociological and psychological conditions that they could hardly have come at any other time.

The Psychology of Dictatorship

A complete analysis of political forces must include not only sociological facts but their relationship to opinion. Although there is always an economic and social aspect to political activity, politics has its roots in psychology. A study of symbols and myths may contribute as much to our knowledge of political institutions as a study of the historical background, economic institutions, and the environmental setting. In any case, there is always the human element which must be understood in assessing political movements. In recent years a number of observers, employing a socio-psychological approach, have deduced interpretations of the nature of man and his reactions to contemporary conditions which help explain the popularity of dictatorships. . . .

Charismatic Leadership

Leadership has always been a great factor in the history of human communities. Carlyle, Maurras, Nietzsche, and Leopold von Ranke saw history as largely the work of great state builders. Charisma is an irrational belief which arises in situations which the average man cannot grasp and understand rationally. In periods of civil strife, religious turmoil, and profound social and economic upheavals, men are often unable to perceive the factors which have caused their misery and distress. Under such circumstances they are likely to look for a leader who will fend off misery and deliver them from destitution. An examination of the idolatrous utterances made by party members, university professors, army officers, business men, and ordinary workers indicates quite clearly that contemporary leaders are revered and that they are thought of as possessing qualities lacking in ordinary mortals. In Nazi Germany hero-worship was formulated into a definite theory, for there were "Führers" for every branch of activity. However, Hermann Goering's description in *Germany Reborn* is similar to the adoration of the person of the dictator in other countries:

[18] For example, the Nazis focused their attention on the Jews, the Communists on the capitalists.

Just as the Roman Catholic considers the Pope infallible in all matters concerning religion and morals, so do we National Socialists believe, with the same inner conviction, that for us the Leader is, in all political and other matters concerning the national and social interests of the people, simply infallible. Wherein lies the secret of this enormous influence which he has on his followers? . . . It is something mystical, inexpressible, almost incomprehensible, which this unique man possesses, and he who cannot feel it instinctively will not be able to grasp it at all. For we love Adolf Hitler, because we believe deeply and unswervingly that God has sent him to us to save Germany.[19]

A similar attitude also existed in Italy where Mussolini was proclaimed as a genius, a creative force who united in his person the irrational elements of the will of history, a man in the Messianic sense who was also the exemplary Italian in whom the people found its representative. . . .

Although the theory of historic materialism denies that an individual can have any influence on the progress of events, the same phenomenon has occurred in the Soviet Union. Although Beatrice and Sidney Webb did not consider Stalin a dictator, they found "the deliberate exploitation by the governing junta of the emotion of hero-worship, of the traditional reverence of the Russian people for a personal autocrat. . . . Scarcely a speech is made or a conference held, without a naïve—some would say a fulsome—reference to 'Comrade Stalin' as the great leader of the people."[20] At the time when the Webbs wrote, the deification of Lenin, which began soon after his death, had become a fixed feature of Soviet national life; . . .

However, extravagant statements of adoration are not confined to rulers in dictatorial countries. One is reminded of the American business man who said that President Franklin D. Roosevelt was "the greatest leader since Jesus Christ."[21] When one reads how thousands wept as they walked in the streets upon the death of Kemal Ataturk, how many of the common people were struck with a sincere grief by the passing of Stalin, or about the emotional feeling of many, if not most, Americans upon the death of President Franklin D. Roosevelt,[22] there can be no doubt about the existence of charisma. Power has a peculiar fascination to the human mind. The masses apparently dote on a leader who by the mystery of magnetism inspires respect, who makes himself into their national symbol, and who makes them feel great through their kinship with him. The belief in one man's power to perform miracles is undoubtedly promoted and encouraged by both the leader and his followers, but there is no question that millions do sincerely believe in it. The fact that the worship of the ruler is a recurring idea in history would also seem to indicate

[19] Hermann Goering, *Germany Reborn* (London, 1934), pp. 79-80.

[20] *Soviet Communism: A New Civilisation?* (New York, Charles Scribner's Sons, 1936), p. 438. For a profound criticism of the Webbs on the ground that their ideas are anti-democratic, see Shirley R. Letwin, "Representation Without Democracy: The Webbs' Constitution," *The Review of Politics,* XVI (July, 1954), 352-375.

[21] John T. Flynn, "Other People's Money," *New Republic,* LXXXV (December 11, 1935), 129.

[22] For a discussion, see Harold Orlansky, "Reactions to the Death of President Roosevelt," *The Journal of Social Psychology,* XXVI (1947), 235-266.

that the masses derive an emotional satisfaction in the experience of hero-worship. The question arises, therefore, as to what are the exigencies in contemporary life responsible for the return of personal leadership and the psychological conditions which have created it. . . .

Even in democratic countries the masses have found it easier to fix their allegiance to a single personality than to a group of legislators whom it is hard to make responsible. Almost everywhere the executive has increased in power and prestige as compared with the legislature; and although this development is to some extent the inevitable result of social and economic changes which have produced a tremendous growth in the functions and activities of government, it has also been furthered by an extension of the suffrage. In both Britain and the United States the exploitation of personality has gone on increasingly as the franchise was widened to include a larger number of citizens. Ever since the days of Gladstone and Disraeli British electors have tended to vote for individual candidates, not on their merits, but in terms of whom they will support to be the prime minister. This development has also been furthered by the increased use of the press and radio. Today everything that a British prime minister or an American president says or does is news. Every party must have a great leader, and in the hands of the publicity experts he becomes almost divinely inspired. . . . In the same manner the eyes of the entire nation are fixed upon the President of the United States. The masses expect him to manage Congress and to secure favorable action on a well-rounded legislative program. Rightly or wrongly they tend to give him all the credit for successes but they also blame him for all the failures or shortcomings during his administration whether they can be attributed to his own personal actions or not. . . .

In so far as the growth of large cities has reduced the opportunity for personal participation by the citizen in local self-government, an important training ground of democracy has been lost; and in so far as modern education has failed to produce a well-rounded individual capable of critically analyzing political issues and devoted to participating in community life and taking an active interest in civic affairs, it has failed to produce the type of man upon which democracy depends.

Freudian Conceptions

Sigmund Freud, the founder of psychoanalysis, developed a theory of human nature and behavior which, when given an application to social problems, has challenged the older forms of social psychology and produced new insights for explaining the emergence of dictatorship.[23] Space does not permit an extensive discussion of Freud's ideas and the social and political implications involved. However, his most important contribution lies in the emphasis he placed upon unconscious motivation and the role of irrational factors in human conduct. His discoveries have caused us to revise our conception of human nature and to see more clearly wherein the democratic theorists of the eighteenth and nineteenth centuries held a much too simple and optimistic view of man and placed too great an emphasis upon his rational nature.

[23] Freud's most important books which make direct contributions to the social sciences are: *Group Psychology and the Analysis of the Ego* (London, 1922); *The Future of an Illusion* (London, 1928); *Civilization and Its Discontents* (London, 1930); and *The Problem of Anxiety* (New York, 1936).

Freud's psychology of society starts from the experience of the individual. There is developed inside the human psyche a father-hatred because it is the father who intervenes and prevents the child from possessing mother completely. In some respects the father is a terrible figure because it is he who brings the element of fear into a child's life through punishment and who teaches him a consciousness of guilt. At the same time, the child has a feeling of respect and admiration for the father, and this hate-love attitude is called ambivalence. The father is the most powerful member of the family; he is generally a kindly and benevolent person; the child is dependent on the father for the necessities of life and indeed thinks of him at first as an all-powerful person.

In the normal family an equilibrium is reached, but in every individual the experience of his early years is entangled with his whole personality. After he becomes an adult, he often wishes that he could return to his childhood when all of his wants were satisfied without effort on his part. After leaving the all-embracing comforts of the home, he is constantly seeking the loving mother and the father whom he respects and admires. Thus the king is an unconscious symbol of the father and the queen of the mother. A successful statesman has frequently been called "the father of his country." It is possible to substitute a symbol or an idea for an individual, but in times of stress and strain a people may not remain content with a "symbolic" leader and demand the destruction of the institutions standing between them and emotional reality. It may be that they will demand a "savior" or a "leader" who will stand in the same emotional relationship to them as that in which a father used to stand. Thus freedom is not really what people want, and dictatorship is merely the effort of a strained people to bring about order. It is the result of an emotional need which people feel, especially at a time when political conditions appear to be outside of human control, for a dominating personality. . . .

If men are cold, hungry, and impoverished and if there is also a vast incomprehensible menace, such as an economic crisis or war, they are seized by a paralyzing fear because the situation seems to leave no room for action. The very nature of the crisis makes an individual feel helpless and like a little child. He is inhibited from taking any action on his own because he does not know what is happening; and even if sources of information are available to the ordinary person, he is incapable of understanding.

> How could the Turkish peasant understand the complications of the world situation in 1922, the Italian the economic crisis, the Russian the famine and civil war which swept over him, the German worker the complex results of war and economic crisis? He is reduced to the position of a child in an incomprehensible world; his reaction resembles that of the ordinary adult in the face of illness.[24]

Evaluation of Present Knowledge

If the conclusions reached in the preceding discussion are sound, dictatorship is the result of an intrinsic weakness of contemporary democracy which

[24] Spearman, *Modern Dictatorship*, p. 104.

is partly institutional but which is mainly psychological and moral. The failure of democratic leadership to muster necessary electoral and legislative support made it impossible for the executive to mobilize the power of the state or to develop and fulfill any broad public policy; and this crisis in authority in turn brought democratic government into contempt even among its supporters and had the effect of strengthening the antidemocratic elements in society. The contemporary crisis of democracy, therefore, is mainly spiritual and psychological. Its roots must be found in the loss of common unity, in the inability of parties and interest groups to achieve agreement on fundamental common aims, and in their failure to find and accept a common moral purpose. . . .

The truth is that democracy has failed where it did not produce satisfactory results. Of all forms of government democracy is the most delicate requiring a long period for maturation and growth and presupposing the inculcation of an appropriate philosophy without which it cannot withstand the forces of disruption. When the pressures impinging on the government's stability are moderate, it can adjust to them and undergo gradual reformation or evolution; but when they are extreme, the desperate civil conflict generally culminates in the elevation of a tyrant.

The "best form of government," as Aristotle said, is relative to circumstances. Under right conditions and favorable circumstances democracy undoubtedly is the best form of government and secures the most satisfactory results. However, when these conditions are not present, democracy may at the same time be one of the worst kinds of government. It is sometimes forgotten that the judgment of both Plato and Aristotle was against democracy; and although they were unfamiliar with modern "representative democracy," the reasons for their adverse judgment and the circumstances out of which it arose may be instructive to us at the present time.

At no time has democracy been widely adopted in practice nor is it likely to be in the future. History does not teach us that men really wish to govern themselves but that they want to be well governed and expect results from the government in power. . . .

Conclusion

It is impossible to state with certainty the future of democracy in the modern world. Man as a free agent has the capacity to choose and the ability to influence his destiny. However, the social sciences lack certainty, and the present state of our knowledge can take us only a small way in determining the outcome.

Emphasis has been placed upon our lack of knowledge and the need for more study because existing theories do not seem to explain adequately political events and because profound changes taking place at the present time are little understood and their significance often ignored. However, there is a sense in which a solution to the crisis does not depend upon more knowledge. As Professor Hans J. Morgenthau has pointed out, "Politics is an art and not a science, and what is required for its mastery is not the rationality of the engineer but the wisdom and moral strength of the statesman."[25] The political con-

[25] *Scientific Man vs. Power Politics* (Chicago, 1946), p. 10.

502   *The Decline of Democracy*

flicts in the modern world are only partially economic; they are not technical problems to be resolved through a blueprint; and they are similar to irrational forces that have previously dominated the aspirations of man. Man is a rational creature, but he is also influenced by prejudice and emotion; and it is impossible to predict with certainty whether the immediate future lies with the democratic leader or the tyrannical demagogue. The question confronting the modern world is whether it has the capacity to produce the statesmen who have the political wisdom to act successfully, who have the moral judgment to choose among expedient actions the least evil ones, and who have the imagination to build a new society which will reconcile man's political nature with his moral aspirations and his weakness with his strength.

~~~~~TOPIC 28

Elitism or Pluralism?

C. WRIGHT MILLS
The Power Elite

The Higher Circles

The power elite is composed of men whose positions enable them to transcend the ordinary environments of ordinary men and women; they are in positions to make decisions having major consequences. Whether they do or do not make such decisions is less important than the fact that they do occupy such pivotal positions: their failure to act, their failure to make decisions, is itself an act that is often of greater consequence than the decisions they do make. For they are in command of the major hierarchies and organizations of modern society. They rule the big corporations. They run the machinery of the state and claim its prerogatives. They direct the military establishment. They occupy the strategic command posts of the social structure, in which are now centered the effective means of the power and the wealth and the celebrity which they enjoy. . . .

Within American society, major national power now resides in the economic, the political, and the military domains. Other institutions seem off to the side of modern history, and, on occasion, duly subordinated to these. No family is as directly powerful in national affairs as any major corporation; no church is as directly powerful in the external biographies of young men in America today as the military establishment; no college is as powerful in the shaping of momentous events as the National Security Council. Religious, educational, and family institutions are not autonomous centers of national power; on the contrary, these decentralized areas are increasingly shaped by the big three, in which developments of decisive and immediate consequence now occur. . . .

Within each of the big three, the typical institutional unit has become

Late professor of sociology, Columbia University. Author, among others, of *White Collar, The Sociological Imagination, Listen Yankee: The Revolution in Cuba,* and *The Marxists.* This essay is abridged from *The Power Elite* (Copyright 1956 by Oxford University Press, Inc.) and from *Power, Politics and People: The Collected Essays of C. Wright Mills* (Copyright 1963 by the Estate of C. Wright Mills) and reprinted by permission of Oxford University Press, Inc., and the author's literary executor, Professor Irving Louis Horowitz.

503

enlarged, has become administrative, and, in the power of its decisions, has become centralized. Behind these developments there is a fabulous technology, for as institutions, they have incorporated this technology and guide it, even as it shapes and paces their developments. . . .

In each of these institutional areas, the means of power at the disposal of decision makers have increased enormously; their central executive powers have been enhanced; within each of them modern administrative routines have been elaborated and tightened up.

As each of these domains becomes enlarged and centralized, the consequences of its activities become greater, and its traffic with the others increases. The decisions of a handful of corporations bear upon military and political as well as upon economic developments around the world. The decisions of the military establishment rest upon and grievously affect political life as well as the very level of economic activity. The decisions made within the political domain determine economic activities and military programs. There is no longer, on the one hand, an economy, and, on the other hand, a political order containing a military establishment unimportant to politics and to money-making. There is a political economy linked, in a thousand ways, with military institutions and decisions. On each side of the world-split running through central Europe and around the Asiatic rimlands, there is an ever-increasing interlocking of economic, military, and political structures.[1] If there is government intervention in the corporate economy, so is there corporate intervention in the governmental process. In the structural sense, this triangle of power is the source of the interlocking directorate that is most important for the historical structure of the present. . . .

At the pinnacle of each of the three enlarged and centralized domains, there have arisen those higher circles which make up the economic, the political, and the military elites. At the top of the economy, among the corporate rich, there are the chief executives; at the top of the political order, the members of the political directorate; at the top of the military establishment, the elite of soldier-statesmen clustered in and around the Joint Chiefs of Staff and the upper echelon. As each of these domains has coincided with the others, as decisions tend to become total in their consequence, the leading men in each of the three domains of power—the warlords, the corporation chieftains, the political directorate—tend to come together, to form the power elite of America. . . .

The political order, once a decentralized set of several dozen states with a weak spinal cord, has become a centralized, executive establishment which has taken up into itself many powers previously scattered, and now enters into each and every cranny of the social structure. . . .

The long-time tendency of business and government to become more intricately and deeply involved with each other has reached a new point of explicitness. The two cannot now be seen clearly as two distinct worlds. It is in terms of the executive agencies of the state that the rapprochement has proceeded most decisively. The growth of the executive branch of the government, with its agencies that patrol the complex economy, does not mean merely

---

[1] Cf. Hans Gerth and C. Wright Mills, *Character and Social Structure* (New York: Harcourt, Brace, 1953), pp. 457 ff.

the 'enlargement of government' as some sort of autonomous bureaucracy: it has meant the ascendancy of the corporation's man as a political eminence.

During the New Deal the corporate chieftains joined the political directorate; as of World War II they have come to dominate it. Long interlocked with government, now they have moved into quite full direction of the economy of the war effort and of the postwar era. This shift of the corporation executives into the political directorate has accelerated the long-term relegation of the professional politicians in the Congress to the middle levels of power. . . .

Executive Power

A small group of men are now in charge of the executive decisions made in the name of the United States of America. These fifty-odd men of the executive branch of the government include the President, the Vice President, and the members of the cabinet; the head men of the major departments and bureaus, agencies and commissions, and the members of the Executive Office of the President, including the White House staff.

Only three of these members of the political directorate[2] are professional party politicians in the sense of having spent most of their working lives running for and occupying elective offices; and only two have spent most of their careers as 'behind-the-scenes' political managers or 'fixers.' Only nine have spent their careers within governmental hierarchies—three of them in the military; four as civil servants in civilian government; and two in a series of appointive positions not under the civil-service system. Thus, a total of only fourteen (or about one-fourth) of these fifty-three executive directors have by virtue of their career been 'professionals' of government administration or party politics.

The remaining three-quarters are political outsiders. At one time or another, several of them have been elected to political offices, and some have entered government service for short periods but, for most of their careers, they have generally worked outside the realms of government and politics. Most of these outsiders—thirty of the thirty-nine in fact—are quite closely linked, financially or professionally or both, with the corporate world, and thus make up slightly over half of all the political directors. The remainder have been active in various other 'professional' fields.

The three top policy-making positions in the country (secretaries of state, treasury, and defense) are occupied by a New York representative of the leading law firm of the country which does international business for Morgan and Rockefeller interests; by a Mid-West corporation executive who was a director of a complex of over thirty corporations; and by the former president of one of the three or four largest corporations and the largest producer of military equipment in the United States.

There are four more members of the corporate rich in the cabinet—two more men from General Motors; a leading financier and director of New England's largest bank; and a millionaire publisher from Texas. The positions of Secretaries of Agriculture and Labor are occupied by professional outsiders, leaving only one cabinet member who is an insider to politics and government

[2] As of May 1953.

—the Attorney-General, who has been both a New York State Assemblyman and a partner in the law firm of Lord, Day and Lord, but has, since 1942, been a political manager for Dewey and later Eisenhower.

Although the Attorney-General and Vice-President are the only political professionals, two other cabinet members have at one time held elective state offices and at least five of the cabinet members were active in the political campaign of 1952. None of them are, in any sense that may be given to the term, civil servants; the President is alone among them as a man trained in a governmental (military) bureaucracy.

On the 'second team' of the political directorate, there is a 'Little Cabinet,' whose members stand in for the first and, who, in fact, handle most of the administrative functions of governing. Among the top thirty-two deputies of the agencies, departments, and commissions, twenty-one are novices in government: many of them never held political office, nor in fact even worked in government, before their present positions. These men usually have had fathers who were big businessmen; twelve attended Ivy League colleges; and they themselves have often been businessmen or bankers or the salaried lawyers of large corporations or members of the big law firms. Unlike professional politicians, they do not belong to the local jamboree of Elk and Legion; they are more often members of quiet social clubs and exclusive country clubs. Their origins, their careers, and their associations make them representative of the corporate rich.

On this 'second team' there is one Rockefeller as well as a former financial adviser to the Rockefellers; there are working inheritors of family power and textile companies; there are bankers; there is a publisher, an airline executive, and lawyers; a representative from the southwestern affiliate of America's largest corporation; and another man from General Motors. There is also Allen Dulles who spent ten years in the diplomatic service, left it (because a promotion in rank offered him no increase above his $8,000 salary) to join the law firm of Sullivan and Cromwell (about the time that his brother became its senior partner) and then returned to the government as its senior spy. On this second team there are also four men who have not been directly associated with the corporate world.

Only seven of the thirty-two members of the second team have been trained in governmental bureaucracies; only four have had considerable experience in party politics. . . .

As a group, the political outsiders who occupy the executive command posts and form the political directorate are legal, managerial, and financial members of the corporate rich. . . . The old-fashioned rich were simply the propertied classes, organized on a family basis and seated in a locality, usually a big city. The corporate rich, in addition to such people, include those whose high 'incomes' include the privileges and prerogatives that have come to be features of high executive position. . . . They are a corporate rich because they depend directly, as well as indirectly, for their money, their privileges, their securities, their advantages, their powers on the world of the big corporations. All the old-fashioned rich are now more or less of the corporate rich, and the newer types of privileged men are there with them. In fact, no one can become rich or stay rich in America today without becoming involved, in one way or another, in the world of the corporate rich. . . .

Power Over the Economy

The economy—once a great scatter of small productive units in autonomous balance—has become dominated by two or three hundred giant corporations, administratively and politically interrelated, which together hold the keys to economic decisions. . . .

In so far as the structural clue to the power elite today lies in the economic order, that clue is the fact that the economy is at once a permanent-war economy and a private-corporation economy. American capitalism is now in considerable part a military capitalism, and the most important relation of the big corporation to the state rests on the coincidence of interests between military and corporate needs, as defined by warlords and corporate rich. Within the elite as a whole, this coincidence of interest between the high military and the corporate chieftains strengthens both of them and further subordinates the role of the merely political men. Not politicians, but corporate executives, sit with the military and plan the organization of war effort. . . .

The corporations are the organized centers of the private property system: the chief executives are the organizers of that system. . . . The chief executives are the men who occupy the top two or three command posts in each of those hundred or so corporations which, measured by sales and capital, are the largest. If, in any one year we list these leading corporations, in all industrial lines, and from their top levels select the presidents and the chairmen of their boards, we shall have listed the chief executives. . . .

Their private decisions, responsibly made in the interests of the feudal-like world of private property and income, determine the size and shape of the national economy, the level of employment, the purchasing power of the consumer, the prices that are advertised, the investments that are channeled. Not 'Wall Street financiers' or bankers, but large owners and executives in their self-financing corporations hold the keys of economic power. Not the politicians of the visible government, but the chief executives who sit in the political directorate, by fact and by proxy, hold the power and the means of defending the privileges of their corporate world. If they do not reign, they do govern at many of the vital points of everyday life in America, and no powers effectively and consistently countervail against them, nor have they as corporate-made men developed any effectively restraining conscience. . . .

Power of the Military

The military order, once a slim establishment in a context of distrust fed by state militia, has become the largest and most expensive feature of government, and, although well versed in smiling public relations, now has all the grim and clumsy efficiency of a sprawling bureaucratic domain. . . .

The most dramatic symbol of the scale and shape of the new military edifice is the Pentagon. The concrete and limestone maze contains the organized brain of the American means of violence. The world's largest office building, the United States Capitol would fit neatly into any one of its five segments. . . .

At the head of the military bureaucracy, below the President of the United States and the Secretary of Defense, whom he appoints, and his assistants, there sits, behind office walls of sheet steel, a military board of directors—the Joint Chiefs of Staff. Immediately below the Joint Chiefs there is a higher circle of generals and admirals which presides over the elaborate and far-flung land, sea, and air forces, as well as the economic and political liaisons held necessary to maintain them, and over the publicity machines. . . .

As the United States has become a great world power, the military establishment has expanded, and members of its higher echelons have moved directly into diplomatic and political circles. . . . In 1942, General Mark Clark dealt with Darlan and Giraud in North Africa; then he commanded the Eighth Army in Italy; then he was occupation commander for Austria; and, in 1952, he became US Commander in newly sovereign Japan, as well as head of the US Far East Command and UN Commander in Korea. General George C. Marshall, after being the President's personal representative to China, became Secretary of State (1947-49), then Secretary of Defense (1950-51). Vice Admiral Alan G. Kirk was Ambassador to Belgium in the late 'forties and then to Russia. In 1947, the Assistant Secretary of State for occupied areas was Major General John H. Hildring who dealt 'directly with the military commanders who control the execution of policy in Germany, Austria, Japan and Korea'; Brigadier General Frank T. Hines was Ambassador to Panama; and General Walter Bedell Smith was Ambassador to Russia. General Smith later became the head of the Central Intelligence Agency (1950-53), then Under Secretary of State (1953-54). As occupation commander in Germany, there was General Lucius D. Clay; of Japan, General MacArthur. And no diplomat, but a former Army Chief of Staff, General J. Lawton Collins, went to troubled Indo-China in 1954 'to restore some order' in an area which he said 'had essential political and economic importance for Southeast Asia and the free world.'[3] . . .

No area of decision has been more influenced by the warlords and by their military metaphysics than that of foreign policy and international relations. . . . The military have become ambassadors as well as special envoys. In many of the major international decisions, the professional diplomats have simply been by-passed, and matters decided by cliques of the high military and political personnel. In the defense agreements signed by the United States and Spain in September of 1953, as in the disposition in 1945 and 1946 of the western Pacific islands captured from the Japanese, the military has set policy of diplomatic relevance without or against the advice of the diplomats.[4] The Japanese peace treaty was not arranged by diplomats but by generals; a peace treaty with Germany has not been made: there have only been alliances and agreements between armies. At Panmunjom, the end of the Korean war was 'negotiated' not by a diplomat but by a General in open collar and without necktie. . . .

Moreover, while still in uniform as well as out of it, high-ranking officers have engaged in policy debate. . . . General Bradley has made numerous speeches which in their context were readily interpreted, by Senator Taft and Hanson Baldwin among others, as relevant to the political issues of the 1952 Presiden-

[3] Hanson W. Baldwin, 'Army Men in High Posts,' *The New York Times,* 12 January 1947; *The New York Times,* 15 November 1954 and 9 November 1954.

[4] See Burton M. Sapin and Richard C. Snyder, 'The Role of the Military in American Foreign Policy' (New York: Doubleday & Co., 1954), pp. 33-4.

tial elections. 'This speech,' wrote Hanson Baldwin, 'helped put General Bradley and the Joint Chiefs of Staff into the political hustings where they have no business to be.' Senator Taft, who accused the Joint Chiefs of Staff of being under the control of the political administration and of echoing their policies rather than rendering merely expert advice, was himself supported by General Albert Wedemeyer, as well as by General MacArthur. Another general, Bonner Fellers, was on the Republican National Committee.

In the 1952 election, in direct violation of U.S. Army Regulation 600-10, General MacArthur, in public speeches, attacked the policies of the duly elected administration, delivered the keynote address at the Republican convention, and made it clear that he was open to the Presidential nomination. . . .

But more important perhaps than the straightforward assumption of political roles, the private advice, or the public speeches, is a more complex type of military influence: high military men have become accepted by other members of the political and economic elite, as well as by broad sectors of the public, as authorities on issues that go well beyond what has historically been considered the proper domain of the military.

Since the early 'forties, the traditional Congressional hostility toward the military has been transformed into something of a 'friendly and trusting' subservience. No witness—except of course J. Edgar Hoover—is treated with more deference by Senators than the high military. 'Both in what it did and in what it refused to do,' we read in an official government account, 'the wartime Congress co-operated consistently and almost unquestioningly with the suggestions and the requests from the Chief of Staff.' And in the coalition strategy, while the President and the Prime Minister 'decided,' theirs were choices approved by the military and made from among alternatives organized and presented by the military.

According to the Constitution, the Congress is supposed to be in charge of the support and governing of the armed might of the nation. During times of peace, prior to World War II, professional politicians in the Congress did argue the details of military life with the military, and made decisions for them, debating strategy and even determining tactics. During World War II, Congressmen 'voted' for such items as the Manhattan Project without having the slightest idea of its presence in the military budget, and when—by rumor—Senator Truman suspected that something big was going on, a word from the Secretary of War was enough to make him drop all inquiry. In the postwar period, the simple fact is that the Congress has had no opportunity to get real information on military matters, much less the skill and time to evaluate it. Behind their 'security' and their 'authority' as experts, the political role of the high military in decisions of basic political and economic relevance has become greatly enlarged. And again, it has been enlarged as much or more because of civilian political default—perhaps necessarily, given the organization and personnel of Congress—than by any military usurpation. . . .

The military establishment has, of course, long been economically relevant. The Corps of Engineers—historically the elite of the West Pointers—has in peacetime controlled rivers and harbor construction. Local economic, as well as Congressional, interests have not been unaware of the pork-barrel possibilities, nor of the chance to have The Corps disapprove of the Reclamation Bureau's plans for multiple-purpose development of river valleys. 'Actually'—we are told by Arthur Maass in his discussion of 'the lobby that can't be licked'—'up to about 1925, the Corps disbursed 12 per cent of the total ordinary expenditures of the government.'

But now the economic relevance of the military establishment is on a qualitatively different scale.[5] The national budget has increased, and within it the percentage spent by and for the military. Since just before World War II, the percentage has never gone below about 30 per cent, and it has averaged over 50 per cent, of the entire government budget. In fact, two out of every three dollars in the budget announced in 1955 were marked for military security. And as the role of government in the economy has increased, so has the role of the military in the government.

We should constantly keep in mind how recent the military ascendancy is. During World War I the military entered the higher economic and political circles only temporarily, for the 'emergency'; it was not until World War II that they intervened in a truly decisive way. Given the nature of modern warfare, they had to do so whether they wanted to or not, just as they had to invite men of economic power into the military. For unless the military sat in on corporate decisions, they could not be sure that their programs would be carried out; and unless the corporation chieftains knew something of the war plans, they could not plan war production. Thus, generals advised corporation presidents and corporation presidents advised generals. 'My first act on becoming Chief of Ordnance on June 1, 1942,' Lt. General Levin H. Campbell, Jr., has said, 'was to establish a personal advisory staff consisting of four outstanding business and industrial leaders who were thoroughly familiar with all phases of mass production.'

During World War II, the merger of the corporate economy and the military bureaucracy came into its present-day significance. The very *scale* of the 'services of supply' could not but be economically decisive: The Services of Supply, *Fortune* remarked in 1942, 'might . . . be likened to a holding company of no mean proportions. In fact—charged with spending this year some $32 billion, or 42 per cent of all that the U.S. will spend for war—it makes U.S. Steel look like a fly-by-night, the A.T. and T. like a country-hotel switchboard, Jesse Jones's RFC or any other government agency like a small-town boondoggle. In all of Washington, indeed, there is scarcely a door—from Harry Hopkins's Munitions Assignments Board on down—in which [General] Somervell or his lieutenants have not come to beg, to borrow, or to steal.'[6] The very *organization* of the economics of war made for the coincidence of interest and the political mingling among economic and military chiefs: 'The Chief of Ordnance has an advisory staff composed of Bernard M. Baruch, Lewis H. Brown of Johns-Manville Corp., K. T. Keller of Chrysler Corp., and Benjamin F. Fairless of United States Steel Corp. Ordnance contracts are placed by four main branches . . . Each branch director . . . [is] assisted by an advisory in-

[5] Between 1789 and 1917, the U.S. government spent about 29½ billion dollars; but in the single fiscal year of 1952, the military alone was allotted 40 billion. In 1913, the cost per capita of the military establishment was $2.25; in 1952, it was almost $250.

[6] 'The S.O.S.,' *Fortune,* September 1942, p. 67.

dustrial group, composed of representatives of the major producers of weapons in which the branch deals.'[7] . . .

After World War II, military demands continued to shape and to pace the corporate economy. It is accordingly not suprising that during the last decade, many generals and admirals, instead of merely retiring, have become members of boards of directors. General Lucius D. Clay, who commanded troops in Germany, then entered the political realm as occupation commander, is now the board chairman of the Continental Can Company. General James H. Doolittle, head of the 8th Air Force shortly before Japan's surrender, is now a vice-president of Shell Oil. General Omar N. Bradley, who commanded the 12th Army group before Berlin, going on to high staff position, then became the board chairman of Bulova Research Laboratories; in February 1955, Chairman Bradley allowed his name to be used—'General of the Army Omar N. Bradley'—on a full-page advertisement in support, on grounds of military necessity, of the new tariff imposed on Swiss watch movements. General Douglas MacArthur, political general in Japan and Korea, is now chairman of the board at Remington Rand, Inc. General Albert C. Wedemeyer, commander of U.S. forces in the China theater, is now a vice-president of AVCO Corporation. Admiral Ben Morell is now chairman of Jones & Laughlin Steel Corp. . . .

It is difficult to avoid the inference that the warlords, in their trade of fame for fortune, are found useful by the corporate executives more because of whom they know in the military and what they know of its rules and ways than because of what they know of finance and industry proper. Given the major contracts that are made by the military with private corporations, we can readily understand why business journalists openly state: 'McNarney knows Convair's best customer, The Pentagon, as few others do—a fact well known to his friend, Floyd Odlum, Convair chairman.' And 'in business circles the word has gone out: Get yourself a general. What branch of the government spends the most money? The military. Who, even more than a five-percenter, is an expert on red tape? A general or an admiral. So make him Chairman of the Board.'

The increased personnel traffic that goes on between the military and the corporate realms, however, is more important as one clue to a structural fact about the United States than as an expeditious means of handling war contracts. Back of this shift at the top, and behind the increased military budget upon which it rests, there lies the great structural shift of modern American capitalism toward a permanent war economy. . . .

In part at least this has resulted from one simple historical fact, pivotal for the years since 1939: the focus of elite attention has been shifted from domestic problems, centered in the 'thirties around slump, to international problems, centered in the 'forties and 'fifties around the war. Since the governing apparatus of the United States has by long historic usage been adapted to and shaped by domestic clash and balance, it has not, from any angle, had suitable agencies and traditions for the handling of international problems. Such formal democratic mechanics as had arisen in the century and a half of national devel-

[7] Major General Lucius D. Clay, General Staff Corps, Assistant Chief of Staff for Material, 'The Army Supply Program,' *Fortune,* February 1943, p. 96.

opment prior to 1941, had not been extended to the American handling of international affairs. It is, in considerable part, in this vacuum that the power elite has grown. . . .

To understand the power elite, we must attend to . . . the psychology of the several elites in their respective milieux. In so far as the power elite is composed of men of similar origin and education, in so far as their careers and their styles of life are similar, there are psychological and social bases for their unity, resting upon the fact that they are of similar social type and leading to the fact of their easy intermingling. This kind of unity reaches its frothier apex in the sharing of that prestige that is to be had in the world of the celebrity; it achieves a more solid culmination in the fact of the interchangeability of positions within and between the three dominant institutional orders. . . .

The power elite is *not* an aristocracy, which is to say that it is not a political ruling group based upon a nobility of hereditary origin. It has no compact basis in a small circle of great families whose members can and do consistently occupy the top positions in the several higher circles which overlap as the power elite. But such nobility is only one possible basis of common origin. That it does not exist for the American elite does not mean that members of this elite derive socially from the full range of strata composing American society. They derive in substantial proportions from the upper classes, both new and old, of local society and the metropolitan 400. The bulk of the very rich, the corporate executives, the political outsiders, the high military, derive from, at most, the upper third of the income and occupational pyramids. Their fathers were at least of the professional and business strata, and very frequently higher than that. They are native-born Americans of native parents, primarily from urban areas, and, with the exceptions of the politicians among them, overwhelmingly from the East. They are mainly Protestants, especially Episcopalian or Presbyterian. In general, the higher the position, the greater the proportion of men within it who have derived from and who maintain connections with the upper classes. The generally similar origins of the members of the power elite are underlined and carried further by the fact of their increasingly common educational routine. Overwhelmingly college graduates, substantial proportions have attended Ivy League colleges, although the education of the higher military, of course, differs from that of other members of the power elite. . . .

There is a kind of reciprocal attraction among the fraternity of the successful—not between each and every member of the circles of the high and mighty, but between enough of them to insure a certain unity. On the slight side, it is a sort of tacit, mutual admiration; in the strongest tie-ins, it proceeds by intermarriage. And there are all grades and types of connection between these extremes. Some overlaps certainly occur by means of cliques and clubs, churches and schools.

If social origin and formal education in common tend to make the members of the power elite more readily understood and trusted by one another, their continued association further cements what they feel they have in common. Members of the several higher circles know one another as personal friends and even as neighbors; they mingle with one another on the golf course, in the gentleman's clubs, at resorts, on transcontinental airplanes, and on ocean liners. They meet at the estates of mutual friends, face each other in front of the TV camera, or serve on the same philanthropic committee; and many are sure to cross one another's path in the columns of newspapers, if not in the exact cafes from which many of these columns originate. . . .

The higher members of the military, economic, and political orders are able readily to take over one another's point of view, always in a sympathetic way, and often in a knowledgeable way as well. They define one another as among those who count, and who, accordingly, must be taken into account. Each of them as a member of the power elite comes to incorporate into his own integrity, his own honor, his own conscience, the viewpoint, the expectations, the values of the others. If there are no common ideals and standards among them that are based upon an explicitly aristocratic culture, that does not mean that they do not feel responsibility to one another.

All the structural coincidence of their interests as well as the intricate, psychological facts of their origins and their education, their careers and their associations make possible the psychological affinities that prevail among them, affinities that make it possible for them to say to one another: He is, of course, one of us. And all this points to the basic, psychological meaning of class consciousness. Nowhere in America is there as great a 'class consciousness' as among the elite; nowhere is it organized as effectively as among the power elite. For by class consciousness, as a psychological fact, one means that the individual member of a 'class' accepts only those accepted by his circle as among those who are significant to his own image of self. . . .

Behind such pyschological and social unity as we may find, are the structure and the mechanics of those institutional hierarchies over which the political directorate, the corporate rich, and the high military now preside. The greater the scale of these bureaucratic domains, the greater the scope of their respective elite's power. How each of the major hierarchies is shaped and what relations it has with the other hierarchies determine in large part the relations of their rulers. If these hierarchies are scattered and disjointed, then their respective elites tend to be scattered and disjointed; if they have many interconnections and points of coinciding interest, then their elites tend to form a coherent kind of grouping.

The unity of the elite is not a simple reflection of the unity of institutions, but men and institutions are always related, and our conception of the power elite invites us to determine that relation. Today in America there are several important structural coincidences of interest between these institutional domains, including the development of a permanent war establishment by a privately incorporated economy inside a political vacuum. . . .

As the business between the big three increases in volume and importance, so does the traffic in personnel. The very criteria for selecting men who will rise come to embody this fact. The corporate commissar, dealing with the state and its military, is wiser to choose a young man who has experienced the state and its military than one who has not. The political director, often dependent for his own political success upon corporate decisions and corporations, is also wiser to choose a man with corporate experience. Thus, by virtue of the very criterion of success, the interchange of personnel and the unity of the power elite is increased. . . .

The unity of the power elite, however, does not rest solely on psychological similarity and social intermingling, nor entirely on the structural coincidences of commanding positions and interests. At times it is the unity of a more explicit co-ordination. To say that these three higher circles are increasingly co-ordinated, that this is *one* basis of their unity, and that at times—as during the wars—such co-ordination is quite decisive, is not to say that the co-ordination is total or continuous, or even that it is very sure-footed. Much less is it to say that willful co-ordination is the sole or the major basis of their unity, or that the power elite has emerged as the realization of a plan. But it is to say that as the institutional mechanics of our time have opened up avenues to men pursuing their several interests, many of them have come to see that these several interests could be realized more easily if they worked together, in informal as well as in more formal ways, and accordingly they have done so.

The Theory of Balance*

The idea of the power elite is of course an interpretation. It rests upon and it enables us to make sense of major institutional trends, the social similarities and psychological affinities of the men at the top. But the idea is also based upon what has been happening on the middle and lower levels of power, to which I now turn.

There are of course other interpretations of the American system of power. The most usual is that it is a moving balance of many competing interests. The image of balance, at least in America, is derived from the idea of the economic market: in the nineteenth century, the balance was thought to occur between a great scatter of individuals and enterprises; in the twentieth century, it is thought to occur between great interest blocs. In both views, the politician is the key man of power because he is the broker of many conflicting powers.

I believe that the balance and the compromise in American society—the 'countervailing powers' and the 'veto groups', of parties and associations, of strata and unions—must now be seen as having mainly to do with the middle levels of power. It is these middle levels that the political journalist and the scholar of politics are most likely to understand and to write about—if only because, being mainly middle class themselves, they are closer to them. Moreover these levels provide the noisy content of most 'political' news and gossip; the images of these levels are more or less in accord with the folklore of how democracy works; and, if the master-image of balance is accepted, many intellectuals, especially in their current patrioteering, are readily able to satisfy such political optimism as they wish to feel. Accordingly, liberal interpretations of what is happening in the United States are now virtually the only interpretations that are widely distributed.

But to believe that the power system reflects a balancing society is, I think, to confuse the present era with earlier times, and to confuse its top and bottom with its middle levels.

By the top levels, as distinguished from the middle, I intend to refer, first of all, to the scope of the decisions that are made. At the top today, these de-

* The balance of this essay is from Mills' *Power, Politics and People: The Collected Essays of C. Wright Mills.* [Eds.]

cisions have to do with all the issues of war and peace. They have also to do with slump and poverty which are now so very much problems of international scope. I intend also to refer to whether or not the groups that struggle politically have a chance to gain the positions from which such top decisions are made, and indeed whether their members do usually hope for such top national command. Most of the competing interests which make up the clang and clash of American politics are strictly concerned with their slice of the existing pie. Labour unions, for example, certainly have no policies of an international sort other than those which given unions adopt for the strict economic protection of their members. Neither do farm organizations. The actions of such middle-level powers may indeed have consequence for top-level policy; certainly at times they hamper these policies. But they are not truly concerned with them, which means of course that their influence tends to be quite irresponsible. . . .

The middle level of politics is not a forum in which there are debated the big decisions of national and international life. Such debate is not carried on by nationally responsible parties representing and clarifying alternative policies. There are no such parties in the United States. More and more, fundamental issues never come to any point or decision before the Congress, much less before the electorate in party campaigns. In the case of Formosa, in the spring of 1955, the Congress abdicated all debate concerning events and decisions which surely bordered on war. The same is largely true of the 1957 crisis in the Middle East. Such decisions now regularly by-pass the Congress, and are never clearly focused issues for public decision.

The American political campaign distracts attention from national and international issues, but that is not to say that there are no issues in these campaigns. In each district and state, issues are set up and watched by organized interests of sovereign local importance. The professional politician is of course a party politician, and the two parties are semi-feudal organizations: they trade patronage and other favours for votes and for protection. The differences between them, so far as national issues are concerned, are very narrow and very mixed up. Often each seems to be forty-eight parties, one to each state; and accordingly, the politician as campaigner and as Congressman is not concerned with national party lines, if any are discernible. Often he is not subject to any effective national party discipline. He speaks for the interests of his own constituency, and he is concerned with national issues only in so far as they affect the interests effectively organized there, and hence his chances of re-election. That is why, when he does speak of national matters, the result is so often such an empty rhetoric. Seated in his sovereign locality, the politician is not at the national summit. He is on and of the middle levels of power. . . .

In the 'thirties, it often seemed that labour would become an insurgent power independent of corporation and state. Organized labour was then emerging for the first time on an American scale, and the only political sense of direction it needed was the slogan, 'organize the unorganized'. Now without the mandate of the slump, labour remains without political direction. Instead of economic and political struggles it has become deeply entangled in administrative routines with both corporation and state. One of its major functions, as a vested interest of the new society, is the regulation of such irregular tendencies as may occur among the rank and file.

There is nothing, it seems to me, in the make-up of the current labour leadership to allow us to expect that it can or that it will lead, rather than merely react. In so far as it fights at all it fights over a share of the goods of a single way of life and not over that way of life itself. The typical labour leader in the U.S.A. today is better understood as an adaptive creature of the main business drift than as an independent actor in a truly national context.

The idea that this society is a balance of powers requires us to assume that the units in balance are of more or less equal power and that they are truly independent of one another. These assumptions have rested, it seems clear, upon the historical importance of a large and independent middle class. In the latter nineteenth century and during the Progressive Era, such a class of farmers and small businessmen fought politically—and lost—their last struggle for a paramount role in national decision. Even then, their aspirations seemed bound to their own imagined past.

This old, independent middle class has of course declined. On the most generous count, it is now 40 per cent of the total middle class (at most 20 per cent of the total labour force). Moreover, it has become politically as well as economically dependent upon the state, most notably in the case of the subsidized farmer.

The *new* middle class of white-collar employees is certainly not the political pivot of any balancing society. It is in no way politically unified. Its unions, such as they are, often serve merely to incorporate it as hanger-on of the labour interest. For a considerable period, the old middle class *was* an independent base of power; the new middle class cannot be. Political freedom and economic security *were* anchored in small and independent properties; they are not anchored in the worlds of the white-collar job. Scattered property holders were economically united by more or less free markets; the jobs of the new middle class are integrated by corporate authority. Economically, the white-collar classes are in the same condition as wage workers; politically, they are in a worse condition, for they are not organized. They are no vanguard of historic change; they are at best a rear-guard of the welfare state. . . .

The agrarian revolt of the 'nineties, the small business revolt that has been more or less continuous since the 'eighties, the labour revolt of the 'thirties—each of these has failed as an independent movement which could countervail against the powers that be; they have failed as politically autonomous third parties. But they have succeeded, in varying degree, as interests vested in the expanded corporation and state; they have succeeded as parochial interests seated in particular districts, in local divisions of the two parties, and in the Congress. What they would become, in short, are well-established features of the *middle* levels of balancing power, on which we may now observe all those strata and interests which in the course of American history have been defeated in their bids for top power or which have never made such bids.

In the classic image, the people are presented with problems. They discuss them. They formulate viewpoints. These viewpoints are organized, and they compete. One viewpoint 'wins out'. Then the people act on this view, or their representatives are instructed to act it out, and this they promptly do.

Such are the images of democracy which are still used as working justifications of power in America. We must now recognize this description as more a fairy tale than a useful approximation. The issues that now shape man's fate are neither raised nor decided by any public at large. The idea of a society that is at bottom composed of publics is not a matter of fact; it is the proclamation of an ideal, and as well the assertion of a legitimation masquerading as fact.

I cannot here describe the several great forces within American society as well as elsewhere which have been at work in the debilitation of the public. I want only to remind you that publics, like free associations, can be deliberately and suddenly smashed, or they can more slowly wither away. But whether smashed in a week or withered in a generation, the demise of the public must be seen in connection with the rise of centralized organizations, with all their new means of power, including those of the mass media of distraction. These, we now know, often seem to expropriate the rationality and the will of the terrorized or—as the case may be—the voluntarily indifferent society of masses. In the more democratic process of indifference the remnants of such publics as remain may only occasionally be intimidated by fanatics in search of 'dis-loyalty'. But regardless of that, they lose their will for decision because they do not possess the instruments for decision; they lose their sense of political be-longing because they do not belong; they lose their political will because they see no way to realize it.

The political structure of a modern democratic state requires that such a public as is projected by democratic theorists not only exist but that it be the very forum within which a politics of real issues is enacted.

It requires a civil service that is firmly linked with the world of knowledge and sensibility, and which is composed of skilled men who, in their careers and in their aspirations, are truly independent of any private, which is to say, corporation, interests.

It requires nationally responsible parties which debate openly and clearly the issues which the nation, and indeed the world, now so rigidly confront.

It requires an intelligentsia, inside as well as outside the universities, who carry on the big discourse of the western world, and whose work is relevant to and influential among parties and movements and publics.

And it certainly requires, as a fact of power, that there be free associa-tions standing between families and smaller communities and publics, on the one hand, and the state, the military, the corporation, on the other. For unless these do exist, there are no vehicles for reasoned opinion, no instruments for the rational exertion of public will.

Such democratic formations are not now ascendant in the power structure of the United States, and accordingly the men of decision are not men selected and formed by careers within such associations and by their performance be-fore such publics. The top of modern American society is increasingly unified, and often seems wilfully co-ordinated: at the top there has emerged an elite whose power probably exceeds that of any small group of men in world history. The middle levels are often a drifting set of stalemated forces: the middle does not link the bottom with the top. The bottom of this society is politically frag-mented, and even as a passive fact, increasingly powerless: at the bottom there is emerging a mass society.

DWIGHT D. EISENHOWER
The Military-Industrial Complex

Three days from now, after half a century in the service of our country, I shall lay down the responsibilities of office as, in traditional and solemn ceremony, the authority of the Presidency is vested in my successor.

This evening I come to you with a message of leave-taking and farewell, and to share a few final thoughts with you, my countrymen. . . .

Throughout America's adventure in free government, our basic purposes have been to keep the peace, to foster progress in human achievement, and to enhance liberty, dignity and integrity among people and among nations. To strive for less would be unworthy of a free and religious people. Any failure traceable to arrogance, or our lack of comprehension or readiness to sacrifice, would inflict upon us grievous hurt both at home and abroad. . . .

A vital element in keeping the peace is our military establishment. Our arms must be mighty, ready for instant action, so that no potential aggressor may be tempted to risk his own destruction.

Our military organization today bears little relation to that known by any of my predecessors in peacetime, or indeed by the fighting men of World War II or Korea.

Until the latest of our world conflicts, the United States had no armaments industry. American makers of plowshares could, with time and as required, make swords as well. But now we can no longer risk emergency improvisation of national defense; we have been compelled to create a permanent armaments industry of vast proportions. Added to this, three and a half million men and women are directly engaged in the defense establishment. We annually spend on military security more than the net income of all United States corporations.

This conjunction of an immense military establishment and a large arms industry is new in the American experience. The total influence—economic, political, even spiritual—is felt in every city, every State house, every office of the Federal government. We recognize the imperative need for this development. Yet we must not fail to comphehend its grave implications. Our toil, resources and livelihood are all involved; so is the very structure of our society.

In the councils of government, we must guard against the acquisition of unwarranted influence, whether sought or unsought, by the military-industrial complex. The potential for the disastrous rise of misplaced power exists and will persist.

We must never let the weight of this combination endanger our liberties or democratic processes. We should take nothing for granted. Only an alert and knowledgeable citizenry can compel the proper meshing of the huge industrial

From "Farewell Radio and Television Address to the American People," January 17, 1961. From *Public Papers of the Presidents: Dwight D. Eisenhower, 1960-61,* (Washington, D. C.: U. S. Government Printing Office, 1961), pp. 1035-1039.

and military machinery of defense with our peaceful methods and goals, so that security and liberty may prosper together.

Akin to, and largely responsible for the sweeping changes in our industrial-military posture, has been the technological revolution during recent decades.

In this revolution, research has become central; it also becomes more formalized, complex, and costly. A steadily increasing share is conducted for, by, or at the direction of, the Federal government.

Today, the solitary inventor, tinkering in his shop, has been overshadowed by task forces of scientists in laboratories and testing fields. In the same fashion, the free university, historically the fountainhead of free ideas and scientific discovery, has experienced a revolution in the conduct of research. Partly because of the huge costs involved, a government contract becomes virtually a substitute for intellectual curiosity. For every old blackboard there are now hundreds of new electronic computers.

The prospect of domination of the nation's scholars by Federal employment, project allocations, and the power of money is ever present—and is gravely to be regarded.

Yet, in holding scientific research and discovery in respect, as we should, we must also be alert to the equal and opposite danger that public policy could itself become the captive of a scientific-technological elite.

It is the task of statesmanship to mold, to balance, and to integrate these and other forces, new and old, within the principles of our democratic system—ever aiming toward the supreme goals of our free society.

DANIEL BELL

Is There a Ruling Class in America?

Power is a difficult subject. Its effects are more observable than its causes; even the power-wielders often do not know what factors shaped their decisions. Its consequences are more refractory to control—and prediction—than any other form of human behavior. C. Wright Mills' *The Power Elite*, because it seeks to locate the sources of power in an identifiable constellation of elites, is one of those rare books in contemporary sociology that deal with the "world of causality" rather than mere description of methodological discussion. It is, in addition, something else: a political book whose loose texture and power rhetoric have allowed different people to read their own emotions into it: for the young neo-Marxists in England (*vide* the group around the *Universities and Left Review*) and the old orthodox Marxists in Poland (*vide* the reception by Adam Schaff, the Party's official philosopher), it has become a primer for the

Professor of Sociology, Columbia University. Author of *The Reforming of General Education* (1966); *The Radical Right* (editor and co-author, 1962); *The End of Ideology* (1960); and *Work and Its Discontents* (1956). This selection is reprinted with permission of The Macmillan Company from pp. 47-74 of *The End of Ideology*, rev. ed. Copyright © 1962 by The Free Press, a Corporation.

understanding of American policy and motives. This is curious, since Mills is not a Marxist, and if anything, his method and conclusions are anti-Marxist. But because it is tough-minded and "unmasks" the naive, populist illusions about power, it has won a ready response among radicals. . . .

Mills' book is molded by direct intellectual progenitors. These are: Veblen, from whom the rhetoric and irony are copied; Weber, for the picture of social structure, not, however, of classes, but of vertical orders, or *Standen;* and, most *crucially,* Pareto, but not for the definition of elite, which is much different from Mills', but the method. While the debts to Veblen and Weber are conscious, that to Pareto is probably not so. Yet there is the same scorn for ideas, and the denial that ideology has any operative meaning in the exercise of power. And by seeing power as an underlying "combination of orders," Mills parallels, in method, what Pareto was doing in seeing social groups as "combinations of residues." This leads, I think, despite the dynamism in the rhetoric, to a static, ahistorical approach.[1] For *The Power Elite* is not an empirical analysis of power in the United States, though many readers have mistaken its illustrations for such an analysis, but a *scheme* for the analysis of power; and a close reading of its argument will show, I think, how confusing and unsatisfactory this scheme is.

The Argument

One can examine Mills' book by an alternate scheme,[2] but as a prior necessity one must write a textual analysis: identify the key terms, see how consistently they are used, and relate evidence to propositions in order to test the coherence of the argument. This, then, is an exercise in hermeneutics.

The argument, as it unfolds in Mills' opening chapter (the others are largely uneven illustrations rather than development or demonstration of the thesis), shuttles perplexingly back and forth on the key problem of how power is wielded. One can show this only by some detailed quotation, a difficult but necessary burden for exposition.[3]

Within American society, says Mills, major national power "now resides in the economic, political and military domains."

[1] My own masters, in this respect, are Dewey and Marx. Dewey, for his insistence on beginning not with structure (habit) but with problems: with the question of why something is called into question, why things are in change and what people did; Marx, for the interplay of ideology and power: for the emphasis on history, on crises as transforming moments, on politics as an activity rooted in concrete interests and played out in determinable strategies.

[2] For one such alternate scheme, see Talcott Parsons' essay-review "The Distribution of Power in American Society," World Politics, October 1957, Vol. X, No. 1. Parsons argues that Mills sees power as a secondary "distributive" concept in a zero-sum game, where the focus is on who has power. Parsons organizes his analysis on the functional, or integrative purpose of power in the ordering of society. Another view, which sees power as a positive force in securing social values for the benefit of society, is advanced by Robert S. Lynd in the symposium edited by Arthur Kornhauser, *Problems of Power in American Democracy,* Wayne State Press, 1958.

[3] All italics, unless otherwise indicated, are mine. They are intended to underline key statements. All citations are from C. Wright Mills' *The Power Elite,* New York, Oxford University Press, 1956.

The way to understand the power of the American elite lies neither solely in recognizing the historical scale of events, nor in accepting the personal awareness reported by men of apparent decision. Behind such men and behind the events of history, linking the two, are the major institutions of modern society. These hierarchies of state and corporation and army constitute the means of power; as such, they are now of a consequence not before equalled in human history—and at their summits, there are now those command posts of modern society which offer us the sociological key to an understanding of the role of the higher circles in America [p. 5].

Thus power, to be power, apparently means control over the *institutions* of power:

By the powerful, we mean, of course, *those who are able to realize their will, even if others resist it.* No one, accordingly, can be truly powerful unless he has access to the command of major institutions, for it is over these institutional means of power that the truly powerful are, in the first instance, powerful [p. 9].

It is shared by only a few persons:

By the power elite, we refer to those political and economic and military *circles* which as an intricate set of overlapping cliques *share decisions having at least national consequences. Insofar as national events are decided, the power elite are those who decide them* [p. 18].

But although these people make the key decisions, they are not the "history makers" of the time. The "power elite" is not, Mills says (p. 20), a theory of history; history is a complex net of intended and unintended decisions.

The idea of the power elite implies *nothing about the process of decision-making as such:* it is an attempt to delimit social areas within which that process, *whatever its character,* goes on. It is a conception of *who* is involved in the process [p. 21].

But historical decisions are made:

In our time the pivotal moment does arise, and at that moment small circles do decide or fail to decide. In either case, they are an elite of power. . . . [p. 22].

Does then the elite make history? Sometimes it is role-determined, sometimes role-determining (pp. 22-25). Mills is obviously wrestling with a contradictory position. For if the power elite are not the history makers, why worry much about them? If they are, it seems to lead to a simple-minded theory of history. Finally Mills resolves the problem:

It was no "historical necessity," but a man named Truman who, with a few other men, decided to drop a bomb on Hiroshima. It was no historical necessity, but an argument within a small circle of men that defeated Admiral Radford's proposal to send troops to Indochina before Dienbienphu fell [p. 24].

If we extract a residue from all this backing and filling, it is that a smaller number of men than ever before holding top positions in government, economic life, and the military, have a set of responsibilities and decision-making powers that are more consequential than ever before in United States history—which, in itself, does not tell us very much.

But it is less the argument than the rhetoric which found an echo, and crucial to Mills' book are a set of operative terms—*institutions* (with which are interchanged freely, *domains, higher circles, top cliques*), *power, command posts,* and *big decisions*—the political use of which gives the book its persuasiveness. These are the key modifiers of the term "elite." What do they mean?

The Terms

(a) *Elite*. Throughout the book, the term elite is used in a variety of ways. Sometimes the term denotes "membership in clique-like sets of people," or "the morality of certain personality types," or "statistics of selected values" such as wealth, political position, etc. In only one place, in a long footnote on page 366, among the notes, Mills explicitly tries to straighten out the confusion created by the profuse interchange of terms. He says that he defines elites primarily on the basis of "institutional position." But what does this mean?

(b) *Institutions, Domains, etc.* Behind men and behind events, linking the two, says Mills, are the major institutions of society: The military, the political, and the economic. But, actually, the military, the economic, the political, as Mills uses these terms, are not institutions but sectors, or what Weber calls *orders*, or vertical hierarchies—each with their enclosed strata—in society. To say that this sector, or order, is more important than that—that in some societies, for example, the religious orders are more important than the political—is to give us large-scale boundaries of knowledge. But surely we want and need more than that.

Such usage as "the military," "the political directorate," etc., is extraordinarily loose. It would be hard to characterize these as institutions. Institutions derive from *particular, established* codes of conduct, which shape the behavior of *particular* groups of men who implicitly or otherwise have a loyalty to that code and are subject to certain controls (anxiety, guilt, shame, expulsion, etc.) if they violate the norms. If the important consideration of power is *where people draw their power from*, then we have to have more particularized ways of identifying the groupings than "institutionalized orders," "domains," "circles," etc.

(c) *Power*. Throughout the book, there is a curious lack of definition of the word power. Only twice, really, does one find a set of limits to the word:

> By the powerful we mean, of course, those who are able to realize their will, even if others resist it [p. 9].

> *All* politics is a struggle for power: the ultimate kind of power is violence [p. 171].

It is quite true that violence, as Weber has said, is the ultimate sanction of power, and in extreme situations (e.g., the Spanish Civil War, Iraq, etc.) control of the means of violence may be decisive in seizing or holding power. But power is not the inexorable, implacable, granitic force that Mills and others make it to be. (Merriam once said: "Rape is not evidence of irresistable power, either in politics or sex.") And is it true to say that *all* politics is a struggle for power? Are there not ideals as a goal? And if ideals are realizable through power—though not always—do they not temper the violence of politics?

Power in Mills' terms is domination. But we do not need an elaborate discussion to see that this view of power avoids more problems than it answers, and particularly once one moves away from the outer boundary of *power as violence* to *institutionalized power,* with which Mills is concerned. For in society, particularly constitutional regimes, and *within* associations, where violence is not the rule, we are in the realm of norms, values, traditions, legitimacy, consensus, leadership, and identification—all the models and mechanisms of command and authority, their acceptance or denial, which shape action in the day-to-day world, *without violence.* And these aspects of power Mills has eschewed.

(d) *The Command Posts.* It is rather striking, too, given Mills' image of power, and politics, as violence, that the metaphor to describe the people of power is a military one. We can take this as a clue to Mills' implicit scheme. But, being little more than a metaphor, it tells us almost nothing about *who* has the power. The men who hold power, he says, are those who run the *organizations* or *domains* which have power. But how do we know they have power, or what power they have? Mills simply takes as postulates: (1) the organization or institution has power; (2) *position in it gives power.* How do we know? Actually, we can only know if power exists by what people *do* with their power.

What powers people have, what decisions they make, how they make them, what factors they have to take into account in making them—all these enter into the question of whether position *can* be transferred into power. But Mills has said: "The idea of the power elite implies nothing about the process of decision-making as such—it is an attempt to delimit the social areas within which that process, *whatever its character,* goes on. It is a conception of who is involved in the process" (p. 21). Thus, we find ourselves stymied. *Who* depends upon positions? But position, as I have argued, is only meaningful if one can define the character of the decisions made with such power. And this problem Mills eschews.[4]

[4] In his extraordinary story of policy conflicts between the Army, Air Force and Navy on strategic concepts—policy issues such as reliance on heavy military bombers and all-out retaliation, against tactical nuclear weapons and conventional ground forces for limited wars, issues which deeply affect the balance of power within the military establishment—General James Gavin provides a striking example of the helplessness of some of the top Army brass against the entrenched bureaucracy within the Defense Department. "With the establishment of the Department of Defense in 1947," he writes, "an additional layer of civilian management was placed above the services. Furthermore, by the law, military officers were forbidden to hold executive positions in the Department of Defense. As a result the Assistant Secretaries of Defense relied heavily on hundreds of civil service employees, who probably have more impact on decision-making in the Department of Defense than any other group of individuals, military or civilian." From *War and Peace in the Space Age* (Harper and Brothers), reprinted in *Life,* August 4, 1958, pp. 81-82.

Mills says, further, that he wants to avoid the problem of the self-awareness of the power holders, or the role of such self-awareness in decisions. ("The way to understand the power of the elite lies neither in recognizing the historic scale of events or the personal awareness reported by men of apparent decision behind the men and the institutions" [p. 15].) But if the power elite is *not* the history-maker (p. 20), as Mills sometimes implies, *then what is the meaning of their position as members of the power elite?* Either they can make effective decisions or not. It is true that many men, like Chanticleer the Cock, crow and believe that they have caused the sun to rise, but if such power is only self-deception, that is an aspect, too, of the meaning of power.

(e) *The Big Decisions.* The power elite comes into its own on the "big decisions." In fact, this is an implicit definition of the power of the elite: only they can effect the "big decisions." Those who talk of a new social balance, or pluralism, or the rise of labor, are talking, if at all correctly, says Mills, about the "middle levels" of power. They fail to see the big decisions.

But, curiously, except in a few instances, Mills fails to specify what the big decisions are. The few, never analyzed with regard to how the decisions were actually made or who made them, are five in number: the steps leading to intervention in World War II; the decision to drop the atom bomb over Hiroshima and Nagasaki; the declaration of war in Korea; the indecisions over Quemoy and Matsu in 1955; the hesitation regarding intervention in Indochina when Dien Bien Phu was on the verge of falling.

It is quite striking (and it is in line with Mills' conception of politics) that all the decisions he singles out as the "big decisions" are connected with *violence*. These are, it is true, the ultimate decisions a society can make: the commitment or refusal to go to war. And in this regard Mills is right. They *are* big decisions. But what is equally striking in his almost cursory discussion of these decisions is the failure to see that they are not made by the power elite. They are the decisions which, in our system, are vested constitutionally in the individual who must bear the responsibility for the choices—the president. And, rather than being a usurpation of the power of the people, so to speak, this is one of the few instances in the Constitution where such responsibility is specifically defined and where accountability is clear. Naturally, a president will consult with others. And in the instances Mills has cited, the president did. Richard Rovere has written a detailed analysis (in the *Progressive,* June, 1956) of the decisions that Mills has cited and, as Mills defines this elite, has broadly refuted the notion that a "power elite" was really involved. Few persons, other than the president, were involved in these decisions: on the atom bomb, Stimson, Churchill, and a few physicists; on Korea, a small group of men whose counsel was divided, like Acheson and Bradley; on Quemoy and Matsu, specifically by Eisenhower; and on Dien Bien Phu, a broader group, the military and the Cabinet: but in this instance, "the" power elite, narrowly defined, was for intervention, while Eisenhower alone was against the intervention and decided against sending in troops, principally, says Rovere, because of the weight of public opinion.

Now it may well be that crucial decisions of such importance should not be in the hands of a few men. But short of a system of national initiative and referendum, such as was proposed in 1938-39 in the Ludlow amendment, or short of reorganizing the political structure of the country to insist on party responsibility for decision, it is difficult to see what Mills' shouting is about. To say that the leaders of a country have a constitutional responsibility to make crucial decisions is a fairly commonplace statement. To say that the power elite makes such decisions is to invest the statement with a weight and emotional charge that is quite impressive, but of little meaning.

The Question of Interests

So far we have been accepting the terms "command posts" and "power elite" in Mills' own usage. But now a difficulty enters: the question not only of *who* constitutes the power elite but how *cohesive* they are. Although Mills contends that he does not believe in a conspiracy theory, his loose account of the centralization of power among the elite comes suspiciously close to it. (It is much like Jack London's *The Iron Heel*—the picture of the American oligarchs —which so influenced socialist imagery and thought before World War I.)

Yet we can only evaluate the meaning of any centralization of power on the basis of what people do with their power. What *unites* them? What *divides* them? And this involves a definition of *interests*. To say, as Mills does: *"All means of power tend to become ends to an elite that is in command of them. And that is why we may define the power elite in terms of power—as those who occupy the command posts"* (p. 23)—is circular.

What does it mean to say that power is an end in itself for the power elite? If the elite is cohesive and is facing another power group, the maintenance of power may be an end in itself. But is the elite cohesive? We do not know without first coming back to the question of interests. And the nature of interests implies a selection of values by a group, or part of a group, over against others, and this leads to a definition of particular privileges, and so on.

Certainly, one cannot have a power elite, or a ruling class, without *community of interests*. Mills implies one: the interest of the elite is in the maintenance of the capitalist system as a *system*. But this is never really discussed or analyzed in terms of the meaning of capitalism, the impact of political controls on the society, or the changes in capitalism in the last twenty-five years.

But even if the interest be as broad as Mills implies, one still has the responsibility of identifying the conditions for the maintenance of the system, and the issues and interests involved. Further, one has to see whether there is or has been a *continuity of interests*, in order to chart the cohesiveness or the rise and fall of particular groups.

One of the main arguments about the importance of the *command posts* is the growing centralization of power, which would imply something about the nature of interests. Yet there is almost no sustained discussion of the forces leading to centralization. These are somewhat assumed, and hover over the book, but are never made explicit. Yet only a sustained discussion of these tendencies would, it seems to me, uncover the *locales* of power and their shifts. For example: the role of technology and increasing capital costs as major factors in the size of enterprise; forces in the federalization of power, such as the need for regulation and planning on a national scale because of increased communication, complexity of living, social and military services, and the managing of the economy; the role of foreign affairs. Curiously, Soviet Russia is not even mentioned in the book, although so much of our posture has been dictated by Russian behavior.

Since his focus is on *who* has power, Mills spends considerable effort in tracing the social origins of the men at the top. But, in a disclaimer toward the end of the book (pp. 280-87) he says that the conception of the power elite does not rest upon common social origins (a theme which underlies, say, Schumpeter's notion of the rise and fall of classes) or upon personal friendship, but (although the presumption is not made explicit) upon their "institutional position." But such a statement begs the most important question of all: *the mechanisms of co-ordination among the power holders.* One can say obliquely, as Mills does, that they "meet each other," but this tells us little. If there are "built-in" situations whereby each position merges into another, what are they? One can say, as Mills does, that the new requirements of government require increased recruitment to policy positions from outside groups.[5] But then, what groups—and what do they do?

At one point Mills says that the Democrats recruited from Dillon, Read, and the Republicans from Kuhn, Loeb. But the point is never developed, and it is hard to know what he means. One could equally say that in the recruitment of science advisors the Democrats took from Chicago and Los Alamos, and the Republicans from Livermore; but if this means anything, and I think it does, one has to trace out the consequences of this different recruitment in the *actions* of the different people. Mills constantly brings the story to the point where analysis has to begin—and stops.

The most extraordinary fact about American foreign policy—the most crucial area of power—has been the lack of co-ordination between the military and foreign-policy officials, and the failure of both to think in political terms. This is exemplified in the lack of liaison in the final days of World War II, and the non-political decisions made by the U.S. generals which have had incalculable consequences for the balance of power in postwar Europe. Unlike the Soviet Union, the United States subordinated all political questions to immediate military objectives. The British, fearful of a postwar Europe dominated by the Soviet Union, were anxious in the final months of the war to push the Allied armies as fast as possible across the North German plain to Berlin— either to beat the Russians or to participate in its capture. But for the U.S. chiefs of staff, Berlin was of secondary importance.

Said General Marshall, chairman of the Joint Chiefs of Staff: "Such psychological and political advantages as would result from the possible capture of Berlin ahead of the Russians should not override the imperative military

[5] One key theoretical point, for Marxists, which Mills, surprisingly, never comes to is the question of the ultimate source of power. Is the political directorate autonomous? Is the military independent? If so, why? What is the relation of economic power to the other two? Mills writes: "Insofar as the structural clue to the power elite today lies in the enlarged and military state, that clue becomes evident in the military ascendency. The warlords have gained decisive political relevance, and the military structure is now in considerable part a political structure." (p. 275) If so, what is one to say then about the other crucial proposition by Mills that the capitalist system in the U.S. is essentially unchanged? [See section below on "The Continuity of Power."]

consideration which, in our opinion, is the destruction and dismemberment of the German armed forces."

And Ray S. Cline in *Washington Command Post: The Operations Division,* a volume in the official army history of World War II, notes the lack of "systematic co-ordination of foreign policy with military planning" and the uncertainty—even in the fall of 1944—of State Department officials "about American foreign policy as applied to the surrender and occupation of Germany." And the Pentagon, which usually is seen as the cold political brains of U.S. foreign policy, in the negotiation on the occupation of Berlin, rejected a British suggestion for a full land corridor from West Germany to Berlin on the ground that the Soviet Union was an ally and that such a corridor was therefore unnecessary. . . .

The European Image

Having defined politics and power in terms of the ultimate sanction of violence, Mill raises the provocative question: Why have the possessors of the means of violence—the military—not established themselves in power more than they have done in the West? Why is not military dictatorship the more normal form of government?

Mills' answer is to point to the role of status. "Prestige to the point of honor, and all that this implies, has, as it were, been the pay-off for the military renunciations of power . . ." (p. 174).

Now, to the extent that this is true, this fact applies primarily to the *European* scene. On the Continent, the military did create and seek to live by a code of honor. Many European works deal with this code, and many European plays, particularly those of Schnitzler, satirize it. But does the concept apply in the United States? Where in the United States has the military (the Navy apart) been kept in check by honor? The military has not had the power—or status—in American life for a variety of vastly different reasons: the original concept of the Army as a people's militia; the populist image of the Army man—often as a "hero"; the "democratic" recruitment to West Point; the reluctance to accept conscription; the low esteem of soldiering as against money-making; the tradition of civil life, etc.

All this Mills sees and knows. But if "honor" and "violence" are not meaningful in our past, why conceptualize the problem of the military in terms of violence and honor as a general category, when the problem does not derive from the American scene in those terms? Unless Mills assumes, as many intellectuals did in the thirties, that we shall yet follow the European experience. . . .

History and Ideas

Now, if one is concerned with the question about changes in the source and style of power, or in the synchronization and centralization of power, one would have to examine the problem historically. Yet except in one or two instances, Mills ignores the historical dimensions. In one place he speaks of a periodization of American history wherein political power has replaced economic power. But this is too loose to be meaningful. In another place—the only concrete discussion of social change in historical terms—he cites an interesting statistic:

> In the middle of the nineteenth century—between 1865 and 1881—only 19 per cent of the men at the top of government began their political career at the national level; but from 1905 to 1953 about one-third of the political elite began there, and in the Eisenhower administration some 40 per cent started in politics at the national level—a high for the entire political history of the U.S. [p. 229].

Even in its own terms, it is hard to figure out the exact meaning of the argument, other than the fact that more problems are centered in Washington than in the states and, for this reason, more persons are drawn directly to the national capital than before. Surely there is a simple explanation for much of this. During World War II, with a great need for both national unity and for specialists, more outsiders were coopted for cabinet posts and the executive branch than before. And, in 1952, since the Republicans had been out of top office for twenty years and would have fewer persons who had a career in government, they would bring in a high proportion of outsiders.

What is interesting in the use of this kind of data is the methodological bias it reveals. In using such data—and variables like lower or national levels—there is a presumption that in the different kind of recruitment one can chart differences in the character of the men at top, and that therefore the *character of their politics* would be different too. (Mills seems to imply this but never develops the point other than to say that, today, the *political outsider* has come into the ascendant. But as a counter-methodology, it would seem to me that one would start not with recruitment or social origins but with the *character of the politics*. Has something changed, and if so, what and why? Is the change due to differences in recruitment (differential class and ethnic backgrounds) or to some other reason? But if one asks these questions, one has to begin with an examination of *ideas and issues*, not social origins.

But Mills, at least here, is almost completely uninterested in ideas and issues. The questions in politics that interest him are: In what way have strategic positions changed, and which positions have come to the fore? Changes in power then are for Mills largely a succession of different positions. As different structural or institutional positions (i.e., military, economic, political) combine, different degrees of power are possible. The circulation of the elite—by which Pareto meant the change in the composition of groups with different "residues" —is transformed here into the succession of institutional positions.

But how does this apply to people? Are people—character, ideas, values —determined by their *positions?* And if so, in what way? More than that, to see political history as a shift in the power position of "institutions" rather than, say, of concrete interest groups, or classes, is to read politics in an extraordinarily abstract fashion. It is to ignore the changes in ideas and interests. This is one of the reasons why Mills can minimize, in the striking way he does, the entire twenty-year history of the New Deal and Fair Deal. For him these twenty years were notable *only* because they fostered the centralizing tendencies of the major "institutions" of society, notably the political.

In this neglect, or even dismissal of ideas and ideologies, one finds a striking parallel in Pareto's explanation of social changes in Italy. For Pareto, the rise of socialism in Italy was a mere change in the "derivations" (i.e., the masks or ideologies) while the basic combination of residues remained.

In effect, the shifts of temper from nationalism to liberalism to socialism reflected shifts in the distribution of class II residues (i.e., the residues of group persistence). Thus changes in the political class meant simply the circulation of sociopsychological types. All ideologies, all philosophical claims, were masks "for mere purposes of partisan convenience in debate. [They are] neither true nor false; [but] simply devoid of meaning."

Similarly, for Mills, changes in power are changes in combinations of constitutional position; and this alone, presumably, is the only meaningful reality.

> Except for the unsuccessful Civil War, changes in the power system of the United States have not involved important challenges to basic legitimations. . . . Changes in the American structure of power have generally come about by institutional shifts in the relative positions of the political, the economic and the military orders [p. 269].

Thus the extraordinary changes in American life, changes in the concepts of property, managerial control, responsibility of government, the changes in moral temper created by the New Deal, will become "reduced" to institutional shifts. But have there been no challenges to basic legitimations in American life? How continuous has been the system of power in the United States?

The Continuity of Power

If in his analysis of politics Mills draws from Pareto, in his image of economic power he becomes a "vulgar" Marxist. Mills notes:

> The recent social history of American capitalism does not reveal any distinct break in the continuity of the higher capitalist class. . . . Over the last half-century in the economy as in the political order, there has been a remarkable *continuity of interests,* vested in the *types* of higher economic men who guard and advance them . . . [p. 137].

Although the language is vague, one can only say that an answer to this proposition rests not on logical or methodological arguments but on empirical grounds, and in Chapter Two [in the *End of Ideology*] on the breakup of family capitalism in America, I have sought to indicate an answer. For the singular fact is that in the last seventy-five years the established relations between the system of property and family, which, Malthus maintained, represented the "fundamental laws" of society, have broken down. And this has meant too the breakup of "family capitalism," which has been the social cement of the bourgeois class system.

In his summation of economic control, Mills paints an even more extraordinary picture:

The top corporations are not a set of splendidly isolated giants. They have been knitted together by explicit associations within their respective industries and regions and in supra-associations such as the NAM. These associations organize a unity among the managerial elite and other members of the corporate rich. They translate narrow economic powers into industry-wide and class-wide power; and they use these powers, first, on the economic front, for example, with reference to labor and its organizations; and second, on the political front, for example in their large role in the political sphere. And they infuse into the ranks of smaller businessmen the views of big business [p. 122].

This is a breath-taking statement more sweeping than anything in the old TNEC reports or of Robert Brady's theory of *Spitzenverbande* (or peak associations) in his *Business as a System of Power*. That there is some co-ordination is obvious; but unity of this scope—and smoothness—is almost fanciful. Mills cites no evidence for these assertions. The facts, actually, point to the other direction. Trade associations in the United States have declined; they were primarily important during wartime as a means of representing industry on government boards. The NAM has become increasingly feckless, and there has been a decline in member interest and contributions. And industry has divided on a wide variety of issues including labor policy (e.g., the large steel and auto companies have been attacked by General Electric and other firms for accepting s.u.b.—supplementary unemployment benefits).

Mills speaks of "their large role in the political sphere." But against whom are the members of the power elite united, and what kinds of issues unite them in the political sphere? I can think of only one issue on which the top corporations would be united: tax policy. In almost all others, they divide. They are divided somewhat on labor. There are major clashes in areas of self-interest, such as those between railroads, truckers, and the railroads and the airlines; or between coal and oil, and coal and natural gas interests. Except in a vague, ideological sense, there are relatively few political issues on which the managerial elite is united.

The problem of *who unites with whom on what* is an empirical one, and this consideration is missing from Mills' work. If such co-ordination as Mills depicts does exist, a further question is raised as to how it comes about. We know, for example, that as a consequence of bureaucratization, career lines within corporations become lengthened and, as a consequence, there is shorter tenure of office for those who reach the top. Within a ten-year period, A.T.&T. has had three executive officers, all of whom had spent thirty to forty years *within* the corporation. If men spend so much time *within* their corporate shells, how do members of the "elite" get acquainted?

In this preoccupation with elite manipulation, Mills becomes indifferent to the problems of what constitutes problems of power in the everyday life of the country. This is quite evident in the way he summarily dismisses all other questions, short of the "big decisions," as "middle level" and, presumably, without much *real* meaning. *Yet are these not the stuff of politics,* the issues which divide men and create the interest conflicts that involve people in a sense of ongoing reality: labor issues, race problems, tax policy, and the like? Is this not the meaning of power to people as it touches their lives?

The use of the term elite poses another question about the utility of its limits for discussing powers. Why use the word *elite* rather than *decision-makers,* or even *rulers?* To talk of *decision-making,* one would have to discuss policy formulation, pressures, etc. To talk of *rule,* one would have to discuss the nature of rule. But if one talks of an elite, one need only discuss institutional position, and one can do so only if, as Mills assumes, the fundamental nature of the system is unchanged, so that one's problem is to chart the circulation at the top. The argument that the fundamental nature of the system—i.e., that of basic legitimations, of continuity of the capitalist class—is unchanged is a curious one, for if power has become so centralized and synchronized, as Mills now assumes, is this not a fundamental change in the system?

Yet, even if one wants to talk in terms of elites, there have been key shifts in power in American society: the breakup of family capitalism (and this is linked to a series of shifts in power in Western society as a whole), but most importantly—and obviously—the decisive role of the political arena.

From Economics to Politics

In the decade before World War I, the growing power of the trusts, the direct influence of the bankers in the economy, the ideological rise of socialism all tended to focus attention on the class system as the hidden but actually decisive element in shaping society and social change. A group of "realistic" historians, notably J. Allen Smith and, most importantly, Charles A. Beard, began the task of reinterpreting the early colonial and constitutional struggles in economic terms. The Beard interpretation, schematically, was roughly this:

The earliest struggles in American history were direct class struggles between the merchant group, represented by the Federalists, and the agrarians, represented by the Democrats. Society was split fairly cleanly between the two groups with antagonistic interests (tariff, cheap money, etc.). The unadorned way in which class conflict was discussed by the "founding fathers" could be strikingly documented in the Federalist papers. As in the later struggle between the English landed gentry and the manufacturing class over the protectionist corn laws, a decisive victory for either would have decided the basic character of the society. But that early American plutocracy, the Eastern merchants, proved to be an unstable social group that was incapable of maintaining the political initiative. So the Federalists lost. Yet the Democrats—in the face of the economic facts of life of a burgeoning capitalism—could not really win, and the "Jeffersonian revolution" was something that Jefferson found easier to promise than to execute.

But later historiography has considerably modified this crude chiaroscuro and has drawn in many subtle tones between the black and the white. As Dixon Ryan Fox, for one, in his study of politics within one state in the first four decades of the nineteenth century, *Yankees and Yorkers,* has written:

"Because of rivalries between English and Dutch, Presbyterian and Anglican, merchants and farmers, and others, party spirit early appeared in New York and persisted in changing manifestations. Yet the party lines were not closely drawn between rich and poor. So assured were the aristocrats of their social place and so various their backgrounds that they did not move as one interest; families faced each other as Capulets and Montagues. As Henry Adams has remarked, 'All these Jays, Schuylers, Livingstones, Clintons, Burrs, had they lived in New England would probably have united, or abandoned the country; but being citizens of New York they quarreled.' When the Tories were removed the Whigs soon split into factions, not merely two, but several, each ready for trade and compromise."

It is at this point that we find the seeds of the peculiarly American party system. The mutual defeat of attempts to establish exclusive domination left the social system undefined from the very start. It was not predominantly mercantile, slave, free, agrarian, industrial, or proletarian. The wealthy families, having lost direct political control, sought to work indirectly through the politician. But in a rapidly shifting society, whose very hugeness casts up a variety of conflicting interests, a politician can succeed only if he is a broker and the party system an agency of mediation.

This is not to deny the existence of classes or the nature of a class system. *But one cannot, unless the society is highly stratified, use the class structure for direct political analysis.* A class system defines the *mode* of gaining wealth and privilege in a society. (This mode can be land [real property], corporate title ["fictitious" property], skill [technical or managerial], mercenaries [*condottieri*], or direct political allocation [party, bureaucracy, or army], and this class system has to be legitimated, in legal forms, in order to assure its continuity. Often this wealth and privilege carries with it power and prestige, but there is no direct correlation.) But most important, whatever the mode, class analysis does not tell us directly *who* exercises the power, nor does it tell us much about the competition within that mode for power. Unless that mode and its legitimations are directly challenged, one rarely sees a class acting as a class in unified fashion. Once a specific mode is established, competition for privilege within the system is high, and various and different interests develop. The growing complexity of society necessarily multiplies those interests, regional or functional, and in an open society the political arena—unless there is a conflict to overthrow the system—is a place where different interests fight it out for advantage. That is why, usually, the prism of "class" is too crude to follow the swift play of diverse political groups. . . .

In the United States, so heterogeneous from the start, and striated even further by diverse ethnic, national, and religious differences, it is difficult to read the political order—which after all became an independent road to privilege for the leaders of minority groups—as a reflection of the economic order. But even where there was some rough correspondence, the play of diverse interests was immense. As late as 1892, Marx's co-worker, Friedrich Engels, wrote in a letter to his friend Sorge: "There is no place yet in America for a *third* party, I believe. The divergence of interests even in the *same* class group is so great in that tremendous area that wholly different groups and interests are represented in each of the two big parties, depending upon the locality, and almost each particular section of the possessing class has its representatives in each of the two parties to a very large degree, though *today* big industry forms the core of the Republicans on the whole, just as the big landowners of the South form that of the Democrats. The apparent haphazardness of this jumbling together is what provides the splendid soil for the corruption and the plundering of the government that flourishes there so beautifully."

At one point in later American history, the dominant business class—the plutocracy, rather than any landed squirearchy—came close to imprinting a clear mark on American politics. By the turn of the twentieth century the growing industrial class had scored a smashing economic victory. With that victory came some efforts to dissolve the structure of group interests by developing a pervasive political ideology which could also serve the emergent national feeling. One such attempt was the doctrine of imperialism in the "manifest destiny" of Beveridge and the "Americanism" of Franklin Giddings. This was alien to a heterogeneous people, or at least premature. The second and more successful effort was in the identification of capitalism with democracy. The early commercial class had feared democracy as a *political* instrument whereby the "swinish multitude" (Burke) would prepare the way for a radical despotism. The ideology of victorious industrial capitalism defined democracy almost completely in agreeable *economic* terms, as liberty of contract.

If the dominant business class was unable to exercise direct political control of the society, it could establish its ideological hegemony. While in the period from 1880 to 1912 the middle class (small farmers and businessmen, and many professionals) had supported the sporadic antitrust and antimonopoly outbursts, such opinions and movements were dissolved by the subsequent two decades of war, prosperity, and propaganda.

This unity burst with the bubble of prosperity because the ideologists of free enterprise, rugged or otherwise, did not understand the realities of the "socialized" economy that had come into being. They had failed to grasp the degree to which this market economy imposes a particular type of dependency upon everyone.

In a pure market society, as Marx once phrased it, each man thinks for himself and no one plans for all. Today it is no longer individual men who are in the market but particular collectivities, each of which tries—by administered prices, farm supports, uniform wage patterns and the like—to exempt itself from the risks of the market; inevitably, the measures each group resorts to for protection provoke governmental concern that the entire economy not be overturned in the anarchic stampede to safety.

De Tocqueville once wrote that historians who live in aristocratic ages are inclined to read all events through the will and character of heroic individuals, whereas historians of democratic times deal perforce with general causes. The dazzling aristocratic glamor of Franklin D. Roosevelt has often confused the efforts to put the New Deal period in historical perspective, and even now we lack an adequate political characterization of the era. There have been many historical analogies inspired by the flavor and verve of Roosevelt himself: e.g., Roosevelt was a temporizing Solon whose political reforms sought to stave off the revolution of propertyless masses; Roosevelt was a Tiberius Gracchus, a patrician who deserted his class to become the people's tribune; Roosevelt was a Louis Napoleon, an ambitious politician manipulating first one class and then another, while straddling them all, to maintain his personal rule. Certainly, they shed little light on the way government action gives rise to new combinations of interests and the operation of these shifting coalitions.

The public face of the New Deal was a set of sweeping social reforms, and, quite naively, some writers, and indeed, Roosevelt himself, have called the New

Deal an assertion of human rights over property rights. But such terms carry little meaning, either philosophically or pragmatically. Are "support prices" for farmers a property right or a human right? In effect, what the New Deal did was to *legitimate* the idea of *group* rights, and the claim of groups, as groups, rather than individuals, for government support. Thus unions won the right to bargain collectively and, through the union shop, to enforce a group decision over individuals; the aged won pensions, the farmers gained subsidies; the veterans received benefits; the minority groups received legal protections, etc. None of these items, in themselves, were unique. Together, they added up to an extraordinary social change. Similarly, the government has always had some role in directing the economy. But the permanently enlarged role, dictated on the one hand by the necessity to maintain full employment, and, on the other, by the expanded military establishment, created a vastly different set of powers in Washington than ever before in our history.

What is amazing, in retrospect, is that while the commitment to a politically managed economy could have been foreseen, we were quite badly deficient in organizing our economic thinking for it. A managed economy requires not only that we have a housekeeping budget for the government as the large spending unit, but also an economic budget that states the major magnitudes of economic interaction for society as a whole—the total amount of goods and services produced in a year's time and the total amount of income paid out. Through these figures we can chart the gaps in consumer spending and in investment and, if necessary, make up the differences by appropriate fiscal measures. Yet it was only in 1936 that the Department of Commerce brought out its first report on national income, and only in 1942 that the other side of the economic balance sheet, the gross national product, was first estimated by government. The two indexes as the pulse beat of economic health were only first combined and published together in President Roosevelt's budget message in 1945.

In the emergence of the political economy, a new kind of decision-making has taken place. In the market society, peoples' wants are registered by their "dollar votes," as part of the automatic interaction of supply and demand. The sum total of individual dollars-and-cents decisions, operating independently of each other, added up, as Bentham thought, to a social decision, e.g., the general consensus. Thus, when decisions on the allocation of resources operated through the market, dollars, not ideology, determined what was to be produced. In this sense, economics was the key to social power, and politics its pale reflection.

But politics, operating through the government, has more and more become the means of registering a social and economic decision. Here, instead of acting independently as in a market, the individual is forced to work through particular collectivities to enforce his will. Since in a managed economy, "politics," not dollars, determines major production, the intervention of the government not only sharpens pressure-group identifications but forces each to adopt an ideology which can justify its claims and which can square with some concept of "national interest."

The Types of Decisions

Ultimately, if one wants to discuss power, it is more fruitful to discuss it in terms of *types of decisions* rather than elites. And curiously, Mills, I would argue, ultimately agrees, for the real heart of the book is a polemic against those who say that decisions are made democratically in the United States. Mills writes:

> More and more of the fundamental issues never came to any point of decision before Congress . . . much less before the electorate [p. 255].

> Insofar as the structural clue to the power elite today lies in the political order, that clue is the decline of politics as genuine and public debates of alternative decisions . . . America is now in considerable part more a formal political democracy [p. 224].

Now, to some extent this is true, but not, it seems to me, with the invidious aspect with which Mills invests the judgment.

In many instances, even the "interested public" feels itself "trapped," so to speak, by its inability to affect events. Much of this arises out of the *security* nature of problems, so that issues are often fought out in a bureaucratic labyrinth. The decision on the H-bomb was one such issue. Here we had groups of scientists versus a section of the military, particularly SAC. Unless one assumes that everyone ever involved in decision-making is a member of the power elite—which is circular—*we have to locate the source of such decisions, for these are the central problems of a sociology of power.*

But another, equally important reason for being unable to affect events is the onset of what one can only call, inaptly, "technical decision making": the fact that once a policy decision is made, or once a technological change comes to the fore, or once some long crescive change has become manifest, a number of other consequences, if one is being "functionally rational," almost inevitably follow. Thus, shifts of power become "technical" concomitants of such "decisions," and a sociology of power must identify the kinds of consequences which follow the different kinds of decisions.

Three short examples may illustrate the point:

(1) *The federal budget as an economic gyroscope.* From 1931 to 1935, in the depth of the depression years, total federal budget expenditures of all kinds averaged 5.2 billion dollars. In the next four years, 1936 to 1940, it reached a new high of 8 billion dollars. (Income during this period was about 60 per cent of expenditures.) Four years later, the federal government was spending, yearly, a staggering total of over 95 billion dollars and accumulating a national debt which more than quintupled the debt of the previous decade. The figures are in constant dollars.

More importantly, these expenditures have to be compared with gross national product (g.n.p.), the sum total of goods and services produced during a year. During the depression decade, despite the then relatively high government spending, the federal budget "consumed" and pumped back between 5 to 10 per cent of g.n.p. During the war, the figure mounted to over 40 per cent. But while this represented an "abnormally" high figure, in the decade and a half since the end of the war, the government has become the "consumer" of nearly one-fourth of the total g.n.p. Except for one year, 1948, the one "peacetime" year in postwar history, when the federal budget reached a "low" of 33 billion dollars (against a g.n.p. of 257 billion), the expenditures in the Korean campaign and the sums required to maintain the arms pace of the cold war have kept the federal budget at record highs. In the last half of the 1950 decade it averaged about 70 billion dollars, with g.n.p. about 325 billion dollars. In 1960, the federal budget will reach over 80 billion (estimated), and g.n.p. over 400 bilion. In the 1950's, the yearly interest alone on the public debt, over 7.2 billion dollars, was greater than the *total* federal government expenditures each year during the depression.

The fact is that this enormous rise in the expenditures of the federal government was not "willed" by any one man or group of men, but arose, inevitably, as a necessary outcome of the war and its effects. And the permanent role of the federal government as the economic gyroscope of the country is due to that fact.

(2) *The "dual economy" of 1950-55*. When the Korean war broke out in 1950, the government was faced with the immediate choice of either converting existing machinery production to war goods or encouraging new plants. The decision rested on an estimate of the type of war. If it seemed as if the Korean war might spread into a general war, then the order to convert civilian facilities could be [construed to lead to the building of] large stockpiles of arms. The decision, based on political-military estimates, was to build a "dual economy." The chief consequence, economically speaking, was the decision to speed new capital expansion by allowing firms to write off the costs of new facilities in five years, as against the normal twenty-five years. (Thus firms could deduct 20 per cent of the new costs from profits and thus gain a considerable tax benefit.) This five-year tax amortization scheme encouraged an extraordinarily high rate of capital investment, undoubtedly spurred the prosperity boom of the mid-fifties, and was responsible for the overexpansion of capacity which was a contributing element to the recession of 1958-59.

(3) *Weapons technology*. The rapid emergence of new weapons decisively affects the relative weight of power and influence within the military, and within each arm of the military, of the different branches. Thus the rise of missiles reduces the importance of the battleship, once the mainstay of the navy, and of the army itself. In the new technology, for example, the missile-carrying submarine becomes a key arm of striking power, while the extension of the range of the missile makes the manned airplane obsolete. These changes in the composition of the armed forces, the requirements of new skill groups, of technicians and of technologists, mean a change in the profile of military power. Research and Development become more important than Operations, and the power of the scientist, the engineer, and the technologist grows accordingly.

All of these consequences grow out of the "big decisions" that Mills has talked about. But the fundamental policy issues which Mills mentions are primarily, as I pointed out before, decisions to be involved in war or not—or, more broadly, the question of foreign policy. And how can one discuss this question, which Mills completely evades, without discussing the cold war, *and the extent to which our posture is shaped by the Russians!* United States foreign policy since 1946—or, more specifically, since Byrnes' Stuttgart speech, which reversed our position on weakening Germany—was not a reflex of any *internal* social divisions or class issues in the United States but was *based on an estimate of Russia's intentions.*

Nor was this estimate made, in the first instance, by "the power elite." It was an estimate made by American scholarly experts, most notably by George Kennan and the policy-planning staff of the State Department. It was a judgment that Stalinism as an ideological phenomenon, and Russia as a geopolitical power, were aggressively, militarily, and ideologically expansionist, and that a policy of containment, including a rapid military build-up, was necessary in order to implement that containment. This underlay Truman's Greco-Turkish policy, and it underlay the Marshall Plan and the desire to aid the rebuilding of the European economy. These policies were not a reflex of power constellations within the U.S. They were estimates of national interest and of national survival.

From the first decision, many others followed: the creation of a long-distance striking arm in the air (SAC), the establishment of a West European Defense Community (EDC, and following its failure, NATO), etc. This is not to say that every strategic step followed inexorably from the first decision (after France rejected EDC, one had to rely more on Germany for military support), *but that the broad imperatives were clear.*

Once these broad lines were laid down, interest groups were affected, and Congress was used—often disastrously—to pass acts which gave pressure groups larger allocations of aid money (e.g., the Bland Act, pressured both by the unions and maritime industry, which provided that 50 per cent of all Marshall Plan aid had to be carried in American bottoms) or to hinder the flexibility of the State Department (e.g., the Battle Act, which forbade trade with the Soviet bloc and, in effect, crippled Ceylon, when it was our ally, by threatening to stop aid if Ceylon sold rubber to China).

To ignore the problems of this type of "imperative" decision-making is, it seems to me, to ignore the stuff of politics as well as the new nature of power in contemporary society. *The theory of the "power elite" implies a unity of purpose and community of interest among the elite that is not proven or demonstrated. It is simply asserted.*

TOPIC 29

Communism and Democracy

V. I. LENIN
State and Revolution

Marx's doctrines are now undergoing the same fate, which, more than once in the course of history, has befallen the doctrines of other revolutionary thinkers and leaders of oppressed classes struggling for emancipation. During the lifetime of great revolutionaries, the oppressing classes have invariably meted out to them relentless persecution, and received their teaching with the most savage hostility, most furious hatred, and a ruthless campaign of lies and slanders. After their death, however, attempts are usually made to turn them into harmless saints, canonizing them, as it were, and investing their name with a certain halo by way of "consolation" to the oppressed classes, and with the object of duping them; while at the same time emasculating and vulgarizing the real essence of their revolutionary theories and blunting their revolutionary edge. At the present time the bourgeoisie and the opportunists within the Labor Movement are co-operating in this work of adulterating Marxism. They omit, obliterate, and distort the revolutionary side of its teaching, its revolutionary soul, and push to the foreground and extol what is, or seems, acceptable to the bourgeoisie. . . .

The State as the Product of the Irreconcilability of Class Antagonisms

Let us begin with the most popular of Engels' works, *The Origin of the Family, Private Property, and the State.* Summarizing his historical analysis Engels says:

> The State in no way constitutes a force imposed on Society from outside. Nor is the State "the reality of the Moral Idea," "the image and reality of Reason" as Hegel asserted. The State is the product of Society at a certain stage of its development. The State is tantamount to an acknowledgment that the given society has become entangled in an insoluble contradiction with itself, that it has broken up into irreconcilable an-

Outstanding leader of the Russian Bolshevik Revolution. First Chairman of the Council of People's Commissars, U.S.S.R. Author of *Imperialism: The Highest Stage of Capitalism* and numerous other books and articles. *State and Revolution*, written in 1917, is presented here in abridged and rearranged form.

tagonisms, of which it is powerless to rid itself. And in order that these antagonisms, these classes with their opposing economic interests, may not devour one another and Society itself in their sterile struggle, some force standing, seemingly, above Society, becomes necessary so as to moderate the force of their collisions and to keep them within the bounds of "order." And this force arising from Society, but placing itself above it, which gradually separates itself from it—this force is the State.

Here, we have, expressed in all its clearness, the basic idea of Marxism on the question of the historical role and meaning of the State. The State is the product and the manifestation of the irreconcilability of class antagonisms. When, where and to what extent the State arises, depends directly on when, where and to what extent the class antagonisms of a given society cannot be objectively reconciled. And, conversely, the existence of the State proves that the class antagonisms *are* irreconcilable. . . .

According to Marx, the State is the organ of class *domination,* the organ of oppression of one class by another. Its aim is the creation of order which legalizes and perpetuates this oppression by moderating the collisions between the classes. But in the opinion of the petty-bourgeois politicians, the establishment of order is equivalent to the reconciliation of classes, and not to the oppression of one class by another. To moderate their collisions does not mean, according to them, to deprive the oppressed class of certain definite means and methods in its struggle for throwing off the yoke of the oppressors, but to conciliate it. . . .

But what is forgotten or overlooked is this:—If the State is the product of the irreconcilable character of class antagonisms, if it is a force standing above society and "separating itself gradually from it," then it is clear that the liberation of the oppressed class is impossible without a violent revolution, and without the destruction of the machinery of State power, which has been created by the governing class and in which this "separation" is embodied. . . .

What does this force consist of, in the main? It consists of special bodies of armed men who have at their command prisons, etc. We are justified in speaking of special bodies of armed men, because the public power peculiar to every State "is not identical" with the armed population, with its "self-acting armed organization." . . .

Bourgeois Democracy

In capitalist society, under the conditions most favorable to its development, we have a more or less complete democracy in the form of a democratic republic. But this democracy is always bound by the narrow framework of capitalist exploitation, and consequently always remains, in reality, a democracy only for the minority, only for the possessing classes, only for the rich. Freedom in capitalist society always remains more or less the same as it was in the ancient Greek republics, that is, freedom for the slave owners. The modern wage-slaves, in virtue of the conditions of capitalist exploitation, remain to such democracy," have "no time for politics"; that, in the ordinary peaceful course an extent crushed by want and poverty that they "cannot be bothered with of events, the majority of the population is debarred from participating in public political life. . . .

Democracy for an insignificant minority, democracy for the rich—that is the democracy of capitalist society. If we look more closely into the mechanism of capitalist democracy, everywhere—in the so-called "petty" details of the suffrage (the residential qualification, the exclusion of women, etc.), in the technique of the representative institutions, in the actual obstacles to the right of meeting (public buildings are not for the "poor"), in the purely capitalist organization of the daily press, etc., etc.—on all sides we shall see restrictions upon restrictions of democracy. These restrictions, exceptions, exclusions, obstacles for the poor, seem slight—especially in the eyes of one who has himself never known want, and has never lived in close contact with the oppressed classes in their hard life, and nine-tenths, if not ninety-nine hundredths, of the bourgeois publicists and politicians are of this class! But in their sum these restrictions exclude and thrust out the poor from politics and from an active share in democracy. Marx splendidly grasped the *essence* of capitalist democracy, when, in his analysis of the experience of the Commune, he said that the oppressed are allowed, once every few years to decide which particular representatives of the oppressing class are to represent and repress them in Parliament! . . .

In a democratic Republic, Engels maintains "wealth wields its power indirectly, but all the more effectively," first, by means of "direct corruption of the officials" (America); second, by means of "the alliance of the government with the stock exchange" (France and America). At the present time, imperialism and the domination of the banks have reduced to a fine art both these methods of defending and practically asserting the omnipotence of wealth in democratic Republics of all descriptions. . . .

We must also note that Engels quite definitely regards universal suffrage as a means of capitalist domination. Universal suffrage, he says (summing up obviously the long experience of German Social-Democracy), is "an index of the maturity of the working class; it cannot and never will, give anything more in the present state." The petty-bourgeois democrats such as our Socialist-Revolutionaries and Mensheviks and also their twin brothers, the Social-Chauvinists and opportunists of Western Europe, all expect a "great deal" from this universal suffrage. They themselves think and instil into the minds of the people the wrong idea that universal suffrage in the "present state" is really capable of expressing the will of the majority of the laboring masses and of securing its realization. . . .

Take any parliamentary country, from America to Switzerland, from France to England, Norway and so forth; the actual work of the State is done behind the scenes and is carried out by the departments, the chancelleries and the staffs. Parliament itself is given up to talk for the special purpose of fooling the "common people." . . .

Two more points. First: when Engels says that in a democratic republic, "not a whit less" than in a monarchy, the State remains an "apparatus for the oppression of one class by another," this by no means signifies that the *form* of oppression is a matter of indifference to the proletariat, as some anarchists "teach." A wider, more free and open form of the class struggle and class oppression enormously assists the proletariat in its struggle for the annihilation of all classes.

Second: only a new generation will be able completely to scrap the ancient lumber of the State—this question is bound up with the question of overcoming democracy, to which we now turn.

Dictatorship of the Proletariat

The forms of bourgeois States are exceedingly various, but their substance is the same and in the last analysis inevitably the *Dictatorship of the Bourgeoisie*. The transition from capitalism to Communism will certainly bring a great variety and abundance of political forms, but the substance will inevitably be: the *Dictatorship of the Proletariat*. . . .

The State is a particular form of organization of force; it is the organization of violence for the purpose of holding down some class. What is the class which the proletariat must hold down? It can only be, naturally, the exploiting class, i.e., the bourgeoisie. The toilers need the State only to overcome the resistance of the exploiters, and only the proletariat can guide this suppression and bring it to fulfillment, for the proletariat is the only class that is thoroughly revolutionary, the only class that can unite all the toilers and the exploited in the struggle against the bourgeoisie, for its complete displacement from power. . . .

But the dictatorship of the proletariat—that is, the organization of the advance-guard of the oppressed as the ruling class, for the purpose of crushing the oppressors—cannot produce merely an expansion of democracy. *Together* with an immense expansion of democracy—for the first time becoming democracy for the poor, democracy for the people, and not democracy for the rich —the dictatorship of the proletariat will produce a series of restrictions of liberty in the case of the oppressors, exploiters and capitalists. We must crush them in order to free humanity from wage-slavery; their resistance must be broken by force. It is clear that where there is suppression there must also be violence, and there cannot be liberty or democracy. . . .

The replacement of the bourgeois by the proletarian State is impossible without a violent revolution. . . . There is [in *Anti-Dühring*] a disquisition on the nature of a violent revolution; and the historical appreciation of its role becomes, with Engels, a veritable panegyric on violent revolution. . . . Here is Engels' argument:

> That force also plays another part in history (other than that of a perpetuation of evil), namely a *revolutionary* part; that, as Marx says, it is the midwife of every old society when it is pregnant with a new one; that force is the instrument and the means by which social movements hack their way through and break up the dead and fossilized political forms—of all this not a word by Herr Dühring. Duly, with sighs and groans, does he admit the possibility that for the overthrow of the system of exploitation force may, perhaps, be necessary, but most unfortunate if you please, because all use of force, forsooth, demoralizes its user! And this is said in face of the great moral and intellectual advance which has

been the result of every victorious revolution! And this is said in Germany where a violent collision—which might perhaps be forced on the people —should have, at the very least, this advantage that it would destroy the spirit of subservience which has been permeating the national mind ever since the degradation and humiliation of the Thirty Years' War. And this turbid, flabby, impotent, parson's mode of thinking dares offer itself for acceptance to the most revolutionary party which history has known!

In the *Communist Manifesto* are summed up the general lessons of history, which force us to see in the State the organ of class domination, and lead us to the inevitable conclusion that the proletariat cannot overthrow the bourgeoisie without first conquering political power, without obtaining political rule, without transforming the State into the "proletariat organized as the ruling class"; and that this proletarian State must begin to wither away immediately after its victory because, in a community without class antagonisms, the State is unnecessary and impossible.

What Is to Replace the Shattered State Machinery?

In 1847, in the *Communist Manifesto,* Marx was as yet only able to answer this question entirely in an abstract manner, stating the problem rather than its solution. To replace this machinery by "the proletariat organized as the ruling class," "by the conquest of democracy"—such was the answer of the *Communist Manifesto.* . . .

Refusing to plunge into Utopia, Marx waited for the experience of a mass movement to produce the answer to the problem as to the exact forms which this organization of the proletariat as the dominant class will assume and exactly in what manner this organization will embody the most complete, most consistent "conquest of democracy." Marx subjected the experiment of the [Paris] Commune, although it was so meagre, to a most minute analysis in his *Civil War in France.* Let us bring before the reader the most important passages of this work. . . .

> The Commune was the direct antithesis of the Empire. It was a definite form . . . of a Republic which was to abolish, not only the monarchical form of class rule, but also class rule itself.

What was this "definite" form of the proletarian Socialist Republic? What was the State it was beginning to create? "The first decree of the [Paris] Commune was the suppression of the standing army, and the substitution for it of the armed people," says Marx. . . . But let us see how, twenty years after the Commune, Engels summed up its lessons for the fighting proletariat. . . .

> Against this inevitable feature of all systems of government that have existed hitherto, viz, the transformation of the State and its organs from servants into the lords of society, the Commune used two unfailing remedies. First, it appointed to all posts, administrative, legal, educational, persons elected by universal suffrage; introducing at the same time the

right of recalling those elected at any time by the decision of their electors. Secondly, it paid all officials, both high and low, only such pay as was received by any other worker. . . .

Thus was created an effective barrier to place-hunting and career-making, even apart from the imperative mandates of the deputies in representative institutions introduced by the Commune over and above this. . . .

The lowering of the pay of the highest State officials seems simply a naive, primitive demand of democracy. One of the "founders" of the newest opportunism, the former Social-Democrat, E. Bernstein, has more than once exercised his talents in the repetition of the vulgar capitalist jeers at "primitive' democracy. Like all opportunists, like the present followers of Kautsky, he quite failed to understand that, first of all, the transition from capitalism to Socialism is impossible without "return," in a measure, to "primitive" democracy. How can we otherwise pass on to the discharge of all the functions of government by the majority of the population and by every individual of the population? And, secondly, he forgot that "primitive democracy" on the basis of capitalism and capitalist culture is not the same primitive democracy as in pre-historic or pre-capitalist times. Capitalist culture has created industry on a large scale in the shape of factories, railways, posts, telephones, and so forth: and *on this basis* the great majority of functions of "the old State" have become enormously simplified and reduced, in practice, to very simple operations such as registration, filing and checking. Hence they will be quite within the reach of every literate person, and it will be possible to perform them for the usual "working man's wage." This circumstance ought to and will strip them of all their former glamour as "government," and, therefore, privileged service.

The control of all officials, without exception, by the unreserved application of the principle of election and, *at any time,* re-call; and the approximation of their salaries to the "ordinary pay of the workers"—these are simple and "self-evident" democratic measures, which harmonize completely the interests of the workers and the majority of peasants; and, at the same time, serve as a bridge leading from capitalism to Socialism. . . .

The dictatorship of the proletariat, the period of transition to Communism, will, for the first time, produce a democracy for the people, for the majority, side by side with the necessary suppression of the minority constituted by the exploiters. Communism alone is capable of giving a really complete democracy, and the fuller it is the more quickly will it become unnecessary and wither away of itself. In other words, under capitalism we have a State in the proper sense of the word: that is, a special instrument for the suppression of one class by another, and of the majority by the minority at that. Naturally, for the successful discharge of such a task as the systematic suppression by the minority of exploiters of the majority of exploited, the greatest ferocity and savagery of suppression is required, and seas of blood are needed, through which humanity has to direct its path, in a condition of slavery, serfdom and wage labor.

Again, during the *transition* from capitalism to Communism, suppression is *still* necessary; but in this case it is suppression of the minority of exploiters by the majority of exploited. A special instrument, a special machine for suppression—that is, the "State"—is necessary, but this is now a transitional State, no longer a State in the ordinary sense of the term. For the suppression of the minority of exploiters, by the majority of those who were *but yesterday* wage slaves, is a matter comparatively so easy, simple and natural that it will cost far less bloodshed than the suppression of the risings of the slaves, serfs or wage laborers, and will cost the human race far less. And it is compatible with the diffusion of democracy over such an overwhelming majority of the nation that the need for any *special machinery* for *suppression* will gradually cease to exist. The exploiters are unable, of course, to suppress the people without a most complex machine for performing this duty; but *the people* can suppress the exploiters even with a very simple "machine"—almost without any "machine" at all, without any special apparatus—by the simple *organization of the armed masses* (such as the Councils of Workers' and Soldiers' Deputies, we may remark, anticipating a little).

Finally, only under Communism will the State become quite unnecessary, for there will be *no one* to suppress—"no one" in the sense of a *class,* in the sense of a systematic struggle with a definite section of the population. We are not utopians, and we do not in the least deny the possibility and inevitability of excesses by *individual persons,* and equally the need to suppress such excesses. But, in the first place, for this no special machine, no special instrument of repression is needed. This will be done by the armed nation itself, as simply and as readily as any crowd of civilized people, even in modern society, parts a pair of combatants or does not allow a woman to be outraged. And, secondly, we know that the fundamental social cause of excesses which violate the rules of social life is the exploitation of the masses, their want and their poverty. With the removal of this chief cause, excesses will inevitably begin to "wither away." We do not know how quickly and in what stages, but we know that they will be withering away. With their withering away, the State will also wither away.

The "Withering Away" of the State

Engels' words regarding the "withering away" of the State enjoy such a popularity, are so often quoted, and reveal so clearly the essence of the common adulteration of Marxism in an opportunist sense that we must examine them in detail. Let us give the passage from which they are taken.

> The proletariat takes control of the State authority and, first of all, converts the means of production into State property. But by this very act it destroys itself, as a proletariat, destroying at the same time all class differences and class antagonisms, and with this, also, the State.

Engels speaks here of the *destruction* of the capitalist State by the proletarian revolution, while the words about its withering away refer to the remains of a *proletarian* State *after* the Socialist revolution. The capitalist State does not wither away, according to Engels, but is *destroyed* by the proletariat in the course of the revolution. Only the proletarian State or semi-State withers away after the revolution. . . .

A general summary of his views is given by Engels in the following words:—

> Thus, the State has not always existed. There were societies which did without it, which had no idea of the State or of State power. At a given stage of economic development which was necessarily bound up with the break up of society into classes, the State became a necessity, as a result of this division. We are now rapidly approaching a stage in the development of production, in which the existence of these classes is not only no longer necessary, but is becoming a direct impediment to production. Classes will vanish as inevitably as they inevitably arose in the past. With the disappearance of classes the State, too, will inevitably disappear. When organizing production anew on the basis of a free and equal association of the producers, Society will banish the whole State machine to a place which will then be the most proper one for it—to the museum of antiquities side by side with the spinning-wheel and the bronze axe.

First Phase of Communist Society: Socialism

It is this Communist society—a society which has just come into the world out of the womb of capitalism, and which, in all respects, bears the stamp of the old society—that Marx terms the first, or lower, phase of Communist society.

The means of production are now no longer the private property of individuals. The means of production belong to the whole of society. Every member of society, performing a certain part of socially-necessary labor, receives a certificate from society that he has done such and such a quantity of work. According to this certificate, he receives from the public stores of articles of consumption, a corresponding quantity of products. After the deduction of that proportion of labor which goes to the public fund, every worker, therefore, receives from society as much as he has given it.

"Equality" seems to reign supreme. . . . But different people are not equal to one another. One is strong, another is weak; one is married, the other is not. One has more children, another has less, and so on.

> With equal labor [Marx concludes] and, therefore, with an equal share in the public stock of articles of consumption, one will, in reality, receive more than another, will find himself richer, and so on. To avoid all this, "rights," instead of being equal, should be unequal.

The first phase of Communism, therefore, still cannot produce justice and equality; differences and unjust differences in wealth will still exist, but the *exploitation* of man by man will have become impossible, because it will be impossible to seize as private property the *means of production,* the factories, machines, land, and so on. . . .

"He who does not work neither shall he eat"—this Socialist principle is *already* realized. "For an equal quantity of labor an equal quantity of products" —this Socialist principle is also already realized. Nevertheless, this is not yet Communism, and this does not abolish "bourgeois law," [for Communism] gives to unequal individuals, in return for an unequal (in reality) amount of work, an equal quantity of products.

This is a "defect," says Marx, but it is unavoidable during the first phase of Communism; for, if we are not to land in Utopia, we cannot imagine that, having overthrown capitalism, people will at once learn to work for society *without any regulations by law;* indeed, the abolition of capitalism does not *immediately* lay the economic foundations for such a change. . . .

The State is withering away in so far as there are no longer any capitalists, any classes, and, consequently, any *class* whatever to suppress. But the State is not yet dead altogether, since there still remains the protection of "bourgeois law," which sanctifies actual inequality. For the complete extinction of the State complete Communism is necessary.

The Higher Phase of Communist Society: Communism

Marx continues:

> In the higher phase of Communist society, after the disappearance of the enslavement of man caused by his subjection to the principle of division of labor; when, together with this, the opposition between brain and manual work will have disappeared; when labor will have ceased to be a mere means of supporting life and will itself have become one of the first necessities of life; when with the all-round development of the individual, the productive forces, too, will have grown to maturity, and all the forces of social wealth will be pouring an uninterrupted torrent— only then will it be possible wholly to pass beyond the narrow horizon of bourgeois laws, and only then will society be able to inscribe on its banner: "From each according to his ability; to each according to his needs."

Only now can we appreciate the full justice of Engels' observations when he mercilessly ridiculed all the absurdity of combining the words "freedom" and "State." While the State exists there can be no freedom. When there is freedom there will be no State.

The economic basis for the complete withering away of the State is that high stage of development of Communism when the distinction between brain and manual work disappears; consequently, when one of the principal sources of modern *social* inequalities will have vanished—a source, moreover, which it is impossible to remove immediately by the mere conversion of the means of production into public property, by the mere expropriation of the capitalists.

This expropriation will make it possible gigantically to develop the forces of production. And seeing how incredibly, even now, capitalism *retards* this development, how much progress could be made even on the basis of modern technique at the level it has reached, we have a right to say, with the fullest confidence, that the expropriation of the capitalists will result inevitably in a gigantic development of the productive forces of human society. But how rapidly this development will go forward, how soon it will reach the point of breaking away from the division of labor, of the destruction of the antagonism between brain and manual work, of the transformation of work into a "first necessity of life"—this we do not and *cannot* know.

Consequently, we are right in speaking solely of the inevitable withering away of the State, emphasizing the protracted nature of this process, and its dependence upon the rapidity of development of the *higher phase* of Communism; leaving quite open the question of lengths of time, or the concrete forms of this withering away, since material for the solution of such questions is not available.

The State will be able to wither away completely when society has realized the formula: "From each according to his ability; to each according to his needs"; that is when people have become accustomed to observe the fundamental principles of social life, and their labor is so productive, that they will voluntarily work *according to their abilities*. "The narrow horizon of bourgeois law," which compels one to calculate, with the pitilessness of a Shylock, whether one has not worked half-an-hour more than another, whether one is not getting less pay than another—this narrow horizon will then be left behind. There will then be no need for any exact calculation by society of the quantity of products to be distributed to each of its members; each will take freely "according to his needs." . . .

Democracy implies equality. The immense significance of the struggle of the proletariat for equality and the power of attraction of such a battlecry are obvious, if we but rightly interpret it as meaning the *annihilation of classes*. But the equality of democracy is *formal equality*—no more; and immediately after the attainment of the equality of all members of society in respect of the ownership of the means of production, that is, of equality of labor and equality of wages, there will inevitably arise before humanity the question of going further from equality which is formal to equality which is real, and of realizing in life the formula, "From each according to his ability; to each according to his needs." By what stages, by means of what practical measures humanity will proceed to this higher aim—this we do not and cannot know. But it is important that one should realize how infinitely mendacious is the usual capitalist representation of Socialism as something lifeless, petrified, fixed once for all. In reality, it is only with Socialism that there will commence a rapid, genuine, real mass advance, in which first the majority and then the *whole* of the population will take part—an advance in all domains of social and individual life.

HERBERT APTHEKER
Is the Soviet Union a Progressive Society?

How shall one define a progressive society? The definition would have to include comparison with other societies and would have to include some firm criteria not themselves wholly relative. That is, if one poses the ques-

National Director of the American Institute for Marxist Studies. This article is the verbatim record of a talk limited to 25 minutes and delivered in a debate format at Howard University, Washington, D. C. Published in *Political Affairs* (April 1963), pp. 45-51. Reprinted by permission of the author.

tion, as we are this evening: Is the Soviet Union a progressive society? our search for an answer must include an effort to compare the present society of the USSR with that which the revolution creating it replaced; it must include an effort to compare that society with the societies which historically have surrounded the European and the Asian components of the USSR; it must include a comparison of that society with the global community as a whole and as it is today, encompassing what are referred to as the "most advanced" societies on earth. It must simultaneously consider whether or not the society reflects a release of the productive capacities within it and whether or not the society enhances the well-being of the members constituting it.

One may also demand of a progressive society today that it be one which is positively associated with the historic efforts to eliminate colonialism and that its general stance in the international arena be one which favors peace and impedes war.

It is my view that the overwhelming weight of all the evidence is in the direction, in all these respects, of an affirmative reply.

Soviet Russia inherited a land whose economy was among the most backward in Europe—and one which had been devastated by war, so that industrial production in 1918 was only 20 per cent of what it had been in 1913. Its population was about 65 per cent illiterate, Church and State had been one and both had been the most medieval in Europe, the Empire had been a prisonhouse of nations with racism, anti-Semitism and colonial-style subjugation, especially of the Asian peoples, all official and chronic and intense features of government and society.

The society inherited by Soviet Russia was one having a death rate comparable to that then afflicting India and China; an educational system of a totally elitist character confined to the barest minority of the top classes and marked by obscurantist emphasis, while the general technical level was among the lowest in the world.

In all these respects—production, health, education, cultural level—the present society is incomparably superior to the one it replaced; we shall bring forward the data demonstrating this in a few minutes. Here we wish to affirm that as to the first test of a progressive society—how it compares with the one it replaced—the evidence leads to the conclusion that the accomplishments of the USSR justify one in saying that its creation was one of the greatest strokes for human advancement in all history.

If one applies another test of the meaning of a progressive society—comparing the USSR with its neighbors—its historic compeers—I think the evidence would confirm that the old Poland and the old Hungary and the old Rumania, and the old Baltic states, and the old Bulgaria—all of them quasi-fascist and monarchical states until the end of World War II, when they, too, were revolutionized—were in every respect really backward and regressive societies. I think that if one compares the USSR with its other neighbors he finds that to the south, "Turkey is in Crisis" to quote the title of the article by Gabriel Gersh in the *Christian Century*, Feb. 20, 1963, where one will read of a land with chronic and massive unemployment, with luxury rampant and starvation widespread, where 65 per cent of the people are illiterate, where half the villages are without schools, and where, as the author summarizes, "the country is in a pre-revolutionary condition." Moving along to Iran and Iraq and Pakistan and India, also neighbors of the USSR—largely the same situation prevails—mass illiteracy, mass poverty, mass hunger—very much like the Russia prior to the USSR! In China—until the revolution of 1949—comparable conditions existed, worsened by chronic warfare and almost incredible governmental corruption and chaos.

These are the neighbors of the USSR and in another test of what is meant by a progressive society—a comparison *vis-à-vis* those nations making up its part of the world—I think again, the evidence indubitably and overwhelmingly supports the proposition that the USSR is such a society and that the Revolution creating it again must be hailed as a decisive event in the forward march of the human race.

How will the USSR fare if it is put to another test—namely, comparing it with the most highly developed and the most advanced of the capitalist nations—our own? Before detailing this, one must state that even posing it—and it is being posed every day now, by the President and the CIA and Congress and every newspaper in the land—is a tremendous tribute to the phenomenal growth of the Soviet Union. It is only thirty years since the United States decided to admit even the existence of the USSR. And while two world wars served to enrich the United States, they—plus the interventions—served to devastate the land of the Soviets. It cannot be overemphasized that in considering the USSR today one is considering a land which for about one-fourth of its life has had to wage war, a land which suffered seventeen million dead in World War Two, a land which saw 50 per cent of its homes, in its European areas, utterly destroyed by the Nazis; let this be burned into the brain of anyone who undertakes a comparison between the United States and the USSR today—for then and only then can he understand what a tribute to the latter such an undertaking actually represents.

The astonishing fact is—and it is a sobering fact for any American—that in a whole series of significant indices the USSR stands today ahead of the USA. Illiteracy is higher in the USA today than in the USSR; the death rate is higher in the USA than in the USSR; the USSR leads the world in the publication of books; the USSR has the highest ratio of libraries per population in the world today; while 40 per cent of all crime in the United States is committed by those under 18, the comparable percentage in the USSR is 5 per cent; while in the "free world" the "call girl" profession and prostitution are institutionalized and spreading, in the USSR they are unknown; while in the USA over 50 per cent of all hospital beds are occupied by the mentally ill, the figure for comparable ailments in the USSR is less than 10 per cent.

The rate of growth of industrial production is about three times greater than that of the USA, and this ratio was maintained again in 1962; the result is that in certain industrial products—steel and cement, for example—the USSR has already caught up with the United States and overall it is closing the gap at a swift pace. Simultaneously, its economy is unmarked by cycles and crises, its working people are unplagued by unemployment, and the development of automation is a blessing rather than a blight and a menace.

While in racism and pornography the United States stands pre-eminent in the world, the USSR has been substantially cleansed of both.

In seeking to eliminate some of the most pressing of its social problems —that of housing, for example—exacerbated as that was by World War II— the USSR leads the world in its massive home-construction program; indeed, in the last five years, it has succeeded in providing new housing for fully one-fourth of its whole population. And in the purification of its legal and political system—especially since the worst abuses associated with the years just before, during and after World War II (with the onset of the Cold War)—the Soviet Union has made impressive advances, according to the testimony of most observers, both American and European. Further, in the direction of enhancing individual freedom and democratic rights, the motion of society in the USSR during the past decade has been a most positive one, in contrast with the situation in the United States, so that, here, too, even in a formal sense, an American will have to exert himself very strongly against the Smith Act and the McCarran Act and the Landrum-Griffin Act and the House Un-American Activities Committee and Senator Eastland's Internal Security Committee, and so forth, if this country of parliamentary democracy and of the Bill of Rights is not to see that tradition utterly trampled into the dust.

Let us present some of the statements from distinguished Americans— clearly non-subversive by any standards other than those set by Mr. Welch.* *On economic advance:* S. L. A. Marshall, in *The New Republic* (Feb. 3, 1958), "The USSR is marching toward superiority in over-all productiveness while we move at a crawl." Walter Lippmann: "The fact of the matter is that the growth of the Soviet economy has been amazing" (column of June 10, 1958).

On Education: Claude M. Fuess, formerly headmaster of Phillips Academy in Massachusetts: "The Russians have realized for some years the necessity of guiding every child as far along the educational path as he is qualified to go, of identifying talent early and cultivating it to the utmost, rewarding scholarship and research, and making teaching a reputable, dignified profession" (*Saturday Review,* Feb. 1, 1958). Alvin C. Eurich, president of the State University of New York: "Soviet education today combines the rigorous European system with the mass education of the United States—a phenomenal attempt. . . . The accomplishments of the Russian educational system are exceedingly impressive" (*The Atlantic,* April 1, 1958). Marc Raeff, professor of history, Clark University in Massachusetts: "Reading [in the USSR] is the national pastime; everybody reads in great amounts, bookstores and libraries are always full, and books literally sell like hot cakes in the streets, in theatres, in museums, stores, railroad stations. Learning is highly valued, thirst for knowledge is great, seriousness of purpose is universal" (*N. Y. Times Magazine,* June 22, 1958). Lawrence G. Derthick, U.S. Commissioner of Education:

> What we have seen has amazed us in one particular. We were simply not prepared for the degree to which the USSR, as a nation, is committed to education as a means of national advancement. Everywhere we went we saw indication after indication of what we could only conclude amounted to a total commitment to education. Our major reaction therefore is one of astonishment—and I choose the word carefully—at the extent to which this seems to have been accomplished (*N. Y. Times,* June 14, 1958).

* Head of the John Birch Society. [Eds.]

On science—in which the evidence before one's eyes is so overwhelming that we offer but one witness—Professor Jerome Wiesner, of MIT, after stating that in science in general the USSR is second to none and that in certain areas— he named meteorology, oceanography and metallurgy—the country has no peer, declared: "The Soviets have a view of science as an integral part of their society. They are pioneers. To the intellectual, the frontier is not the land but the mind, and the Soviet leaders seem to understand this. Because they appreciate the long-term implications of the development of science for the growth of their society, they are able to make determined long-range commitments to train people, build universities, laboratories, and institutes on a grand scale" (essay in *Soviet Progress and American Enterprise,* New York, 1958).

On health, official UN data show: the mortality rate in the USSR is lower than in the USA; longevity in the USSR is equal to that in the USA; in the number of physicians in proportion to population the USSR is far ahead of the USA; and in the number of hospital beds, while the USSR is still behind, her rate of growth has been more than twice as rapid as has been that in the USA.

The testimony as to the particularly favored position of *children* in the USSR is universal and uncontradicted so far as I know. *The advanced position of women*—who have achieved a status of equality never approached before by any society—also is a matter of fact universally agreed to and again, so far as I know, uncontroverted. On this last point, one of the most recent American reporters to confirm it was Mrs. Jewell R. Mazique, a distinguished graduate of this University, and columnist for the *Afro-American* chain of newspapers.

The developing *role of trade unions* in the Soviet Union, and their active and real participation in the political and economic and productive life of the nation, has been confirmed and documented at length in the book issued by the International Labor Office of Geneva after a study on the spot and published in 1960.

As to *culture,* one has had in the USSR the most colossal revolution in all history, for a people hitherto largely illiterate have been brought not only to full literacy, but they have been raised to the highest cultural level in the world. As Ossia Trilling, vice-president of the International Association of Theatre Critics, stated: "In no city in the world can one see so much Shakespeare, Ibsen, Wilde, Schiller, Ostrovsky, Chekhov, and so on, in one week as in Moscow" (*N. Y. Times,* Jan. 26, 1958). Wrote Howard Taubman of the *N. Y. Times* in the summer of 1958, after an extended stay in the USSR: "There is a genuine dedication to artistic ideals in the Soviet Union. There is a pervasive love of beauty. There is an exhilaration in the skill and virtuosity of highly trained performers. There is respect for the creative vocation. The people are being taught unremittingly to take pride in art as in learning. . . . To be cultured is regarded as one of the highest goods."

In *international affairs,* I think the record proves, from the Decree of Peace issued as its first act by the revolutionary Soviet Russia in 1917 to its leadership in getting the United Nations to adopt unanimously in 1959 the declaration for general and complete disarmament, the USSR has been in the forefront of the battle against war and against fascism. Her record in the international sphere—from Italy's rape of Ethiopia to fascism's ravishment of Spain to Japanese imperialism's war upon China, to her decisive role in breaking the back of fascism when that monster was led under Hitler's banners—consistently has been a record of support of the forces of democracy and peace and opposition to the forces of reaction and war. This was true in her struggle against war in 1917, and it is true in her support of the Cuban Revolutionary Government against the attacks, invasions, insults, and provocations of the United States. I think that the works of Professors J. P. Morray, F. L. Schuman, D. F. Fleming, and Arnold Toynbee sufficiently demonstrate this truth; I have myself labored to document it in the recent work, *American Foreign Policy and The Cold War* (New York, 1962).

The "secret" explaining the basic domestic and international record of the USSR—it is a secret alas, only in the United States—is the fact that socialism exists there; the private ownership of the means of production has been eliminated—the exploitation of man by man has been terminated. Heaven did not result, nor did hell, but great improvement did result, and a considerable fragment of this globe was revolutionized. The system triumphant there has brought great progress to its people, helped save humanity, and is being instituted—of course, with necessary national differences—in other parts of Europe, in Asia, and now, in America.

Of course, one's evaluation of the Soviet Union is not simply an academic exercise. Mr. Richard Nixon, in 1957, when he was Vice-President, affirmed that the USSR was civilization's main threat and insisted that "we are in a war today" with that threat. Vice-Admiral Charles R. Brown, addressing the Navy League in October, 1958, said: "World War III has long since started, whether we'll admit it or not," and the Admiral went on to name the USSR as the foe.

The Admiral and the former Vice-President may be impatient to attempt the destruction of the USSR. But is that country—described by leading American figures and eyewitnesses in the terms already brought before you—is that country really the enemy of the peoples of the United States?

Rather, in the case of most of those who have described the tremendous advances made in the Soviet Union, the conclusion drawn has been that these advances should stimulate us to improve ourselves. Certainly, this is the conclusion which was drawn by the late Mrs. F. D. Roosevelt; by Walter Lippmann, by Howard Taubman, by Professor Marc Raeff.

Professor Harold J. Berman, of Harvard University—an outstanding authority on Soviet law, and recently having lectured at the University of Moscow —has said that the main point in the world as it is today, given the forward sweep of its socialist sector, is that here in our own country we must concentrate on the achievements of "justice, mercy and morality," and that we must match in a way consonant with our own national genius, "the spirit of service, self-sacrifice, and common purpose," that the peoples of the USSR in their way have brought to their country.

Here is a kind of contest that is worthy of the finest national feeling and profoundest love of country of which any of us—citizens of the USA or of the USSR—are capable. Come, let us see, as friends and brothers, who can contribute most to the happiness and well-being of mankind!

AN OFFICIAL SOVIET VIEW
Dictatorship or Democracy?

By making the mills and factories, railways and banks the property of the people and by abolishing private ownership in land in the very first months of its existence, the Soviet state created the conditions for ensuring genuine democracy. You may speak all you want about the democratic rights of the people, freedom and equality for all citizens, but if alongside these rights you place the right of private ownership of the means of production and defend its inviolability, then democracy will inevitably remain merely a paper democracy. By gradually turning the means of production into the property of the people, the Soviet state has created the economic basis of genuine democracy. It is on this basis that the people have gained freedom from exploitation, from economic crises and unemployment, freedom from poverty and other freedoms which are of incomparably greater importance to people than legal rights. It is these freedoms that give the people a real possibility of showing what they can do, of developing their abilities and becoming active participants in political life, which is the most important feature of true democracy. . . .

The main distinguishing feature of Soviet socialist society is that it is not divided into antagonistic, hostile classes, for it no longer has any exploiting classes. A person travelling across the country from end to end will nowhere find any landed estates, factories or mills belonging to capitalists, and will encounter no peasants working on fields belonging to landlords or kulaks, or workers toiling for a boss. . . .

How the Soviet State Is Organized and How It Functions

Now let us see Soviet democracy in action. For this we first have to get an idea of how the Soviet state is organized and how it functions.

State power in the USSR belongs to the Soviets of Working People's Deputies. Article 2 of the Constitution of the USSR reads: "The political foundation of the USSR is the Soviets of Working People's Deputies, which grew and became strong as a result of the overthrow of the power of the landlords and capitalists and the conquest of the dictatorship of the proletariat." The Soviets form a well-knit system of organs of state power. The highest level of this system is the USSR Supreme Soviet, which is the highest organ of state power in the Soviet Union. Next come the Supreme Soviets of the Union Republics, the constituent members of the Union of Soviet Socialist Republics and the Supreme Soviets of the Autonomous Republics. Local organs of state power are the territorial, regional, district, city, rural and other Soviets of Working People's Deputies, of which there are close to 60,000 in the country.

All these organs of state power are elected by the people directly for a

From *The U.S.S.R., A Socialist State of Workers and Peasants*, 1958, *passim.*

554   Communism and Democracy

term of from 2 to 4 years, in accordance with the fixed basis of representation. Elections in the USSR are universal, direct and equal by secret ballot. . . . The election procedure ensures the complete secrecy of voting: the ballots are not numbered and are filled in by the voters in special booths, to which no one is admitted except the voter. This precludes any pressure on the electorate.

Candidates are nominated by public meeting of factory and office workers, by general membership meetings of collective farmers, etc. The right to nominate candidates is secured to public organizations and societies of the working people: Communist Party organizations, trade unions, co-operatives, youth organizations and cultural societies. All who wish can take part in discussing the merits or demerits of the nominees.

The turnout at the polls in the USSR is much higher than in any non-socialist country. For example, in the elections to local Soviets in 1957, 99.9 per cent of the electors went to polls in a number of republics. The proportion of ballots cast for the candidates is also very high. This is explained by the fact that candidates are nominated jointly by Party and non-Party organizations which enjoy great prestige among the people. . . .

In the Soviet Union there is no class enmity between the director of an establishment and the workers. Although a factory director is appointed by the state, he does not consider himself unaccountable to the people. The plant community controls the work of the management in various ways. Such right is possessed in the first place by the plant's Party organization, which consists of the most active and politically conscious part of the personnel. The trade-union organization, which usually embraces all workers and other employees, also has considerable rights. The relations between the management and the workers are governed by a collective agreement concluded annually by the trade-union committee and the management. The agreement stipulates the mutual obligations of the sides for carrying out the production plan, improvement in the organization of work and safety measures, wages and work quotas, satisfaction of the material and cultural needs of the workers, etc. Trade unions exercise regular control over the fulfilment of the collective agreement. If the management systematically violates the agreement, the trade union can take it to task by turning to a higher economic organization or take the matter to court. . . .

Slightly less than half of the entire population of the Soviet Union consists of peasants united in collective farms. A collective farm is not only an economic enterprise but also a social community. Unlike state enterprises, which are owned by the whole people, collective farms are owned by their members in common. The members themselves elect the board and the chairman, and they themselves settle all of the farm's important questions. General meetings of the collective farm's members are usually held two or three times a year, and the meetings elect delegates to check on the work of the board and decide some important problems in the interval between meetings. This, as it were, is a collective-farm *parliament*.

And so, real democracy, which actually obtains, is expressed not alone in democratic forms of state organization. It is also expressed in that the working people manage production both through their representatives and directly, by taking part in production conferences, meetings of workers and collective farmers. Business-like criticism of shortcomings at all levels, from the USSR

Supreme Soviet to a workers' or collective farmers' meeting, is a real embodiment of socialist democracy.

Some people are accustomed to seeing democracy only in countries where there is an organized opposition to the government. Their idea of a model democracy is a system under which anyone can make a speech at a square or in a park, whether he preaches religious dogmas or criticizes the government. But do supporters of such a view ever think how effective such a form of democracy is and what influence it has on life? It is by no means our intention to deny traditional forms of democracy existing in other countries, but we categorically reject them as the sole criterion of democracy.

It is understandable, for example, that organized opposition to the government is of great importance in countries where there are antagonistic classes, where the government does not express the interests and aspirations of a considerable part or the majority of the population. This compels these sections to defend their interests through opposition to the government's policy. But what significance can such a criterion have for a socialist country, where there are no antagonistic classes, where the government considers itself and actually is the servant of the people? Obviously, under these conditions the dissatisfaction of one part of the population or another with shortcomings in the work of state organs is expressed in a different form, in the form of criticism and self-criticism.

The view that democracy implies the existence of many parties is a rather widespread delusion abroad. "If you have only one party, the Communist Party," we are told, "you can have no genuine democracy! In what way is the will of the people expressed if they are deprived of the possibility of setting up other parties?"

Our answer to this line of reasoning is first that it is wrong to think that the degree of democracy is determined everywhere and at all times by the existence of several parties. It is quite natural that in countries where a struggle is going on between antagonistic classes many political parties arise, expressing and defending the interests of different classes. But this is no real guarantee of democracy. The degree of democracy is determined not by the number of parties in a country but by what class is actually in power, by the *policy* pursued by the government. Only a state in which the ruling party follows a policy that accords with the interests of the people may be called a truly democratic state. . . .

The Communist Party of the Soviet Union unites now in its ranks close to eight million men and women. These are not a kind of privileged stratum of Soviet society, but the finest representatives of all strata who consider their membership in the Party as a duty to be in the front ranks everywhere, on the most difficult tasks. As the ruling party, the Communist Party gives guidance to state organs, including the USSR Government. But this guidance is not in the nature of some back-stage dictation. It is done through Communists who are members of state bodies and who decide questions with full observance of the standards set by the USSR Constitution. If we are to speak not of the formal aspects but the essence of the matter, we must stress that the Communist Party's guidance makes it possible to reflect and bring out the will of the people most fully in the activity of state organs. The Communist Party, which is a public organization, the advanced detachment of the working people, listens very attentively to the voice of the masses, expresses their aspirations and embodies in its decisions solutions to urgent problems of social development. Indicative, for example, is the fact that it was on the initiative of the Central Committee of the CPSU that the question of reorganizing industrial management, a question that had fully matured for Soviet society, was submitted for discussion to the whole people. . . .

Cooperation of Nations

Tsarism and capitalism left a terrible legacy to the young Soviet Republic: not only colonial backwardness of the borderlands in which non-Russian peoples lived, but also bitter strife between the peoples, discord between the nations. Long years of national oppression engendered among many peoples mistrust of everything Russian; on top of this came strife between the oppressed peoples themselves: between Georgians and Armenians and Azerbaijans, and so on. Matters reached such lengths that in 1919-1920, when the Mensheviks, Mussavatists and Dashnaks[1] dominated in Transcaucasia, wars were fought between Georgia and Armenia and between Azerbaijan and Armenia; there were even wars within the republics as, for example, the defeat and sacking of South Ossetia by the Georgian Mensheviks, etc.

How did the Soviet state succeed in cutting this Gordian Knot, in solving the problem of relations between nationalities, which according to the French writer Henri Barbusse was a "sanguinary vicious circle in all modern history"? . . . This is a new multi-national state without precedent in history. Its salient feature is first that it is founded on the *voluntary* unity of the peoples. The voluntary nature of the union is underscored by the fact that under the Constitution of the USSR each Union Republic retains the right of secession from the USSR. The equality of all peoples is another cornerstone of the multi-national Socialist state. All Soviet Socialist Republics making up the USSR enjoy equal rights. The Constitution of the USSR precludes national inequality. It proclaims the equality of citizens of the USSR, irrespective of nationality or race, in all spheres of economic, government, cultural, political and other public activities. Any direct or indirect restriction of the right of, or conversely, the establishment of any direct or indirect privileges for citizens on account of their race or nationality, as well as any advocacy of racial or national exclusiveness or hatred are declared a crime punishable by law.

But the concept of equality, which seems so simple, has two aspects. One is equality under the law, proclaimed in the USSR at the very inception of Soviet power, and the other is actual equality, which depends on the degree of economic, political and cultural development of a people. If Soviet power had limited itself to the proclamation of legal equality, the equality would have remained only formal since many peoples and tribes, owing to their backwardness, would have been unable to exercise the rights granted them by law. But in this, as in other spheres, Soviet power provided the peoples the material conditions to enable them to exercise the democratic rights proclaimed in the Con-

[1] Mussavatists were members of a bourgeois-landlord nationalist party in Azerbaijan, Dashnaks were members of an Armenian bourgeois-nationalist party.

stitution. It has accomplished a truly titanic task in eliminating the economic, political and cultural backwardness inherited by many peoples from the old system. This required great effort and even sacrifices on the part of the Russian people, as the most developed people in Russia. Thanks to its fraternal, unselfish assistance the peoples in the borderlands were able swiftly to develop their industry and agriculture and to create their own culture, national in form and Socialist in content. . . .

The State and Freedom of the Individual

The economic foundation of the Socialist system is public ownership of the means of production, which far from disuniting, unites people, helps to bring them closer together. Relations of comradely co-operation and Socialist mutual assistance of people free from exploitation are created in the process of collective labour. This eliminates the "war of all against all" and ends the operation of the jungle law of capitalist competition. . . .

The rights of the individual are secured in a special chapter (Chapter X) of the USSR Constitution. Here we find the rights and freedoms which are usually recorded in constitutions of democratic states, for example, freedom of speech, of the press and of assembly, inviolability of the person, inviolability of the home, etc., but in addition there are also rights which are usually not found in constitutions of non-Socialist states. These are the rights of USSR citizens to work, i.e., the right to guaranteed employment and payment for their work in accordance with its quantity and quality; the right to rest and leisure; the right to maintenance in old age and also in case of sickness or disability; the right to education.

The rights of citizens to work, to rest and leisure, education and material maintenance, secured to them by the USSR Constitution, reflect the great gains of Socialism. But these rights are important not only by themselves. Still more important is the confidence of Soviet citizens in the feasibility of these rights, in that the steady development of the Socialist economic system will ensure them in the future, as today, the possibility of working fruitfully and improving their living standards. The Soviet citizen knows that he is threatened neither by economic crisis, nor unemployment, nor the danger of being evicted from his home because of inability to pay rent. He knows that in case of sickness the state will provide him free medical aid and state social insurance agencies will pay him sick benefits. He knows that his children will be able to receive an education.

All this gives the Soviet citizen firm confidence in the morrow and creates favourable conditions for the development of his personal abilities and talents. . . . Only in Socialist society where there is no private ownership of the means of production, no exploitation of man by man, no crises and unemployment, are the common people able to develop their talents, to find application for them, to display their initiative.

REINHOLD NIEBUHR
What Is Evil in Communism

The real tragedy of our age lies in the fact that the Marxist alternative to the injustices of our society should have generated cruelties and injustices so much worse than those which Marxism challenged, and should nevertheless be able to gain the devotion of millions of desperate people in Europe and particularly in Asia upon the basis of the original dream, as if the dream had not turned into a nightmare.[1]

What makes communism so evil and what are the sources of its malignancy? We are bound to ask the question because we are fated as a generation to live in the insecurity which this universal evil of communism creates for our world. The timid spirits ask another question: is communism really as evil as we now think; or are we tempted by the tensions of our conflict with it to exaggerate our negative judgments about it, somewhat as we did in judging the Kaiser's Germany, which we erroneously regarded as evil as Hitler's Germany subsequently proved to be.

It is important to analyze the nature of the communist evil both for the sake of those who take its evil for granted but do not bother to diagnose its nature or trace its sources; and for the sake of those deluded spirits who imagine that communism is but a different version of a common democratic creed, a difference which might be resolved if a dissipation of the war psychosis would permit us to engage in the enterprise. We must analyze it too for the sake of those who assess the degree of evil in communism correctly but prove their confusion in regard to its nature by comparing it with something much less evil than itself, as for instance the former State Department official who asserted that communism was "nothing but" the old Russian imperialism in a new form. This judgment obscured the difference between the comparative ordinate and normal lust for power of a great traditional nation and the noxious demonry of this worldwide secular religion.

Monopoly of Power

If we seek to isolate more specifically the various causes of an organized evil which spreads terror and cruelty throughout the world and confronts us everywhere with faceless men who are immune to every term of moral and

Professor Emeritus, Union Theological Seminary. Author of *The Children of Light* and *The Children of Darkness*, *Moral Man and Immoral Society*, fifteen other books, and numerous articles. This compilation is taken from the writings of Reinhold Niebuhr cited at the end of each selection below. A substantial portion of this article is also reprinted in *Reinhold Niebuhr on Politics* edited by Harry R. Davis and Robert C. Good (New York, Charles Scribner's Sons, 1960).

[1] "The Soviet Reality," *Nation*, Vol. CLXXI (September 23, 1950), p. 270. By permission.

political persuasion we must inevitably begin with the monopoly of power which communism established. Disproportions of power everywhere in the human community are fruitful of injustice, but a system which gives some men absolute power over other men results in evils which are worse than injustice. Marxism did not indeed plan the highly centralized power structure of communism, but Marx did plan for a "dictatorship of the proletariat"; and the progressive moral deterioration of such a dictatorship was inevitable rather than fortuitous for two reasons.

The *first* is that when society is divided into the powerful and the powerless there is no way of preventing the gradual concentration of the monopoly of power. The monopoly of a class becomes the monopoly of the party which claims to be the vanguard of the whole class; the monopoly of the party becomes the monopoly of a small oligarchy who speaks at first for the class to other classes who have been robbed of power. But their authority inevitably degenerates into a monopoly of power exercised over their party and class because no one in the whole community has the constitutional means to challenge and check the inevitable extension of power after which the most powerful grasp. The dictatorship of the oligarchy further degenerates into the dictatorship of a single tyrant.[2]

Let us recall how this tyranny developed. The Marxist dogma provided for a "dictatorship of the proletariat.' According to the dogma, this dictatorship was necessary because the messianic class, the workers, was bound to be insecure until its class enemies were "liquidated." . . . The theory was that the workers would exercise a dictatorship to eliminate their class enemies, but they would enjoy a perfect brotherhood among themselves. They would not need courts and policemen because they would put down any anti-social behavior by spontaneous action.

It is well to note the utopian touch in the vision of a democracy within a dictatorship, because it is the first clue to the question why the Marxist utopia turned into a hell. The visionaries did not consider the ordinary problems of a community, the competition of interests, the arbitration of rights, the adjudication of conflict. The only cause for conflict, namely property, was abolished. But meanwhile, the community on the other side of the revolution needed to be organized. It could not rely on spontaneous action. The embryo of the dictatorship lay in the party. The dogma assumed that, while the workers were the messianic class, they needed the party to inform them of the logic of history and what good things it intended for them. The workers had an essential righteousness, but evidently no wisdom. Lenin declared that they, left to themselves, could not rise above a "trade union psychology." How right he was. The Marxist dogma would always outrage the common sense of common men. It could be believed only by the ideologists. These were the secular prophets who became the priest-kings of the utopian state.

So we proceed from the dictatorship of the workers to the dictatorship of the party. But the party must also be organized. Everywhere the need for government which the dogma had defined as merely an instrument of oppression, makes itself felt. Without integration, the masses are merely a mob. The

[2] *Christian Realism and Political Problems,* pp. 34, 35. Copyright 1953 Charles Scribner's Sons. By permission of Charles Scribner's Sons.

party must have a "central committee." The committee is even now the governing group in theory. But the committee was too large for executive action. The
ruling group within the committee was first a mere class war improvisation.
But naturally, its powers grew rather than diminished. The real oligarchs
emerged. They had the power. It is this "democratic centralism" of Lenin to
which the present oligarchs would fain return, after experiencing the baneful
effects of absolute tyranny. It must be observed, however, that Lenin, while
more subtle than Stalin, was potentially a dictator. He did not allow real discussion even within the ruling group. Above all, he did not allow "factions."
He was the charismatic leader who knew the logic of history better than his
colleagues. Had he not prophesied correctly?

But without real freedom, either within the party or in the community,
there was nothing to prevent a shrewd manipulator, Stalin, from bringing all
the organs of power into his single hands, from liquidating even the oldest
prophets who did not agree with him, and from terrorizing a whole generation
of newer oligarchs—many of whom owed their positions to his favor and had
helped to eliminate his foes. It is this absolute monopoly of power which
proved to be so vicious and which is now defined by the euphemism, "the cult
of personality." The present oligarchs would like to eliminate the possibility of
a return to such a tyranny, yet meanwhile they try to maintain their own power
and preserve the dogma which sanctifies it.[3]

Togliatti, the Italian Communist leader, the French Communists, and
even the lowly American Communist Party dare to criticize the present leadership and ask the embarrassing question: "What were the present leaders doing
when all these atrocities of Stalin were perpetrated?" Khrushchev has asserted
that no one could protest, for fear of his life. Nothing can change the impact of
this confession.[4]

One must confess, incidentally, an ironic satisfaction in observing orthodox
Marxists, who believe that history moves only in terms of "objective conditions,"
placing all the blame for a horrible tyranny upon the failure of a single individual. They have practiced "the cult of the individual" in reverse. Meanwhile
the "objective conditions" which generated the evil are still with them. It is the
monopoly of power which proved even more grievous in a revolutionary movement than all history proved it to be when it was used to defend the status quo.[5]

The Marxist Theory of the State

A *second* reason for the excessive concentration of power is that the
Marxist theory wrongly assumes that economic power inheres solely in the
ownership of property and obscures the power of the manager of property. It
therefore wrongly concludes that the socialization of property causes economic
power to evaporate when in fact it merely gives a *single oligarchy a monopoly
of both economic and political power.*[6]

[3] "Is This the Collapse of a Tyranny?" *Christianity and Society,* Vol. XVI (July
9, 1956), p. 5. By permission.
[4] *Ibid.,* p. 4.
[5] "Nikita Khrushchev's Meditation on Josef Stalin," *Christianity and Crisis,* Vol.
XVI (July 9, 1956), p. 90. By permission.
[6] *Christian Realism and Political Problems,* p. 36.

The Marxian theory of the state is very simple. The state is the instrument of class oppression. It will therefore disappear with the disappearance of classes. "In the course of its development," declared Marx, "the working class will replace the old bourgeois society . . . and there will no longer be any real political power, for political power is precisely the official expression of class antagonisms in bourgeois society." Lenin, proclaiming the same faith, says, "We do not expect the advent of an order of society in which the principle of the subordination of the minority to the majority will not be observed. But striving for socialism, we are convinced that it will develop into communism, . . . all need for force will vanish, and for the subjection of one man to another, and one part of the population to another, since people will grow accustomed to observing the elementary conditions of social existence without force and without subjection." One might multiply such citations indefinitely. They all look forward to a kind of anarchistic Utopia despite the explicit disavowals of utopianism that are found in Marxism.

Obviously the crucial point in this interpretation of the function of force in society is that it is regarded not as a necessity of social cohesion but simply as an instrument of class oppression. This implies that human egoism is not congenital but merely the product of a particular class organization of society. Nothing is more paradoxical in Marxian theory than that it prompts its adherents to a cynically realistic analysis of human motives in the present instance and yet persuades them to look forward to a paradise of brotherhood after the revolution. For the period after the revolution every orthodox Marxian is a liberal. The eighteenth-century faith in the perfectibility of man is expressed with the greater abandon for having been tentatively veiled and qualified. . . .

Stalin's power is a double refutation of the Marxian theory of the state. The fact that the power is necessary refutes the Communists, who regard the growth of an oligarchy as merely the fruit of Stalin's perfidy. Every society must finally define its course and assert its will not only against foreign foes but against dissenters within its own household. In a socialist society, such dissent is derived not merely from remnants of capitalist ideology but from varying interpretations of the purpose and program of socialism made by different schools of Marxist thought. The instincts of self-preservation within a great community will generate an irrefutable logic of their own against which doctrinaire creeds are powerless. In exactly the same way, French ideals of a bourgeois world revolution were compounded with patriotism in the period after the French Revolution.

But the degree of Stalin's power, its irresponsible and autocratic character, refutes the Marxian theory of the state in another sense. The Marxian thesis that the state will wither away after the capitalist enemies of socialism are destroyed prompts Marxists to maximize the power of the state and to relax ordinary human precautions against the exercise of irresponsible power. Since the state is involved in a process of self-destruction, it is believed that its power can safely be increased. This power will supposedly enhance the efficiency of the Communist community in defeating its internal and external foes; and when this has been done, the state will wither away.

Every government is tempted to confuse its own prejudices with the general welfare and to corrupt its rule by the lust for power. "Power tends to corrupt," declared Lord Acton quite truly, "and absolute power corrupts absolutely." The validity of this observation escapes utopians, who imagine that they have found a way to eliminate power and coercion from society. Hence they allow the power of their state to grow unduly, vainly imagining that the heart which beats under the tunic of a commissar is of different stuff from the hearts of ancient kings.[7]

Imperialism

Around a central dogma which ascribes all historic evil to the institutions of property and promises redemption from every ill through the socialization of property are clustered a whole series of ancillary and derivative dogmas.[8]

Marxism projects an ideal community in which the rivalry between nations will be abolished because that rivalry is ascribed purely to economic causes. Therefore, the socialization of property is expected to guarantee not only a classless national community but also a harmonious international community.[9]

The vexatious and tyrannical rule of Russia over the smaller communist states is completely obscured and denied by the official theory. Hamilton Fish Armstrong reports Bukharin's interpretation of the relation of communist states to each other as follows: "Bukharin explained at length that national rivalry between Communist states was 'an impossibility by definition.' 'What creates wars,' he said, 'is the competition of monopoly capitalism for raw materials and markets. Capitalist society is made up of selfish and competing national units and therefore is by definition a world at war. Communist society will be made up of unselfish and harmonious units and therefore will be by definition a world at peace. Just as capitalism cannot live without war, so war cannot live with Communism.' " It is difficult to conceive of a more implausible theory of human nature and conduct.[10]

Nations, as individuals who are completely innocent in their own esteem, are insufferable in their human contacts. The whole world suffers from the pretensions of the communist oligarchs.[11] The result of such a delusion is a meretricious compound of Russian nationalism with Communist dreams of world dominion; and the creation of a tyrannical oligarchy devoid of either internal or external checks upon its power.[12] The illusions enable communists to pose as liberators of every class or nation which they intend to enslave; and to exploit every moral and political weakness of the civilized world as if they had the conscience of civilization in their keeping.[13] The thesis that imperialism is purely the fruit of "capitalism" and therefore noncapitalist nations are non-

[7] "Russia and Karl Marx," *Nation*, Vol. CXLVI (May 7, 1938), pp. 530, 531. By permission.

[8] *Christian Realism and Political Problems*, p. 46.

[9] *The Structure of Nations and Empires*, p. 240. Copyright 1959 Charles Scribner's Sons. By permission of Charles Scribner's Sons.

[10] *The Irony of American History*, p. 20. Copyright 1952 Charles Scribner's Sons. By permission of Charles Scribner's Sons.

[11] *Ibid.*, p. 42.

[12] "Hazards and Resources," *Virginia Quarterly Review*, Vol. XXV (Spring 1949), p. 204. By permission.

[13] *Christian Realism and Political Problems*, p. 37.

imperialistic and internationalist "by definition" has been refuted through the flagrant imperialism of Russia.[14]

The Manipulation of Destiny

Another pretension of communism is usually obscured by the stock criticism against Marxism. It is rightly accused of being deterministic, that is, of underestimating the freedom of man and of emphasizing the determined character of his culture and of his convictions, which are said to be rooted in his economic interest. The determinism is at least half true and not nearly as dangerous as a supplementary and contradictory dogma according to which history works toward a climax in which the proletarian class must by a "revolutionary act" intervene in the course of history and thereby change not only history but the whole human situation. For after this act man is no longer both creature and creator of history but purely the creator who "not only proposes but also disposes." This idea involves monstrous claims of both omnipotence and omniscience which support the actual monopoly of power and aggravate its evil. Molotov illustrated the pretensions of omniscience when he declared that the communists, guided by "Marxist-Leninist science" know not only the inner meaning of current events but are able to penetrate the curtain of the future and anticipate its events. This tendency of playing God to human history is the cause for a great deal of communist malignancy.

The seemingly opposite tendency to regard men as the product of economic circumstance supports the pretension; for it makes it possible for an elite to pretend to be the manipulators of the destiny of their fellow men. The pretension reveals the similarity between the Nazi evil, based upon the pretension of Nietzsche's "superman," who makes his power self-justifying, and this kind of superman whose power is ostensibly justified by the fate which appoints him as the creator of historical destiny. Some of the communist fury is the consequence of the frustration of the communist oligarchs, when they discover history to be more complex than anticipated in their logic and find that opposing forces, which are marked for defeat in their apocalypse, show a more stubborn strength and resistance than they anticipated.

The Dominion of Dogma Over Facts

The Marxist dogmatism, coupled with its pretensions of scientific rationality, is an additional source of evil. The dogmas are the more questionable because the tyrannical organization prevents a re-examination of the dogmas when the facts refute them. Thus communist irrationality and dogmatism consist of a rigorous adhesion to dogma in defiance of the fact. The communists test every historical fact with ostensible precision and coolness, but their so-called science looks at the world through the spectacles of inflexible dogma which alters all the facts and creates a confused world picture. The greatest danger of communist policy comes from the fact that the communists do not know what kind of a world they live in, and what their foes are like. Their own rigorous dogma obscures the facts and their tyrannical system prevents, for

[14] *Ibid.*, p. 46.

motives of fear, the various proconsuls of their imperium from apprising the men in the Kremlin of the truth.

The rigor of the communist dogmatism creates an ideological inflexibility, consonant with the monolithic political structure. The combination of dogmatism and tyranny led to shocking irrationalities in communist trials, where the victims were made to confess to the most implausible charges. Since the communist dogma allows for no differences of opinion among the elect, every deviation from orthodoxy is not only branded as treason but is attributed to some original sinful social taint.

It is instructive that the actual monopoly of power accentuates the evil in the ideological pretensions of communism while these pretensions give a spiritual dimension to the evils which flow from a monopoly of power. Thus the evil of communism flows from a combination of political and "spiritual" factors, which prove that the combination of power and pride is responsible for turning the illusory dreams of yesterday into the present nightmare, which disturbs the ease of millions of men in our generation.[15]

Communism and Nazism

It is deeply ironic that our modern culture, which dreams of the gradual elimination of "methods of force" in favor of "methods of mind" and of the progressive triumph of democratic government over all forms of tyranny, should encounter two worms of tyranny in one generation. It is baffling, as well as ironic, that the two forms of tyranny, Nazism and communism, should be so similar in practice and yet so dissimilar in theory. Unless we are perfectly clear how such contradictory theories of man's moral and political problem can issue in practically identical political institutions and moral behavior, we will not fully comprehend the breadth and depth of our contemporary crisis.

Nazism was the fruit of moral cynicism. Communism is the product of moral and political utopianism. Nazism believed (or believes) that a nation has the right to declare that there are no standards of justice beyond its own interest. Communism dreams of a universal society in which all nations will be related to each other in a frictionless harmony, if indeed nations will not disappear entirely in a universal brotherhood. Nazism raises the self-worship, to which all ethnic groups are prone, to explicit proportions in its theory of a "master race." Communism believes that ethnic distinctions are irrelevant in an ideal society.

Nazism regards power as the final justification of any action. According to its theory a nation which has the power to organize an imperial society beyond its own borders, proves its right to do so by its success. Communism dreams of an ideal society in which the state "will wither away" and in which every form of coercion, force and power will gradually become irrelevant. Nazism believes in an elite class which manages the affairs of the mass of men. Communism is fiercely equalitarian in theory and hopes for the abolition of all class distinctions. The "dictatorship of the proletariat" is, in theory, pro-

[15] *Christian Realism and Political Problems,* pp. 39-42, as rewritten in *Reinhold Niebuhr on Politics,* edited by Harry R. Davis and Robert C. Good. By permission of Charles Scribner's Sons.

visional. For the dictatorship of a small oligarchy, which has in fact established itself in the communist state, there is no place at all in communist theory.

The contrast in theory between the two systems is practically complete. The question is how almost identical political institutions can develop from these contradictory theories. Nazi theory and practice are consistent. The practice follows by logical necessity from the theory. Communism boasts that it has created a new unity of theory and practice. Yet it presents the modern world with the most shocking disparity between the two.

We have seen that the root of communist utopianism lies in the Marxist analysis of the cause of human egoism. If it should be true that a particular economic institution (private property) is the cause of all human egoism, it would follow of course that the elimination of that institution would make men completely social and would abolish all frictions and competitions in human society. A propertyless society would have no use for the coercive functions of the state. It would wither away. If it should be true that this desirable end cannot be achieved without a world-wide revolution of the propertyless classes against the property owners, the idyllic paradise to be attained would seem to justify the ruthless policies pursued in the conflict. It would seem also to justify a provisional dictatorship, which will give cohesion and striking power to the cohorts of redemption. If this provisional dictatorship seems to have inordinate power, the utopian need not worry over-much about the perils of such power, because, according to his theory, all political power will atrophy in the day when a complete victory has been won.

Thus, communism, as we know it, is a political system in which a provisional moral cynicism, which countenances the defiance of the moral experience of the human race, is justified by a moral utopianism which dreams of the achievement of an ideal world in which property, government, nationality and ethnic distinctions will all disappear. Since the communist hope is an illusion, the objective observer must recognize the provisional cynicism as no different than the basic cynicism of the Nazis even as he knows that a supposedly provisional dictatorship follows the same practices as one which claimed permanent tenure.

While it is important to recognize that diametrically opposite conceptions of human nature may thus produce common unscrupulous and ruthless political practices and despotic political institutions, it is nevertheless important to bear the differences in basic theory in mind. One reason for doing this is that the corruption of an ideal may be politically more dangerous than a frankly cynical political program.[16] Most of our polemic against communism sounds like something left over from the propaganda warfare against Nazism. We think we are making the ultimate condemnation of communism if we insist that its totalitarianism is identical with that of Nazism. Thereby we obscure its greater danger, which is derived from the fact that it is a corruption of a utopian dream and does not stem from the pure moral cynicism which the Nazis avowed.[17]

The Nazis were, for instance, frustrated in their senseless self-worship. It is ridiculous to ask a subject people to violate their sense of self-respect by

[16] "Two Forms of Tyranny," *Christianity and Crisis,* Vol. VIII (February 2, 1948), pp. 3, 4. By permission.
[17] "The Soviet Reality," *op. cit.,* p. 270.

holding the conqueror in religious veneration. The Russian will-to-power is more subtly related to the communist cause. Russia comes to every nation, which it intends to subjugate, as a "liberator" from "fascist" and "imperialist" oppression. Russian nationalism was related to the liberal dream of the eighteenth century. The difference between the nationalism of the Nazis and the nationalism of the Russian communists is the difference between the "honest" moral cynic and the misguided or self-deceived idealist, who fails to recognize to what degree self-interest corrupts even the most ideal motives. A corrupted ideal may be more potent than a frank defiance of all ideal values. The proof of that higher potency is given by the fact that Russia's so-called "fifth columns" in the Western world are composed not of the miserable traitors who constituted the Nazi-dominated "Bund," nor yet of mere Communist Party hacks. They contain thousands of misguided idealists, who still think that Russia is the midwife of an ideal society, about to be born.

But here is an even more important reason for noting the difference between the utopian and the cynical bases of these two forms of tyranny. It will not do to fight a despotism, which had its inspiration in utopianism, merely by calling attention to the crass corruption of the original ideal. It is necessary for a democratic civilization to recognize the weakness in its own life which gave power and plausibility to this dream.[18]

Communism and Liberalism

The fact is that Marxism, in its pure form, has been the most potent critic of liberal illusions. Who understands the pretensions of "rational objectivity" in social conflict better than a real Marxist? Or for that matter the invalidity of an absolute distinction between the covert and the overt use of force? Yet the provisional realism of the Marxists quickly results in new illusions and confusions.[19] Those of us who once used Marxist collectivism to counter the error of liberal individualism, Marxist catastrophism to counter false liberal optimism, and Marxist determinism to challenge the sentimentality of liberal moralism and idealism, must now admit that the "truths" which we used to challenge "error" turned out to be no more true (though also no less true) than the liberal ones. But they were more dangerous.[20]

For example, our liberal or democratic culture, which maintained a critical attitude toward political power, became increasingly uncritical toward economic power, assuming it to be the source of justice. Thus property rights were made more absolute in an industrial and commercial society than they were in the older agrarian society despite the fact that a technical civilization created new perils of economic power which did not exist in an agrarian civilization. It was this error which invited, in a sense, first the legitimate criticism, but then the counter-error, of Marxism. For a religious veneration of the institution of

[18] "Two Forms of Tyranny," *op. cit.,* pp. 4, 5.

[19] *Christianity and Power Politics,* p. 91. Copyright 1940 Charles Scribner's Sons. By permission of Charles Scribner's Sons.

[20] "Communism and the Clergy," *Christian Century,* Vol. LXX (August 19, 1953), p. 937. Copyright 1953 Christian Century Foundation. Reprinted by permission.

property led to a new religion which sought the redemption of mankind through the abolition of property. Since Marxism erroneously assumed that economic power inhered altogether in the ownership of property, failing to recognize that the power of the manager of economic process would persist even in a society devoid of private property, its policy of socialization merely resulted in turning both economic and political power over to a single oligarchy, thus increasing the danger of tyranny. This error, added to all of its other miscalculations of human nature and history, accentuated its drift toward despotism.[21]

The Open Society

A democratic or open society is not a perfect society; on the contrary it allows its imperfections to be published abroad. It is a society which permits and even encourages criticism of itself in the light of universal standards. Such a society has at hand the means of peaceful self-correction. Such a society keeps alive the concern for objective truth and it can never be deceived into substituting the fiat of the state for objective truth. Such a society enables persons to keep their integrity as persons without constant fear of the secret police. Such a society permits minorities to organize for the purpose of changing its policies and even its structure. Such a society is uncorrupted by officially planned terror against its most independent minds and its bravest spirits.[22] Yet we are committed even to the proposition that there are no human institutions, including religious ones, which can safely be made immune to democratic criticism and which can be allowed to dictate the terms and the limits of the unity of the culture. We are committed to democracy as a method of holding all sources of power under restraint and all sources of authority under criticism.[23] The reason this final democratic freedom is right is that there is no historical reality, whether it be church or government, whether it be the reason of wise men or specialists, which is not involved in the flux and relativity of human existence; which is not subject to error and sin, and which is not tempted to exaggerate its errors and sins when they are made immune to criticism.[24]

[21] "Two Forms of Tyranny," *op. cit.,* p. 5.

[22] "What Is at Stake?" *Christianity and Crisis,* Vol. I (May 19, 1941), p. 1. By permission.

[23] "The Contribution of Religion to Cultural Unity," Hazen Pamphlet No. 13 (1945), p. 4. By permission.

[24] *The Children of Light and the Children of Darkness,* pp. 70, 71. Copyright 1944 Charles Scribner's Sons. By permission of Charles Scribner's Sons.

Defense of Democracy

H. B. MAYO
Justification of Democracy

In this discussion, I propose to examine the values which are inherent in or implied by *any* democracy; those values which follow logically or emerge from the actual working of a democratic system. Those values will then constitute a large part of the justification for democracy. . . .

Democracy Is "For" the People

One broad implication of democracy almost inevitably follows from the system: government by the people is likely to aim also at government *for* the people, and not only because democracy is partly so defined, as in Lincoln's well-known phrase. . . .

Of itself, this does not take us very far—it merely puts the emphasis on the *people*. In some way, what is done to and for them is most important of all; the sights are trained on them, and not upon a collectivity, an organic state, a divine monarch, a particular class, or the like. The utilitarians in their emphasis on the happiness of the greatest number, and all democratic politicians in stressing the welfare or service of the people, belong in some sense to the same tradition of government for the people. Some of the support for democracy, and the opposition too, has come from those who hoped or feared, as the case might be, that it would turn out to be *for* the people.

So much has the idea of government *for* the people sunk into the modern mind that dictators nowadays profess to rule for the benefit of their people, a method of justification for despotism used far less often in earlier days. The definition of democracy given by Soviet spokesmen usually follows this line: if the policies of a government are for the benefit of the people, instead of for "their most bitter enemies," then the government is a democracy. But this definition will not do. It abolishes the distinction entirely between benevolent despotism and democracy, while in the absence of the political freedoms and effective choice—which are distinguishing features of democracy—we have only the dictator's word for it that his policies are in fact for the people.

Professor of Political Science, University of Western Ontario. Author of *An Introduction to Marxist Theory*. The selection is from *An Introduction to Democratic Theory* by Henry B. Mayo. © 1960 by Oxford University Press, Inc. Reprinted by permission.

The Soviet definition leads into two ancient errors: one is that the wishes of the people can be ascertained more accurately by some mysterious methods of intuition open to an elite rather than by allowing people to discuss and vote and decide freely. The other error goes deeper: that in some way the rulers know the "real" interest of the people better than the people and their freely chosen leaders would know it themselves. All fanatics believe the same.

When Aristotle spoke of the state continuing that men might live well and said that the purpose of the *polis* was to promote the "good" life, he too laid the democrat's emphasis on *"for* the people" (though in this case on a concept of their virtue). Historical experience shows, I think, a rather high positive correlation between rule *by* and *for* as representative democracy has broadened. After votes for women were secured, more women's-rights legislation of all kinds followed; with every widening of the franchise, more legislation followed to benefit the enfranchised voters. Common sense and a knowledge of political methods would confirm this: after all, a politician comes to office by bidding for votes, by offering something he believes the voters want. He has room for "statesmanship" in the debate and competition, which give him the chance to persuade them to want what he thinks they need. The cynic might call this mass bribery, but it scarcely rivals the class bribery of the earlier limited franchise. There is too much evidence that special-interest legislation was a corrupt and delicate art, brought to a much finer flower of perfection in the days before universal suffrage.

Yet this first implication—that democracy works out for (or is designed for) the people—is undeniably vague. What sectional interest or policy, after all, is not defended on the ground that it is *for* the people? Yet vague as it is, it is not useless, and may be said to constitute one of the values of democracies, a value which many people rate highly. In this context, however, I shall treat it as a highly general, preliminary value, and proceed to identify more specific values of democracy.

The Specific Values of a Democratic System

The values of democracy are two-fold: (a) those underlying the principles considered separately; and (b) the values of the system as a whole. The task is to identify the values in both cases, so that, these being isolated, we may see what values we are committed to when we embrace democracy. In isolating these values we are not, of course, committing ourselves to every institution in every democracy, since obviously any actual democracy contains much that is unique and adventitious derived from its particular history. . . .

(1) *The first value is the peaceful voluntary adjustment of disputes.* Life in any human society contains a perpetual conflict of interests and opinions, whether the conflict is suppressed or conducted openly. If anyone doubts this, let him look around him or read history. A democracy is unique in recognizing the political expression of such conflicts as legitimate, and in providing for their peaceful adjustment through the negotiations of politics, as an alternative to their settlement by force or fiat. Every political theory either provides means for this peaceful settlement within a political system, or else it must call upon a *deus ex machina* to impose order, an authority from outside the system of con-

flict, as Hobbes expected the monarch of the Leviathan to rule, as Bolingbroke looked to his Patriot King, as Plato looked to his Guardians, as the Germans looked to the Führer and as Marx once or twice spoke of the state as standing "above society."

Democracy makes unique provision for the peaceful adjustment of disputes, the maintenance of order, and the working out of public policies, by means of its "honest broker" or compromise function. The policy compromises are worked out as the representatives bid for electoral support, amid the constant public debate, agitation, and politicking that go on in the context of political liberties, until in time many policies pass from dispute to virtual unanimity in settled law. . . .

Democracy is thus institutionalized peaceful settlement of conflict (ballots for bullets, a counting instead of a cracking of heads), a settlement arrived at *pro tem* with the widest possible participation because of the adult suffrage and the political freedoms. It is distinguished from elite systems or borderline cases (with *some* freedoms, *some* choice, etc.) by the difference in degree, by the recognition of the legitimacy of many diverse political interests and the extent of public participation in the settlement of disputes.

Here, then, is a value, characteristic of democracy, which will be prized by all who prefer voluntary to imposed adjustment and agreement. It is not a value, however, to those (if there are any such) who believe that force is preferable; nor would democracy be valued by those who believe that the ideally best policies are always preferable even if they have to be imposed from above.

(2) *The second value is that of ensuring peaceful change in a changing society.* This is so closely related that it may be regarded as an application of the first to the special circumstances of the modern world. The value makes a stronger appeal today than in earlier, more static, periods, that is, it has a greater element of plausibility now, because we accept the normality, even inevitability, of rapid technological change. Tomorrow the stars. (In suggesting that technology is an independent variable, initiating social and political changes though not fully determining their extent or direction, we need not ignore other determinants such as population changes or such mechanisms as the entrepreneurial function.)

We know from experience that social changes of many kinds inevitably follow the technological. The democratic political method—flexible, responsive to public opinion and to the influence of leadership, open to controversy—ensures political adaptation to this determinant of change. Almost by definition, because of the electoral changes of policy-makers, there is less "political lag" in the many adjustments which are required in law and policy to meet rapidly changing circumstances. . . .

(3) *The third value is the orderly succession of rulers.* Democracy not only presides over social conflict and change, but at the same time solves an even older political problem: that of finding, peacefully, legitimate successors to the present rulers. Hobbes, for instance, thought that the problem of succession was the chief difficulty with a monarchical system. Democracy is preeminently an answer to the question which no alternative system can answer convincingly in the modern climate of opinion: how to find and change the rulers peaceably and legitimately. The methods of self-appointment, of heredi-

tary succession, of co-option by an elite, and of the *coup d'état* are not con-
temporaneously plausible in their philosophic justifications, apart altogether
from the practical difficulties inherent in them, to which abundant historical
experience testifies.

It was with these three social values in mind—peaceful adjustment, change,
succession—that Judge Learned Hand could write of democracy and free elections:

> It seems to me, with all its defects our system does just that. For,
> abuse it as you will, it gives a bloodless measure of social forces—blood-
> less, have you thought of that?—a means of continuity, a principle of
> stability, a relief from the paralyzing terror of revolution.[1]

(4) *The fourth value is that of the minimum of coercion.* A fourth value
may be constructed by reference to the extent and quality of coercion involved
in a democracy. . . . It is not only that almost by definition the greater number approves of the policy decisions, so that always the smaller number is
coerced. This is the least of the argument, which depends much more on the
existence of political freedoms and the way in which policies are made. For one
thing there is great value in a safety valve, in being able to let off steam and
to contribute to the debate and the politicking even though one is finally out-
voted. We may follow the fashion and call it a catharsis, a working-off harm-
lessly of buried feelings of aggression, guilt, or the like. An ill-treated minority
does normally feel differently—less coerced—if political equality is recognized
and if it has to give only conditional obedience to policies which it may criticize
and which it can entertain a reasonable hope of altering either by persuasion or
by political influence. (This does not, however, always satisfy "permanent"
minorities. . . .)

We may go further. The normal democratic policy is in a sense a decision
which gives no claimant everything he asks for; is not a mere mechanical
compromise but a new policy, shaped from the continuing dialogue and struggle
of the political process. Some go so far as to call the method "creative discussion." From this it is only a short step to saying that there is more value in
decisions which we make, or help to make, than in having "wiser" decisions
made *for* us, and which we must be compelled to obey.

> To try to force people to embrace something that is believed to be good
> and glorious but which they do not actually want, even though they may
> be expected to like it when they experience its results—is the very hall-
> mark of anti-democratic belief.[2]

One might plausibly assume then that nearly everybody would accept this
value—that *ceteris paribus,** it is better to coerce fewer people than more, to
get voluntary observance rather than coerced obedience, to substitute what

[1] Learned Hand, *The Spirit of Liberty,* ed. Irving Dillard, New York, 1952 and
1959, p. 76.
[2] Cf. A. D. Lindsay, *The Modern Democratic State,* Oxford, 1943, pp. 45, 241,
275. Schumpeter, *Capitalism, Socialism and Democracy* (New York, 1950), p. 237.
* Other things being equal. [Eds.]

Wordsworth called the "discipline of virtue" for the "discipline of slavery": "order else cannot subsist, nor confidence nor peace." The notion of willing obedience reasonably, freely, and conditionally given would also agree with ideas of self-discipline, responsibility, and the like, of which we hear so much.

(5) *The fifth value is that of diversity.* The argument here depends initially on whether diversity of beliefs and action, and a wider area of choice, are of themselves good. Many will dispute their value, since diversity and variety can result in more of both the good and the bad, and free choice implies the freedom to choose badly. Ruskin thought that liberty of choice destroyed life and strength, and hence democracy was destructive. Human freedom has destructive as well as creative possibilities. But is there not at least some prima facie case for diversity and variety per se, as there is for freedom?

In the first place there is always diversity in any society, even if not to the extent of as many opinions as there are men. Democracy merely recognizes its existence, and legitimatizes the different opinions and interests. . . .

In the second place, the value of open channels and political liberties is that by implication an inevitable variety will result. Here, too, as far as ideas are concerned, we may fall back upon the arguments used by Mill in his defense of liberty of opinion. We do rightly, on grounds of experience, to be suspicious of man's ability to know beforehand what new idea or proposal or way of behaving should be strangled at birth by the authorities and what allowed to live. The true and the good often repel in their very novelty.

In the third place, however, we can only say that "other things being equal," a wider choice is *ipso facto* good; it is a necessary condition for moral improvement, for reaching closer to the truth (so long as we assume we have not already reached perfection or the *summum bonum*). . . .[3]

By maintaining an open society, democracy may then be called good because its freedoms give flexibility and a wide variety of choice. The argument may rest not only on the formal principles of democracy, but also on the empirical tendency for the political freedoms to extend beyond the purely political. The tendency is strong and ever present since political discussion includes the very topic of what is political, and because in their bidding for votes, parties and candidates tend to compete in granting substantive favors, including repeal of restrictive laws in some fields, and promotion of positive policies in others, e.g., on behalf of education, the arts and sciences. It is partly because of this tendency that democracy is sometimes called a "way of life." . . .

(6) *The sixth value is the attainment of justice.* Justice has been rated highly by political philosophers as a value to be attained in many societies. Its achievement is often regarded as the central core of political morality, and the defense of democracy on this ground must be that it is the system best able to produce justice. There are several relevant points in the case.

First, let us grant that the best we can hope for in any practicable political

---

[3] A subsidiary value from diversity may be formulated: a wider range of temptations gives more opportunities of strengthening the character. For this reason Morris Cohen could write: "the very essence of civilization [is] that we should increase the temptation and with it the power of self-control." *Reason and Law,* Glencoe, Ill., 1950, p. 52. Rousseau started from the same point: morality for the individual implies liberty of choice. Unfortunately, he tended to merge individual liberty in the community, though in this he was not far from one of the ideals of the Greek city-state.

system is not that injustice will never be committed (a perfectionist ideal) but that it can be seen, corrected if possible, and avoided the next time beforehand. (The dilemma could perhaps be avoided if democracy were by definition, or could be in practice, unanimous rule. There would then be no others within the system to judge the decisions to be unwise or unjust. But even then, a later generation could pass such judgment, as could persons in other states. Unanimity or universality is no guarantee of rightness or justice. The link with democracy lies in the political liberties—the procedures, the publicity, and possibilities of redress. What the U.S. Supreme Court once said of liberty may be true of justice too: "the history of liberty has largely been the history of the observance of procedural safeguards."

No political system, lacking perfection, can be entitled to unconditional allegiance. There may come a time when any individual may feel bound in conscience to withhold his obedience; and it comes to much the same thing to say that no political system can lay down, beforehand, the institutional rules for justified disobedience or rebellion. In this respect, democracy again makes perhaps the best claim for obedience to an unjust law because of the political freedoms, provisional obedience, and chances of redress. It is certainly not illogical to obey a particular bad law if it is part of a general system of which we approve, and where we have the liberty of protest and persuasion, and the reasonable hope for redress. We must beware of posing the problem of obeying bad laws too sharply, and on this we may look to Locke for some sensible observations. Allegiance and obedience are never explainable on the ground that the political system gives us, as individuals, everything that we want.

Second, the likelihood of injustice under democracy is much less than where the political freedoms are suppressed, and where none of the usual political safeguards exist. Democracy provides some representation of all substantial groups and interests (though not always strictly in proportion to their numbers, and still less to their "importance"); injured interests, being vocal and able to muster power through influencing votes and through many other recognized and legitimate ways, are seldom likely to be ignored when policy decisions are being made. . . .

Third, democracy involves political compromise or harmony by the adjustment of conflicting claims. This may fairly enough be called "relative" justice, even though it does not approach the kind of harmony or "right relationship" of classes which constituted so much of Plato's idea of justice. In any case "absolute" justice is an ideal beyond the reach of democratic politics, partly because it involves less than full satisfaction of some claims (or "rights") but also partly because absolute justice in any other sense is beyond any system of government. Only relative justice, the relative attainment of any of our highest ideals, is feasible in any political system. The best word to use perhaps is equity, with its connotation of both justice and flexibility. . . .

(7) [*Another*] *value consists of the freedoms found in a democracy.* . . .

The case for democracy, on the ground that it promotes freedoms, is chiefly in terms of the political freedoms. Whether freedoms will be extended to other spheres is not guaranteed by the logic of the democratic system, but is merely a likelihood or probability, a tendency for the political freedoms to carry over into other spheres. The presumption is extremely strong that they will do so, as they did in Athens if we may take the word of Pericles on the social freedom which the citizens enjoyed. It is the same sort of (weaker) tendency by which equality tends to be carried over from the political to other spheres. As Duverger puts it:

> The history of the development of civil rights in France shows a link between the existence of a liberal regime and that of a democratic regime with free elections. This same link is to be found in most of the countries in the world, so that the following general statement may be formulated: civil rights in a country exist in direct proportion to the degree of democracy to be found there. This is not a logical connection but one based on actual fact.[4]

The case can go somewhat deeper. The inescapable conditions of social life impose restrictions on one's freedom of action: freedoms conflict with other goods which we value highly, and sometimes with one another. The essential function of co-ordinating freedoms with one another and with other goods is performed by all governments, but the claim on behalf of democracy is that democratic co-ordination maximizes freedoms. And—paradoxical though it may sound—the maximizing of freedoms does not necessarily mean that the laws are few. To protect and even extend freedoms may demand an elaborate network of laws. We may start with Hobbes's dictum about the silence of the law, but a political theory cannot end there.

It is perhaps worth mentioning again that the political freedoms of a democracy may be valued highly in their own right, and not only for the instrumental reason that they give citizens a share in political power, or are necessary to promote social welfare. There is eloquent testimony that such freedoms may be valued intrinsically, given by many refugees from Nazi Germany and from the Soviet Union and its satellites. Those of us living in democracies, having been born free, and never having been deprived, must often make a greater effort in order to appreciate our birthright. To those who value political freedoms, for whatever reason, the justification for democracy is strong; to those who place a higher intrinsic value upon *other* freedoms, it can at least be said that democracy has a marked tendency to extend the freedoms from the political to other spheres if only because there are channels for the political extension of freedoms.

(8) *Finally, a value may be constructed for democracy from the deficiencies of alternative systems.* Any alternative is inevitably a system in which some kind of minority makes the policy decisions—always of course a properly qualified minority, since no one advocates that the numerical minority should rule merely *because* they are a minority.

In the contemporary world there is a strong, almost universal aversion to the idea that any kind of minority has any right or title to rule. Not only are the almost unrecognized postulates of our political thinking against it, but also the rational objections: What minority? What credentials? Who will judge the credentials? Nor must we make the mistake of merely assuming that because democracy is imperfect, any minority alternative is better because it is made so

---

[4] Maurice Duverger, *The French Political System* (Chicago, 1958), p. 161.

by definition. We cannot get from a definition to a feasible and perfect political system.

Obviously, only those who prize those values listed above, and who believe they are inseparable from or most likely to be promoted by a democracy, will find the values cogent arguments for a democratic system. Thus, apart altogether from considerations of the social and other empirical conditions necessary for democracy, we have not proved that democracy is logically always and everywhere the best political system. I do not think it can be proved, in any logical sense of proof, and that is why I have not attempted it. Instead we may agree with Aristotle that the best form of government is relative to circumstances. The case for democracy is a case, not a demonstration like a Euclidean theorem. By taking this attitude we avoid making a political system itself into an absolute value, as well as the mistake of completely identifying any existing democracy with the theoretical model.

Again, all the values noted are not always and only found in actual democratic systems. Political systems do not always work as their distinguishing principles might lead us to think. Absolute monarchies, for instance, may occasionally be noted for the freedoms and diversity which they permit, as in the rich literary, artistic, and scientific life of eighteenth-century France. But those values noted above follow from the logic of a democratic system, whereas they do not follow from the logic of other systems. . . .

Some Criticisms of Democracy

A common opinion has it that democracy has lost much of its appeal in the modern world because its attitudes or character are thought not to agree with the findings of psychology. At any rate, there is a substantial corpus of pessimistic writing to that effect.

For one thing, it is alleged that a whole body of psychological doctrine, starting with Freud, has undermined belief in the rationality of man by showing that much of our behavior is determined at the unconscious mental level. If political decisions cannot be partly rational—in both the economic sense of means to ends and the sense of choosing ends—it is hard to see how we can justify democracy. Another fashionable school of thought purports to show that people are "naturally" and not "culturally" afraid of what Gide called the "anguish of freedom"—of choice, self-discipline, and the responsibility that the democratic method presupposes.

Then, again, so it is said, sociology and the discovery of "iron laws of oligarchy" in virtually every type of large-scale social organization including political parties tend to the same pessimistic conclusion of the inherent unsuitability of democratic principles and attitudes for any large-scale organization, and *a fortiori* for one as large as a political system. This kind of social determinism is seen at its most determinist and pessimistic in the classic by Michels on *Political Parties:* the iron law of oligarchy is "the fundamental sociological law of political parties." No remedy can be found: all organizations in time will become oligarchic. The charge of inevitable oligarchy, or something very similar, is brought not only by Michels but also by writers such as Pareto, Mosca, and Burnham, and is supported by much empirical evidence drawn from the study of political parties, trade unions, and business organizations. The charge is based on different concepts such as that of the "managerial elite," the inevitable trends to bureaucracy, the "organization man," the nature of large-scale technology, and so forth. The concept of the "sociology of knowledge" has contributed also to the same end—e.g., here and there in the works of Karl Mannheim—by suggesting that social factors determine man's beliefs and actions.

What are we to say to these impressive arguments? For myself, I do not find that they support the anti-democratic conclusions so often drawn. Take the "iron law of oligarchy." There is nothing in democratic theory which cannot come to terms with leadership in organizations, political or any other kind. It is no great news that large-scale organizations are led by the leaders. This sociological finding, for which so many—sometimes conflicting—causes are given and from which different conclusions are drawn, is only devastating to a primitive or direct type of democratic system, and scarcely affects a representative system. A democracy does not require everyone to be politically active, or show all the democratic attitudes, and can make full allowance for the realities of leadership and parties. (A democracy does, however, presuppose that political action is not determinist, but that human choice and attitudes do count, causally; that human choice can control and mold the impersonal forces at work in society, and within limits shape them to human ends.)

A fuller answer may be attempted to the charge based upon psychology. We can, in the first place, readily admit that any democracy may contain a proportion of undemocratic personalities, judged by the standards set forth above or by other standards. How high the proportion can get before a democracy becomes unworkable, we simply do not know. Doubtless the proportion will vary with the kind of political circumstances at different times, including the urgency and magnitude of the policies to be made, the quality of political leadership, and so forth. We do know, however, that democracy need not presuppose any large proportion of the politically active, or even a high proportion of voters. Despite Aristotle, not every man is (or need be) a political animal.

Then, too, we can point to the going democracies, some of which have been successful for a considerable time; and to the many attempts at self-government—even those that have failed—all of which must be explained away by the psychological pessimists. Those who assert that man is not psychologically able to work democracy often forget that full representative democracy is, for all practical purposes, a comparatively new political system. It takes time for the masses of men to adjust to new political forms, and to adapt to the ideas and the moral climate which accompanies democracy—the autonomy, the discussion, the political equality and freedoms, and the majority principle—until they become "second nature." Life in the past seems to have been lived more by "instinct" (or custom) and government has been more readily accepted with resignation, instead of approached with the idea that it can be popularly created and controlled. Every democracy trails clouds of these older traditions into the present. Democracy, as Morley said, "stands for a remarkable revolution in human affairs." Then, too, there is still the cogent point that so much of man's "unfitness" for democracy may be simply his "unfitness" for, or painful adjustment to, a scientific and industrial urban way of living.

In pointing thus to experience with democracy and self-government, we do not need to posit any primitive "instinct to freedom," nor yet to assume any universal psychological or other needs which only democracy can satisfy. There is a set of psychological *wants* that are democratic, but they are a function of the values of democracy, i.e., they are culturally learned and (as yet) certainly not universal. Men may come to democracy to fulfill different needs—as they go to religion for different reasons. It is enough if the needs thus fulfilled, in their overt expression as wants, are compatible with democracy. (Those who have been led to take a pessimistic view of man's capacity for democracy have, I think, been led astray by making two additional mistakes: first, by founding their psychological theory upon clinical experience with the unfit; and second, by assuming that democracy presupposes that all, or even a large proportion of, citizens need be politically active. They have been better at their psychology, their technical expertise, than in their understanding of politics.

We can also point to the psychological evidence in *favor* of man's capacity for democracy—including those persons who value the procedures of democracy more highly than any of its substantive objectives. While it may be true that "every man bears within himself a dormant fascist," it is equally true that we are all animals in our unconscious. It is what is in our consciousness that counts, and the business of any society is to make a civilized consciousness.

Our conclusions can be modest. We need conclude only that there is nothing in the demands which democracy makes upon men, or in the kind of personality which it requires and promotes, that is at variance with what we know with a fair degree of reliability of psychology. This may not be saying much, because we may not know much for certain; most psychology is local and western and not universal. On the other hand, if we do not know much, it is hard to feel that arguments drawn from psychological theories are very damaging to democracy. We must assume, however, that the democratic character "does not form against the grain" in enough people [to make it impossible] to work the system successfully. Compatibility, then, is a justifiable assumption, and a quite sufficient one. "Man has no nature: what he has is . . . history." (And it may help to recall that anthropology finds something very like democracy in some early primitive societies, whence some assert that democracy is the oldest form of government, while some make the cheerful assumption that democracy is the norm at which the political animal most naturally will arrive.) . . .

The Charge of Incompetence

The second class of contemporary criticism, commanding a wide following, may for convenience be grouped under the head of "incompetence." A host of such specific charges used to be directed at the existing democracies before World War II, most of them being associated with Fascism and Nazism, both of which despised democracy but avoided the Marxist diagnosis of putting the blame on the capitalists and the economic system. The charges were focused instead around the allegation that democracy is incompetent and inefficient—in dealing with serious economic problems, in its unstable domestic and foreign policies, and in its inability to prepare for war. The breakdown of democracy in Germany and Italy, and its relative economic failure everywhere in the depression of the 1930's, was usually adduced as supporting evidence of incompetence. (The Marxist criticism is almost the opposite, that democracy *is* efficient in terms of its own "real" underlying principles—giving the *bourgeoisie* their way, and maintaining class rule for the time being.)

The alleged incompetence of democracy is accounted for in several ways. For one thing, the democratic system is inevitably slow—taking too long to act, to hammer out a policy in the endless debates, electioneering, and politicking. The slow method is quite unsuited for dealing with emergencies requiring quick decision. Nothing gets done, except during a war, and then only at the cost of suspending democracy.

For another, the political system of democracy is said to be inherently unsuited to the complexities and large scale of the modern world, whatever may perhaps have been its usefulness in a simpler age, when political units were small or when *laissez faire* prevailed and the services provided by government were few. When a government does a few things, mistakes hardly matter; but when many things, failures are always serious and may be calamitous. This particular criticism is indeed made the basis of pessimistic predictions of the prospects of democracy by both its friends and its enemies: by its friends who fear that "increasing" government may destroy democracy, and by its enemies who hope that it will do so.

Then again, democracy is said to fail on the score of leadership. The talents for vote-getting are not those of ruling—of making "wise" decisions. Democracy emphasizes and rewards the former, and bonuses opportunism of parties and politicians as they have the money or cunning to influence the votes. But good government, wise policies, are needed to ensure the success of any system, and only good leaders can provide these desiderata.

Moreover, even if competent leaders should occasionally find themselves in office—combining the roles of politicians and statesmen—they are hopelessly handicapped by the methods of democratic politics. Democracy diffuses responsibility for policies, whereas responsibility must be concentrated in order to "get things done," i.e., to decide policies, to make them into a consistent pattern, and to see they are carried out efficiently. A casual reference to the near-chaos or deadlock in some multi-party systems—usually that of France—is taken to be enough to document the case against democratic leadership.

The very principle of compromise which is, so to speak, built into the democratic system further militates against efficiency, consistency, and "good" government. Compromise is also made the basis of the charge that democracy lacks "principle" (compromise is said to be the exaltation of "no principle"), while in addition it stands for and invites unlimited sectionalism, pressures, and group selfishness. Alternatively, democracy is sometimes accused of being organized deceit and hypocrisy—professing high principles and the public interest but always deviating from them in the compromises of politics—an inevitable tendency (so it is said), since, not being able to accomplish anything important, politicians must pretend that the trivial things they actually do are important.

Democracy is also confusing to the citizens, who cannot understand the complexities and subtleties of its policy-making or methods of operation. It has, moreover, no ideology, no body of agreed and simple doctrine, no great aims or purposes, by which to inspire devotion and sacrifice and to command the enthusiastic loyalty, if not the understanding, of the masses. The result is bound to be disillusion and apathy among the public, and in the end a collapse of the system from its own defects—to give way to more militant, inspiring, and demanding faiths, supporting other newer systems which are the "wave of the future." Where the democratic system has worked, after a fashion, its success is accounted for by extraneous or fortuitous factors which have, as it were, managed to keep a bumbling and incompetent system afloat in spite of its defects.

The case is familiar and at first sight formidable. (I pass over the virtues sometimes grudgingly granted to democracy, e.g., that it solves the problem of peaceful succession of rulers.) And it would obviously be foolish to deny an element of truth here and there in these criticisms. Before coming to grips with the main charge of incompetence, two oft-forgotten points of considerable importance should be recalled.

(a) Much of democratic government—though by no means all—is conducted in the white glare of publicity, and faults are exaggerated. The very function of an opposition is to oppose, and to do so as noisily and as effectively as possible. Because of the political liberties allowed, every democracy produces critics of the system and of its most fundamental principles. Mistakes of policy and abuses of the system, both real and imaginary, are freely ventilated—often to loud and profitable applause. By contrast, only praise and flattery are allowed in a dictatorship, and since the mistakes and evils go uncriticized, one tends to assume they are nonexistent. The old observation is still true that under a popular government everyone speaks ill of the people with freedom and without fear; whereas no one speaks of an absolute prince without a thousand fears and precautions.

(b) The critics of democracy all too often fail to apply the same standards to democracy as to its rivals. The very highest, often perfectionist, standards are used to judge democracy—as when moral purists attack the United States for the mote and make generous excuses for the Soviet beam, or denounce the scandals of democratic politics, forgetting the institutionalized corruption of other political systems. (This kind of criticism also subtly shifts the ground of attack from incompetence to moral turpitude.)

Nevertheless, even when due allowance has been made for the exaggeration of faults and the use of the double standard, the charge of incompetence raises a question which goes to the very root of the theory of democratic politics. Incompetence, or the lack of political wisdom, constitutes in fact the gravamen of the most serious charge (other than the Marxist) and is also the oldest of the criticisms against democracy—modern versions being seldom more than glosses on Plato, with a few topical illustrations added. In the end, the quasi-Platonic criticism is directed against the principle of political equality, and rests upon a particular view of the nature of politics. This principle of political equality, so it is said, is based on the assumption of equality of political wisdom among the citizens—which is absurd. Political wisdom is distributed unequally, and some obviously know more than others. The masses of the citizens are ignorant, and even if most of them can be made technically literate, their judgment on public policy (if it can be called judgment) is necessarily incomplete and faulty.

Whatever validity Plato's critique of the assumption of equal political wisdom had against Athenian democracy, the modern version has far less force against the indirect, representative democracy with which we are familiar. Political wisdom of a high order on every complex issue is not required of all citizens in a system where the people do not make the policy decisions, but instead elect and authorize representatives to do this for them. The wisdom is needed by the leaders (though there is admittedly the problem of how the leaders may persuade the citizens to follow them). The modern criticism ought, then, to be directed against the democratic method of choosing its leaders (politicians). And often it is in fact so directed—as when it becomes an attack upon the universal suffrage, which is alleged to have been responsible for the rise of Hitler, to make the conduct of enlightened foreign policy impossible, to lower and destroy moral and cultural values alike.[5]

Democracy, like any other political system, must produce "adequate" leaders, adequate to ensure the continuance of the system, and thus to realize its values; adequate to meet the short- and long-term problems, whether economic or international or whatever they may be. Democracy obviously stands or falls by its method of selecting its leaders, and rests on the explicit assumption that elections are the best, or least bad, method of choosing the wisest and best. Behind the elections there is, of course, the pre-selection of candidates by parties—using all the political criteria of "availability," electoral appeal, and so forth; an elaborate and severely competitive pre-selection process that is usually ignored by the critics.

Let us grant that we need more investigations into democratic leadership: how it is in fact found and brought forward; in what political "talent" consists; whether there is a large stock of "talent"; whether the system does in fact make good use of its "talent"; whether a traditional ruling class is necessary (as Schumpeter argued); whether businessmen as a class are inherently poor political leaders (as Adam Smith believed); whether democratic leadership tends to compare unfavorably with leadership in other systems, and many similar questions. H. L. Mencken was much more severe than Adam Smith on what he called the plutocracy. Bryce too, a friendly critic, thought that the chief fault of democracy was "The power of money to pervert administration or legislation."

The theoretical argument against democratic wisdom is not, however, to be turned aside by empirical studies of leadership, even if their results should happen to be favorable to democracy. Questions of philosophy and principle are also at stake. Plato, it will be recalled, supported his critique by extended argument on the kind of knowledge required, and hence on the difficulty of acquiring wisdom, and on the training and qualifications of the guardians. The philosopher-rulers were to be an aristocracy in the better sense of the word, who by a combination of experience and knowledge received their title to rule just because they *were* qualified.

[5] For a survey of the criticisms of democracy on cultural grounds by Carlyle, Ruskin, Arnold, Stephen, Maine, and Lecky see Benjamin E. Lippincott, *Victorian Critics of Democracy*, Minneapolis, 1938. De Tocqueville and Henry Adams should also be consulted.

Fundamentally, two quite different views of the nature of politics and government—the question of what politics and political leadership are *about*—are involved. In the one case, the "proper end" and the implementing policies can only be known with difficulty, by the philosophers; in the democratic view the ends and policies are many and conflicting, the task of ruling is not conceived as holding society, willy-nilly, to the highest ideals, but of achieving the tolerable and the acceptable for the time being, of permitting progress to whatever ideals may be cherished and which the public may be persuaded to accept. Knowledge of the *summum bonum* is not excluded from a democracy, but it must be married to political persuasion in the politician or pressure group.

It is, however, when we come to consider practical minority-rule alternatives to democracy that the nature of the elite critique is more clearly revealed. Not only do all such critiques start by assuming differences in political capacity and wisdom—so much is admitted to exist—but they go on to assert that the "wise elite" can be identified and their rule validated. This is precisely the insuperable difficulty, since there are no accepted credentials for such wisdom.

> Nor will I forsake the faith of our fathers in democracy, however I must transmute it, and make it unlovely to their eyes, were they here to see their strangely perverse disciple. If you will give me scales by which to weigh Tom and Dick and Harry as to their fitness to rule, and tell me how much each shall count, I will talk with you about some other kind of organization. Plato jumped hurdles that are too high for my legs. . . .[6]

Even if an elite is once selected, methods of continuing its recruitment and training must be invented. (The nearest approach to a dominant elite today is the self-selected communist party in some countries.)

The selection of an elite cannot be done by mass voting, or else we should be back again at democracy, yet somehow the whole of the citizens must be able to recognize the presence of such wisdom and the rulers who have it; and must accept and continue to accept the validity of their rule, i.e., its legitimacy. It is no wonder that even Plato flinched at this task, and resorted to his "myths" and "conditioning" once the initial philosopher-kings were installed. Nor can it be seriously maintained today that we can accept the rule of some kind of aristocracy based on and validated by wealth, blood, intellect, military prowess, or priestly power. (Think of the difficulty of getting an I.Q. rating accepted as conferring a right to rule.) We know that none of these is necessarily accompanied by political wisdom.

Further, the elite alternative assumes that the wisest and best, once found, will accept rule and responsibility, and will continue to exercise it wisely, their virtue and judgment alike remaining incorruptible by power. These are large assumptions, for which we are not in the market. Architects of Utopia may ignore the peril, but we know too much today about the corrupting influence of power upon those aloof from and out of touch with the governed, exacting obedience, yet unaccountable to anyone except their consciences or their God. It is for this reason that it seems so true that "Great men are nearly always bad men." In the end such rulers can only reduce the stature of their subjects, and

[6] Learned Hand, *op. cit.* p. 77. See also Charles E. Merriam, *Systematic Politics,* Chicago, 1945, pp. 187ff.

they are left trying vainly—as Mill put it—to "do great things with little people." Only a democracy provides institutional safeguards against the corruption of power in an elite, by its freedoms and elections answering the old question *quis custodiet ipsos custodes?** Elites and dictators, both good and bad, are shrewd enough not to take chances by asking for a free renewal of their mandate. They fall a prey to all the evils of the "cult of the individual," having "no remedy for the personality defects which they may bring into their exalted station."[7]

* Who will watch over the rulers? [Eds.]
[7] F. Hermens, *The Representative Republic,* Notre Dame, 1958, p. 83.

✍Section XII

THE BASES OF AMERICAN FOREIGN POLICY

On what premises and assumptions should American foreign policy be based? Should we agree with Wilson that "we dare not turn from the principle that morality and not expediency is the thing that must guide us, and that we will never condone iniquity because it is most convenient to do so"? Or, must we distinguish between "moral sympathies and the political interests which [we] must defend"? Or, should we seek a "coincidence between national self-interest and supranational ideals"? The issue is discussed by Professors Hans J. Morgenthau and Robert E. Osgood.

After considering to what extent "national interests" and moral or ideological considerations should determine American foreign policy the final topic in this book presents three different points of view on the highly controversial issue of our relations with Communist China.

〜〜〜〜TOPIC 31

Ideals and National Interest

HANS J. MORGENTHAU
The Primacy of the National Interest

Moral principles and the national interest have contended for dominance over the minds and actions of men throughout the history of the modern state system. The conduct of American foreign affairs in particular has from its very beginning been deeply affected by the contest between these two principles of political action. Perhaps never before or after have the practical alternatives which flow from these two principles been stated with greater acumen and persuasiveness than in the Pacificus articles of Alexander Hamilton, and it is for the light which Hamilton's arguments shed upon our problem —as well as for the analogy between the situation to which they apply and some of the situations with which American foreign policy must deal in our time— that we might dwell at some length upon the situation which gave rise to the Pacificus articles, and upon the philosophy which they express.

In 1792 the War of the First Coalition had ranged Austria, Prussia, Sardinia, Great Britain and the United Netherlands against revolutionary France, which was tied to the United States by a treaty of alliance. On April 22, 1793, Washington issued a Proclamation of Neutrality, and it was in defense of that proclamation that Hamilton wrote the Pacificus articles. Among the arguments directed against the Proclamation were three derived from moral principles. Faithfulness to treaty obligations, gratitude toward a country which had lent its assistance to the colonies in their struggle for independence, and the affinity of republican institutions, were cited to prove that the United States must side with France. Against these moral principles, Hamilton invoked the national interest of the United States:

There would be no proportion between the mischiefs and perils to which the United States would expose themselves, by embarking in the

Professor of Political Science, The City College of the City University of New York. Author of *Scientific Man vs. Power Politics, Politics Among Nations, In Defense of the National Interest,* and of many articles in the field of international relations. The selection is from Hans J. Morgenthau, "The Primacy of the National Interest," *The American Scholar,* Vol. 18 (Spring, 1949), pp. 207-210 and from "Another 'Great Debate': The National Interest of the United States," *The American Political Science Review,* Vol. XLVI (December, 1952), pp. 961-988. Reprinted by permission of *The American Scholar* and of *The American Political Science Review.*

war, and the benefit which the nature of their stipulation aims at securing to France, or that which it would be in their power actually to render her by becoming a party.

This disproportion would be a valid reason for not executing the guaranty. All contracts are to receive a reasonable construction. Self-preservation is the first duty of a nation; and though in the performance of stipulations relating to war, good faith requires that its ordinary hazards should be fairly met, because they are directly contemplated by such stipulations, yet it does not require that extraordinary and extreme hazards should be run. . . .

The basis of gratitude is a benefit received or intended which there was no right to claim, originating in a regard to the interest or advantage of the party on whom the benefit is, or is meant to be, conferred. If a service is rendered from views relative to the immediate interest of the party who performs it, and is productive of reciprocal advantages, there seems scarcely, in such a case, to be an adequate basis for a sentiment like that of gratitude. . . . It may be affirmed as a general principle, that the predominant motive of good offices from one nation to another, is the interest or advantage of the nation which performs them.

Indeed, the rule of morality in this respect is not precisely the same between nations as between individuals. The duty of making its own welfare the guide of its actions, is much stronger upon the former than upon the latter; in proportion to the greater magnitude and importance of national compared with individual happiness, and to the greater permanency of the effects of national than of individual conduct. Existing millions, and for the most part future generations, are concerned in the present measures of a government; while the consequences of the private actions of an individual ordinarily terminate with himself, or are circumscribed within a narrow compass. . . .

The philosophy of this discussion provided the guiding principles of American foreign policy for more than a century. That philosophy has found expression in the *Federalist* and Washington's Farewell Address, no less than in many diplomatic documents. It was eclipsed by a conception of foreign policy whose main representatives were McKinley, Theodore Roosevelt and Admiral Mahan. In that second period, moral principles were invoked side by side with the national interest to justify American expansion within and outside the Western hemisphere. Yet, as before with Gladstone's similar emphasis upon the moral obligations of British foreign policy, it so happened that by a felicitous coincidence what the moral law demanded of the United States was always identical with what its national interest seemed to require.

It is a distinctive characteristic of the third conception of American foreign policy, propounded by Woodrow Wilson, that this identity between the national interest and moral principles is consciously abandoned, and that the sacrifice of the national interest for compliance with moral principles is made the earmark of a worthy foreign policy. In his address at Mobile on October 27, 1913, Wilson declared: "It is a very perilous thing to determine the foreign policy of a nation in the terms of material interest. It not only is unfair to those with whom you are dealing, but it is degrading as regards your own actions. . . . We dare not turn from the principle that morality and not expediency is the thing that must guide us, and that we will never condone iniquity because it is most convenient to do so."

"Only a free people . . ." he said in his message of April 2, 1917, "prefer the interest of mankind to any interest of their own. . . . We have no selfish ends to serve. . . . We are but one of the champions of the rights of mankind." And in his message of January 22, 1917, he had opposed "a peace that will serve the several interests and immediate aims of the nations engaged."

It stands to reason that no statesman in actual performance could have lived up to such principles without ruining his country. Whenever, therefore, Wilson had to apply these moral principles to situations, especially in the Western hemisphere, where the national interest was of long standing and well-defined, he applied them in actions which might as well have been justified in terms of the national interest. Where, however, the national interest was new and not yet clearly defined—as with regard to Europe at the end of the First World War—Wilson started with the assumption, which was a subtly isolationist one, that no specific national interest of the United States was affected by any particular settlement of European issues, and ended up with half-hearted, uneasy compromises between moral principles and the national interests of the more influential European states. Such compromises could not fail to shock the adherents of the Wilsonian principles, to disappoint the nations whose interests had not been fully satisfied, and to remain unintelligible to those sectors of the American public which, following the Federalist tradition of the national interest, had not been affected by the idealism of Wilson's "new diplomacy."

Thus the twenties witnessed a revival of the conception of the national interest, however erroneously defined. Under Franklin D. Roosevelt, Wilsonianism was revived in the foreign policy of Cordell Hull, while the President came closest to identifying the national interest with moral principles, the characteristic of the second period of American foreign policy. It is with the Truman Doctrine that a fourth conception of foreign policy has come to dominate the conduct of American foreign affairs. The Truman Doctrine is Wilsonian in that it proclaims universal moral principles—such as promotion of free and democratic governments everywhere in the world—as standards of American foreign policy. It is within the Federalist tradition in that it finds the containment of Russian power at some point required by the national interest. Yet, by defining that point in terms of its moral principles and not in those political and military terms which the national interest would demand, it vitiates its consideration of the national interest and cannot help being eclectic and immature as a philosophy, and halfhearted, contradictory and threatened with failure in actual operation. . . .

The man in the street, unsophisticated as he is and uninformed as he may be, has a surer grasp of the essentials of foreign policy and a more mature judgment of its basic issues than many of the intellectuals and politicians who pretend to speak for him and cater to what they imagine his prejudices to be. During the recent war the ideologues of the Atlantic Charter, the Four Freedoms, and the United Nations were constantly complaining that the American soldier did not know what he was fighting for. Indeed, if he was fighting for some utopian ideal, divorced from the concrete experiences and interests of the country, then the complaint was well grounded. However, if he was fighting for the territorial integrity of the nation and for its survival as a free country where he could live, think, and act as he pleased, then he had never any doubt about what he was fighting for. Ideological rationalizations and justifications are indeed the indispensable concomitants of all political action. Yet there is something unhealthy in a craving for ideological intoxication and in the inability to act and to see merit in action except under the stimulant of grandiose ideas and far-fetched schemes. Have our intellectuals become, like Hamlet, too much beset by doubt to act and, unlike Hamlet, compelled to still their doubts by renouncing their sense of what is real? The man in the street has no such doubts. It is true that ideologues and demagogues can sway him by appealing to his emotions. But it is also true, as American history shows in abundance and as the popular success of Ambassador Kennan's bcoks demonstrates, that responsible statesmen can guide him by awakening his latent understanding of the national interest.

Yet what is the national interest? How can we define it and give it the content which will make it a guide for action? This is one of the relevant questions to which the current debate has given rise.

It has been frequently argued against the realist conception of foreign policy that its key concept, the national interest, does not provide an acceptable standard for political action. This argument is in the main based upon two grounds: the elusiveness of the concept and its susceptibility to interpretations, such as limitless imperialism and narrow nationalism, which are not in keeping with the American tradition in foreign policy. The argument has substance as far as it goes, but it does not invalidate the usefulness of the concept.

The concept of the national interest is similar in two respects to the "great generalities" of the Constitution, such as the general welfare and due process. It contains a residual meaning which is inherent in the concept itself, but beyond these minimum requirements its content can run the whole gamut of meanings which are logically compatible with it. That content is determined by the political traditions and the total cultural context within which a nation formulates its foreign policy. The concept of the national interest, then, contains two elements, one that is logically required and in that sense necessary, and one that is variable and determined by circumstances.

Any foreign policy which operates under the standard of the national interest must obviously have some reference to the physical, political and cultural entity which we call a nation. In a world where a number of sovereign nations compete with and oppose each other for power, the foreign policies of all nations must necessarily refer to their survival as their minimum requirements. Thus all nations do what they cannot help but do: protect their physical, political, and cultural identity against encroachments by other nations.

It has been suggested that this reasoning erects the national state into the last word in politics and the national interest into an absolute standard for political action. This, however, is not quite the case. The idea of interest is indeed of the essence of politics and, as such, unaffected by the circumstances of time and place. Thucydides' statement, born of the experiences of ancient Greece, that "identity of interest is the surest of bonds whether between states or individuals" was taken up in the nineteenth century by Lord Salisbury's remark that "the only bond of union that endures" among nations is "the absence of all clashing interests." The perennial issue between the realist and utopian schools of thought over the nature of politics, to which we have referred before, might well be formulated in terms of concrete interest *vs.* abstract principles. Yet while the concern of politics with interest is perennial, the connection between interest and the national state is a product of history.

The national state itself is obviously a product of history and as such destined to yield in time to different modes of political organization. As long as the world is politically organized into nations, the national interest is indeed the last word in world politics. When the national state will have been replaced by another mode of organization, foreign policy must then protect the interest in survival of that new organization. For the benefit of those who insist upon discarding the national state and constructing supranational organizations by constitutional fiat, it must be pointed out that these new organizational forms will either come into being through conquest or else through consent based upon the mutual recognition of the national interests of the nations concerned; for no nation will forego its freedom of action if it has no reason to expect proportionate benefits in compensation for that loss. This is true of treaties concerning commerce or fisheries as it is true of the great compacts, such as the European Coal and Steel Community, through which nations try to create supranational forms of organization. Thus, by an apparent paradox, what is historically relative in the idea of the national interest can be overcome only through the promotion in concert of the national interest of a number of nations.

The survival of a political unit, such as a nation, in its identity is the irreducible minimum, the necessary element of its interest vis-à-vis other units. Taken in isolation, the determination of its content in a concrete situation is relatively simple; for it encompasses the integrity of the nation's territory, of its political institutions, and of its culture. Thus bipartisanship in foreign policy, especially in times of war, has been most easily achieved in the promotion of these minimum requirements of the national interest. The situation is different with respect to the variable elements of the national interest. All the cross currents of personalities, public opinion, sectional interests, partisan politics, and politicial and moral folkways are brought to bear upon their determination. In consequence, the contribution which science can make to this field, as to all fields of policy formation, is limited. It can identify the different agencies of the government which contribute to the determination of the variable elements of the national interest and assess their relative weight. It can separate the long-range objectives of foreign policy from the short-term ones which are the means for the achievement of the former and can tentatively establish their rational relations. Finally, it can analyze the variable elements of the national interest in terms of their legitimacy and their compatibility with other national values and with the national interest of other nations. . . .

We have said before that the utopian and realist positions in international affairs do not necessarily differ in the policies they advocate, but that they part company over their general philosophies of politics and their way of thinking about matters political. It does not follow that the present debate is only of academic interest and without practical significance. Both camps, it is true, may support this same policy for different reasons. Yet if the reasons are unsound, the soundness of the policies supported by them is a mere coincidence, and these very same reasons may be, and inevitably are, invoked on other occasions in support of unsound policies. The nefarious consequences of false philosophies and wrong ways of thinking may for the time being be concealed by the apparent success of policies derived from them. You may go to war, justified by your nation's interests, for a moral purpose and in disregard of considerations of power; and military victory seems to satisfy both your moral aspirations and your nation's interests. Yet the manner in which you waged the war, achieved victory, and settled the peace cannot help reflecting your philosophy of politics and your way of thinking about political problems. If these are in error, you may win victory on the field of battle and still assist in defeat of both your moral principles and the national interest of your country.

Any number of examples could illustrate the real yet subtle practical consequences which follow from the different positions taken. We have chosen two: collective security in Korea and the liberation of the nations that are captives of Communism. A case for both policies can be made from both the utopian and realist positions, but with significant differences in the emphasis and substance of the policies pursued.

Collective security as an abstract principle of utopian politics requires that all nations come to the aid of a victim of aggression by resisting the aggressor with all means necessary to frustrate his aims. Once the case of aggression is established, the duty to act is unequivocal. Its extent may be affected by concern for the nation's survival; obviously no nation will commit outright suicide in the service of collective security. But beyond that elemental limitation no consideration of interest or power, either with regard to the aggressor or his victim or the nation acting in the latter's defense, can qualify the obligation to act under the principle of collective security. Thus high officials of our government have declared that we intervened in Korea not for any narrow interest of ours but in support of the moral principle of collective security.

Collective security as a concrete principle of realist policy is the age-old maxim, "Hang together or hang separately," in modern dress. It recognizes the need for nation A under certain circumstances to defend nation B against attack by nation C. That need is determined, first, by the interest which A has in the territorial integrity of B and by the relation of that interest to all the other interests of A as well as to the resources available for the support of all those interests. Furthermore, A must take into account the power which is at the disposal of aggressor C for fighting A and B as over against the power available to A and B for fighting C. The same calculation must be carried on concerning the power of the likely allies of C as over against those of A and B. Before going to war for the defense of South Korea in the name of collective security, an American adherent of political realism would have demanded an answer to the following four questions: First, what is our interest in the preservation of the independence of South Korea; second, what is our power to defend that independence against North Korea; third, what is our power to defend that independence against China and the Soviet Union; and fourth, what are the chances for preventing China and the Soviet Union from entering the Korean War?

In view of the principle of collective security, interpreted in utopian terms, our intervention in Korea was a foregone conclusion. The interpretation of this principle in realist terms might or might not, depending upon the concrete circumstances of interest and power, have led us to the same conclusion. In the execution of the policy of collective security the utopian had to be indifferent to the possibility of Chinese and Russian intervention, except for his resolution to apply the principle of collective security to anybody who would intervene on the side of the aggressor. The realist could not help weighing the possibility of the intervention of a great power on the side of the aggressor in terms of the interests engaged and the power available on the other side.

The Truman administration could not bring itself to taking resolutely the utopian or the realist position. It resolved to intervene in good measure on utopian grounds and in spite of military advice to the contrary; it allowed the military commander to advance to the Yalu River in disregard of the risk of the intervention of a great power against which collective security could be carried out only by means of a general war, and then refused to pursue the war with full effectiveness on the realist grounds of the risk of a third world war. Thus Mr. Truman in 1952 was caught in the same dilemma from which Mr. Baldwin could extricate himself in 1936 on the occasion of the League of Nations sanctions against Italy's attack upon Ethiopia only at an enormous loss to British prestige. Collective security as a defense of the *status quo* short of a general war can be effective only against second-rate powers. Applied against a major power, it is a contradiction in terms, for it means necessarily a major war. Of this self-defeating contradiction Mr. Baldwin was as unaware in the 'thirties as Mr. Truman seemed to be in 1952. Mr. Churchill put Mr. Baldwin's dilemma in these cogent terms: "First, the Prime Minister had declared that sanctions meant war; secondly, he was resolved that there must be no war; and thirdly, he decided upon sanctions. It was evidently impossible to comply with these three conditions." Similarly Mr. Truman had declared that the effective prosecution of the Korean War meant the possibility of a third world war; he resolved that there must be no third world war; and he decided upon intervention in the Korean War. Here, too, it is impossible to comply with these three conditions.

Similar contradictions are inherent in the proposals which would substitute for the current policy of containment one of the liberation of the nations presently the captives of Russian Communism. This objective can be compatible with the utopian or realist position, but the policies designed to secure it will be fundamentally different according to whether they are based upon one or the other position. The clearest case to date for the utopian justification of such policies has been made by Representative Charles J. Kersten of Wisconsin who pointed to these four "basic defects" of the "negative policy of containment and negotiated coexistence":

> It would be immoral and unchristian to negotiate a permanent agreement with forces which by every religious creed and moral precept are evil. It abandons nearly one-half of humanity and the once free nations

of Poland, Czechoslovakia, Hungary, Rumania, Bulgaria, Albania, Lithuania, Latvia, Estonia and China to enslavement of the Communist police state.

It is un-American because it violates the principle of the American Declaration of Independence, which proclaims the rights of all people to freedom and their right and duty to throw off tyranny.

It will lead to all-out World War III because it aligns all the forces of the non-Communist world in military opposition to and against all the forces of the Communist world, including the 800,000,000 peoples behind the Iron Curtain.

The policy of mere containment is uneconomic and will lead to national bankruptcy.

This statement is interesting for its straightforwardness and because it combines in a rather typical fashion considerations of abstract morality and of expediency. The captive nations must be liberated not only because their captivity is immoral, unchristian, and un-American, but also because its continuation will lead to a third world war and to national bankruptcy. To what extent, however, these considerations of expediency are invalidated by their utopian setting will become obvious from a comparison between the utopian and the realist positions.

From the utopian point of view there can be no difference between the liberation of Estonia or Czechoslovakia, of Poland or China; the captivity of any nation, large or small, close or far away, is a moral outrage which cannot be tolerated. The realist, too, seeks the liberation of all captive nations because he realizes that the presence of the Russian armies in the heart of Europe and their cooperation with the Chinese armies constitute the two main sources of the imbalance of power which threatens our security. Yet before he formulates a program of liberation, he will seek answers to a number of questions such as these: While the United States has a general interest in the liberation of all captive nations, what is the hierarchy of interests it has in the liberation, say, of China, Estonia, and Hungary? And while the Soviet Union has a general interest in keeping all captive nations in that state, what is the hierarchy of its interests in keeping, say, Poland, Eastern Germany, and Bulgaria captive? If we assume, as we must on the historic evidence of two centuries, that Russia would never give up control over Poland without being compelled by force of arms, would the objective of the liberation of Poland justify the ruin of western civilization, that of Poland included, which would be the certain result of a third world war? What resources does the United States have at its disposal for the liberation of all captive nations or some of them? What resources does the Soviet Union have at its disposal to keep in captivity all captive nations or some of them? Are we more likely to avoid national bankruptcy by embarking upon a policy of indiscriminate liberation with the concomitant certainty of war or by continuing the present policy of containment?

It might be that in a particular instance the policies suggested by the answers to these questions will coincide with Representative Kersten's proposals, but there can be no doubt that in its overall character, substance, emphasis, and likely consequences a utopian policy of liberation differs fundamentally from a realist one.

The issue between liberation as a utopian principle of abstract morality *vs.* the realist evaluation of the consequences which a policy of liberation would have for the survival of the nation has arisen before in American history. Abraham Lincoln was faced with a dilemma similar to that which confronts us today. Should he make the liberation of the slaves the ultimate standard of his policy even at the risk of destroying the Union, as many urged him to do, or should he subordinate the moral principle of universal freedom to considerations of the national interest? The answer Lincoln gave to Horace Greeley, a spokesman for the utopian moralists, is timeless in its eloquent wisdom. "If there be those," he wrote on August 22, 1862,

> who would not save the Union unless they could at the same time save slavery, I do not agree with them. If there be those who would not save the Union unless they could at the same time destroy slavery, I do not agree with them. My paramount object in this struggle *is* to save the Union, and is *not* either to save or destroy slavery. If I could save the Union without freeing *any* slave I would do it, and if I could save it by freeing *all* the slaves, I would do it; and if I could save it by freeing some and leaving others alone I would also do that. What I do about slavery, and the colored race, I do because I believe it helps to save the Union; and what I forbear, I forbear because I do *not* believe it would help to save the Union. I shall do *less* whenever I shall believe what I am doing hurts the cause, and I shall do *more* whenever I shall believe doing more will help the cause. I shall try to correct errors when shown to be errors; and I shall adopt new views so fast as they appear to be true views.
>
> I have here stated my purpose according to my view of *official* duty; and I intend no modification of my oft-expressed *personal* wish that all men everywhere could be free.

The foregoing discussion ought to shed additional light, if this is still needed, upon the moral merits of the utopian and realist positions. . . .

The realist recognizes that a moral decision, especially in the political sphere, does not imply a simple choice between a moral principle and a standard of action which is morally irrelevant or even outright immoral. A moral decision implies always a choice among different moral principles, one of which is given precedence over others. To say that a political action has no moral purpose is absurd; for political action can be defined as an attempt to realize moral values through the medium of politics, that is, power. The relevant moral question concerns the choice among different moral values, and it is at this point that the realist and the utopian part company again. If an American statesman must choose between the promotion of universal liberty, which is a moral good, at the risk of American security and, hence, of liberty in the United States, and the promotion of American security and of liberty in the United States, which is another moral good, to the detriment of the promotion of universal liberty, which choice ought he to make? The utopian will not face the issue squarely and will deceive himself into believing that he can achieve both goods at the same time. The realist will choose the national interest on both moral and pragmatic grounds; for if he does not take care of the national interest nobody else will, and if he puts American security and liberty in jeopardy the cause of liberty everywhere will be impaired.

Finally, the political realist distinguishes between his moral sympathies and the political interests which he must defend. He will distinguish with Lincoln between his *"official* duty" which is to protect the national interest and his *"personal* wish" which is to see universal moral values realized throughout the world. . . .

The contest between utopianism and realism is not tantamount to a contest between principle and expediency, morality and immorality, although some spokesmen for the former would like to have it that way. The contest is rather between one type of political morality and another type of political morality, one taking as its standard universal moral principles abstractly formulated, the other weighing these principles against the moral requirements of concrete political action, their relative merits to be decided by a prudent evaluation of the political consequences to which they are likely to lead.

These points are re-emphasized by the foregoing discussion. Which attitude with regard to collective security and to the liberation of the captive nations, the utopian or the realist, is more likely to safeguard the survival of the United States in its territorial, political, and cultural identity and at the same time to contribute the most to the security and liberty of other nations? This is the ultimate test—political and moral—by which utopianism and realism must be judged.

ROBERT ENDICOTT OSGOOD
Ideals and Self-Interest

There is no virtue in a nation's being able to achieve its ends if those ends are not worth achieving. Obviously, I am not just interested in the stability and effectiveness of America's foreign relations as one might be interested in the adjustment of the Hopi Indians to their social and physical environment, without passing any judgment on the moral purpose and consequence of such an adjustment. . . .

Self-Interest Without Ideals is Self-Defeating

Fundamentally, there is no justification for ideals beyond the ideals themselves. They are matters of faith, not empirical propositions. But, if one assumes the worth of the Christian-liberal-humanitarian ideals, as this essay does, then it is relevant to understand that the calculation and pursuit of national self-interest without regard for universal ideals is not only immoral but self-

Professor, School of Advanced International Studies, and Director, Washington Center of Foreign Policy Research, Johns Hopkins University. This selection is from Robert Endicott Osgood, *Ideals and Self Interest in America's Foreign Relations* (Chicago, University of Chicago Press, 1953), pp. 20, 442-444, 446-451, and 23.

defeating. Any assessment of the conditions for achieving a nation's international ends which ignores this fact is unrealistic.

If one believes that the enrichment of the individual's life, and not the aggrandizement of the state, is the ultimate goal of politics, if one believes that the object of survival is not mere breathing but the fulfillment of the liberal and humane values of Western civilization, then the preservation and the promotion of American power and interests cannot be an end in itself; it is but a means to an end. This is not just a theoretical consideration. It has practical implications for the conduct of America's foreign relations, and for her domestic affairs too, in the present time of troubles.

National security, like danger, is an uncertain quality; it is relative, not absolute; it is largely subjective and takes countless forms according to a variety of international circumstances. Under the complex circumstances of a worldwide power conflict the bounds of self-preservation are vastly extended, until there is scarcely any aspect of foreign policy that does not involve the nation's safety. Under the impact of persistent fear and tension national security becomes even more protean and nebulous, so that the notion of self-defense tends to become absorbed in the notion of self-assertion, and the assertion of national pride, honor, prestige, and power tends to become an end in itself. But when the preservation or aggrandizement of national power becomes an end in itself, the search for security will have defeated its very purpose; for according to the values which America professes to exemplify, power is meaningless unless it is a means to some ultimate goal.

If American power becomes an end in itself, American society, no less than international society, will suffer; for unless American security is measured by ideal standards transcending the national interest, it may take forms that undermine the moral basis of all social relations. If the Christian, humanitarian, and democratic values, which are the basis of America's social and political institutions, are valid at all, they are as valid outside American borders as within. Consequently, if they cease to compel respect in America's foreign relations, they will, ultimately, become ineffective in her domestic affairs. The resulting destruction of America's moral fiber through the loss of national integrity and the disintegration of ethical standards would be as great a blow to the nation as an armed attack upon her territory.

I do not mean that the standard of conduct in America's internal affairs varies in direct proportion with her standard in foreign relations. Clearly, this is not the case, for the relative anarchy of international society imposes severe limitations upon human morality, which, fortunately, do not apply to relations among groups and individuals within the structure of American society. Nevertheless, since the validity of the moral and ethical principles which form the bonds of American society is derived from their universal applicability, it would be unrealistic to suppose that the American people can maintain the vitality of these principles within their national borders while they are allowed to languish outside. If national self-interest becomes an all-consuming end in America's outlook upon international relations, it will necessarily jeopardize the strength and stability of liberal and humane values within the United States.

Woodrow Wilson and other American idealists understood the profound moral and psychological bond between America's international and her national behavior. Their mistake was in confusing what was ideally desirable with what was practically attainable. To expect nations to conform to the moral standards obeyed by groups and individuals within nations is not only utopian but, as Theodore Roosevelt asserted, ultimately destructive of both universal principles and the national advantage. But it is equally true that to reduce what is ideally desirable to what is practically attainable is to deprive the popular conscience of a standard of moral judgment which is indispensable to the progress and stability of all social relations, whether within or among nations. This is the moral dilemma posed by the impact of man's egoism upon his desire for perfection. In the past, American Realists have been too prone to ignore this dilemma by investing the unpleasant realities of national egoism with the character of normative principles. . . .

Human Nature Demands that Ideals Supplement Reason

A view of international relations which imagines that nations can in the long run achieve a stable and effective foreign policy solely by a rational calculation of the demands of national self-interest is based upon an unrealistic conception of human nature, for it is certainly utopian to expect any great number of people to have the wit to perceive or the will to follow the dictates of enlightened self-interest on the basis of sheer reason alone. Rational self-interest divorced from ideal principles is as weak and erratic a guide for foreign policy as idealism undisciplined by reason. No great mass of people is Machiavellian, least of all the American people. Americans in particular have displayed a strong aversion to the pursuit of self-interest, unless self-interest has been leavened with moral sentiment.

A genuine realist should recognize that the transcendent ideals expressed in the traditional American mission, no less than America's fundamental strategic interests, are an indispensable source of stability in America's foreign relations. The vitality and the persistence of the liberal strain of American idealism —whether manifested in anti-imperialism, the peace movement, internationalism, the search for disarmament, or anti-fascism—is evidence of this fact. However naive or misguided the proponents of this central strain of American idealism may have been during the last half-century, they have, nevertheless, tenaciously preserved its vital core, which constitutes its universal validity; and their continual reassertion of that vital core of moral purpose—a reassertion kindled by a lively conscience and a profound faculty for self-criticism— has been one of the strongest, most consistent, and most influential aspects of America's international conduct. If American idealism has, at times, been an unsettling influence upon foreign policy, it is because it has lacked the discipline of political realism; but this is largely due to America's relative isolation and security in the past, not to any fatal antithesis between realism and idealism. One can well imagine American idealism being moderated by a less utopian view of international politics—indeed signs of this development are already apparent—but a steady and effective foreign policy devoid of moral appeal is scarcely conceivable.

If the present international tension puts a premium upon a rational comprehension of the thrust of national power and self-interest in world politics, it equally demands an unwavering devotion to ideal ends transcending the national interest in order that reason be given direction and purpose. For example, we have observed that, according to a realistic view of international relations, the American people must be prepared to compromise their ideals in the short run in order to preserve and promote them in the long run. We have stated that compromise will become increasingly necessary, the longer the polarized power struggle persists; and that, therefore, the need for clear, calm reason will become correspondingly great. However, unless the people realize that reason is only the instrument for effecting compromises and not the standard for judging their effectiveness, some anxious citizens, in their growing concern for the national security, may become so habituated to compromise that they will lose sight of the ideal criteria of judgment which determine whether a compromise achieves its purpose. They may blindly settle upon the half-loaf or reject the loaf altogether, when three-quarters of the loaf is available. As fear may constrict ideals to an inflexible pattern, reason may so continually stretch ideals to suit expediency that they will lose all shape and elasticity. The end result will be the same: the undermining of that idealistic element of stability in foreign relations, which reason alone cannot supply. . . .

A preoccupation with expediency leads men to seek the minimum risk and effort in the expectation of a limited return; it dulls imagination and saps initiative. A purely selfish attitude tends to confine attention to those manifestations of power which bear directly and immediately upon the national interest; it tends to obscure those positive, constructive measures which cope with the basic social and psychological conditions behind such manifestations. Rational self-interest, by itself, fails to inspire boldness or breadth of vision. It may even corrode the national faith and paralyze the will to resist. In a sense, the collapse of France was the collapse of pure rational expediency, as expressed in the popular slogan "Why die for Danzig?" It is no accident that those American isolationists in the period preceding Pearl Harbor who were most insistent that the United States shape its foreign relations strictly according to its selfish interests were also the ones who were most blind to the real requirements of American self-interest, and the least willing to take measures that recognized the dependence of American security upon the survival of Great Britain and France; whereas those idealists who were most sensitive to the Fascist menace to Western culture and civilization were among the first to understand the necessity of undertaking revolutionary measures to sustain America's first line of defense in Europe.

In other words, a realistic conception of human nature must recognize that national egoism unenlightened by idealism may lead men to view America's self-interest too narrowly to achieve or preserve security itself, for idealism is an indispensable spur to reason in leading men to perceive and act upon the real imperatives of power politics. It limbers the imagination and impels men to look beyond the immediate circumstances of the power struggle. It places the status quo in the perspective of ultimate goals. It frees the reason to examine broadly and perceptively the variety of means for adjusting the instruments of national purpose to the ever-changing international environment. Idealism illuminates the basic human aspirations common to all people and thus sharpens men's insight into the psychological sources of national power. It excites the human sympathies which inspire men to enlarge the area of mutual national interest among peoples sharing common values. Idealism is the driving force, the dynamic element, which can dispel the inertia of habit and move men to adopt the bold, constructive measures necessary for surmounting the present crisis and the crises beyond. In the long run, it is the only impulse that can sustain the people's willingness to make the personal and national sacrifices that are indispensable for sheer survival.

The Expediency of Idealism

A true realist must recognize that ideals and self-interest are so closely interdependent that, even on grounds of national expediency, there are cogent arguments for maintaining the vitality of American idealism.

Ideals are as much an instrument of national power as the weapons of war. All manifestations of national power, including the threat of coercion, operate by influencing the thoughts and actions of human beings, whether by frightening them or by converting them. Since men are motivated by faith and moral sentiment as well as by fear and the instinct of self-preservation, the strength of America's moral reputation and the persuasiveness of the American mission are as vital a factor in the power equation as planes, ships, and tanks. One has only to recall the consequences of the rise and fall of America's moral reputation during and after World War I to understand the force of American idealism among foreign peoples.

The persuasiveness of the American mission is especially significant under the present circumstances, when the competition of ideologies is such a conspicuous feature of the power struggle between the Russian and the American orbits and when the effectiveness of American policy depends so heavily upon winning the moral and intellectual allegiance of vast numbers of people in the throes of social and nationalistic revolution. If in the eyes of millions of people living in underdeveloped areas of the world the United States ceases to stand for a positive and constructive program of social and material progress, if American ideals no longer mean anything beyond smug generalities and hypocritical rationalizations of selfish national advantage, then all the wealth and military power the United States can muster will not render these people an asset to the free world. If the nations within the Western Coalition conclude that America has lost all passion for improving the lot of common people for the sake of the people themselves, if they believe that Americans have lost interest in the vision of world peace in their overriding concern for their national self-interest, then no display of shrewd power politics will win for the United States the popular trust and admiration which American leadership requires.

Moreover, no coalition can survive through a common fear of tyranny without a common faith in liberty. If the leader of the Western Coalition ceases to sustain that faith, then who will sustain it? Because the United States is unavoidably thrust into a position of global leadership, her standards of conduct must, inevitably, have a great influence in setting the moral tone of international relations in general. Consequently, it behooves America to conduct its foreign relations in a way that will encourage the kind of international environment compatible with its ideals and interests.

That kind of environment cannot exist apart from a widespread respect for the universal ideals of peace, brotherhood, and the essential dignity of the individual. To perceive this one has but to imagine the unmitigated anarchy that would ensue if every nation identified the interests of all nations with its own interests and pursued its own independent security as a self-sufficient end without relation to universal goals; for if every nation made expediency its sole guide in foreign relations, and if every nation anticipated that every other nation was motivated solely by the improvement of its own welfare, the only bond among nations would be the concurrence of their interests. But there is no automatic harmony of interests among nations, and unadorned reason is a weak instrument for achieving the tolerance and fair play indispensable to a contrived harmony. If national self-interest were the sole standard of conduct common to nations, an improvement in the power position of one nation would set off a wave of distrust among the rest; and, eventually, the pressure of international conflict would loosen what moral and ethical restraints man has succeeded in placing on his collective behavior; international society would disintegrate into a Hobbesian state of anarchy. In the light of this prospect, it is apparent that America's moral leadership is an indispensable instrument of her survival.

We may admit the expediency of America's reputation for idealism, but we should not imagine that America's ability to gain the moral and intellectual allegiance of foreign peoples is merely a problem in the technique of propaganda. To be sure, skilful propaganda can make a vast difference in the effectiveness of America's leadership. American ideals must be interpreted with resourcefulness and imagination, according to the particular needs and aspirations of different peoples. But, no matter how clever American propaganda may be, if it is not consistent with American actions, it will be of little value as an instrument of policy and may well alienate its intended converts. At the same time, the actions of the United States must, in the long run, reflect the actual state of American opinion; for no foreign program, least of all one of international benevolence, will survive long in a democracy if it is contrary to public opinion, and it would be extremely unrealistic to expect Americans to support such a program for its propagandistic worth if they did not also believe in its moral worth. It follows that a sincere and widespread devotion to positive ideals of human betterment is a prerequisite for effective propaganda, for Americans cannot pretend to be idealists without being truly idealistic. American idealism cannot be exported like American machinery and weapons. The United States is a democracy, and, therefore, official propaganda, in its broad outlines, must be believed to be effective. Otherwise, it will be undermined at home, foreign peoples will see that it is undermined, and American idealism will be marked down as deception and hypocrisy. Therefore, genuine conviction becomes necessary in order to sustain the appearance of idealism demanded by sheer national expediency. It is fortunate for the survival of democratic government that this paradox exists. . . .

To recognize the points of coincidence between national self-interest and supranational ideals is one of the highest tasks of statesmanship. The last half-century of Anglo-American relations demonstrates that men can recognize and even multiply the points of coincidence by patiently building upon a foundation of mutual self-interest to enlarge the area of international confidence and respect. It seems likely that the greatest advances in international morality in the foreseeable future will be brought about by men with enough vision and good will to temper the more immediate or extreme demands of national self-interest with the superior demands of a long-run interest in international compromise and the rational, peaceful settlement of differences. In this imperfect world it is neither too much nor too little to expect that man's recognition of the coincidence of ideals with national self-interest may mitigate and enlighten the thrust of national egoism.

✍✍✍TOPIC 32

China and U.S. Foreign Policy

EDWARD M. KENNEDY
We Must Seek a New Policy

For twenty years, our China policy has been a war policy. For far too long, we have carried out hostile measures of political, diplomatic, and economic antagonism toward one of the world's most important nations.

Now we must turn away from our policy of war and pursue a policy of peace. We must seek a new policy, not because of any supposed weakness in our present position or because we are soft on China, but because it is in our own national interest and the interest of all nations. By its sheer size and population, China deserves a major place in the world. As a nuclear power and a nation of 750 million citizens—likely to exceed one billion by the 1980's—China demands a voice in world efforts to deal with arms control and population control, with Asian security and international economic development, with all the great issues of our time.

Yet sixteen years after the end of the Korean War, we do not trade with China. We have no scientific or cultural exchanges. We oppose the representation of China in the United Nations. We refuse to give any sort of diplomatic recognition to the Communist regime on the mainland, and continue to recognize the Nationalist regime of Chiang Kai-Shek on Taiwan as the government of all China. Instead of developing ways to coexist with China in peace, we assume China will attack us as soon as she can, and we prepare to spend billions to meet that threat.

By some cruel paradox, an entire generation of young Americans and young Chinese have grown to maturity with their countries in a state of suspended war toward one another. Tragically, the world's oldest civilization and the world's most modern civilization, the world's most populous nation and the world's richest and most powerful nation, glare at each other across the abyss of nuclear war.

The division between us goes back to American support of the Chinese Nationalist regime during World War II, and to the immediate post-war struggle between the Communists and the Nationalists. In the beginning, our policy

United States Senator from the state of Massachusetts. The following is from a speech delivered by Senator Kennedy on March 20, 1969 before the National Committee on United States-China Relations.

was uncertain. The Communists gained power over the mainland in 1949. Between then and the outbreak of the Korean War in 1950, the United States seemed to be preparing to accept the fact of the Chinese Revolution. After the retreat of the Nationalists to Taiwan, our government refused to go to their aid and refused to place the American Seventh Fleet in the Taiwan Strait to prevent a Communist takeover of the island. To do so, we said, would be to intervene in the domestic civil war between the Communists and the Nationalists.

This policy was fully debated by the Congress and the public. Although we deplored the Communist rise to power, we recognized we could do nothing to change it. We anticipated that we would soon adjust to the new Asian reality by establishing relations with the Communist regime.

This situation changed overnight on June 25, 1950, when North Korea attacked South Korea. Fearing that the attack foreshadowed a Communist offensive throughout Asia, the United States ordered the Seventh Fleet into the Taiwan Strait and sent large amounts of military aid to the weak Nationalist Government on the island. To the Communists, the meaning was clear. We would use force to deny Taiwan to the new mainland government, even though both the Communists and the Nationalists agreed the island was Chinese.

Shortly thereafter, in response to the attempt of our forces to bring down the North Korean Government by driving toward the Chinese border, China entered the Korean War. With hindsight, most experts agree that China's action in Korea was an essentially defensive response, launched to prevent the establishment of a hostile government on her border. At the time, however, the issue was far less clear. At the request of the United States, the United Nations formally branded China as an aggressor, a stigma that rankles Peking's leaders even today.

While we fought the Chinese in Korea, we carried out a series of political and economic actions against their country. We imposed a total embargo on all American trade with the mainland. We froze Peking's assets in the United States. We demanded that our allies limit their trade with China. We conducted espionage and sabotage operations against the mainland, and supported similar efforts by the Nationalists. We began to construct a chain of bases, encircling China with American military power, including nuclear weapons.

It is not my purpose here to question the merits of the actions we took while fighting China in Korea. We all remember the climate of those times and the great concern of our country with Chinese military actions. Today, however, sixteen years after the Korean armistice was signed, we have taken almost no significant steps to abandon our posture of war toward China and to develop relations of peace.

Let us look at our policy from the viewpoint of Peking: China's leaders see the United States supporting the Nationalists' pretense to be the government of the mainland. They see thousands of American military personnel on Taiwan. American warships guard the waters between the mainland and Taiwan. American nuclear bases and submarines ring the periphery of China. The United States supports Nationalist U-2 flights over the mainland, as well as Nationalist guerrilla raids and espionage. Hundreds of thousands of American soldiers are fighting in Vietnam to contain China. America applies constant diplomatic and political pressure to deny Peking a seat in the United Nations, to deny it diplomatic recognition by the nations of the world, and to deny it freedom of trade. We turn our nuclear warheads toward China. And now we prepare to build a vast ABM system to protect ourselves against China. In light of all these facts, what Chinese leader would dare to propose anything but the deepest hostility toward the United States?

With respect to the ABM question, I am strongly opposed for many reasons to the deployment of the Pentagon's system. For the purpose of the present discussion, however, one of its most significant drawbacks is that it is likely to be seen in Peking as a new military provocation by the United States. Our overwhelming nuclear arsenal already provides adequate deterrence against any temptation by Peking to engage in a first strike against the United States. From the Chinese perspective, the only utility of an American ABM system is to defend the United States against whatever feeble response Peking could muster after an American first strike against China. Far from deterring aggression by China, therefore, deployment of the ABM system will simply add fuel to our warlike posture toward China. It will increase Chinese fears of American attack and will encourage China's leaders to embark on new steps in the development of their nuclear capability. Apart from the technical and other policy objections that exist against the ABM system, I believe it makes no sense from the standpoint of a rational Asia policy for America.

In large part, our continuing hostility toward China after the Korean War has rested on a hope that is now obviously forlorn, a hope that under a policy of military containment and political isolation the Communist regime on the mainland would be a passing phenomenon and would eventually be repudiated by the Chinese people. Few of us today have any serious doubt that Communism is permanent for the foreseeable future on the mainland. There is no believable prospect that Chiang Kai-Shek and the Nationalists will return to power there, however regrettable we may regard that fact.

Surely, in the entire history of American foreign policy, there has been no fiction more palpably absurd than our official position that Communist China does not exist. For twenty years, the Nationalists have controlled only the two million Chinese and eleven million Taiwanese on the island of Taiwan, one hundred miles from the mainland of China. How long will we continue to insist that the rulers of Taiwan are also the rulers of the hundreds of millions of Chinese on the millions of square miles of the mainland? It is as though the island of Cuba were to claim sovereignty over the entire continent of North America.

The folly of our present policy of isolating China is matched by its futility. Almost all other nations have adjusted to the reality of China. For years, Peking has had extensive diplomatic, commercial and cultural relations with a number of the nations in the world, including many of our closest allies. Outside the United Nations, our policy of quarantine toward China has failed. To the extent that the Communist regime is isolated at all, it is isolated largely at China's own choosing, and not as a consequence of any effective American policy.

Our actions toward China have rested on the premise that the People's

Republic is an illegitimate, evil and expansionist regime that must be contained until it collapses or at least begins to behave in conformity with American interests. Secretary of State Dulles was the foremost exponent of this moralistic view, carrying it to the extent that he even refused to shake hands with Chou En-Lai at the Geneva Conference in 1954. That slight has not been forgotten.

The Communist regime was said to be illegitimate because, we claimed, it had been imposed on the supposedly unreceptive Chinese people by agents of the Soviet Union. Communist China, according to this view, was a mere Soviet satellite. One Assistant Secretary in the State Department called it a Soviet Manchukuo, suggesting that China's new leaders were no more independent than were the Chinese puppets whom Japan installed in Manchuria in the 1930's. This evaluation grossly exaggerated the extent to which Soviet aid was responsible for the Communist takeover of China, and the events of the past decade—amply confirmed by the intense hostility of the current border clashes—have shattered the myth of Soviet domination of China.

The Communist regime was said to be evil because of the great violence and deprivation of freedom that it inflicted on millions of people who opposed its rise to power. Obviously, we cannot condone the appalling cost, in human life and suffering, of the Chinese Revolution. Yet, in many other cases, we have recognized revolutionary regimes, especially when the period of revolutionary excess has passed. Even in the case of the Soviet Union, the United States waited only 16 years to normalize relations with the revolutionary government.

Unfortunately, we have tended to focus exclusively on the costs of the Chinese revolution. We have ignored the historical conditions that evoked it and the social and economic gains it produced. We have ignored the fact that the Nationalists also engaged in repressive measures and deprivations of freedom, not only during their tenure on the mainland, but also on Taiwan. We have created a false image of a struggle between "Free China" and "Red China," between good and evil. Given our current perspective and the greater understanding of revolutionary change that has come with time, we can now afford a more dispassionate and accurate review of the Chinese Revolution.

Finally, there is the charge that the Communist regime is an expansionist power. At bottom, it is this view that has given rise to our containment policy in Asia, with the enormous sacrifices it has entailed. The charge that the Communist regime is expansionist has meant different things at different times. On occasion, American spokesmen have conjured up the image of a "Golden Horde" or "Yellow Peril" that would swoop down over Asia. Today, most leaders in Washington employ more responsible rhetoric, and it is the Russians who perpetuate this image of China.

Virtually no experts on China expect Peking to commit aggression, in the conventional sense of forcibly occupying the territory of another country—as the Soviet Union recently occupied Czechoslovakia. Such action is in accord with neither past Chinese actions nor present Chinese capabilities. Despite their ideological bombast, the Chinese Communists have in fact been extremely cautious about risking military involvement since the Korean War. The Quemoy crises of the 1950's and the 1962 clash with India were carefully limited engagements. The struggle over Tibet is widely regarded as reassertion of traditional Chinese jurisdiction over that remote area. China has not used force to protect the overseas Chinese in the disturbances in Burma, Malaysia, or Indonesia. Her navy and air force are small. She can neither transport her troops nor supply them across the long distances and difficult terrain of a prolonged war of aggression.

Obviously, our concern today is not so much the danger of direct Chinese aggression as the danger of indirect aggression, based on Chinese efforts to subvert existing governments and replace them with governments friendly to Peking. Yet, until Vietnam led to our massive involvement in Southeast Asia, Peking enjoyed only very limited success in its attempts to foster "wars of national liberation." Although China of course will claim to play a role wherever political instability occurs in Asia, Africa and even Latin America, its record of subversion is unimpressive. On the basis of the past, it is very likely that nations whose governments work for equality and social justice for their people will be able to overcome any threat of Chinese subversion.

Furthermore, we can expect that time will moderate China's revolutionary zeal. Experience with the Soviet Union and the Eastern European Communist nations suggests that the more fully China is brought into the world community, the greater will be the pressure to behave like a nation-state, rather than a revolutionary power.

Ironically, it is Communist China's former teacher, the Soviet Union, that is now determined to prevent any moderation of Chinese-American hostility. We cannot accept at face value the current Soviet image of China, for the Soviets have far different interests in Asia than we do. Although we must persist in our efforts to achieve wider agreement with Moscow, we must not allow the Russians to make continuing hostility toward Peking the price of future Soviet-American cooperation. Rather than retard our relations with Moscow, a Washington-Peking thaw might well provide the Soviet Union with a badly needed incentive to improve relations with us.

We must not, however, regard relations with Peking and Moscow as an "either/or" proposition. We must strive to improve relations with both. We must be alert, therefore, to any opportunity offered by the escalating hostility between China and the Soviet Union to ease our own tensions with those nations.

Both of us—Chinese and Americans alike—are prisoners of the passions of the past. What we need now, and in the decades ahead, is liberation from those passions. Given the history of our past relations with China, it is unrealistic to expect Peking to take the initiative. It is our obligation. We are the great and powerful nation, and we should not condition our approach on any favorable action or change of attitude by Peking. For us to begin a policy of peace would be a credit to our history and our place in the world today. To continue on our present path will lead only to further hostility, and the real possibility of mutual destruction.

Of course, we must not delude ourselves. Even if the United States moves toward an enlightened China policy, the foreseeable prospects for moderating Chinese-American tensions are not bright. It is said that there is no basis for hope so long as the current generation of Communist Chinese leaders remains in power. This may well be true. Yet, Peking's invitation last November to resume the Warsaw talks, although now withdrawn, suggests the possibility that China's policy may change more rapidly than outside observers can now anticipate.

We must remember, too, that the regime in Peking is not a monolith. As the upheavals of the Great Leap Forward and the Cultural Revolution have shown, China's leaders are divided by conflicting views and pressures for change. We must seek to influence such change in a favorable direction. We can do so by insuring that reasonable options for improved relations with the United States are always available to Peking's moderate or less extreme leaders.

The steps that we take should be taken soon. Even now, the deterioration of Chinese-Soviet relations in the wake of the recent border clashes may be stimulating at least some of the leaders in Peking to re-evaluate their posture toward the United States and provide us with an extraordinary opportunity to break the bonds of distrust.

What can we do to hasten the next opportunity? Many of us here tonight are already on record as favoring a more positive stand. We must actively encourage China to adopt the change in attitude for which we now simply wait. We must act now to make clear to the Chinese and to the world that the responsibility for the present impasse no longer lies with us.

First, and most important, we should proclaim our willingness to adopt a new policy toward China—a policy of peace, not war, a policy that abandons the old slogans, embraces today's reality, and encourages tomorrow's possibility. We should make clear that we regard China as a legitimate power in control of the mainland, entitled to full participation as an equal member of the world community and to a decent regard for its own security. The policy I advocate will in no way impede our ability to respond firmly and effectively to any possibility of attack by the Chinese. What it will do, however, is emphasize to China that our military posture is purely defensive, and that we stand ready at all times to work toward improvement in our relations.

Second, we should attempt to reconvene the Warsaw talks. At the time the talks were cancelled, I wrote the Secretary of State, asking the Administration to make an urgent new attempt to establish the contact that we so nearly achieved at Warsaw, and to do so before the air of expectancy that hung over the talks is completely dissipated. If the talks are resumed, we should attempt to transform them into a more confidential and perhaps more significant dialogue. The parties might meet on an alternating basis in their respective embassies, or even in their respective countries, rather than in a palace of the Polish Government. Whether or not the talks are resumed, more informal official and semi-official conversations with China's leaders should be offered.

Third, we should unilaterally do away with restrictions on travel and nonstrategic trade. We should do all we can to promote exchanges of people and ideas, through scientific and cultural programs and access by news media representatives. In trade, we should place China on the same footing as the Soviet Union and the Communist nations of Eastern Europe. We should offer to send trade delegations and even a resident trade mission to China, and to receive Chinese trade delegations and a Chinese trade mission in this country. Finally, we should welcome closer contacts between China and the rest of the world, rather than continue to exert pressure on our friends to isolate the Peking regime.

Fourth, we should announce our willingness to re-establish the consular offices we maintained in the People's Republic during the earliest period of Communist rule, and we should welcome Chinese consular officials in the United States. Consular relations facilitate trade and other contacts. They frequently exist in the absence of diplomatic relations, and often pave the way for the establishment of such relations.

Fifth, we should strive to involve the Chinese in serious arms control talks. We should actively encourage them to begin to participate in international conferences, and we should seek out new opportunities to discuss Asian security and other problems.

Sixth, we should seek, at the earliest opportunity, to discuss with China's leaders the complex question of the establishment of full diplomatic relations. For the present, we should continue our diplomatic relations with the Nationalist regime on Taiwan and guarantee the people of that island against any forcible takeover by the mainland. To Peking at this time, the question of diplomatic recognition seems to be unavoidably linked to the question of whether we will withdraw recognition from the Nationalists and the question of whether Taiwan is part of the territory of China. Both the Communists and the Nationalists claim Taiwan as part of China, but our own government regards the status of the island as undefined, even though we maintain diplomatic relations with the Nationalists.

We have failed to agree on solutions involving other divided countries and peoples—as in Germany—and we cannot be confident of greater success in the matter of Taiwan. There are critical questions that simply cannot now be answered:

• Will the minority regime of the Chinese Nationalists continue to control the island's Taiwanese population?
• Will the Taiwanese majority eventually transform the island's government through the exercise of self-determination?
• Will an accommodation be worked out between a future Taiwan Government and the Peking regime on the mainland?

To help elicit Peking's interest in negotiations, we should withdraw our token American military presence from Taiwan. This demilitarization of Taiwan could take place at no cost to our treaty commitments, or to the security of the island. Yet, it would help to make clear to Peking our desire for the Communists, the Nationalists, and the Taiwanese to reach a negotiated solution on the status of the island.

A dramatic step like unilateral recognition of Peking would probably be an empty gesture at this time. As the experience of France implies, unilateral recognition of Peking is not likely to be effective unless it is accompanied by the withdrawal of our existing recognition of the Nationalists. And, as the case of Great Britain suggests, Peking may insist on our recognition of the mainland's claim to Taiwan before allowing us to establish full ambassadorial relations. These problems will have to be negotiated, and we should move now to start the process.

Seventh, without waiting for resolution of the complex question of Taiwan, we should withdraw our opposition to Peking's entry into the United Nations as the representative of China, not only in the General Assembly, but also in the Security Council and other organs. The Security Council seat was granted to China in 1945 in recognition of a great people who had borne a major share of the burden in World War II, thereby making the United Nations possible. It was not a reward for the particular political group that happened to be running the country at the time.

In addition, we should work within the United Nations to attempt to assure representation for the people on Taiwan that will reflect the island's governmental status. It may be that the Chinese Nationalists can continue to enjoy a seat in the General Assembly. Or, if an independent republic of Taiwan emerges, it might be admitted into the United Nations as a new state. Possibly, if a political accommodation is reached between the Communist regime on the mainland and the government on Taiwan, the people of Taiwan might be represented in the United Nations as an autonomous unit of China, by analogy to the present status of Byelorussia and the Ukraine in the United Nations as autonomous provinces of the Soviet Union.

From its inception, the United Nations has displayed remarkable flexibility in adjusting to political realities. There are many possible solutions to the China problem in the United Nations. Without insisting on any one, we should move now to free the United Nations to undertake the long-delayed process of adjusting to the reality of the People's Republic of China, and we should clearly indicate to Peking our willingness to discuss these questions.

In dealing with the problems of diplomatic recognition and United Nations representation, I have placed primary emphasis on the need to initiate discussions with Peking in these areas. Since it is impossible to predict when or how the Chinese will respond to a change in American policy, we cannot maintain a hard and fast position on these questions. We cannot afford to close any options by endorsing detailed schemes at this time. What we can do, however, is act now on the broad range of initiatives I have mentioned, and make clear to Peking that our views are not rigid on even the most difficult issues that have divided us so bitterly in recent years.

We will have to be patient. Peking's initial reaction to serious initiatives on our part will probably be a blunt refusal. But, by laying the groundwork for an improved relationship in the Seventies and beyond, we will be offering the present and future leaders in Peking a clear and attractive alternative to the existing impasse in our relations.

Many outstanding authorities on China are here tonight. Perhaps I can sum up my central theme in terms that you may find appropriate. According to Chinese tradition, the model Confucian gentleman was taught that, whenever involved in a dispute, he should first examine his own behavior, ask himself whether he bears some responsibility for the dispute, and take the initiative to try to arrive at a harmonious settlement.

It may prove futile for us to follow this advice when dealing with Chinese who claim to reject many of China's great traditions. But we will never know unless we try. If nothing changes, we Americans will have to live with the consequences of arms and fear and war. We owe ourselves, we owe the future, a heavy obligation to try.

DEAN RUSK
Statement of the United States Policy

Mr. Chairman, during the last month and a half this distinguished committee and its corresponding members in the other house have heard testimony on Communist China from a number of prominent scholars and distinguished experts on Asia.

I welcome these hearings. For Communist China's policies and intentions, in all their aspects, need to be examined—and reexamined continually.

The Department of State and other agencies of the Government do collect, study, and analyze continually with the greatest care all the information obtainable on Communist China in order to make—and, when the facts warrant, revise —judgments of Peiping's intentions and objectives. . . .

Three Caveats

Before going further, I would like to enter three caveats:

First, the experts do not always agree, especially in their estimates of Chinese Communist intentions.

Second, the leaders we are discussing are both Chinese and Communist. Some of their words and acts can perhaps be best understood in terms of Chinese background—Chinese traits or historic Chinese ambitions. Others can perhaps be better understood in terms of their beliefs and ambitions as Communists. They are deeply committed to a body of Communist doctrine developed by Mao Tse-tung. Still other words and acts may be consistent with both the Chinese and doctrinaire Communist factors.

We have faced a similar problem over the years with respect to the Soviet leadership. Some of their words and acts could be explained chiefly in terms of historic Russian imperial ambitions or Russian traits or practices. Others have been clearly attributable to Marxist-Leninist doctrine, or to interpretations of that doctrine by Stalin and more recent leaders. Some sovietologists put more emphasis on the traditional or imperial factors, others put more on the Marxist-Leninist factors. There is no way to determine the exact weight which ought to be given to each of these two influences.

Likewise, with regard to the Chinese Communists, there has been considerable disagreement over the respective dimensions of the two streams of influence: Chinese and Marxist-Leninist-Maoist. Over the years some of the experts on China may not have appreciated adequately Marxist-Leninist-Maoist doctrine. Likewise, some of the experts on Chinese Communist doctrine may tend

Formerly U.S. Secretary of State, now associated with the Rockefeller Foundation. This is from a statement made by then Secretary of State Rusk before the Far East and Pacific Subcommittee of the House Foreign Affairs Committee, March 16, 1966.

to underestimate the Chinese factors in the behavior and intentions of the Peiping regime.

The third caveat is this: Predicting what the Chinese Communists will do next may be even more hazardous than usual at this juncture. They themselves appear to be taking stock. . . .

Chinese Communist Setbacks

We know—the whole world knows—that the Chinese Communists have suffered some severe setbacks internationally during the past 14 months. They were unable to persuade the Afro-Asians to accept their substantive views on the Second Bandung Conference. They have found themselves in difficulty in several African countries. Their diplomatic missions have been expelled from Burundi, Dahomey, and the Central African Republic. Their technicians have been expelled from Ghana. The Governments of Kenya and Tunisia have warned them against promoting revolution in Africa.

During the fighting between India and Pakistan, the Chinese Communists marched up hill and down again. They have been disappointed by the Tashkent agreement and the steps taken in accord with it. They were strongly opposed to the agreement between Japan and the Republic of Korea, which was ratified by both countries. They have suffered a major setback in Indonesia—the Indonesian Communist Party has been decimated.

Generally, in their struggle with Moscow for leadership of the world Communist movement, the Chinese Communists appear to have lost ground. Even their relations with Castro's Cuba have sunk to the level of mudslinging.

And, probably most important of all, Peiping sees the power of the United States committed in Southeast Asia to repel an aggression supported—and actively promoted—by Peiping.

Will the Chinese Communist reaction to all these setbacks be a wild lashing out? Or will it be a sober decision to draw back and even to move toward peaceful coexistence?

We, of course, hope it will be the latter. But we cannot be sure what Peiping intends to do. We do not expect the worst but we must be prepared for it.

Our Relations With Peiping

I will not try here today to review in detail the record of our relations with the Peiping regime. In the months after the Chinese Communist takeover in 1949 we watched to see whether the initial demonstration of intense hostility toward the United States and toward Americans who were still resident in China was momentary, or reflected a basic Peiping policy. Then came the aggression against the Republic of Korea, to which, at a second stage, the Chinese Communists committed large forces, thus coming into direct conflict with the United Nations and the United States.

We have searched year after year for some sign that Communist China was ready to renounce the use of force to resolve disputes. We have also searched for some indication that it was ready to abandon its premise that the United States is its prime enemy.

The Chinese Communist attitudes and actions have been hostile and rigid. But a democracy, such as ours, does not accept rigidity. It seeks solutions to problems, however intractable they may seem.

We have discussed various problems with the Chinese Communists at international conferences such as the Geneva conferences of 1954 and 1962.

In 1955 we began with them a series of bilateral conversations at the level of ambassadors, first in Geneva and later in Warsaw. It was our hope that by direct, systematic communication we might be able to reduce the sharpness of the conflict between us. There now have been 129 of these meetings, the latest of which took place in Warsaw today.

These exchanges have ranged widely, covering many subjects affecting our two countries. At first there was a little progress in dealing with small specific issues, such as the release of Americans being held in Communist China. Although an understanding was reached in this limited area, Peiping refused to fulfill its commitment to release all the Americans.

I think it is accurate to say that no other non-Communist nation has had such extensive conversations with the Peiping regime as we have had. The problem is not lack of contact between Peiping and Washington. It is what, with contact, the Peiping regime itself says and does.

Although they have produced almost no tangible results, these conversations have served and still serve useful purposes. They permit us to clarify the numerous points of difference between us. They enable us to communicate in private during periods of crisis. They provide an opening through which, hopefully, light might one day penetrate. But the talks have, so far, given no evidence of a shift or easing in Peiping's hostility toward the United States and its bellicose doctrines of world revolution. Indeed, the Chinese Communists have consistently demanded, privately as well as publicly, that we let them have Taiwan. And when we say that we will not abandon the 12 or 13 million people on Taiwan, against their will, they say that, until we change our minds about that, no improvement in relations is possible.

Today we and Peiping are as far apart on matters of fundamental policy as we were 17 years ago.

The Basic Issues

In assessing Peiping's policies and actions, and the problems they present to American foreign policy and to the free peoples of the world, we must ask ourselves certain key questions:

What does Peiping want, and how does it pursue its objectives?

How successful has it been, and how successful is it likely to be in the future?

Is it on a collision course with the United States?

What are the prospects for change in its policies?

What policies should the United States adopt, or work toward, in dealing with Communist China?

First, the Chinese Communist leaders seek to bring China on the world stage as a great power. They hold that China's history, size, and geographic position entitle it to great-power status. They seek to overcome the humiliation of 150 years of economic, cultural, and political domination by outside powers.

Our concern is with the way they are pursuing their quest for power and influence in the world. And it is not only our concern but that of many other countries, including in recent years the Soviet Union.

Peiping is aware that it still lacks many of the attributes of great-power status, and it chafes bitterly under this realization.

The Chinese Communists are determined to rectify this situation. They already have one of the largest armies in the world. They are now developing nuclear weapons and missile delivery systems. They are pouring a disproportionately large proportion of their industrial and scientific effort into military and military-related fields.

What is all this military power for? Some believe it to be for defensive purposes alone:

To erect a token "deterrent" nuclear capability against the United States or the U.S.S.R.;

To demonstrate symbolically that "China must be reckoned with";

To react to an imaginary, almost pathological, notion that the United States and other countries around its borders are seeking an opportunity to invade mainland China and destroy the Peiping regime.

But such weapons need not serve a defensive role. They can be used directly by Peiping to try to intimidate its neighbors, or in efforts to blackmail Asian countries into breaking defense alliances with the United States, or in an attempt to create a nuclear "balance" in Asia in which Peiping's potentially almost unlimited conventional forces might be used with increased effect.

These weapons can ultimately be employed to attack Peiping's Asian neighbors and, in time, even the United States or the Soviet Union. This would be mad and suicidal, as Peiping must know, despite cavalier statements that mainland China can survive nuclear war. Nevertheless, a potential nuclear capability, on top of enormous conventional forces, represents a new factor in the equilibrium of power in Asia that this country and its friends and allies cannot ignore.

Peiping's use of power is closely related to what I believe are its second and third objectives: dominance within Asia and leadership of the Communist world revolution, employing Maoist tactics. Peiping is striving to restore traditional Chinese influence or dominance in South, Southeast, and East Asia. Its concept of influence is exclusive. Foreign Minister Ch'en Yi reportedly told Prince Sihanouk recently that his country's "friendship" with Cambodia would be incompatible with Cambodian ties with the United States. Peiping has tried to alienate North Viet Nam and North Korea from the Soviet Union. It has had uneven success in such maneuvers. But it has not abandoned this objective. Where Peiping is present, it seeks to exclude all others. And this is not only true in its relations with its neighbors but in the Communist world as well.

Peiping has not refrained from the use of force to pursue its objectives. Following Korea, there were Tibet and the attacks on the offshore islands in the Taiwan Straits. There have been the attacks on India. It is true that, since Korea, Peiping has moved only against weaker foes and has carefully avoided situations which might bring it face to face with the United States. It has probed for weaknesses around its frontier but drawn back when the possibility of a wider conflict loomed.

While the massive and direct use of Chinese Communist troops in overt aggression cannot be ruled out, Peiping's behavior up to now suggests it would approach any such decision with caution.

If the costs and risks of a greater use of force were reduced by, for example, our unilateral withdrawal from the region, Peiping might well feel freer to use its power to intimidate or overwhelm a recalcitrant opponent or to aid directly insurgent forces.

Mao's Doctrine of World Revolution

As I have said, the Chinese Communist leaders are dedicated to a fanatical and bellicose Marxist-Leninist-Maoist doctrine of world revolution. Last fall, Lin Piao, the Chinese Communist Minister of Defense, recapitulated in a long article Peiping's strategy of violence for achieving Communist domination of the world. This strategy involves the mobilization of the underdeveloped areas of the world—which the Chinese Communists compare to the "rural areas"— against the industrialized or "urban" areas. It involves the relentless prosecution of what they call "people's wars." The final stage of all this violence is to be what they frankly describe as "wars of annihilation."

It is true that this doctrine calls for revolution by the natives of each country. In that sense it may be considered a "do-it-yourself kit." But Peiping is prepared to train and indoctrinate the leaders of these revolutions and to support them with funds, arms, and propaganda, as well as politically. It is even prepared to manufacture these revolutionary movements out of whole cloth.

Peiping has encouraged and assisted—with arms and other means—the aggressions of the North Vietnamese Communists in Laos and against South Viet Nam. It has publicly declared its support for so-called national liberation forces in Thailand, and there are already terrorist attacks in the remote rural areas of northeast Thailand. There is talk in Peiping that Malaysia is next on the list. The basic tactics of these "wars of liberation" have been set forth by Mao and his disciples, including General Giap, the North Vietnamese Communist Minister of Defense. They progress from the undermining of independent governments and the economic and social fabrics of society by terror and assassination, through guerrilla warfare, to large-scale military action.

Peiping has sought to promote Communist coups and "wars of liberation" against independent governments in Africa and Latin America as well as in Asia.

Some say we should ignore what the Chinese Communist leaders say and judge them only by what they do. It is true that they have been more cautious in action than in words—more cautious in what they do themselves than in what they have urged the Soviet Union to do. Undoubtedly, they recognize that their power is limited. They have shown, in many ways, that they have a healthy respect for the power of the United States.

But it does not follow that we should disregard the intentions and plans for the future which they have proclaimed. To do so would be to repeat the catastrophic miscalculation that so many people made about the ambitions of

Hitler—and that many have made at various times in appraising the intentions of the Soviet leaders.

I have noted criticism of the so-called analogy between Hitler and Mao-Tse-tung. I am perfectly aware of the important differences between these two and the countries in which they have exercised power. The seizure of Manchuria by Japanese militarists, of Ethiopia by Mussolini, and of the Rhineland, Austria, and Czechoslovakia by Hitler, were laboratory experiments in the anatomy and physiology of aggression. How to deal with the phenomenon of aggression was the principal problem faced in drafting the United Nations Charter, and the answer was: collective action. We do ourselves no service by insisting that each source of aggression or each instance of aggression is unique. My own view is that we have learned a good deal about this phenomenon and its potentiality for leading into catastrophe if the problem is not met in a timely fashion.

The bellicosity of the Chinese Communists has created problems within the Communist world as well as between Peiping and the non-Communist world.

Recently a leading official of a Communist state said to me that the most serious problem in the world today is how to get Peiping to move to a policy of "peaceful coexistence."

Chinese Communist Fear of Attack

At times the Communist Chinese leaders seem to be obsessed with the notion that they are being threatened and encircled. We have told them both publicly and privately, and I believe have demonstrated in our actions in times of crisis and even under grave provocation, that we want no war with Communist China. The President restated this only last month in New York. We do not seek the overthrow by force of the Peiping regime; we do object to its attempt to overthrow other regimes by force.

How much Peiping's "fear" of the United States is genuine and how much it is artificially induced for domestic political purposes only the Chinese Communist leaders themselves know. I am convinced, however, that their desire to expel our influence and activity from the western Pacific and Southeast Asia is not motivated by fears that we are threatening them.

I wish I could believe that Communist China seeks merely a guarantee of friendly states around its borders, as some commentators have suggested. If it was as simple as this, they would have only to abandon their policies which cause their neighbors to seek help from the United States.

The trouble is that Peiping's leaders want neighboring countries to accept subordination to Chinese power. They want them to become political and economic dependencies of Peiping. If the United States can be driven from Asia, this goal will be in their grasp. The "influence," therefore, that Peiping's present leaders seek in Asia is indeed far reaching.

Dominance in the Communist Movement

. . .

One of Peiping's most fundamental differences with Moscow centers on its desire to maintain the sharpest possible polarization between the Communist world and the United States. Peiping argues that we are the "enemy of all the people in the world." Its national interests in Asia are served by maximizing Communist (and world) pressure on us and by attempting to "isolate" us. For this reason alone the Chinese would probably have opposed any Soviet attempts to reach understandings with us. In addition there are ideological and psychological reasons for Sino-Soviet rivalry:

The intense and deadly antagonisms that have always characterized schisms in the Marxist world; Mao's belief that after Stalin's death the mantle of world Communist leadership should rightfully have passed to him and the Chinese Communist party; Peiping's obsession, also held or professed by the leaders of the Soviet Union during the 30 years after the Bolshevik revolution, with a fear of being threatened and encircled; the mixture of the psychology of the veterans of the long march and Chinese traditional attitudes which has led Peiping's leaders to believe that through a combination of patience, struggle, and "right thinking" all obstacles can be conquered; and Peiping's professed belief that the Soviets are joining with the United States in keeping China in a position of inferiority and subordination: all these have merged to give the Sino-Soviet dispute a flavor and an intensity which rival even the current Chinese Communist antagonism for the United States itself.

How Successful Has Peiping Been?

We can see that the Communist Chinese have set vast goals for themselves, both internally and externally. The disastrous results of the so-called great leap forward have forced them to acknowledge that it will take them generations to achieve their goals.

They have wrought considerable changes on the mainland of China. Perhaps their greatest feat has been to establish their complete political authority throughout the country. They have made some progress in industrialization, education, and public health—although at the expense of human freedom, originality, and creativity. But their efforts to improve agriculture and to mold the Chinese people into a uniform Marxist pattern have been far less successful.

The economic, political, and social problems still confronting the Chinese Communist leaders today are staggering.

Peiping's economic power will almost certainly increase over the coming years. But even with relatively effective birth control programs the population of mainland China may reach 1 billion by 1985.

Where is the food to come from? Where are the resources for investment to come from? Can the rapidly increasing military and economic costs of great-power status be carried by Chinese society at the same time that other economic tasks vital to China's economic survival are carried out? I do not denigrate in the slightest native Chinese ingenuity and capacity for incredibly hard work when I suggest that the solutions to these problems are in the gravest doubt.

Even more important to Peiping's leaders than these economic problems, however, are the will and morale of their own people. The current leaders—Mao, Liu Shao-ch'i, Chou En-lai, and others—are in intensely committed group of men whose entire lives symbolize their willingness to postpone the satisfactions of the present for the promised glory of the future.

Every generation is suspicious that the youth of today is not what it was in the good old days. But this has become another obsession of Peiping's old men. Their comments to visitors, as well as the reports of refugees, have all emphasized their distrust of the youth of the country. They fear that their grand designs and goals—both domestic and foreign—will not be pursued with zeal by the next generation.

I believe their concern may be both genuine and warranted. How pleased can young college graduates be to be sent off to rural China for years for ideological hardening? How attractive is it to the Chinese peasant and worker to be called on for years of sacrifice to bring revolution to Africa or Latin America? Will Chinese scientists accept the dogma that scientific truth can be found only in the pages of Mao Tse-tung's writings? How can professional Chinese Communist army officers and soldiers be persuaded that the words of Mao represent a "spiritual atomic bomb" more powerful than any material weapon?

I am unaware of any new revolution brewing on the Chinese mainland. I have no evidence that the current regime does not, in practical terms, control effectively all of mainland China. But there is evidence of a growing psychological weariness that in years to come could produce a significant shift in the policies of a new generation of leaders.

The dramatic succession of foreign policy failures during the last year, both in the Communist and non-Communist world, must be having some effect on the confidence of the people in the wisdom of their leaders and even on the leaders themselves.

I do not predict any quick changes in China. Nor are there simple solutions. Peiping's present state of mind is a combination of aggressive arrogance and obsessions of its own making. There are doubtless many reasons, cultural, historical, political, for this state of mind. Psychologists have struggled for years in an effort to characterize what is a normal personality. The definition of what a normal state personality might be is beyond my abilities. I would be inclined, however, to advance the view that a country whose behavior is as violent, irascible, unyielding, and hostile as that of Communist China is led by leaders whose view of the world and of life itself is unreal. It is said that we have isolated them. But to me they have isolated themselves—both in the non-Communist and Communist world.

We have little hope of changing the outlook of these leaders. They are products of their entire lives. They seem to be immune to agreement or persuasion by anyone, including their own allies.

It is of no help in formulating policy to describe Peiping's behavior as neurotic. Its present policies pose grave and immediate problems for the United States and other countries. These must be dealt with now. The weapons and advisers that Peiping exports to promote and assist insurrections in other countries cannot be met by psychoanalysis. At the present time there is a need for a counterweight of real power to Chinese Communist pressures. This has had to be supplied primarily by the United States and our allies.

We should be under no illusion that by yielding to Peiping's bellicose demands today we would in some way ease the path toward peace in Asia. If Peiping reaps success from its current policies, not only its present leaders but those who follow will be emboldened to continue them. This is the path to increased tension and even greater dangers to world peace in the years ahead.

We expect China to become some day a great world power. Communist China is a major Asian power today. In the ordinary course of events, a peaceful China would be expected to have close relations—political, cultural, and economic—with the countries around its borders and with the United States.

It is no part of the policy of the United States to block the peaceful attainment of these objectives.

More than any other Western people, we have had close and warm ties with the Chinese people. We opposed the staking out of spheres of influence in China. We used our share of the Boxer indemnity to establish scholarships for Chinese students in the United States. We welcomed the revolution of Sun Yat-sen. We took the lead in relinquishing Western extraterritorial privileges in China. We refused to recognize the puppet regime established by Japan in Manchuria. And it was our refusal to accept or endorse, even by implication, Japan's imperial conquests and further designs in China that made it impossible for us to achieve a *modus vivendi* with Japan in 1940-41.

We look forward hopefully—and confidently—to a time in the future when the government of mainland China will permit the restoration of the historic ties of friendship between the people of mainland China and ourselves.

Elements of Future Policy

What should be the main elements in our policy toward Communist China?

We must take care to do nothing which encourages Peiping—or anyone else—to believe that it can reap gains from its aggressive actions and designs. It is just as essential to "contain" Communist aggression in Asia as it was, and is, to "contain" Communist aggression in Europe.

At the same time, we must continue to make it plain that, if Peiping abandons its belief that force is the best way to resolve disputes and gives up its violent strategy of world revolution, we would welcome an era of good relations.

More specifically, I believe, there should be 10 elements in our policy.

First, we must remain firm in our determination to help those Allied nations which seek our help to resist the direct or indirect use or threat of force against their territory by Peiping.

Second, we must continue to assist the countries of Asia in building broadly based effective governments, devoted to progressive economic and social policies, which can better withstand Asian Communist pressures and maintain the security of their people.

Third, we must honor our commitments to the Republic of China and to the people on Taiwan, who do not want to live under communism. We will continue to assist in their defense and to try to persuade the Chinese Communists to join with us in renouncing the use of force in the area of Taiwan.

Fourth, we will continue our efforts to prevent the expulsion of the Republic of China from the United Nations or its agencies. So long as Peiping follows its present course it is extremely difficult for us to see how it can be held to fulfill the requirements set forth in the charter for membership, and the United States opposes its membership. It is worth recalling that the Chinese

Communists have set forth some interesting conditions which must be fulfilled before they are even willing to consider membership:
- The United Nations resolution of 1950 condemning Chinese Communist aggression in Korea must be rescinded;
- There must be a new United Nations resolution condemning U.S. "aggression";
- The United Nations must be reorganized;
- The Republic of China must be expelled;
- All other "imperialist puppets" must be expelled. One can only ask whether the Chinese Communists seriously want membership, or whether they mean to destroy the United Nations. We believe the United Nations must approach this issue with the utmost caution and deliberation.

Fifth, we should continue our efforts to reassure Peiping that the United States does not intend to attack mainland China. There are, of course, risks of war with China. This was true in 1950. It was true in the Taiwan Straits crises of 1955 and 1958. It was true in the Chinese Communist drive into Indian territory in 1962. It is true today in Viet Nam. But we do not want war. We do not intend to provoke war. There is no fatal inevitability of war with Communist China. The Chinese Communists have, as I have already said, acted with caution when they foresaw a collision with the United States. We have acted with restraint and care in the past and we are doing so today. I hope that they will realize this and guide their actions accordingly.

Sixth, we must keep firmly in our minds that there is nothing eternal about the policies and attitudes of Communist China. We must avoid assuming the existence of an unending and inevitable state of hostility between ourselves and the rulers of mainland China.

Seventh, when it can be done without jeopardizing other U.S. interests, we should continue to enlarge the possibilities for unofficial contacts between Communist China and ourselves—contacts which may gradually assist in altering Peiping's picture of the United States.

In this connection, we have gradually expanded the categories of American citizens who may travel to Communist China. American libraries may freely purchase Chinese Communist publications. American citizens may send and receive mail from the mainland. We have in the past indicated that if the Chinese themselves were interested in purchasing grain we would consider such sales. We have indicated our willingness to allow Chinese Communist newspapermen to come to the United States. We are prepared to permit American universities to invite Chinese Communist scientists to visit their institutions.

We do not expect that for the time being the Chinese Communists will seize upon these avenues of contact or exchange. All the evidence suggests Peiping wishes to remain isolated from the United States. But we believe it is in our interests that such channels be opened and kept open. We believe contact and communication are not incompatible with a firm policy of containment.

Eighth, we should keep open our direct diplomatic contacts with Peiping in Warsaw. While these meetings frequently provide merely an opportunity for a reiteration of known positions, they play a role in enabling each side to communicate information and attitudes in times of crisis. It is our hope that they might at some time become the channel for a more fruitful dialogue.

Ninth, we are prepared to sit down with Peiping and other countries to discuss the critical problems of disarmament and non-proliferation of nuclear weapons. Peiping has rejected all suggestions and invitations to join in such talks. It has attacked the test ban treaty. It has advocated the further spread of nuclear weapons to non-nuclear countries. It is an urgent task of all countries to persuade Peiping to change its stand.

Tenth, we must continue to explore and analyze all available information on Communist China and keep our own policies up to date. We hope that Peiping's policies may one day take account of the [wish of the] people of Asia and her own people for peace and security. We have said, in successive administrations, that when Peiping abandons the aggressive use of force and shows that it is not irrevocably hostile to the United States, then expanded contacts and improved relations may become possible. This continues to be our position.

These, I believe, are the essential ingredients of a sound policy in regard to Communist China.

I believe that they serve the interests not only of the United States and of the free world as a whole—but of the Chinese people. We have always known of the pragmatic genius of the Chinese people, and we can see evidence of it even today. The practices and doctrines of the present Peiping regime are yielding poor returns to the Chinese people. I believe that the Chinese people, no less than their neighbors and the American people, crave the opportunity to move toward the enduring goals of mankind: a better life, safety, freedom, human dignity, and peace.

WALTER H. JUDD
Quarantine the Aggressor

From what I have seen in the press, most of the changes in American policy toward Communist China proposed by various witnesses before this committee appear to be based on certain assumptions which do not seem to me to be justified:

1. That the Communist regime now in control of the China mainland is here to stay.

But the same was said of Hitler, of Khrushchev, of Sukarno, of Nkrumah. People are not so sure now that Castro will last forever. Despots generally appear invincible—"until the last 5 minutes."

2. That the United States is stubbornly keeping Red China isolated and therefore we are responsible for its hostility and belligerence. The reverse is the truth; it is Red China's hostility and belligerence in its international attitudes and actions, that are responsible for its isolation.

General George Marshall wrote on January 7, 1947, after he had spent a

Dr. Judd served in the House of Representatives in the 78th to 87th Congresses as a Republican from Minnesota. He was an American delegate to the 12th General Assembly of the United Nations. The following is an excerpt from a statement made by Dr. Judd before the Senate Foreign Relations Committee on March 28, 1966.

year trying the very policies now being recommended of friendliness, conciliation, bringing the Chinese Communists into the Chinese Government and into
the world community:

> I wish to state to the American people that in the deliberate mis-
> representation and abuse of the action, policies, and purposes of our
> Government this propaganda (against the United States) has been with-
> out regard for the truth, without any regard whatsoever for the facts, and
> has given plain evidence of a determined purpose to mislead the Chinese
> people and the world and to arouse a bitter hatred of Americans. . . .

We must not do anything to strengthen Red China. Secondly, we must do
all we properly can to strengthen the countries around China that are resisting
its expansion. Mr. Chairman, I don't believe the American people will ever
accept the assumption that any tyranny is here to stay, or that we will accept as
permanent the subjugation of any people, no matter how powerful the despots
may look at the moment.

The cause of Red China's hostility is not its isolation, but the Communist
doctrine of the necessity for use of armed force to achieve world revolution.
To remove China's isolation now would prove that the doctrine is correct and
should be adhered to by them even more tenaciously.

3. That there is a better hope of getting Red China to change its attitudes
and activities by giving in to it on matters like diplomatic recognition, trade,
and admission to the United Nations than by resolute continuance of the policy
of containment as long as Red China refuses to act like a responsible member
of civilized society.

4. That changing our policy vis-a-vis Red China just might start an evolutionary process there.

But, of course, it might just as easily reduce the chances of such an evolutionary process. Everybody desires and hopes for "evolution" in Red China.
The debate should be over what measures are most likely to produce it.

For example (a) giving Red China greater prestige, influence, entree; that
is, making it stronger? Or keeping it as weak and isolated as possible?

(b) Concessions from its intended victims—like the United States? Or
pressures from its present victims—the Chinese within Red China, those on
Taiwan and in southeast Asia, Muslims in Indonesia and Malaysia, et cetera?

(c) Proving that Red China's truculence and stubborn defiance of the
world succeeds? Or showing that it will fail?

(d) Taking the mountain—United Nations—to Mao? Or patiently and non-
belligerently insisting that Mao come to the mountain of better international
conduct if he wants the benefits to Red China of membership in the international community?

What has caused the reported mellowing and evolution inside Yugoslavia,
Rumania, the Soviet Union? Influences from without? Or their failures within?

If economic and other pressures from within and without are compelling
some Communist governments to moderate their policies, at least toward their
own people, shouldn't we keep the pressures up rather than reduce them by
helping those Governments to solve their problems?

Changes in China Policy

Let us look now at the changes in policy toward Red China suggested by some. They are mostly three: official diplomatic recognition by the United States, expansion of trade relations, and admission of Communist China to the United Nations. What would be the probable results of such changes, the gains, and the losses?

Almost no one, so far as I have seen, goes further than to express the vague hope that some time after these steps, perhaps after Mao dies or in another generation or two, Red China may "mellow, moderate, mature, evolve." But there is no evidence on which to base the hoped-for changes.

What benefits, economic or political, has Great Britain received from her granting of diplomatic recognition in 1950? Or France 2 years ago?

Prime Minister Nehru of India recognized Communist China in 1949 and worked out with Chou En-lai the "Five Principles of Peaceful Coexistence." He remarked to me that we Americans didn't get along very well with the Chinese Communists because we are not Asians, implying that he being a fellow Asian could. I replied that I feared he would find that the Chinese Communists will not act as Asians but as world revolutionists. He was Red China's chief apologist and advocate—at the U.N. and elsewhere. How did his fellow Asians in Peking respond to his being their best friend? They invaded India, and left Mr. Nehru a broken man.

It is suggested that with diplomatic recognition we might get more information about conditions in Red China. But we have been getting plenty of information by a variety of means, especially from the thousands of escapees each year. Red China has not allowed newspaper correspondents of any nationality to travel freely in that land unless it had reason to believe in advance that they were generally favorable. Our trouble is not lack of information but erosion of our steadfastness, our patience, our will—as Mao boasted would be the case.

Resulting Losses

In contrast, there is no uncertainty as to the losses that would result from the suggested weakening of American policy.

Here are some:

1. It would pull the rug out from under our loyal allies on Taiwan. The Chinese are a realistic, even fatalistic, people. With no hope for reunion in freedom with their brethren on the China mainland, they would have little or no choice but to prepare for the inevitable.

Americans who advocate admitting Red China and then add glibly, "Of course we would support the defense of Taiwan," may be salving their own consciences but I think no Asians will be deceived. Twelve million Chinese could hardly maintain indefinitely the will or the capacity to resist 700 million, with the world organization for peace itself rejecting the 12 million and accepting the 700 million. . . .

2. With weakening or loss of Taiwan our Pacific island chain of defenses would be breached. It is doubtful that the Philippines could long resist Com-

munist pressures and blandishments. Filipinos remember that it was from Taiwan that their country was invaded by the Japanese. It would take vast intervention with American forces to save that new nation for which we certainly have a special responsibility in the Pacific. I have not found any responsible Filipino leaders who favor recognition of Communist China, or its admission to the U.N.

3. The 15 million or so Chinese living in southeast Asia would be shaken. They occupy key positions of power and influence in Vietnam, Malaya, Thailand, Burma, Indonesia, the Philippines. The governments of those countries could not refuse to recognize Communist China once we did. That would mean every Chinese embassy and consulate in southeast Asia, and the world for that matter, would become a protected center of Communist espionage, propaganda, sabotage and subversion of the host government—as recently exposed in Indonesia and Ghana. Through these embassies and consulates the Chinese minorities would be under direct and almost irresistible pressure to support the aggressive policies of the Mao regime. The stability of the strategic countries of southeast Asia would inevitably be weakened.

4. If the United States were to show that it is not a dependable ally in Asia, our allies elsewhere, including those in Europe, would know they cannot count on us either. What would happen to the whole system of collective security we have been building at such cost and effort, and which this committee has taken such effective leadership in developing, and which is absolutely indispensable to our own survival as a free nation? Why should any country anywhere stand by us if it is not sure we will stand by it?

5. It would tell the neutrals and "uncommitted" nations that they were right all along and that they might as well give in to the winning side at once.

6. Perhaps worst of all, it would tell the 700 million people on the China mainland that we are accepting their subjugation, that we think there is more hope for peace for ourselves in deals with their oppressors than in standing steadfastly with them, the oppressed. . . .

Resumption of Trade Relations

What would be the gains from resumption of trade relations? Based on the experience of others and on the announced purposes of the Communists, the gains would be minimal.

The Communists themselves have made clear on numerous occasions that their unwavering purposes are:

First, to get military and industrial equipment and supplies which they cannot yet obtain within the Communist bloc—not in order that they can trade more with us in the future, but so that they can become self-sufficient and not need to trade with us at all.

Second, to take advantage of a favorable trade or price situation wherever there is one that they cannot match even by exploitation of their own people and of their satellites.

Third, to induce countries to become more and more dependent on trade with the Soviet bloc, and therefore more at its mercy. This applies particularly to Germany and Japan.

Fourth, to divide the free world powers.

Our own objectives in trade are to improve the lives of people, to improve relations between the countries involved, to promote peace and prosperity in the world, and in the process earn a profit much of which becomes capital for further expansion of production and trade with further improvements of living standards.

But none of these is or can be the objective of a Communist regime. All trade is conducted by Communist state organizations and monopolies that have as their single objective the strengthening of the state. They cannot trade under the accepted rules of the free world without ceasing to be Communist. They cannot cease to be Communist without their movement collapsing. Trade is as much a weapon of their expansionism as are missiles. It is to be expanded or contracted, to be directed here or shifted there, as those at the top determine to be advantageous in promoting the Communist world revolution.

This was dramatically illustrated some years ago when Japan established trade relations with Communist China. It soon found that Red China would not actually carry on trade unless Japan bowed to Red China's political wishes.

In 1953 when Pakistan appeared to be veering toward the United States, Red China cut its purchases of Pakistan cotton from $84 million to $7 million in 1 year.

Where trade between Communist China and other countries does exist, it is only on sufferance of the Communist government and will be extinguished when it has served its purpose. This has never been denied by the Chinese Communist leaders. On the contrary, they have avowed on numerous occasions that complete nationalization of industries and trade and collectivization of agriculture has to come, but in stages—which means just as fast as they feel themselves strong enough to impose it. Would it be in our interest, economic or otherwise, to help them do it faster? . . .

In summary, seating of Red China in the United Nations would be illegal. It would require violation of the organization's charter.

It would be immoral. It would almost certainly mean removal of a member that abides by the charter to seat a nonmember that brazenly refuses to abide by the Charter. It would abandon 700 million people to Communist subjugation. It would properly be regarded as an attempt to buy peace for ourselves by sacrificing our principles and other people's freedom.

And it would bring no practical benefits. On the contrary, there would be definite and disastrous losses—with our allies; with the neutrals; with the peoples of Asia and everywhere else who desire to retain their freedom; and with the long-suffering millions now under Communist rule who long to regain their freedom. Do not break the hearts of the oppressed and their continued will to resist from within by accepting their oppressors.

Free Asia will crumble once it believes the Communists are winning. Admission of Red China to the United Nations would mean to much of Asia, as it should mean to us, that the Communists have all but won.

Having spent more than $100 billion to strengthen the will and capacity of free nations and peoples to resist communism, would it make sense now to strengthen communism?

The whole Communist movement worldwide is in serious trouble today.

Why change the policies that have contributed to its difficulties both abroad and at home, and thereby provided the free world its first ray of hope in years? We must always keep the door open to any genuine change on their part—as proved by deeds. We must keep the door resolutely closed to Communist threats, tricks, or promises not supported by performance.

Mr. Chairman, this is the time to stand fast for the basic containment policies that have proved sound and more successful during the last 15 years than most people believed possible. There is no course that does not involve serious risk: we are dealing with a ruthless and resourceful enemy. But such a course as outlined involves, I believe, far less risk.

Unless someone can suggest policies that offer better prospects of success, based on something more substantial than speculation, wishful thinking, or just hope, I can see no sound, sensible, or logical reason to change present policies and every reason to continue them, always being flexible in our tactics as required by developments as they come along.